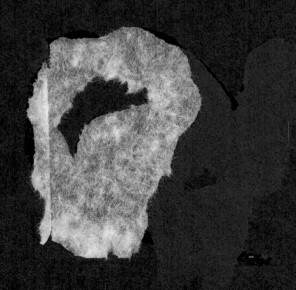

DISSENT
IN THE
SUPREME
COURT

DISSENT
IN THE
SUPREME
COURT

A CHRONOLOGY
BY PERCIVAL E. JACKSON

THE UNIVERSITY OF OKLAHOMA PRESS : NORMAN

BY PERCIVAL E. JACKSON

Law of Cadavers (New York, 1936, 1950)
Look at the Law (New York, 1940)
What Every Corporation Director Should Know
(New York, 1949)
Corporate Management (Charlottesville,
Virginia, 1955)
Justice and the Law (Charlottesville, Virginia, 1960)
The Wisdom of the Supreme Court (Norman, 1962)
Dissent in the Supreme Court (Norman, 1969)

STANDARD BOOK NUMBER: 8061-0839-8

LIBRARY OF CONGRESS CATALOG CARD NUMBER: 69-10621

“But after all whither do his doctrines tend? He has wrought confusion, he overthrows beliefs that have existed since the beginning, he speaks of new virtues which must be recognized and sought for, he speaks of a Divinity hitherto unknown to us. The blasphemer, he deems himself wiser than the gods! No, 'twere better we remain true to the old gods whom we know. They may not always be just, sometimes they may flare up in unjust wrath . . . but did not our ancestors live with them in the peace of their souls . . . . And now . . . the old virtue is out of joint. What does it all lead to?”

Vladimir G. Korolenko, "The Shades,"
Best Russian Short Stories, Modern Library.

Preface

SINCE THE SUPREME COURT, to quote Justice Miller, has "no patronage and no control of purse or sword" and "since its power and influence rest solely upon the public sense of the necessity for the existence of a tribunal to which all may appeal for the assertion and protection of rights guaranteed by the Constitution and by the laws of the land, and on the confidence reposed in the soundness of (its) decisions and purity of (its) motives," the creation of a sound public opinion is important so that healthy development of the law may be encouraged and unhealthy inroads on our institutions may be restrained.

But while the nine members of the Court are acquainted with what the electorate says, the electorate, except for what may be described as a tiny minority, is unacquainted with what the Court says. According to *The New York Times* of April 16, 1967, a survey made by Dr. John P. Robinson of the University of Michigan Survey Research Center concludes that "one-third of the United States population, that portion with less than a high school education and an annual income of less than $7,500, knows little about world affairs and is insulated from information about them." Dr. Robinson reported that "poorer people with little education rarely come in contact with any printed materials" . . . which deal with world events.

Gilbert Cranberg, editorial writer for the Des Moines, Iowa, *Register and Tribune,* in an article entitled "What Did the Supreme Court Say?" in the *Saturday Review of Literature* of April 8, 1967, reported that "scarcely anybody" reads the official publications of the Supreme Court of the United States:

> The total circulation of Supreme Court opinions is probably no more than 20,000. Most of the texts are located in forbidding legal libraries and inaccessible private law offices. Because there are no more than 300,000 lawyers in the United States, it's apparent that even many of the nation's attorneys do not actually read the Court's opinions.
>
> Yet . . . the alternative of poring over Supreme Court texts seemed about

as inviting as an evening of wading through a technical manual. Indeed, the deadly, all-but-indigestible legalese I expected to find was there in abundance, but to my delighted surprise there was also a gold mine of information and often exciting, absorbing reading. . . .

The wholesale shunning of what the Court says . . . leaves most of the country dependent on second-hand reports. It would be difficult to devise handicaps more devastating to an understanding of the Court than those that hobble news reporting of its rulings. . . . Where Congressmen, subordinate administrators, and Presidents are frequently eager to explain and to defend their policies, Justices of the Supreme Court emerge from isolation only to read their opinions. . . . No Justice is available to discuss or clarify the opinion he has written.

Mr. Cranberg quoted Justice Clark as saying, "The newspaperman is pushed to even get the result, much less the reasoning back of each judgment. . . . The news media announcements . . . were not complete. As one commentator said, 'The trouble is that the Court—like the old complaint of the wife—is never understood.' "

Mr. Cranberg also quoted a columnist who said a decade ago that the Supreme Court was "the worst reported and the worst judged institution in the American system of government. . . ." And he quoted Chief Justice Warren as rating "public understanding of the Supreme Court far below the level of public understanding of the Executive and Legislative branches of government."

He concluded, "Exposure to the texts of Supreme Court opinions will not convince the reader of the 'correctness' of a ruling—some of the Court's closest followers are its severest critics. But the thoughtful American who puts the Supreme Court on his reading list will be persuaded that exposure to the authentic voice of the Court has given him unique insight into this remote and least understood of institutions that speaks to the people only through its opinions."

It is to be noted that the Association of American Law Schools has recognized the problem to which Mr. Cranberg called attention, and for the past several years its Special Committee on Supreme Court Decisions has sent out memoranda concerning forthcoming Supreme Court decisions. This effort emphasizes the need for this volume.

As what constitutes a brief history of the Court, written by the pens of its members, travels along its 175-year road, there emerges the sententious foundation-building phrases of Marshall, their democratic overlay by Taney, the prescience of Waite, Miller, and Harlan, the wit and wisdom of Holmes, the learning of Brandeis, Hughes, and Stone, the realism of Jackson, the scintillations of Frankfurter, and finally, and of immediate import, the epochal conclusions of their ultimate successors. From these springs arise reflections of the clashes of a dynamic society, of crime detection and punishment, of racial discrimination, of church and state separation, of equality of franchise, the grist of today's news and controversy.

In an effort to enlarge the area of understanding of the Court and its work, to increase the potential of public opinion that may influence the Court's attitude and strengthen its support, I have sought to mirror the acts and actions of its members, their strengths and weaknesses, restraints and excesses, philosophies and idiosyncrasies. Earlier cases, largely of historic value, have been subordinated to permit more extended quotation from current-day issues and controversies. Thus readers, informed, may themselves judge whether the voices that presently predominate, more often than not by a majority of one, are voices of power or of reason, of prescience or of blind activism, of republicanism or of an overriding nationalism, and thus form that core of intelligent opinion that is the sole, lasting bulwark of an effective court. On that score, it might be added that *The New York Times* reported on July 10, 1968, that a Gallup poll had found the high court in disfavor, three to two, with public approval dropping in the past year.

PERCIVAL E. JACKSON

New York, New York
April 1, 1969

Contents

Preface   *page vii*

PART I: THE EARLIER YEARS   I

Chapter
   I   The Anatomy of Dissent   3
   II   William Johnson: Dissenter of the Marshall Court   20
   III Judicial Conflict in the Slavery Era   41
   IV The Civil War and Reconstruction Years   61
   V   The Fourteenth Amendment and the
      Period of Judicial Restraint   79
   VI The Court as a Superlegislature—1   98
   VII The Court as a Superlegislature—2   130
   VIII The Court as a Superlegislature—3   146
   IX The Roosevelt Era—1   171
   X   The Roosevelt Era—2   188
   XI The Post-New Deal Court   202
   XII The Era of the Wild Horses—1   221
   XIII The Era of the Wild Horses—2   242
   XIV The Years of the Witch-Hunt—1   259
   XV The Years of the Witch-Hunt—2   280

PART II: THE LAST DECADE   295

   XVI The Fourth Amendment   297
   XVII The Negro Racial Issue—1   324
   XVIII The Negro Racial Issue—2   341
   XIX Crime and the Criminal Law: Confessions and Counsel—1   359
   XX Crime and the Criminal Law—2   381
   XXI Censorship and Obscenity   400
   XXII Reapportionment and Literacy in Voting   416

XXIII The First Amendment   439
XXIV Labor   461
XXV Antitrust and Other Issues   480
XXVI The Incidence of Dissent   497
XXVII The Final Term of the Warren Court   514
XXVIII Commentary   520

Table of Cases   531

Index   548

PART ONE
The Earlier Years

CHAPTER I

The Anatomy of Dissent

W HILE "DISSENT" AND "DISSENTER" conform to their Latin etymologic heritage, "dissenter" in England came to denominate a member of a religious body which had separated from the established church and, eventually, to one of the "Protestant Dissenters" named in a 1688 act of the British Parliament. Other religious dissenters were known as "dissidents" and, in later years, as "nonconformists."

Here in modern America "dissenter" has come to bear legal connotations, with reminders of Oliver Wendell Holmes, the "Great Dissenter," who, in a day now held to be one of legal reaction, preached nonconformity.

The American dissenter, in the tradition of his predecessors, is primarily a nonconformist. The dissident mantles of Galileo, Luther, and others fell, in the newly won nation, on Thomas Paine and Patrick Henry, who advocated and fostered revolution from the mother country. They were succeeded by Thomas Jefferson, who advanced the dogma of democracy, and Wendell Phillips, who preached the abolition of the existing order of slavery that marred it.

Generally the dissenter has viewed the core of mass acceptance with skepticism and found it wanting. He has supplied the "con" in the debate that lies at the basis of modern democracy. He has borne the scorn of the herd whose collective thinking he challenges. He is the heretic whose heresy may not stand the rays of established thought or the spectrum of time. Or he may be the prophet whose heresy of today becomes the dogma of tomorrow.

In a nation that emerged from the womb of dissent, where progress grew from free thought, from diversity of opinion, from challenge of majority concurrence, conformity that banishes challenge becomes a dead hand that seeks to stay evolution—a dead hand that beckons to oppression and stagnation.

In the streets, on the campuses, from the reams poured out by the printing presses, dissent may be synonymic with nonconformity. Nonconformity may spring from the farseeing, from the weak who cannot fit into the patterns of conformity, or from the idealists whose gaze is fixed upward. Similarly, dissent in our courts may be little more than the reflection of the growth of extramural dissent, of a changing current of public opinion beyond the outer peripheries of our courtrooms, or it may be an awakening stimulated by the baton of past legal leadership. "Conflicts which have divided the Justices always mirror a conflict which pervades society," said Justice Jackson.[1] As dissent outside the courtroom may represent the struggle to modify existing patterns to newly acquired knowledge, or to resist untried experiment, so its reflection in the courtroom may represent the galloping of legal activists or the reins of legal conformists seeking to slow the ruptures of established precedents.

The antisegregation school decisions in Brown v. Board of Education,[2] which struck down the earlier Plessy decision,[3] followed by over half a century the dissenting lead of the elder Harlan, as the welter of overruling cases in the Hughes and Stone courts followed the prophetic, farseeing earlier dissents of Holmes and Brandeis. These represented the posthumous triumphs of the day's nonconformists in contrast to today's dissents of the younger Harlan, of Stewart, of White, and sometimes of Clark, which seek to stem the victorious inroads of the Warren liberal majorities upon the established legal order.

That ferment, challenge, skepticism, denial are the order of the day admits of little contention. The rise of the working class through unionization, once a minority view promoted by the prescience of Brandeis, the advancement of the rights of the Negro, once advocated by the elder Harlan, the growth of personal liberties and their constitutional protection, as extolled by Holmes, Brandeis, and Stone, have been followed by greater advocacy of and demands for minority rights. Though the courts are notorious laggards, we find a corresponding legal fermentation that produces a spew of heightened dissent.

Dissent is endemic in a country won by blood spilled for conscience and expression. It is natural, essential, and inevitable. Its absence marks a graveyard of conformity, to paraphrase Justice Jackson. And its value and inevitability is no less within the precincts of the law.

It is "in the nature of Supreme Court litigation" that explanation "must be sought for the large incidence of dissent," said Justice Frankfurter.[4] Chief Justice Hughes expressed surprise "that in the midst of controversies on every conceivable subject, one should expect unanimity upon difficult legal questions."[5] Judge (later Justice) Cardozo pointed out that a percentage of cases, "not large indeed, and yet not so small as to be negligible, . . . might be decided

---

1 Robert H. Jackson, *The Struggle for Judicial Supremacy* (New York, Alfred A. Knopf, 1941), 312–13.

2 347 U.S. 483 (1954); 349 U.S. 294 (1955).

3 Plessy v. Ferguson, 163 U.S. 537 (1896).

4 Felix Frankfurter, "Holmes and the Constitution," 41 *Harvard Law Review* 121–22.

4

either way," since "reasons plausible and fairly persuasive might be found for one conclusion as for another."[6]

Over the years, there has been no lack of justification for legal dissent. Justice Story said in an early case:

> It is a matter of regret that in this conclusion I have the misfortune to differ from a majority of the court, for whose superior learning and ability I entertain the most entire respect. But I hold it an indispensable duty not to surrender my own judgment, because a great weight of opinion is against me—a weight which no one can feel more sensibly than myself. Had this been an ordinary case I should have contented myself with silence; but believing that no more important or interesting question ever came before a prize tribunal, and that the national rights suspended on it are of infinite moment to the maritime world, I have thought it not unfit to pronounce my own opinion.[7]

On occasion, even Marshall found need to dissent. In constitutional cases, opinions seriatim, including concurrences as well as dissents, have invariably been approved.

Inquiry concerning the rocks upon which unanimity of opinion founders, to borrow from Justice Cardozo, must begin with exposition of the divergencies of and the conflicts between philosophies of the arbiters of legal controversies. One cannot better the mellifluous words of Cardozo, philosopher, statesman, and jurist:

> More subtle are the forces so far beneath the surface that they cannot reasonably be classified as other than subconscious. . . . every one of us has in truth an underlying philosophy of life . . . which gives coherence and direction to thought and action. Judges cannot escape that current any more than other mortals. . . . inherited instincts, traditional beliefs, acquired convictions . . . a conception of social needs . . . which, when reasons are nicely balanced, must determine where choice shall fall. . . . In this mental background every problem finds its setting. We may try to see things as objectively as we please. None the less, we can never see them with any eyes except our own.[8]

Indeed, justices of our high court are frequently selected for their bents. President Lincoln wrote to George S. Boutwell, concerning the former's choice of a chief justice to succeed Taney: ". . . we wish for a Chief Justice who will

[5] Address, 13 Amer. Law Inst. Proceedings (1936), 61, 64, quoted in Felix Frankfurter, *Of Law and Men* (New York, Harcourt, Brace & Co., 1956), 42.

[6] Benjamin N. Cardozo, *The Nature of the Judicial Process* (New Haven, Yale University Press, 1921), 164–65.

[7] The Nereide, 9 Cranch 388, 455 (1815).

[8] Cardozo, *The Nature of the Judicial Process*, 11–13.

sustain what has been done in regard to emancipation and the legal tenders. We cannot ask a man what he will do. . . . Therefore, we must take a man whose opinions are known."[9] President Theodore Roosevelt selected Chief Justice Holmes of the Massachusetts Supreme Court, believing he would reflect the President's antitrust views on the high court bench; that he was disappointed when Holmes joined what Roosevelt considered a reactionary majority[10] reflected only the latter's misjudgment. Later President Franklin D. Roosevelt substituted the selection of the liberals Black and Douglas for his stillborn court-packing plan designed to overcome the reactionary majority that had circumvented his New Deal.

The range of opportunity for disagreement in our high court is almost limitless. The legal breaker system that sifts out from the Court all but the most controversial issues requires the skill of a John Marshall and the acquiescence of his far-gone day to avoid dissidence. The ever-present struggle between the desire for and the need of certainty and the demands of progress takes its toll of unanimity. Like vegetating humans who die but remain unburied, rules that have outlived their usefulness tend to continue to struggle for nostalgic acceptance. Concepts that have ruled human destinies cling to their scepters, despite revolutionary discoveries and advances in learning. Property rights close ranks against advocates of personal liberties and privileges. Even mere definitions assert vested rights and refuse to yield to ravages of public acceptance.

Page after page of our Supreme Court reports reveal clash of subjectivity and objectivity that produces difference and dissent. Where the judicial and legislative functions meet, we find Justice Holmes saying, in upholding a legislative act over the dissent of his confreres, "It by no means is true that every law is void which may seem to the judges who pass upon it excessive, unsuited to its ostensible end, or based upon conceptions of morality with which they disagree."[11]

In the field of constitutional interpretation, Judge Learned Hand said:

> What is "freedom of speech and of the press"; what is the "establishment of religion and the free exercise thereof"; what are "unreasonable searches," "due process of law," and "equal protection of the law"; all these are left wholly undefined. . . . Indeed, these fundamental canons are not jural concepts at all, in the ordinary sense; and in application they turn out to be no more than admonitions of moderation, as appears from the varying and contradictory interpretations that the judges themselves find it necessary to put upon them.[12]

[9] George S. Boutwell, *Reminiscences of Sixty Years in Public Affairs* (New York, McClure, Phillips & Co., 1902), 29.

[10] Northern Securities Co. v. United States, 193 U.S. 197 (1904).

[11] Otis v. Parker, 187 U.S. 606, 608 (1903).

[12] Irving Dilliard, ed., *The Spirit of Liberty—Papers and Addresses of Learned Hand* (New York, Vintage Books, 1959), 211.

6

Established rule, precedents, the rule of stare decisis vis-à-vis the need for re-examination and change create a fruitful area for philosophic disharmony, another Charybdis sundering judicial unanimity. Justice Holmes inveighed against the sanctity of rule having only the claim of age.[13] Justice Frankfurter decried "an excessive regard for formalism."[14] Justice Cardozo advocated discarding rules that no longer function.[15] "We do not realize how large a part of our law is open to reconsideration in the habit of the public mind," said Justice Holmes.[16] The books are strewn with overruled and overruling cases.

Justice Cardozo also called attention to new conceptions of the significance of constitutional provisions, of concepts of personal liberties, of public use, and of regulation of property. "New times and new manners may call for new standards and new rules," he said.[17]

In applying the law to the facts, in the area of determining what rule of law is called for by the facts of the case, in interpreting and drawing conclusions from the facts, all of which determine the great majority of legal controversies, the personal idiosyncrasies of individual judges and consequent differences get full play. "In the excitement produced by ardent controversy, gentlemen view the same object through such different media that minds not unfrequently receive therefrom precisely opposite impressions," said Chief Justice Marshall.[18] And, in the words of Justice William Johnson, "We pretend not to more infallibility than other courts composed of the same frail materials which compose this."[19]

In evaluating evidence five justices found a federal agent had joined in an unlawful search before it was concluded;[20] three of the four dissenters accepted the trial court's view to the contrary, the fourth, Justice Reed, upon his own examination, so found and joined in dissent. In a more recent case[21] the claim was made that three boys accused of rape had been denied due process because of suppressed and perjured evidence. In more than fifty pages of text, three justices joined in an opinion vacating the conviction and remanding the case to the state court; another justice concurred after devoting some thirteen pages to a review of the evidence; a fifth justice concurred for reasons which actuated the lower court judge who had granted a new trial but whose decision had been reversed by the state court of appeals, while four dissenting justices joined

---

[13] Oliver Wendell Holmes, *Collected Legal Papers* (New York, Harcourt, Brace & Co., 1920), 187.

[14] Great Northern Life Ins. Co. v. Read, 322 U.S. 47, 57–58 (1944).

[15] Cardozo, *The Nature of the Judicial Process,* 100.

[16] Oliver Wendell Holmes, "The Path of the Law," 10 *Harvard Law Review* 457, 466.

[17] Cardozo, *The Nature of the Judicial Process,* 88.

[18] Mitchel v. United States, 9 Pet. 711, 723, (1835).

[19] Martin v. Hunter's Lessee, 1 Wheat. 304, 364 (1816).

[20] Lustig v. United States, 338 U.S. 74 (1949).

[21] Giles v. Maryland, 386 U.S. 66 (1967).

in an opinion saying that "on the basis of the trial record, it would be difficult to imagine charges more convincingly proved."[22]

Where a bench consists of minorities of the Court which vary from time to time, the sitting justices on one day may well decide an issue one way while their sitting associates may hold the contrary a week later, unless the second minority suppress their different view in obeisance to judicial decorum and the interests of consequent certainty. Witness, for example, a high court majority exculpating Cummings and Garland while, with the death of one of the majority that so ruled, a later equal division affirming a lower court decision to the contrary.

Justice Frankfurter deprecated the Court's "giving fair ground for the belief that the law is the expression of chance, for instance, of unexpected changes in the Court's composition and the contingencies in the choice of successors."[23]

A source of deviation of opinion results, at least with open-minded justices, when factual data are made available that lay at rest long-accepted myths and shibboleths. Justice Brandeis pointed the way for such rejection with word and act. In an address given before the Chicago Bar Association in 1916,[24] he maintained that the law had not shifted "from legal justice to social justice"; that "legal science . . . was largely deaf and blind"; that the law "had not kept pace with the rapid development of our political, economic, and social ideals." He ascribed this lag of the law to the judges' and lawyers' lack of "the necessary knowledge of economic and social science." He added that the ignorance and prejudices of the judges had been responsible for their constitutional constructions. He documented his statements by reference to the notorious Lochner decision striking down New York's attempt to limit the daily stint of bakers to ten hours and to the similar determination of the New York Court of Appeals in the Williams case,[25] striking down an act seeking to limit the hours of labor for women.

But Brandeis did not confine himself to polemics. In 1907 he accepted a retainer from the state of Oregon to defend its ten-hour law for women. The one-hundred-page brief he submitted to the Court argued that "the facts of common knowledge of which the court may take judicial notice establish . . . conclusively that there is reasonable ground for holding that to permit women in Oregon to work in a 'mechanical establishment, or factory, or laundry' more than ten hours in one day is dangerous to the public health, safety, morals or welfare."[26]

22 *Ibid.*, 102.
23 United States v. Rabinowitz, 339 U.S. 56, 86 (1950).
24 Louis D. Brandeis, "The Living Law," 10 *Illinois Law Review* 461.
25 People v. Williams, 189 N.Y. 131 (1907).
26 Muller v. Oregon, 208 U.S. 412, 416 (1908).

8

"The facts of common knowledge"—a statement not intended to be ironical—were supplied to the Court in that case by way of "extracts from over ninety reports of committees, bureaus of statistics, commissioners of hygiene, inspectors of factories, both in this country and in Europe, to the effect that long hours of labor are dangerous for women."[27] Justice Brewer, writing for a unanimous court sustaining the legislation, said that the "opinions referred to in the margin may not be, technically speaking, authorities . . . yet they are significant."[28]

However, not all judges are to be moved by "facts of common knowledge" that disturb their long-accepted dogma; thus dissent is bred. For example, in subsequent cases, where the voluminous Brandeis type of factual presentation was made by the Brandeis successor—the then Professor Felix Frankfurter—success was achieved only by reason of the acquiescence of a majority in the one case,[29] and by reason of an equally divided court in the other.[30]

The Brandeis technique has become commonplace, not only in lawyers' brief-writing but also in judges' opinion-writing. As a judge Brandeis frequently resorted to it as in New State Ice Co. v. Liebmann.[31] Justice Frankfurter employed it frequently, as in the case of Wolf v. Colorado,[32] where he turned back—though for a time only—those who sought to make the Fourth Amendment applicable to the states. In a later case,[33] in denying Justice Black's historical thesis that the Fourteenth Amendment is "shorthand" for the first eight amendments of the Bill of Rights, he annexed an appendix summarizing the constitutional provisions of the ratifying and subsequently admitted states vis-à-vis the provisions of the Fifth, Sixth, and Seventh amendments of the federal Constitution. Justice Douglas quotes liberally from extrajudicial sources, even in one case, a recent antitrust suit, he reproduced a column written by Art Buchwald, well-known newspaper humorist.

Even definitions may claim vested rights and take their toll of agreement. Without the legal pale, as within its circumference, the hub of controversy is frequently found to rest upon mere variance of definition. "There is at present no theory of Definition capable of practical application under normal circumstances," say Ogden and Richards, apropos of general fields of meaning.[34] "The meaning of today is not the meaning of tomorrow," said Justice Car-

[27] *Ibid.,* 419n.

[28] *Ibid.,* 420.

[29] Bunting v. Oregon, 243 U.S. 426 (1917).

[30] Stettler v. O'Hara, 243 U.S. 629 (1917).

[31] 285 U.S. 262 (1932).

[32] 338 U.S. 25 (1949).

[33] Bartkus v. Illinois, 359 U.S. 121 (1959).

[34] C. K. Ogden and L. A. Richards, *The Meaning of Meaning* (New York, Harcourt, Brace & Co., 1923), 109.

dozo.[35] "A word is not a crystal, transparent and unchanged; it is the skin of a living thought and may vary greatly in color and content according to the circumstances and the time in which it is used," declared Justice Holmes.[36] And in the words of Chief Justice Marshall: "In common language the same word has various meanings, and the peculiar sense in which it is used in any sentence is to be determined by the context."[37] The complexity of legal definition is attested by the multitudinous pages of the Black and other legal dictionaries.

In the area of advance and resistance we find scientific attacks upon subjects of criminal prosecution, such as drug addiction, alcoholism, and sex deviation, claimed to be illnesses, contentions which, at best, only gradually meet with favor and meanwhile produce skepticism, denial, and dissent. Changing mores concerning prison recidivism, attempted rehabilitation of prisoners, crime, and criminal administration generally take their toll of unanimity. Psychiatry and social research challenge accepted beliefs; a recent denial that erotica leads to antisocial acts is cited to alleviate such rigor as remains respecting obscenity. Pending general acceptance, these contentions must necessarily breed division in disparate minds fed by disparate backgrounds.

Justice Douglas, on an application for a writ of certiorari in Pierce v. Turner, 386 U.S. 947, said, "Denial of certiorari is proper in this case. . . . The underlying question is whether the M'Naghten test of legal insanity is a constitutionally permissible test of criminal liability in light of the contemporary state of knowledge on the problems of insanity. Should that test give way to the 128 years of experience in the fields of psychiatry and psychology since its formulation? Should it be replaced by the more sophisticated and realistic Durham test (Durham v. United States, 214 F.2d 862) or some other test more in keeping with due process?"

Justice Jackson linked various areas of dissent: "personal impressions," obsolescence of "precedents and authorities," "that words no longer mean what they have always meant," and "that the law knows no fixed principles."[38]

Justice Brandeis upheld stare decisis with the oft-quoted statement that it was more important that the rule of law be settled than that it be settled right,[39] while he was expatiating on the need for flexibility in application of settled rule.[40] Justice Roberts, on an impassioned occasion, likened the Court's ephemeral decisions to a "restricted railroad ticket, good for this day and train only."[41]

[35] Cardozo, *The Nature of the Judicial Process,* 84.
[36] Towne v. Eisner, 245 U.S. 418, 425 (1918).
[37] Cherokee Nation v. Georgia, 5 Pet. 1, 19 (1831).
[38] Brown, Speller, Daniels v. Allen, 344 U.S. 443, 535 (1953).
[39] Burnet v. Coronado Oil & Gas Co., 285 U.S. 393, 406 (1932).
[40] *Ibid.,* 406–408.

Over the years clash of judicial review and legislative prerogative furnishes cogent evidence of the tempests engendered by objective judicial consideration meeting subjective judicial predilection. When the Fuller and later courts departed from the Waite court's policy of moderation in judicial supervision of legislative action, the way was paved, according to Justice Frankfurter's count, to the knell of 228 legislative acts between 1890 and 1937 in support of the unenlightened property-rights interpretation of the provisions of the Fourteenth Amendment. Justice Brewer's frank pronunciamento that "the paternal theory of government is to me odious" was the key to the property-rights commitment that overcame the democratic process. Its destruction was foretold by Justice Holmes in his initial effort on the high court bench, and the Hughes and succeeding courts effected the demise of the superlegislative function of the high court as it returned to the Marshall and Waite concept of the Court's province.

The principal exponents of latter-day personal idealogy that defies rule and stimulates dissent have been Justices Black and Douglas. The latter has made no secret of his contempt for stare decisis, saying *"Stare decisis* has . . . little place in American constitutional law. . . .*[42] This re-examination of precedent in constitutional law is a personal matter for each judge who comes along."[43] His attitude on the bench has given no lie to his pronouncements.

While Justice Black, upon his accession to the bench, failed to dissent from Justice Cardozo's moderate "unifying" rule in the Palko case that denied that the Fourteenth Amendment made the Fifth applicable *in toto* to the states, Justice Black raised and carried on high thereafter the banner of contention that the Fourteenth Amendment incorporated the Bill of Rights. In so doing, he has maintained that his conclusion has been the result of his "study of the historical events that culminated in the Fourteenth Amendment," which, he argued, had "never received full consideration or exposition in any opinion of this Court interpreting the Amendment."[44]

In making his contention and repeating it at every possible opportunity, as has been his wont, Justice Black has not only ignored solid expert refutation, but has shed the shackles of rule and judicial decorum. In his pursuit he has ignored the repeated contrary assertions of his associates,[45] who found over the years that the application of Justice Cardozo's moderate stance in the Palko case had effected a just and adequate means of enforcing the substance which

[41] Smith v. Allwright, 321 U.S. 649, 669, (1944).

[42] William O. Douglas, *We the Judges* (Garden City, N.Y., Doubleday & Co., 1956), 429.

[43] *Ibid.*, 431.

[44] Adamson v. California, 332 U.S. 46, 71–72 (1947).

[45] E.g., Twining v. New Jersey, 211 U.S. 78 (1908); Frankfurter, J., in Bartkus v. Illinois, 359 U.S. 121 (1959); Griswold v. Connecticut, 381 U.S. 479, 492 (1965).

due process was designed to protect, without relying on a fallacious and repudiated historical concept.

In his quest Justice Black has never lacked for collaboration; Justice Douglas was Black's early adherent. In his *We the Judges,* Justice Douglas said flatly, "I have always thought that the Fourteenth Amendment made the Bill of Rights applicable to the States,"[46] though he admitted that a case to the contrary could be made out. And over the years he has stood by the side of his battling mentor on the generality[47] and on specifics.[48] Indeed, in the last mentioned case he cited a previous case[49] as justifying his claim that the Fourteenth Amendment made the cruel and unusual punishment clause of the Eighth Amendment applicable to the states, though the claim was of doubtful verity.

But, withal, Justice Black's war of attrition has been marked by victories on the field of battle (*see* Chapter XII). The First Amendment had fallen before Justice Black took up arms.[50] But with Justice Clark defecting, the Fourth Amendment could hold out for less than three decades after the initial Black assault.[51] Only fragments of the Fifth and Sixth amendments were left undefeated.[52] It was Justice Harlan, dissenting for himself and Justice Clark in the Malloy-Hogan case, who proved Cassandra-like for the dissenters when he said that a continuing re-examination of due process would be called for "and development of the community sense of justice may in time lead to expansion of the protection which due process affords."[53]

Not all Justice Black's essays, however, have met with equal success. No more startling expression of personal view—one disregarding half a century of precedent—is to be found in the Supreme Court archives than that of freshman Black who, dissenting in 1938, maintained that the protections of the Fourteenth Amendment did not accrue to corporations.[54] In a later case Justice Douglas joined him in this iconoclasm.[55]

In that case Justice Jackson, after writing for the Court, wrote separately and critically of the dissent, saying, *inter alia,* "...in at least two cases this Court,

[46] Page 264.

[47] E.g., Poe, Doe & Buxton v. Ullman, 367 U.S. 497 (1961); Malloy v. Hogan, 378 U.S. 1 (1964).

[48] NAACP v. Williams, 359 U.S. 550 (1959).

[49] Louisiana v. Resweber, 329 U.S. 459 (1947).

[50] Gitlow v. New York, 268 U.S. 652 (1925).

[51] Mapp v. Ohio, 367 U.S. 643 (1961).

[52] Malloy v. Hogan, 378 U.S. 1 (1964); Escobedo v. Illinois, 378 U.S. 478 (1964); Gideon v. Wainwright, 372 U.S. 335 (1963); Pointer v. Texas, 380 U.S. 400 (1965); Douglas v. Alabama, 380 U.S. 415 (1965); Griffin v. California, 380 U.S. 609 (1965); Miranda v. Arizona, 384 U.S. 436 (1966).

[53] Malloy v. Hogan, 378 U.S. 1, 15 (1964).

[54] Connecticut Gen. Life Ins. Co. v. Johnson, 303 U.S. 77, 87, (1938).

[55] Wheeling Steel Corp. v. Glander, 337 U.S. 562, 576 (1949).

joined by both Justices now asserting that corporations have no rights under the Fourteenth Amendment, recently has granted relief to corporations by striking down state action as conflicting with corporate rights under that amendment." He cited the two prior cases.[56] The rule Justice Black was so boldly attacking had been first declared by the Waite court in 1886 and had not been questioned during the ensuing half century.

Throughout their terms of service, the effort to advance the cause of personal beliefs has been endemic with Justices Black and Douglas, and its path has been marked with monuments of disregard for precedent, not only of relics of the past but of the breath of the present.

The free-wheeling attitude of Black and Douglas contrasts notably with that of Holmes who deprecated "persistent expressions of opinions that do not command the agreement of the Court" as reaching "obvious limits of propriety."[57] Their disrespect for past wisdom likewise contrasts with the Holmes obeisance. A per curiam opinion included the following: "The Chief Justice and Mr. Justice Holmes . . . if they exercised their independent judgment, would be for affirmance; [they] nevertheless concur in the conclusion now announced by the Court because they consider that they are constrained to it in virtue of the controlling effect of the previous decisions . . . cited in the opinion of the Court."[58]

Another example of judicial deference to precedent was furnished by Chief Justice Taney when, in a conflict between Rhode Island and Massachusetts over boundaries,[59] the Court overruled Massachusetts' claim that it lacked jurisdiction, and Taney dissented. When, finally, the Court found for Massachusetts on the merits and dismissed Rhode Island's suit, Taney concurred in the dismissal, still contending that the Court lacked jurisdiction.

Later, when a boundary dispute between Iowa and Missouri, which had threatened armed conflict (Missouri had put 1,500 armed men and Iowa 1,100 on the disputed boundary line), came to the Court and was decided in favor of Iowa,[60] the Chief Justice relinquished dissent in compliance with the precedent set by the Court in the earlier case.

Contrasting present-day manners, it might be noted in a quite recent case that a five-to-four decision found that a Maryland health inspector might inspect premises without a search warrant to find evidence of rodent infestation.[61] In a similar and simultaneous case from Ohio where certiorari was

---

[56] Times-Mirror Co. v. Superior Court, 314 U.S. 252 (1941); Pennekamp v. Florida, 328 U.S. 331 (1946).

[57] Federal Trade Commission v. Beechnut Co., 257 U.S. 441, 456 (1922).

[58] United States v. Lehigh Valley R.R., 254 U.S. 255 (1920).

[59] Rhode Island v. Massachusetts, 12 Pet. 657 (1838).

[60] Missouri v. Iowa; Iowa v. Missouri, 7 How. 660 (1849).

[61] Frank v. Maryland, 364 U.S. 253 (1960).

sought, the dissenters refused to be bound by the decision just rendered and voted probable jurisdiction. This sufficed to put the Ohio case on the calendar for argument. Thereupon, since Justice Stewart, one of the five-man majority in the earlier case, disqualified himself in the subsequent case, an equal division in the voting resulted that served to affirm the conviction below and follow the previous ruling. However, four of the dissenters later persisted and succeeded in inducing Justices White and Fortas to rally to their cause, whereupon the original Maryland decision was overruled.

A glaring and similar breach of respect for a prior decision occurred during the 1967 term when the Court affirmed the convictions in cases where habitual criminal statutes of Texas were challenged.[62] Justice Harlan wrote for four members of the Court and Justice Stewart concurred. Chief Justice Warren, joined by Justice Fortas, wrote, dissenting in two of the cases. Justice Brennan, joined by Justice Douglas, wrote, dissenting in all three cases. These decisions were handed down on January 23, 1967.

On February 13 following, the Court denied certiorari in ten cases,[63] in each of which Justice Douglas dissented "for the reasons stated in the dissenting opinion of Mr. Justice Brennan in Spencer v. Texas" (one of the prior cases), and on the same day, in nine other cases, the Chief Justice and Justices Douglas and Fortas dissented for the reasons stated "in the dissenting opinion of the Chief Justice in the same case."[64] Then on February 20, the Chief Justice and Justices Douglas and Fortas added two more cases to this list of dissents,[65] and Justice Douglas dissented in eight other disassociated denials of certiorari.[66] Nevertheless Justice Brennan, who had written in dissent in the Spencer case and who had joined in the dissent of the Chief Justice, respected the proprieties his dissenting brothers ignored.

Attesting the intransigency of the dissenters and the viability of the Court, we find Justice Douglas, writing for six members of the Court, including the dissenters in the last-mentioned Spencer case. He held, over the dissents of Justices Harlan, Black, and White, that, although enhanced punishment had not been imposed under the recidivist statutes and even though the trial court had instructed the jury not to consider prior offenses for any purpose, the admission in evidence of prior convictions where the record did not disclose the defendant had been represented by counsel, required reversal of a conviction.[67] Chief Justice Warren characterized the case as "the frightful progeny of Spencer and of that decision's unjustified deviation from settled principles

[62] Spencer v. Texas, 385 U.S. 554 (1967).
[63] 386 U.S. 926–27 (1967).
[64] Ibid., 928–29.
[65] Ibid., 938.
[66] Ibid., 937.
[67] Burgett v. Texas, 389 U.S. 109 (1967).

14

of fairness." He also said, "Today we have placed a needed limitation on the Spencer rule, but nothing except an outright rejection would truly serve the cause of justice."[68]

In fairness, it must be noted that Justices Clark, Harlan, and Stewart, who ordinarily evidenced respect for the previous opinions of majorities in cases where they dissented, followed the lead of the Chief Justice and of Justices Douglas and Fortas. In one case they dissented for the reasons set forth in Justice Harlan's dissenting opinion in Spevak v. Klein, 385 U.S. 511,[69] and in another for the reasons stated in Justice Harlan's dissent in the Spevak case and in Garrity v. New Jersey, 385 U.S. 493.[70] Justice White dissented in both cases for the reasons stated in his dissenting opinion in the Spevak and Garrity cases.

Dissent can be avoided as the French avoid it, by having the decision announced by the presiding judge, who "speaks for the whole Court, whether a decision be unanimous or by a bare majority. A dissent is unthinkable. The ethics of the *Magistrature* never permit it."[71] But our system leaves free the avenues of dissent, as does the English seriatim system, although both determine cases by a majority vote, with a tie vote constituting no vote.

Hence, while there is nothing to restrain judicial "wild horses"—Chief Justice Stone's characterization of his associates[72]—or to prevent the assertion "of the highly individualistic traits characteristic of liberalism"—a phrase culled from *Newsweek*[73]—mitigating measures can be tried. Thus, dissent need not be provoked by careless choice of words or by superfluity of language or argument in the opinion for the Court. The judge who writes for the Court must not roam the fields; on the contrary, he must weigh his words within an ambit of discretion so that he may secure agreement from his fellows. He must avoid confusion and uncertainty not only to obtain unanimity but also to command respect from the bar and the public for the decision of the Court. It is the dissenter who dares to be outspoken, at times to the point of recklessness. Judge Cardozo, in extolling form in judicial opinions, quoted a French novelist as saying, "There was only one example of the perfect style, and that was the Code Napoleon; for there alone everything was subordinated to the exact and complete expression of what was to be said."[74]

Similarly, the judge who would avoid dissent must hew close to substance

[68] *Ibid.*, 120.

[69] Zuckerman v. Greason, 386 U.S. 15 (1967).

[70] Kaye v. Co-ordinating Committee, 386 U.S. 17 (1967).

[71] William L. Burdick, *The Bench and Bar of Other Lands* (Brooklyn, N.Y., Metropolitan Law Book Co., 1939), 289.

[72] Alpheus Thomas Mason, *Harlan Fiske Stone: Pillar of the Law* (New York, Viking Press, 1956), 580.

[73] December 8, 1941, p. 23, quoted in Mason, *ibid.*

[74] Benjamin N. Cardozo, *Law and Literature* (New York, Harcourt, Brace & Co., 1931), 4.

and dare not go afield. A striking example is found in a 1959 case,[75] with Justice Brennan writing for six members of the Court and the Chief Justice and Justices Black and Douglas dissenting. The Court had considered discussion of an alternate theory advanced by the government as unnecessary while Justice Brennan considered its implications to be so disturbing as to require comment. This he supplied by following his opinion for the Court with a separate opinion rejecting the government's alternate contention. He justified this procedure by quoting from a prior case,[76] in which Justice Jackson delivered the opinion of the Court over the dissent of Justices Black and Douglas and followed it with a separate opinion in which he said, "The writer of the Court's opinion deems it necessary to complete the record by pointing out why, in writing by assignment for the Court, he assumed without discussion that the protections of the Fourteenth Amendment are available to a corporation. . . . It cannot be suggested that in cases where the author is the mere instrument of the Court he must forego expression of his own convictions. Mr. Justice Cardozo taught us how Justices may write for the Court and still reserve their own positions, though overruled," he added, citing a prior case.[77]

An example of an extreme concession to obtain a majority vote is found in Camara v. Municipal Court, decided in 1967. In order to give five votes to hold that a health inspector had to obtain a warrant before inspecting the premises of an objecting householder in the face of a prior 1959 decision to the contrary, Justice White watered down the constitutional requirement of showing probable cause before a warrant could issue to a point where Justice Clark termed the lessened requirements prostitution of the command of the Fourth Amendment.[78]

But when and where "angry passions" rage, a term employed by Justice Johnson,[79] the first of our noted dissenters, or where minds unaccustomed to the same habit of thinking cannot be reconciled,[80] there is little to be done to still dissent.

On the other hand, dissent may properly be justified. Justice Johnson defended his dissent in one case by unwillingness to have ambiguities ascribed to him in a matter of momentous importance.[81] Concurring in Cherokee Nation v. Georgia,[82] he said, "In pursuance of my practice in giving an opinion on all constitutional questions, I must present my views on this."

[75] Abbate v. United States, 359 U.S. 187 (1959).
[76] *Ibid.*, 196 n. 1, citing Wheeling Steel Corp. v. Glander, 337 U.S. 562, 576 (1949).
[77] Wheeling Steel Corp. v. Glander, 337 U.S. 562, 574, 576 (1949); Helvering v. Davis, 301 U.S. 619, 639 (1937).
[78] Camara v. Municipal Court, 387 U.S. 523 (1967).
[79] Martin v. Hunter's Lessee, 1 Wheat. 304, 377 (1816).
[80] *Ibid.*, 362.
[81] Marine Ins. Co. v. Young, 5 Cranch 187, 191 (1809).
[82] 5 Pet. 1, 20 (1831).

Justice Frankfurter dissented from a course to which his "purely personal attitude" led him since it represented "the thought and action of a lifetime," because he found his personal beliefs and predilections irrelevant to a determination of the controversy.[83]

Justice Story "ever thought" that upon constitutional questions it was his "duty to give a public expression" of his opinions, "when they differed from that of the Court,"[84] for he believed that "upon constitutional questions, the public have a right to know the opinion of every judge who dissents from the opinion of the Court and the reasons of his dissent."[85]

Justice Sutherland maintained that every judge had taken an individual oath and that he could not satisfy it "by an automatic acceptance of the views of others which have neither convinced, nor created a reasonable doubt in his mind."[86]

However, justification for dissent finds wider ground. The pages of history testify to the need and the value of dissent. "Dissent is essential to an effective judiciary in a democratic society," said Justice Frankfurter.[87] It "record(s) prophecy and shape(s) history," he said elsewhere.[88] It "sounds a warning note that legal doctrine must not be pressed too far," said Chief Justice Stone.[89] Justice Cardozo put it thus in his mellifluous Victorian prose, "The voice of the majority may be that of force triumphant, content with the plaudits of the hour and recking little of the morrow. The dissenter speaks of the future, and his voice is pitched to a key that will carry through the years."[90] And Chief Justice Hughes remarked, "A dissent in a court of last resort is an appeal to the brooding spirit of the law, to the intelligence of a future day, when a later decision may possibly correct the error into which the dissenting judge believes the court to have been betrayed."[91]

Of course, these encomia were largely tributes to the edifice erected in the first three decades of the twentieth century by Justice Holmes and buttressed by Justice Brandeis. While this monument pierced the obscuring mists of the moment and pointed to the path of the future, other lesser notables had erected milestones along the way. The elder Justice Harlan marked the way for the later Warren court when he dissented in 1896 with the statement that "our

[83] West Virginia State Board of Education v. Barnette, 319 U.S. 624, 646–47 (1943).

[84] Briscoe v. Bank of Kentucky, 11 Pet. 257, 329 (1837).

[85] *Ibid.*, 350.

[86] West Coast Hotel Co. v. Parrish, 300 U.S. 379, 401–402 (1937).

[87] Ferguson v. Moore-McCormack Lines, 352 U.S. 521, 528 (1957).

[88] Frankfurter, "Holmes and the Constitution," 41 *Harvard Law Review* 162.

[89] Mason, *Harlan Fiske Stone*, 591.

[90] Cardozo, *Law and Literature*, 36.

[91] Charles Evans Hughes, *The Supreme Court of the United States* (New York, Columbia University Press, 1928), 68.

Constitution is color-blind."[92] Justices White, Harlan, Jackson, and Brown prophesied the way of the future in the 1895 Income Tax cases,[93] with Justice White saying, "It (the decision) takes invested wealth and reads it into the Constitution as a favored and protected class of property, which cannot be taxed without apportionment, whilst it leaves the occupation of the minister, the doctor, the professor, the lawyer, the inventor, the author, the merchant, the mechanic, and all other forms of industry upon which the prosperity of a people must depend, subject to taxation without that condition." While some of these justices did not live to see their prophetic foresight vindicated by history, Justice Stone had to wait only three years to see the Court adopt his dissenting views in the first of the Jehovah's Witnesses cases.[94]

But in truth, each such dissent is a *rara avis*; the overwhelming majority of dissents might quite as well not have been written. Justice Holmes, sometimes described as the "Great Dissenter" (without too much justification numerically), deprecated unnecessary dissent. In his first dissent, the one that provoked his sponsor, President Theodore Roosevelt, to wrath, he said he thought it "useless and undesirable as a rule, to express dissent."[95] And later he said that he dissented from decisions which he regretted and as to which he felt deeply.[96]

Unnecessary dissent can be harmful. Justice White said, "The only purpose which an elaborate dissent can accomplish, if any, is to weaken the effect of the majority, and thus engender want to confidence in the conclusions of courts of last resort."[97] "There are times when an insistence upon a division is not in the interests of the best administration of justice," said Justice Jackson.[98]

Certainly, an excess of dissent justifies inquiry, especially when there have been major variances in the incidence of dissent over the years. In the following pages we consider the incidence of dissent from time to time. Here we might draw general conclusions from the undeniable fact that throughout the early years of the Republic, when so many cases of first impression were being presented to the Court and when partisan feelings ran high and infected the members of the Court, the maximum of dissent (during the Taney regime) was no more than 25 per cent of the decisions rendered, half of which were by a single justice; that during the Fuller and White terms, with the "Great Dissenter" on the bench, 1913 matched 1892 with less than 1 per cent of dissents;

92 Plessy v. Ferguson, 163 U.S. 537 (1896).
93 Pollock v. Farmers' Loan & Trust Co.; Hyde v. Continental Trust Co., 158 U.S. 601 (1895).
94 Minersville School Dist. v. Gobitis, 310 U.S. 586 (1940).
95 Northern Securities Co. v. United States, 193 U.S. 197, 400 (1904).
96 Oliver Wendell Holmes, *His Book Notices and Uncollected Letters and Papers* (New York, Central Book Co., 1936), 196.
97 Pollock v. Farmers Loan & Trust Co., 157 U.S. 429, 608 (1895).
98 United States v. Swift & Co., 318 U.S. 442, 446 (1943).

18

that during the era of Holmes, Brandeis, and Stone dissents never exceeded 21 per cent; while since 1942, dissent invariably is found in more than half the cases decided. During the controversial pre-1937 period, when the reactionary Four Horsemen (Sutherland, McReynolds, Butler, and Van Devanter) prevailed and gradually went down to defeat, dissent never exceeded one in five, while following the accession of Black and Douglas they gradually rose to today's level of more than three in five.

CHAPTER II

William Johnson:
Dissenter of the Marshall Court

THAT DISSENT WAS NOT UNKNOWN to the American judicial system prior to 1789 is attested by a 1786 case in the High Court of Errors and Appeals of Pennsylvania.[1] Chief Justice McKean wrote for the Court on an appeal from the Court of Admiralty, reversing that court, and awarding appellants some £3,795. Justices Atlee and Rush dissented. Respondent's motion for a rehearing was granted and in an opinion by Justice Shippen, the appellant's recovery was reduced to some £948. Justice Rush wrote in dissent, saying he would have affirmed the judgment below, adding, "However disposed to concur with my brethren in this cause, I have not been able to do it. Unanimity in courts of justice, though a very desirable object, ought never to be attained at the expense of sacrificing the judgment."[2]

During the 1792 term of the United States Supreme Court, a motion was denied because the Court was divided in opinion on the powers and duties of the Attorney General's office.[3] At the 1793 term of the high court, in Georgia v. Brailsford,[4] Justice Iredell led off with the statement: "It is my misfortune to dissent from the opinion entertained by the rest of the court upon the present occasion; but I am bound to decide, according to the dictates of my own judgments." Justice Blair followed, saying: "My sentiments have coincided, till this moment, with the sentiments entertained by the majority of the court; but a doubt has just occurred, which I think it my duty to declare."[5] Finally, Chief Justice Jay wrote for "all the court, except the judges who have just delivered their sentiments."[6]

These dissents were recorded while the Court was at times following the prevailing English practice of delivering opinions seriatim. During the August, 1792, term, in considering the adoption of rules, the Court considered "the

1 Purviance v. Angus, 1 Dallas 180 (1786).
2 *Ibid.*, 494.
3 Hayburn's Case, 2 Dallas 409 (1792).
4 2 Dallas 415 (1793).
5 *Ibid.*, 417–18.
6 *Ibid.*, 418.

practice of the courts of King's Bench and Chancery in England, as affording outlines for the practice of this court"; and added "that they will, from time to time, make such alterations therein, as circumstances may render necessary."[7]

In passing upon an application for an injunction, in a suit by Georgia against two citizens of South Carolina to stay payment of a debt until an adjudication could be had respecting its ownership, "The judges delivered their opinions seriatim."[8] And in a most important case holding that a citizen of one sovereign state could sue another sovereign state,[9] a decision overruled by a prompt proposal to amend the Constitution followed by the passage of the Eleventh Amendment in 1798,[10] it was noted that the judges "delivered their opinion seriatim."[11]

On one occasion after "the judges delivered their opinions seriatim, . . ."[12] Justice Chase complained, "The judges agreeing unanimously in their opinion, I presumed that the sense of the court would have been delivered by the president; and therefore, I have not prepared a formal argument on the occasion."[13]

Incidentally, Charles Warren, the leading Supreme Court historian, contended, on the basis of this statement by Chase, that Marshall was not the initiator of the practice of having the opinions of the Court delivered by the Chief Justice as charged by Jefferson in the 1820's.[14] Nevertheless, it is undeniable that Marshall appreciated that seriatim opinions bred dissent and uncertainty and that unity of opinion was essential if the Court, lacking other resource, was to corral and gain strength from popular support. It is undeniable that in the first case in which he participated and which he decided, following his accession to the bench,[15] Marshall undertook to put the English seriatim practice, which had theretofore been followed by the Court, at rest, by writing for the Court.

Of forty-seven cases found in the first two volumes of Cranch's reports (1801–1805), following Marshall's appointment, the Chief Justice wrote for the Court in twenty-eight cases; he did not participate in two, the Court acted or spoke per curiam in sixteen, and one was left for future reargument. During this four-year period there were no dissents, and only one concurring opinion by Justice Chase.[16] There was also a separate opinion by Justice Washington

---

[7] Rule, 2 Dallas 411 (1792).

[8] Georgia v. Brailsford, 2 Dallas 402, 405 (1792).

[9] Chisholm v. Georgia, 2 Dallas 419 (1793).

[10] Hollingsworth v. Virginia, 3 Dallas 378 (1798).

[11] Chisholm v. Georgia, 2 Dallas 419, 429 (1793).

[12] Bas v. Tingy, 4 Dallas 37 (1800).

[13] *Ibid.*, 43.

[14] Charles Warren, *The Supreme Court in United States History* (3 vols., Boston, Little, Brown & Co., 1922), II, 114.

[15] Talbot v. Seeman, 1 Cranch 1 (1801).

[16] Head & Amory v. Providence Ins. Co., 2 Cranch 127, 169 (1804).

(who did not participate in the decision of the case since he evidently had participated in the circuit court decision which the Court was reversing) in explanation of the lower court decision. He said:

> Although I take no part in the decision of this cause, I feel myself justified by the importance of the question in declaring the reasons which induced the Circuit Court of Pennsylvania to pronounce the opinion which is to be re-examined here.
>
> In any instance where I am so unfortunate as to differ with this Court, I cannot fail to doubt the correctness of my own opinion. But if I cannot feel convinced of the error, I owe it in some measure to myself . . . to show at least that the opinion was not hastily or inconsiderately given.[17]

Marshall continued his practice of writing for the Court to a point where he rendered the Court's opinion in almost half of the nearly one thousand decisions it handed down during his regime. Thus he sought not only to avoid dissent but also, by the trend of his argument and choice of his language, to foreclose the expression of differences with the reasoning he employed to lead to an agreed-upon result, a syndrome of concurring opinions.

In a letter signed with a nom de plume and published by a Federalist newspaper, the *Union of Philadelphia*, Marshall explained and defended his practice by saying: "The course of every tribunal must necessarily be, that the opinion which is to be delivered as the opinion of the court, is previously submitted to the consideration of all the judges; and, if any part of the reasoning be disapproved, it must be so modified as to receive the approbation of all, before it can be delivered as the opinion of all."[18] Marshall insisted that he did not control the Court, that the other judges were free to dissent if they chose, and he cited the dissents in the case of the Nereide.[19] Beveridge said of Marshall's alleged control: "His control of the court was made so easy for the Justices that they never resented it; often, perhaps, they did not realize it."[20]

Justice William Johnson's analysis of the "real cause" was disclosed in a letter to Jefferson: "Cushing was incompetent, Chase could not be got to think or write—Paterson was a slow man and willingly declined the Trouble, and the other two (Marshall and Washington) are commonly estimated as one Judge."[21]

---

[17] United States v. Fisher, 2 Cranch 358, 397–98 (1804).

[18] Albert J. Beveridge, *John Marshall* (4 vols., Boston and New York, Houghton Mifflin Co., 1919), IV, 320.

[19] 9 Cranch 388 (1815).

[20] Beveridge, *John Marshall*, IV, 89.

[21] Johnson to Jefferson, December 10, 1822, from *Jefferson Papers*, Library of Congress, quoted in Donald G. Morgan, "Mr. Justice William Johnson and the Constitution," 57 *Harvard Law Review* 328, 334 n.23.

Jefferson's estimate appeared in a letter to President Madison, on the occasion of the latter's selection of a replacement on the bench: "It will be difficult to find a character of firmness enough to preserve his independence on the same bench with Marshall."[22] However, when Marshall did not participate, his confreres frequently resorted to the seriatim practice, thus breaking the silence the Chief Justice sought to impose upon them.

In Johnson's last-cited letter to Jefferson, he wrote: "While I was on our State-bench I was accustomed to delivering seriatim Opinions in our Appellate Court, and was not a little surprised to find our Chief Justice in the Supreme Court delivering all the opinions in Cases in which he sat . . . I remonstrated in vain; the Answer was he is willing to take the trouble and it is a Mark of Respect to him."[23]

It might be noted that as late as 1939 Justice Frankfurter characterized the English seriatim practice, which still prevails, as a "healthy" one, although he felt that the volume of business before the Court no longer permitted it to subscribe to that practice.[24]

The practice of stating views in constitutional cases has long been justified in our courts, as witness Judge Story's statement, those of Justices McLean and Woodbury,[25] and that of Justice Frankfurter in recent years[26] justifying the seven opinions, six concurring and one dissenting, in denying the President's authority to take over the steel mills to avoid a threatened strike. Even as far back as 1847, the seriatim practice was in effect indulged in when differences of opinion occasioned six opinions in the License Cases and eight opinions aggregating 250 pages in the Passenger Cases. Of course, within recent years we are no longer shocked by a multiplicity of opinions in a single case, as, for example, seven opinions stating varying views in a recent obscenity case.[27]

Jefferson not only was an exponent of the English seriatim practice but also was convinced that Marshall's ability to have the Court avoid it resulted in many of the important decisions with which he differed. In a letter to Johnson, Jefferson maintained that the public was entitled to a statement of each justice's convictions in leading cases. He referred to the practice in England, where the courts, except under Lord Mansfield, had resorted to this practice. He contended that the Marshall practice shielded "the lazy, the modest and the incompetent" and avoided the judge's individual responsibility.[28] He com-

[22] Jefferson to Madison, May 25, 1810, in Paul Leicester Ford, ed., *Writings of Thomas Jefferson* (10 vols., New York, G. P. Putnam's Sons, 1892 *et seq.*), IX, 274–76.

[23] Johnson to Jefferson, 57 *Harvard Law Review* 334 n.21.

[24] Graves v. New York, 306 U.S. 466, 487 (1939).

[25] West River Bridge v. Dix, 6 How. 507, 536, 539 (1848).

[26] Graves v. New York, 306 U.S. 466, 487 (1939).

[27] Memoirs v. Massachusetts, 383 U.S. 413 (1966).

[28] October 27, 1822, Ford, ed., *Writings of Thomas Jefferson*, X, 223.

plained that "an opinion is huddled up in conclave, perhaps by a majority of one, delivered as if unanimous, and with the silent acquiescence of lazy or timid associates, by a crafty chief judge."[29]

Actuated also by his dislike for Marshall, Jefferson prodded Johnson, whom he had appointed to the bench at the tender age of thirty-two, to subscribe to the English practice. He continued to press Johnson[30] and induced Madison, who doubted the practice could be changed, to share his views.[31] Finally Johnson wrote agreeing "to adopt your suggestion on all subjects of general interest; particularly Constitutional questions."[32]

Marshall not only deprecated dissent but personally went to great lengths to avoid it. In an early case he said: "I have been convinced that I was mistaken, and I have receded from this first opinion. I acquiesce in that of my brethren."[33]

On two occasions, in extreme situations, the Chief Justice dissented. In the Dandridge case he said: "I should now, as is my custom, when I have the misfortune to differ from this Court, acquiesce silently in its opinion, did I not believe that the judge of the Circuit Court of Virginia gave general surprise to the profession and was generally condemned."[34] So he came to his support with a dissent from the overruling decision of the Court and continued: "I have stated the view which was taken by the Circuit Court of this case. I have only to add, that the law is now settled otherwise, perhaps to the advancement of public convenience."

In the second case the justices delivered their opinions seriatim: first Washington; then Johnson, followed by Thompson; then Trimble, followed by Marshall, who stated the case for the minority, consisting of himself, Story, and Duvall; and finally by Johnson, who had been "instructed by the majority of the court finally to dispose of this cause."[35] However, the other three members of the majority dissented from Johnson's last opinion, and the Chief Justice and Justices Duvall and Story assented to the judgment of affirmance. This was the first time Marshall had dissented on a constitutional question. The lower court was affirmed by a four-to-three vote, the various opinions docu-

---

[29] Letter to Thomas Ritchie, December 25, 1820, *ibid.,* 169, 171; letter to James Pleasants, December 26, 1821, *ibid.,* 197, 199.

[30] Letter to Johnson, March 4, 1823, *ibid.,* 246; letter to Johnson, June 12, 1823, Andrew A. Lipscomb, ed., *The Writings of Thomas Jefferson* (20 vols., Washington, D.C., The Thomas Jefferson Memorial Association), XV, 422, 451.

[31] Letter to Jefferson, January 15, 1823, William Cabell Rives, ed., *Letters and Other Writings of James Madison* (4 vols., Philadelphia, J. B. Lippincott & Co., 1865), III, 292.

[32] Johnson to Jefferson, April 11, 1823, quoted in Morgan, "Mr. Justice William Johnson and the Constitution," 57 *Harvard Law Review* 334 n.27.

[33] Little v. Barreme, 2 Cranch 170, 179 (1804).

[34] Bank of United States v. Dandridge, 12 Wheat. 64, 90 (1827).

[35] Ogden v. Saunders, 12 Wheat. 213, 358 (1827).

menting the conclusion that seriatim opinions breed confusion and uncertainty.

That, to avoid dissent and to obtain acquiescence in his opinions for the Court, Marshall "so modified his views as to receive the approbation of all" there can be no doubt. Indeed, Justice Johnson said that "in some cases Marshall wrote for the Court even when the opinion was contrary to his own Judgment and Vote."[36] Professor Crosskey, calling attention to the fact that "nearly all of Marshall's constitutional opinions were delivered for a Court with a hand-picked Jeffersonian majority upon it," expressed doubt that "everything in these opinions represents Marshall's own views and hence Federalist views."[37] While it is true that Justices Thompson, McLean, and Baldwin tended to be antipathetic to Marshall's constitutional dogma, Story thought as Marshall did, and Johnson and Duvall's nationalism was paramount to their republicanism. So that when nationalism and republicanism clashed, the Chief Justice started with a majority of the votes.

Johnson chafed under Marshall's restrictions and Jefferson's criticism. Writing to Jefferson, he said:

Some Case soon occurred in which I differed from my Brethren, and I felt it a thing of Course to deliver my Opinion. But, during the rest of the Session I heard nothing but Lectures on the Indecency of Judges cutting at each other, and the Loss of Reputation which the Virginia appellate court had sustained by pursuing such a Course. At length I found that I must either submit to Circumstances or become such a Cypher in our Consultations as to effect no good at all. I therefore bent to the Current, and persevered until I got them to adopt the Course they now pursue, which is to appoint some one to deliver the Opinion of the Majority, but to leave it to the rest of the Judges to record their Opinions or not ad libitum.[38]

Considering the courteous manner of the day, one wonders what the Chief Justice might have said when the second Justice Harlan dissented thus:

This run-of-the-mill negligence case presents no new question of law or departure from established legal principles. The question is whether there was enough evidence to take the case to the jury.

A total of 12 New York judges . . . have held that the evidence was not sufficient to warrant submission of the case to the jury.

To bring such a case here for review by nine more Justices seems to me a

[36] Johnson to Jefferson, quoted in Morgan, "Mr. Justice William Johnson and the Constitution," 57 *Harvard Law Review* 334 n.21.

[37] Allison Dunham and Philip B. Kurland, eds., *Mr. Justice* (Chicago, The University of Chicago Press, 1956), 20–21.

[38] Johnson to Jefferson, quoted in Morgan, "Mr. Justice William Johnson and the Constitution," 57 *Harvard Law Review* 334 n.21.

most futile expenditure of judicial time. Having reflected on the oral argument, briefs, and record, I conclude that the only terms on which this reversal can be justified is that anything a jury says goes.[39]

Or one wonders what Marshall might have said when Justice Clark opened his dissent in a case involving Chinese possession of narcotics with the statement that "the Court has made a Chinese puzzle out of this case."[40]

Justice William Johnson, who became a pioneer and the principal dissenter of the Marshall court, was born in South Carolina in 1771. He was graduated from the College of New Jersey (now Princeton), was elected to the South Carolina House of Representatives in 1794 at the age of twenty-three, and became a judge of the Court of Common Pleas five years later.[41] He served on the Supreme Court bench from 1804, when Jefferson appointed him as the first Jeffersonian Republican on the Court, until his death in 1834.

Johnson proved to be able and independent—independent of Marshall as almost half of the seventy dissents cast and the sixty concurring opinions written during the Marshall regime attested, and independent of Jefferson when Johnson's nationalism and Jefferson's republicanism clashed, as Johnson's failure to dissent in the Marshall landmark cases attested. Despite the fact that he wrote separately only three times from 1819 to 1822,[42] Johnson proved to be the most voluble of the judges on the Marshall court—excepting, of course, Marshall; in one-third of his opinions he either dissented or concurred separately.[43]

The Marshall court's first dissent came from Justice William Paterson in 1805, challenging an opinion written by the Chief Justice.[44] Johnson's first opinion was one of concurrence,[45] and it was not until 1808, three years later, that he read his first dissent in a case where a prize court sitting in Santo Domingo had ordered a cargo of coffee sold after being captured by a French privateer.[46] When the coffee arrived in Charleston, South Carolina, it was libeled by the original owner and the question arose whether the condemnation by the Santo Domingo prize court was effective in the United States. Marshall, in an opinion for the majority, said "yes"; Johnson, dissenting, said "no." But that had its limitations, as demonstrated in the Burr case. On occasion, Johnson's dissents could be ascribed to his republicanism, or perhaps more properly, to his loyalty to Jefferson.

The effort of President Jefferson to fasten upon Aaron Burr a charge of

[39] Basham v. Pennsylvania R.R., 372 U.S. 699, 701 (1963).
[40] Wong Sun v. United States, 371 U.S. 471, 498 (1963).
[41] Morgan, "Mr. Justice William Johnson and the Constitution," 57 *Harvard Law Review* 329.
[42] *Ibid.*, 332.
[43] *Ibid.*, 329.
[44] Simms & Wise v. Slacum, 3 Cranch 300 (1806).
[45] Huidekoper's Lessee v. Douglass, 3 Cranch 1 (1805).
[46] Rose v. Himely, 4 Cranch 241 (1808).

treason found its prologue when General James Wilkinson, army commander at New Orleans, caused the arrest of Samuel Swartwout and Erick Bollman, agents of Burr, charged with treason. Wilkinson had been a close associate of Burr, whose influence had had him appointed governor of Upper Louisiana. Now Wilkinson undertook to aid Jefferson in pinning a badge of treason on Burr. The arrest of Swartwout and Bollman was the first step in the campaign. Having arrested them, Wilkinson had them put on a warship for delivery to Jefferson at Washington.

Once they were in Washington and confined to a military prison, an application was made to the federal court of the District of Columbia for a writ of habeas corpus. With the active aid of Jefferson, the United States Attorney General and the federal District Attorney sought to have the defendants held. Judge William Cranch, a Federalist, voted to discharge them; his associates, two Republicans, overruled him.

Now application was made to Chief Justice Marshall for a writ. To thwart the high court, the Jeffersonians in Congress introduced a bill to suspend the privilege of the writ in cases of treason for a period of three months. It was passed by the Senate, but the House rejected it. Thereupon the Supreme Court held that it had jurisdiction to issue a writ, and Republican Justice Johnson dissented, with the concurrence of Justice Chase.[47] Johnson said that he had "submitted in silent deference to the decision of my brethren" in the case of Burford, decided in 1806,[48] which, Johnson admitted, "was . . . strictly parallel to the present."[49] However, he said, "The gentleman who argued that cause confined himself strictly to those considerations which ought alone to influence the decisions of this court. No popular observations on the necessity of protecting the citizen from executive oppression, no animated address calculated to enlist the passions or prejudices of an audience . . . imposed on me the necessity of vindicating my opinion."[50] (It is noteworthy that counsel for the petitioners, referring to the Burford case, had said flatly that it "was wholly unconnected with political considerations, or party feelings,"[51] thus throwing the gage at Johnson's feet.)

Following the assertion of jurisdiction, Marshall defined treason *in extenso,* as was his wont, and said that he would not rely on precedent, since "a case that cannot be tested by principle is not law."[52] He finally held that in "the opinion of a majority of the court . . . in the case of Samuel Swartwout there is not sufficient evidence of his levying war against the United States to justify

---

[47] *Ex parte* Bollman, 4 Cranch 75 (1807).
[48] *Ibid.,* 107.
[49] *Ibid.,* 104.
[50] *Ibid.,* 107.
[51] *Ibid.,* 88.
[52] *Ibid.,* 104.

his commitment on the charge of treason" and that "against Erick Bollman there is still less testimony." He directed their discharge and invited the authorities to prosecute them where the offense charged was committed.[53]

The aftermath was the apprehension of Burr, his trial before Marshall, and his ultimate acquittal, despite the active intervention and participation of Jefferson in the prosecution.

It is interesting to note that the prototype of the reasons that have moved the Warren court to reverse convictions in communities inflamed by publicity prejudicing defendants is to be found in the summation of Benjamin Botts, a young, able, and courageous lawyer representing Burr in his trial before Marshall.

Botts charged that

> "the moving force back of the prosecution [was] the rescue of the prestige of Jefferson's administration . . . . It has not only been said here but published in all the newspapers throughout the United States, that if Aaron Burr should be acquitted it will be the severest satire on the government; and that the people are called upon to support the government by the conviction of Colonel Burr; . . . even jurymen have been taught by the common example to insult him."
>
> No lie was too contemptible to be published about him. . . . "every man who dares to look at the accused with a smile or present him the hand of friendship" is "denounced as a traitor."
>
> [Botts] dwelt on the devices resorted to for inflaming the people against Burr, and after they had been aroused, the demand that public sentiment be heeded and the accused convicted.[54]

In contradiction to his own stance in the previous Burford case, Johnson gave Jefferson token support in dissenting from Marshall's holding that the Court had jurisdiction to issue a writ in the Bollman case, but he stood with Marshall in finding no evidence of treason against Swartwout and Bollman. And in the next clash with his sponsor, he left no doubt concerning his judicial independence.

The Embargo Act of 1808 had required collectors of customs to detain ships which they suspected of carrying cargo to United States ports with intent to evade the Act. Jefferson sought to strengthen the Act by instructing collectors to detain all vessels, thus attempting to supersede any exercise of a collector's discretion. The presidential authority to do this was challenged by a shipowner who asked Justice Johnson, sitting in circuit, for a writ of mandamus directed to the collector at Charleston. Johnson granted the writ, holding that the President had no authority to direct the detention of the vessel, saying: "The of-

---

[53] *Ibid.*, 135–36.
[54] Beveridge, *John Marshall*, III, 499–500.

ficers of our Government, from the highest to the lowest, are equally subjected to legal restraint."[55]

Here Johnson was moved by two favored principles—that of legislative superiority and that of nationalism—as he upheld congressional power over that of the executive and struck down a state statute as violative of the superior national jurisdiction over commerce.

Jefferson, construing Johnson's decision as a personal attack upon him, had the Attorney General issue an opinion challenging it, and this opinion, released to the press, caused Johnson to take the equally unusual step of replying in kind.[56] Later Johnson could find justification in the holding of the Court, in which he participated, that even the bestowal of power by Congress upon the President to employ military and naval forces to enforce a seizure, when necessary, would not empower him to issue an order to a civil officer to seize a ship.[57]

Johnson's republicanism again asserted itself in dissent in the notorious case involving the Yazoo land speculations,[58] a case where constitutionality served expediency, as so often happens. Here Marshall's court had occasion to pass on the validity of an annulling act adopted by a Georgia legislature after a previous legislature had authorized the sale by the state of Georgia's interest in some thirty-five million acres of land (which ultimately became the states of Alabama and Mississippi). The sale price was $500,000, something less than one and a half cents an acre. The Georgia legislature had been led to authorize the sale by flagrant corruption of some of the members of the legislature and by coercion and duress exercised upon others. The Governor had reluctantly signed the authorization bill on January 7, 1805. The transaction was labeled "Yazoo," in keeping with that of a highly questionable sale of lands by Georgia some years before.

There were some justifications for the sale, among others, the desperate financial need of the state and the fact that the state's title was subject to those of the occupying Indians—Creeks, Choctaws, and Cherokees. These titles could not be extinguished by the state, since only the national government had the power of dealing with the Indian tribes.

However, the passage of the authorizing bill by the legislature had been preceded by the completion in February, 1804, by Eli Whitney, of a model of his cotton gin, which he intended to "lodge at Philadelphia in the Secretary of State's office, when he takes out his patent."[59] By March, 1804, Whitney had

---

[55] Gilchrist v. Collector, 10 Fed. Cas. 355, #5420.

[56] Warren, *The Supreme Court in United States History*, I, 329–30.

[57] Gelston v. Hoyt, 3 Wheat. 246 (1818).

[58] Fletcher v. Peck, 6 Cranch 87 (1810).

[59] Jeanette Mirsky and Allan Nevins, *The World of Eli Whitney* (New York, The Macmillan Company, 1952), 78.

received his patent,[60] and Phineas Miller, who became his partner in the venture, advertised in the *Gazette* of the state of Georgia on March 6, 1804, that he would undertake "to gin" cotton "in a manner equal to picking by hand" and that ginning machines "will actually be erected in different parts of the country."[61] (Miller, it might be remarked, participated heavily in the Yazoo speculation.)

By the time the legislature acted to authorize the Yazoo land sales, knowledge of the cotton gin and its efficiency was widespread throughout Georgia, and by the spring of 1795 unscrupulous adventurers were duplicating it. Consequently, its use by the planters had become common, and cotton land values increased. In particular the value of the land affected by the Yazoo speculation and the shares of the purchasing corporations mounted appreciably.[62] This rise in speculative values, accompanied by dissemination of knowledge of the corruption that attended the action of the Georgia legislature, generated a tide of state-wide indignation.[63] As a result, most of those who sought election to the succeeding legislature had pledged that they would undertake to undo the fraudulently induced transaction, and after the election the legislature promptly declared the act of the previous legislature null and void.[64]

Meanwhile, those who had acquired the shares originally—the insiders— were "hedging their bets" by reselling land and shares to those who, because the contrary could not be proved, could claim to be "innocent purchasers for value."[65] Most of these purchasers were New Englanders and other northerners. The average resale price was at the rate of fourteen cents an acre,[66] thus showing a rise in speculative value approximating 1,000 per cent.

When the Georgia legislature undertook to void the sales, the northern investors, fearful of losing their investments, organized to protect their interests. An opinion was obtained from Alexander Hamilton, who declared the repudiation by the subsequent legislature void since it impaired the obligation of contract protected by the Constitution.[67]

After much maneuvering, a friendly suit was brought in the Massachusetts Federal Court by John Peck, who claimed to have sold 15,000 acres of his Georgia holdings to Robert Fletcher for the unpaid sum of three thousand dollars, for which Peck sought judgment. Ultimately the suit reached the Supreme Court, and Joseph Story, soon to be appointed one of its justices,

---

[60] *Ibid.,* 79.
[61] *Ibid.,* 95–96.
[62] Beveridge, *John Marshall,* III, 555–56.
[63] *Ibid.,* 559.
[64] *Ibid.,* 563.
[65] *Ibid.,* 566.
[66] *Ibid.,* 567.
[67] *Ibid.,* 569.

argued, on behalf of Peck, that the repudiation was invalid. Finally, Marshall wrote an opinion so holding, on the constitutional ground originally advanced by Hamilton; thus the Court, for the first time, declared a state act unconstitutional.

In the course of his opinion Marshall held that the rights of the Indian tribes did not prevent the state from claiming the fee of the land. Johnson, while affirming the main and vital point in the case, i.e., the invalidity of the legislative repudiation, dissented from Marshall's holding respecting the Indian titles. In addition he said: "I have been very unwilling to proceed to the decision of this cause at all. It appears to me to bear strong evidence, upon the face of it, of being a mere feigned case. It is our duty to decide on the rights, but not on the speculations of parties."[68]

However, Jefferson and Madison found Marshall's decision satisfactory,[69] so Judge Johnson's republicanism showed, when instead of voting to dismiss the suit as having been improperly brought, he said: "My confidence, however, in the respectable gentlemen who have been engaged for the parties, has induced me to abandon my scruples, in the belief that they would never consent to impose a mere feigned case upon this court."[70]

The opinion of Marshall aided the claimants in finally receiving an award of five million dollars appropriated by Congress to reimburse the Yazoo speculators, a consequence of doubtful justification, at least concerning many of the not-so-innocent purchasers.

In the case of the Nereide,[71] in which Story cast a rare dissent from a Marshall opinion, the question was whether the Court should reverse the circuit court's declaration of a forfeiture of a cargo owned by a neutral carried in a belligerent vessel or find that the facts justified forfeiture as an exception to the general rule. Marshall was able to induce only two associates to join in his opinion invoking the general rule; Justice Story, dissenting, commanded two votes, and the responsibility of decision lay with Johnson, who wrote concurring in the result advocated by Marshall. Johnson's concurrence gave him another opportunity to implement his favorite theory of the strength of legislative power and to distinguish it from the judicial power. He said: "To the legislative power alone it must belong to determine when the violence of other nations is to be met by violence; to the judiciary to administer law and justice as it is, not as it is made to be by the folly or caprice of other nations."[72] (It could be noted that he might have equally distinguished the executive and the

[68] Fletcher v. Peck, 6 Cranch 87, 147 (1810).
[69] Beveridge, *John Marshall*, III, 592–93.
[70] Fletcher v. Peck, 6 Cranch 87, 148 (1810).
[71] 9 Cranch 388 (1815).
[72] *Ibid.*, 432.

legislative powers in this day of travail.) Later, attesting judicial recognition of precedent, the same basic question resulted in affirmation of the general rule without dissent. Again Johnson concurred.[73]

A minor dissent by Johnson to an opinion for the Court, Marshall and Washington not participating, was followed by a controversy between the Supreme Court and the Virginia Court of Appeals, which ended in a declaration of supremacy of the Supreme Court over the state courts. The case involved a controversy between a land syndicate, in which the Chief Justice and his brother were interested, and one David Hunter, concerning title to certain waste and unappropriated land in the northern neck of Virginia, which had been granted to Lord Fairfax by royal charters. The Marshall land syndicate had purchased the land from the heir of Lord Fairfax. However, five years previously, the state of Virginia had granted the property to David Hunter, who sued Fairfax's devisee for the recovery of the land. The district court decided against Hunter, who appealed to the court of appeals. Sixteen years after the lower court decision, the court of appeals reversed it. Thereupon the Fairfax devisee appealed to the United States Supreme Court. Because of the family interest Marshall declined to sit. The majority of the Court, in an opinion by Justice Story, reversed the Virginia court. Justice Johnson dissented.[74]

The judges of the Virginia Court of Appeals, including Judge Roane, a bitter enemy of Marshall who had expected to replace him had the Chase impeachment succeeded, refused to obey the mandate of Marshall's court. They denied the Court's power to re-examine the decision of the state court, whereupon the Marshall land interests took the case back to the Supreme Court. Again without Marshall's participation, the Court overruled the Virginia court. An opinion by Justice Story asserted the supremacy of the national court.[75]

Justice Story avoided a clash with the Virginia court by saying: "We have not thought it incumbent on us to give any opinion upon the question, whether this court has authority to issue a writ of mandamus to the Court of Appeals to enforce the former judgments, as we do not think it necessarily involved in the decision of this cause."[76] Instead, the high court sent its mandate to the district court which had rendered the opinion the Supreme Court was now affirming.

The Republicans had made the issue between the courts a *cause célèbre*, and they maligned Story, a Republican, for his apostasy. With the "out" supplied by Story, Johnson, a nationalist and believer in the Marshall credo of supremacy of the Court, satisfied his republicanism by an ambivalent opinion,

[73] The Atlanta, 3 Wheat. 409 (1818).
[74] Fairfax's Devisee v. Hunter's Lessee, 7 Cranch 603 (1813).
[75] Martin v. Hunter's Lessee, 1 Wheat. 304 (1816).
[76] *Ibid.*, 362.

fixing on the Court's failure to assert its right to "issue compulsory process to the state courts,"[77] while declaiming the supremacy of the national court. In fact, he really wrote a concurring opinion on the vital issue.

It is noteworthy, and a tribute to Marshall, that the decisions which form the cornerstone of national judicial supremacy lacked dissent with one exception, a dissent noted without opinion by the inconsequential Justice Duvall. Of these decisions, Beveridge said:

> On March 2, 1824, Marshall delivered that opinion which has done more to knit the American people into an indivisible nation than any other one force in our history, excepting only war. In Marbury v. Madison[78] he established that fundamental principle of liberty that a permanent written Constitution controls a temporary Congress; . . . in the Dartmouth College case,[79] he asserted the sanctity of good faith; in McCulloch v. Maryland[80] and Cohens v. Virginia[81] he made the Government of the American people a living thing; but in Gibbons v. Ogden,[82] he welded that people into a unit by the force of their mutual interest.[83]

In the first of these decisions, he coined the cogent phrase, "A law repugnant to the Constitution is void."[84] In the second is found the oft-repeated definition: "A corporation is an artificial being, invisible, intangible, and existing only in contemplation of law . . . . It possesses only those properties which the charter of its creation confers upon it . . . . Among the most important are immortality, and . . . individuality."[85] In the third he said, "It is a Constitution we are expounding,"[86] and he added that it was one "intended to endure for ages to come, and consequently, to be adapted to the various crises of human affairs,"[87] with the dicta, "Let the end be legitimate . . . and all the means which are appropriate which are not prohibited . . . are constitutional."[88] In the fourth he waxed eloquent in saying: "A constitution is framed for ages to come and is designed to approach it. Its course cannot always be tranquil. It is exposed to storms and tempests, and its framers must be unwise statesmen indeed,

[77] *Ibid.*

[78] 1 Cranch 137 (1803). Judicial supremacy was asserted earlier in the case of Bayard & Wife v. Singleton, 1 Martin (North Carolina) 42 (1797), in which the Carolina court found a legislative act void as contravening the Constitution.

[79] 4 Wheat. 518 (1819).

[80] 4 Wheat. 316 (1819).

[81] 6 Wheat. 264 (1821).

[82] 9 Wheat. 1 (1824).

[83] Beveridge, *John Marshall*, IV, 429–30.

[84] Marbury v. Madison, 1 Cranch 137, 180 (1803).

[85] Dartmouth College v. Woodward, 4 Wheat. 518, 636 (1819).

[86] McCulloch v. Maryland, 4 Wheat. 316, 407 (1819).

[87] *Ibid.*, 415.

[88] *Ibid.*, 421.

if they have not provided it . . . with the means of self-preservation from the perils it may be destined to encounter."[89] And in the fifth he defined commerce as traffic and added, "But it is something more; it is intercourse."[90]

Johnson's failure to dissent in these landmark cases was the subject of complaint by Jefferson,[91] which, however, did not dilute Johnson's nationalism.

Indeed, while Marshall, in Gibbons v. Ogden, found it unnecessary to hold the federal commerce power exclusive, since he found Congress had acted, Johnson, concurring, went all the way in declaring the congressional power exclusive, whether or not Congress had acted. With this holding the Court later agreed, in a case which also announced the "original package" doctrine, i.e., that a state could not tax imported goods at least until the goods were sold in their original packages.[92]

In connection with the decision in McCulloch v. Maryland, Charles Warren points out that the decision might have been anticipated ten years before with cogent consequences had Johnson not denied jurisdiction (with affirmation by the Marshall court) in a suit brought by the Bank of United States to determine the right of Georgia to tax the bank.[93] Jurisdiction was denied by reason of the then prevailing rule that in a suit in which a corporation was a party the diversity of residence rule looked to the residence of stockholders of the corporation instead of to its place of incorporation, as was later held.[94]

Following the McCulloch decision, Ohio government officials decided to disregard it and to enforce collection of taxes previously imposed by the Ohio legislature from the Bank of United States. The Bank retaliated by obtaining a temporary injunction from the federal court; Osborn, the state auditor, ignored the injunction and caused his assistant, John L. Harper, to seize some $120,000 of the Bank's funds. The Bank started suit against the state officials and obtained judgment and, for his failure to pay, caused the state treasurer to be committed for contempt.

Ultimately the case was submitted to the Supreme Court, which, as might have been expected, followed the McCulloch decision. The Chief Justice, writing for the Court, held that the language of the act incorporating the Bank entitled it to bring the action and distinguished that language from that of the act incorporating the former bank involved in the previous Deveaux action.[95] Justice Johnson, dissenting, took issue with that conclusion and

---

[89] Cohens v. Virginia, 6 Wheat. 264, 387 (1821).

[90] Gibbons v. Ogden, 9 Wheat. 1, 189 (1824).

[91] Morgan, "Mr. Justice William Johnson and the Constitution," 57 *Harvard Law Review* 333.

[92] Brown v. Maryland, 12 Wheat. 419 (1827).

[93] Bank of United States v. Deveaux, 5 Cranch 61 (1809); Hope Ins. Co. v. Boardman, 5 Cranch 57 (1809).

[94] E.g., Muller v. Dows, 4 Otto 444 (1877).

[95] Osborn v. Bank of United States, 9 Wheat. 738, 817 (1824).

relied on the Deveaux decision.[96] He said he could not persuade himself "that the constitution sanctions the vesting of the right of action in this bank, in cases in which the privilege is exclusively personal."[97] He deprecated the rash of state bank creations which had "inundated the country with a new description of bills of credit, against which it was obvious that the provisions of the constitution opposed no adequate inhibition."[98]

Hence, when the Court was called upon to determine the validity of bills of credit issued by a loan office in the state of Missouri established pursuant to a legislative act, Johnson, joined by Justices Thompson and McLean, dissented from an opinion delivered by the Chief Justice, holding the act void under Article 1, Section 10, 1 of the federal Constitution declaring that "no State shall emit bills of credit."[99] Johnson maintained that the certificates represented a borrowing and were not bills of credit as the term was understood at the time of the adoption of the Constitution.[100]

At the close of the 1834 term Chief Justice Marshall announced that, for want of the concurrence of a majority, Briscoe v. Commonwealth Bank of Kentucky, which involved the question of the constitutionality of certificates of indebtedness issued by the bank, which was wholly owned by the state, as well as two other cases,[101] would be deferred until the following term. Marshall said, "The practice of this Court is not (except in cases of absolute necessity) to deliver any judgment in cases where constitutional questions are involved unless four judges concur in opinion, thus making the decision that of a majority of the whole Court."[102]

Then on February 12, 1835, Marshall announced a further deferment, since it was not known "whether there will be a full court during the term,"[103] the Court then consisting of only six Judges.

Following the deaths of the Chief Justice and Justice Johnson, the Court, now consisting of Chief Justice Taney and Justices Story, Thompson, McLean, Baldwin, Wayne, and Barbour, in an opinion written for the Court by Justice McLean, distinguished Craig v. Missouri and held that the certificates did not violate the constitutional inhibition.[104] Justice Story dissented, saying that "when this cause was formerly argued before this court, a majority of the judges, who then heard it, were decidedly of opinion that the act of Kentucky was unconstitutional and void. . . . In principle it was thought to be

[96] *Ibid.*, 871.
[97] *Ibid.*, 874.
[98] *Ibid.*, 873.
[99] Craig v. Missouri, 4 Pet. 410 (1830).
[100] *Ibid.*, 444.
[101] Briscoe v. Bank of Kentucky, 8 Pet. 118 (1834); Mayor v. Miln, 8 Pet. 118, 120 (1834).
[102] Mayor v. Miln, 8 Pet. 118, 122 (1834).
[103] Briscoe v. Bank of Kentucky, Mayor v. Miln, 9 Pet. 85 (1835).
[104] Briscoe v. Bank of Kentucky, 11 Pet. 257 (1837).

decided by the case of Craig v. State of Missouri. . . . Among that majority was the late Mr. Chief Justice Marshall."[105] Since Johnson was one of the three dissenters in the Craig case, with McLean and Thompson, it might be assumed that the Briscoe decision vindicated his previous dissent and theirs.

The opinion of Chief Justice Marshall, for a unanimous court, found that a state had authority to pass a bankruptcy law, provided it did not impair the obligation of contracts within the meaning of the Constitution and provided no act of Congress was in force to establish a uniform system of bankruptcy conflicting with such a law. The Chief Justice said at the end of his opinion, "This opinion is confined to the case actually under consideration."[106]

The decision created much confusion in the business world and pointed up the need for a federal bankruptcy law. Lacking such an overriding statute, the Court found itself faced, in 1827, with much the same questions it had dealt with in the Sturges case, the essential difference, as stated by the Chief Justice, being that in the Sturges case "the law acted on a contract which was made before its passage; in this case, the contract was entered into after the passage of the law."[107] However, another cleavage of opinion in the subsequent case prevented clarification of the confusion bred by the Sturges decision; instead, it created a confusion of its own.

Initially four judges, Washington, Johnson, Thompson, and McLean, held that the New York bankruptcy statute, enacted in the absence of a federal act, was valid and did not impair the obligation of contract, as had been held in the Sturges case, because the contract postdated the statute. To this holding the Chief Justice and Justices Story and Duvall dissented, relying on their Sturges decision. Following additional argument on the question of the extraterritorial effect of a New York bankruptcy discharge, Justice Johnson, who had been "instructed by the majority of the court finally to dispose of this cause," said that "the present majority is not the same which determined the general question" and that "I now stand united with the minority on the former question, and therefore feel it due to myself and the community to maintain my consistency."

Thereupon Johnson held that the New York discharge could not be pleaded to bar recovery in the Louisiana court and that the recovery for the plaintiff in the lower court should be affirmed. Now, since the Chief Justice and Justices Story and Duvall contended that the New York discharge was invalid at best, they joined with Justice Johnson in affirming the judgment below.[108]

Immediately thereafter, the Court, over the dissent of Justice Washington,

---

[105] Ibid., 329.
[106] Sturges v. Crowninshield, 4 Wheat. 122, 207 (1819).
[107] Ogden v. Saunders, 12 Wheat. 213, 333 (1827).
[108] Ibid., 369.

held that the states had a right to regulate or abolish imprisonment for debt and that the insolvency law of a state could so provide. Justice Washington took the position that, while he favored the abolition of imprisonment for debt, the Sturges case required a holding that a law operating retroactively upon a contract impaired the obligation of the contract.[109]

While Justice Johnson joined Justice Thompson in dissenting from a finding of jurisdiction to strike down what the majority considered a tax imposed by the city of Charleston on federal indebtedness, he affirmed his nationalism, saying: "The exercise of a power which, under the mask of imposing a tax, may defeat or impede the operation of the government of the United States in borrowing money, could not be tolerated."[110] His democratic views when finding the tax an income tax are interesting:

> I consider the case, therefore, as one of a tax upon income arising from the interest of money, a very unwise and suicidal tax unquestionably, . . .
>
> Why should not the stock of the United States when it becomes mixed up with the capital of its citizens, become subject to taxation in common with other capital? Or why should one who enjoys all the advantages of a society purchased at a heavy expense, and lives in affluence upon an income derived exclusively from government stock, be exempt from taxation?[111]

Later, in the 1860's, the Court unanimously followed the decision, holding that stock of the United States, constituting a part of the whole of the capital stock of a bank organized under state law, was not subject to state taxation, even though the tax was on the aggregate of the taxpayer's property.[112] In turn, a later Court held the last mentioned case decisive in subsequent attempts to tax banks.[113]

A century later we find Justice Sutherland writing to hold that a Massachusetts state tax, however small, on securities issued by the United States or income derived therefrom, was invalid: "The principle set forth a century ago in Weston v. Charleston, 2 Pet. 449, 468 . . . has never since been departed from by this court."[114] Justice Stone, joined by Justices Brandeis and Holmes, dissenting, contended that, since the tax was for the privilege of doing business and was upon net and not upon gross income, it was an excise tax, as the state courts had found, and, as such, was valid. Later Chief Justice Hughes joined the conservatives to void a Missouri statute taxing corporate net worth, the

[109] Mason v. Haile, 12 Wheat. 370, 379, (1827).
[110] Weston v. Charleston, 2 Pet. 449, 472 (1829).
[111] *Ibid.,* 473.
[112] People *ex. rel.* Bank of Commerce v. Commissioners, 2 Black 620 (1863).
[113] People *ex. rel.* Bank of Commonwealth v. Commissioners, 2 Wall. 200 (1865) (Bank Tax Cases).
[114] Macallen v. Massachusetts, 279 U.S. 620, 624 (1929).

assets including federal government securities. Again the same three liberals dissented (Justice Sanford had died).[115]

Still later, in 1931, Justice Stone wrote for a majority, including the Chief Justice and middle-of-the-roader Roberts, sustaining a corporate franchise tax based on net income collected in part from royalties derived from federal copyrights.[116] To satisfy possible dissenters, Stone distinguished and did not attempt to overrule the previous Massachusetts case. Justices Sutherland, Van Devanter, and Butler dissented, relying on the Massachusetts case.

A year later Stone succeeded in getting the same majority to subscribe to his ruling that a state franchise tax on the entire net income of a corporation, including income from tax exempt bonds, was constitutional.[117] Again Sutherland, Van Devanter, and Butler dissented. And again, in thus overruling the Massachusetts case, Stone tried but was unable to induce the Chief Justice to go along with a statement that the case was being overruled, because he was fearful that, with such a statement, a majority could not be obtained.[118]

It might be noted that the New York Court of Appeals, in the closing days of 1967, held that banks with national charters were not federal instrumentalities but private corporations and, as such, were not immune from paying state and local sales taxes. In so holding, the Court found obsolete the exemptions to the contrary in the days of the early Bank of United States, as found in McCulloch v. Maryland.[119]

However, at the close of the 1967 term, a five-man majority of the Supreme Court, over the dissent of Justices Marshall, Harlan, and Stewart, overruled the Massachusetts Supreme Court, holding that the state could not collect sales and use taxes on a federal bank's purchases of equipment since Congress had not specifically authorized such state taxation.[120]

Another set of repercussions from the century-old Weston case came when Justice Holmes, writing in 1922 for a six-man majority, held that the income of a lessee of Indian lands derived from oil and gas revenues could not be taxed. Citing the Weston case, he said that a tax upon income would be the same as a tax upon leases, which would be "a direct hamper upon the effort of the United States to make the best terms that it can for its wards."[121] This was one of the rare instances when Holmes and Brandeis parted company. Dissenting with Brandeis were Pitney and Clarke.

[115] Missouri v. Gehner, 281 U.S. 313 (1930).
[116] Educational Films Corp. v. Ward, 282 U.S. 379 (1931).
[117] Pacific Co. v. Johnson, 285 U.S. 480 (1932).
[118] Mason, *Harlan Fiske Stone,* 308–309.
[119] Liberty National Bank v. Buscaglia, 21 N.Y. 2d 357 (1967).
[120] First Agricultural National Bank v. State Tax Commission, 392 U.S. 339 (1968).
[121] Gillespie v. Oklahoma, 257 U.S. 501, 506 (1922).

Justice Stone, who came on the bench later, wrote in a subsequent 1931 case for a unanimous Court, including Justice Holmes, with Justice Roberts not participating, that the Government could tax oil and gas income derived from lands purchased from the state, property which had completely passed to the buyer.[122]

Then, after Justice Cardozo succeeded Holmes, Justice McReynolds wrote for a majority, holding that the federal government could not tax oil and gas income derived by a lessee of state lands where the state had a percentage interest in the revenue derived, expressly following the Holmes decision.[123] Justice Stone wrote in dissent, joined by Justices Brandeis, Cardozo, and Roberts, maintaining that his decision in the previous case and not the Holmes decision should be followed and the Holmes decision overruled.

Finally in 1938, Chief Justice Hughes wrote, upholding federal taxation upon the income derived by a lessee of state school lands from operations under his lease and overruling the Holmes and McReynolds decisions. He distinguished the Weston case.[124]

When the Cherokee Nation of Indians sought an injunction to prevent the execution of certain acts of the legislature of Georgia, the complainant maintained that the Court had jurisdiction because the Cherokee Nation was a "foreign state" and therefore was entitled to sue a domestic state under the terms of the Constitution. In an opinion written by Marshall, a majority held that the Cherokee Nation was not a "foreign state" and that, consequently, the Court could not entertain the suit.[125] Again Justice Story cast one of his rare dissents to a Marshall decision, in which he was joined by Justice Thompson.

However, while the suit was pending and before the Court rendered its decision, an application was made to the Court for a writ of error to review the state court conviction for the murder of a Cherokee Indian named George Tassels. An order signed by Marshall directed Georgia to appear and answer the writ. The Georgia legislature adopted a resolution instructing state officers to disregard the writ and to execute the prisoner. The sheriff did so.

Following Marshall's decision in the Cherokee Nation suit, the question of the rights of Georgia respecting the Cherokees again came to the Court. The occasion was the indictment of a Vermont minister named Worcester who, in company with other missionaries, went into the Cherokee country and refused to leave, whereupon he and another minister were arrested and charged with violating a Georgia statute regulating residence by whites in

[122] Group No. 1 Oil Corp. v. Bass, 283 U.S. 279 (1931).
[123] Burnet v. Coronado Oil & Gas Co., 285 U.S. 393 (1932).
[124] Helvering v. Mountain Producers Corp., 303 U.S. 376, 386 (1938).
[125] Cherokee Nation v. Georgia, 5 Pet. 1 (1831).

Indian territory. From the conviction and sentence, Worcester appealed. The high court reversed, holding the Georgia legislative acts unconstitutional. Justice Baldwin dissented on a technical ground.[126]

The officials and the people of the state of Georgia were outraged by the decision. President Jackson, who had contributed to the result by removing Worcester as a government postmaster, was also resentful of Marshall's opinion and the decision of the Court. It was on this occasion that Jackson was claimed to have said, "John Marshall had made his decision; now let him enforce it."[127]

Without the aid of the federal government, the Court could do nothing to enforce its judgment. Georgia ignored it, and Worcester remained in jail until, after serving a year of his four-year sentence, he was pardoned by the Governor. Georgia succeeded too, against the Cherokees; Jackson had them moved to the Indian Territory.

However, the consequence of Georgia's success in defying the Court and of Jackson's support of the Georgia assertions of state sovereignty vis-à-vis the supremacy of the Court, proved for President Jackson to be chickens coming home to roost. It encouraged the nullificationists to the point of compelling the unpredictable Jackson to counter the South Carolina Nullification Ordinance declaring the Tariff Acts of 1828 and 1832 null and void by issuing a nullification proclamation. In his proclamation Jackson, adopting Marshall's views, upheld the Court as the ultimate arbiter of constitutionality, saying: "There are two appeals from an unconstitutional act passed by Congress—one to the judiciary, the other to the people and the States. . . . our social compact, in express terms, declares that the laws of the United States, its Constitution, and the treaties made under it are the supreme law of the land," and, for greater caution, he added that "the judges in every State shall be bound thereby, anything in the constitution or laws of any State to the contrary notwithstanding."[128]

During the last term of Marshall's service the Court handed down forty opinions. Of these, only three met with dissent, Thompson and McLean each dissenting once and Baldwin twice. Johnson was incapacitated much of the time. Of the Court's forty opinions, Marshall, despite his age, his ill-health, his growing despondency, and the inroads the accession of Jackson and the growth of the democratic spirit had made upon his federalism, wrote thirteen for a unanimous Court.

126 Worcester v. Georgia, 6 Pet. 515 (1832).
127 Beveridge, *John Marshall*, IV, 551.
128 James D. Richardson, ed., *Messages and Papers of the Presidents* (20 vols., New York, Bureau of National Literature, 1897). III, 1205 (1832).

CHAPTER III

Judicial Conflict in the Slavery Era

CHIEF JUSTICE TANEY TOOK OFFICE at the opening of the 1837 term, following the death of Chief Justice Marshall. Over the years, the record discloses, the members of the Taney court did not overstress dissent. There were two issues that caused sharp divisions of the Court; one reflected the facets of the slavery question, and the other mirrored the growing public fears of the growth of power of corporations and public resentment of its attendant abuses. While the Court was generally nationalistic-minded, it recognized the changing and progressive social, economic, and political conditions of the country and the need of recognizing the police power of the states. Much of this made for agreement rather than disagreement except where the two principal issues were involved.

Perhaps typical of the record of the Court respecting dissent, it appears that during the 1854 December term the Court announced seventy-two decisions, of which 25 per cent bore dissents. However, half of these were by a single justice and only one was a five-to-four decision. Justice Daniel, with nine dissents, was the principal dissenter. He was alone in four of his dissents, while Justice Campbell dissented seven times, in three of which he was alone. The Chief Justice and Justice McLean each dissented four times; Taney, once by himself and three times with Daniel.

The 1855 December term registered twenty dissents of a total of ninety-five decisions (over 20 per cent), of which but one was a five-to-four split. Again, 50 per cent of the dissents were by a single justice, of which eight of a total of sixteen were Daniel's. Justice Campbell joined him in five of the other eight. Of the other justices, Catron had three dissents and each of the others only two, excepting McLean, who had but one.

Taney, no less than Marshall, proved an advocate of the judicial supremacy of a powerful court, despite his reputed involvement, as President Jackson's Attorney General, in Jackson's veto message. That veto in 1832 killed the recharter of the Bank of the United States—a message in which the ambivalent Jackson said:

It is maintained by the advocates of the Bank that its constitutionality . . . ought to be considered as settled by precedent and by the decision of the Supreme Court. To this conclusion I cannot assent. . . .

If the opinion of the Supreme Court covered the whole ground of this act, it ought not to control the coordinate authorities of this Government. The Congress, the Executive, and the Court must each for itself be guided by its own opinion of the Constitution. . . . The opinion of the judges has no more authority over Congress than the opinion of Congress has over the judges, and on that point the President is independent of both.[1]

Jackson's dictum no more bound Taney, assuming he played a part in its formulation, than it did Jackson, who took back his words when he issued his nullification proclamation.

The fact that three of the early decisions of the Taney court held over from the Marshall court[2] met with dissents at the hands of Story as alter ego for the deceased Marshall, pointed up the change from Marshall and the Marshall court to Taney and what was to be the Taney court. Marshall was the great Federalist conservative; Taney was to be the great democratic Jacksonian liberal. Marshall had been devoted to the federalist promotion of individual property rights; Taney was to be devoted to the social and economic rights of the people under the aegis of the police powers of the state.

Taney's opinion in the first of these cases made the disparity clear, as did the result.[3] In the course of holding that a charter authorizing the construction of a toll bridge did not prevent a subsequent legislature from granting a charter for the construction of a free bridge paralleling the toll bridge, the new Chief Justice wrote:

> The object and end of all government is to promote the happiness and prosperity of the community by which it is established; and it can never be assumed that the government intended to diminish its power of accomplishing the end for which it was created. And in a country like ours, free, active, enterprising, continually advancing in numbers and wealth, new channels of communication are daily found necessary, both for travel and trade, and are essential to the comfort, convenience, and prosperity of the people. . . .[4]
>
> While the rights of private property are sacredly guarded, we must not forget that the community also have rights, and that the happiness and well being of every citizen depends on their faithful preservation.[5]

Justice McLean said he believed the Court lacked jurisdiction, although

---

[1] James D. Richardson, *Messages and Papers of the Presidents* (20 vols., New York, Bureau of National Literature, 1897), III, 1144–45 (1832).

[2] Briscoe v. Bank of Kentucky; Mayor v. Miln, 9 Pet. 85 (1835); Charles River Bridge v. Warren Bridge, 11 Pet. 420 (1837).

[3] Charles River Bridge v. Warren Bridge, 11 Pet. 420 (1837).

[4] *Ibid.*, 547.   [5] *Ibid.*, 548.

he felt the merits were on the side of the complainant, Justice Story, with the concurrence of Justice Thompson and the posthumous concurrence of Chief Justice Marshall, stood on the strict doctrine of the Dartmouth College case, denying the Taney court's holding that, though a corporate charter constituted a contract, as the Dartmouth College case held, it was to be strictly construed in favor of the state so that implied powers might not be claimed.

A second case (Miln) in this trilogy[6] reflected the beginning of a clash between state police powers and the commerce clause of the Constitution. Here the state-minded Taney court collided with the nationalistic view of the Marshall court. The case involved an act of the New York legislature requiring masters of vessels bringing immigrants into the port of New York to report their passengers and permitting the mayor of the city to require bonds to assure they would not become charges. The suit was for penalties under the act. Justice Barbour wrote for the majority. He distinguished Brown v. Maryland and said that the law fell within the police powers of the state and thus did not conflict with the federal Constitution. He added that, had it been necessary, he would have been prepared to declare the statute valid in view of the fact that Congress had not legislated in the area.

Justice Story dissented, saying: "I have the consolation to know that I had the entire concurrence, upon the same grounds of that great constitutional jurist, the late Mr. Chief Justice Marshall. Having heard the former arguments, his deliberate opinion was that the act of New York was unconstitutional, and that the present case fell directly within the principles established in the case of Gibbons v. Ogden."[7]

Later, in the Passenger Cases, another phase of the statute considered in the Miln case came to the Court and was found repugnant to the Constitution and laws of the United States and therefore void.[8] Then New York amended the statute to avoid the effect of the decision, and, as amended, it came back to the Court. Thereupon the Court again held the statute void, as it did similar statutes of Louisiana and California, saying the subject was within the exclusive control of Congress.[9] The Court added that it did not undertake to decide whether or not a state may, in the absence of all legislation by Congress on the same subject, pass a statute strictly limited to defending itself against paupers, convicted criminals, and others of that class, but was of the opinion that to Congress rightfully and appropriately belongs the power of legislating on the whole subject.[10]

[6] Mayor v. Miln, 11 Pet. 102 (1837).

[7] *Ibid.*, 161.

[8] Smith v. Turner; Norris v. Boston, 7 How. 283 (1849) (Passenger Cases).

[9] Henderson v. Wickham, Mayor of New York; Commissioners of Immigration v. North German Lloyd, 2 Otto (92 U.S.) 259 (1876); Chy Lung v. Freeman, 2 Otto (92 U.S.) 275 (1876).

[10] Henderson v. Wickham, Mayor of New York, 2 Otto (92 U.S.) 259, 274 (1876).

Meanwhile, however, Chief Justice Taney persisted in maintaining that, though Congress controlled commerce on public navigable streams, the Court had no jurisdiction to declare a bridge a public nuisance and order its removal in the absence of congressional legislation on the subject.[11] Justice Daniel also dissented from the decision to the contrary. The dissenters little knew, nor could they or the majority imagine, for that matter, how Congress was to use the commerce clause in the closing years of the century and thereafter to increase and centralize the national power.

However, despite his state-mindedness and his resort to the police powers to permit states some measure of interference with immigration, Taney went all the way in sustaining the federal jurisdiction as against that of the states in dealing with foreign nations. A question arose when the Supreme Court of Vermont affirmed the act of the Governor who had ordered the delivery to Canadian authorities of George Holmes, a Canadian citizen charged in Canada with murder, despite the fact that there was no extradition treaty in existence between the United States and Canada. An appeal to the high court from the Vermont Supreme Court was dismissed for want of jurisdiction, when the Court divided equally (four to four) on the issue.[12] The Chief Justice and Justices Story, McLean, and Wayne rendered a sound opinion asserting the exclusive federal right of extradition, but the equal division made it ineffectual.

In the Miln case Justice Barbour had defined "police power" as "not only the right, but the bounden and solemn duty of a State, to advance the safety, happiness and prosperity of its people, and to provide for its general welfare, by any and every act of legislation which it may deem to be conducive to these ends; where the power over the particular subject, or the manner of its exercise is not surrendered or restrained."[13]

Earlier, in 1846, Taney had had occasion to define police power in deciding a group of three license cases argued and decided together.[14] Here the states of Massachusetts, New Hampshire, and Rhode Island, by respective state statutes, had endeavored to regulate the sale of liquor. Chief Justice Taney wrote the principal opinion finding the laws constitutional as within the police powers of the states, as might have been expected. He held that the privilege of Congress to regulate commerce did not extend to the "internal traffic" of the states; that "every State . . . may regulate its own internal traffic, according to its own judgment and upon its own views of the interest

---

[11] Pennsylvania v. Wheeling Bridge Co., 13 How. 518, 580 (1851).

[12] Holmes v. Jennison, 14 Pet. 540 (1840).

[13] Mayor v. Miln, 11 Pet. 102, 139 (1837).

[14] Thurlow v. Massachusetts; Fletcher v. Rhode Island; Pierce v. New Hampshire, 5 How. 504 (1847) (License Cases).

and well-being of its citizens."[15] He went on to define police powers as "nothing more or less than the powers of government inherent in every sovereignty to the extent of its dominations . . . . It is by virtue of this power that it legislates."[16]

In these cases, the brief submitted by Messrs. Webster and Choate pointed to the language of the Court in Gibbons v. Ogden concerning statutes within the police powers: "They form a portion of that immense mass of legislation which embraces everything within the territory of a State, not surrendered to the general government; all of which can be most advantageously exercised by the State itself."[17]

The third early case in which the Taney court differed from Marshall's previous holding and definition of "bills of credit" concerned notes issued by the Bank of the Commonwealth of Kentucky. The Marshall court had held certificates authorized by a Missouri legislature invalid as not constituting "bills of credit." Again Justice Story had dissented, saying: "Mr. Chief Justice Marshall is not here to speak for himself, and knowing full well the grounds of his opinion, in which I concurred, that this act is unconstitutional, I have felt an earnest desire to vindicate his memory from the imputation of rashness, or want of deep reflection. Had he been living, he would have spoken in the joint names of both of us."[18]

Justice Baldwin, who voted with the majority in the three cases which bore the Marshall dissent, proved himself the prototype of Justice Black, when he submitted statements comprising 197 pages[19] to explain what he felt "may be deemed my peculiar views of the Constitution."[20] That Justice Baldwin was no conformist was demonstrated when he excepted to approval of a Court resolution declining an invitation to attend, in its official capacity, the funeral of a congressman who had been killed in a duel with another congressman.[21]

Another unusual type of dissent that might be more properly termed disagreement was evidenced when Richard Peters, the Court reporter, who had served since 1828, was removed without notice or inquiry and replaced by Benjamin C. Howard, by a vote of four to three, on January 27, 1843, at a time when Justices Story and McKinley were absent. Justice Story wrote

[15] *Ibid.*, 574.
[16] *Ibid.*, 583.
[17] 9 Wheat. 1, 203 (1824).
[18] Briscoe v. Bank of Kentucky, 11 Pet. 257, 350 (1837).
[19] Hon. Henry Baldwin, "A General View of the Origin and Nature of the Constitution and Government of the United States," 9 U.S. Sup. Ct. Reports (Lawyers Ed.), 871 *et seq.*
[20] *Ibid.*, 873.
[21] Charles Warren, *The Supreme Court in United States History* (3 vols., Boston, Little, Brown & Co., 1922), II, 323.

saying that he had "seldom been more pained" and that he "no longer ever expected to see revived the kind and frank courtesy of the old Court."[22]

In a case that involved a conflict between the legislative, judicial, and executive powers, a majority of the Court held that the circuit court had jurisdiction to order the Postmaster General to pay certain claims approved by the Solicitor of the Treasury pursuant to a congressional order.[23] The Postmaster General claimed to be subject only to the orders of the President. When the Court held the contrary, the Chief Justice, joined by Justices Catron and Barbour, dissented, denying the power of the circuit court to mandamus the Postmaster General. Thus Taney subscribed to the stand taken by President Jackson and later by President Van Buren.[24]

Despite the issue that was going to divide the court in the future, i.e., the growing power of corporations and the abuses engendered thereby, the Court held that a corporation incorporated in one state had power to contract in another if its certificate and the state of incorporation permitted. The question came to the Court in three cases.[25] Judge McKinley, who, sitting in circuit, had held the contrary, to the dismay of the country's business interests, dissented.

The first decision handed down at the January, 1842, term involved a comparatively innocuous question of liability on a note.[26] When, however, the Court came to apply a rule of law and looked at Section 34 of the Judiciary Act, Justice Story came to the conclusion that the congressional command to follow the state law meant only that the Court was enjoined to respect the statutory and not the substantive law of the state. Justice Washington, in 1814, had pointed out the "injustice" and "absurdity" of having the federal courts in a state following a federal rule while the state courts were following another. Such a practice, he declared, would result in a conflict of result in the various federal courts and leave the appellate courts to affirm or reverse, incontinently depending on the rule in the state where the litigation originated.

On the other hand, with a uniform rule for all the federal courts, there would be conflicts in various states between federal and local rules and leave it to plaintiffs who, by virtue of diversity of citizenship or other irrelevancies, could make a choice to select the more favorable jurisdiction. The problem was really one for Congress (except as Brandeis later raised an issue of constitutionality); it had indubitably enjoined the federal courts to follow state

22 *Ibid.*, 380–81.

23 Kendall v. United States, 12 Pet. 524 (1838).

24 Richardson, *Messages and Papers of the Presidents*, IV, 1720–21 (1838).

25 Bank of Augusta v. Earle; Bank of United States v. Primrose; New Orleans v. Earle, 13 Pet. 519 (1839).

26 Swift v. Tyson, 16 Pet. 1 (1842).

statutes. By the same power, it could define "law" as including substantive law, which is truly as much law as statutory law.

As Justice Washington made his choice so Justice Story made his. He decided to follow Cicero, who said that the law is not one thing at Rome and another at Athens, an apothegm of doubtful appositiveness when one realizes the years of effort, frequently fruitless, to get uniform statutory law in the states.

Behind the façade of his construction of the Judiciary Act, Justice Story, with a unanimous court behind him (Justice Catron disagreed on a minor point, but the major dissents came later) ruled that "the decisions of the local tribunals . . . are entitled to and will receive the most deliberate attention and respect of this Court; but they cannot furnish positive rules, or conclusive authority by which our own judgments are to be bound up or governed."[27]

Thus Justice Story launched a bark that rode a far from calm sea for almost a century until, in 1938, by a vote of seven to two,[28] in another otherwise insignificant case, a court about to embark on a journey of finding previous courts mistaken decided to put into a more satisfactory haven.

Meanwhile, Justice Story's venture encountered some rough seas. Dissents from its application or extension were registered in 1845 by two of its original sponsors, Chief Justice Taney and Justice McKinley,[29] followed by half a dozen dissents from the 1840's to 1870. Justice Field attacked the rule;[30] so did Justice Holmes,[31] who, writing to his correspondent, the noted British legal authority Sir Frederick Pollock, characterized it as "an established though very fishy principle started by Story."[32]

Justice Brandeis had, in the past, evidenced his dislike of the rule. That it lent itself to chicanery there could be no doubt. An outstanding and notorious example was a Kentucky case well publicized for its bald use of the Tyson case and its consequent success.[33] In that case the Brown & Yellow Taxicab Co., a Kentucky corporation, had had a contract with the Louisville and Nashville Railroad giving the taxicab company exclusive rights at the railroad's station. The Black & White Taxicab & Transfer Company, also a Kentucky corporation, aware that the Kentucky law would declare the contract void as creating a monopoly, infringed on the Brown & Yellow Company's rights at the railroad station. Brown & Yellow Company's lawyer, aware that

27 *Ibid.,* 19.
28 Erie R.R. v. Tompkins, 304 U.S. 64 (1938).
29 Lane v. Vick, 3 How. 464 (1845).
30 Baltimore & Ohio R.R. v. Baugh, 149 U.S. 368 (1893).
31 Kuhn v. Fairmont Coal Co., 215 U.S. 349 (1910).
32 Prigg v. Pennsylvania, 16 Pet. 539 (1842).
33 Black & White Taxi Co. v. Brown & Yellow Taxi Co., 276 U.S. 518 (1928).

47

the Kentucky federal court would not respect the Kentucky state court monopoly rule (since under the Tyson rule it did not have to do so), had the owners of Brown & Yellow Company form a similarly named company in Tennessee, to which the Kentucky Brown & Yellow Company transferred all its assets. Then he arranged to have the railroad give the Tennessee company a similar contract for the exclusive rights at the railroad station.

That put the Tennessee corporation in a position to sue in the Kentucky federal court to prevent the Black & White Company from infringing upon the exclusive rights which had been granted it by the railroad, since, as a citizen of Tennessee, it could sue a citizen of Kentucky in the Kentucky federal court under the diversity of citizenship rule.

As its lawyer had predicted, Brown & Yellow won its case in the federal district court, in the United States Circuit Court and finally, by a vote of six to three, in the United States Supreme Court. In that case Holmes, with the concurrence of Brandeis and Stone, said in his dissenting opinion that though he would leave the Tyson case undisturbed, he "would not allow it to spread the assumed dominion into new fields."[34]

While this was a particularly brazen example of the perversion which the Swift v. Tyson rule countenanced, it had been a common practice over the years for one injured through the alleged negligence of a railroad to shop about to pick a federal court with rules to his liking in one of the various states in which the railroad operated and start his suit there. Thus he could avoid a more stringent home-state rule.

An example of this practice was furnished when a Mr. Tompkins, a citizen of Pennsylvania, went to the federal court in New York and there recovered a verdict of $30,000 against the Erie Railroad Company for its negligence, under the federal rule, which was more advantageous to his cause than the Pennsylvania state rule was. But when the case reached the Supreme Court, Justice Brandeis, who had expressed his dissent from the Tyson rule in the Brown & Yellow case just discussed, on behalf of six members of the Court, decided that the time had come to put an end to "injustice and confusion incident to the doctrine of Swift v. Tyson" and to try the other expedient, *i.e.*, that of having the federal court bound by not only the statutory but also by the substantive law of the state in which it sits.[35]

Justice Brandeis acted reluctantly, saying that "if only a question of statutory construction was involved, we should not be prepared to abandon a doctrine so widely applied throughout nearly a century." But he found Justice Story's expedient unconstitutional in that, though Section 34 of the Judiciary Act was not of itself unconstitutional, it was unconstitutional for the lower

[34] *Ibid.*, 535.
[35] Erie R.R. v. Tompkins, 304 U.S. 64 (1938).

courts to invade "rights which in our opinion are reserved by the Constitution to the several States."[36]

What thus amounted to a dissent from Justice Story's majority opinion met with a dissent of its own by the remainder of the 1930 rear guard, Justices Butler and McReynolds. Justice Butler said rightly, "No constitutional question was suggested or argued below or here."[37] Justice Reed, agreeing to overrule Swift v. Tyson, disagreed with Justice Brandeis' conclusion that unconstitutionality required its demise.

Justice Jackson, in his work on the Supreme Court, said that the Brandeis decision had "declared thousands of decisions of federal courts, which are no longer subject to correction, were wrongly decided" and adjudged "federal courts for almost a century guilty of taking the property of one and giving it to another without warrant of law."[38] However, except as to Tompkins, the new rule was not retroactive. As to him, the Court might well have applied the prospective overruling rule.[39]

During the 1966 term the Court, by a six-man majority, held that state adjudications respecting inheritance taxes due the federal government were not binding on federal courts under the doctrine of Erie v. Tompkins.[40] Justice Douglas dissented upon the ground that a federal court cannot "ignore a state court judgment when federal taxation depends upon property rights and property rights rest on state law."[41] Justice Harlan, joined by Justice Fortas, also dissented.

Another case in which dissent was deferred until a later date involved a construction of the will of Stephen Girard.[42] Girard, a native of France, came to the United States shortly before the issuance of the Declaration of Independence. A resident of Philadelphia, he died in 1831. He left an estate of between five and ten million dollars. His survivors were a brother and several nieces.

By his will Girard left the bulk of his estate in trust to the city of Philadelphia for the purpose of founding and maintaining a college for "poor white male orphans, between the ages of six and ten years."[43] He imposed certain restrictions, including one that barred from the college any "ecclesiastic, missionary, or minister of any sect" in any capacity, including that of a visitor, so as "to keep the tender minds of the orphans . . . free from the excitement

---

[36] *Ibid.*, 80.

[37] *Ibid.*, 82.

[38] *The Struggle for Judicial Supremacy* (New York, Alfred A. Knopf, 1941), 283.

[39] Great Northern R.R. v. Sunburst Oil Co., 287 U.S. 358 (1932).

[40] Commissioner v. Bosch Estate, 387 U.S. 456 (1967).

[41] *Ibid.*, 466.

[42] Vidal v. Mayor of Philadelphia, 2 How. 127 (1844).

[43] *Ibid.*, 131.

which clashing doctrines and sectarian controversy are so apt to produce."[44]

Girard's relatives maintained that the trusts in the will were void upon various grounds, one of which was that "the foundation of the college upon the principles and exclusions prescribed by the testator, is derogatory and hostile to the Christian religion."[45] Justice Story, writing for a unanimous Court, overruled the objections.

But while the restrictions on religion furnished the nub of the contemporary controversy, the inclusion of "white" provided the ground of conflict in the following century. Now following the Court's ruling that school segregation was unconstitutional, the Court held that the "Board of Directors of City Trusts of the City of Philadelphia," which, by virtue of an act of the Pennsylvania legislature, was administering the Girard trust and operating the college which was founded after the will had been sustained, was an agency of the state. Hence, its refusal to enroll two Negroes, despite the restrictions in the Girard will, constituted discrimination forbidden by the Fourteenth Amendment. So the Court, reversing the Pennsylvania Supreme Court, now denied Girard's 1831 right to put nonwhite restrictions on the use of his money.[46]

Following the Supreme Court decision, the State Orphans' Court removed the trustees and appointed substitute trustees whose acts of continued exclusion of Negroes, it held, were not acts of the state.[47] The Supreme Court of Pennsylvania affirmed the decision of the Orphans' Court.[48] Thereafter, application was made to the federal district court to enjoin the trustees from continuing their policy of exclusion upon the ground that it was forbidden by the State Public Accommodations Act vitiating racial discrimination. The district court granted the application,[49] but the circuit court of appeals reversed upon the ground that the issue had been previously decided by the state court adversely to the complainant. The case having been remanded to the district court, District Judge Lord heard argument and granted a permanent injunction on the complainant's charge that the exclusion violated the equal protection clause of the Fourteenth Amendment.[50]

The circuit court affirmed, saying: "Given everything we know of Mr. Girard, it is inconceivable that in this changed world, he would not be quietly happy that his cherished project had raised its sights with the times and joy-

---

[44] *Ibid.*, 133.

[45] *Ibid.*, 132.

[46] Pennsylvania v. Board of Directors, 353 U.S. 230 (1957).

[47] Fiduciary Reporter (Pennsylvania), 555, 606.

[48] Girard College Trusteeship, 391 Pa. 434 (1958).

[49] Pennsylvania v. Brown, 260 F. Supp. 323, 329 (1966).

[50] Pennsylvania v. Brown, 373 F. 2d 771 (1967); Pennsylvania v. Brown, 276 F. Supp. 782 (1967).

fully recognized that all human beings are created equal."[51] Thereafter, on May 20, 1968, the Supreme Court denied certiorari and the trustees declared the litigation and their rejection of Negroes at an end.

The corporate issue that divided the country and the parties found reflection in the Court in 1854. Over the years the Democrats had been attacking the exemptions from taxation granted by legislatures in corporate charters, many of which were claimed to have been induced by intensive lobbying and malpractices, including wholesale bribery of legislators. The Republicans aligned themselves with the business interests seeking to maintain their tax exemptions and found themselves in conflict with later legislatures elected by an aroused populace seeking to vitiate the exemptions. The constitutionality of such later legislation, as well as the power of subsequent legislatures to void exemptions granted by previous legislatures, became the legal issues.

These legal issues were posed in a case in which the Ohio Supreme Court had sustained the action of the Ohio legislature, which had enacted legislation taxing the Piqua Branch of the State Bank of Ohio, which had a charter giving it tax exemption. Justice McLean, writing for five members of the Court, held that the language of the exemption was "so explicit" that it was not of "doubtful meaning"; that, as the Dartmouth College case had held, it constituted a contract; and that the action of the subsequent legislature was void under the federal Constitution as impairing the obligation of contract.[52] Chief Justice Taney and Justices Catron, Daniel, and Campbell, all Democrats, dissented.

Concurrently the Court affirmed the action of the Ohio Supreme Court in holding valid taxation of the Ohio Life Insurance Company upon the ground that the language of its charter did not constitute a tax exemption.[53] The majority thus holding consisted of the four dissenters in the previous case, with Justice Grier joining in an opinion by the Chief Justice, which he also made applicable to the previous case.

Taney's opinion stated the Democratic case for the people. Saying that in the charters granted the various banks by the legislatures "the rule of construction, as held in the Charles River Bridge case," required strict construction, he adverted to the fact, of which the court could take judicial notice,

> that almost every bill for the incorporation of banking companies, insurance and trust companies, railroad companies, or other corporations, is drawn originally by the parties who are personally interested in obtaining the charter; and that they are often passed by the Legislature in the last days of its session, when, from the nature of our political institutions, the business is unavoidably transacted in a hurried manner, and it is impossible that every member can delib-

[51] Pennsylvania v. Brown, 392 F. 2d 120 (1968).
[52] Piqua Branch Bank v. Knoop, 16 How. 369 (1853).
[53] Ohio Life Ins. Co. v. Debolt, 16 How. 416 (1853).

erately examine every provision in every bill upon which he is called on to act.

On the other hand, those who accept the charter have abundant time to examine and consider its provisions, before they invest their money.[54]

Justice Catron said:

When I take into consideration . . . the unparalleled increase of corporations throughout the Union within the last few years; the ease with which charters, containing exclusive privileges and exemptions are obtained; the vast amount of property, power, and exclusive benefits, prejudicial to other classes of society that are vested in and held by these numerous bodies of associated wealth, I cannot but feel the grave importance of being called on to sanction the conclusion that they hold their rights of franchise and property under the Constitution of the United States, and practically under this Court, and stand above the state government creating them.[55]

Justice Daniel added:

I never can believe in that, to my mind suicidal doctrine, which confers upon one Legislature, the creatures and limited agents of the sovereign people, the power, by a breach of duty and by transcending the commission with which they are clothed, to bind forever and irrevocably their creator . . . to consequences however mischievous or destructive.[56]

Justice Campbell, whose conscience and states' rights southern sympathies were such as to call upon him to resign when the Civil War broke out, was unequivocally frank. "The discussions before this court in the Indiana Railroad and the Baltimore Railroad cases exposed to us the sly and stealthy arts to which state Legislatures are exposed, and the greedy appetites of adventurers, for monopolies and immunities from the state right of government."[57]

The Ohio Supreme Court was so outraged by the Court's reversal of its decision in the Piqua Bank case that, for two years thereafter, it refused to enter the high court's mandate.[58]

Chief Justice Taney's opinion expressing his stand on state sovereignty had said that "no one Legislature can disarm their successors of any of the powers or rights of sovereignty confided by the people to the legislative body, unless they are authorized to do so by the constitution under which they are elected."[59]

[54] *Ibid.*, 435–36.
[55] *Ibid.*, 442–43.
[56] *Ibid.*, 443.
[57] Piqua Branch Bank v. Knoop, 16 How. 369, 412 (1853).
[58] Warren, *The Supreme Court in United States History*, II, 530.
[59] Ohio Life Ins. Co. v. Debolt, 16 How. 416, 431 (1853).

Taney having thus pointed the way, the irate people of Ohio voted to amend their constitution so as to provide for taxation of banks. Nevertheless, the high court, following its Piqua decision, held that even a subsequent state constitutional provision would not suffice to avoid the federal constitutional inhibition against impairing the obligation of contract. The Chief Justice joined the majority; Justices Campbell, Daniel, and Catron held to their states' rights stance.

Writing for the dissenters, Justice Campbell denied the right of Woolsey, a stockholder of the bank, to maintain the suit to prevent the bank from paying the tax; in addition the dissenters persisted in the opinions they had expressed in the Piqua suit. Campbell repeated the Democratic argument that moved so many of the people:

> The courts cannot look to the corruption, the blindness, nor mischievous effects of state legislation, to determine its binding operation . . . . The court, therefore, becomes the patron of such legislation, by furnishing motives of incalculable power to the corporations to stimulate it, and affording stability and security to the successful effort. Where, then, is the remedy for the people? They have none in their state government nor in themselves, and the federal government is enlisted by their adversary.[60]

It might be noted that the later inability of the people of Tennessee to get their legislature to change the state voting patterns ultimately led the Court to abandon its refusal to concern itself with political problems and to take jurisdiction.

Meanwhile, the antagonism of the Ohio Supreme Court was further evidenced by a decision of its Chief Justice denying the validity of the appellate jurisdiction of the high court under the Judiciary Act.[61] Previously, the California Supreme Court had refused to permit an appeal to the high court, likewise denying its jurisdiction to overrule the California court.[62]

The California legislature, during the following session, passed an act negating its state court's decision and two years later, the Court itself thought better of its action and with Judge (later Justice) Field on the bench, over the objection of the Chief Justice, David S. Terry (who was to die at the hands of Field's marshal) reversed its previous emotional ruling.

It might be noted that, in an earlier case (striking down a legislative statute as violative of the obligation of contract contained in a grant of charter powers), two of the ardent states' righters, the Chief Justice and Justice Daniel

[60] Dodge v. Woolsey, 18 How. 331, 371 (1856).
[61] Stunt v. Steamboat Ohio, 3 Ohio Decisions Reprint 362 (1865).
[62] Johnson v. Gordon, 4 Cal. 368 (1854).

53

dissented. The latter said his judgment repelled the annulling of "a legislative act of a sovereign State."[63]

Later the Court considered the impairment of contract doctrine of the Dartmouth College case in a number of cases. A state tax that increased the taxes of a bank beyond the amount specified in its charter was held void as impairing the obligation of contract.[64] The opinion of the majority, represented by Justice Swayne, stressed reliance on the Dartmouth College case. Justice Strong's dissent held that the legislative intent to relinquish the right to tax must clearly appear; that the presumptions are to the contrary. He was joined by Justices Clifford and Field.

A majority held that the contract to conduct a business of manufacturing liquor embodied in the corporate charter did not prevent a later exercise of the police power to terminate the use as a nuisance. Justice Miller said he felt there should be condemnation and payment. Justice Strong said the contract was protected by the Dartmouth College case.[65]

In another case a unanimous Court held, through the Chief Justice, that while the Dartmouth College doctrine was embedded in the law, it was not the charter but the contract contained therein that was protected and that the protection is restricted to those contracts that relate to property but not to governmental rights.[66] Also, he added, one legislature cannot bargain away the police powers of the state to prevent a subsequent one from exercising those powers. Hence, though a company was chartered to operate lotteries for a term of years, a subsequent legislature was held to have the power to decide, during the granted term, to abolish lotteries in the exercise of the police powers of the state.

The second divisive issue that rocked the country and was reflected in the Court stemmed from the same source as that which pitted legislative acts against the federal constitutional protection of contracts and grant of power over commerce. The rights of the states vis-à-vis the federal government was the issue then as it remains an issue now. It appeared in its most virulent form when issues primarily resulting from slavery shook the Court and the nation.

It was natural that judicial dispassion should be rent when the justices found themselves tempted to behave like the men they were. The Chief Justice was the son of a slaveowner and had himself owned slaves. In 1832 he had said: "The African race in the United States even when free, are everywhere a degraded class . . . The privileges they are allowed to enjoy,

---

63 Planters' Bank v. Sharp; Baldwin v. Payne, 6 How. 301 (1848).
64 Farrington v. Tennessee, 5 Otto (95 U.S.) 679 (1878).
65 Boston Beer Co. v. Massachusetts, 7 Otto (97 U.S.) 25 (1878).
66 Stone v. Mississippi, 11 Otto (101 U.S.) 814 (1880).

are accorded to them as a matter of kindness and benevolence rather than of right. They are the only class of persons who can be held as mere property, as slaves."[67] One might view this with Chief Justice Marshall's finding in a previous case that a slave who had drowned in an accident on a steamboat "resembles a passenger, not a package of goods."[68]

Nor was Taney the only Democrat of strong convictions born of birth and a lifetime of experience who was serving on the Court. Justices Wayne, Campbell, Catron, and Daniel shared his views and feelings, as the later Dred Scott decision attested. Nor was it coincidence that Democrats and the South should be represented on the Court.

An early slavery case posed the question whether a note given for the purchase of slaves after May 1, 1833, was valid.[69] From this date the Mississippi Constitution prohibited the introduction of slaves. In turn, this raised the question of whether the provision in the Mississippi Constitution violated the commerce clause of the federal Constitution and, finally and basically, the question of whether slaves were persons or articles of commerce—a question it took a war, and not Taney in the Dred Scott case, to settle.

A court majority of four (Justice Catron did not sit, and Justice Barbour died before the decision was handed down) found itself able to evade these issues in holding that the Mississippi constitutional provision was ineffectual in the absence of statutory supplement. Justice McLean, admitting that he was writing dicta, said, "The power over slavery belongs to the States," which led the Chief Justice to agree.[70] Justices McKinley and Story dissented, holding the notes void, but agreed that the commerce clause of the federal Constitution did not conflict with the provision of the Mississippi Constitution involved in the case. Justice Baldwin then felt it necessary to state his view that "slaves are property in every constitutional sense." Manifestly, these expressions were syndromes of the prevailing public conflict then building up to an explosive conclusion.

Some years later the same question was presented to the Court.[71] However, the Mississippi Supreme Court in the meantime had disagreed with the high court, holding that the Mississippi Constitution provision was self-executing. This was urged on the Court as a reason for departing from its Groves opinion, but the Court refused to be moved by the ruling of the Mississippi court, with Justice Daniel dissenting.

Controversies concerning fugitive slaves brought to the Court issues that

---

[67] Allison Dunham and Philip B. Kurland, eds., *Mr. Justice* (Chicago, The University of Chicago Press, 1956), 213.

[68] Boyce v. Anderson, 2 Pet. 150 (1829).

[69] Groves v. Slaughter; Brown v. Slaughter, 15 Pet. 449 (1841).

[70] Groves v. Slaughter, 15 Pet. 449, 508 (1841).

[71] Rowan v. Runnels, 5 How. 134 (1847).

were generally plaguing the country. So, when a Mr. Prigg found and seized a fugitive slave in Pennsylvania, and was refused a certificate for her removal as required by the Pennsylvania law, he defied the law and took her back to Maryland. Thereupon he was indicted and convicted under the Pennsylvania law. On appeal, the high court justices were able to agree that the attempt by Pennsylvania to legislate was unconstitutional since the exclusive right lay with the national Congress.[72] However, other differences of opinion concerning slavery throughout the nation found their way into the deliberations of the Court. The result was that, in addition to the majority opinion by Justice Story, there were seven concurring opinions, as was noted by Justice Wayne.[73] The principal difference expressed by the Chief Justice was that the states could legislate in aid of the return of fugitives but could not legislate to retard their return.

That the necessity of antislavery judges thwarting fugitive slaves was painful was expressed by Justice Woodbury five years later, when the Court upheld the federal Fugitive Slave Law of 1793.[74] "This court has no alternative . . . ," he said, "but to stand by the Constitution and laws with fidelity to their duties and their oaths. Their path is a straight and narrow one, to go where that Constitution and the laws lead, and not to break both, by traveling without or beyond them."[75]

The dissent of the abolitionists was so fervid, despite the fact that Justice Story, a known antislavery man, wrote the Prigg opinion for the Court and that Justice Woodbury was also known to be of that persuasion, that Justice McLean wrote to an abolitionist editor defending Justice Story and the Court.[76]

The second, and a most vital, decision overruling a congressional statute came when Dred Scott, a Negro slave, sued,[77] alleging that his master had taken him to Illinois and the Louisiana Territory (afterward Minnesota) by reason of which, under the Northwest Territory Ordinance of 1787 and the Missouri Compromise Act, he had become free. He sought an adjudication to that effect and also holding that he had remained free though thereafter he had been taken to Missouri, a slave state. The case reached the Supreme Court from a circuit court denial of his contention. Before the case was argued, Congress passed the Kansas-Nebraska Act, which repealed the Missouri Compromise Act and expressly denied the congressional intent to legislate concerning slavery in any state or territory.

While the case was pending before the Court, debate was raging in Con-

---

[72] Prigg v. Pennsylvania, 16 Pet. 539 (1842).
[73] Ibid., 637.
[74] Jones v. Van Zandt, 5 How. 215 (1847).
[75] Ibid., 231.
[76] Warren, The Supreme Court in United States History, II, 430–31.
[77] Dred Scott v. Sanford, 19 How. 393 (1857).

gress concerning slavery and it was apparent that a court decision upon the power of Congress could have momentous effects upon the vital issue of legislation respecting slavery in the territories. On the other hand, the Court could readily avoid any opinion on the constitutionality of the Missouri Compromise Act by leaving the determination of Scott's status to the laws of Missouri. This apparently the judges had agreed to do, and Justice Nelson had been assigned to write the opinion, when Justice McLean and later Justice Curtis indicated their intention to write sustaining the constitutionality of the Act. Thereupon Justice Wayne decided he could quell the raging fires by writing that the Act was unconstitutional and persuaded the Chief Justice to write such an opinion in which Justices Campbell, Catron, and Daniel would join.

In order to induce Justice Grier to concur, Catron wrote President-elect Buchanan asking him to consent to settle the issue one way or the other by an affirmative decision of the Court. Buchanan wrote to Justice Grier, who replied saying that "we [Grier, Wayne, and Taney] fully appreciate and concur in your [Buchanan's] views as to the desirableness at this time of having an expression of the opinion of the Court on this troublesome question." Grier went on to give Buchanan "in confidence the history of the case . . . with the probable result."[78]

The Court's opinion holding the Missouri Compromise Act unconstitutional was read by the Chief Justice and was concurred in by five of the eight Justices. Justices McLean and Curtis dissented.

Justice Wayne's judgment that the Court's determination would settle the issue could not have been more mistaken. The decision, with the Chief Justice and the four concurring justices each writing an opinion, fanned the northern abolitionist flames with disastrous results to the prestige of the Court and especially to that of its Chief Justice. Though, as so frequently has been charged, the decision did not cause the Civil War, it did, with the aid of Senator Douglas' espousal of its doctrine in the debates in the 1860 presidential race, help to elect President Lincoln.

The invective heaped upon the Court ranged from charges that it had abused its powers to the perennial recurrence of denials that it had them. However, Lincoln affirmed its jurisdiction while characterizing its decision as erroneous and trusting that it would be overruled.

In his first inaugural address, Lincoln said:

I do not forget the position assumed by some that constitutional questions must be binding in any case upon the parties to a suit as to the object of that suit, while they are also entitled to very high respect and consideration in all parallel

78 Warren, *The Supreme Court in United States History*, III, 15 *et seq.*

cases by all other departments of the Government. And while it is obviously possible that such decisions may be erroneous in any given case, still the evil effect following it, being limited to that particular case, with the chance that it may be overruled and never become a precedent for other cases, can better be borne than could the evils of a different practice. At the same time, the candid citizen must confess that if the policy of the Government upon vital questions affecting the whole people is to be irrevocably fixed by decisions of the Supreme Court, the instant they are made in ordinary litigation between parties in personal actions, the people will have ceased to be their own rulers, having to that extent practically resigned their Government into the hands of that eminent tribunal. Nor is there in this view any assault upon the court or the judges. It is a duty from which they may not shrink to decide cases properly brought before them, and it is no fault of theirs if others seek to turn their decisions to political purposes.[79]

Wisconsin was among the many states dissatisfied with the high court. After one Booth had been convicted of a violation of the federal Fugitive Slave Act, the state court granted Booth a writ of habeas corpus, and the Supreme Court of Wisconsin sustained it on the ground that the federal law was unconstitutional[80]—a case of man biting dog.

The United States Attorney General obtained a writ of error from the high court, but the clerk of the Wisconsin Supreme Court, on orders from the judges, refused to file the record with the high court.[81] Nevertheless, the latter took the case and after argument by the Attorney General, Wisconsin having failed to appear, Chief Justice Taney wrote an opinion reversing the judgment of the state court and, in ringing tones that might have been those of Marshall, asserted federal judicial supremacy.[82] The Wisconsin legislature adopted "defiant resolutions,"[83] and the supreme court of the state refused to obey the mandate of the high court.

A United States marshal then rearrested Booth, who again sought a writ of habeas corpus in the state court. Finally, in 1861, after the Civil War had started, the Wisconsin Supreme Court fell into line and acknowledged the supremacy of the federal jurisdiction.[84]

There was still another disapproving reaction to the Court's approval of the federal Fugitive Slave Law. This one came from Ohio, where a United States marshal was imprisoned by a state court for rearresting a fugitive slave

---

[79] Richardson, *Messages and Papers of the Presidents,* VII, 3210–11 (1861).

[80] Warren, *The Supreme Court in United States History,* II, 532–33.

[81] *Ibid.,* III, 54.

[82] Ableman v. Booth; United States v. Booth, 21 How. 506 (1859).

[83] Warren, *The Supreme Court in United States History,* III, 62–63.

[84] Arnold v. Booth, 14 Wis. 180 (1861).

whom the state court had taken from the marshal's custody. Justice McLean ordered the marshal's release.[85]

While it was too much to expect the judges to be less than human on the burning states' rights question, they demonstrated their ability to put aside prevailing Democratic partisanship in refusing jurisdiction of a political dispute which arose out of the effort of Thomas W. Dorr of Rhode Island to broaden the suffrage of disenfranchised Rhode Island voters. Rhode Island had never adopted a constitution; it was still operating under the anachronistic charter granted by Charles II in 1663. Dorr became the leader of the radical Democrats of Rhode Island who met in convention in 1841 and adopted a constitution for the state. Thereafter, at the gubernatorial election of 1842, the radical Democrats elected Dorr governor, while the existing organization recognized by the legislature, elected one King. Dorr's forces having taken to arms, Dorr was indicted for treason, convicted, and sentenced to life imprisonment.

The authorities held him incommunicado, and friends appealed in his behalf to the Supreme Court for a writ of habeas corpus. The Court held it lacked jurisdiction to grant the writ under the existing circumstances.[86]

However, in 1845 the issue came back to the Court as a result of a suit brought by a citizen and his wife, whose premises had been invaded by members of the state militia acting under martial law declared by the King regime. A majority of five (three justices not participating) joined in an opinion written by the Chief Justice and handed down after a delay of almost a year after final argument. Justice Woodbury dissented on a minor issue. The majority held that it was for Congress to determine what government was the established one for a state and that its decision was binding on every other department of the government and "could not be questioned in a judicial tribunal."[87]

The decision of the Court was rendered despite the fact that the case had become a *cause célèbre* in which Democrats throughout the nation supported Dorr, who had accomplished his main purpose: Rhode Island's first constitution, which enfranchised most of the theretofore disenfranchised citizens, was adopted by the ruling authorities in 1841. Later, Dorr was pardoned and his rights restored by the Democrats.

The two vital issues that brought out the division produced by the composition of the Taney court resulted in bloc, rather than in individual dissent. It resulted, too, on occasion, in a multiplicity of opinions that smacked of the seriatim practice. For example, in the three license cases argued and decided

---

[85] Warren, *The Supreme Court in United States History*, III, 66.

[86] *Ex parte* Dorr, 3 How. 103 (1845).

[87] Luther v. Borden, 7 How. 1, 42 (1849).

together, the members of the Court disagreeing "in the principles upon which these cases are decided,"[88] no less than six opinions were read. In the Passenger Cases[89] eight of the nine justices wrote a collection of views comprising over 250 pages in the law report, which took seven hours to read.[90] The justices were no doubt accustomed to the tautology which was endemic among the members of the Court and to which Marshall was no stranger, but the *Baltimore Sun* found the "excess of words . . . a great grievance," and the *New York Journal of Commerce* pronounced "these separate opinions . . . a great nuisance."[91]

Finally, the vote in two companion cases might be referred to in which Chief Justice Taney wrote affirming the judgment below, "The majority of the Court who give this judgment do not altogether agree in the principles upon which it ought to be maintained."[92] Justice Grier concurred in Taney's opinion. Justices Catron and Daniel wrote separately, each concurring in the result.[93] Justice Campbell said plaintively, "I find myself unable to decide the case."[94] Apparently Justice McLean found himself in the same situation, for he wrote ambiguously, without expressly indicating concurrence or dissent.[95] Justices Wayne and Curtis dissented, Justice Nelson concurring with Curtis.

[88] Thurlow v. Massachusetts; Fletcher v. Rhode Island; Pierce v. New Hampshire, 5 How. 504, 573 (1847).

[89] Smith v. Turner; Norris v. Boston, 7 How. 283 (1849).

[90] Warren, *The Supreme Court in United States History*, II, 452.

[91] *Ibid.*, 453.

[92] Ohio Life Ins. Co. v. Debolt, 16 How. 416, 427 (1853).

[93] *Ibid.*, 441, 443.

[94] *Ibid.*, 444.

[95] *Ibid.*

CHAPTER IV

The Civil War and Reconstruction Years

FOLLOWING THE DRED SCOTT DECISION, the Court, which until the slavery issue became crucial had enjoyed popular support and esteem, reached its all-time nadir in the minds and hearts of the people of the North. Taney was not merely criticized; he was castigated and condemned. The Court was termed "a mere party machine."[1] *The New York Times* said the decision had "done much to divest it of moral influence and to impair the confidence of the country."[2]

South Carolina took the slavery issue from the Court to the battlefield on April 12, 1861. Meanwhile, Justice Daniel had died, and some two weeks after the outbreak of war Justice Campbell resigned, feeling it his duty to do so in view of his southern sympathies. The Chief Justice, however, stayed on, though by now he was in his eighties and in poor health. However, his mind was active, as he demonstrated when, some six weeks after the war had begun, a man named Merryman was arrested by the military and sought a writ of habeas corpus from Taney, sitting in the circuit court. Taney granted the writ, but the military refused to honor it, since the President had authorized the suspension of the writ for reasons of public safety. Taney's effort to punish the military officer for contempt was thwarted by the latter, whereupon he wrote and filed an opinion denying the constitutional authority of the President to suspend the writ, even in time of war.[3]

Lincoln's reaction was of a piece with that expressed by President Jackson anent the decision of Chief Justice Marshall denying Georgia's power in the case of the Cherokee Indians. He justified his action and continued his policy, contending that the situation was within constitutional exceptions, because it was required by considerations of public safety in the face of rebellion.[4]

[1] Charles Warren, *The Supreme Court in United States History* (3 vols., Boston, Little, Brown & Co., 1922), III, 29–30, quoting Gen. Webb, owner of *New York Courier*, March 7, 1857.

[2] March 8, 1857, quoted in Warren, *ibid.*, 31.

[3] *Ex parte* Merryman, 17 F. Cas. #9487 (1861).

[4] Letter to Erastus Corning and others, June 12, 1863, John Nicolay and John Hay, eds., *Complete Works of Abraham Lincoln* (12 vols., New York, The Lamb Publishing Co., 1905), VIII, 298.

Again Taney was the subject of popular castigation. While he was both correct and courageous in his Merryman decision, as was attested by the later Milligan decision, he was properly criticized for his failure to resign, not alone because of his age, ill-health, and consequent inability to give full attention to his duties but also because of the low state in the public mind his continued presence helped to inflict on the Court.

The death of McLean left the Court with three vacancies, and finally the President appointed Noah H. Swayne of Ohio, Samuel F. Miller of Iowa, and David Davis of Illinois. Thus, when the December, 1862, term opened, the administration was represented by three appointees. During this term, the court decided the Prize Cases, which involved the question of applying the rules of war to neutrals who sought to violate the blockade of Southern ports the Union was attempting to maintain.[5] The situation, like that in Vietnam, was complicated by the fact that the Union was unwilling to concede that it was at war with a belligerent; instead, it maintained that it was dealing with an insurrection, and Secretary of State Seward had officially maintained that no state of war existed. However, the Court held that though a civil war is never publicly proclaimed and may be termed an insurrection, it is nonetheless a civil war, with belligerent parties in hostile array, and the proclamation of blockade is official and conclusive evidence that a state of war exists; this is similar to a determination of recent import concerning the blockade of the Gulf of Aqaba by Egypt and the retaliatory action by the state of Israel.

There were fears that Taney's court, upon which there were only three Lincoln appointees, might prove a hindrance to the administration and its pursuit of the war. However, the fears proved unfounded; by a five-to-four vote, with the Chief Justice dissenting, the Union position was upheld. With rare exception, that proved to be the attitude of the Court throughout the conflict, although the Lincoln appointees did not constitute a majority of the Court until after 1864.

The Chief Justice died on October 12, 1864, following the creation by Congress of a tenth judicial circuit, thus increasing the membership of the Court to ten. To this post the President appointed Stephen J. Field of California. Thereafter, following the appointment of Salmon P. Chase, Lincoln's secretary of the treasury, as Chief Justice, Justice Catron died. In the subsequent year, after President Lincoln's death, Congress reduced the Court's membership to nine to avoid an appointment by President Johnson. When Justice Wayne died on July 5, 1867, Congress reduced the Court's membership to eight, again to avoid the seating of a Johnson appointee. Parenthetically and

5 Preciat, John Currie, Miller, William Currie v. United States, 2 Black 635 (1863) (Prize Cases).

reminiscently, in 1968 Republicans in the Senate filibustered to prevent the confirmation of Johnson appointees.

Of the Lincoln appointees, Justices Miller and Field were to prove especially able and independent. With Justice Bradley, later appointed by President Grant, they became three of the more important members of the Court through the period of physical and economic expansion of the country during the years following the Civil War.

Justice Miller was forty-six years old when he was appointed at the instance of the representatives in Congress from Iowa, his adopted state, who caused 28 of the 32 senators and 120 members of the House of Representatives probably three-fourths of those in attendance) to petition President Lincoln to select him.[6] He was the first justice appointed to the Court from beyond the Mississippi,[7] and, except for his belated career at the bar, his record could hardly have justified his selection, since, after he had graduated in medicine, he had spent the next ten years of his life practicing as a country doctor in Kentucky. His interest in the law had been aroused by the fact that, as a doctor, he shared an office with a lawyer, and his law training was confined to "reading law,"[8] as was the case with Marshall.

In view of the fact that he served while the Court was considering and limiting the rights of Negroes under the Fourteenth Amendment, it is interesting to note that while he was a resident of Kentucky he owned slaves and that he moved to Iowa because he no longer wanted to live in a slave state and, once in Iowa, freed his slaves. Justice Miller was to succeed Justice Johnson as the principal dissenter on the Court; he wrote some seven hundred opinions during his twenty-eight years on the bench, and, interestingly enough, his first opinion was a dissent.[9]

Justice Stephen Field was about the same age as Justice Miller when appointed. He was the son of David Dudley Field, a New England Congregational minister of early American ancestry. One of Stephen Field's brothers was David Dudley Field, named for his father, who became one of the country's outstanding lawyers; another was Cyrus W. Field, who laid the cable spanning the Atlantic Ocean. Stephen Field's sister was the mother of David P. Brewer, who became a justice of the Supreme Court and sat on the bench with his uncle. Field had practiced law in California and had served in the state legislature and on the state supreme court bench, finally becoming Chief Justice.

The appointment of Chief Justice Chase created an equal division of Repub-

---

[6] Charles Noble Gregory, "Samuel Freeman Miller," 17 *Yale Law Journal* 422, 426–27.

[7] *Ibid.*, 427.

[8] *Ibid.*, 424.

[9] *Ibid.*, 428; *and see* Calais S. Co. v. Van Pelt's Adm'r, 2 Black 372 (1863).

licans and Democrats while the bench remained at ten. After Justice Catron's death, the Lincoln appointees constituted a majority. That fact did not prevent the Lincoln-appointed justices from joining with the others to hold illegal the action of a military commission that convicted Milligan,[10] thus affirming the correctness of Chief Justice Taney's decision in the Merryman case from which President Lincoln had dissented.

The Milligan decision, written by Justice Davis, Lincoln's appointee, close personal friend, and later executor, marked the involvement of the Court in the struggle between Thaddeus Stevens' radical Republicans in Congress and President Johnson over Reconstruction policies.

Milligan had been convicted of violating the laws of war by a military commission and had been sentenced to be hanged. He sought a writ of habeas corpus from the Indiana Circuit Court, which referred the application to the Supreme Court. Granting the writ, Justice Davis wrote the much-quoted words: "The Constitution . . . is a law for rulers and people, equally in war and in peace," and he said its provisions cannot "be suspended during any of the great exigencies of government. . . . Martial law can never exist where the Courts are open."

However, to his dicta, subscribed to by four of the other judges, that neither the President nor Congress could authorize military commissions except in the actual theater of war where civil courts were not available, the remaining four justices dissented. The Chief Justice said: "The power of Congress to authorize trials for crimes against the security and safety of the National forces may be derived from its constitutional authority to raise and support armies and to declare war, if not from its constitutional authority to provide for governing the National forces."[11]

Subsequently, in passing upon the contention of seven German saboteurs that they could not be tried by court-martial on the authority of the Milligan case, a unanimous Court held that the Milligan case had no application to belligerents.

In a World War II case before the Court following the attack on Pearl Harbor,[12] the Territorial Governor, with the concurrence of the President, declared martial law and the commanding general proclaimed himself military governor and undertook the defense of the Territory and the maintenance of order. The civil courts were closed down, and military tribunals were established.

Eight months later a stockbroker was arrested, charged with embezzlement. Two years after the attack on Pearl Harbor a civilian shipfitter was

[10] *Ex parte* Milligan, 4 Wall. 2 (1866).
[11] *Ibid.*, 142.
[12] Duncan v. Kahanomoku; White v. Steer, 327 U.S. 304 (1946).

64

arrested, charged with brawling with two armed Marine sentries. Military tribunals tried both men, though by the time of the trial of the latter the courts were again open, but the military courts retained jursidiction of an assault upon military personnel.

The Court granted habeas corpus, holding that power to declare martial law did not include the power to supplant courts by military tribunals, where conditions are not such as to prevent the enforcement of the laws by the courts. The Chief Justice and Justice Murphy concurred, the latter citing the previous Milligan case. Justices Burton and Frankfurter dissented.

Almost one hundred years after Milligan, in 1955, we find Justice Black citing the case in holding that an ex-serviceman could not be tried by court-martial after his discharge on a charge of murder committed in Korea. Writing for a majority of six, Justice Black said: "This assertion of military authority over civilians cannot rest on the President's power as commander-in-chief, or on any theory of martial law."[13] Justice Reed, writing for himself and Justices Minton and Burton in dissent, maintained that the prosecution was not "an effort to make a civilian subject to military law"; that would violate the rule of two other cases.[14]

Again quoting the Milligan case, Justice Black, writing for himself, the Chief Justice, and Justices Douglas and Brennan, held that a Mrs. Smith, the wife of an Army officer, could not be tried by court-martial in Japan for the murder of her husband committed in that country, nor could a Mrs. Covert, the wife of an Air Force sergeant, be tried by court-martial in England for the murder of her husband committed in that country.[15] Justices Frankfurter and Harlan concurred, limiting their concurrence to capital cases. Justices Clark and Burton dissented, Justice Clark having previously written for five justices affirming the conviction of Mrs. Smith,[16] and of Mrs. Covert.[17] Thereafter reargument had been granted with the results stated above.

Later, again with Justice Clark writing for five members of the Court, it was held that a soldier's wife could not be tried by court-martial for manslaughter—a noncapital offense—committed abroad. Justices Whittaker and Stewart concurred but restricted their holding to "civilian dependents," as distinguished from "civilian employees," of the armed forces. Justices Harlan and Frankfurter dissented, maintaining that the Constitution did not prevent such trials on noncapital charges.[18] In a companion case the conviction of a civilian employee charged with murder but convicted of manslaughter (a lesser

[13] United States v. Quarles, 350 U.S. 11, 13 (1955).
[14] Duncan v. Kahanomoku, 327 U.S. 304 (1946); ex parte Endo, 323 U.S. 283 (1944).
[15] Reid v. Covert; Kinsella v. Krueger, 354 U.S. 1 (1957).
[16] Kinsella v. Krueger, 351 U.S. 470 (1956).
[17] Reid v. Covert, 351 U.S. 487 (1956).
[18] Kinsella v. United States ex rel. Singleton, 361 U.S. 234 (1960).

degree) was reversed.[19] Once more Justice Clark wrote for five members of the Court, with Justices Harlan and Frankfurter concurring because the trial originally was for a capital offense. Justices Whittaker and Stewart dissented, maintaining that such a trial was constitutional respecting "civilian employees." Finally, the Court split five to four in holding that a civilian employee in Morocco and a civilian auditor in Germany could not be tried for noncapital offenses, with Justices Harlan, Frankfurter, Whittaker, and Stewart dissenting.[20]

The earlier Milligan decision was greeted with dismay by the radical Republicans who sought to punish the rebellious southern states, and their dismay turned to anger when President Johnson viewed the decision as enabling him to undertake to speedily end military government in the South. In addition, with the precedent of Milligan, he ordered dismissal of pending military trials of southern civilians; and similar action was taken by a Delaware district judge respecting four civilians convicted of the murder of Union soldiers in South Carolina.[21] There were also congressional demands for impeachment of some of the high court judges or for a court-packing reorganization of the Court, for the Thaddeus Stevens group of radical Republicans feared the fate of their reconstruction legislation before the existing Court.

In the midst of this furor, which produced none of the threatened legislation, Congress enacted a number of laws providing for military government in the southern states. After veto by the President, who urged constitutional objections, the Congress re-enacted these laws by the necessary two-thirds.[22]

Immediately thereafter, a motion was made in the Court, on behalf of the state of Mississippi, for leave to sue for an injunction to prevent President Johnson, his agents, and the military from acting under the congressional acts. The Court promptly denied the motion, holding that where acts required the exercise of executive discretion the Court had "no jurisdiction . . . to enjoin the President in the performance of his official duties."[23]

A subsequent attempt, this time to enjoin Secretary of War Stanton and General Grant from proceeding under the provisions of the Reconstruction Acts, met with a like fate; the Court held that the suits were political in nature and that it lacked jurisdiction of such controversies.[24] However, when Mississippi's counsel sought to amend its bill seeking the injunction that had been denied, the Court divided equally, four to four, thus denying the application.[25]

[19] Grisham v. Hagan, 361 U.S. 278 (1960).
[20] McElroy v. United States ex rel. Guagliardo; Wilson v. Bohlender, 361 U.S. 281 (1960).
[21] Warren, *The Supreme Court in United States History*, III, 164–65.
[22] *Ibid.*, 177.
[23] Mississippi v. Johnson, 4 Wall. 475, 502 (1867).
[24] Georgia v. Stanton, 6 Wall. 50 (1868).

66

Two five-to-four opinions decided the fates of a priest and a lawyer. John A. Cummings, a Roman Catholic priest, was indicted and convicted in Missouri of the crime of teaching and preaching without first having taken an oath that he had not been "in armed hostility to the United States" and that he had not "by act or word" manifested his adherence to the cause of the enemies of the United States. Justice Field, writing for the majority, said that the oath

> embraces more than thirty distinct affirmations or tests. . . . All men have certain inalienable rights—that among these are life, liberty and the pursuit of happiness; and that in the pursuit of happiness all avocations, all honors, all positions are alike open to everyone, and that in the protection of these rights all are equal before the law. Any deprivation or suspension of any of these rights for past conduct is punishment.[26]

Thus finding, since obviously the oath could not be taken by those guilty of the proscribed past acts, Field concluded that punishment without trial for such past acts necessarily followed, with the result that the provisions in the Constitution against ex post facto laws and bills of attainder were violated.

In the case of A. H. Garland, an attorney who had been admitted to practice in 1860, the Court was faced with a congressional statute denying the right to practice law without taking an oath that one had never taken arms against the United States. The Court had amended its rules to conform to the congressional act. Garland moved for permission to practice before the Court and produced a pardon signed by President Johnson for any offenses committed by him during the Rebellion. Before holding that the pardon sufficed to fully exculpate Garland, Field said:

> The attorney and counselor being, by the solemn judicial act of the court, clothed with his office, does not hold it as a matter of grace and favor. The right . . . is something more than a mere indulgence, revocable at the pleasure of the court, or at the command of the Legislature. It is a right of which he can only be deprived by the judgment of the court, for moral or professional delinquency.[27]

The Chief Justice and Justices Miller, Swayne, and Davis dissented in both cases.

Cummings and Garland were fortunate in that their cases were decided before Justice Wayne died. In his absence, in 1870, when a similar Missouri question came to the Court, the Court divided four and four, with the same

[25] Warren, *The Supreme Court in United States History*, III, 185–86.
[26] Cummings v. Missouri, 4 Wall. 277, 321–22 (1867).
[27] *Ex parte* Garland, 4 Wall. 333, 379 (1867).

four dissenters voting to affirm a decision below favorable to the statute. This time the statute was upheld, and the petitioner's right to vote, in the absence of his statutory oath, was denied.[28]

As late as 1966 the Court was still struggling with the various questions posed by the requirements of loyalty oaths. These and other such emanations are facets of the agitation and hysteria that accompany and follow every war, as is attested by Vietnam excesses. Common incidents include criminal statutes and prosecutions, requirements for loyalty oaths, and loyalty reviews for government employees. The Gitlow prosecution and the Schwimmer naturalization case persecutions and other such abuses marked World War I; the anti-Communist cold war McCarthyism, which still persists, followed World War II.

In 1947 President Truman, by executive order, established a so-called loyalty security program that laid out procedures to be followed respecting government employees suspected or accused of disloyalty. Congress included in the Management Labor Relations Act of 1947 a provision requiring officers of unions to file affidavits (1) denying membership in the Communist party and (2) attesting their loyalty by denying membership in or support for any organization that believed in or taught the overthrow of the Government. In 1950 five members of the Court (the Chief Justice and Justices Reed, Burton, Frankfurter, and Jackson) held the provision valid.[29] Of the six judges who sat, only Black dissented *in toto*. Three members of the Court found the second requirement valid, but as to that, Justices Frankfurter and Jackson dissented. These two justices, with Justice Black, produced an equal division that resulted in a declaration of validity for that portion also.

The following year, by a vote of five to four, the Court upheld a city ordinance requiring a public employee to take an oath and make an affidavit to the effect that he had not been a member of or become affiliated with any group advocating the violent overthrow of the Government. Justices Burton, Frankfurter, Douglas, and Black dissented.[30]

Justice Black distinguished the case from a prior decision at the same term, in which a unanimous Court upheld a Maryland statute requiring a candidate for public office to take an oath that he was not a subversive.[31] He likened the situation to previous decisions of the Court striking down loyalty oaths,[32] which, Justice Douglas contended, governed the case.[33] He maintained the ordinance was void as a bill of attainder and as an ex post facto law.

28 Blair v. Ridgely, unreported.
29 American Com. Assoc. v. Douds; United Steelworkers v. NLRB, 339 U.S. 382 (1950).
30 Garner v. Board of Pub. Works, 341 U.S. 716 (1951).
31 Gerende v. Board of Supervisors, 341 U.S. 56 (1951).
32 Cummings v. Missouri, 4 Wall. 277 (1867); *ex parte* Garland, 4 Wall. 333 (1867).
33 Garner v. Board of Pub. Works, 341 U.S. 716, 732 (1951).

A veteran denied a property tax exemption because of a refusal to file a loyalty oath, as required by the California Constitution, sued to recover taxes paid under protest and for a declaratory judgment. Justice Brennan, writing for six members of the Court, found that the statutory provisions denied the veteran freedom of speech without due process and reversed the adverse decision of the state courts.[34] Justice Burton concurred in the result. Justice Clark dissented. The Chief Justice did not participate. Companion cases[35] received similar treatment.

In 1966 the issue of constitutionality of a statute requiring an oath by Arizona state employees, challenged by a teacher, had been remanded to the state court for reconsideration[36] in the light of a prior decision.[37] The Arizona court reaffirmed its finding of validity of the statute. Over the dissent of Justices White, Clark, Harlan, and Stewart, five members of the Court, in an opinion by Justice Douglas, struck down the statute. Douglas held that the statute subjected to prosecution for perjury and for discharge from public office anyone who took the oath, a standard form of allegiance, and who knowingly and willfully became or remained a member of the Communist party or of any subordinate or other organization having for one of its purposes the overthrow of the government of Arizona.[38]

The majority maintained that those who joined an organization without sharing in its unlawful purposes pose no threat to constitutional government and that to presume conclusively that those who join a subversive organization share its unlawful aims is forbidden.

The minority defended the statute on the ground that the penalties were restricted to those having knowledge of the unlawful purposes of the organization and maintained that the Court should not forbid Arizona from conditioning employment upon the oath but should limit itself to invalidating only the portions of the statute that invoked criminal penalties.

In another case[39] the Court struck down an Oklahoma statute requiring state employees on the staff and faculty of a state college to take a loyalty oath, distinguishing the situation from the prior cases upon the ground that it created a conclusive presumption of disloyalty by reason of association with an organization, regardless of the innocence of the person accused. Justices Black and Douglas concurred, maintaining the statute violative of First Amendment rights. Justices Frankfurter and Burton also concurred; Justice Jackson did not participate.

[34] Speiser v. Randall, 357 U.S. 513 (1958).
[35] Valley Unitarian Church, First Unitarian Church v. Los Angeles, 357 U.S. 545 (1958).
[36] Elfbrand v. Russell, 378 U.S. 127 (1964).
[37] Bagget v. Bullitt, 377 U.S. 360 (1964).
[38] Elfbrand v. Russell, 384 U.S. 11 (1966).
[39] Wieman v. Updegraff, 344 U.S. 183 (1952).

During the 1967 term, Justice Douglas, writing for six members of the Court, held that the Maryland requirement for a loyalty oath to be taken by a faculty member of the University of Maryland, when read with reference to other provisions of the Maryland statute defining a "subversive" and a "subversive organization," was unconstitutionally vague.

Justice Harlan, joined by Justices Stewart and White, maintained that the oath should be considered on its own basis and that, as such, it was valid in that it required no more than an answer to the question of whether the affiant was "now, in one way or another engaged in an attempt to overthrow the Government by force and violence."[40]

Another situation was presented when, by statutes and administrative regulations, in an effort to keep its school system free of subversives, New York required personnel to certify, *inter alia,* that they were not Communists. The constitutionality of the plan was challenged in 1952, but the high court upheld it. Ten years later, in 1962, members of the faculty of a privately owned and operated university, which merged into and became part of the State University of New York, refused to certify, as required by the state plan, that they were not Communists and again resorted to the courts to challenge the constitutionality of the plan. In an opinion during the 1966 term by Justice Brennan for five members of the Court, he found that the issue of vagueness of certain sections of the statutes had not been passed upon by the Court in the previous case, that those sections were too vague for enforcement, and that, in consequence, they were invalid in so far as they proscribed mere knowing membership without any showing of specific intent to further the unlawful aims of the Communist party.[41]

Justice Clark, joined by Justices Harlan, Stewart, and White, wrote in dissent, saying:

> The blunderbuss fashion in which the majority couches "its artillery of words," together with the morass of cases it cites as authority and the obscurity of their application to the question at hand, makes it difficult to grasp the true thrust of its decision.
>
> The certificate and statement once required by the Board of Trustees of the State University and upon which appellants base their attack were, before the case was tried, abandoned by the Board and are no longer required to be made. Despite this fact the majority proceeds to its decision. . . . It does not explain how the statute can be applied to appellants under procedures which have been for almost two years a dead letter. The issues posed are, therefore, purely abstract and entirely speculative in character. The Court under such

40 Whitehill v. Elkins, 389 U.S. 54 (1967).

41 Adler v. Board of Education, 342 U.S. 485 (1952); Keyishian v. Board of Regents, 385 U.S. 589, 609–10 (1967).

circumstances has in the past refused to pass upon constitutional questions. . . .
No court has ever reached out so far to destroy so much with so little. . . .
This Court has again and again, since at least 1951, approved procedures either identical or at the least similar to the ones the Court condemns today. [Clark cited Garner v. Board of Public Works.[42]]

The majority says that the Feinberg Law is bad because it has an "overbroad sweep." I regret to say—and I do so with deference—that the majority has by its broadside swept away one of our most precious rights, namely, the right of self-preservation.[43]

An interesting dissent by Chief Justice Chase and Justice Clifford pointed up the Court's lack of appreciation of the potentialities of the commerce clause, though its immediate application was unnecessary. Nevada had attempted to tax persons leaving the state by railroad or stagecoach. A majority of the Court held that the right of passing through a state by a citizen of the United States is one guaranteed to him by the Constitution and that hence the taxing statute was unconstitutional.[44] The majority opinion said that "as the tax does not itself institute any regulation of commerce of a national character, or which has a uniform operation over the whole country, it is not easy to maintain . . . that it violates the clause of the Federal Constitution."[45]
Dissenting, Justice Clifford wrote:

I hold that the Act of the State Legislature is inconsistent with the power conferred upon Congress to regulate commerce among the several States, and I think the judgment of the court should have been put exclusively on that ground . . . I am clear that the State Legislature cannot impose any such burden upon commerce among the several States. Such commerce is secured against such legislation in the States by the Constitution, irrespective of any Congressional action.[46]

During the 1941 term the Court struck down a California statute seeking to restrain the entry of indigents into the state. The Court held, in an opinion by Justice Byrne, that the statute violated the commerce clause. Justice Byrne said that "poverty and immorality are not synonymous."[47]
However, four of the justices were not pleased with the ground upon which the majority placed the decision. Therefore, Justice Douglas, concurring, said:

[42] 341 U.S. 716 (1951).
[43] Keyishian v. Board of Regents, 385 U.S. 589, 620–28 (1967).
[44] Crandall v. Nevada, 6 Wall. 35 (1867).
[45] *Ibid.*, 43.
[46] *Ibid.*, 49.
[47] Edwards v. California 314 U.S. 160, 177 (1941).

The right of persons to move freely from State to State occupies a more protected position in our constitutional system than does the movement of cattle, fruit, steel and coal across state lines. . . . The right to move freely from State to State is an incident of national citizenship protected by the privileges and immunities clause of the Fourteenth Amendment against state interference.[48]

Justices Black and Murphy joined in the Douglas opinion, and Justice Jackson, also concurring, said:

The migration of a human being of whom it is charged that he possesses nothing that can be sold and has no wherewithal to buy, does not fit easily into my notions as to what is commerce. . . .

This clause (privileges and immunities) was adopted to make United States citizenship the dominant and paramount allegiance among us. The return which the law had long associated with allegiance was protection. The power of citizenship as a shield against oppression was widely known from the example of Paul's Roman citizenship, which sent the centurion scurrying to his higher-ups with the message: "Take heed what thou doest: for this man is a Roman."

"Indigence" in itself is neither a source of rights nor a basis for denying them. The mere state of being without funds is a neutral fact—constitutionally an irrelevance, like race, creed, or color. . . .

Property can have no more dangerous, even if unwitting, enemy than one who would make its possession a pretext for unequal or exclusive civil rights.[49]

However, in a previous 1920 case, with but Justice Clarke dissenting, the Court held an observation made in Twining v. New Jersey "to the effect that it had been held in the Crandall case that the privilege of passing from state to state is an attribute of National citizenship may here be put out of view as inapposite."[50]

The Court went on to apply the Slaughter House doctrine to hold that defendants who had driven other citizens out of Arizona into New Mexico and threatened them with death or grave bodily injury if they returned could not be punished under federal law, since the privileges and immunities guaranteed by Article 4, Section 2, of the Constitution were enforceable only against adverse action by the states. "No basis is accorded for contending that the wrongful prevention by an individual of the enjoyment by a citizen of one state in another of rights possessed in that state by its own citizens was a violation of the right afforded by the Constitution."[51] Nor were the acts complained of found to have burdened interstate commerce.

Another phase of the application of Article 4, Section 2, of the Constitu-

48 *Ibid.*, 178.
49 *Ibid.*, 182, 184–85.
50 United States v. Wheeler, 254 U.S. 281, 299 (1920).
51 *Ibid.*, 298.

tion holding that "the Citizens of each State shall be entitled to all Privileges and Immunities of Citizens in the several States," as well as the privileges and immunities and other clauses of the Fourteenth Amendment were involved when citizens of one state claimed they, as nonresidents of another, were discriminated against in being charged license fees for hunting and fishing in excess of those charged to residents. An early case[52] had held that such discrimination was permissible since a state owned the wild animals found within its boundaries and the soil and waters from which they were taken by hunters and fishermen. However, though this view prevailed for some years, Justices Frankfurter and Jackson announced the later and more modern view[53] which was followed in a subsequent case to strike down a discriminatory Alaska statute[54] upon the ground that while a state may require nonresidents to compensate for an added enforcement burden or for any conservation expenditures borne by residents, it may not otherwise discriminate against nonresidents, in fixing license fees because of the constitutional protection afforded them.

Just how far the constitutional privileges and immunities of the citizens of another state vis-à-vis a state may be stretched will call for a high court determination of a 1967 divided ruling of a Connecticut district court. It held that the state of Connecticut could not constitutionally require a stated term of prior residence before admitting a nonresident who had entered and taken residence in the state to the welfare rolls, since such a requirement would burden the right of free interstate passage. The Court said, "The right of interstate travel also encompasses the right to be free of discouragement of interstate movement." The high court has the question undecided but under review at this writing.

One might well be of the opinion that the right to receive welfare monies is a privilege, at least to nonresidents of a state, and that the right of interstate travel does not encompass the privilege of selecting a state with the greatest possible welfare benefits. However, one might also conclude that lower courts would enlarge the rights of welfare clients in view of the "war on poverty" and the availability of free legal representation for the indigent. And such conclusion would be borne out by the decision of an Alabama court holding unconstitutional the state "substitute father" welfare rule, which there and in eighteen other states denies welfare benefits to the children of women who engage in extramarital sexual relations, a decision which the highest court affirmed in the closing days of the 1967 term.[55] Other lower

[52] Corfield v. Coryell (1823 Pa.), 4 Wash. C.C. 371, F. Cas. #3233.
[53] Toomer v. Witsell, 334 U.S. 385 (1948).
[54] Mullaney v. Anderson, 342 U.S. 415 (1952).
[55] King v. Smith, 392 U.S. 309 (1968).

court decisions have established precedents foreign to past points of view, which ultimately will come before the Supreme Court for final determination.[56]

Over the dissent of Justices Miller, Swayne, and Grier, an opinion by Chief Justice Chase, for the majority, held that the rebellion by Texas did not cause it to lose its status as a state: "The Constitution, in all its provisions, looks to an indestructible Union, composed of indestructible States. When, therefore, Texas became one of the United States, she entered into an indissoluble relation."[57]

As a war measure, Congress in 1862 passed the first of the acts making paper currency issued by the Treasury legal tender. Challenge of the validity of the act came before the Court in 1863,[58] but the Court disclaimed jurisdiction (a decision which in 1872 it found erroneous).[59] The question reached the Court again in 1865 but was not argued finally until December 10, 1869. According to Justice Chase, when the "cause was decided in conference," Justice Grier voted to declare the Act unconstitutional. However, Justice Grier was notoriously senile and was induced to resign on February 1, 1870. His resignation reduced the sitting Court to seven, and the Chief Justice was able to bring the situation within the ambit of Chief Justice Marshall's injunction that a constitutional decision should not be rendered without a majority of four. So, on February 7, Chase announced the Hepburn decision holding the Acts unconstitutional by a majority of four, Justices Miller, Swayne, and Davis dissenting.[60]

However, on the same day, President Grant appointed two new members of the Court, William Strong and Joseph P. Bradley, Congress having increased the membership to nine now that President Johnson was out of the way. Thereupon the Court set for reargument the Legal Tender Cases (Knox v. Lee and Parker v. Davis), which had been argued previously on November 17, 1869, and they were reargued on February 23 and April 18 and 19, 1871. Two weeks later, Justice Strong, with the concurrence of the newly appointed Bradley and the three dissenters from the opinion of the Chief Justice in the Hepburn case, overruled that decision and held the Legal Tender Acts constitutional. Now the Chief Justice and Justices Clifford, Field, and Nelson, who had held the Acts unconstitutional in the Hepburn case, dissented.[61]

Chief Justice Chase sought to justify his finding of unconstitutionality of acts which he, as Secretary of the Treasury, and the President, who had

56 *New York Times*, September 26, 1967.
57 Texas v. White, 7 Wall. 700, 725–26 (1869).
58 Roosevelt v. Meyer, 1 Wall. 512 (1863).
59 Trebilcock v. Wilson, 12 Wall. 687 (1872).
60 Hepburn v. Griswold, 8 Wall. 603, 626 (1870).
61 Knox v. Lee; Parker v. Davis, 12 Wall. 457 (1871) (Legal Tender Cases).

appointed him, had sponsored, by ascribing the latter to "the tumult of the late civil war, and under the influence of apprehensions for the safety of the Republic."[62] Similarly, Justice Strong undertook to justify overruling the recent Hepburn decision of the Court by the circumstances under which that decision was made.[63] Beyond that, had the Knox v. Lee decision not been rendered, the dissent of Justice Miller in the Hepburn case, holding that "if the act to be considered is in any sense essential to the execution of an acknowledged power, the degree of that necessity is for the Legislature and not for the court to determine," would have pointed the way for future determinations.[64]

Indeed, the Hepburn case would have been overruled and the dissent sustained later, when the Court had occasion to pass on an act of Congress which forbade the further retirement of legal tender notes and directed that, when returned to the Treasury, they should be reissued and kept in circulation. On this occasion, one Julliard sued one Greenman for payment for goods sold and delivered and Greenman alleged that he had tendered payment in legal tender notes which Julliard had refused to accept.

The issue thus presented to the Court was whether, the Court having found congressional power to issue such notes in time of war, it had the power to do so in time of peace. The majority said "yes"; Justice Field, faithful to his Hepburn and Knox v. Lee stance, said "no," adding: "What was in 1862 called the 'medicine of the Constitution' has now become its daily bread. So it always happens that whenever a wrong principle of conduct, political or personal, is adopted on a plea of necessity, it will be afterwards followed on a plea of convenience."[65] And he concluded in a spirit of prophecy: "Why pay interest on the millions of dollars of bonds now due, when Congress can in one day make the money to pay the principal? And why should there be any restraint upon unlimited appropriations by the government for all imaginary schemes of public improvement, if the printing press can furnish the money that is needed for them?"[66]

In overruling its denial of jurisdiction in Roosevelt v. Meyer, the Court, in the Trebilcock case held that a contract calling for payment of dollars, "in specie," could not be satisfied by payment in legal tender notes, but required payment in "gold or silver dollars." Justices Bradley and Miller consistent with their Hepburn stand dissented, Bradley saying that "only in those cases in which gold and silver are stipulated for as bullion can they be demanded

---

[62] Hepburn v. Griswold, 8 Wall. 603, 625 (1870).

[63] Knox v. Lee, 12 Wall. 457, 553-54 (1871).

[64] Hepburn v. Griswold, 8 Wall. 603, 639 (1870).

[65] Julliard v. Greenman, 110 U.S. 421 (1884) (Legal Tender Cases).

[66] *Ibid.*, 470.

in specie."[67] Justice Miller, too, wrote briefly in support of the Hepburn decision, a precursor to the five-to-four opinion to follow sixty years later authorizing payment of gold bonds in depreciated legal tender notes.[68]

Justice Bradley dissented from the decision of his brethren who held that the "supremacy of the General Government . . . cannot be maintained," and that "the two governments (state and federal) are upon an equality"; hence they concluded that it was unconstitutional for the national government to attempt to tax the salary of a judicial officer of a state.[69] Justice Bradley said in reply that

> the General Government has the same power of taxing the income of officers of the State Governments as it has of taxing that of its own officers. It is the common government of all alike. . . . No man ceases to be a citizen of the United States by being an officer under the State Government. . . . The taxation by the State Governments of the instruments employed by the General Government in the exercise of its powers, is a very different thing. Such taxation involves an interference with the powers of a government in which other States and their citizens are equally interested.[70]

Gradually,[71] the force of Justice Bradley's dissent "gathered rather than lost strength with time"[72] until in 1939, over the dissent of Justices Butler and McReynolds, a majority held that New York could tax the officers of the Home Owners' Loan Corporation, a federal instrumentality,[73] as it had previously held it could tax employees of the Port of New York Authority, a bistate agency.[74] Thus the Court laid at rest the concept that a tax on income is a tax on its source, and, in so holding, the Court expressly overruled two cases[75] and implicitly overruled two others so far as they recognized an implied constitutional immunity from income taxation of the salaries of officers or employees of the national or of a state government or of their instrumentalities.[76]

Incidentally, in one respect at least, Justice Nelson, writing for the majority,

[67] Trebilcock v. Wilson, 12 Wall. 687, 699 (1872).
[68] Norman v. Baltimore & Ohio R.R., United States v. Bankers Trust Co., 294 U.S. 240 (1935) (Gold Clause Cases).
[69] Collector v. Day, 11 Wall. 113 (1871).
[70] Ibid., 128–29.
[71] Helvering v. Gerhardt; Helvering v. Wilson; Helvering v. Mulcahy, 304 U.S. 405 (1938).
[72] Frankfurter, J., in Graves v. New York, 306 U.S. 466, 489, (1939).
[73] Ibid.
[74] Helvering v. Gerhardt, 304 U.S. 405 (1938).
[75] Collector v. Day, 11 Wall. 113 (1871); New York ex rel. Rogers v. Graves, 299 U.S. 401 (1937).
[76] Dobbins v. Commissioners, 16 Pet. 435 (1842); Brush v. Commissioner, 300 U.S. 352 (1937).

was correct in saying that both governments were on a par, for ultimately, following the lead of Justices Holmes and Brandeis, the Court and Congress agreed that even federal judges were not tax-exempt.

In a later case[77] Justice Frankfurter wrote for himself and Justice Rutledge, holding that the federal government could levy taxes on proceeds arising out of sales by the state of mineral water taken from Saratoga Springs, New York. The state contended that it was engaged in a nontaxable governmental activity in that it was selling part of a natural resource. Justice Frankfurter said that "on the basis of authority the case is quickly disposed of."[78] He relied on denials of immunity in prior cases involving proceeds arising from conduct by a state of the liquor business,[79] and a state's operation of a street railway.[80] "We certainly see no reason for putting soft drinks in a different constitutional category from hard drinks," Justice Frankfurter wrote,[81] citing a prior case.[82] He said that "the views of Mr. Justice Bradley have been . . . vindicated by time and experience."[83]

The opinion defined limitation of the states' immunity: "There are, of course, State activities and State-owned property that partake of uniqueness from the point of view of intergovernmental relations. These inherently constitute a class by themselves . . . so long as Congress generally taps a source of revenue by whomsoever earned and not uniquely capable of being earned only by a State, the Constitution of the United States does not forbid it merely because its incidence falls also on a State."[84] And it added: "If Congress desires, it may of course leave untaxed enterprises pursued by States for the public good while it taxes like enterprises organized for private ends."

Justice Rutledge, joining in Justice Frankfurter's opinion, said, "The shift from immunity to taxability has gone too far."[85] Justice Douglas, dissenting with Justice Black, contended that "the notion that the sovereign position of the states must find its protection in the will of a transient majority of Congress is foreign to and a negation of our constitutional system."[86] Chief Justice Stone and Justices Reed, Murphy, and Burton concurred in the result. Justice Jackson did not participate.

(It might be noted that the prevailing philosophy dictated federal tax aggrandizement; today a different attitude might well evolve, since there

---

[77] New York v. United States, 326 U.S. 572 (1946).
[78] Ibid., 574.
[79] South Carolina v. United States, 199 U.S. 437 (1905).
[80] Ohio v. Helvering, 292 U.S. 360 (1933).
[81] New York v. United States, 326 U.S. 572, 575 (1946).
[82] Allen v. University System, 304 U.S. 439 (1937).
[83] New York v. United States, 326 U.S. 572, 577 n.5 (1946).
[84] Ibid., 582.
[85] Ibid., 584.
[86] Ibid., 594.

exists growing disenchantment with national growth and action, coupled with recognition of the need for a substitution of state and local action that requires enhancement of state and local revenues, that might well support the position of the dissenters.)

During the December, 1866, term the Court handed down eighty decisions, to only seven of which there were dissents, a little more than 8 per cent. Of the seven dissents, six were by a single justice and one by two justices. There were no four-to-four or five-to-three decisions. Justice Miller dissented three times, each time alone, and of the others, Justices Davis, Nelson, Field, Swayne, and Grier each dissented once.

During the following term (1867), 109 decisions (excluding multiple cases) were handed down. These registered eleven dissents, less than 10 per cent, of which four were by a single Justice and four were by five to three. The prevailing practice was not, as at present, to hand down memorandum decisions. Of the total of eleven dissents, Justice Miller had seven, two with the Chief Justice, four with Grier, and two with Field. The Chief Justice filed four dissents, two with Miller, three with Grier, and one each with Clifford, Field, and Swayne. Grier, with six dissents, had two with Field and one each with Clifford and Swayne. Clifford had three dissents, one alone and one each with Chase, Grier, and Field. Field, with three dissents, shared with others as above stated, while Swayne dissented only once with Chase and Grier.

Obviously, despite the raging passions of the day and the divisions among radical Republicans, Republicans, and Democrats, the justices formed no blocs and acted in a spirit of compromise. And with Chase, Field, and Miller on the bench, the unanimity displayed could hardly be attributed to weakness, as Justice Johnson had charged respecting acquiescent justices on the Marshall Court.

The noteworthy dissent, in the light of subsequent decisions, was that of Justices Bradley and Miller in the Hepburn case, so promptly vindicated in the Legal Tender Cases.

CHAPTER V

The Fourteenth Amendment and
The Period of Judicial Restraint

IN THE CLOSING DAYS of Chase's incumbency, the Court, in the so-called Slaughter House Cases, faced a problem of the construction of the Fourteenth Amendment that was to plague it for over half a century.[1] Though there was little doubt that one of the purposes of radical Republicans in enacting the Fourteenth Amendment was to broaden the national powers over dissident states, the Court moved away from its previous nationalistic attitude to limit the scope of the Amendment and to broaden the police powers of the states.

The principal issue raised by former Supreme Court Justice Campbell for the opponents of the legislation was whether the granting of a slaughter house monopoly to a corporation abridged "the privileges or immunities" of New Orleans butchers, or denied them "the equal protection of the laws," as provided by the Amendment. Justice Miller, writing for the five-man majority and faced with the contention that might have, in practical effect, reduced the states to what the majority evidently feared would be complete subordination to the federal power, found that the privileges and immunities clause protected by the Amendment were those of national, not of state citizenship. And the former he defined as limited to those that owed their being to the federal government, its national character, its Constitution, and its laws, while the latter comprised all others. These, he said, were left to the state governments for security and protection.

He found that the Thirteenth, Fourteenth, and Fifteenth amendments had as "the one pervading purpose . . . the freedom of the slave race, the security and firm establishment of that freedom, and the protection of the newly made freeman and citizen from the oppressions of those who had formerly exercised unlimited domination over him."[2] And concerning the police powers of the state and the fear of the effect upon them of excessive nationalism, Miller said that a broader construction of the Fourteenth Amendment "would constitute this court a perpetual censor upon all legislation of the States, on the

[1] Butchers' Assoc. v. Crescent City Co., 16 Wall. 36 (1873).
[2] *Ibid.*, 71.

civil rights of their own citizens, with authority to nullify such as it did not approve as consistent with those rights, as they existed at the time of the adoption of this Amendment."[3]

Of the dissenters (the Chief Justice, and Justices Field, Swayne, and Bradley), the latter said:

> It is futile to argue that none but persons of the African race are intended to be benefited by this Amendment. They may have been the primary cause of the Amendment, but its language is general, embracing all citizens, and I think it was purposely so expressed. . . . The Amendment was an attempt to give voice to the strong national yearning for that time and that condition of things, in which American citizenship should be a sure guaranty of safety, and in which every citizen of the United States might stand erect in every portion of its soil, in the full enjoyment of every right and privilege belonging to a freeman, without fear of violation or molestation.[4]

Justice Swayne, also writing in dissent, said:

> The first eleven Amendments to the Constitution were intended to be checks and limitations upon the government which that instrument called into existence. . . . These Amendments (the Thirteenth, Fourteenth, and Fifteenth) are a new departure, and mark an important epoch in the constitutional history of the country. They trench directly upon the power of the States. . . . They are in this respect, at the opposite pole from the first eleven[5] . . . .
>
> These Amendments are all consequences of the late civil war. The prejudices and apprehension as to the central government which prevailed when the Constitution was adopted were dispelled by the light of experience. The public mind became satisfied that there was less danger of tyranny in the head than of anarchy and tyranny in the members. . . . This court has no authority to interpolate a limitation that is neither expressed nor implied. Our duty is to execute the law, not to make it. The protection provided was not intended to be confined to those of any particular race or class, but to embrace equally all races, classes and conditions of men. . . . To the extent of that limitation it turns, as it were, what was meant for bread into a stone.[6]

While former Justice Campbell made reference to the equal protection and the due process clauses of the Amendment, Justice Miller said that these points had not been pressed, and he dismissed them rather summarily, with no notion that the dissenting language would soon provoke successful reliance

[3] *Ibid.*, 78.
[4] *Ibid.*, 123.
[5] *Ibid.*, 124–25.
[6] *Ibid.*, 128–29.

on these clauses and accomplish the application of the Amendment which the Court was now denying.

In 1884 the Court passed on a successful application for an injunction granted by a lower court to the successful Crescent City Company, to restrain a beneficiary of a municipal ordinance of New Orleans which opened to general competition the right to build slaughter houses and other structures. The ordinance, in effect, repealed the exclusive grant of 1869 which the Court had sustained in the previous case. Now the Court held that one legislature could not so exercise its police powers as to restrain a subsequent legislature and that the Crescent City Company could not continue to enjoy its monopoly of the business. Justice Bradley, with the concurrence of Justices Harlan and Woods, concurred in the result for the reason that he believed the original grant violated the privileges and immunities clause of the Fourteenth Amendment. Justice Field concurred on both grounds.[7]

Chief Justice Chase, having dissented from Justice Miller's limitation of the scope of the Fourteenth Amendment in the Slaughter House Cases, again dissented, but without opinion, when the other members of the Court, including his former dissenting confreres, held that the right to practice law was not a right of a citizen of the United States protected by the Fourteenth Amendment but a right to be granted and protected by virtue of state citizenship. Hence, said Justice Miller, the Court could do nothing for Myra Bradwell, a married woman who claimed the Fourteenth Amendment protected her right to demand admission to the bar of the state of Illinois. All the other former Slaughter House dissenters, except the Chief Justice, went along with Justice Miller's Slaughter House limitation; however, Justice Bradley, concurring, rushed in where angels should have feared to tread by defending the legislative right to believe that there were some occupations for which delicate womanhood was not fitted and that the practice of the law was one of them. He made a distinction between married women, whose "paramount destiny and mission . . . are to fulfill the noble and benign offices of wife and mother . . . the law of the Creator," and unmarried women, who are "not affected by any of the duties, complications, and incapacities arising out of the married state." But these, he said, "are exceptions to the general rule."[8] These, of course, were obvious dicta, since the petitioner was a "Mrs." Whatever motivated silent Chief Justice Chase to dissent, whether gallantry or a belief in the broader scope of the Fourteenth Amendment, he set the pattern for the future.

[7] Butchers' Assoc. v. Crescent City Co., 111 U.S. 746 (1884).

[8] Bradwell v. Illinois, 16 Wall. 130 (1870). A later unanimous opinion held that a state could deny women the privilege of suffrage, since it was not secured to a "citizen" by the Fourteenth Amendment.

The Slaughter House Cases were decided on April 14, 1873. The Chief Justice, who had dissented, died a month later. A subsequent case[9] was submitted in December, 1873, and decided on March 4, 1874, the day Chase's successor took office. Here the Court of eight justices was presented with the question of whether the conviction of a defendant, a citizen of the United States and of Iowa, for selling intoxicating liquor in violation of an Iowa statute, violated the due process clause of the Amendment. A unanimous Court affirmed the conviction. Justice Miller, who wrote the Slaughter House opinion, said that no immunity existed prior to the Fourteenth Amendment that would prevent state regulation or even prohibition of the sale of liquor; hence, the case fell within the purview of the Slaughter House Cases. However, he said that if the defendant was the owner of the liquor sold at the time the state first prohibited its sale, a question of whether the owner was being deprived of his property without due process of law would arise. But he said that question was not presented, and the Court noted that the Iowa statute preceded the Fourteenth Amendment.

Justices Bradley, Swayne, and Field explained their concurrence by distinguishing the situation from that in the Slaughter House Cases, thus maintaining the positions they had taken in their dissents.

Morrison R. Waite of Ohio succeeded Chief Justice Chase on March 4, 1874. The Court he headed was a strong one, including as it did justices of the caliber of Miller, Field, and Bradley, There was no change of personnel until 1877, when John Marshall Harlan of Kentucky succeeded Justice Davis. Four years later, Stanley Matthews of Ohio replaced Justice Swayne, and during the same year, 1881, Horace Gray of Massachusetts replaced Justice Clifford. In the following year Samuel Blatchford of New York succeeded Justice Hunt, and finally in 1887, Lucius Q. C. Lamar of Mississippi replaced Justice Woods.

Chief Justice Waite's term of service was a period of great economic expansion of the country, which marked a concurrent period of expansion of the business of the Court. The Court enlarged state powers under the Fourteenth Amendment while it enlarged the national power under the commerce clause. It negated the civil rights of Negroes under the Fourteenth Amendment, as it diminished the national powers of enforcement of the Reconstruction Acts. It permitted legislative rate regulation and decried judicial scrutiny. It lent no aid to defaulting states and political subdivisions that sought to repudiate bonded indebtedness.

The history of the Waite term of office marked the first phase of the application of due process under the Fourteenth Amendment; the excesses of the Fuller, White, and Taft courts, unrestrained by the dissents of Holmes and

[9] Bartmeyer v. Iowa, 18 Wall. 129 (1874).

Brandeis, constituted its second phase; and finally, the twentieth-century resurrection of the Waite restraints became its third phase.

The path the Court was to take respecting the Fourteenth Amendment had been set by the Slaughter House Cases. On this path the Court set its feet in 1877, when it decided the Granger Cases,[10] which, with the companion Munn case,[11] became a monument marking direction for the future clash of legislative action and judicial supervisory power.

By the early 1870's the resentment against the arrogant practices of the railroads, exceeding those of the corporations which had created divisions in the Taney court twenty years before, had reached a point where the Grange movement in the Middle West had been initiated to combat the power and practices of railroads and associated enterprises, such as warehouses and grain elevators. The results of the awakened popular indignation found expression in legislative acts in middle western states fixing maximum rates for railroad charges and in Illinois fixing the charges for grain elevators.

Railroads and other corporations started suits to declare the legislation unconstitutional. While the suits were pending, the depression of 1873 seriously affected the railroad earnings, thus making successful prosecution of the suits more likely.

The Munn case affirming the Illinois statute regulating the charges for storage of grain and the Granger Cases were decided on March 1, 1877, after the lapse of a year following argument. Chief Justice Waite wrote the opinion for the Court in both cases. In the Munn case he held that the railroads and grain elevators were property that had been clothed with a public interest, and as such, the common good required that they be regulated by legislative action. He said that, though the power of regulation might be abused by the legislature, "for protection against abuses by Legislatures, the people must resort to the polls, not to the Courts."[12] Justices Field and Strong dissented. On the same day the Chief Justice wrote for the Court in the Granger Cases, also with Justices Field and Strong dissenting.

In the Munn case Justice Field argued that grain elevators were not clothed with a public interest. He interposed the protection of the Fourteenth Amendment:

All that is beneficial in property arises from its use, and the fruits of that use, and whatever deprives a person of them deprives him of all that is desirable

[10] Chicago B. & Q. R.R. v. Iowa, 4 Otto (94 U.S.) 155, 183 (1877); Peik v. Chicago & N. W. R.R.; Lawrence v. Paul, 4 Otto (94 U.S.) 164 (1877); Chicago M. & St. P. R.R. v. Ackley, 4 Otto (94 U.S.) 179 (1877); Winona & St. P. R.R. v. Blake, 4 Otto (94 U.S.) 180 (1877); Stone v. Wisconsin, 4 Otto (94 U.S.) 181 (1877). (Granger Cases).

[11] Munn v. Illinois, 4 Otto (94 U.S.) 113 (1877) (Granger Cases).

[12] *Ibid.*, 134.

or valuable in the title and possession. If the constitutional guaranty extends no further than to prevent a deprivation of title and possession, and allows a deprivation of use and the fruits of that use, it does not merit the encomiums it has received.[13]

Field argued against legislative price-fixing:

> It is only where some right or privilege is conferred by the government or municipality upon the owners, which he can use in connection with his property, or by means of which the use of his property is rendered more valuable to him, or he thereby enjoys an advantage over others, that the compensation to be received by him becomes a legitimate matter of regulation. . . . When the privilege ends the power of regulation ceases.[14]

Agreeing with the latter view, Field said, in dissenting in the Granger Cases:[15]

> There is no doubt about the power of the Legislature to prescribe in the charter of any corporation the compensation it may receive for services rendered, or to reserve the power to regulate such compensation subsequently. The power to prescribe the conditions of use and enjoyment necessarily accompanies the power to grant. . . .
> Of what avail is the constitutional privilege that no State shall deprive any person of his property except by due process of law, if the State can, by fixing the compensation which he may receive for its use, take from him all that is valuable in the property? . . . If the State can, in the face of a charter provision authorizing a company to charge reasonable rates, prescribe what rates shall be deemed reasonable for services rendered?[16]

Field also said that, if under the reserved power to alter charters the legislature could regulate charges, at least that power should not "in common honesty, be so used as to destroy or essentially impair the value of mortgages and other obligations executed under express authority of the State."[17]

The Munn and Granger opinions of Chief Justice Waite stand as landmarks of recognition of legislative power, while Justice Field's dissents forecast the exercise of the judicial power of supervision and the conflict that produced varying restraints and abuses from time to time, in one direction or the other. The extremism of the Waite view found frequent dilution. Indeed, so much of the Granger opinion as gave the state control of domestic

[13] *Ibid.*, 141.
[14] *Ibid.*, 146–67.
[15] Stone v. Wisconsin, 4 Otto (94 U.S.) 181, 185 (1877).
[16] *Ibid.*, 186.
[17] *Ibid.*

railroad rates, although they affected interstate traffic, was practically over-ruled by a divided court, Justices Bradley and Gray and the Chief Justice dissenting, with the majority compelled to attempt to distinguish the Munn and Granger cases.[18]

Also in 1886, in the case of a Mississippi statute, the Court indicated that it might be for the Court, not for the voters, as Waite had said previously, to correct abuse by the legislature.[19] And in the following year, in a case sustaining a Kansas prohibition statute,[20] Justice Harlan, writing for the Court, said that the Court might well look at the legislative act to determine whether, in truth, it "is to be accepted as a legitimate exertion of the police power of the State." There are, he added, "of necessity, limits beyond which legislation cannot rightfully go."[21]

Likewise, when a majority of the Court approved a Pennsylvania statute regulating the manufacture and sale of oleomargarine, after the Court had refused to permit the defendant to prove that it was a perfectly healthful product, Justice Field, dissenting, said that the regulation was arbitrary and had no relation to exertion of the police power.[22]

The restrictions placed upon the privileges or immunity clause by the Slaughter House decision had an effect in turning litigants to the due process clause. Justice Miller, in writing for the Court[23] and holding that due process was not violated by assessments reviewed by a fair trial in a court of justice, said, respecting the words "due process of law":

It is not a little remarkable, that while this provision has been in the Constitution of the United States, as a restraint upon the authority of the Federal Government, for nearly a century, and, while, during all that time, the manner in which the powers of that Government have been exercised has been watched with jealousy, and subjected to the most rigid criticism in all its branches, this special limitation upon its powers has rarely been invoked in the judicial forum. . . . But while it has been a part of the Constitution, as a restraint upon the power of the States, only a few years, the docket of this court is crowded with cases in which we are asked to hold that State Courts and State Legislatures have deprived their own citizens of life, liberty or property without due process of law. There is here abundant evidence that there exists some strange misconception of the scope of this provision as found in the XIVth Amendment. In fact, it would seem, from the character of many of the cases before us, and

[18] Wabash R.R. v. Illinois, 118 U.S. 557 (1886).

[19] Stone v. Farmers' Loan & Trust Co., 116 U.S. 307; Stone v. Illinois Cent. R.R., 116 U.S. 347; Stone v. New Orleans R.R. 116 U.S. 352 (1886) (Railroad Commission Cases).

[20] Mugler v. Kansas; Kansas v. Ziebold, 123 U.S. 623 (1887).

[21] *Ibid.*, 661.

[22] Powell v. Pennsylvania, 127 U.S. 678 (1888).

[23] Davidson v. New Orleans, 6 Otto (96 U.S.) 97 (1878).

the arguments made in them, that the clause under consideration is looked upon as a means of bringing to the test of the decision of this court the abstract opinions of every unsuccessful litigant in a State Court of the justice of the decision against him, and of the merits of the legislation on which such a decision may be founded.[24]

Justice Miller said that despite the first definition of "due process" as the "law of the land" in an 1855 case,[25] he felt that "there is wisdom . . . in the ascertaining of the intent and application of such an important phrase . . . by the gradual process of judicial inclusion and exclusion, as the cases presented for decision shall require, with the reasoning on which such decisions may be founded."[26]

Previously a majority of the Court had said:[27]

A State cannot deprive a person of his property without due process of law; but this does not necessarily imply that all trials in the state courts affecting the property of persons must be by jury. . . . Due process of law is process due according to the law of the land. This process in the States is regulated by the law of the State. Our power over that law is only to determine whether it is in conflict with the supreme law of the land; that is to say, with the Constitution and laws of the United States made in pursuance thereof, or with any treaty made under the authority of the United States.

Justices Clifford and Field dissented.

Justice Miller was concerned about the number of cases brought to the Court under claims of lack of due process. But while there were seventy Fourteenth Amendment cases between 1873 and 1888, the duration of the Waite court, there were 725 such cases brought during the subsequent thirty years.[28]

Later, in 1884, Justice Matthews had occasion to determine whether California might charge a person with murder upon an information, without indictment by a grand jury.[29] The contention there made was that "due process" meant "settled usage." To which Justice Matthews replied: ". . . to hold that such a characteristic is essential to due process of law, would be to deny every quality of law but its age, and to render it incapable of progress or improvement. It would be to stamp upon our jurisprudence the unchange-

24 *Ibid.*, 103–104.

25 Den, *ex dem.*, Murray v. Hoboken Co., 18 How. 272 (1856).

26 Davidson v. New Orleans, 6 Otto (96 U.S.) 97, 104 (1878).

27 Walker v. Sauvinet, 2 Otto (92 U.S.) 90 (1876).

28 Charles Warren, *The Supreme Court in United States History*, III, 320–21 (3 vols., Boston, Little, Brown & Co., 1922).

29 Hurtado v. California, 110 U.S. 516 (1884).

ableness attributed to the laws of the Medes and the Persians." The Constitution of the United States was ordained "for an undefined and expanding future."[30] Justice Harlan dissented, and Justice Field did not participate.

Over the dissent of Justice Harlan, the Court held that a New York statute providing for the taxation of foreign insurance companies at the same rate as the respective foreign state taxed New York companies did not constitute a denial of equal protection under the Fourteenth Amendment.[31]

Again Justice Harlan dissented when the Court upheld Missouri legislation fixing the number of challenges in a jury trial and varying the number, in the legislative discretion, by conditions in various localities, over an equal protection claim.[32]

The public dissatisfaction with the rapacities of the railroads in one situation moved the government to act. The Union Pacific and Central Pacific railroads had been built with the aid of loans of government money and donations of government lands. The builders of the roads, acting in the dual and conflicting capacities of directors of the companies and stockholders of the construction companies building the roads, caused the railroads to pay the construction companies exorbitant prices and in other ways mulcted the railroad corporations of enormous sums of money. The result was a national scandal and a congressional investigation, followed by the enactment of an act directing the Attorney General to sue to compel reimbursement either to the government or to the defrauded railroad corporations.

A suit had previously been brought to recover interest on second mortgage bonds, without avail.[33] Now the government, in the District of Connecticut, sued the Union Pacific Railroad Company, the Wyoming Coal Company, the Credit Mobilier Company and some one hundred and fifty individual defendants. The circuit court dismissed the bill. The high court affirmed.[34] Writing for the Court, Justice Miller held that while the acts alleged in the bill were frauds for which a court of equity would give relief, it was the railroad and not the government (which was a creditor, not a stockholder) that could have such relief, and that since the railroad or its stockholders were not the plaintiffs, the suit must fail. Justices Swayne and Harlan dissented.

Pending the previous suit, Congress had passed an act amending the charter of the Union Pacific and establishing a sinking fund requiring the Company to lay by a portion of its current net income to meet its debts when they fell due, thus preventing existing stockholders from depleting the treasury for their own benefit at the expense of those who were to come after

---

[30] *Ibid.*, 529, 530–31.
[31] Fire Assoc. v. New York, 119 U.S. 110 (1886).
[32] Hayes v. Missouri, 120 U.S. 68 (1887).
[33] United States v. Union Pac. R.R., 1 Otto (91 U.S.) 72 (1875).
[34] United States v. Union Pac. R.R., 8 Otto (98 U.S.) 569 (1879).

them. The Secretary of the Treasury was constituted the sinking fund agent and the Treasury of the United States the depository. The railroad maintained that the Act was violative of the due process clause of the Fifth Amendment. Chief Justice Waite held to the contrary. Justices Strong, Field, and Bradley dissented.[35]

As time went on, the commerce clause of the Constitution increasingly engaged the attention of the Court. Up to 1840 the Court had had only five cases dealing with the commerce clause; up to 1860 it had had twenty cases; up to 1870, thirty cases; up to 1880, 77 cases; and in its last decade, to 1890, it rendered decisions in 148 cases.[36]

The Chase court, during its last days, struck down a Pennsylvania statute seeking to tax freight passing through the state, or carried out of it, as violative of the commerce clause.[37] Justices Swayne and Davis dissented. However, the Court held that a tax levied upon the gross receipts of the railroad was not a tax upon interstate transportation and could be sustained.[38] To this ruling, Justices Miller, Hunt, and Field dissented.

Similarly, the Waite court held valid a charter of the Baltimore and Ohio Railroad that required the road to pay to the state a portion of fare received, despite the fact that the charter authorized constructing and operating a branch between Baltimore, Maryland, and Washington, D.C.[39] Justice Miller dissented.

However, when Shelby County undertook to tax drummers who offered goods for sale in the county by sample, the Court struck the ordinance down.[40] The Chief Justice and Justices Field and Gray dissented, saying they were not deciding whether or not taking orders by drummers without samples was valid. The Court had previously invalidated a Missouri statute which imposed a license tax on peddlers who sold goods manufactured out of the state as being a tax on the goods themselves.[41]

A Florida grant of an exclusive license to a telegraph company was held not to preclude the Western Union Telegraph Company from infringing the monopoly, upon the ground that, in the promotion of interstate commerce, Congress had provided for the "convenient transmission of intelligence from place to place," and had said that "the erection of telegraph lines shall, so far as state interference is concerned, be free to all . . . and that corporations

---

[35] Union Pac. R.R. v. United States, 9 Otto (99 U.S.) 700 (1879); Central Pac. R.R. v. Gallatin, *ibid.*, 727 (Sinking Fund Cases).

[36] Warren, *The Supreme Court in United States History,* III, 347.

[37] Reading R.R. v. Pennsylvania, 15 Wall. 232 (1873).

[38] *Ibid.*, 284.

[39] Baltimore & Ohio R.R. v. Maryland, 21 Wall. 456 (1875).

[40] Robbins v. Shelby County Tax Dist., 120 U.S. 489 (1887).

[41] Welton v. Missouri 1 Otto (91 U.S.) 275 (1876).

organized under the laws of one state . . . shall not be excluded."[42] Justice Field dissented solely on a construction of the statute, holding it was restricted to telegraphic construction on military and post roads in the domain of the federal government.

The Court denied the power of a state to forbid a common carrier to bring intoxicating liquor into the state, though it admitted, as it had previously held, the power of the state to control the intrastate manufacture and sale within its police powers.[43] Justice Field, concurring, made the distinction first made in Brown v. Maryland and announced by the Court in that Original Package Case: "The absence of regulations as to interstate commerce with reference to any particular subject is taken as a declaration that the importation of that article into the states shall be unrestricted. It is only when the importation is completed with and becomes a part of the general property of the state, that its regulations can act upon it, except insofar as may be necessary to insure safety in the disposition of the import until it is mingled."[44] Justices Gray, Harlan, and the Chief Justice dissented, with Justice Harlan writing, saying that the decision "may impair, if not destroy the power of a state to protect her people against the injurious consequences that are admitted to flow from the general use of intoxicating liquors." He insisted that "the reserved power of the states to guard the health, morals and safety of their people is more vital to the existence of society than their power in respect to trade and commerce having no possible connection with these subjects."[45]

Following the accession of Fuller to the chief justiceship, the Court affirmed the holding of the Bowman case, in what also became known as an Original Package Case, with Justices Harlan, Gray, and Brewer dissenting and standing on the doctrine of police power.[46] Ultimately Congress upheld the views of the dissenters by passing the Webb-Kenyon Act of 1913, prohibiting the transportation of intoxicating liquor, whether in the original package or not, to states barring it.

The Court's record in reconstruction and civil rights cases was in keeping with the mores of the day. With his unquestioned liberality and his brave words in the Slaughter House Cases, Justice Miller was one of a majority that said that though the Fifteenth Amendment did not confer the right of suffrage, it did forbid discrimination in the elective franchise on account of race, color or previous condition of servitude and it found that Congress might enforce that prohibition by "appropriate legislation."

[42] Pensacola v. Western Union, 6 Otto (96 U.S.) 1 (1878).
[43] Bowman v. Chicago & N. W. R.R., 125 U.S. 465 (1888) (Original Package case).
[44] Ibid., 508.
[45] Ibid., 513–14.
[46] Leisy v. Hardin, 135 U.S. 100 (1890) (Original Package case).

However, considering an indictment found against two inspectors of election for refusing to receive and count the vote of William Garner, a Negro, the Court began the process of whittling down the provisions of the Amendment by holding that the Act of 1870 was not such "appropriate legislation." Instead of being limited to refusal to receive and count votes by reason of the limited discrimination by race or color provided for by the Amendment, it imposed penalties on all discrimination, which, it said, the Amendment did not authorize. Justice Clifford concurred in the view that the indictment was bad on the ground of vagueness. Justice Hunt dissented and, *inter alia,* said cogently:

> The existence of a large colored population in the Southern States, lately slaves and necessarily ignorant, was a disturbing element in our affairs. It could not be overlooked. It confronted us always and everywhere. Congress determined to meet the emergency by creating a political equality . . . . It was believed that the newly enfranchised people could be most effectually secured in the protection of their rights . . . by giving to them that greatest of rights among freemen,—the ballot. . . . Just so far as the ballot to . . . the freedman is abridged, in the same degree is their importance and their security diminished.[47]

On the same day it handed down this decision, the Court held invalid indictments of more than one hundred members of mobs in Louisiana for conspiring to prevent Negroes from assembling and voting by threatening and beating them. It held that the Fourteenth Amendment afforded protection only against the actions of a state and not against the actions of private persons and that such protection was limited to racial discrimination.

The opinion of the Chief Justice, for the entire Court, excepting only Justice Clifford who concurred in a separate opinion, held that all the other rights claimed to have been violated were not rights springing from the federal Constitution and hence not the subject of protection under the Amendment. The Chief Justice found the indictment too vague; so did Justice Clifford, who concurred in the result on that ground alone.[48]

The Court also held invalid a statute of Louisiana forbidding discrimination because of race or color on any conveyance operating within the state in pursuance of a similar provision in the Louisiana Constitution, because, in the case of a steamboat on the Mississippi, it operated interstate and thus the statute imposed a burden on interstate commerce.[49] Justice Clifford, concurring, took the opportunity to justify the doctrine of segregation, saying: "Substantial equality of right is the law of the State and of the United States;

47 United States v. Reese, 2 Otto (92 U.S.) 214, 247–48 (1876).
48 United States v. Cruikshank, 2 Otto (92 U.S.) 542 (1876).
49 Hall v. DeCuir, 5 Otto (95 U.S.) 485 (1878).

but equality does not mean identity, as in the nature of things identity in the accommodation afforded to passengers, whether colored or white, is impossible .... Adult male passengers are never allowed a passage in the ladies' cabin."[50] Clifford anticipated the Plessy case when he said: "Equality of rights does not involve the necessity of educating white and colored persons in the same school ... and ... any classification which preserves substantially equal school advantages is not prohibited by either the State or Federal Constitution."[51]

Conformably, the Court dismissed indictments found under the congressional anti-Ku Klux Klan Act of 1871 against twenty members of a mob that had taken Negro prisoners from the custody of a sheriff and beaten them, because the statute was not "appropriate legislation," since it was broader than was authorized by the Amendment which was limited to action by the state.[52]

However, the Court did hold that a Negro charged with murder who petitioned the West Virginia court to permit removal of his case to the federal court upon the ground that the West Virginia statutes excluded Negroes from service on grand and petit juries, was entitled to such removal. Accordingly, the Court voided his conviction, over the dissent of Justices Clifford and Field, who wrote no opinion.[53]

In a companion case two Negroes charged with the murder of a white man sought removal to the federal court. Their motion having been denied, they were tried. One was convicted; the jury disagreed as to the other. Now they petitioned the federal circuit court, which granted habeas corpus and took them from the custody of the state authorities. Thereupon the state of Virginia sought a mandamus to compel the return of the defendants from federal custody. The Court granted the writ, holding that the statutes of Virginia did not discriminate, as charged, against the service of Negroes as jurors, and that if, as claimed, a state officer took it upon himself to exclude Negroes as jurors, that fact should be put to the state court in the first instance, subject to ultimate appeal to the high court, should that be necessary. Justice Strong, writing the majority opinion, distinguished between a claim of exclusion of Negroes and a contention that the defendants were entitled to have a percentage of Negroes on the jury.[54]

In a third case, decided on the same day, the Court was asked to grant habeas corpus to a Virginia state judge who had been indicted for excluding Negroes from the grand and petit juries in his county because of their race and color. The Court held that he had no exemption as a judge because, in

[50] *Ibid.*, 503.
[51] *Ibid.*, 504.
[52] United States v. Harris, 16 Otto (106 U.S.) 629 (1883).
[53] Strauder v. West Virginia, 10 Otto (100 U.S.) 303 (1880).
[54] *Ex parte* Virginia, 10 Otto (100 U.S.) 313 (1880).

selecting jurors, he was merely performing a ministerial act and that since a state must act by agents, he, as an agent of the state, was bound to obey the requirements of the Fourteenth Amendment and the congressional statutes adopted thereunder. With Justices Field and Clifford dissenting, the majority denied the application. Justice Field maintained that Section 4 of the Civil Rights Act of 1875, under which the judge was indicted, was unconstitutional. Ultimately, the judge was tried and, of course, acquitted,[55] a consequence that remains today a southern custom in civil rights cases, with gradually growing exceptions.

In a subsequent case, though the Delaware Constitution restricted voting and service as jurors to whites, Justice Harlan, writing for a majority, held that the subsequent passage of the Fourteenth Amendment raised a presumption that the state constitution stood as if amended and would not be deemed discriminatory. However, a defendant charged with rape had moved to quash his indictment on the ground that subordinate officers of the state had, in fact, excluded Negroes from the jury and offered to make proof of the fact. Without denial by the authorities, the state court denied his motion, and, after trial, he was convicted. The high court voided the conviction. The Chief Justice and Justice Field dissented, the latter saying flatly that he did not believe that the Fourteenth Amendment was applicable to a claim of discrimination in the selection of jurors.[56]

Finally, carrying its concept of the amendments to its logical conclusion, the Court laid to rest the provisions of the Civil Rights Act, adopted by Congress in 1875, which forbade racial discrimination in conveyances, hotels, theaters, and other places, as not being authorized by the Thirteenth and Fourteenth Amendments.[57] These cases involved refusal of accommodations at a hotel, in a railroad car, and in theaters, one in San Francisco and another in New York. Justice Bradley, writing for a majority that excluded only Justice Harlan, said:

> When a man has emerged from slavery, and by the aid of beneficent legislation has shaken off the inseparable concomitants of that state, there must be some stage in the progress of his elevation when he takes the rank of a mere citizen, and ceases to be the special favorite of the laws, and when his rights, as a citizen or a man, are to be protected in the ordinary modes by which other men's rights are protected.[58]

[55] Ibid., 339.

[56] Neal v. Delaware, 13 Otto (103 U.S.) 370 (1881).

[57] United States v. Stanley; United States v. Ryan; United States v. Nichols; United States v. Singleton; Robinson v. Memphis R.R., 109 U.S. 3 (1883) (Civil Rights cases).

[58] Ibid., 25.

This was too much for Justice Harlan, who, dissenting, said stridently:

I cannot resist the conclusion that the substance and spirit of the recent Amendments of the Constitution have been sacrificed by a subtle and ingenious verbal criticism . . . Constitutional provisions, adopted in the interest of liberty, and for the purpose of securing, through national legislation, if need be, rights inhering in a state of freedom, and belonging to American citizenship, have been so construed as to defeat the ends the people desired to accomplish, which they attempted to accomplish, and which they supposed they had accomplished. . . .[59]

I hold that since slavery . . . was the moving or principal cause of the adoption of that Amendment [the 13th] and since that institution rested wholly upon the inferiority, as a race, of those held in bondage, their freedom necessarily involved immunity from, and protection against, all discrimination against them, because of their race, in respect of such civil rights as belong to freemen of other races. . . .[60]

The 13th Amendment alone obliterated the race line, so far as all rights fundamental in a state of freedom are concerned . . . .[61]

A keeper of an inn is in the exercise of a quasi public employment. . . . The public nature of his employment forbids him from discriminating against any person asking admission as a guest on account of the race or color of that person. . . .

. . . places of public amusement . . . are such as are established and maintained under direct license of the law. The authority to establish and maintain them comes from the public. The colored race is a part of that public. The local government granting the license represents them as well as all other races within its jurisdiction. A license from the public . . . imports, in law, equality of right, at such places, among all the members of that public. . . .[62]

It is, I submit, scarcely just to say that the colored race has been the special favorite of the laws. The statute of 1875, now adjudged to be unconstitutional, is for the benefit of citizens of every race and color. . . . It was not deemed enough "to help the feeble up, but to support him after." The one underlying purpose of Congressional legislation has been to enable the black race to take the rank of mere citizens . . . . At every step, in this direction, the nation has been confronted with class tyranny, which a contemporary English historian says is, of all tyrannies, the most intolerable. . . . Today, it is the colored race which is denied. . . . At some future time, it may be that some other race will fall under the ban of race discrimination. If the constitutional amendments be enforced, according to the intent with which, as I conceive, they were adopted, there cannot be, in this republic, any class of human beings in practical sub-

59 *Ibid.*, 26.
60 *Ibid.*, 36.
61 *Ibid.*, 40.
62 *Ibid.*, 41.

jection to another class, with power in the latter to dole out to the former just such privileges as they may choose to grant.[63]

The last of the civil rights cases to come before the Waite court involved the right to indict and convict eight Georgians for conspiring to beat and intimidate a Negro voter respecting a congressional election. Without dissent, a unanimous court upheld the conviction and denied an application for a writ of habeas corpus.[64]

Following the Civil War there occurred a spate of attempted repudiations of their bonded indebtedness by various southern states. The Waite court had two hundred cases involving debt repudiation by states and political subdivisions brought to it.[65] Among these debtors, Virginia was prominent. In 1871 the Virginia General Assembly passed an act to provide for the funding and payment of the public debt, by which two-thirds of the amount due on old bonds might be funded in new bonds, with interest coupons attached which were expressly made receivable for taxes. However, the following year the General Assembly passed an act forbidding taxing officers from taking such coupons in payment of taxes. When, in 1880, the latter act was challenged, the Court held the act void as impairing the obligation of contract.[66]

Thereafter, in 1882, the state renewed its effort to avoid use of interest coupons in payment of taxes, under the guise that forged bonds were outstanding and that the authenticity of coupons had to be checked. It also changed the form of remedy available to the taxpayer who sought to enforce his rights. The Court, though reiterating its opinion that the attempt to repudiate the state's obligation was void, held that the change of remedy was not unconstitutional. Justice Matthews concurred on another ground, and Justices Bradley, Woods, and Gray concurred with both the majority and Justice Matthews' opinion. Justice Field dissented, holding that the change of remedy also violated the taxpayer's constitutional rights.[67]

It might be noted that the repudiating states took refuge behind the Eleventh Amendment, which prohibits a suit against a state by a citizen of another state. The Eleventh Amendment had been passed to overcome the decision in Chisholm v. Georgia,[68] which held that a state could be sued by a citizen of another state. The principle of the Amendment had been stated

---

[63] *Ibid.*, 61–62.
[64] *Ex parte* Yarborough, 110 U.S. 651 (1884).
[65] Warren, *The Supreme Court in United States History*, III, 400.
[66] Hartman v. Greenhow, 12 Otto (102 U.S.) 672 (1881).
[67] Antoni v. Greenhow, 17 Otto (107 U.S.) 769 (1883).
[68] 2 Dallas 419 (1793).

in a later case,[69] which supplied the prohibition that the Amendment lacked, i.e., that a state could not be sued by one of its own citizens.

This refuge was availed of in cases brought against Louisiana, Georgia, and South Carolina, in some of which the Court found itself powerless because of the Amendment.[70] Even in a case where bondholders assigned their claims to New Hampshire to avoid the effect of the Amendment, the Court held itself prohibited from entertaining the suit.[71] However, it finally found a way of acting. In an opinion by Justice Matthews,[72] it held that a suit against a tax collector was not a suit against the state and that the acts of the General Assembly of Virginia prohibiting the acceptance of bond coupons and similar statutes were void as impairing the obligations of contracts. Justice Matthews distinguished the previous Greenhow case. The Chief Justice and Justices Bradley, Miller, and Gray dissented in this and in three companion Virginia bond cases.

Similarly, in the case of bonds issued by a municipality, the Court held that legislative enactments which repealed the charter of the city of Mobile and incorporated a successor corporation, the Port of Mobile, which took the property of its predecessor, but which made no provision for the recognition of the previous bond issue, were ineffectual to alter the rights of the bondholder who, the Court unanimously held, was entitled to a peremptory writ of mandamus to be issued against the Port of Mobile.[73]

Anticipating default, the Court struck down a legislative authorization for a town to issue its bonds in aid of a manufacturing enterprise operated by individuals because taxes could not be levied to pay the bonds, since that would constitute a transfer of monies from taxpayers to individuals.[74] Justice Clifford dissented. (A later practice that grew to disproportionate extents involved the leasing of property to manufacturing concerns and the issuance by towns of tax-exempt revenue bonds, secured by the rentals under the lease. During 1968, as part of a tax bill, Congress denied exemption to such bonds issued in amounts exceeding five million dollars.)

Of historic interest is the consequence of a suit brought by George W. P. C. Lee to recover a parcel of some eleven hundred acres of land, known as the Arlington Estate, which he had inherited from his grandfather, George Washington Parke Custis, after the death of Custis' daughter, the wife of

[69] Hans v. Louisiana, 134 U.S. 1 (1890).

[70] Louisiana v. Jumel; Elliott v. Wiltz, 17 Otto (107 U.S.) 711 (1883); Cunningham v. Macon & Brunswick R.R., 109 U.S. 446 (1883).

[71] New Hampshire v. Louisiana; New York v. Louisiana, 108 U.S. 76 (1883).

[72] Poindexter v. Greenhow, 114 U.S. 270 (1885).

[73] Port of Mobile v. Watson, 116 U.S. 289 (1886).

[74] Savings & Loan Assoc. v. Topeka, 20 Wall. 655 (1875).

General Robert E. Lee. The property had, for a period of ten years, been held by officers and agents of the federal government as public property and used as a military station and as a national cemetery, (Arlington), established for the burial of deceased soldiers and sailors. The defendants, the agents of the federal government, claimed title under a tax sale certificate issued by commissioners who had bid the property in.

The Attorney General of the United States maintained that the suit was, in truth, against the government and therefore could not be maintained. The plaintiff contended that the tax sale was invalid. Justice Miller, writing for a majority, sustained the plaintiff's position on both counts. He wrote these stirring words:

> While by the Constitution the judicial department is recognized as one of the three great branches among which all the powers and functions of the Government are distributed, it is inherently the weakest of them all.
>
> Dependent as its courts are for the enforcement of their judgments, upon officers appointed by the Executive and removable at his pleasure, with no patronage and no control of purse or sword, their power and influence rest solely upon the public sense of the necessity for the existence of a tribunal to which all may appeal for the assertion and protection of rights guaranteed by the Constitution and by the laws of the land, and on the confidence reposed in the soundness of their decisions and purity of their motives.
>
> From such a tribunal no well founded fear can be entertained of injustice to the Government, or purpose to obstruct or diminish its just authority.[75]

Justice Gray wrote in dissent, supported by the Chief Justice and by Justices Bradley and Woods.

Despite the problems consequent upon the social and economic expansion of the nation during the period of the Waite incumbency, and despite the strong individual personalities, the Court attained a reasonable degree of unanimity, not only among the Justices but with Congress. During its service, the Court held only eight congressional acts unconstitutional, of which three were reconstruction enactments. As the Court said, in instructing Congress of the difference between patents and inventions and trademarks: "A due respect for a coordinate branch of the government requires that we shall decide that it has transcended its power only when that is so plain that we cannot avoid the duty."[76]

The October, 1876, term witnessed 129 decisions (treating the six Grange decisions as one), of which there were dissents in twenty-five, approximately

---

[75] United States v. Lee; Kaufman v. Lee, 16 Otto (106 U.S.) 196 (1882).

[76] United States v. Steffens; United States v. Witteman; United States v. Johnson, 10 Otto (100 U.S.) 82, 196 (1879) (Trade-Mark Cases).

20 per cent. Of the dissents, twelve, or 50 per cent, were by a single Justice, of which Justice Clifford had seven. There were three five-to-four decisions, two of which were in a patent case and its companion case. Justice Clifford was a principal dissenter, sharing one dissent each with Hunt, Davis, and Swayne and two with Strong. Justice Strong had eight dissents, two alone, four with the Chief Justice, one with Field, and two each with Clifford, Bradley, and Miller. Of the others, the Chief Justice and Miller each had four, Bradley and Field each three, Swayne and Hunt each two, and Davis only one. The bloc evil was not present.

The Court's subsequent record of dissents did not vary. The decisions for the October, 1882, term reported in 17 Otto came to a total of seventy-five. Of these, there were seven dissents (a little more than 9 per cent), two by single justices, one by a five-to-four vote. Justice Field dissented five times, the Chief Justice and Harlan each three, Justice Gray two, and Justices Bradley, Matthews, and Miller each one.

The notable dissents of the period, those in the Slaughter House Cases, were Justice Field's in the Munn and Chicago B. & Q. cases, Justice Harlan's in the Original Package and particularly, in the civil rights cases, and that of Justice Hunt in the Reese case. Justice Harlan's prescient civil rights dissents might have been written by his grandson, three-quarters of a century later.

CHAPTER VI

The Court as a Superlegislature—1

FOLLOWING THE DEATH OF CHIEF JUSTICE WAITE on March 23, 1888, Melville Weston Fuller of Illinois was appointed Chief Justice. He served until his death in 1910. It was during Fuller's tenure and those of his successors, Chief Justices White and Taft, that the Court not only remained conservative but became extremely nationalistic. This trend was pronounced in the application of the due process clause of the Fourteenth Amendment as the Court viewed state legislation and the exercise of state police powers with the jaundiced, laissez-faire eyes of Justice Brewer (a nephew of Justice Field), who said revealingly in 1892: "The paternal theory of government is to me odious. The utmost possible liberty to the individual, and the fullest possible protection to him and his property, is both the limitation and duty of government."[1]

Between 1890 and 1937, as pointed out by Professor (later Justice) Frankfurter, the Court set aside 228 legislative acts by recourse to the provisions of the Fourteenth Amendment.[2] New York Circuit Judge Hough dated this "flood" from a decision by the Court in 1890.[3] In that case Justice Blatchford, drawing sustenance from a prior decision,[4] said: "The question of the reasonableness of a rate or charge for transportation by a railroad company, involving as it does the element of reasonableness both as regards the company and as regards the public, is eminently a question for judicial investigation, requiring due process of law for its determination."[5]

Justice Miller, concurring, refined the Blatchford generality:

Neither the Legislature, nor such commission . . . can establish arbitrarily and without regard to justice and right a tariff of rates for such transportation,

[1] Budd v. New York; People *ex rel.* Annan v. Walsh; People *ex rel.* Pinto v. Walsh, 143 U.S. 517, 551 (1892).

[2] Felix Frankfurter, *Mr. Justice Holmes and the Supreme Court* (Cambridge, Harvard University Press, 1938), Appendix I.

[3] Chicago, M. & St. P. R.R. v. Minnesota, 134 U.S. 418 (1890).

[4] Stone v. Farmers' Loan & Trust Co., 116 U.S. 307; Stone v. Illinois Cent. R.R., 116 U.S. 347; Stone v. New Orleans R.R., 116 U.S. 352 (1886). (Railroad Commission Cases).

[5] Chicago M. & St. P. R.R. v. Minnesota, 134 U.S. 418, 458 (1890).

which is so unreasonable as to practically destroy the value of property of persons engaged in the carrying business on the one hand, nor so exorbitant and extravagant as to be in utter disregard of the rights of the public . . . on the other.[6]

Justice Bradley, dissenting, put the matter in what was to prove to be the proper light, saying that the decision practically overruled Munn v. Illinois and then added: "It is urged that what is a reasonable charge is a judicial question. On the contrary, it is pre-eminently a legislative one, involving considerations of policy as well as of remuneration."[7] "I do not mean to say that the Legislature, or its constituted Board of Commissioners, or other legislative agency, may not so act as to deprive parties of their property without due process of law . . . but . . . the invasion should be clear and unmistakable."[8] Justices Gray and Lamar joined in the dissent.

The floodgates had been opened by two decisions of the Waite court: the first, when it held in 1886 that a corporation was a "person" entitled to "equal protection" under the Fourteenth Amendment[9]—a rule which it established and Justice Black challenged so boldly half a century later. As a result, a corporation was entitled to invoke the due process clause of the Amendment.[10]

A second crucial decision harked back to the Chisholm case,[11] disposed of by the Eleventh Amendment,[12] and held that a suit against a state officer to compel him to do what a statute required him to do was not a suit against the state within the meaning of the Eleventh Amendment and hence could be maintained.[13] So no bar remained to prevent suits in equity from restraining state officers from enforcing state-made rates, regulations, and orders claimed to violate the due process clause of the Fourteenth Amendment.[14]

Thus was again posed, as Justice Bradley pointed out, the issue of who was to supervise the exercise of legislative police powers, the voters or the Court. As Chief Justice Waite maintained that the proper repository of such supervisory powers lay with the voters, the Fuller court now proclaimed nationalistic powers of overriding control in the Court. But that emendating assertion did not lack challenge.

[6] *Ibid.*, 459.

[7] *Ibid.*, 462.

[8] *Ibid.*, 465.

[9] Santa Clara Co. v. Southern Pac. R.R.; California v. Cent. Pac. R.R.; California v. Southern Pac. R.R., 118 U.S. 394 (1886).

[10] Minneapolis & St. L. R.R. v. Beckwith, 129 U.S. 26 (1889).

[11] Chisholm v. Georgia, 2 Dallas 419 (1793).

[12] Hans v. Louisiana, 134 U.S. 1 (1890).

[13] Rolston v. Crittenden, 120 U.S. 390 (1887).

[14] Reagan v. Farmers' Loan & Trust Co., 154 U.S. 362 (1894); Smyth v. Ames, 169 U.S. 466 (1898); Prout v. Starr, 188 U.S. 537 (1903).

Immediately following his appointment on December 8, 1902, to replace Justice Gray, Oliver Wendell Holmes, formerly Chief Justice of the Massachusetts Supreme Court, took his stand. He delivered his first utterance on the subject in a case argued a few days after he had taken his seat on the bench.[15] Writing for a seven-man majority, he took issue with the extremists:

> While the courts must exercise a judgment of their own, it by no means is true that every law is void which may seem to the judges who pass upon it excessive, unsuited to its ostensible end, or based upon conceptions of morality with which they disagree. . . . No court would declare a usury law unconstitutional, even if every member of it believed that Jeremy Bentham had said the last word on that subject, and had shown for all time that such laws did more harm than good. The Sunday laws, no doubt, would be sustained by a bench of judges, even if every one of them thought it superstitious to make any day holy.[16]

But thereafter the extremists rallied a five-man majority to strike down a New York statute limiting bakery workers to a ten-hour day, in what was to prove the notorious Lochner decision—one which brought forth the first of Holmes's notable dissents.[17] It was of the tenor of his first opinion and of the one that would prove to be his last dissent.

The Court had previously found valid a Utah statute which limited miners to an eight-hour day, although the specious opposing argument had been made that the statute interfered with the miners' "freedom of contract,"[18] a freedom to bargain with a dominant employer that a workman of that day, lacking unionization, must have found ironic. In the Lochner case, however, the term was again employed and was found credible and acceptable to a conservative majority.

In the Utah case, the Court had found the legislature properly exerting the police power to ensure the health and safety of its citizens, although Justice Brown said: "We have no disposition to criticize the many authorities which hold that state statutes restricting the hours of labor are unconstitutional."[19] Justices Brewer and Peckham dissented.

Now, in the Lochner case, the Utah dissenter, Justice Peckham, wrote for the five-man majority. He found the statutes "meddlesome interference with the rights of the individual, and they are not saved from condemnation by the claim that they are passed . . . upon the subject of the health of the indi-

[15] Otis v. Parker, 187 U.S. 606 (1903).
[16] *Ibid.*, 608, 609.
[17] Lochner v. New York, 198 U.S. 45 (1905).
[18] Holden v. Hardy, 169 U.S. 366 (1898).
[19] *Ibid.*, 397–98.

vidual whose rights are interfered with."[20] He said that the bakery trade had "never been regarded as an unhealthy one."[21] He defined the "freedom of contract," which he was upholding, as "part of the liberty of the individual protected by the Fourteenth Amendment."[22]

Justice Harlan, dissenting, asserted:

> I take it to be firmly established that what is called the liberty of contract may, within certain limits, be subjected to regulations designed and calculated to protect the general welfare, or to guard the public health, the public morals, or the public safety. . . .[23]
>
> It is plain that this statute was enacted in order to protect the physical welfare of those who work in bakery and confectionery establishments. It may be that the statute had its origin, in part, in the belief that employers and employees in such establishments were not upon an equal footing, and that the necessities of the latter often compelled them to submit to such exactions as unduly taxed their strength. . . . Whether or not this be wise legislation it is not the province of the Court to inquire.[24]

Justices White and Day joined in the dissent. However, Holmes felt that something more was needed and said:

> This case is decided upon an economic theory which a large part of the country does not entertain. If it were a question whether I agreed with that theory, I should desire to study it further and long before making up my mind. But I do not conceive that to be my duty, because I strongly believe my agreement or disagreement has nothing to do with the right of a majority to embody their opinions in law. . . . The Fourteenth Amendment does not enact Mr. Herbert Spencer's Social Statics.[25]

But the conservative Canutes on the bench could not withstand the rising tide of public opinion. Three years later the Court unanimously approved an Oregon limitation of ten hours for women.[26] And thereafter, the Court approved an Illinois child labor law[27] and a fifty-four-hour work week for Massachusetts women.[28] Two similar California laws were approved in 1915.[29]

[20] Lochner v. New York, 198 U.S. 45, 61 (1905).
[21] *Ibid.,* 59.
[22] *Ibid.,* 53.
[23] *Ibid.,* 67.
[24] *Ibid.,* 69.
[25] *Ibid.,* 75–76.
[26] Muller v. Oregon, 208 U.S. 412 (1908).
[27] Sturges v. Beauchamp, 231 U.S. 320 (1913).
[28] Riley v. Massachusetts, 232 U.S. 671 (1914).
[29] Miller v. Wilson, 236 U.S. 373 (1915); Bosley v. McLaughlin, 236 U.S. 385 (1915).

Finally the Court approved an Oregon limitation of working hours for men in industries on the theory that excessive labor was unhealthful,[30] a case in which the then Professor Frankfurter submitted a Brandeis brief. Here, there were three dissenters, the Chief Justice and Justices Van Devanter and McReynolds.

The "freedom of contract" doctrine employed to deny labor benefits was preceded by the technique of the injunction to avoid and to end strikes. In the case of an Idaho strike against a mining company, an injunction that proved unsuccessful in its effect was sought to be supplemented by an indictment for a conspiracy to commit an offense against the United States, i.e., "to corruptly and by force and threats obstruct and impede the due administration of justice in the aforesaid United States Circuit Court."[31] The Chief Justice, for the majority, found the indictment not borne out by the facts and ordered it quashed. However, the temper of the times was reflected in dissents by Justices Brown and Brewer.

A later case[32] had its genesis in the notable strike against the Pullman Company in 1894 and its consequent violence. This enabled President Cleveland to intervene with troops and to obtain an injunction restraining interference with transportation of the mails and forbidding incitement or encouragement to strike. Eugene V. Debs, who was heading the strike, defied the injunction and was adjudged guilty of contempt and sentenced to six months' imprisonment. The high court unanimously denied an application for a writ of habeas corpus and upheld the injunction, since it was "only to restrain forcible obstructions of the highways along which interstate commerce travels and the mails are carried. And the facts set forth at length are only those facts which tended to show that the defendants were engaged in such obstructions."[33]

Thereafter, when a coal company signed contracts with its employees making nonunion membership a condition of employment (so-called "yellow-dog contracts"), a majority of the Court, which had held in the Adair and Coppage cases that such contracts could not be invalidated by legislative action, now protected them by upholding an injunction barring the union from seeking to enroll the workers who had signed such contracts as members.[34]

Justice Brandeis, dissenting, said:

It is urged that a union agreement curtails liberty of the operator. Every agreement curtails the liberty of those who enter into it.[35] ... Coercion, in a legal

30 Bunting v. Oregon, 243 U.S. 426 (1917).
31 Pettibone v. United States, 148 U.S. 197 (1893).
32 In re Debs, 158 U.S. 564 (1895).
33 Ibid., 598.
34 Hitchman v. Mitchell, 245 U.S. 229 (1917).

sense, is not exerted when a union merely endeavors to induce employees to join a union with the intention thereafter to order a strike unless the employer consents to unionize his shop.[36]

In this and a concurrent case[37] Justices Holmes and Clarke joined Brandeis in dissent when Pitney, for the majority, held that an employer was entitled to be protected from unjustifiable interference with the good will of his employees and that a labor organization might not instigate nonunion workers to strike.

In an unpublished dissent in this case, Holmes said: "I have no doubt that when the power of either capital or labor is exercised in such a way as to attack the life of the community, those who seek their private interest at such costs are public enemies and should be dealt with as such."[38]

In a later (1921) labor case, the Court held that the anti-injunction provisions of the 1914 Clayton Act did not forbid enjoining pickets conducting a secondary boycott.[39] With the support of Holmes and Clarke, Justice Brandeis wrote in dissent:

> The conditions developed in industry may be such that those engaged in it cannot continue their struggle without danger to the community. But it is not for judges to determine whether such conditions exist, nor is it their function to set the limits of permissible contest, and to declare the duties which the new situation demands. This is the function of the legislature which . . . may substitute processes of justice for the more primitive method of trial by combat.[40]

Congress agreed with Brandeis and in 1932 enacted the Norris–La Guardia Anti-injunction Act.

Unionization, designed to make the "freedom of contract" doctrine something less than a euphemism, lay at the base of the spawn of labor conflict that reached the Court. In 1908 in the Adair case,[41] *mirabile dictu,* Justice Harlan dignified the odious freedom-of-contract doctrine by writing for the Court and striking down a congressional statute making it a criminal offense for an officer or agent of an interstate carrier to discharge an employee for being a member of a labor organization as violative of the due process clause of the Fifth

---

[35] *Ibid.,* 270.

[36] *Ibid.,* 271.

[37] Eagle Glass & Mfg. Co. v. Rowe, 245 U.S. 275 (1917).

[38] Mark de Wolfe, ed., *Holmes-Pollock Letters* (2 vols., Cambridge, Harvard University Press, 1941), II, 28.

[39] Duplex Print. Co. v. Deering, 254 U.S. 443 (1921).

[40] *Ibid.,* 488.

[41] Adair v. United States, 208 U.S. 161 (1908).

Amendment. The statute also prohibited the carrier from requiring an employee to agree not to join a labor union during the period of his employment under penalty of dismissal, but the Court did not pass on that clause until later in the Coppage case.

Justices McKenna and Holmes dissented, the latter writing:

> I suppose that it hardly would be denied that some of the relations of railroads with unions of railroad employees are closely enough connected with commerce to justify legislation by Congress. If so, legislation to prevent the exclusion of such unions from employment is sufficiently near. . . .
>
> The section is, in substance, a very limited interference with freedom of contract, no more . . . . I confess that I think that the right to make contracts at will that has been derived from the word "liberty" in the Amendments has been stretched to its extreme by the decisions. . . . Where there is, or generally is believed to be, an important ground of public policy for restraint, the Constitution does not forbid it, whether this Court agrees or disagrees with the policy pursued. . . . I could not pronounce it unwarranted if Congress should decide that to foster a strong union was for the best interest, not only of the men, but of the railroads and the country at large.[42]

Thereafter, in 1915, the Court, by a vote of six to three, struck down a Kansas statute as infringing upon the rights of personal liberty and property of a railroad by providing criminal penalties for requiring an employee, as a condition of employment, to agree not to join a labor union while so employed (the yellow-dog contract).[43] Justice Pitney, writing for the majority, leaned heavily upon the Adair decision, finding it in accord with the almost unbroken current of authorities in the state courts. Accordingly, he concluded that both principle and authority found the statute repugnant to the due process clause of the Fourteenth Amendment. Justice Holmes, dissenting, said bluntly that he believed that the Adair case should be overruled and wrote:

> In present conditions a workman not unnaturally may believe that only by belonging to a union can he secure a contract that shall be fair to him. . . .
> If that belief, whether right or wrong, may be held by a reasonable man, it seems to me that it may be enforced by law in order to establish the equality of position between the parties in which liberty of contract begins.[44]

Justice Day also wrote, dissenting, and Justice Hughes, who was later to write an opinion overruling these cases,[45] joined in the dissent.

42 *Ibid.,* 190–92.
43 Coppage v. Kansas, 236 U.S. 1 (1915).
44 *Ibid.,* 26–27.

However much Brandeis was wedded to the union cause, it is not to be thought that he was not prepared to deal fairly with a situation. Thus we find him saying in a 1926 case: "A strike may be illegal because of its purpose, however orderly the manner in which it is conducted."[46]

With the Duplex decision holding that the Clayton anti-injunction provision added nothing to the theretofore existing rules of substantive law, Chief Justice Taft, early in his judicial career, wrote for a majority, which included Justice Holmes, with Justice Brandeis concurring and only Justice Clarke dissenting. Taft distinguished between peaceful picketing seeking to influence by persuasion and appeal and picketing armed with threat and violence seeking success through force, intimidation, or obstruction.[47] Hence, the Court modified an injunction granted the employer to permit the former and deny the latter. Justice Brandeis said he concurred in substance in the opinion and in the judgment.

However, immediately thereafter, the Chief Justice joined four brethren to strike down an Arizona statute prohibiting injunctions forbidding peaceful picketing as violating the equal protection provision of the Fourteenth Amendment.[48] Truax, an Arizona restaurant owner, sought an injunction because picketing by striking employees, though peaceful, was causing him to suffer loss of business and profits. The Arizona legislature had provided that injunctions should not be granted against peaceful picketing, except to prevent injuries for which there was no legal redress. The Arizona court had followed the statute. The high court reversed.

Not only did Justices Clarke, Brandeis, and Holmes dissent, but Justice Pitney, who had written the majority Duplex opinion, joined them. Brandeis, as was his wont, wrote statistically and at length. Holmes, on his favorite Fourteenth Amendment ground, said:

> Legislation may begin where an evil begins. If, as many intelligent people believe, there is more danger that the injunction will be abused in labor cases than elsewhere, I can feel no doubt of the power of the legislature to deny it in such cases. . . .[49]

> There is nothing that I more deprecate than the use of the Fourteenth Amendment beyond the absolute compulsion of its words to prevent the making of social experiments that an important part of the community desires, in the insulated chambers afforded by the several states, even though the experiments

[45] Phelps Dodge v. NLRB, 313 U.S. 177 (1941).
[46] Dorchy v. Kansas, 272 U.S. 306, 311 (1926).
[47] American Steel v. Tri-City, 257 U.S. 184 (1921).
[48] Truax v. Corrigan, 257 U.S. 312 (1921).
[49] *Ibid.,* 343.

may seem futile or even noxious to me and to those whose judgment I most respect.[50]

The Court had less difficulty in applying the Sherman Anti-Trust Act to labor than it had in enforcing it against business. Thus a unanimous Court found a labor union, which had set up a boycott against a hat company in an effort to unionize it, liable for treble damages.[51] While this decision, which wrecked the Danbury Hatters' Union, could be justified, egalitarian treatment would not have justified the results accorded property rights in the Standard Oil and American Tobacco cases.

Later, when the Coronado Coal Company and others sued the international and local coal unions for treble damages under the Sherman Act, the Court reverted to the Knight decision to hold that coal mining was an intrastate business. The Chief Justice, writing for a unanimous court, vacated a recovery by the plaintiff and ordered a new trial.[52] When the case came back, after a verdict for the defendants, the Court found that the plaintiffs had furnished proof of the destruction of their mines and that the purpose of the destruction was to stop the production of nonunion coal and to prevent its shipment in interstate commerce. Hence, the Court concluded, the local union was liable for treble damages under the Sherman Act.[53]

Still later the Court upheld an injunction to restrain a union from conspiring to commit acts in restraint of trade in violation of the Sherman Act.[54] The acts complained of were the instigation and encouragement of a boycott of the plaintiff's products by union labor, and, since the boycott was effective in states other than that in which plaintiff operated, the Court held that the Duplex decision applied. Justice George Sutherland of Utah, who by now had replaced Justice Clarke, writing the opinion for the majority, found the similarity so close that, he said, the opinion in that case would serve here.

Justice Stone said he concurred only because his views had been rejected on the authority of the Duplex case. Justice Holmes went along with Brandeis, who dissented because, he said, referring to the Standard Oil decision as his authority, the Sherman Act prohibited only unreasonable restraints of trade, and he did not consider the union's boycott unreasonable.[55]

Another phase of the recurrent labor litigation arose from legislative efforts to fix minimum wages. Thus, following affirmation by the Court of an Oregon minimum wage law[56] in consequence of an equal division re-

[50] *Ibid.*, 344.
[51] Loewe v. Lawlor, 208 U.S. 274 (1908).
[52] United Mine Workers v. Coronado Coal Co., 259 U.S. 344 (1922).
[53] United Mine Workers v. Coronado Coal Co., 268 U.S. 295 (1925).
[54] Bedford Cut Stone Co. v. Journeyman Stone Cutters' Assoc., 274 U.S. 37 (1927).
[55] *Ibid.*, 58.

sulting from the failure of Brandeis, who had defended the law in 1914, to sit, Congress created a board to fix minimum wages for women in the District of Columbia. When in the Adkins case the District of Columbia Minimum Wage Law came to the Court in 1923, Justice Sutherland wrote the opinion for the five-man majority striking it down.[57] The majority included the arch-conservative Butler. With McReynolds and Van Devanter, Butler and Sutherland were to form the reactionary bloc that was to make the Court a conservative cynosure for a decade or more. The Van Devanter stance aroused dissent from the Chief Justice, no radical, as well as from Sanford and Holmes. Brandeis, as in the Oregon minimum wage case, did not sit.

Holmes wrote a dissenting opinion and even the conservative Chief Justice, with whom Sanford joined, did the same. Holmes said, *inter alia*: "To me . . . the power of Congress seems absolutely free from doubt. The end, to remove conditions leading to ill health, immorality and the deterioration of the race, no one would deny to be within the scope of constitutional legislation."[58]

Labeling it a "dogma," Holmes cited innumerable instances of allowable infringement of "liberty of contract." ". . . pretty much all law consists in forbidding men to do some things they want to do, and contract is no more exempt from law than other acts," he said.[59]

Later, in 1936, the reactionary Four Horsemen (still intact) with the aid of Justice Roberts, overcame a minority of four in holding a New York minimum wage law unconstitutional.[60] However, the following year, with Chief Justice Hughes writing the opinion and with the aid of Roberts, who abandoned his conservative compatriots, the Court held constitutional a Washington state minimum wage law[61] which differed immeasurably from the New York law Roberts and his four associates had struck down the previous year. And the Court expressly overruled the Adkins case.

Another phase of the struggle affecting labor that pitted legislatures against the Court was the state effort to control employment agencies. When a Washington State statute made it a criminal offense to collect fees from workers seeking employment, although it permitted such payments by employers, a majority of five, in an opinion by Justice McReynolds, held the statute unconstitutional under the Fourteenth Amendment.[62]

This was the sort of issue in which Brandeis reveled and excelled. In a dissenting opinion he recited the history of abuses stemming from employ-

---

[56] Stettler v. O'Hara, 243 U.S. 629 (1917).
[57] Adkins v. Children's Hospital, 261 U.S. 525 (1923).
[58] *Ibid.*, 567.
[59] *Ibid.*, 568.
[60] Morehead v. Tipaldo, 298 U.S. 587 (1936).
[61] West Coast Hotel Co. v. Parrish, 300 U.S. 379 (1937).
[62] Adams v. Tanner, 244 U.S. 590 (1917).

ment agencies, the problems involved and the regulation attempted. He quoted a Bureau of Labor report that said: "The business as a whole reeks with fraud, extortion and flagrant abuses of every kind."[63] With Holmes, Brandeis maintained that legislative acts were entitled to a presumption of constitutionality and that legislatures were entitled to exercise their judgment, so long as it was not clearly unjustified or arbitrary. Clarke, whose liberal views comported, joined in the dissent. Justice McKenna made a fourth.

Some ten years later, New Jersey undertook to license and regulate employment agencies and, in the course of regulation, to fix their charges. A majority of the Court held the attempt to fix prices unconstitutional.[64] Justice Sanford joined the majority, saying he felt he was bound by a prior decision denying New York the right to fix charges of a theater ticket agency. Justice Stone, supported by Holmes and Brandeis, wrote a dissenting opinion, repeating to a great extent what Justice Brandeis had written in the Washington case.

In turn, this Ribnik decision was overruled when the Court unanimously approved a Nebraska statute limiting the fees that could be charged by a private employment agency to an applicant for employment.[65]

Another labor phase—workmen's compensation for injuries received in the course of employment burst the seams of the Court's unanimity. A 1919 opinion, in which Holmes concurred, approving an Arizona Workmen's Compensation Act, which required, in certain hazardous industries, compensation from funds wholly contributed by employers, met with four conservative dissents.[66] The dissenters' statement that the Fourteenth Amendment protected the employer's immunity from liability for no fault, a right "inherent in free government," led Holmes, in a concurring opinion, to say:

> If it is thought to be public policy to put certain voluntary conduct at the peril of those pursuing it, whether in the interest of safety and upon economic or other grounds, I know nothing to hinder....[67]
>
> If a business is unsuccessful it means that the public does not care enough for it to make it pay. If it is successful the public pays its expenses and something more. It is reasonable that the public should pay the whole cost of producing what it wants, and a part of that cost is the pain and mutilation incident to production. By throwing that loss upon the employer in the first instance we throw it upon the public in the long run and that is just.[68]

63 *Ibid.*, 602.
64 Ribnik v. McBride, 277 U.S. 350 (1928).
65 Olsen v. Nebraska, 313 U.S. 236 (1941).
66 Arizona Copper Co. v. Hammer; Arizona Copper Co. v. Bray; Ray Cons. Copper Co. v. Veazey; Inspiration Cons. Copper Co. v. Mendez; Superior Copper Co. v. Tomich, 250 U.S. 400 (1919) (Arizona Employers' Liability Cases).
67 *Ibid.*, 432.
68 *Ibid.*, 433.

Holmes's correspondent, Sir Frederick Pollock, when apprised of this decision, characterized as "amazing to my English mind that four judges of your Court should be found to assert a constitutional right not to be held liable in a civil action without actual fault." With this Holmes agreed, adding that the opinion of Justice Pitney, "which I agreed to make the opinion of the Court in order to get something that could be called that, was but a flabby performance."[69]

What was also amazing about the dissent was the fact that it came two years after the Court had approved New York, Washington State, and Iowa workmen's compensation acts, with Justice Pitney writing for the Court in each case. The Washington case was the bellwether; the vote was five to four, Chief Justice White and Justices McKenna, Van Devanter, and McReynolds joining in dissent.[70] In the New York case Justice Pitney wrote: "Liability without fault is not a novelty in the law."[71] The New York and the Iowa decisions bore no notation of dissent,[72] the minority doubtless recognizing that they were bound by the Washington decision. At least the Chief Justice recognized the obligation to respect a precedent when he concurred in a 1920 decision approving an Ohio workmen's compensation statute, although Justice McReynolds repeated his obdurate dissent.[73]

At times the touchstone of determination of legislative power rested on a conclusion of whether the "public interest" justified legislative interference. For example, by a vote of five to three, the Court held that the Kansas legislature could find the business of writing fire insurance affected with a public interest and consequently could regulate rates.[74] Justice Lamar, dissenting, extolled the Munn case: "The Munn case is a landmark in the law. It is accepted as an authoritative statement of the principles on which the right to fix rates is based."[75]

A five-to-four decision in 1927 struck down a New York statute that undertook to regulate the prices ticket agencies could charge for theater tickets.[76] Justices Holmes and Brandeis were joined in dissent by Justices Stone and Sanford. Holmes wrote:

> . . . the constitutional requirement of compensation when property is taken cannot be pressed to its grammatical extreme; . . . property rights may be

[69] De Wolfe, *Holmes-Pollock Letters*, II, 21–22.
[70] Mountain Timber Co. v. Washington, 243 U.S. 219 (1917).
[71] New York Cent. R.R. v. White, 243 U.S. 188 (1917).
[72] Hawkins v. Bleakley, 243 U.S. 210 (1917).
[73] Thornton v. Duffy, 254 U.S. 361 (1920).
[74] German Alliance Ins. Co. v. Lewis, 233 U.S. 389 (1914).
[75] *Ibid.*, 424–25.
[76] Tyson Bros. v. Banton, 273 U.S. 418 (1927).

taken for public purposes without pay if you do not take too much. . . . some play must be allowed to the joints if the machine is to work. . . .[77]

. . . the notion that a business is clothed with a public interest and has been devoted to the public use is little more than a fiction intended to beautify what is disagreeable to the sufferers. The truth seems to me to be that, subject to compensation when compensation is due, the legislature may forbid or restrict any business when it has a sufficient force of public opinion behind it. Lotteries were thought useful adjuncts of the State a century or so ago; now they are believed to be immoral and they have been stopped. Wine has been thought good for man from the time of the Apostles until recent years. But when public opinion changed it did not need the Eighteenth Amendment, notwithstanding the Fourteenth, to enable a state to say that the business should end. . . . What has happened to lotteries and wine might happen to theaters in some moral storm of the future, not because theaters were devoted to a public use, but because people had come to think that way.[78]

But if we are to yield to fashionable conventions, it seems to me that theaters are as much devoted to public use as anything well can be. We have not that respect for art that is one of the glories of France. But to many people the superfluous is the necessary, and it seems to me that government does not go beyond its sphere in attempting to make life livable for them. I am far from saying that I think this particular law a wise and rational provision. That is not my affair. If the people of the state of New York speaking by the authorized voice say that they want it, I see nothing in the Constitution of the United States to prevent their having their will.[79]

The "public use" argument employed by the majority in the theater ticket agency case was employed similarly to prevent New Jersey from fixing charges for employment agencies which, a majority held, were not devoted to a "public use."

"Public interest" also came to the fore in the Rent Law Cases, one a statute adopted by Congress to control rents in the District of Columbia[80] and the other a New York Rent Control Act adopted by the legislature.[81] Both these decisions were written for the five-man majority by Holmes with the Chief Justice and Justices McKenna, Van Devanter, and McReynolds dissenting. Justice Holmes, writing in the District of Columbia case, said: "Housing is a necessary of life. All the elements of a public interest justifying some degree of control are present.[82] Assuming the end in view otherwise justified the means adopted by Congress, we have no concern, of course, whether those

[77] *Ibid.*, 445–46.
[78] *Ibid.*, 446.
[79] *Ibid.*, 447.
[80] Block v. Hirsh, 256 U.S. 135 (1921).
[81] Marcus Brown Holding Co. v. Feldman, 256 U.S. 170 (1921).
[82] Block v. Hirsh, 256 U.S. 135, 156 (1921).

means were the wisest, whether they may not cost more than they come to, or will effect the result desired."[83]

Six members of an eight-man Hughes court held that the business of manufacturing, selling, and distributing ice was not so charged with a public use as to justify an Oklahoma licensing statute. The opinion was written by Sutherland, with the support of the Chief Justice and Roberts.[84] The recurrent issue of whether the legislative discretion or the high court's estimate that the legislative will was arbitrary lay between the Chief Justice, Justice Roberts, and the confirmed conservatives on the one hand and Justices Stone and Brandeis, awaiting Cardozo, on the other.

Now the Brandeis dissent was augmented by the shadow of the depression. Brandeis said: "The people of the United States are now confronted with an emergency more serious than war. Misery is wide-spread, in a time, not of scarcity, but of overabundance. The long-continued depression has brought unprecedented unemployment, a catastrophic fall in commodity prices and a volume of economic losses which threatens our financial institutions.[85] Thus was sounded a note of which more was to be heard within the classic portals of the Court in the near future.

The superlegislative function of the Court, which had been nurtured by the Fuller and White courts, waxed with the consolidation of the conservatives, Sutherland, McReynolds, Butler, and Van Devanter, termed the Four Horsemen. Unremittingly Holmes's dissents rang the knell of their pronouncements for the future. And while Holmes was presuming legislative knowledge and intent, Brandeis was demonstrating it. After Stone supplanted McKenna in 1925, the dissenting twosome frequently became a threesome.

The diversity of subjects touched by Court disagreement was considerable. And disagreement was not infrequent. Even Holmes and Brandeis, on occasion, failed to see eye to eye. One of those occasions was to be found, *inter alia,* in two cases[86] which came to the Court in 1923 after state legislatures had forbidden the teaching of any language but English in the primary schools. With the incitement of war passions, the legislators sought to ban the teaching of German. The Court held the acts unconstitutional as violative of the Fourteenth Amendment. Holmes, joined by Sutherland, dissented, saying—in the Bartels case:

It is with hesitation and unwillingness that I differ from my brethren with

[83] *Ibid.,* 158.
[84] New State Ice Co. v. Liebmann, 285 U.S. 262 (1932).
[85] *Ibid.,* 306.
[86] Meyer v. Nebraska, 262 U.S. 390 (1923); Bartels v. Iowa; Bohning v. Ohio; Pohl v. Ohio; Nebraska Dist. v. McKelvie, 262 U.S. 404 (1923).

regard to a law like this but I cannot bring my mind to believe that in some circumstances, and circumstances existing it is said in Nebraska, the statute might not be regarded as a reasonable or even necessary method of reaching the desired result. . . . Youth is the time when familiarity with a language is established and if there are sections in the State where a child would hear only Polish or French or German spoken at home I am not prepared to say that it is unreasonable to provide that in his early years he shall hear and speak only English at school. . . . I think I appreciate the objection to the law but it appears to me to present a question upon which men reasonably might differ and therefore I am unable to say that the Constitution of the United States prevents the experiment being tried.[87]

These cases were followed by another involving an attempt by an organization operating a Roman Catholic school to enjoin enforcement of an Oregon statute requiring attendance at public schools.[88] Although Justice McReynolds, writing for a unanimous Court, discussed the issue from a standpoint of destruction of the Society's property rights, he followed the first of the two cases last discussed—the Meyer case—while saying: "The child is not a mere creature of the state; those who nurture him and protect his destiny have the right, coupled with the high duty, to recognize and prepare him for additional obligations."[89]

When the Court held unconstitutional a Nebraska statute regulating the weight of bread, Brandeis, dissenting, delivered a typical Brandeis opinion discussing the history of such regulation and lectured his associates of the majority in schoolmasterish fashion: "Unless we know the facts on which the legislators may have acted, we cannot properly decide whether they were (or whether their measures are) unreasonable, arbitrary, or capricious. Knowledge is essential to understanding; and understanding to judging."[90] And he concluded: ". . . to decide, as a fact, that the prohibition of excess weights is not necessary . . . is, in my opinion, an exercise of the powers of a superlegislature . . . not the performance of the constitutional function of judicial review."[91] Holmes concurred in the Brandeis opinion.

In a 1925 case we find Holmes dissenting from a decision holding unconstitutional a statute providing that gifts within six years of a donor's death should be conclusively presumed to have been made in contemplation of death. Holmes said: "I think that with the States as with Congress, when the means are not prohibited and are calculated to effect the object, we ought not to inquire into the degree of the necessity for resorting to them."[92]

[87] Ibid., 412.
[88] Pierce v. Society of Sisters, 268 U.S. 510 (1925).
[89] Ibid., 535.
[90] Burns Baking Co. v. Bryan, 264 U.S. 504, 520–21 (1924).
[91] Ibid., 534.

Justices Brandeis and Stone joined Holmes when he opposed a finding that the Pennsylvania legislature might not prohibit the use of shoddy in bedding. Holmes wrote with prescience of today's allergy concepts:

> If the Legislature of Pennsylvania was of opinion that disease is likely to be spread by the use of unsterilized shoddy in comfortables, I do not suppose that this Court would pronounce the opinion so manifestly absurd that it could not be acted upon. If we should not, then I think that we ought to assume the opinion to be right for the purpose of testing the law.... On these premises, if the Legislature regarded the danger as very great and inspection and tagging as inadequate remedies, it seems to me that in order to prevent the spread of disease, it constitutionally could forbid any use of shoddy for bedding and upholstery.[93]

He added, "I think we are pressing the Fourteenth Amendment too far."[94]

In 1926 the majority struck down a California statute providing for the licensing and regulation of those transporting persons or property over a regular route on the public highways for compensation, on the ground that the real purpose of the legislature was an ulterior one. Holmes, in a dissenting opinion, with Justices McReynolds and Brandeis also dissenting, maintained that the only question was one of legislative power and said, "... with reference to the reasons that may have induced the legislature to pass it [the Act],... if a warrant can be found in such reasons they must be presumed to have been the ground."[95]

Again, when the majority struck down a Pennsylvania statute seeking to regulate chain drugstores thereafter opened or acquired, Holmes wrote a dissent, in which Brandeis joined.[96] Holmes said:

> A standing criticism of the use of corporations in business is that it causes such business to be owned by people who do not know anything about it. Argument was not supposed to be necessary in order to show that the divorce between the powers of control and knowledge is an evil. The selling of drugs and poisons calls for knowledge in a high degree, and Pennsylvania after enacting a series of other safeguards has provided that in that matter the divorce shall not be allowed. . . .[97] The Constitution does not make it a condition of preventive legislation that it should work a perfect cure. But for

[92] Schlesinger v. Wisconsin, 270 U.S. 230, 242 (1926).
[93] Weaver v. Palmer Bros. Co., 270 U.S. 402, 415 (1926).
[94] *Ibid.*, 416.
[95] Frost v. California, 271 U.S. 583, 600 (1926).
[96] Liggett Co. v. Baldridge, 278 U.S. 105 (1928).
[97] *Ibid.*, 114.

decisions to which I bow, I should not think any conciliatory phrase necessary to justify what seems to me one of the incidents of legislative power.[98]

In another Pennsylvania case,[99] later overruled,[100] a seven-man majority struck down a Pennsylvania statute requiring the licensing of persons selling steamship tickets to foreign countries on the ground that it burdened or interfered with foreign commerce. Brandeis wrote a dissenting opinion, in which Holmes concurred, saying:

> The statute is an exertion of the police power of the State. Its evident purpose is to prevent a particular species of fraud and imposition found to have been practiced in Pennsylvania upon persons of small means, unfamiliar with our language and institutions. A similar statute has been enacted in New York . . . and similar laws have been enacted in other States.[101] . . . If Pennsylvania must submit to see its citizens defrauded, it is not because Congress has so willed, but because the Constitution so commands. I cannot believe that it does.[102]

In still another Pennsylvania case, a six-man majority held that Pennsylvania could not discriminate in imposing taxes on gross receipts of operators of taxicabs between corporations on the one hand and individuals and partnerships on the other. Holmes said in dissent, "I see no reason why the larger business may not be taxed and the small ones disregarded."[103]

Previously the Court had voided a Pennsylvania statute forbidding the mining of coal under private dwellings, streets, or cities for the purpose of avoiding subsidence. Justice Holmes wrote for the Court, holding that the statute called for a taking of property without due process of law. He said: "What makes the right to mine coal valuable is that it can be exercised with profit. To make it commercially impracticable to mine certain coal has very nearly the same effect for constitutional purposes as appropriating or destroying it. This we think we are warranted in assuming the statute does."[104]

In a letter to Pollock Holmes explained that the ground of his thinking was "that the public only got on to this land by paying for it and that if they saw fit to pay only for a surface right, they can't enlarge it because they need it now any more than they could have taken the right of being there in the first place."[105]

[98] *Ibid.*, 115.
[99] Di Santo v. Pennsylvania, 273 U.S. 34 (1927).
[100] California v. Thompson, 313 U.S. 109 (1941).
[101] Di Santo v. Pennsylvania, 273 U.S. 34, 38 n.1 (1927).
[102] *Ibid.*, 39.
[103] Quaker City Cab Co. v. Pennsylvania, 277 U.S. 389, 403 (1928).
[104] Pennsylvania Coal Co. v. Mahon, 260 U.S. 393, 414–15 (1922).
[105] De Wolfe, *Holmes-Pollock Letters*, II, 109.

When Holmes said that the subsurface should be condemned and paid for, his role as a protector of private property rights was challenged by, of all people, his confrere Brandeis, who, dissenting, said: "Restriction imposed to protect the public health, safety, or morals from dangers threatened is not . . . a taking. The restriction here in question is merely the prohibition of a noxious use."[106]

A 1928 decision, over the dissent of Holmes, Brandeis, Sanford, and Stone, struck down a Kentucky statute that imposed a recording tax on mortgages that matured in more than five years.[107] The majority held that the classification was illegal in that it violated the Fourteenth Amendment guarantee of equal protection. Justice Brandeis wrote a typical Brandeis dissertation. Holmes said:

> When a legal distinction is determined, as no one doubts that it may be, between night and day, childhood and maturity, or any other extremes, a point has to be fixed or a line has to be drawn, or gradually picked out by successive decisions, to mark where the change takes place. Looked at by itself without regard to the necessity behind it, the line or point seems arbitrary. It might as well or might nearly as well be a little more to the one side or the other. But when it is seen that a line or point there must be, and that there is no mathematical or logical way of fixing it precisely, the decision of the legislature must be accepted unless we can say that it is very wide of any reasonable mark. . . .
>
> I hardly think it would be denied that the large transactions of the money market reasonably may be subjected to a tax from which small ones for private need are exempted.[108]

With McReynolds dissenting, the Court held unconstitutional as denying equal protection a provision in the Arizona constitution requiring every employer of more than five workers at any one time to employ not less than 50 per cent of qualified electors or native-born citizens.[109]

The views of Holmes prevailed over dissents in two cases worthy of note. In holding valid the Migratory Bird Treaty Act that authorized a treaty with Canada as not infringing the rights of states, over the dissents of Justices Van Devanter and Pitney, Holmes wrote:

> When we are dealing with words that also are a constituent act, like the Constitution of the United States, we must realize that they have called into life a being the development of which could not have been foreseen complete

106 Pennsylvania Coal Co. v. Mahon, 260 U.S. 393, 417 (1922).
107 Louisville Gas Co. v. Coleman, 277 U.S. 32 (1928).
108 Ibid., 41.
109 Truax v. Raich, 239 U.S. 33 (1915).

by the most gifted of its begetters. It was only for them to realize or to hope that they had created an organism; it has taken a century and has cost their successors much sweat and blood to prove that they created a nation. . . .[110]

Wild birds are not in the possession of any one; and possession is the beginning of ownership. The whole foundation of the states' rights is the presence within their jurisdiction of birds that yesterday had not arrived, tomorrow may be in another State, and in a week a thousand miles away.[111]

In the second case, Holmes, over the dissent of Justice Butler, held that a state might sterilize imbeciles, saying:

We have seen more than once that the public welfare may call upon the best citizens for their lives. It would be strange if it could not call upon those who already sap the strength of the State for these lesser sacrifices. . . . It is better for all the world, if instead of waiting to execute degenerate offspring for crime, or to let them starve for their imbecility, society can prevent those who are manifestly unfit from continuing their kind. . . . Three generations of imbeciles are enough.[112]

With the division on the Hughes court, the Fourteenth Amendment issue was bound to recur frequently. And so, when the question arose about the right of Missouri to claim inheritance taxes on the value of bank deposits and personal property in Missouri owned by an Illinois decedent, the Chief Justice joined the conservatives to deny the state's claim.[113]

Now, when Mr. Justice Oliver Wendell Holmes, aged eighty-nine, after a service of almost three decades, stood at his old-fashioned desk to write what was to be his penultimate dissenting opinion, he must have felt that he had spent his aging years in an exercise of futility. For, as he wrote, he must have remembered the words of his first utterance on the Court: "While the courts must exercise a judgment of their own, it by no means is true that every law is void which may seem to the judges who pass upon it excessive, unsuited to its ostensible end, or based upon conceptions of morality with which they disagree."

And now, after witnessing violation after violation of that salutary principle for more than two and a half decades, he was writing:

I have not yet adequately expressed the more than anxiety that I feel at the ever increasing scope given to the Fourteenth Amendment in cutting down what I believe to be the constitutional rights of the States. As the decisions now

[110] Missouri v. Holland, 252 U.S. 416, 433 (1920).
[111] Ibid., 434.
[112] Buck v. Bell, 274 U.S. 200, 207 (1927).
[113] Baldwin v. Missouri, 281 U.S. 586 (1930).

stand, I see hardly any limit but the sky to the invalidating of those rights if they happen to strike a majority of this Court as for any reason undesirable. I cannot believe that the Amendment was intended to give us *carte blanche* to embody our economic or moral beliefs in its prohibitions. Yet I can think of no narrower reason that seems to me to justify the present and the earlier decisions to which I have referred.[114]

He had written his friend Pollock in 1928: ". . . as long as one continues to write, the question is always of tomorrow and not of yesterday, and tomorrow one may show what a fool one is."[115] But he need not have been concerned, for history vindicated his words of dissent as it has swept away those of his heedless brethren.

While the Court, during these terms (Fuller through Taft), was denigrating the legislative exercise of the police power of the states, it was protecting them from the inroads of the federal Constitution. So, in 1908, it denied the claim of two bank directors that a state trial judge violated their rights of immunity from self-incrimination in commenting upon their failure to take the stand in their own defense. It was not argued, said Justice Moody,

> that the defendants are protected by that part of the Fifth Amendment which provides that "no person . . . shall be compelled in any criminal case to be a witness against himself," for it is recognized by counsel that, by a long line of decisions, the first ten Amendments are not operative on the states. . . . But it is argued that this privilege is one of the fundamental rights of national citizenship, placed under national protection by the Fourteenth Amendment, and it is specially argued that the "privileges and immunities of citizens of the United States," protected against state action by that Amendment, include those fundamental personal rights which were protected against national action by the first eight Amendments. . . . These arguments are not new to this court and the answer to them is found in its decisions."[116]

The Court held that neither the privileges and immunities clause nor the due process clause of the Fourteenth Amendment made the self-incrimination clause of the Fifth Amendment applicable to the states. Justice Harlan dissented.

Later, in 1937, Palko, a defendant convicted of murder in a Connecticut state court on a second trial, after a previous second-degree conviction had been appealed by the state and reversed, pleaded that his right of immunity from double jeopardy under the Fourteenth Amendment had been violated. Over the dissent of Justice Butler, in an opinion by Justice Cardozo, the Court

[114] *Ibid.,* 595–96.
[115] De Wolfe, *Holmes-Pollock Letters,* II, 211.
[116] Twining v. New Jersey, 211 U.S. 78, 93 (1908).

overruled the defendant's contention.[117] Justice Cardozo said: "The argument for appellant is that whatever is forbidden by the Fifth Amendment is forbidden by the Fourteenth also...."[118] His thesis is even broader. Whatever would be a violation of the original bill of rights [Amendments I to VIII] if done by the federal government is now equally unlawful by force of the Fourteenth Amendment if done by a state. There is no such general rule.[119]

However, reviewing the cases pro and con, Justice Cardozo found "a unifying principle." It was embodied in the answer to his question: "Does it [the act complained of] violate those 'fundamental principles of liberty and justice' which lie at the base of all our civil and political institutions?"[120] He was quoting a prior case.[121]

It might be noted that Justice Black, then a freshman who had been sworn in two months previously, and who was to become the principal exponent of the contention advanced by the appellant and overruled by the Court, did not dissent from the ruling. However, he took up and continued to wield these cudgels later.

Over the years, in a variety of cases, the Court adhered to the Cardozo compromise, as enunciated in the Palko case, resisting the Black contention that the Fourteenth Amendment had imported the Fifth into intrastate law administration.

In 1947, in affirmation of the Palko doctrine, the Court held that "the power to free defendants in state trials from self-incrimination . . . [was] beyond the scope of the privileges and immunities clause of the Fifth Amendment." Hence the Court rejected the contention that a California law permitting the failure of a defendant to explain or deny evidence against him to be commented upon by court and counsel and to be considered by court and jury was invalid as violating the due process clause of the Fourteenth Amendment.[122] Justice Reed, writing for the Court, said, "The purpose of due process is not to protect an accused against a proper conviction but against an unfair conviction."[123] Justice Frankfurter concurred; Justices Black, Douglas, and Murphy dissented.

In his concurring opinion Justice Frankfurter called the roll of judges "alert in safeguarding and promoting the interests of liberty and human dignity through law" who had denied the thesis that the Fourteenth Amendment "was a shorthand summary of the first eight Amendments." He said

117 Palko v. Connecticut, 302 U.S. 319 (1937).
118 *Ibid.*, 322.
119 *Ibid.*, 323.
120 *Ibid.*, 328.
121 Hebert v. Louisiana, 272 U.S. 312 (1926).
122 Adamson v. California, 332 U.S. 46, 52 (1947).
123 *Ibid.*, 57.

that the scope of the Amendment had been passed upon by forty-three judges and that, "of all these judges, only one, who may respectfully be called an eccentric exception, ever indicated" such a belief.[124]

Justice Black, dissenting, wrote at length, saying that his "study of the historical events that culminated in the Fourteenth Amendment" had persuaded him that "the provisions of the Amendment's first section, separately, and as a whole, were intended to . . . make the Bill of Rights, applicable to the states."[125]

Subsequently, a man named Konigsberg refused to answer questions put to him by a California bar committee, which was passing upon his application for admission to the bar. The committee refused to approve him, and the California court supported the committee. Five members of the high court reversed and remanded the case for further proceedings.[126] When the case came back, the four dissenters in the previous case were able to command the majority,[127] and Justice Harlan said that "the Fourteenth Amendment's protection against arbitrary state action does not forbid a State from denying admission to a bar applicant so long as he refuses to provide unprivileged answers to questions having a substantial relevance to his qualifications."[128] Chief Justice Warren and Justices Black, Douglas, and Brennan dissented.

Simultaneously, the same majority, over the same dissent, upheld an Illinois refusal to admit an applicant to practice as a lawyer for his refusal to answer questions respecting his Communist party membership.[129]

On the same day, the same five-man majority, over the dissent of the same four members, upheld the disbarment of a New York lawyer who refused to answer relevant questions upon an "ambulance-chasing" investigation conducted by a judge.[130]

These cases were decided while the conservatives were able to command a bare majority to reject erosion of the Palko principle. However, once more Canutes could not turn back the eroding liberal tide.

So in still another Connecticut case, where Malloy, a witness in a state inquiry into gambling and other crimes, had invoked his privilege against self-incrimination and had been convicted of contempt, he sought a writ of habeas corpus and when it was denied appealed to the high court. Now the Court held the Fourteenth Amendment made the Fifth Amendment privilege against self-incrimination applicable to the states in an opinion by Justice

124 *Ibid.*, 62.
125 *Ibid.*, 71–72.
126 Konigsberg v. State Bar, 353 U.S. 252 (1957).
127 Konigsberg v. State Bar, 366 U.S. 36 (1961).
128 *Ibid.*, 44.
129 *In re* Anastaplo, 366 U.S. 82 (1961).
130 Cohen v. Hurley, 366 U.S. 117 (1961).

Brennan for five members of the Court. Justice Douglas concurred, reiterating his opinion that the Fourteenth Amendment incorporated the Bill of Rights. Justice Harlan, supported by Justice Clark, dissented. Justice White, joined by Justice Stewart, dissented and wrote only respecting the finding that the petitioner's claim should have been upheld.[131] Justice Brennan relied on the Mapp decision respecting the Fourth Amendment.

Justice Harlan, dissenting, said:

> Believing that the reasoning behind the Court's decision carries extremely mischievous, if not dangerous, consequences for our federal system in the realm of criminal law enforcement, I must dissent. . . .[132]
>
> I can only read the Court's opinion as accepting in fact what it rejects in theory: the application to the States via the Fourteenth Amendment, of the forms of federal criminal procedure embodied within the first eight Amendments to the Constitution. . . .[133]
>
> The ultimate result is compelled uniformity, which is inconsistent with the purpose of our federal system and which is achieved either by encroachment on the States' sovereign powers or by dilution in federal law enforcement of the specific protections found in the Bill of Rights.[134]
>
> As recently as 1961, this Court reaffirmed that "the Fifth Amendment's privilege against self-incrimination," . . . was not applicable against the States. . . .[135] Until today it has been regarded as settled law that the *Fifth Amendment* privilege did not, by any process of reasoning, apply *as such* to the States. . . .
>
> Certainly there has been no intimation until now that Twining has been tacitly overruled.[136]
>
> Mr. Justice Cardozo made the independence of the Due Process Clause from the provisions of the first eight Amendments explicit. . . .[137]
>
> The Court's undiscriminating approach to the Due Process Clause carries serious implications for the sound working of our federal system in the field of criminal law. . . .
>
> About all that the Court offers . . . is the observation that it would be "incongruous" if different standards governed. . . . Such "incongruity," however, is at the heart of our federal system. The powers and responsibilities of the state and federal governments are not congruent; under our Constitution, they are not intended to be. . . .[138]
>
> The Court's reference to a federal standard is, to put it bluntly, simply an

131 Malloy v. Hogan, 378 U.S. 1 (1964).
132 *Ibid.*, 14–15.
133 *Ibid.*, 15.
134 *Ibid.*, 16–17.
135 Cohen v. Hurley, 366 U.S. 117 (1961).
136 Malloy v. Hogan, 378 U.S. 1, 17 (1964).
137 *Ibid.*, 23.
138 *Ibid.*, 27.

excuse for the Court to substitute its own superficial assessment of the facts and state law for the careful and better informed conclusions of the state court.[139]

Now that the Fifth Amendment bars were down and the Twining case had been tacitly overruled, as Justice Harlan had said in the Malloy case, there was no option when the Twining contention came to the Court at the instance of Eddie Dean Griffin, who had been convicted of murder in a California state court. Here, both Court and counsel had commented on the defendant's failure to testify respecting facts which he could reasonably be expected to deny or explain because they were within his knowledge, as permitted by the California constitution. Writing for five members of the Court, Justice Douglas held that the Fourteenth Amendment made the Fifth Amendment applicable to the states and reversed the conviction. Justices White and Stewart dissented; the Chief Justice did not participate.[140]

Justice Harlan, concurring, said he could see no escape from the decision of the majority since the previous case of Malloy v. Hogan had made the Fifth Amendment applicable to the states. He added:

I do so [concur], however, with great reluctance, since for me the decision exemplifies the creeping paralysis with which this Court's recent adoption of the "incorporation" doctrine is infecting the operation of the federal system. . . .[141]

Justice Stewart, supported by Justice White, said in dissent: "No claim is made that the prosecutor's argument or the trial judge's instructions to the jury in this case deprived the petitioner of due process of law as such. This Court long ago decided that the Due Process Clause of the Fourteenth Amendment does not of its own force forbid this kind of comment on a defendant's failure to testify. . . .[142]

We must determine whether the petitioner has been compelled . . . to be a witness against himself. Compulsion is the focus of the inquiry. . . . When a suspect was brought before . . . the Star Chamber, he was commanded to answer. . . . He declined to answer on pain of incarceration, banishment, or mutilation. . . . Faced with this formidable array of alternatives, his decision to speak was unquestionably coerced.

Those were the lurid realities which lay behind enactment of the Fifth Amendment, a far cry from the subject matter of the case before us. I think that the Court in this case stretches the concept of compulsion beyond all reasonable bounds, and that whatever compulsion may exist derives from the defendant's choice not to testify, not from any comment by court or counsel. In support of its conclusion . . . the Court has only this to say: "It is a penalty

[139] Ibid., 33.
[140] Griffin v. California, 380 U.S. 609 (1965).
[141] Ibid., 615–16.
[142] Ibid., 619.

imposed by courts for exercising a constitutional privilege. It cuts down on the privilege by making its assertion costly." Exactly what the penalty imposed consists of is not clear. It is not . . . that the jury becomes aware that the defendant has chosen not to testify, . . . for the jury will, of course, realize this quite evident fact, even though the choice goes unmentioned. . . .

How can it be said that the inferences drawn by a jury will be more detrimental to a defendant under the limiting and carefully controlling language of the instruction here involved than would result if the jury were left to roam at large with only its untutored instincts to guide it, to draw from the defendant's silence broad inferences of guilt? . . .[143]

I think the California comment rule is not a coercive device . . . but rather a means of articulating and bringing into the light of rational discussion a fact inescapably impressed on the jury's consciousness. . . .

The California rule . . . is hardly an idiosyncratic aberration. The Model Code of Evidence and the Uniform Rules of Evidence both sanction the use of such procedures. The practice has been endorsed by resolution of the American Bar Association and the American Law Institute, and has the support of the weight of scholarly opinion. . . .[144]

The formulation of procedural rules to govern the administration of criminal justice in the various States is properly a matter of local concern. . . .[145]

Before the Court had held the California constitutional rule invalid in the Griffin case, one Chapman and others were convicted in a California state court of kidnapping and murder. Pending their appeal, the Griffin case was decided. The high court reversed because it held the state had not shown, beyond a reasonable doubt, that the repetitive comments of the prosecutor and the trial court's instructions to the jury respecting defendants' failure to take the stand did not contribute to their convictions.[146]

Justices Stewart and Harlan differed respecting the majority view concerning the application of the "harmless error" rule.

Also before the Griffin decision, five members of the Court had reversed a murder conviction because the prosecutor asked the defendant, who had taken the stand in his own defense, though he had not done so on two previous trials: "This is the first time you have gone on the stand, isn't it?"[147] The Court argued that the rule that failure of a defendant to testify in his own behalf shall not create any presumption against him, had been violated. Justice Frankfurter, supported by Justices Harlan and Whittaker, dissenting, said:

---

[143] *Ibid.,* 620–21.
[144] *Ibid.,* 622.
[145] *Ibid.,* 623.
[146] Chapman v. California, 386 U.S. 18 (1967); Anderson v. Nelson, 390 U.S. 523 (1968).
[147] Stewart v. United States, 366 U.S. 1 (1961).

The result which the Court draws from its account of the trial seems not unreasonable. But by force of what the Court does not relate, there is such disparity between its account and the almost nine hundred pages of the trial transcript that, in fairness, the Court's opinion hardly conveys what took place before the jury and what must, therefore, rationally be evaluated in attributing any influence on the jury's verdict to the questions which the Government now concedes were improperly asked. . . . "To turn a criminal appeal into a quest for error no more promotes the ends of justice than to acquiesce in low standards of criminal prosecution." . . .

What emerges from the transcript, at the outset, is that Willie Lee Stewart's killing of Harry Honikman was practically never in issue. The testimony of two eyewitnesses who positively identified Stewart as the killer was not seriously challenged. A third witness had examined in Stewart's hands, shortly before the killing, the gun which unimpugned ballistic evidence established fired the lethal shots. The testimony of a fingerprint expert, also unimpugned, linked Stewart to the killing. Nowhere in their opening or closing statements did experienced defense counsel ask the jury to doubt that Stewart was the killer; the whole of the defense was that Stewart was not responsible because insane.

Insanity was not merely, as the Court says, Stewart's chief defense; it was his defense. His lawyer put it aptly: "(The prosecutor) knows as well as I, as anybody in this courtroom, the only defense we have is insanity." Thus, there is not involved in this case the danger that the jury, being told as laymen of the defendant's previous failure to testify in his own behalf, reasoned that if Stewart did not do the acts with which he was charged he would have said so. Here, those acts were not contested.[148]

Justice Clark, joined by Justice Whittaker, said:

It may be that Willie Lee Stewart "had an intelligence level in the moronic class," but he can laugh up his sleeve today for he has again made a laughing-stock of the law. This makes the third jury verdict of guilt . . . that has been set aside since 1953. It was in that year that Willie walked into Harry Honikman's little grocery store here in Washington, bought a bag of potato chips and a soft drink, consumed them in the store, ordered another bottle of soda, and then pulled out a pistol and killed Honikman right before the eyes of his wife and young daughter.[149]

Since one inroad leads to another, incursions tend to become epidemic. Police officers, questioned during a state investigation of fixing traffic tickets, had testified after being warned that refusal to answer would result in discharge under a state statute. The testimony thus elicited was used later to

148 *Ibid.*, 12.
149 *Ibid.*, 22.

convict them in criminal proceedings. Justice Douglas and his four liberal confreres held that their testimony was coerced by the threat of removal of office and vacated the convictions.[150] Justice Douglas disregarded but quoted Justice Holmes's oft-repeated statement that "the petitioner may have a constitutional right to talk politics, but he has no constitutional right to be a policeman. There are few employments for hire in which the servant does not agree to suspend his constitutional right of free speech, as well as of idleness, by the implied terms of his contract. The servant cannot complain, as he takes the employment on the terms which are offered him. On the same principle, the city may impose any reasonable condition upon holding offices within its control."[151]

Justice Douglas held that "the question in this case, however, is not cognizable in those terms. Our question is whether the Government, contrary to the requirement of the Fourteenth Amendment, can use the threat of discharge to secure incriminatory evidence against an employee."[152]

Referring to a prior case,[153] which held that a public school teacher could not be discharged merely because he had invoked the Fifth Amendment privilege before a congressional committee, he said, "We conclude that policemen, like teachers and lawyers, are not relegated to a watered-down version of constitutional rights."[154] The same majority consistently overruled a prior case[155] and held that a lawyer could not be disbarred for refusal to produce records called for in a state ambulance-chasing investigation.[156]

Justice Harlan wrote in dissent in both cases and was joined by Justices Clark and Stewart. Justice White wrote in dissent in both cases with an opinion in the second case.

Justice Harlan argued that the facts disclosed that the statements of the policemen were voluntary and that the defendants had not contended that they were involuntary in fact but only that the threat of dismissal made them involuntary in law. As to that, Justice Harlan said:

> ... nothing in the logic or purposes of the privilege demands that all consequences which may result from a witness' silence be forbidden merely because the silence is privileged. The validity of a consequence depends both upon the hazards, if any, it presents to the integrity of the privilege and upon the urgency of the public interests it is designed to protect.

150 Garrity v. New Jersey, 385 U.S. 493 (1967).
151 McAuliffe v. New Bedford, 155 Mass. 216, 220 (1892).
152 Garrity v. New Jersey, 385 U.S. 493, 499 (1967).
153 Slochower v. Board of Education, 350 U.S. 551 (1956).
154 Garrity v. New Jersey, 385 U.S. 493, 500 (1967).
155 Cohen v. Hurley, 366 U.S. 117 (1961).
156 Spevack v. Klein, 385 U.S. 511 (1967).

It can hardly be denied that New Jersey is permitted by the Constitution to establish reasonable qualifications and standards of conduct for its public employees. Nor can it be said that it is arbitrary or unreasonable for New Jersey to insist that its employees furnish the appropriate authorities with information pertinent to their employment.... Finally, it is surely plain that New Jersey may in particular require its employees to assist in the prevention and detection of unlawful activities by officers of the state government. The urgency of these requirements is the more obvious here, where the conduct in question is that of officials directly entrusted with the administration of justice.[157]

Harlan quoted the following, which merely paraphrased Justice Holmes, from a California case[158]:

Duty required them to answer. Privilege permitted them to refuse to answer. They chose to exercise the privilege, but the exercise of such privilege was wholly inconsistent with their duty as police officers. They claim that they had a constitutional right to refuse to answer under the circumstances, but ... they had no constitutional right to remain police officers in the face of their clear violation of the duty imposed upon them.[159]

In the Spevack case, Justice Harlan wrote:

This decision, made in the name of the Constitution, permits a lawyer suspected of professional misconduct to thwart direct official inquiry of him without fear of disciplinary action. What is done today will be disheartening and frustrating to courts and bar associations throughout the country in their efforts to maintain high standards at the bar. . . . And, still more pervasively, this decision can hardly fail to encourage oncoming generations of lawyers to think of their calling as imposing on them no higher standards of behavior than might be acceptable in the general marketplace.[160]

Referring to prior cases,[161] Harlan said:

These cases . . . make plain that so long as state authorities do not derive any imputation of guilt from a claim of the privilege, they may in the course of a bona fide assessment of an employee's fitness for public employment require that the employee disclose information reasonably related to his fitness, and may order his discharge if he declines....[162]

[157] Garrity v. New Jersey, 385 U.S. 493, 507 (1967).
[158] Christal v. Police Commissioner, 33 Cal. App. 2d 564.
[159] Garrity v. New Jersey, 385 U.S. 493, 509 n.32 (1967).
[160] Spevack v. Klein, 385 U.S. 511, 520–21 (1967).
[161] Slochower v. Board of Education, 350 U.S. 551 (1956); Beilan v. Board of Pub. Educ., 357 U.S. 399 (1958); Lerner v. Casey, 357 U.S. 468 (1958); Nelson v. Los Angeles, 362 U.S. 1 (1960).
[162] Spevack v. Klein, 385 U.S. 511, 528 (1967).

... nothing in New York's efforts in good faith to assure the integrity of its judicial system destroys, inhibits, or even minimizes the petitioner's constitutional privilege.... it suffices that the State is earnestly concerned with an urgent public interest, and that it has selected methods for the pursuit of that interest which do not prevent attainment of the privilege's purpose.[163]

Subsequently, five members of the Court vacated the judgments below and remanded the cases for reconsideration where lawyers had been called upon to testify under threat of disbarment in light of the Spevack case. Justices Clark, Harlan, Stewart, and White dissented, as they had in the Spevack case. Later, on January 29, 1968, the complaining lawyers, who upon reconsideration below, had been suspended from practice, were denied certiorari, only Justices Black and Douglas dissenting.[164]

In two cases the Court held unanimously that a provision in the New York City charter requiring dismissal of public employees who refused to sign waivers of immunity from prosecution before testifying before a grand jury were unconstitutional as requiring them to waive their constitutional immunity from self-incrimination under the Fifth Amendment.[165] This extension of the earlier Garrity decision was qualified by the reservation that public employees might be dismissed "if they refuse to account for their performance of their public trust," and the proceedings do "not involve an attempt to coerce them to relinquish their constitutional rights."[166]

However, the Court held, over the dissent of Justices Black and Douglas, that New York City might blacklist a company whose officer refused to sign a waiver of immunity respecting testimony before a grand jury, since the constitutional privilege was not available to a corporation.[167]

In 1967-term decisions, with the Chief Justice dissenting and Justice Marshall not participating, the Court voided the conviction of two gamblers who had failed to register as professional gamblers and obtain and display the necessary stamp certifying to the registration upon the ground that such action involved a confession of guilt prohibited by the Fifth Amendment.[168] Simultaneously, it voided, by the same vote, a section of the National Firearms Act that made it a crime to possess an unregistered sawed-off shotgun, machine

163 *Ibid.*, 530.
164 Zuckerman v. Greason, 386 U.S. 15 (1967); Kaye v. Co-ordinating Committee, *ibid.*, 17; Zuckerman v. Greason; Allison v. Greason; Resnicoff v. Assoc. of the Bar, 390 U.S. 925 (1968).
165 Gardner v. Broderick, 392 U.S. 273 (1968); Uniformed Sanitation Men's Assoc. v. Commissioner of Sanitation, *ibid.*, 280.
166 Uniformed Sanitation Men's Assoc. v. Commissioner of Sanitation, 392 U.S. 280, 285 (1968).
167 Campbell Painting Co. v. Reid, 392 U.S. 286 (1968).
168 Marchetti v. United States, 390 U.S. 39 (1968); Grosso v. United States, 390 U.S. 62 (1968).

gun, or other weapon subject to federal regulation, upon the ground that the law made it a felony to possess such a weapon not properly registered.[169] Chief Justice Warren maintained that the decisions would result in "a new wave of attacks on a number of Federal registration statutes whenever the registration requirement touches upon allegedly illegal activities."[170]

In applying the self-incrimination prohibitions of the Fifth Amendment to these situations, the Court was holding consistently with its previous decision that the Communist party need not register pursuant to the order of the Subversive Activities Control Board,[171] to say nothing of the Fifth Amendment case involving policemen[172] and lawyers[173] who received similar exculpation.

In giving its blessing to the gambler Marchetti, the Court overruled two previous cases[174] and distinguished a third.[175]

The repercussions of decisions such as that in the Marchetti case find illustration in the fact that dismissals of indictments in no less than twenty-three similar cases were recorded in the per curiam decisions of March 4, 1968.

And the repercussions caused ripples in outlying waters. So in a 1968 case[176] the petitioner maintained that the trial court had improperly permitted at his trial testimony he had given on a previous application to suppress evidence. Justice Harlan, writing for six judges (Justice Marshall not participating), held that he had testified that he owned a suitcase containing incriminating evidence to obtain a "benefit" under the Fourth Amendment; that his choice was to forego that "benefit" or risk incriminating himself under the Fifth Amendment and that, under such circumstances, his choice was so limited as to require the Court to find the former testimony inadmissible.[177]

Justices Black and White dissented, the former saying, with the approval of the latter:

> The Court makes new law in reversing Garrett's conviction on the ground that it was error to allow the Government to use against him testimony he had given upon his unsuccessful motion to suppress evidence allegedly seized in violation of the Fourth Amendment. The testimony used was Garrett's statement in the suppression hearing that he was the owner of a suitcase which contained money wrappers taken from the bank that was robbed. . . . this

[169] Haynes v. United States, 390 U.S. 85 (1968).
[170] Grosso v. United States, 390 U.S. 62, 83 (1968).
[171] Albertson v. Subversive Activities Control Board, 382 U.S. 70 (1965).
[172] Garrity v. New Jersey, 385 U.S. 493 (1967).
[173] Spevack v. Klein, 385 U.S. 511 (1967).
[174] United States v. Kahriger, 345 U.S. 22 (1953); Lewis v. United States, 348 U.S. 419 (1955).
[175] Shapiro v. United States, 335 U.S. 1 (1948).
[176] Simmons v. United States, 390 U.S. 377 (1968).
[177] Ibid., 394.

testimony, along with the statements of the eyewitnesses against him, showed beyond all question that Garrett was one of the bank robbers. The question then is whether the Government is barred from offering a truthful statement made by a defendant at a suppression hearing in order to prevent the defendant from winning an acquittal on the false premise that he is not the owner of the property he has already sworn that he owns. My answer to this question is "No." The Court's answer is "Yes" on the premise that "a defendant who knows that his testimony may be admissible against him at trial will sometimes be deterred from presenting the testimonial proof of standing necessary to assert a Fourth Amendment claim."[178]

The standard of proof necessary to convict in a criminal case is high, and quite properly so, but for this reason highly probative evidence such as that involved here should not lightly be held inadmissible. For me the importance of bringing guilty criminals to book is a far more crucial consideration than the desirability of giving defendants every possible assistance in their attempts to invoke an evidentiary rule which itself can result in the exclusion of highly relevant evidence. . . .

This leaves for me only the possible contention that Garrett's testimony was inadmissible under the Fifth Amendment because it was compelled. . . .[179] The reason why the Fifth Amendment poses no bar to acceptance of Garrett's testimony is not . . . that a promise of benefit is not generally fatal. Rather, the answer is that the privilege against self-incrimination has always been considered a privilege that can be waived, and the validity of the waiver is, of course, not undermined by the inevitable fact that by testifying, a defendant can obtain the "benefit" of a chance to help his own case by the testimony he gives. When Garrett took the stand at the suppression hearing, he validly surrendered his privilege with respect to the statements he actually made at that time, and since these statements were therefore not "compelled," they could be used against him for any subsequent purpose.

The consequence of the Court's holding . . . is but to permit lawless people to play ducks and drakes with the basic principles of the administration of criminal law.[180]

Similarly, by a vote of six to two, Justices Black and White dissenting and Justice Marshall not participating, the Court vitiated a conviction for transporting a kidnapped person across a state line under the terms of a statute, enacted in 1932 as a result of the kidnapping of the infant son of Charles A. Lindbergh.

The statute was amended in 1934 to provide that the death penalty might be imposed "if the kidnapped person has not been liberated unharmed, and if the verdict of the jury shall so recommend." The amendment was prompted

178 *Ibid.*, 396–97.
179 *Ibid.*, 397.
180 *Ibid.*, 398.

by opponents of capital punishment who felt that defendants could avoid the death penalty by choosing to waive a jury trial. However, experience demonstrated that even though defendants undertook to waive jury trials, the Court had the power to call in a jury and, hence, the only way a defendant could be assured of avoiding the death penalty was to plead guilty before the judge.

Justice Stewart, writing for the majority and affirming the opinion of Connecticut District Judge Timbers that the death penalty clause was unconstitutional, reasoned that the compulsion on a defendant to waive a jury trial violated the Sixth Amendment guaranty of a right to a jury trial, that the pressure upon a defendant to plead guilty violated his rights under the self-incrimination clause of the Fifth Amendment, and that this choice constituted "an impermissible burden upon the exercise of a constitutional right."[181]

The dissenters maintained that judges could refuse to accept guilty pleas or waivers of jury trials if they found them compelled by the threat of a jury verdict of death.[182]

Also, the Court held, over the dissents of Justices Harlan, Black, and White, that a defendant's testimony at an earlier trial, seeking to avoid a confession which was later declared invalid, was inadmissible at his second trial.[183]

[181] United States v. Jackson, 390 U.S. 570 (1968); *see also* Pope v. United States 392 U.S. 651 (1968).

[182] United States v. Jackson, 390 U.S. 570, 592 (1968).

[183] Harrison v. United States, 392 U.S. 219 (1968).

The Court as a Superlegislature—2

THE CLASH OF COURT AND LEGISLATURE inevitably involved the impact of the commerce clause in considering the application of the Sherman and Clayton acts. In this area the Fuller court subordinated its nationalism to a states' rights attitude worthy of the Taney court and contrasting glaringly with its superlegislative role. And, for that matter, its concept of the commerce clause was narrow even for that era.

So, in considering the Sherman Anti-Trust Act, passed by Congress in 1890 to curb corporate rapacities, the Court decided, in the Knight case, that monopoly of intrastate production was a matter for states to curb under their police powers and that Congress not only had not intended to interfere by passing the Sherman Act but lacked the power to do so.[1]

In that case it appeared that the American Sugar Refining Company controlled 63 per cent of all the sugar refined in the United States. Four Pennsylvania companies controlled 33 per cent. A Boston company controlled another 2 per cent. American undertook to buy control of the Pennsylvania companies, thus giving it 98 per cent of all sugar refined in the country. The government invoked the Sherman Act. The Court said "no." Justice Harlan was the only dissenter.

He stated this opinion in a manner reminiscent of the Taney Democrats' anticorporate feeling:

> If this combination . . . cannot be restrained or suppressed under some power granted to Congress, it will be cause for regret that the patriotic statesmen who framed the Constitution did not foresee the necessity of investing the national government with power to deal with gigantic monopolies holding in their grasp, and injuriously controlling in their own interest, the entire trade among the states in food products that are essential to the comfort of every household in the land. . . .[2]

---

[1] United States v. E. C. Knight Co., 156 U.S. 1 (1895). Two years later a five-to-four decision held an agreement in restraint of interstate trade void. United States v. Trans-Missouri Freight Assoc., 166 U.S. 290 (1897).

In my judgment, the citizens of the several states composing the Union are entitled, of right, to buy goods in the state where they are manufactured, or in any other state, without being confronted by an illegal combination whose business extends throughout the whole country, which by the law everywhere is an enemy to the public interests, and which prevents such buying, except at prices arbitrarily fixed. I insist that the free course of trade among the states cannot coexist with such combinations. . . .[3]

It [the Constitution] gives to Congress, in express terms authority to enact all laws necessary and proper for carrying into execution the power to regulate commerce. . . . Let the end be legitimate, let it be within the scope of the Constitution, and all means which are appropriate, which are plainly adapted to that end, which are not prohibited, but consistent with the letter and spirit of the Constitution, are constitutional.[4]

The Knight concept of the narrow scope of the commerce clause became a dead letter; but the decision intensified the popular demand for "trust-busting," and President Theodore Roosevelt made it his slogan. One of his *bêtes noires* was the merger of the Great Northern and Northern Pacific Railroads that the railroad magnates Harriman and Hill sought to effect by a common acquisition of the stock of both. So when Justice Gray died and Roosevelt looked about for a replacement, he had in mind naming a liberal who would cast a vote against the merger. But his choice, Justice Holmes, voted with the dissenters when a five-man majority struck down the transaction.[5] Roosevelt never forgave Holmes for thus disappointing him.

In the presidential campaign of 1912, in addition to inveighing against the "trusts," Roosevelt called for the recall of judicial decisions by act of Congress, akin to what Marshall, in his moment of weakness, had suggested.

Nevertheless, Holmes's dissent is worthy of repetition. He said:

Great cases, like hard cases, make bad law. For great cases are called great, not always by reason of their real importance in establishing the law of the future, but because of some accident of immediate overwhelming interest which appeals to the feelings and distorts the judgment. These immediate interests exercise a kind of hydraulic pressure which makes what previously was clear seem doubtful, and before which even well-settled principles of law will bend. . . .[6]

When their [judges'] task is to interpret and apply the words of a statute, their function is merely academic to begin with, and to read English intelli-

---

[2] *Ibid.*, 19.
[3] *Ibid.*, 37.
[4] *Ibid.*, 39.
[5] Northern Securities Co. v. United States, 193 U.S. 197 (1904).
[6] *Ibid.*, 400–401.

gently—and a consideration of consequences comes into play, if at all, only when the meaning of the words used is open to reasonable doubt. . . .[7]

There is a natural feeling that somehow or other the statute meant to strike at combinations great enough to cause just anxiety on the part of those who love their country more than money, while it viewed such little ones as I have supposed with just indifference. This notion, it may be said, somehow breathes from the pores of the act, although it seems to be contradicted in every way by the words in detail. . . .[8]

I repeat, if the restraint on the freedom of the members of a combination, because of their entering into a partnership, is a restraint of trade, every such combination, as well the small as the great, is within the act. . . .[9]

I am happy to know that only a minority of my brethren adopt an interpretation of the law which, in my opinion, would make eternal the *bellum omnium contra omnes* and disintegrate society so far as it could into individual atoms. If that were its intent I should regard calling such a law a regulation of commerce as a mere pretense. It would be an attempt to reconstruct society. I am not concerned with the wisdom of such an attempt, but I believe that Congress was not intrusted by the Constitution with the power to make it, and I am deeply persuaded that it has not tried.[10]

The contradictions involved in the Knight and the Northern Securities cases respecting the commerce clause were emphasized when the Chief Justice, who voted with the majority in both cases, joined to make a fourth dissenter when the majority held that Congress might prohibit the transport of lottery tickets by express, as well as through the mails.[11]

A dissent by Justice Harlan challenged as judicial legislation a majority construction of the Sherman Act as forbidding only undue restraint of interstate and foreign trade or commerce, thus announcing "a rule of reason."[12] While the Knight case had held sugar refining to be an intrastate activity and, as such, not subject to the Act, that distinction had not availed in the Northern Securities case.

While the majority, with the concurrence of Harlan, found the facts compelling and directed dissolution of the offending companies, Harlan dissented from the insertion in Justice White's opinion of the "rule of reason," saying that this was "an attempt, by interpretation, to soften or modify what some regard as a harsh public policy."[13]

[7] *Ibid.*, 401.
[8] *Ibid.*, 407.
[9] *Ibid.*, 410–11.
[10] *Ibid.*, 411.
[11] Champion v. Ames, 188 U.S. 321 (1903).
[12] Standard Oil Co. v. United States, 221 U.S. 1 (1911); United States v. American Tobacco Co., *ibid.*, 106 (1911).
[13] Standard Oil Co. v. United States, 221 U.S. 1, 104 (1911).

"I am impelled," he said, "to say there is abroad in our land a most harmful tendency to bring about the amendment of Constitutions and legislative enactments by means alone of judicial construction. . . . To overreach the action of Congress merely by judicial construction, that, by indirection, is a blow to the integrity of our governmental system, and in the end will prove most dangerous to all."[14]

He called attention to the opinion of Justice White, who, with Holmes, dissented in the Northern Securities case and who there said that the Act, in contradiction to what he was now saying, "prohibited any contract in restraint of interstate commerce...whether...reasonable or unreasonable." And he called attention to Holmes's statement: "For it cannot be too carefully remembered that the clause applies to 'every' contract of the forbidden kind."[15] In the American Tobacco case, Justice Harlan said the "rule of reason" was *obiter dicta,* pure and simple."[16]

Holmes also had occasion to write a dissenting opinion in a Sherman Anti-Trust case involving price maintenance agreements between a manufacturer and retailers. The majority held the agreements void as violative of the Act.[17] Holmes, the sole dissenter, wrote, expressing a timely opinion in view of present-day discount houses and the various controversies respecting fair trade laws:

> I think we greatly exaggerate the value and importance to the public of competition in the production or distribution of an article...as fixing a fair price. What really fixes that is the competition of conflicting desires. We, none of us, can have as much as we want of all things that we want. Therefore we have to choose. As soon as the price of something that we want goes above the point at which we are willing to give up other things to have that, we cease to buy it and buy something else. Of course, I am speaking of things that we can get along without. There may be necessaries that sooner or later must be dealt with like short rations in a shipwreck....I cannot believe that in the long run the public will profit by this Court permitting knaves to cut reasonable prices for some ulterior purpose of their own and thus to impair, if not to destroy, the production and sale of articles which it is assumed to be desirable that the public should be able to get.[18]

Early in the subsequent Taft court's first term came the recurrent antitrust litigation. In the first case, a majority of the Court held that the practices of a trade association in collecting and disseminating information among

[14] *Ibid.,* 105.
[15] *Ibid.,* 96.
[16] United States v. American Tobacco Co., 221 U.S. 106, 193 (1911).
[17] Dr. Miles Medical Co. v. Park, 220 U.S. 373 (1911).
[18] *Ibid.,* 412.

its members concerning demand, production, prices, and similar items constituted a violation of antitrust laws.[19] Holmes, Brandeis, and McKenna dissented vis-à-vis the majority of six.

Brandeis wrote in dissent:

> The cooperation which is incident to this plan does not suppress competition. On the contrary, it tends to promote all in competition which is desirable. But substituting knowledge for ignorance, rumor, guess, and suspicion, it tends also to substitute research and reasoning for gambling and piracy, without closing the door to adventure, or lessening the value of prophetic wisdom.... The evidence in this case, far from establishing an illegal restraint of trade, presents, in my opinion, an instance of commendable effort by concerns engaged in chaotic industry, to make possible its intelligent conduct under competitive conditions.[20]

This decision was followed by another to the same effect in 1923.[21] However, in 1925, Justice Stone, who succeeded Justice McKenna in that year, wrote in two cases[22] approving like practices by trade associations, thus justifying the previous Holmes-Brandeis dissents. Justice Stone did not expressly overrule the previous two decisions, though in effect he did, leaving the Chief Justice and Justice Sanford to say that since the authority of these two cases was not questioned in the opinions of the majority of the Court, they dissented on the basis of that authority. Justice McReynolds dissented separately.

As the Sherman Act was keyed to interstate commerce, so the question of child labor was made dependent upon the flow of goods between the states. In 1918 Holmes wrote, in the Dagenhart case, dissenting from a five-man finding of unconstitutionality of an act of Congress. The act prohibited interstate shipment of goods produced in a United States cotton mill in which within thirty days before the removal of the product children under fourteen had been employed, or children between fourteen and sixteen had been employed more than eight hours in a day, or more than six days in any week, or between seven in the evening and six in the morning.[23] The objection urged was that "the States have exclusive control over their methods of production and that Congress cannot meddle with them."[24] Five members of the Court agreed; four, including Holmes and Brandeis, disagreed.

[19] American Column & Lumber Co. v. United States, 257 U.S. 377 (1921).

[20] Ibid., 418.

[21] United States v. American Linseed Oil Co., 262 U.S. 371 (1923).

[22] Maple Flooring Mfrs. Assoc. v. United States, 268 U.S. 563 (1925); Cement Mfrs. Assoc. v. United States, 268 U.S. 588 (1925).

[23] Hammer v. Dagenhart, 247 U.S. 251 (1918).

[24] Ibid., 277.

Holmes said:

The notion that prohibition is any less prohibition when applied to things now thought evil I do not understand. But if there is any matter upon which civilized countries have agreed—far more unanimously than they have with regard to intoxicants and some other matters over which this country is now emotionally aroused—it is the evil of premature and excessive child labor. I should have thought that if we were to introduce our own moral conceptions where in my opinion they do not belong, this was pre-eminently a case for upholding the exercise of all its powers by the United States....[25]

The national welfare as understood by Congress may require a different attitude within its sphere from that of some self-seeking State.[26]

Later, neither Holmes nor Brandeis dissented from a 1922 decision holding unconstitutional a congressional statute that imposed a tax of 10 per cent as a penalty upon an employer who used child labor under certain prescribed conditions, although Justice Clarke did dissent without opinion.[27]

In 1924 Congress undertook to overcome the Dagenhart decision by proposing a constitutional amendment. However, it failed to command the necessary votes of the states. Then, in 1938, Congress enacted the Fair Labor Standards Act, which prohibited the shipment or delivery for shipment in commerce of any goods in or about which children under sixteen years of age were employed. Thereafter, in 1941, Justice Stone, writing for a unanimous court, sustained the constitutionality of the Act.[28] Thus was overruled the discredited Dagenhart decision, which, during the 1938 term, had been relied on by Justices Butler and McReynolds in dissenting from an opinion by Justice Roberts for a six-man majority holding that the marketing provisions of the Agricultural Adjustment Act of 1938 were constitutional under the powers conferred upon Congress by the commerce clause.[29]

However, the vicissitudes of the efforts to end child labor survived the enactment of the Fair Labor Standards Act of 1938 when the statute was held inapplicable to the business of collecting, transmitting, and delivering telegraphic messages. This was accomplished over the dissent of Justices Murphy, Black, Douglas, and Rutledge.[30] In an opinion by Justice Jackson, five members of the Court, construing the statute, held that boys under sixteen, constituting 12 per cent of the messenger force, concededly engaged in "oppressive child labor" as defined by the federal statute, were not within its language, because

[25] *Ibid.*, 280.
[26] *Ibid.*, 281.
[27] Bailey v. Drexel Furniture Co., 259 U.S. 20 (1922).
[28] United States v. Darby, 312 U.S. 100 (1941).
[29] Mulford v. Smith, 307 U.S. 38 (1939).
[30] Western Union Tel. Co. v. Lenroot, 323 U.S. 490 (1945).

the telegraph company was not a "producer" of telegraphic messages, nor was it engaged in "shipping" messages.[31]

Justice Murphy, dissenting, said, "Oppressive child labor in any industry is a reversion to an outmoded and degenerate code of economic and social behavior."[32]

Admitting the conclusion that Western Union did not "ship" goods, as provided in the Act, Justice Murphy said that "proper respect for the legislative intent and the interpretative process does not demand fastidious adherence to linguistic purism."[33]

Relying on the national power over interstate commerce, the Court held, over the dissent of three justices, that Congress could fix an eight-hour day and temporarily regulate wages for railroad employees to avoid a strike and concurrent interruption of interstate commerce. Dissenter McReynolds said:

> Considering the doctrine now formed by a majority of the Court as established, it follows as a matter of course that Congress has power to fix a maximum as well as a minimum wage for trainmen; to require compulsory arbitration of labor disputes which may seriously and directly jeopardize the movement of interstate traffic; and to take measures effectively to protect the free flow of such commerce against any combination, whether of operatives, owners, or strangers.[34]

The income tax decision that compelled a constitutional amendment (the Sixteenth) stemmed from blandishments of the persuasive Joseph H. Choate and, after much maneuvering, from the vote of a single justice. When the cases were first decided, the Court held the congressional act invalid in so far as it attempted to tax the income derived from real estate and from municipal bonds; it divided equally as to the income from personal property. Justices White and Harlan dissented respecting the tax on real estate income.[35] Though the personnel creating the division respecting the income from personal property was not disclosed, it became common knowledge that those voting for constitutionality, in addition to Justices White and Harlan, included Justices Brown and Shiras. The illness and absence of Justice Jackson had produced this unsatisfactory result, and so the Court set the cases down for further argument and reconsideration.

The final judgment, by a vote of five to four, held taxes on income derived from both real and personal property unconstitutional and void. Though Justice Jackson voted for constitutionality, Justice Shiras, who had so voted

---

[31] *Ibid.*, 504–506.
[32] *Ibid.*, 510.
[33] *Ibid.*, 512.
[34] Wilson v. New, 243 U.S. 332, 389 (1917).
[35] Pollock v. Farmers' Loan & Trust Co.; Hyde v. Continental Trust Co., 157 U.S. 429 (1895).

in rendering the previous decision, switched to vote with the four who had previously voted to strike down the tax on income from personal property.[36]

The Chief Justice wrote for the majority, saying: "If it be true that the Constitution should have been so framed that a tax of this kind could be laid, the instrument defines the way for its amendment."[37]

In concurring in the earlier opinion, Justice Field declared:

> The income tax law under consideration is marked by discriminating features which affect the whole law. It discriminates between those who receive an income of four thousand dollars and those who do not. It thus vitiates, in my judgment, by this arbitrary discrimination, the whole legislation. . . . The legislation, in the discrimination it makes, is class legislation. Whenever a distinction is made in the burdens a law imposes or in the benefits it confers on any citizens by reason of their birth, or wealth, or religion, it is class legislation, and leads inevitably to oppression and abuses, and to general unrest and disturbance in society.[38]

Justice Harlan, dissenting, said:

> . . . the court . . . declares that our government has been so framed that, in matters of taxation for its support and maintenance, those who have incomes derived from the renting of real estate . . . or who own invested personal property . . . have privileges that cannot be accorded to those having incomes derived from the labor of their hands, or the exercise of their skill, or the use of their brains. . . .[39]

> Every one, I take it, will concede that Congress, in taxing incomes, may rightfully allow an exemption in some amount. . . . Such exemptions rest upon grounds of public policy. . . . The basis upon which such exemptions rest is that the general welfare requires that in taxing incomes, such exemptions should be made as will fairly cover the annual expenses of the average family, and thus prevent the members of such families becoming a charge upon the public. . . .[40]

> . . . the real friends of property are not those who would exempt the wealth of the country from bearing its fair share of the burdens of taxation, but rather those who seek to have every one, without reference to his locality, contribute from his substance, upon terms of equality with all others, to the support of the government. . . . There is no tax which, in its essence, is more just and equitable than an income tax, if the statute imposing it allows only such exemptions as are demanded by public considerations and are consistent with the recognized principles of the equality of all persons before the law, and, while

[36] Pollock v. Farmers Loan & Trust Co., 158 U.S. 601 (1895).
[37] *Ibid.*, 635.
[38] Pollock v. Farmers' Loan & Trust Co., 157 U.S. 429, 596 (1895).
[39] Pollock v. Farmers' Loan & Trust Co., 158 U.S. 601, 672 (1895).
[40] *Ibid.*, 675–76.

providing for its collection in ways that do not unnecessarily irritate and annoy the taxpayer, reaches the earnings of the entire property of the country, except governmental property and agencies, and compels those, whether individuals or corporations, who receive such earnings, to contribute therefrom a reasonable amount for the support of the common government of all.[41]

Previously, in March, 1863, Chief Justice Taney had written Secretary of the Treasury Chase, saying he found that an act of Congress imposing a tax of 3 per cent on the salaries of all officers in the employ of the United States was being construed by the Treasury to embrace judicial officers and that the amount of the tax had been deducted from judges' salaries. The Chief Justice called the attention of Secretary Chase to the fact that the Constitution (Art. 3, Sec. 1) provided that the compensation of judges was not to "be diminished during their continuance in office," and that the deduction of a tax from the salary of a judge violated that provision. The Chief Justice explained that since all judges were interested in the issue, there was no mode of settling the question in a judicial proceeding; hence his letter.[42]

Later, in 1920, following the passage of the Revenue Act of 1919, a Kentucky federal judge raised the same question and found seven high court justices who agreed with Chief Justice Taney.[43] However, neither Justice Holmes nor Justice Brandeis could find anything in the Constitution "to indicate that the judges were to be a privileged class free from bearing their share of the cost of the institutions upon which their well-being, if not their life, depends."[44] And Holmes found his conclusion buttressed by the fact that the Sixteenth Amendment laid a tax "on incomes, from whatever source derived."[45] In 1925 the Court held that judges who were appointed after the income tax was levied could claim a like exemption; whereupon Congress vetoed their exemption.[46]

Finally, a federal circuit judge contended that his salary was not subject to the federal income tax because, though he was appointed on a date subsequent to the effective date in the federal statute for taxation of judges' salaries, he had been appointed a district judge prior to the effective date. A majority of the Court held to the contrary.[47] Justice Butler dissented; Justice McReynolds did not sit. The Court disapproved the prior decision and overruled the second.[48]

[41] Ibid., 676.
[42] Appendix, 158 U.S. (39 U.S. Supreme Court Reports; Lawyers' Ed., p. 1155).
[43] Evans v. Gore, 253 U.S. 245 (1920).
[44] Ibid., 265.
[45] Ibid., 267.
[46] Miles v. Graham, 268 U.S. 501 (1925).
[47] O'Malley v. Woodrough, 307 U.S. 277 (1939).
[48] Evans v. Gore, 253 U.S. 245 (1920); Miles v. Graham, 268 U.S. 501 (1925).

138

Concluding his dissent, Justice Butler said nostalgically: "For one convinced that the judgment now given is wrong, it is impossible to acquiesce or merely to note dissent. And so this opinion is written to indicate the grounds of opposition and to evidence regret that another landmark has been removed."[49]

The Waite court's attitude in the area of civil rights also reflected the spirit of the times. In the wake of treaties with China, the Court sustained congressional treaty violations in two cases. The decision in the second case moved Justice Field, no great friend of the Chinese, to dissent, with the support of his nephew, Brewer, saying that there was a vast difference between denying entry to aliens, as in the prior case, where he had written the opinion, and deporting them, which he characterized as a cruel and unusual punishment and beyond all reason in its severity.[50]

In 1896 the Court wrote a corollary to the decisions of the Waite court disposing of the congressional efforts to implement the Fourteenth Amendment's provisions for the benefit of the Negroes. For twenty years Congress had remained apathetic while the southern states were active in advancing segregation and other discriminatory practices. So when Homer Adolph Plessy undertook to challenge a Louisiana statute requiring railroad segregation and was convicted for its violation, the Court was called upon to take a stand. It did so, upholding the law.[51]

The Court held the law a reasonable exercise of the police power of the state; it said that it did not violate the Thirteenth Amendment. Justice Brown, writing for the Court, said:

> We consider the underlying fallacy of the plaintiff's argument to consist in the assumption that the enforced separation of the two races stamps the colored race with a badge of inferiority. If this be so, it is . . . solely because the colored race chooses to put that construction upon it . . . The argument also assumes that social prejudices may be overcome by legislation, and that equal rights cannot be secured to the Negro except by an enforced commingling of the two races. We cannot accept this proposition. If the two races are to meet on terms of social equality, it must be the result of natural affinities, a mutual appreciation of each other's merits and a voluntary consent of individuals. . . . Legis-

---

[49] O'Malley v. Woodrough, 307 U.S. 277, 299 (1939).

[50] Chae Chan Ping v. United States, 130 U.S. 581 (1889); Fong Yue Ting v. United States; Wong Quan v. United States; Lee Joe v. United States, 149 U.S. 698 (1893). (According to an article in *The New York Times* of September 20, 1966, the House of Representatives voted the day before to repeal so-called "trade laws." According to the article, "the House Judiciary Committee contended that the laws serve 'no useful purpose and present an unnecessary and disparaging reminder of a past historical period which potentially could be the cause of misunderstanding as to the present relationships between the people of the United States and the peoples of Oriental countries.'")

[51] Plessy v. Ferguson, 163 U.S. 537 (1896).

lation is powerless to eradicate racial instincts or to abolish distinctions based upon physical differences, and the attempt to do so can only result in accentuating the difficulties of the present situation. If the civil and political rights of both races be equal, one cannot be inferior to the other civilly or politically. If one race be inferior to the other socially, the Constitution of the United States cannot put them upon the same plane.[52]

Justice Harlan, dissenting, might have been writing in 1954 when he said:

In respect of civil rights, common to all citizens, the Constitution of the United States does not, I think, permit any public authority to know the race of those entitled to be protected in the enjoyment of such rights....I deny that any legislative body or judicial tribunal may have regard to the race of citizens when the civil rights of those citizens are involved.[53]

It is one thing for railroad carriers to furnish, or be required by law to furnish, equal accommodations....It is quite another thing for government to forbid citizens of the white and black races from traveling in the same public conveyance....if this statute...is consistent with the personal liberty of citizens, why may not the state require the separation in railroad coaches of native and naturalized citizens...or of Protestants and Roman Catholics?[54] ... in view of the Constitution, in the eye of the law, there is in this country no superior, dominant, ruling class of citizens. There is no caste here. Our Constitution is color-blind. In respect of civil rights, all citizens are equal before the law. The humblest is the peer of the most powerful. The law regards man as man....

In my opinion, the judgment this day rendered will, in time, prove to be quite as pernicious as the decision made by this tribunal in the Dred Scott case...

Sixty millions of whites are in no danger from the presence here of eight millions of blacks. The destinies of the two races in this country are indissolubly linked together and the interests of both require that the common government of all shall not permit the seeds of race hate to be planted under the sanction of law....

This question is not met by the suggestion that social equality cannot exist. ...that argument...is scarcely worthy of consideration, for social equality no more exists between two races when traveling in a passenger coach...than when members of the same races sit by each other in a street car or in the jury box....

If evils will result from the commingling of the two races upon public highways established for the benefit of all, they will be infinitely less than those that will surely come from state legislation regulating the enjoyment of civil rights upon the basis of race.[55]

52 *Ibid.*, 551–52.
53 *Ibid.*, 554.
54 *Ibid.*, 558
55 *Ibid.* 559.

In the face of the fact that the complexion of the Court had changed during the regime of Chief Justice White, resulting in a new and somewhat more liberal alignment, Justice Holmes joined the ultraconservative Lurton in an inexplicable dissent.

An Alabama Negro named Bailey had signed a contract to work for a company for a year for a wage of twelve dollars a month. The company had advanced him fifteen dollars. After working for a little over a month, he quit but failed to return the fifteen dollars advanced. Thereupon he was arrested, charged under an Alabama statute which provided that failure to refund the advance under such circumstances was prima facie evidence of intent to injure an employer, for which a fine would be imposed.

After a trial Bailey was found guilty and fined thirty dollars and costs, and in default of payment was sentenced to serve a prison term at hard labor. When his case was appealed to the Supreme Court, a majority held the statute unconstitutional as creating peonage violative of the Thirteenth Amendment. Justices Holmes and Lurton dissented. Holmes wrote an opinion that defies either quotation or explanation.[56]

A subsequent Alabama peonage case was found to involve possible recurring obligations to labor to satisfy the demands of the employer. The Court found the statute violative of the Thirteenth Amendment, and Justice Holmes concurring, said that on the ground of successive terms of labor he was "inclined to agree."[57]

Concurrently with the last-mentioned decision, Justice Hughes wrote for five members of the Court holding that, pursuant to the Plessy decision, a state might, without infringing the Fourteenth Amendment, require separate but equal accommodations for the white and Negro races. He held that so much of the statute as permitted carriers to provide sleeping cars, dining cars, and chair cars exclusively for white persons, without providing similar accommodations for Negroes, denied equal protection under the Amendment. However, because none of the petitioners had actually been denied accommodations, the Court affirmed the dismissal of the bill for an injunction.[58] Chief Justice White and Justices Holmes, Lamar, and McReynolds concurred. Justice Harlan, who had loosed the harbinger of the later Brown case by his dissent in the Plessy case, was no longer on the bench.

In the few other cases of note involving Negroes that came before the Court, no complaint could be made by the Negroes concerning its attitude. So, when Oklahoma attempted to enfranchise illiterate whites while dis-

---

[56] Bailey v. Alabama, 219 U.S. 219 (1911).

[57] United States v. Reynolds; United States v. Broughton, 235 U.S. 133, 150 (1914).

[58] McCabe v. Atchison T. & S. F. R.R., 235 U.S. 169 (1914); see also Mitchell v. United States, 313 U.S. 80 (1941).

criminating against illiterate Negroes by providing that those who were entitled to vote on January 1, 1866, and their descendants were exempted from taking a literacy test (the so-called "grandfather clause"), the Court struck down the exemption as violative of the Fifteenth Amendment.[59] Justice White, writing for the Court, asserted: "It cannot be said that there was any peculiar necromancy in the time named which engendered attributes affecting the qualifications to vote which would not exist at another and different period unless the Fifteenth Amendment was in view."[60]

In companion cases the Court struck down a Maryland grandfather clause, the result of which effected a waiver of various qualifications affecting whites but denied equal protection to Negroes.[61]

When, to promote racial harmony, a municipality adopted an ordinance forbidding whites to move into a colored neighborhood and forbidding Negroes to move into white neighborhoods, the Court held the ordinance discriminatory and void under the Fourteenth Amendment.[62] Those seeking to uphold the ordinance relied on the Plessy case and another upholding the doctrine of educational segregation.[63] Justice Day, writing for the Court, pointed to a Georgia case striking down a similar ordinance.[64] He said:

> That there exists a serious and difficult problem arising from a feeling of race hostility which the law is powerless to control, and to which it must give a measure of consideration, may be freely admitted. But its solution cannot be promoted by depriving citizens of their constitutional rights and privileges.
>
> As we have seen, this court has held laws valid which separated the races on the basis of equal accommodations. . . . But . . . such legislation must have its limitations. . . .
>
> The right which the ordinance annulled was the civil right of a white man to dispose of his property if he saw fit to do so to a person of color, and of a colored person to make such disposition to a white person. . . .
>
> It is said that such acquisition by colored persons depreciate property owned in the neighborhood by white persons. But property may be acquired by undesirable white neighbors, or put to disagreeable though lawful uses with like results.[65]

In 1926 the Court invalidated a Texas statute denying Negroes the right to vote in a Democratic party primary.[66] Thereupon the Texas legislature

[59] Guinn v. United States, 238 U.S. 347 (1915).
[60] *Ibid.*, 365.
[61] Myers v. Anderson; Myers v. Howard; Myers v. Brown, 238 U.S. 368 (1915).
[62] Buchanan v. Warley, 245 U.S. 60 (1917).
[63] Berea College v. Kentucky, 211 U.S. 45 (1908).
[64] Carey v. Atlanta, 143 Ga. 192 (1915).
[65] Buchanan v. Warley, 245 U.S. 60, 80, 82 (1917).
[66] Nixon v. Herndon, 273 U.S. 536 (1927).

gave political parties the power to prescribe the qualifications of their members and, pursuant thereto, the Democratic party re-enacted the proscription against Negroes voting in the primaries. Later, as a member of the Hughes court, Justice Cardozo, writing for a majority of five, including the Chief Justice and Roberts, and over the dissent of the Sutherland bloc, held the statute invalid, saying that the Fourteenth Amendment protected the Negroes from such discrimination at the hands of a group deriving its authority from the state.[67]

Ironically, the Four Horsemen, who for years had been deprecating the power of the states and enlarging that of their superlegislature, found themselves relying on the adjudications of the Texas statutory and substantive law.

Later, in 1934, an unanimous court, in an opinion by Justice Roberts, distinguished the Condon decision, saying that in the Grovey case then before it the restriction against Negroes voting in Democratic primaries was the party's will voted at a convention of its delegates and therefore was not voided by the Fourteenth Amendment.[68]

In 1941 the newly formed Civil Rights Division of the Attorney General's office successfully prosecuted Louisiana primary election officials for violation of the old 1870 Civil Rights Act.[69] The Court held unanimously that the right to choose a federal official was guaranteed by the Constitution and that that right extended to primary as well as to general elections. The dissent of three of the justices did not go to this facet of the ruling.

This decision overruled the 1921 decision that exculpated Truman H. Newberry, a Michigan candidate for the senate, who had been convicted of a violation of a congressional statute fixing a maximum that could be spent in a primary election.[70] It also paved the way for a 1944 decision which, in effect, disposed of the incredible unanimous opinion in the Grovey case.[71] Eight justices agreed that the Louisiana decision had disposed of the issue and the Grovey case, but Roberts, who felt he had been "taken" in going along with the Classic decision, dissented, saying:

> Not a fact differentiates (the Grovey case) from this except the names of the parties. . . . If this Court's opinion in the Classic case discloses its method of overruling earlier decisions, I can only protest that, in fairness, it should have adopted the open and frank way of saying what it was doing . . . though those less sapient never realized the fact. . . . The instant decision tends to bring

[67] Nixon v. Condon, 286 U.S. 73 (1932).
[68] Grovey v. Townsend, 295 U.S. 45 (1935).
[69] United States v. Classic, 313 U.S. 299 (1941).
[70] Newberry v. United States, 256 U.S. 232 (1921).
[71] Smith v. Allwright, 321 U.S. 649 (1944).

adjudication of this tribunal into the same class as a railroad ticket, good for this day and train only.[72]

Akin to the racial prejudice in the case of Negroes was that manifested by Georgians in the case of one Leo M. Frank, a Jew, who was accused of the murder of a girl worker in a factory of which he was manager. His trial in a Georgia state court was conducted in an atmosphere of hatred, prejudice, and threat of mob violence that attracted nation-wide attention. Following his conviction and a denial of relief by the Georgia Supreme Court, Frank sought habeas corpus in the district court and from its denial he appealed to the high court, contending that he had been denied due process under the Fourteenth Amendment. A majority of the Court affirmed the denial of the writ.[73] Thereafter, and before he could be executed, Frank was seized, taken from the prison, and lynched by a mob.

Justices Holmes and Hughes dissented. After reciting the facts, which demonstrated, as petitioner alleged, that "the trial was dominated by a hostile mob and was nothing but an empty form,"[74] Holmes wrote:

> Whatever disagreement there may be as to the scope of the phrase "due process of law," there can be no doubt that it embraces the fundamental conception of a fair trial, with opportunity to be heard. Mob law does not become due process of law by securing the assent of a terrorized jury....[75] . . . it is our duty ... to declare lynch law as little valid when practiced by a regularly drawn jury as when administered by one elected by a mob intent on death.[76]

Some years later, Justice Holmes wrote for a majority of the Court and, relying on his dissent in the Frank case, held that where, in a trial of Negroes charged with murder and convicted,

> the whole proceeding is a mask,—that counsel, jury and judge were swept to the fatal end by an irresistible wave of public passion, and that the state courts failed to correct the wrong,—neither perfection in the machinery for correction nor the possibility that the trial court and counsel saw no other way of avoiding an immediate outbreak of the mob can prevent this court from securing to the petitioners their constitutional rights.[77]

Justices McReynolds and Sutherland dissented, the former saying that he thought the doctrine of the Frank case was "right and wholesome."[78]

[72] *Ibid.*, 669.
[73] Frank v. Mangum, 237 U.S. 309 (1915).
[74] *Ibid.*, 346.
[75] *Ibid.*, 347.
[76] *Ibid.*, 350.
[77] Moore v. Dempsey, 261 U.S. 86, 91 (1923).

It might be noted that it is a far cry from the circumstances that rendered the Frank trial an "empty form" and the publicity attendant upon the Shepherd trial or the televising of the Estes trial, which denied the constitutional guarantee of fair trials and resulted in reversals of convictions. Nor had the Sixth Amendment then been held applicable to the states, as it was, at least in part, later. Also to be noted is the affinity between Holmes's philosophy in the Frank dissent and that of Cardozo in the later Palko decision.

[78] *Ibid.*, 93.

CHAPTER VIII

The Court as a Superlegislature—3

It was the World War I Espionage Act and war-inflamed public opinion that ultimately brought out the best in Holmes and Brandeis in defense of the right to dissent, a right which, as a result, today encounters the usual xenophobic resistance in Congress and other more volatile places but finds no responsible challenge.

It was in connection with these cases that Holmes wrote his friend Pollock, "Some of our subordinate Judges seem to me to have been hysterical during the war,"[1] a diagnosis not inapplicable today.

In the first of the wartime convictions under the Espionage Act of 1917, Charles T. Schenck, a Socialist, was charged with circulating matter designed to induce draftees to be insubordinate and otherwise to obstruct the recruiting and enlistment service.[2] The Court upheld the conviction. Holmes wrote for a unanimous court and, in conjunction with Brandeis,[3] worked out a formula in the following words:

> We admit that in many places and in ordinary times the defendants in saying all that was said in the circular would have been within their constitutional rights. But the character of every act depends upon the circumstances in which it is done. . . . The most stringent protection of free speech would not protect a man in falsely shouting fire in a theater and causing a panic. . . . The question in every case is whether the words are used in such circumstances and are of such a nature as to create a clear and present danger that they will bring about the substantive evils that Congress has a right to prevent. It is a question of proximity and degree.[4]

Immediately following the Schenck case came that of Frowerk[5] and that of Eugene Debs, the head of the Socialist movement in the United States.[6]

1 Mark de Wolfe, ed., *Holmes-Pollock Letters* (Cambridge, Harvard University Press, 1941), II, 28–29.

2 Schenck v. United States, 249 U.S. 47 (1919).

3 Alpheus T. Mason, *Brandeis: A Free Man's Life* (New York, The Viking Press, 1946), 562.

4 Schenck v. United States, 249 U.S. 47, 52 (1919).

Hoping to soften criticism, no doubt, the Chief Justice assigned the task of writing the Court's opinion affirming the convictions to Holmes, who writing Pollock concerning the assignment, said: "It is one of the ironies that I, who probably take the extremest view in favor of free speech (in which, in the abstract, I have no very enthusiastic belief, though I hope I would die for it), that I should have been selected for blowing up."[7]

Holmes justified the conviction of Frowerk by the rule he established in the Schenck case, commenting that, on the record, "it is impossible to say that it might not have been found that the circulation of the paper was in quarters where a little breath would be enough to kindle a flame."[8]

In the Debs case, Holmes justified the conviction of Debs for a speech in which he allied himself with and defended other Socialist agitators who had been convicted under the Espionage Act, by saying that "the jury were most carefully instructed that they could not find the defendant guilty for advocacy of any of his opinions unless the words used had as their natural tendency and reasonably probable effect to obstruct the recruiting services, etc., and unless the defendant had the specific intent to do so in his mind."[9]

Thereafter, Holmes wrote Pollock:

Debs, a noted agitator, was rightly convicted of obstructing the recruiting service so far as the law was concerned. I wondered that the Government should press the case to a hearing before us, as the inevitable result was that fools, knaves, and ignorant persons were bound to say he was convicted because he was a dangerous agitator and that obstructing the draft was a pretence.[10]

I hope that the President will pardon him and some other poor devils with whom I have more sympathy. Those whose cases have come before us have seemed to me poor fools whom I should have been inclined to pass over if I could."[11]

The conviction and jailing of Debs, then an old man, had martyred him to a point where Holmes's wish was realized, and in 1921 President Harding turned him loose.

These three cases marked the limits of Holmes's and Brandeis' tolerance in acting and speaking out of character, for when the government undertook to justify a twenty-year sentence for an inconsequential garment worker and his associates—"alien anarchists" the Court called them—who had published

[5] Frowerk v. United States, 249 U.S. 204 (1919).
[6] Debs v. United States, 249 U.S. 211 (1919).
[7] De Wolfe, *Holmes-Pollock Letters*, II, 29.
[8] Frowerk v. United States, 249 U.S. 204, 209 (1919).
[9] Debs v. United States, 249 U.S. 211, 216 (1919).
[10] De Wolfe, *Holmes-Pollock Letters*, II, 7.
[11] *Ibid.*, 11.

two leaflets, Justice Clarke shed his liberal garment and wrote for a seven-man majority.[12] But Holmes and Brandeis had had enough.

With the support of Brandeis, Holmes wrote:

> In this case sentences of twenty years' imprisonment have been imposed for the publishing of two leaflets that I believe the defendants had as much right to publish as the government has to publish the Constitution of the United States now vainly invoked by them.... the defendants are to be made to suffer not for what the indictment alleges, but for the creed that they avow—a creed that I believe to be the creed of ignorance and immaturity....[13]
>
> Persecution for the expression of opinions seems to me perfectly logical. ... But when men have realized that time has upset many fighting faiths, they may come to believe even more than they believe the very foundation of their own conduct that the ultimate good desired is better reached by free trade in ideas—that the best test of truth is the power of the thought to get itself accepted in the competition of the market, and that truth is the only ground upon which their wishes safely can be carried out. That at any rate is the theory of our Constitution.[14]

Then came an appeal to the Court from wartime convictions of newspaper publishers and others for printing in their German paper derisive articles concerning the war activities of the United States.[15] The appeal resulted in affirmances as to some of the defendants. Holmes, Brandeis, and Clarke dissented, Brandeis and Clarke writing opinions. Brandeis said the clear and present danger rule enunciated in the Schenck case "is a rule of reason. Correctly applied, it will preserve the right of free speech both from suppression or tyrannous, well-meaning majorities, and from abuse by irresponsible, fanatical minorities. ... Convictions such as these, besides abridging freedom of speech, threaten freedom of thought and of belief."[16]

The fifth of these cases in the high court involved a pamphlet entitled *The Price We Pay,* written by Irwin St. John Tucker, an Episcopal clergyman who, Justice Brandeis said, was prominent enough to be given space in the 1916–17 *Who's Who.* The pamphlet had been sent to various Socialist locals for distribution, but the local in question had doubts of the legality of the pamphlet which was at issue in a case pending before a Baltimore judge. After the Judge dismissed the indictment, saying he found nothing actionable in the pamphlet, members of the local began to distribute it. Pierce, one of the distributors was indicted and convicted upon the ground that statements in the

---

[12] United States v. Abrams, 250 U.S. 616 (1919).
[13] *Ibid.,* 629.
[14] *Ibid.,* 630.
[15] Schaefer, Vogel, Werner, Darkow, Lemke v. United States, 251 U.S. 466 (1920).
[16] *Ibid.,* 482, 495.

pamphlet were false. A seven-man majority affirmed the conviction. Brandeis, dissenting with Holmes, said: "Statements like that here charged to be false are in essence matters of opinion and judgment, not matters of fact....[17] The fundamental right of free men to strive for better conditions through new legislation and new institutions will not be preserved, if efforts to secure it by argument to fellow-citizens may be considered as criminal incitement."[18]

Later, in 1925, Holmes and Brandeis joined in dissenting from the conviction of a prominent Socialist named Gitlow. Holmes wrote, saying that the criterion the Court had accepted in the Schenck case had been discarded in the Abrams case. He added:

> The convictions I expressed in that case are too deep for it to be possible for me as yet to believe that it (has) settled the law. . . . It is said that this manifesto ... was an incitement. Every idea is an incitement. It offers itself for belief.... The only difference between the expression of an opinion and an incitement . . . is the speaker's enthusiasm for the result. Eloquence may set fire to reason.[19]

Brandeis joined in the opinion.

However, the Gitlow case did settle the law in one important respect, as Justice Sanford, writing for the majority, intimated: "For present purposes we may and do assume that freedom of speech and of the press—which are protected by the First Amendment from abridgment by Congress—are among the fundamental personal rights and 'liberties' protected by the due process clause of the Fourteenth Amendment from impairment."[20]

Concerning this case, Holmes wrote Pollock: "My last performance . . . was a dissent . . . in favor of the rights of an anarchist (so-called) to talk drool in favor of the proletarian dictatorship. But the prevailing notion of free speech seems to be that you may say what you choose if you don't shock *me*."[21]

Almost half a century later, on a three-count conviction, the defendant Epton was convicted for conspiring to riot, advocating criminal anarchy, and conspiring to engage in such anarchy. He was sentenced to serve concurrent one-year terms. The Court denied certiorari. Justice Stewart concurred because the riot conviction presented no substantial federal question and the other sentences were concurrent. However, he and Justice Douglas, who dissented, felt that the Court's decision in the Gitlow case should be reviewed and that the

[17] Pierce v. United States, 252 U.S. 239, 269 (1920).
[18] *Ibid.*, 273
[19] Gitlow v. New York, 268 U.S. 652, 673 (1925).
[20] *Ibid.*, 666.
[21] De Wolfe, *Holmes-Pollock Letters*, II, 163.

question considered of whether the New York anarchy statutes violated the First and Fourteenth amendments.[22]

A Minnesota statute prohibited interfering with or discouraging the enlistment of a man in the military or naval service of the state or federal government. With the concurrence of Justice Holmes, the Court upheld the statute.[23] The Chief Justice dissented on the ground that the subject was within the exclusive power of Congress. Justice Brandeis, differing with Holmes and the majority, said that the measure was not a war measure; that it related to teaching of pacifism; and that, as such, it abridged freedom of speech and invaded the privacy and freedom of the home where parents would be forbidden to "follow the promptings of religious belief, or conscience of conviction, and teach son or daughter the doctrine of pacifism."[24]

He added that, as an "incident of its power to declare war, it (Congress) may, when the public safety demands . . . to avert a clear and present danger, prohibit interference."[25]

As a war measure, Postmaster General Burleson ordered that the *Milwaukee Leader*, a newspaper published by Victor Berger, a prominent Socialist agitator opposed to the war, should be denied the second-class mailing privileges extended to newspapers. The Supreme Court affirmed the Postmaster General's order by a seven-man majority.[26] Justices Brandeis and Holmes dissented. Holmes found that the Espionage Act under which the Postmaster General acted gave him the right only to refuse to transmit papers that violated the Act and not to refuse to extend the second-class rate to such publications. In so holding, Holmes said: "The United States may give up the Post Office when it sees fit, but while it carries it on, the use of the mails is almost as much a part of free speech as the right to use our tongues; and it would take very strong language to convince me that Congress ever intended to give such a practically despotic power to any one man."[27]

Justice Brandeis maintained that the Postmaster General had never been authorized to exercise prior restraint of a particular newspaper. He said, "In 1890 Tolstoi's *Kreutzer Sonata* had been excluded from the mails as indecent."[28] He concluded, "In every extension of governmental functions lurks a new danger to civil liberty."[29]

The following year, 1922, the Postmaster General issued a fraud order,

22 Epton v. New York, 390 U.S. 29, 30 (1968).
23 Gilbert v. Minnesota, 254 U.S. 325 (1920).
24 *Ibid.*, 335–36.
25 *Ibid.*, 336.
26 Milwaukee Publishing Co. v. Burleson, 255 U.S. 407 (1921).
27 *Ibid.*, 437.
28 *Ibid.*, 422.
29 *Ibid.*, 436.

prohibiting the delivery of mail or payment of money orders to a man named Leach, and directing the disposition of mail which should be addressed to him, upon the ground that his advertising was fraudulent. The Court sustained the order by a vote of seven to two, the two being Justices Brandeis and Holmes.[30] Justice Holmes said:

> ...this form of communication with people at a distance is through the post office alone; and, notwithstanding all modern inventions, letters still are the principal means of speech with those who are not before our face. I do not suppose that anyone would say that the freedom of written speech is less protected by the First Amendment than the freedom of spoken words. Therefore I cannot understand by what authority Congress undertakes to authorize anyone to determine in advance, on the grounds before us, that certain words shall not be uttered. Even those who interpret the Amendment most strictly agree that it was intended to prevent previous restraints.... Usually private swindling does not depend upon the post office.[31]

In a letter to Pollock Holmes said that he thought that the stoppage of letters by the Postmaster General was "used to stop communications that would seem all right to a different mode of thought."[32]

At a later term Chief Justice Hughes held that a Minnesota statute authorizing a court to enjoin the publication of a newspaper printing obscene or malicious, scandalous or defamatory matter, as a public nuisance, violated the freedom of the press guaranteed by the Fourteenth Amendment.[33] The newspaper, the *Saturday Press*, had been regularly publishing malicious, scandalous, and defamatory articles concerning the principal public officers, leading newspapers, many private persons, and the Jewish race. Nevertheless, the majority, over the dissent of the obdurate four, held that previous restraint upon publication constituted an unconstitutional censorship. The decision affirmed the Holmes-Brandeis contention in the last mentioned *Milwaukee Leader* newspaper case respecting the unconstitutionality of prior restraints.

During subsequent terms (1930–31, 1931–32), the Court, headed by Chief Justice Hughes, was concerned with some rather important and interesting civil rights issues. The noted MacIntosh case split the Court.[34] Justice Sutherland, writing the opinion for the majority, held that the Schwimmer case[35] required that the Court deny citizenship to Douglas Clyde MacIntosh, a Canadian and a professor of divinity at Yale University, who, seeking

---

[30] Leach v. Carlile, 258 U.S. 138 (1922).
[31] *Ibid.*, 140–41.
[32] De Wolfe, *Holmes-Pollock Letters*, II, 90.
[33] Near v. Minnesota, 283 U.S. 697 (1931).
[34] United States v. Macintosh, 283 U.S. 605 (1931).
[35] United States v. Schwimmer, 279 U.S. 644 (1929).

naturalization, "would not promise in advance to bear arms in defense of the United States unless he believed the war to be morally justified."[36] Justice Roberts joined the four conservatives to form a five-man majority. Chief Justice Hughes joined the three-man liberal bloc, Holmes, Brandeis, and Stone. Justice Hughes wrote the dissent, which he placed upon the narrow ground that Congress had not required a promise to bear arms as a condition of granting naturalization, concluding that "the judgment in United States v. Schwimmer . . . stands upon the special facts of that case."[37]

The Schwimmer case had denied naturalization to Rosika Schwimmer, a Hungarian Jewess, who said in no uncertain terms that she was a pacifist, did not believe in nationalism, was opposed to the use of force, and would not bear arms. Justice Holmes wrote in dissent; Justice Brandeis joined in Holmes's opinion, and Justice Sanford also dissented.

Justice Holmes said he could hardly see how the adequacy of her oath was affected by her statement that she would not bear arms, "inasmuch as she is a woman over fifty years of age, and would not be allowed to bear arms if she wanted to."[38] He said that she "thoroughly believes in organized government and prefers that of the United States to any other in the world." He contended that "it cannot show a lack of attachment to the principles of the Constitution that she thinks it can be improved," adding, "I suppose that most intelligent people think that it might be."[39] Holmes continued:

> Some of her answers might excite popular prejudice, but if there is any principle of the Constitution that more imperatively calls for attachment than any other it is the principle of free thought—not free thought for those who agree with us but freedom for the thought that we hate. I think that we should adhere to that principle with regard to admission into, as well as to life within, this country. And, recurring to the opinion that bars this applicant's way, I would suggest that the Quakers have done their share to make the country what it is, that many citizens agree with the applicant's belief, and that I had not supposed hitherto that we regretted our inability to expel them because they believe more than some of us do in the teachings of the Sermon on the Mount.[40]

Referring to MacIntosh's scruples against unjust wars, Chief Justice Hughes said, with aptness to present-day controversy: "There is nothing new in such an attitude. Among the most eminent statesmen here and abroad have been those who condemned the action of their country in entering into wars they thought to be unjustified."[41]

[36] United States v. Macintosh, 283 U.S. 605, 613 (1931).
[37] *Ibid.*, 635.
[38] United States v. Schwimmer, 279 U.S. 644, 653–54 (1929).
[39] *Ibid.*, 654.
[40] *Ibid.*, 654–55.
[41] United States v. Macintosh, 283 U.S. 605, 635 (1931).

Here Hughes spoke in Holmesian fashion: ". . . in the forum of conscience, duty to a moral power higher than the state has always been maintained. . . . The essence of religion is belief in a relation to God involving duties superior to those arising from any human relation."[42]

The MacIntosh case was considered and decided with that of Marie Averil Bland,[43] another Canadian seeking naturalization, who was unwilling to take the oath of allegiance without adding "as far as my conscience as a Christian will allow," and was accordingly denied admission. Those who had dissented in the MacIntosh case also dissented from Sutherland's opinion for the majority.

Holmes's correspondent, Sir Frederick Pollock, wrote Holmes saying, apropos of the MacIntosh decision and referring to "the post-war State jingoism mania": "Apart from the particular merits it seems to me all wrong to make naturalization a judicial or quasi-judicial matter: it is better dealt with by administrative discretion. Not that I believe it ever occurred to the Home Secretary here to ask an applicant whether he (let alone she) had scruples of conscience about bearing arms for the defense of the realm."[44]

Subsequently, during the 1944 term, a five-to-four vote sustained the refusal of Illinois to admit an applicant to practice as a lawyer upon the ground that he had refused to take the required oath to support the Illinois Constitution, despite the fact that his refusal was based upon his conscientious objection to violence and his consequent unwillingness to bear arms, as required by the Illinois Constitution.[45] The majority relied on the doctrine of the Schwimmer case, refusing naturalization for unwillingness to pledge military service, saying that "even the powerful dissents which emphasized the deep cleavage in this Court on the issue of admission to citizenship did not challenge the right of Congress to require military service from every able-bodied man."[46]

Justice Black wrote, dissenting, with the support of Justices Douglas, Murphy, and Rutledge. Justice Black said:

> . . . the probability that Illinois would ever call the petitioner to serve in a war has little more reality than an imaginary quantity in mathematics.
>
> I cannot agree that a state can lawfully bar from a semi-public position a well-qualified man of good character solely because he entertains a religious belief which might prompt him at some time in the future to violate a law which has not yet been and may never be enacted.[47]

During the next term, over the dissent of the Chief Justice and Justices Reed

[42] *Ibid.*, 634–35.
[43] United States v. Bland, 283 U.S. 636 (1931).
[44] De Wolfe, *Holmes-Pollock Letters*, II, 299–300.
[45] *In re* Summers, 325 U.S. 561 (1945).
[46] *Ibid.*, 572–73.
[47] *Ibid.*, 577.

and Frankfurter, in an opinion by Justice Douglas, the Court subscribed to the dissent of Justice Holmes in overruling the Schwimmer, MacIntosh, and Bland cases and holding that one unwilling to take up arms in the country's defense would not be deprived of citizenship.[48]

The Chief Justice, who had "dissented in the MacIntosh and Bland cases, for reasons which the Court now adopts as ground for overruling them,"[49] now dissented, maintaining that he believed that Congress had adopted and confirmed the Court's earlier construction of the naturalization statutes.

Ironically, when the Court upheld removal from a state to a federal court of a trial for murder alleged to have been committed by a federal deputy collector of internal revenue acting in the discharge of his duties, Justices Clifford and Field dissented.[50] Similarly, when the Court held constitutional a congressional act making it a crime to obstruct deputy marshals of the United States in the performance of their duties at congressional elections, both Justice Field and Justice Clifford dissented.[51]

Some years later Judge David S. Terry, once chief justice of the California Supreme Court and an associate of Justice Field, was shot and killed by David Neagle, a United States marshal assigned to protect Field, in consequence of threats made against him by Terry. Terry's antagonism to Field arose as a result of Terry's having been jailed by Field for contempt of court, in the course of unsuccessful litigation pursued by Terry's wife.

At Fresno, California, the Terrys had boarded a train on which Field and Neagle were traveling. While Field and Neagle were in the dining car, the Terrys entered. Seeing Field, Mrs. Terry returned to her seat to get a satchel containing a revolver. While she was gone, Terry came up to Field and struck him. When Neagle called on him to stop, he thrust his hand in his bosom, where he was known to carry a bowie knife. Thereupon Neagle shot and killed him.

Neagle was arrested and charged with murder in the state court. The federal court issued a writ of habeas corpus and directed his release. On appeal, the high court affirmed. Justice Lamar and the Chief Justice dissented upon the ground that the state court had jurisdiction of the offense and should have been permitted to try the case. However, Justice Lamar concluded: ". . . we cannot permit ourselves to doubt that the authorities of the state of California are competent and willing to do justice; and that even if the appellee had been indicted, and had gone to trial upon this record, God and his country would have given him a good deliverance."[52]

[48] Girouard v. United States, 328 U.S. 61 (1946).
[49] *Ibid.,* 72.
[50] Tennessee v. Davis, 10 Otto (100 U.S.) 257 (1880).
[51] *Ex parte* Siebold, 10 Otto (100 U.S.) 371 (1880).
[52] Cunningham v. Neagle, 135 U.S. 1, 99 (1890).

In 1918 a five-man majority sustained a contempt conviction against a company publishing the *Toledo News-Bee*. The paper had attacked suitors before the Court and the Judge himself. Finally, after suffering these attacks for a period of six months, the Judge initiated contempt proceedings against the publishing company. He conducted a summary hearing, found it guilty, and fined it heavily. Holmes and Brandeis dissented.[53]

Holmes said that the statute in force "confined the power of the Court in cases of this sort to where there had been 'misbehavior of any person in their presence, or so near thereto as to obstruct the administration of justice.'" He found that the statute contemplated the "present protection of the Court from actual interference, and not to postponed retribution for lack of respect for its dignity."[54] He went on: ". . . a judge of the United States is expected to be a man of ordinary firmness of character,"[55] and he confessed that he could not find "anything that would have affected a mind of reasonable fortitude."[56]

In 1941 the Holmes view was accepted and the majority decision overruled while the Court was holding that inducing, by improper means, a plaintiff to discontinue his suit did not constitute obstructing justice within the meaning of the applicable statute. The defendant's conviction was affirmed, however, because on that issue the Court divided evenly.[57]

During the next term, a California newspaper, the *Times-Mirror,* and Harry Bridges, a nationally known labor leader, were adjudged guilty of civil contempt by a California judge. The newspaper had published three editorials calling on the Court to punish two members of a labor union who had been found guilty of assaulting nonunion truck drivers because it was claimed the editorials had had a "reasonable tendency" to interfere with the orderly administration of justice. A majority in an opinion by Black held the contrary.

Bridges was convicted of publishing a telegram to the Secretary of Labor that referred to a judge's decision as "outrageous" and was construed as a statement that if the court's decree was enforced there would be a strike. Both convictions were reversed, Black quoting Holmes's dissent respecting a judge's "fortitude" in the Toledo Newspaper case.[58] The Chief Justice and Justices Frankfurter, Roberts, and Byrnes dissented.

Justice Black, writing for the majority, put the decision on the ground that free speech should not be restrained in the absence of a clear and present danger. Justice Frankfurter, writing in dissent, held that protection of the court's administration of justice was paramount in the instant situation and

[53] Toledo Newspaper Co. v. United States, 247 U.S. 402 (1918).
[54] *Ibid.,* 423.
[55] *Ibid.,* 424.
[56] *Ibid.,* 425.
[57] Nye v. United States, 313 U.S. 33 (1941)
[58] Bridges v. California; Times-Mirror Co. v. Superior Court, 314 U.S. 252 (1941).

said that, if the majority felt that what was done was too weak to coerce the court, it ought to say so.[59]

Later Bridges was ordered deported by the Immigration and Naturalization Service upon the ground of affiliation with the Communist party. A majority granted habeas corpus on the ground that the term "affiliation" as used in the statute had been misinterpreted and that the hearing on the question of Bridges' membership in the Communist party had been unfair.[60]

Justice Jackson did not participate. Justice Murphy, concurring, wrote: "The record in this case will stand forever as a monument to man's intolerance of man. Seldom if ever in the history of this nation has there been such a concentrated and relentless crusade to deport an individual because he dared to exercise the freedom that belongs to him as a human being and that is guaranteed to him by the Constitution."[61] The Chief Justice and Justices Roberts and Frankfurter dissented.

Following this disposal of the attempt to deport him, Bridges, with two witnesses, appeared in the superior court in San Francisco, testified that he had never been a member of any organization advocating the overthrow of the government by force or violence and, with the aid of two witnesses who vouched for his loyalty, was naturalized as a citizen. More than three years later, in 1949, he and his witnesses were indicted, charged with conspiracy to defeat the administration of the naturalization laws. The Court reversed the conviction upon the ground that the statute of limitations barred the prosecution and that the Wartime Suspension of Limitations Act applied only to frauds of a pecuniary nature or of a nature concerning property.[62]

Justice Burton wrote for four members of the Court; the Chief Justice and Justices Reed and Minton dissented; Justices Clark and Jackson did not participate. In 1955 the government sought unsuccessfully to revoke Bridges' naturalization. At present writing he is still with us and an important figure in the labor movement.

Later the Court reversed a contempt adjudication of a Florida newspaper which had published two editorials and a cartoon critical of the administration of criminal justice in cases pending before a Florida court. The majority based its decision on the clear and present danger rule as applied in Bridges v. California. Justices Frankfurter, Murphy, and Rutledge concurred. Justice Frankfurter, who had dissented in the Bridges case, said that "clear and present danger," as used by Justice Holmes, was "a literary phrase not to be distorted by being taken out of context."[63] He maintained that the cases referred to

---

[59] *Ibid.*, 280.
[60] Bridges v. Wixon, 326 U.S. 135 (1945).
[61] *Ibid.*, 157.
[62] Bridges v. United States, 346 U.S. 209 (1953).
[63] Pennekamp v. Florida, 328 U.S. 331, 353 (1946).

were no longer "pending" and therefore the publications "could not have disturbed the trial court in the sense of fairness but only in its sense of perspective."[64]

These were acts committed wholly without the courtroom and its peripheries. But even closer range, it was held, must have been shown to be an obstruction to come within the borders of the statute.[65] So, in a 1919 case, it was held that perjury must have been shown to have had an obstructive effect to constitute contempt within the statute.[66] Holding thus respecting perjury committed before a grand jury, Justice Black explained:

> All perjured relevant testimony is at war with justice, since it may produce a judgment not resting on truth. Therefore it cannot be denied that it tends to defeat the sole ultimate objective of a trial. It need not necessarily, however, obstruct or halt the judicial process. For the function of trial is to sift the truth from a mass of contradictory evidence, and to do so the fact finding tribunal must hear both truthful and false witnesses. It is in this sense, doubtless that this Court spoke when it decided that perjury alone does not constitute an "obstruction"[67]

So a lawyer's statement that he would continue a line of questioning the judge had ruled out until he was stopped by the bailiff was held, by a vote of five to two, not to constitute an "obstruction" supporting a contempt adjudication.[68]

As late as the 1965 term, we find the court divided on application of the general principle laid down by cases it cited[69] and which had been codified in Rules 42 (a) and (b) of the Rules of Criminal Procedure. In an earlier case the conservative members of the Court had held that a witness before a grand jury who refused to answer questions after being directed to do so by the district judge could be punished summarily for criminal contempt.[70] The liberals, the Chief Justice and Justices Black, Douglas, and Brennan dissented.

Then, in the 1965 term, the liberals got the upper hand, and with Justices Stewart, Clark, Harlan, and White dissenting, they overruled the previous case and held the witness entitled to notice and a hearing.[71] Justice Stewart, dissenting, objected to the Court's overturning "a settled construction,"[72]

---

[64] *Ibid.*, 369.
[65] United States Judicial Code, Sec. 268.
[66] *Ex parte* Hudgins, 249 U.S. 378 (1919).
[67] *In re* Michael, 326 U.S. 224, 227–28 (1945).
[68] *In re* McConnell, 370 U.S. 230 (1962).
[69] *Ex parte* Terry, 128 U.S. 289 (1888); Cooke v. United States, 267 U.S. 517 (1925).
[70] Brown v. United States, 359 U.S. 41 (1959).
[71] Harris v. United States, 382 U.S. 162 (1965).
[72] *Ibid.*, 168.

although he knew how little stability could be looked for in a five-to-four court.

Later in the term Justice Clark, writing for the Court, held that witnesses who refused to answer questions posed before a grand jury were guilty of a civil, not a criminal, contempt, because, when committed, it was provided they could purge themselves and be released when they decided to answer the questions and thus "carried the keys of their prison in their own pockets."[73] He held further that, since the grand jury was no longer in session and the witness could no longer purge himself, he was entitled to be discharged. Justice Black concurred in the result. Justice White did not participate. Justice Harlan, concurring in the following, a companion, case, included dissent in the instant case with these words, "I see no reason why a fixed sentence with an automatic purge clause should be deemed impermissible."[74]

In the companion case the defendant violated an injunction pendente lite issued following a Federal Trade Commission cease-and-desist order and, after his demand for a jury trial was denied, was sentenced to six months in jail for contempt.[75] Justice Clark wrote in affirmance for himself, the Chief Justice, and Justices Brennan and Fortas, holding that even though the defendant was found guilty of criminal contempt a right of jury trial did not attach to "petty offenses" such as the one in the instant case. However, he held that a sentence of over six months would call for a jury trial. Justices Harlan and Stewart concurred, maintaining, however, that the prosecution of criminal contempts was not subject to grand and petit jury requirements on the authority of a prior case.[76] Justice White did not participate.

Justice Douglas, supported by Justice Black, dissented, maintaining, as he had in the prior case cited by Justice Harlan, that criminal contempt was a "crime" which entitled the defendant to trial by jury under the Sixth Amendment. He objected to defining "petty" by the length of the sentence imposed.

Later, in March, 1967, Justice Black had occasion to dissent from denial of certiorari where an attorney who lied to a judge, saying he had been ill in an effort to avoid a dismissal of his client's cause, had been sentenced to six-months imprisonment for contempt.[77]

Later, during the 1968 term, the Court held, over the dissent of Justice Harlan, that it would require a jury trial where a defendant was charged with criminal contempt and was sentenced to a two-year prison term, since

[73] Shillitani v. United States; Pappadio v. United States, 384 U.S. 364 (1966).

[74] Cheff v. Schnackenberg, 384 U.S. 373, 384 (1966).

[75] Ibid.

[76] Green v. United States, 356 U.S. 165 (1958).

[77] Temple v. United States, 386 U.S. 961 (1967).

any offense including criminal contempt, punishable by a two-year term, was to be deemed a "serious crime."[78] Simultaneously, it denied a jury trial where a state statute provided for a maximum sentence of ten days imprisonment and a fine of $150, thus denominating the offense as a petty one.[79]

Here, Justice Black dissented, maintaining that "the word 'petty' has no exact meaning and until it is given a better definition than that which the Court gives it today, I do not desire to condemn the right of trial by jury to such an uncertain fate."[80]

An interesting series of five-to-four bloc votes occurred when the members of the Fuller court undertook, after the Spanish-American War, to determine the status of Puerto Rico, Hawaii, and the Philippines in their relationship to the United States. The Court divided into two groups, one consisting of the Chief Justice and Justices Harlan, Brewer, and Peckham, the other composed of Justices Gray, McKenna, Shiras, and White. There were five decisions in 1901, and Justice Brown made the fifth man of a five-man majority in each of them. He joined the Chief Justice's group in three of the cases,[81] leaving Justices Gray, McKenna, Shiras, and White to constitute a minority. However, in two of the cases[82] he joined the Gray minority, leaving the Chief Justice and his temporary associates to fill the minority role.

In a 1903 case concerning Hawaii, Holmes and Day joined with Brown (who wrote the opinion), McKenna, and White, thus relegating the Chief Justice's group to the minority position.[83] However, the following year, the Brown group lost Day, so that Holmes, White, McKenna, and, for once, Brown, found themselves in the minority.[84] But over all, Brown was the key man, as Roberts was to be three decades later.

A conspiracy of amazing magnitude, "to import, possess and sell liquor unlawfully" was revealed by evidence largely obtained by intercepting messages on the telephones of the conspirators by four federal prohibition officers, who, however, did not trespass upon the property of the defendants. The latter pleaded the immunities granted by the Fourth Amendment. Chief Justice Taft, writing for a majority of five, held that wiretapping did not come within the purview of its protections despite the fact that the state statute made it a crime. He reiterated the common law rule respecting admissibility of evidence, however obtained, and held it applied in the instant case. He held, also, that

[78] Duncan v. Louisiana, 391 U.S. 145 (1968).
[79] Dyke v. Taylor Implement Co., 391 U.S. 216 (1968).
[80] *Ibid.*, 223.
[81] De Lima v. Bidwell, 182 U.S. 1 (1901); Dooley v. United States, 182 U.S. 222 (1901); Fourteen Diamond Rings v. United States, 183 U.S. 176 (1901).
[82] Downes v. Bidwell, 182 U.S. 244 (1901); Dooley v. United States, 182 U.S. 222 (1901).
[83] Hawaii v. Mankichi, 190 U.S. 197 (1903).
[84] Kepner v. United States, 195 U.S. 100 (1904).

"without the sanction of congressional enactment, [the court could not] subscribe to the suggestion that the courts have a discretion to exclude evidence, the admission of which is not unconstitutional, because unethically secured."

"A standard," he said, "which would forbid the reception of evidence if obtained by other than nice ethical conduct by government officials would make society suffer and give criminals greater immunity than has been known heretofore."[85]

Justices Holmes, Brandeis, Stone, and Butler dissented, Holmes and Brandeis writing noted dissents. Holmes said:

> It is desirable that criminals should be detected, and to that end that all available evidence should be used. It also is desirable that the government should not itself foster and pay for other crimes, when they are the means by which the evidence is to be obtained.... We have to choose, and for my part I think it a less evil that some criminals should escape than that the government should play an ignoble part....
>
> If the existing code does not permit district attorneys to have a hand in such dirty business, it does not permit the judge to allow such iniquities to succeed.[86]

Justice Brandeis said: "Our government is the potent, the omnipresent, teacher. For good or ill, it teaches the whole people by its example. Crime is contagious. If the government becomes a law-breaker, it breeds contempt for the law; it invites every man to become a law unto himself; it invites anarchy."[87]

Congress agreed with Justices Holmes and Brandeis and, in 1934, enacted 47 U.S. Code, Sec. 605, which prohibited interception of communication by wire (wiretapping) or radio and the divulging of its content without the authority of the sender, as well as the disclosure or use of such information by one who knowingly received it. In consequence, it has been held that wiretapping by federal or state authorities is illegal and that evidence so procured may not be received.[88]

Although the wiretapping prohibition did not except federal agents, a recent Senate investigation revealed that government agents did not consider wiretapping forbidden for them provided the information obtained was not divulged outside the government. However, as a result of the investigation, President Johnson issued a directive in 1965 forbidding wiretapping in all but national security cases; later, in 1968, following the assassination of Senator

85 Olmstead v. United States; McInnis v. United States; Green v. United States, 277 U.S. 438 (1928).

86 *Ibid.,* 470.

87 *Ibid.,* 485.

88 Nardone v. United States, 302 U.S. 379 (1937); Benanti v. United States, 355 U.S. 126 (1957).

Robert F. Kennedy, Congress passed the Administrations' "Crime Bill," which authorized wiretapping on a widened basis.

At the close of the 1967 term, over the dissents of Justices Harlan, White, and Black, the majority ruled that criminal evidence obtained by police who eavesdropped on a party-line telephone conversation was inadmissible as a violation of the Federal Communications Act.[89]

The development of electronic eavesdropping devices has broadened the area of detection far beyond that contemplated by the wiretapping statute. As a result, the Supreme Court has been called upon to consider the right to introduce evidence obtained by eavesdropping other than by wiretapping.

In an early case agents had trespassed to install a transmitter inside a defendant's hotel room to enable them to eavesdrop. It did not work, but the defendant was overheard through a detectaphone placed on the outer wall of his hotel room. The Court held that evidence admissible because such eavesdropping was not barred by the wiretapping statute and because, though it would have been barred by a listening device that involved a trespass, placing the detectaphone on the outer wall did not involve a trespass.[90] The Court ignored the initial trespass to install the first device, so it may be assumed that the trespass was rendered nugatory because the device did not work. However, a 1967 case vitiated "the presence or absence of a physical intrusion."

In a subsequent case, by a five-to-four vote, the Court affirmed the conviction of Chin Foy, a Chinese laundryman who was found dealing in proscribed opium. He had been convicted as a result of evidence of a conversation he had had with a Chinese "friend," who had been induced by federal agents to wear a radio transmitter which enabled the agents to overhear his conversation with Chin Foy. Following the Goldman case just discussed, Justice Jackson, writing for the majority, held that the use of the transmitter did not constitute wiretapping and that it did not violate either the Fourth or Fifth Amendments. He said: "It would be a dubious service to the genuine liberties protected by the Fourth Amendment to make them bedfellows with spurious liberties imposed by far-fetched analogies."[91] He quoted Justice Stone, who said in another case: "A criminal prosecution is more than a game in which the Government may be checkmated and the game lost merely because its officers have not played according to rule."[92]

Justice Jackson continued:

The trend of the law in recent years has been to turn away from rigid rule of

[89] Lee v. Florida, 392 U.S. 378 (1968).

[90] Goldman (Martin) v. United States; Shulman v. United States; Goldman (Theodore) v. United States, 316 U.S. 129 (1942).

[91] On Lee v. United States, 343 U.S. 747, 754 (1952).

[92] McGuire v. United States, 273 U.S. 95, 99 (1927).

incompetence in favor of admitting testimony and allowing the trier of the fact to judge the weight to be given it.

However unwilling we as individuals may be to approve conduct such as that of Chin Foy, such disapproval may not be thought to justify a social policy of the magnitude necessary to arbitrarily exclude otherwise relevant evidence. We think the administration of justice is better served if stratagems such as we have here are regarded as raising, not questions of law, but issues of credibility.[93]

Then, as now, Justice Douglas dissented from such an expression of policy. He wanted to overrule previous decisions that held wiretapping did not violate the Fourth and Fifth amendments. He said that though he had joined with Justice Roberts in holding the contrary in the previous Goldman case, he now thought he had been wrong in so doing. Justices Frankfurter and Burton also dissented; they felt that surreptitious transmission of a private conversation amounted to an unreasonable search and seizure. Justice Frankfurter said, "Lawlessness begets lawlessness."[94]

In a succeeding case,[95] the officers used a so-called "spike-mike," an electronic device that penetrated a party wall separating their observation post from the premises next door used for gambling. It made contact with a heating duct in the adjoining premises. This enabled the officers to eavesdrop and obtain evidence of gambling on which convictions were obtained. A unanimous court voided the convictions, saying, "At the very core (of the Fourth Amendment) stands the right of a man to retreat into his own home and there be free from unreasonable governmental intrusion."[96]

It is worthy of note that the "home" into which the defendants "retreated" was the headquarters of a gambling operation and that the officers had a search warrant obtained upon what the government contended were "ample grounds." However, again it is to be noted that, under a 1967 ruling, trespass becomes nugatory as a factor in these cases.

In a 1962 case the prosecution offered evidence obtained as a result of electronically intercepted and recorded conversations between the defendant and his brother while the former was in jail. The defendant claimed the benefit of the Fourth Amendment, with an argument that might be said to be that, to a jailbird, a public jail was the equivalent of a "home" or of Edmund Burke's "Englishman's castle."[97] That was too much for the Court, though Justices Douglas, Brennan, and the Chief Justice deprecated the inclusion of what they termed unnecessary dicta taking a jail outside the protection of the Fourth Amendment.

[93] On Lee v. United States, 343 U.S. 747, 757 (1952).
[94] Ibid., 760.
[95] Silverman v. United States, 365 U.S. 505 (1961).
[96] Ibid., 511.
[97] Lanza v. New York, 370 U.S. 139 (1962).

In 1963 the Court permitted evidence supplied by a recording of a conversation between a federal agent and a defendant, in the course of which the latter offered the agent a bribe. The Court found that the recording "was used only to obtain the most reliable evidence possible of a conversation in which the Government's own agent was a participant and which that agent was fully entitled to disclose."[98]

In two recent cases involving James R. Hoffa, the president of the Teamsters Union, the Fourth Amendment was invoked. In the one, Hoffa's "friend" Partin had testified to statements made in his presence by Hoffa which the latter claimed should have been barred under the Fourth Amendment. Justice Stewart, writing for the majority, said: "Neither this Court nor any member of it has ever expressed the view that the Fourth Amendment protects a wrongdoer's misplaced belief that a person to whom he voluntarily confides his wrongdoing will not reveal it. Indeed, the Court unanimously rejected that very contention less than four years ago in Lopez v. United States."[99] The Chief Justice dissented on other grounds.

While no issue of electronic eavesdropping was raised in Hoffa's case, in a companion case an informer was furnished with a recording device which recorded conversations with Osborn, Hoffa's lawyer, charged with endeavoring to bribe a juror. The use of the concealed recorder had been authorized by two of the judges of the federal district court. Justice Stewart said, "There could hardly be a clearer example of 'the procedure of antecedent justification before a magistrate that is central to the Fourth Amendment' as 'a precondition of lawful electronic surveillance.'"[100] Dissenting, Justice Douglas said, "I would . . . bar the use of all testimonial evidence obtained by wiretapping or by an electronic device."[101]

Finally, at the end of the 1966 term, the Court struck down the New York law which enabled the police to obtain judicial warrants authorizing them to place microphones in the premises of criminal suspects. The case did not involve the New York wiretapping law which permits judicially authorized wiretapping by the police authorities. Justice Clark, writing for the majority, held that the New York statute was unconstitutional because its prescribed procedures did not contain specific safeguards against violations of the Fourth Amendment. As usual, the majority opinion was the voice of five, while Justices Harlan, Black, and White dissented. Justice Stewart held the statute constitutional but concurred in the result because he did not believe the affidavits in the particular instance were sufficient.[102]

[98] Lopez v. United States, 373 U.S. 427, 439 (1963).

[99] Hoffa, Parks, Campbell, King v. United States, 385 U.S. 293 (1966); see also Miller v. California, 392 U.S. 616 (1968).

[100] Osborn v. United States, 385 U.S. 323, 330 (1966).

[101] Ibid., 352.

[102] Berger v. New York, 388 U.S. 41 (1967).

Justice Clark said: "In any event we cannot forgive the requirements of the Fourth Amendment in the name of law enforcement. This is no formality that we require today but a fundamental rule that has long been recognized as basic to the privacy of every home in America. . . .[103]

"Our concern with the statute here," he added, "is whether its language permits a trespassory invasion of the home, by general warrant, contrary to the command of the Fourth Amendment. As it is written, we believe it does."[104]

Justice Douglas said he thought that "at long last it (the decision) over-rules sub silentio Olmstead v. United States. . . . There persists my overriding objection to electronic surveillance, viz., that it is a search for 'mere evidence' which, as I have maintained on other occasions . . . is a violation of the Fourth and Fifth Amendments, no matter the nicety and precision with which a warrant may be drawn."[105]

Justice Stewart said, "I think that 'electronic eavesdropping, *as such,* or as it is permitted by the statute is not an unreasonable search and seizure."[106]

Justice Black, a stickler for constitutional enforcement, dissenting, said:

Evidence obtained by such electronic eavesdropping was used to convict the petitioner here of conspiracy to bribe the chairman of the State Liquor Authority. . . . without this evidence a conviction could not have been obtained, and it seems apparent that use of that evidence showed petitioner to be a briber beyond all reasonable doubt. Notwithstanding petitioner's obvious guilt, however, the Court now strikes down his conviction in a way that plainly makes it impossible ever to convict him again. . . . it seems obvious to me that its (the Court's) holding, by creating obstacles that cannot be overcome, makes it completely impossible for the State or the Federal Government ever to have a valid eavesdropping statute. All of this is done, it seems to me, in part because of the Court's hostility to eavesdropping as "ignoble" and "dirty business" and in part because of fear that rapidly advancing science and technology is making eavesdropping more and more effective. . . . Neither of these, nor any other grounds that I can think of, are sufficient in my judgment to justify a holding that the use of evidence secured by eavesdropping is barred by the Constitution. . . .[107]

Eavesdroppers have always been deemed competent witnesses in English and American courts. The main test of admissibility has been relevance and first-hand knowledge, not by whom or by what method proffered evidence was obtained. . . . the traditional common-law rule [was] that relevant evi-

[103] *Ibid.*, 62–63.
[104] *Ibid.*, 64.
[105] *Ibid.*
[106] *Ibid.*, 68.
[107] *Ibid.*, 70–71.

dence is admissible, even though obtained contrary to ethics, morals or law. And, for reasons that follow, this evidentiary rule is well adapted to our Government, set up, as it was, to "insure domestic tranquility" under a system of laws. . . .[108]

. . . it is noticeable that this Amendment (the Fourth) contains no appropriate language, as does the Fifth, to forbid the use and introduction of search and seizure evidence even though secured "unreasonably." . . . the Amendment itself provides no sanctions to enforce its standards of searches, seizures, and warrants. This was left for Congress to carry out if it chose to do so. . . .[109]

It is impossible for me to think that the wise framers of the Fourth Amendment would ever have dreamed about drafting an Amendment to protect the "right of privacy." That expression, like a chameleon, has a different color for every turning. In fact, use of "privacy" as the keyword in the Fourth Amendment simply gives this Court a useful new tool, as I see it, both to usurp the policy-making power of the Congress and to hold more state and federal laws unconstitutional when the Court entertains a sufficient hostility to them. . . .[110]

Honest men may rightly differ on the potential dangers or benefits inherent in electronic eavesdropping and wiretapping. But that is the very reason that legislatures, like New York's, should be left free to pass laws about the subject rather than be told that the Constitution forbids it on grounds no more forceful than the Court has been able to muster in this case.[111]

Reminiscent of Justice Wayne's mistaken notion that the Court could settle the slavery question by superseding Congress' jurisdiction, Justice Harlan, dissented thus:

Despite the fact that the use of electronic eavesdropping devices as instruments of criminal law enforcement is currently being comprehensively addressed by the Congress and other bodies in the country, the Court has chosen, quite unnecessarily, to decide this case in a manner which will seriously restrict, if not entirely thwart, such efforts, and will freeze further progress in this field, except as the Court may itself act or a Constitutional Amendment may set things right. In my opinion what the Court is doing is very wrong.[112]

The confusion and doubts engendered by the last-mentioned Berger case were clarified by a 1967 opinion written by Justice Stewart for seven members of the Court,[113] over the dissent of Justice Black. Justice Marshall did not participate.

[108] *Ibid.*, 71–72.
[109] *Ibid.*, 75.
[110] *Ibid.*, 77.
[111] *Ibid.*, 88–89.
[112] *Ibid.*, 89–90.
[113] Katz v. United States, 389 U.S. 347 (1967).

In that case the defendant, Katz, had been convicted on evidence of conversations he had had while in a telephone booth. These were overheard by FBI agents employing electronic listening and recording devices attached to the outside of the booth. The government maintained, in pursuance of earlier decisions of the Court, that, in the absence of a physical trespass, the interception was legal. The defendant argued that a telephone booth was "a constitutionally protected area." The Court denied both contentions by holding that eavesdropping comes within the search and seizure provisions of the Fourth Amendment—a thesis which Justice Black logically denied. Hence, said Justice Stewart, the Fourth Amendment protects "persons," not "places," while overruling the trespass distinctions upon which previous decisions rested (Olmstead v. United States), and wound up by declaring, in contradiction to the implications of the Berger case, that the states could authorize eavesdropping under the protections found in the Fourth Amendment.

It might be noted that the decision would seem to be a further retreat by the Court in the face of publicity concerning rising crime rates and the court-afforded protections of the admittedly guilty.

One further line of recent relevant cases needs to be mentioned. In consequence of the Senate investigation previously referred to, the Supreme Court called on the governmental authorities for information concerning electronic eavesdropping and wiretapping in pending cases. In consequence of such information, upon disclosure that the FBI had recorded conversations between a defendant and his counsel, though the government maintained that nothing overheard had been employed to convict the defendant, a conviction was vacated and a new trial ordered.[114] Justices Harlan and Stewart dissented, arguing that the case should be remanded for investigation.

A similar result was ordered by a majority, over a similar dissent, in a later case.[115] Here the dissenters distinguished a previous case where a conviction had been vacated upon the ground that the government had conceded that the evidence was tainted.[116]

In still another case the Court found insufficient justification for a new trial but vacated the judgment of the court of appeals and remanded the case for an evidentiary hearing by the district court, following which it was either to reinstate the conviction or to order a new trial.[117] Justice Black dissented.

In a later case,[118] over the dissent of Justice Black and without the participation of Justice Marshall, the Court departed from a previously acceptable

[114] Black v. United States, 385 U.S. 26, (1966).
[115] O'Brien v. United States, 386 U.S. 345 (1967).
[116] Schipani v. United States, 385 U.S. 372 (1966).
[117] Hoffa v. United States, 387 U.S. 231 (1967); *see also* Roberts v. United States, 389 U.S. 18 (1967), citing United States v. Wade, 388 U.S. 218, 243 (1967).
[118] Kolod v. United States, 390 U.S. 136 (1968).

practice and refused to accept the assurance of the Solicitor General that no overheard conversation in which any of the defendants participated was relevant to the prosecution. Instead seven members of the Court vacated the judgment below and remanded the case to the district court for a determination in an adversary proceeding of the relevance of the information obtained through the unlawful eavesdropping.

To go back three-quarters of a century, we may note that, on the score of dissent, the Fuller court's record justified no complaint. At the October, 1892, term, a total of 126 decisions appearing in Volumes 147 and 148 of the United States Reports disclosed only eight dissents (a percentage of six-tenths of 1 per cent), of which six were by a single justice and the others by seven-to-two votes. Of the total, four were filed by Justice Brown, three by Field, two by Brewer and one by the Chief Justice.

During the October, 1906, term, of a total of 199 opinions, there were dissents in 36, approximately 19 per cent. Of these, sixteen were by a single justice, and two were five-to-four decisions. Only one out of four dissents was accompanied by an opinion, generally brief. The leading dissenters were Brewer with thirteen dissents, of which five were sole; Harlan with an equal number, of which four were sole; and Peckham with twelve, of which all but one were with other justices. The Chief Justice dissented nine times; Justice Day, eight. Justice White dissented but once and that once with Harlan. Holmes, the "Great Dissenter," dissented only three times, one of which was sole. Brewer and Peckham saw eye to eye in dissent six times; Harlan and the Chief Justice were aligned five times. These were the noticeable alignments. Obviously there were no blocs.

The value and strength of the dissents during this period were attested by that of Justice Bradley in the Chicago Railroad case; that of Holmes in the Lochner case, later sustained in a number of cases; those of Holmes in Adair and Coppage, both cases later overruled, and that of Harlan in the Knight case, with his concept of the commerce clause destined to supplant the narrowness of that of the Knight decision. Again, there was that of Harlan in the Pollock case, to be adopted by the states as the law of the land; and finally there was the expression by Justice Harlan in 1894 of the mid–twentieth century view of the racial problem in the Plessy case, vindicated when Plessy was overruled in 1954.

Chief Justice Edward Douglas White of Louisiana, who had served as a justice since 1894, was confirmed on December 12, 1910, following the death of Chief Justice Fuller on July 4, 1910. During the latter half of Justice Fuller's term President Roosevelt appointed three justices, Oliver Wendell Holmes of Massachusetts, William R. Day of Ohio, and William H. Moody, also of Massachusetts. Later President Taft appointed Horace H. Lurton of Tennessee, Charles Evans Hughes of New York, Joseph R. Lamar of Georgia, and Mahlon Pitney of New Jersey. Then, when Justice Lurton died, President Wilson appointed James Clark McReynolds of Tennessee, and in place of deceased Justice Lamar, he appointed Louis D. Brandeis of Massachusetts. Finally, when Justice Hughes resigned to oppose Wilson for the presidency, the latter appointed John H. Clarke of Ohio.

During the October, 1913, term, the White court handed down 158 decisions, to which there were only eleven dissents, none of which was supported by an opinion. This was less than 1 per cent. Of these dissents, eight were by a single justice. There were no five-to-four decisions. The Chief Justice dissented five times, Justice Hughes on four occasions, Justice Holmes twice, and Justices McKenna and Day one each.

It would have been difficult to match this 1913 record, but the statistics of the 1918 term were nothing to be ashamed of. Of the amazing work load represented by a total of 225 decisions (treating associated decisions as one), twenty-four drew dissents, approximately 10 per cent. Of these, five, or 2 per cent of the total, were by votes of five to four. There were concurrences with the result in the case of six decisions, though only two of these were accompanied by opinions. An interesting fact is that these 225 cases, including the preliminary arguments of counsel, occupied 1600 pages in the reports, a remarkably low average of seven pages per case.

The principal dissenters were Clarke and Van Devanter, each with eleven dissents; Brandeis had nine, and Pitney, McKenna, and McReynolds had seven each. The Chief Justice, Holmes, and Day each dissented three times. While Brandeis and Holmes differed on occasions, Holmes's three dissents were with Brandeis. The future close association between Van Devanter and McReynolds was not made apparent by the 1918–19 record (they joined in dissent only twice); the association of Holmes, writing sparingly, as though writing a constitution to be filled in by an understanding reader, and Brandeis, a master of prolix detail, was plainly to be seen.

The years of this Court, and of the preceding and the following ones, might well be termed the era of qualitative dissent, as those of later years became the eras of quantitative dissent. Noted dissent during the reign of White was almost exclusively the function of Holmes and Brandeis, and their dissenting opinions cast beams that lighted the subsequent ways of the law.

So Justices Holmes and Hughes furnished the prologue in the Frank case for Holmes's majority opinion in the Moore case. And it was Holmes and Brandeis whose dissents in the child labor case found later affirmation by Congress and the Court; whose dissent in the Washington and New Jersey employment agency cases became the law in a subsequent case; whose dissent in the Adair, Coppage, Hitchman, and Eagle cases was supported by Congress and the Court when Adair was overruled in 1941; whose clear and present danger rule became the Court's guidance in the nineteen forties; and whose contempt of court rule was adopted when the decision to which they excepted was overruled. Truly the White court attested the need and value of dissent.

Following the death of Chief Justice White, former President Taft realized his ambition and became Chief Justice on June 30, 1921. During his term of office, Justices Clarke, Day, and Pitney, who resigned in 1922, were replaced by Justices George Sutherland of Utah, Pierce Butler of Minnesota, and Edward T. Sanford of Tennessee. Later, when Justice McKenna resigned, President Coolidge appointed Justice Harlan Fiske Stone of New York. The Taft court continued in the conservative tradition of its immediate predecessors. The struggle concerning police and judicial powers in the aura of the Fourteenth Amendment continued. Labor continued to be the judicial underdog in its contest to defeat the injunction. Holmes and Brandeis, and later Stone, continued to build their structure of dissent for subsequent acceptance.

It is not to be thought that, because of the deep philosophic gulf between the two opposing blocs on the scope of the commands of the Fourteenth Amendment and respecting some civil rights issues, the Court was a bedlam of dissent.

During the October, 1921, term (257, 258, 259 United States Reports) of a total of 169 decisions, there were thirty-six dissents, a percentage of more than 21 per cent. Of these, only two were five-to-four decisions. Justice Clarke led with fifteen dissents; Brandeis followed with thirteen, as did McReynolds; McKenna followed with eleven. Then came Holmes and Van Devanter, each with eight, the Chief Justice with six, and Pitney and Day, each with four. In seven of his eight dissents, Holmes was associated with Brandeis, who also shared seven with Clarke. McReynolds and Van Devanter, who were later to join in an ultraconservative bloc, were associated in six of Van Devanter's eight dissents.

Of 131 decisions handed down during the October, 1928, term, there are to be found in Volumes 278 and 279 of the United States Reports only eighteen dissents (plus 14 per cent). Of these, one-third were by a single justice, four by McReynolds, one by Holmes, and one by Brandeis. Brandeis registered the greatest number of dissents, eight, of which two were cast with Holmes alone, three with Holmes and Stone, one with Holmes and Sanford, and one with McReynolds. Brandeis dissented without Holmes twice. Holmes delivered seven dissents, one alone, six with Brandeis, three with Stone, and one with Sanford. Stone dissented four times, of which three were with Holmes and Brandeis and one each with Sutherland, Butler, and Sanford. Of those in the other camp, Van Devanter dissented three times, two of these with Taft, one with Sutherland, and three with Butler. Butler dissented five times, with Taft twice, with Sutherland twice, and with Van Devanter three times. Sutherland dissented three times, once with each of Stone and Sanford, three with Van Devanter, and twice with Butler. The Chief Justice dissented only twice, each time with Butler and Van Devanter.

The Court under Chief Justice Taft completed a trilogy of conservatism comprised of itself and the two preceding courts, those of Chief Justice Fuller and Chief Justice White. Its conservative philosophy advanced by the weld of Van Devanter, Butler, McReynolds, and Sutherland was to continue during the early years of the next regime until dissipated in a welter of Roosevelt liberalism. The Court took, when labor issues did not intervene, a reasonable and at least moderately enlightened view in the area of civil rights, as witness its criminal syndicalism decisions in a time of agitation against the I.W.W.[119] In both the Whitney and the Gitlow cases, it expressed adherence to enlightened doctrines that transcended the particular results. On the other hand, it nurtured a conservative bloc that was to feed a later fire of liberalism.

[119] Whitney v. California, 274 U.S. 357 (1927); Fiske v. Kansas, 274 U.S. 380 (1927).

CHAPTER IX

The Roosevelt Era—1

CHARLES EVANS HUGHES, formerly governor of New York, who served as a member of the White court but resigned to run for President in 1916 and thereafter served as secretary of state, was sworn in as Chief Justice on February 24, 1930, succeeding Chief Justice Taft. His court comprised the liberals, Holmes, Brandeis, and Stone; the so-called Four Horsemen, the aging conservatives, Sutherland, Van Devanter, McReynolds, and Butler, three of whom were over seventy, with Owen J. Roberts of Pennsylvania, who replaced Justice Sanford during the closing days of the October 1929 term, making the ninth. Justice Holmes at 89 was approaching retirement and was replaced as a justice and a liberal by Benjamin Cardozo, chief judge of the New York Court of Appeals, early in 1932.

Roberts was essentially a conservative; his sponsor had been Senator George Wharton Pepper of Pennsylvania, an archconservative. The Chief Justice was a civil rights liberal but an economic conservative. As the decisions of the Court demonstrated, for a time Roberts proved to be the dominant figure in determining how the Court went in a given case. When he joined the four conservatives, a five-man majority was assured and the Chief Justice could either make it six or increase the dissenting group to four. On the other hand, when Roberts went liberal, the Chief Justice was hard put to it to do less (although on occasion he did), and a liberal majority was assured. And so it went for the first half dozen years of the reign of Hughes, which thus, in effect, became the reign of Roberts.

A box score on the closely divided decisions during the 1930 term showed the Chief Justice voting with the conservative bloc on three occasions and with the liberal bloc on eight. Justice Roberts voted with the conservatives on three occasions and with the liberals on seven. Before Roberts joined the Court, the Chief Justice voted with the conservatives twice. After Roberts joined the Court, he voted conservative on one occasion when the Chief Justice did not participate; on another occasion, he voted liberal when the Chief Justice voted conservative, and on two other occasions, in the MacIntosh and Bland cases, he joined the conservatives while Hughes was dissenting with the liberals.

So, facing a New Jersey statute limiting commissions allowable by fire insurers, the aid of Roberts and the Chief Justice saved the statute over the en bloc dissent of the conservatives, who said that the freedom of contract concept "settled by the decisions of this court and . . . no longer open to question,"[1] required voiding of the enactment. As authority for this conclusion, they cited the discredited Adkins case.

With the Chief Justice and Roberts moving from side to side, bloc voting made decisions akin to a game of chess. Thus we find the Chief Justice joining the conservatives to strike down a statute imposing an inheritance tax because it was enacted after the execution of an irrevocable trust deed.[2] We also find both the Chief Justice and Roberts joining the conservatives to strike down, over liberal dissent, a state tax on the combined incomes of husband and wife who had filed separate returns,[3] an inheritance tax by a state of incorporation on stock owned by a decedent,[4] a congressional statute taxing *inter vivos* transfers within two years of death as having been made in contemplation of that finality,[5] destruction of existing causes of action by repeal of a constitutional provision creating them,[6] and Florida state taxation discriminating against chain stores.[7]

For another example, the Interstate Commerce Commission did not fare well at the hands of Justice Roberts. In five cases, in two of which the Chief Justice joined, Roberts and the conservatives overruled the Interstate Commerce Commission.[8] In one of these, the Milwaukee case, the majority denied the right of the Commission to pass on fees of reorganization managers and other insiders; later Congress came to the rescue with statutory authority.

At the end of the 1930 term both Roberts and the Chief Justice, standing between the two committed blocs, might be described as bearing toward future adherence to the liberal side. However, Stone had misgivings concerning Roberts.[9] As for Hughes, in a 1937 article in the *New Republic* entitled "How Liberal is Justice Hughes" the author said:

[1] O'Gorman & Young v. Hartford Ins. Co., 282 U.S. 251, 267 (1931).
[2] Coolidge v. Long, 282 U.S. 582 (1931).
[3] Hoeper v. Tax Commission, 284 U.S. 206 (1931).
[4] First National Bank v. Maine, 284 U.S. 312 (1932).
[5] Heiner v. Donnan, 285 U.S. 312 (1932).
[6] Coombes v. Getz, 285 U.S. 434 (1932).
[7] Liggett Co. v. Lee, 288 U.S. 517 (1933).
[8] United States v. Chicago, M., St. P. & Pac. R.R., 282 U.S. 311 (1931); Chicago, R.I. & P. R.R. v. United States, 284 U.S. 80 (1931); United States v. Baltimore & Ohio R.R., 284 U.S. 195 (1931); Arizona Groc. Co. v. Atchison, T. & S. F. R.R., 284 U.S. 370 (1932); Texas & Pac. R.R. v. United States, 289 U.S. 627 (1933).
[9] Alpheus T. Mason, *Harlan Fiske Stone: Pillar of the Law* (New York, The Viking Press, 1956), 310–11.

When Charles Evans Hughes is a liberal, he proclaims it to the world. When he is a reactionary, he votes silently and allows somebody else to be torn to pieces by the liberal dissenters. . . . One can only wonder what the reputation of Mr. Hughes would be, if, in the fifty-one cases in which he helped to create a reactionary majority, he had exposed himself sixteen times to the dissenting logic of Mr. Justice Stone.[10]

Pusey, Hughes's biographer, said that "out of approximately 350 opinions that Hughes wrote for the court as Chief Justice, thirty-nine are especially significant in their bearing upon the powers of the states. In thirty-two of these he sustained the state law or action that was challenged; in seven (including four tax cases) he administered a lethal dose of constitutionalism. Three times he dissented because a majority liquidated state laws he believed to be valid."[11]

The 1931–32 tally showed an unpromising near future for the liberal point of view. A trend was discernible which was to be borne out by the averages. Of fourteen split decisions, the reputedly liberal Chief Justice voted with the conservatives thirteen times. Of fifteen votes, Roberts cast twelve with the conservatives and three with the liberals, one of which occurred when the Chief Justice was absent.

Clues to the philosophy of the Chief Justice and Roberts are also found in the fact that they both voted with the conservative bloc to strike down orders of the Interstate Commerce Commission, to deny state rights to tax, to exert the due process clause of the Fourteenth Amendment to deny congressional taxing power, and to uphold the principle of res judicata against manifest individual injustice and consequent restitution. However, they parted company in the Coronado case on the issue of stare decisis.[12]

In his dissenting opinion in the Coronado case is found Brandeis' much quoted exposition of the rule of stare decisis:

> Stare decisis is not, like the rule of res judicata, a universal inexorable command.[13] . . . "Whether it shall be followed or departed from is a question entirely within the discretion of the court, which is again called upon to consider a question once decided." . . . Stare decisis is usually the wise policy, because in most matters it is more important that the applicable rule of law be settled than that it be settled right.[14] . . . in cases involving the Federal Constitution, where correction through legislative action is practically impossible, this Court

[10] *Ibid.*, 316.

[11] Merlo J. Pusey, *Charles Evans Hughes* (2 vols., New York, The Macmillan Company, 1952), II, 696.

[12] Burnet v. Coronado Oil & Gas Co., 285 U.S. 393 (1932).

[13] *Ibid.*, 405.

[14] *Ibid.*, 406.

has often overruled its earlier decisions.[15] The Court bows to the lessons of experience and the force of better reasoning, recognizing that the process of trial and error, so fruitful in the physical sciences, is appropriate also in the judicial function.[16]

Despite his words, Brandeis could be moved by hardship even to disregard the "universal inexorable command" of res judicata, as when the liberal three joined in dissent while the Chief Justice and Roberts joined Sutherland and others in holding that "the mischief which would follow the establishment of a precedent for so disregarding this salutary doctrine [res judicata] would be greater than the benefit which would result from relieving some case of individual hardship."[17] The hardship was obvious, for a man named Allen had claimed the ownership of money in the hands of a man named Walker which the latter had collected from rentals of certain real property devised by the will of Silas Holmes, Allen's grandfather. The Court found against Allen and in favor of collateral relatives. Allen appealed, and while the appeal was pending, the collateral relatives, on the strength of the decision against Allen, sued for possession of the real property from which the rents in dispute had arisen. The Court awarded them possession, and Allen failed to appeal from that judgment. Then the first decision was reversed, and Allen was awarded the rents. Now Allen sued to recover the real estate which had been taken from him on the basis of the first upset decision.

Justice Cardozo, advocating the return of the property to Allen, wrote:

> The judicial process has been moulded with an anxious effort to put an end as speedily as may be to wrongs originating in judicial errors.[18] . . . The entry of a second judgment, instead of being a circumstance fastening the rivets of injustice, was merely an additional reason why the rivets should be broken.[19] . . . A system of procedure is perverted from its proper function when it multiplies impediments to justice without the warrant of clear necessity.[20]

Dissents during the 1931 term were at the reasonable rate of 15 per cent, a total of 22 out of 149 decisions. Only two of the split decisions were by a five-to-four vote, one by a vote of four to two. Justice Brandeis was the leading dissenter with twelve dissents, of which eleven were cast with Justice Stone, five with Holmes, three with Cardozo, and two with Roberts. Stone also had twelve dissents, four with Holmes, four with Cardozo, and two with Roberts.

[15] *Ibid.,* 407.
[16] *Ibid.,* 408.
[17] Reed v. Allen, 286 U.S. 191, 199 (1932).
[18] *Ibid.,* 204.
[19] *Ibid.,* 205.
[20] *Ibid.,* 209.

Holmes had five dissents, four with Stone and all five with Brandeis. Cardozo dissented four times; each one with Stone, three with Brandeis, and one with Roberts.

Indicating predominance, Van Devanter had four dissents, one alone, one with Sutherland, one with McReynolds, and three with Butler. Butler dissented five times, of which one was with McReynolds and two were with Sutherland. McReynolds dissented four times, three alone and one with Sutherland, Butler, and Van Devanter. Sutherland had three dissents as noted.

During this term the Chief Justice wrote twenty-three opinions, of which five drew dissents, three of which—two by McReynolds and one by Butler—were sole.

The most important happening of the 1932–33 term was the election of Franklin Delano Roosevelt as President of the United States. That occurrence was destined to turn the Court from the path of conservatism and to speed up its change of course.

During the term there were twenty-eight dissents (17 per cent) out of a total of 168 decisions. Three of the dissents were by a five-to-four court. Justice Stone led with thirteen dissents, followed by Cardozo with twelve. Brandeis dissented nine times. Of the conservatives, Butler dissented eleven times, McReynolds had eight dissents, and Van Devanter and Sutherland each had four. The control of the middlemen was attested by the fact that Roberts had occasion to dissent only twice, and the Chief Justice only three times. Of nineteen split decisions where the conservative and liberal blocs were at odds, each of the two middlemen voted with the conservatives ten times, though not always together.

Stone dissented with Cardozo eleven times and with Brandeis seven times. He dissented with Roberts once, with Hughes twice, once with Butler, and once with McReynolds. Cardozo dissented with Brandeis five times, three times with Hughes, and once each with Roberts, Butler, McReynolds, and Van Devanter. Brandeis dissented once with Roberts, once with Hughes, and once with Butler.

Of the conservatives, Butler dissented alone three times, with McReynolds four times, with Sutherland four times, and with Van Devanter three times. McReynolds dissented with Sutherland once and with Van Devanter twice. Sutherland dissented with Van Devanter twice.

There were two cases during the 1932 term which betokened a gathering storm of corporate stockholder resentment that was to result in a congressional investigation and the creation of the Securities and Exchange Commission.[21]

Richard Reid Rogers, a New York lawyer, was a stockholder of the American Tobacco Company which, under the dictatorial aegis of George Washing-

---

[21] Rogers v. Guaranty Trust Co., 288 U.S. 123 (1933); Rogers v. Hill, 289 U.S. 582 (1933).

ton Hill, had grown fat in business and profits. Rogers, like other New York lawyers who were close to the corporate scene, had been aware of the corporate practices of the astigmatic corporate giants of the twenties that were unconscious of the fiduciary duties owed ignored stockholders. Rogers started a stockholder's suit in the New York federal court to cancel stock which he alleged had been wrongfully issued by the company to its officers and directors. Noted counsel for the defendants urged the New York court to dismiss the suit upon the ground that the Tobacco Company was a New Jersey corporation and, as such, should be sued there. The New York court acquiesced, and the Supreme Court affirmed by a vote of five to three. The Chief Justice voted with the majority despite his experience with the fraud of the New York insurance companies that had made him New York's governor. Justice Roberts did not participate. Justices Stone and Cardozo, with an awareness of what had been taking place in corporate circles, wrote dissenting opinions, with which Justice Brandeis concurred.

Justice Stone said: "Their [the directors'] business competence did not confer on them the privilege of making concealed or unauthorized profits or relieve them of the elementary obligation which the law imposes on all corporate directors to deal frankly and openly with stockholders."[22] Justice Cardozo wrote: "Consent will not protect if reason and moderation are not made to mark the boundaries of what is done under its shelter."[23]

But Rogers had also instituted another suit—this one on behalf of the Tobacco Company to recover bonuses that the officers and directors had caused the corporation to pay them pursuant to a bylaw they adopted entitling them to a stated percentage of the net earnings of the company. Rogers contended that the bonuses paid, which aggregated in excess of three million dollars over a ten-year period, had not been earned and bore no relationship to the services performed. The New York federal court had dismissed the suit. But Justice Butler, who had written the opinion in the previous case, held that corporate bonuses had to bear a reasonable relationship to services rendered and the Court remanded the case to the district court for further proceedings.

The decision, and especially the dissenting opinions of Justices Stone and Cardozo in the previous case, concerning the much neglected fiduciary duties of corporate officers and directors, aroused widespread attention, and coming, as they did, when the incidence of the depression had caused huge stockholder losses, investigations and stockholder suits followed with the results noted.

Apparently the eloquence of Cardozo and Stone had also convinced Justice Van Devanter (though it had not moved Roberts), for he joined with the Chief Justice and the three liberals to enable Cardozo to write for a five-man

[22] Rogers v. Guaranty Trust Co., 288 U.S. 123, 143 (1933).
[23] Ibid., 150.

majority assessing promotors of a corporate enterprise for losses sustained by the corporation.[24] Justice Cardozo said: "The promotors and their confederates pocketed the spoils. . . .[25] Promotors of a corporation stand in a fiduciary relation to it to this extent at least, that they will be chargeable as trustees if they deal with it unconscionably or oppressively."[26] Justice Roberts, McReynolds, Sutherland, and Butler dissented. Again, the decision of the majority spurred the growing public dissatisfaction with the corporate practices of Wall Street promoters and their co-operators.

As in other matters of moment, the Chief Justice and Roberts determined whether the cast of the Court should be liberal or conservative in a number of civil rights cases.

Following reversal of the convictions of eight of the nine Negro boys charged with rape in the so-called Scottsboro cases[27] for lack of adequate representation by counsel, over the dissent of Justices Butler and McReynolds, the Court reviewed the second conviction of Norris, one of the eight. It reversed his conviction upon the ground that Negroes had been excluded from grand and petit juries.[28]

Simultaneously, the Court considered the case of Patterson, another of the eight. He had been convicted a second time but the judge had set the verdict aside as against the weight of evidence. The Court reviewed his third conviction and reversed it on the same ground as in the case of Norris.[29] This time Butler went along, and McReynolds was absent.

Roberts and Hughes joined the conservatives in deciding that Herndon, a Communist, convicted in Georgia of an attempt to incite insurrection could have no relief "for the reason that no federal question was seasonably raised in the court below."[30] Justice Cardozo wrote a dissenting opinion, in which he said,

> Here is an unequivocal rejection of the test of clear and present danger. . . . Will men "judging in calmness" . . . say of the defendant's conduct as shown forth in the pages of this record that it was an attempt to stir up revolution through the power of his persuasion and within the time when that persuasion might be expected to endure? If men so judging will say yes, will the Constitution of the United States uphold a reading of the statute that will lead to that response? Those are the questions that the defendant lays before us after

[24] McCandless v. Furland, 296 U.S. 140 (1935).
[25] Ibid., 155.
[26] Ibid., 156.
[27] Powell v. Alabama, 287 U.S. 45 (1932).
[28] Norris v. Alabama, 294 U.S. 587 (1935).
[29] Patterson v. Alabama, 294 U.S. 600 (1935).
[30] Herndon v. Georgia, 295 U.S. 441 (1935).

conviction of a crime punishable by death in the discretion of the jury. I think he should receive an answer.[31]

Brandeis and Stone joined.

The next term, Herndon returned for a hearing which the Court had previously denied him over the objection of the three liberals and for the answers that Justice Cardozo said he was entitled to receive. He received them when a five-man majority voided the conviction.[32]

Justice Roberts, over the dissents of his four former associates, gave the answers in words that reflected those of Holmes and Brandeis when he said:

> The power of a state to abridge freedom of speech and of assembly is the exception rather than the rule and the penalizing even of utterances of a defined character must find its justification in a reasonable apprehension of danger to organized government. . . .[33]
>
> And where a statute is so vague and uncertain as to make criminal an utterance or an act which may be innocently said or done with no intent to induce resort to violence . . . a conviction under such a law cannot be sustained. . . .[34]
>
> The statute, as construed and applied, amounts merely to a dragnet which may enmesh anyone who agitates for a change of government. . . . So vague and indeterminate are the boundaries thus set of the freedom of speech and assembly that the law necessarily violates the guaranties of liberty embodied in the Fourteenth Amendment.[35]

Ignoring for the moment cases that might have been affected by a New Deal cast, labor also had to guess how Roberts would go at a particular time.

He committed a crowning indignity when he joined the conservatives to strike down a New York minimum wage law over the dissents of the Chief Justice and the three liberals.[36] Butler and his conservative associates voted as they had in the past. Now, writing the opinion for the majority, Butler said, "The Adkins case, unless distinguishable, requires affirmance of the judgment."[37] Chief Justice Hughes's dissenting opinion reflected little credit to him, since he argued that the statutes in the Adkins and Morehead cases differed, instead of taking the position he took in the following term that the long-since-discredited Adkins decision should be overruled. Roberts, at the moment an established conservative, discredited himself by going along with the reactionaries on Fourteenth Amendment issues long since exploded by

[31] *Ibid.*, 455.
[32] Herndon v. Lowry, 301 U.S. 242, 263–64 (1937).
[33] *Ibid.*, 258.
[34] *Ibid.*, 259.
[35] *Ibid.* 264.
[36] Morehead v. Tipaldo, 298 U.S. 587 (1936).
[37] *Ibid.*, 604.

the dissenting opinions of Holmes and then, in the following term, sheepishly following Hughes in overruling the decision he was now supporting. Stone, in his dissent, took the Chief Justice to task and demolished the evasions of Butler when he said: "I know of no rule or practice by which the arguments advanced in support of an application for certiorari restrict our choice between conflicting precedents in deciding a question of constitutional law."[38]

On December 16 and 17 of the following term there was argued before the Court the constitutionality of a Washington statute fixing a minimum wage for women and minors. The West Coast decision, written by Chief Justice Hughes for a five-man majority consisting of himself, Justice Roberts, and the three liberals, over the dissent of the Sutherland four, affirmed its constitutionality and overruled the decision to the contrary for which Justice Roberts had been responsible at the previous term.[39]

However, Roberts' about-face in these minimum wage cases were as naught compared with his later gyrations resulting from his New Deal turnabouts, for while the routine business of the Court was droning on during the 1932 and 1933 terms, a storm of activity was raging outside. Franklin D. Roosevelt, the newly inaugurated President, had called for action, quick action, national action to restore the economy, to furnish jobs for the unemployed, to provide customers for the farmers, to reopen the banks, which precautionarily had been closed by national decree. Within a week after his inauguration, the President called on Congress to act; all over the country the people were calling on their state legislatures to relieve their plights, and "New Dealers" invaded Washington with visions of statutory panaceas. Congress responded by converting their ideas, their nostrums, into legislation.

The first of the depression cases reached the Court during the 1933–34 term.[40] It involved the Minnesota Mortgage Moratorium Law, which provided for certain deferments of sales and extensions of periods of redemption for mortgages in default. The statute was challenged as repugnant to the contract clause of Article 1 and to the due process and equal protection clauses of the Fourteenth Amendment. Thus the issues of the past came into conflict with the needs of the future, and the liberal three, with the aid of Hughes and Roberts, routed, for the moment, the hardened-arterial four who were unaware of the winds of change blowing outside their ivory tower.

The Chief Justice wrote quotably when he said: "Emergency does not create power, [but] emergency may furnish the occasion for the exercise of power.[41] . . . there has been a growing appreciation of public needs and of

---

[38] *Ibid.,* 636.
[39] West Coast Hotel Co. v. Parrish, 300 U.S. 379 (1937).
[40] Home Bldg. & L. Assoc. v. Blaisdell, 290 U.S. 398 (1934).
[41] *Ibid.,* 426.

the necessity of finding ground for a rational compromise between individual rights and public welfare. . . . It is no answer to say that this public need was not apprehended a century ago, or to insist that what the provision of the Constitution meant to the vision of that day it must mean to the vision of our time."[42]

The second opportunity to discover on which side Roberts would fall from his tightrope came when the New York Milk Law came before the Court in the form of a conviction of the proprietor of a small grocery store for selling two quarts of milk and a loaf of bread for eighteen cents, although the Milk Control Board had fixed a price of nine cents a quart for milk.[43]

Now Roberts not only wrote for the majority upholding the law, but with Hughes, he was the majority, since the Van Devanter group voted as a bloc in support of McReynolds' shrill and indignant dissent. The defendant, he said, "was convicted of a crime for selling his own property—wholesome milk—in the ordinary course of business at a price satisfactory to himself and the customer."[44]

Justice Roberts listed the cases in which the Court had sanctioned state action consistent with due process.[45] Despite his vote striking down the Oklahoma statute in the Ice case, Roberts now said, "The phrase 'affected with a public interest' can, in the nature of things, mean no more than that an industry, for adequate reason, is subject to control for the public good."[46] However, he failed to make reference to Holmes's opinion in the Tyson theater ticket case. Later Justice Cardozo wrote for a unanimous court, limiting the Milk Control Act to intrastate activities.[47]

Roberts' ambivalence made him utterly unpredictable. Following his liberal stance in the Minnesota Moratorium and the Milk Control cases, he joined the conservatives to strike down a Federal Trade Commission order, with the Chief Justice aligned with the liberals in dissent,[48] and to strike down an Illinois tax statute as denying equal protection, with the three liberals dissenting.[49] The Chief Justice did not participate.

That the conservative bloc did not intend to strain the Constitution was announced by Justice Sutherland, when, speaking for his group in a case where the four concurred in striking down an Arkansas statute as impairing contractual obligations, he said: "We were unable then, as we are now, to

[42] Ibid., 442.
[43] Nebbia v. New York, 291 U.S. 502 (1934).
[44] Ibid., 543-44.
[45] Ibid., 525 et seq.; and see footnotes.
[46] Ibid., 536.
[47] Baldwin v. Seelig, 294 U.S. 511 (1935).
[48] Arrow-Hart & H. Co. v. Federal Trade Commission, 291 U.S. 587 (1934).
[49] Concordia Fire Ins. Co. v. Illinois, 292 U.S. 535 (1934).

concur in the view that an emergency can ever justify . . . a nullification of the constitutional restriction upon state power in respect of the impairment of contractual obligations . . . . The power of this court is not to amend but only to expound the Constitution."[50]

Despite the deep philosophic differences between the liberal and conservative blocs respecting constitutional fundamentals, the 1934–35 term saw an unbroken string of thirty-eight decisions without a single dissent. Then the volatile Roberts joined Butler in two dissents.

However, the recalcitrants did go along in approving a Maryland statute, adopted to stem a flood of mortgage foreclosures resulting from the depression, calling for consent of the holders of 25 per cent of mortgage participation certificates in order to foreclose.[51]

But when the early New Deal case involving congressional delegation of power to the President to prohibit the transportation of oil exceeding state allowances (so-called "hot oil"), only Justice Cardozo dissented from a ruling that such delegation by Section 9 (c) of the National Industrial Recovery Act (NIRA) was unconstitutional.[52]

Roberts, with the Chief Justice, stayed with the liberals to overcome the Sutherland bloc in upholding the validity of the congressional resolution repudiating obligations to pay in gold.[53] There were two companion suits; the principal suit was brought by the holder of a bond of the Baltimore & Ohio Railroad Company which called for payment "in gold coin of the United States of America of or equal to the standard of weight and fineness existing on February, 1930," to recover on an interest coupon. As against the $22.50 face of the coupon, the plaintiff alleged that the value of the gold coin called for was $38.10. The Court upheld the repudiation upon the ground of the power of Congress to establish a monetary system under the Constitution.

The third of the Gold Clause Cases presented the question of whether the holder of $106,000 of gold certificates issued by the government was entitled to receive gold or its equivalent value of $170,000 in currency.[54] The Court said "no," basing its answer on the fact that Congress had called in all gold in public hands and that the holder of it, if he received it in payment of his certificates, could do nothing with it since there was no free market in gold in the United States, and under the law he could not sell it elsewhere.

The fourth of these cases was a suit by the holder of a $10,000 Liberty bond issued by the government and calling for payment in gold.[55] While

[50] Worthen v. Thomas, 292 U.S. 426, 434–35 (1934).
[51] United States Mortgage Co. v. Matthews, 293 U.S. 232 (1934).
[52] Panama Refining Co. v. Ryan, 293 U.S. 388 (1935).
[53] Norman v. Baltimore & Ohio R.R.; United States v. Bankers Trust Co., 294 U.S. 240 (1935).
[54] Nortz v. United States, 294 U.S. 317 (1935).
[55] Perry v. United States, 294 U.S. 330 (1935).

the Court agreed that Congress lacked the power to repudiate the governmental obligation to pay in gold, or its equivalent, it took recourse in the conclusion that the holder suffered no damage when the government refused to pay in gold for the reason given in the prior case. Justice McReynolds wrote in dissent for his group, saying fruitlessly, "Loss of reputation for dishonorable dealing will bring us unending humiliation; the impending legal and moral chaos is appalling."[56]

Later, with the aid of the Chief Justice and Justice Roberts, the liberals were able to command majorities to affirm a repudiation of a gold clause in a lease,[57] to approve a call for redemption of Liberty bonds with payment in currency,[58] to deny a claim for Dutch guilders equal in value to gold where gold bonds were also payable in guilders and other foreign currencies,[59] and to hold consistently in the case of bonds issued by the Bethlehem Steel Company, with similar multiple provisions, which had been marketed abroad.[60]

The balance of the 1934 term saw three New Deal acts voided. The first of these was the Railroad Retirement Act of June 27, 1934, by which Congress undertook to establish a compulsory retirement system for railroad employees.[61] It was the unpredictable Roberts who gave the Act the coup de grâce to make a fifth with the conservative bloc, while the Chief Justice joined the dissenting liberals. "The gravest aspect of the decision is that it does not rest simply upon a condemnation of particular features of the Railroad Retirement Act, but denies to Congress the power to pass any compulsory pension act for railroad employees," said the Chief Justice, dissenting.[62]

The next New Deal debacle concerned the most ambitious and far-reaching of the New Deal projects. This was embodied in the NIRA, which was designed to cure all economic ills by the co-operation of business and government: to prevent overproduction, to regulate competition, to raise wages, and to eliminate substandard working conditions. The method of accomplishing all these beneficences was to have each industry adopt a code and by action of the President, enact that code into law. Like other overambitious and idealistic projects, the NIRA soon demonstrated, among other things, as in the case of socialistic panaceas, that its benefits could not exceed the abilities of available fallible human administration.

---

56 *Ibid.*, 381.

57 Holyoke Water Power Co. v. American Writ. Paper Co., 300 U.S. 324 (1937).

58 Smyth v. United States; Dixie T. Co. v. United States; United States v. Machen, 302 U.S. 329 (1937).

59 Guaranty Trust Co. v. Henwood; Chemical Bank & Trust Co. v. Henwood, 307 U.S. 247 (1939).

60 Bethlehem Steel Co. v. Zurich Ins. Co., 307 U.S. 265 (1939).

61 Railroad Retirement Board v. Alton R.R., 295 U.S. 330 (1935).

62 *Ibid.*, 374–75.

The New Dealers had, with prescience, feared the reaction of the Court, and they delayed putting the statute to the test. By the time they did, its proponents had lost heart, and its performance had caused the public and business to lose faith to a point where it was rumored that prominent lawyers were competing for the privilege of attacking it.

So when some inconsequential chicken dealers were convicted of violations of the poultry code and took an appeal to the high court, the stage was set for a unanimous ruling that Congress had improperly delegated legislative power to the President, as it had in the previous Hot Oil Case, and this over-ambitious project found the fate it deserved.[63] Justice Cardozo, concurring, wrote: "The delegated power of legislation which has found expression in this code is not canalized within banks that keep it from overflowing. It is unconfined and vagrant."[64]

On the same day another New Deal catastrophe occurred. A unanimous Court, in an opinion by Brandeis, filed a dissent to the congressional Frazier-Lemke Amendment to the National Bankruptcy Act upon the ground that it violated the Fifth Amendment.[65] The Act had been designed to aid mortgagors in default, but, as Justice Brandeis wrote,

> . . . the Fifth Amendment commands that, however great the Nation's need, private property shall not be . . . taken even for a wholly public use without just compensation. If the public interest requires, and permits, the taking of property of individual mortgagees in order to relieve the necessities of individual mortgagors, resort must be had to proceedings by eminent domain; so that, through taxation, the burden of the relief afforded to the public interest may be borne by the public.[66]

The final setback for the Administration during this term came when the Court held that the President's power to remove a member of the Federal Trade Commission was limited to those causes which Congress had specified in the Federal Trade Commission Act, since such a commissioner was not an executive officer.[67] Justice Sutherland, writing for a unanimous court, distinguished the previous Myers case.

A review of the depression and New Deal legislation passed upon by the Court during the 1934 term showed Hughes and Roberts making the liberal three a majority of five in upholding three state statutes and in approving the Gold Clause Cases but striking down a state statute or ruling, over the dissent

[63] Schechter v. United States, 295 U.S. 495 (1935).
[64] Ibid., 551.
[65] Louisville Bank v. Radford, 295 U.S. 555 (1935).
[66] Ibid., 602.
[67] Humphrey's Executor v. United States; Rathbun v. United States, 295 U.S. 602 (1935).

of the liberals, in three cases. Then Roberts is to be found making a fifth to strike down a state statute over the liberal dissent, with Hughes not sitting, and making a fifth to strike down a federal commission order over the dissent of Hughes and the liberals. Both Hughes and Roberts joined an eight-man court to strike down the Hot Oil section of the NIRA (Cardozo dissenting) and joined with the other members of the Court to strike down the NIRA and the Frazier-Lemke Act. Roberts joined the conservatives, with Hughes voting with the liberals, in striking down the Railroad Retirement Act. At this point, it looked as if Hughes was more likely to vote liberal than Roberts and would be less likely to vote conservative when Roberts did not.

The last phase of the reign of the four reactionaries opened when, during the first half of the 1935 term, the question of the constitutionality of the Agricultural Adjustment Act of 1933 was argued. This was the New Deal solution for the plight of the farmers; it levied a processing tax on wheat, corn, cotton, and other farm products to provide funds to induce farmers to limit their acreage. The act had been operative for better than two years before being submitted to the Court. The objection was made that the Act invaded the rights of the states and, as such, was unconstitutional. Within a month of the argument, by a vote of six to three, in an opinion written by Roberts for the Chief Justice and the four conservatives, the majority so held, and it held also that the taxing power of Congress could not be employed to raise money to enforce by economic pressure a compliance with a congressional regulation of a matter respecting which Congress had no authority.[68] Justice Stone wrote in dissent for himself and Justices Brandeis and Cardozo:

> The power of courts to declare a statute unconstitutional is subject to two guiding principles of decision. . . . One is that courts are concerned only with the power to enact statutes, not with their wisdom. The other is that while unconstitutional exercise of power by the executive and legislative branches of the government is subject to judicial restraint, the only check upon our own exercise of power is our own sense of self-restraint. For the removal of unwise laws from the statute books appeal lies, not to the courts, but to the ballot and to the processes of democratic government.[69]
>
> That the Governmental power of the purse is a great one is not now for the first time announced. . . .[70]
>
> The suggestion that it must now be curtailed by judicial fiat because it may be abused by unwise use hardly rises to the dignity of argument. So may judicial power be abased. "The power to tax is the power to destroy," but we do not, for that reason, doubt its existence. . . . The power to tax and spend

[68] United States v. Butler, 297 U.S. 1 (1936).
[69] *Ibid.*, 78–79.
[70] *Ibid.*, 86.

is not without constitutional restraints. One restriction is that the purpose must be truly national. Another is that it may not be used to coerce action left to state control. Another is the conscience and patriotism of Congress and the Executive. . . .[71]

It was rumored about Washington that the Chief Justice had joined the majority to avoid another five-to-four decision; however, he labelled the rumor as "manifestly absurd."[72]

The Court's decision in this and in the NIRA case provoked President Roosevelt to an outburst of criticism, in the course of which he accused the Court of reaction that would prevent the national government from dealing with the country's social and economic problems. Nevertheless, the Court proceeded on its reactionary way under the leadership of Roberts, now wedded to the conservative bloc.

Another phase of the controversy concerning the New York Milk Law came before the Court.[73] Despite the shedding of his liberal skin meanwhile, Roberts adhered to his former stance, writing the opinion, with the result that the challenged provision in the Act was approved by a five-to-four vote, the four dissidents standing their ground.

However, a moment later, chameleon-like Roberts read another opinion holding a different provision of the Act unconstitutional and said whether that rendered the statute wholly inoperative was a matter for the state courts.[74] Now he was joined by the four irreconcilables, as well as by the Chief Justice, leaving it for Justice Cardozo to read a dissenting opinion, in which Brandeis and Stone joined.

Only Justice McReynolds dissented from the Court's approval of the construction of the Wilson Dam at Muscle Shoals in the Tennessee River (the TVA project).[75]

Again the Chief Justice and Roberts joined the conservatives in denying the power of the Securities and Exchange Commission to compel J. Edward Jones, who had filed a registration statement to enable him to sell certain securities, to appear for examination and investigation after he had withdrawn his registration statement. Mild-mannered Justice Cardozo, dissenting, waxed indignant. "Recklessness and deceit do not automatically excuse themselves by notice of repentance," he said.[76] He continued, ". . . when wrongs such as these have been committed or attempted, they must be dragged to

71 *Ibid.*, 87.
72 Pusey, *Charles Evans Hughes*, II, 744.
73 Borden's Farm Prod. Co. v. Ten Eyck, 297 U.S. 251 (1936).
74 Mayflower Farms v. Ten Eyck, 297 U.S. 266 (1936).
75 Ashwander v. TVA, 297 U.S. 288 (1936).
76 Jones v. SEC, 298 U.S. 1, 30 (1936).

light and pilloried."[77] "A Commission which . . . can only inquire and report . . . is likened with denunciatory fervor to the Star Chamber of the Stuarts. Historians may find hyperbole in the sanguinary simile," he concluded.[78] And Brandeis and Stone agreed.

Roberts and Hughes joined the Sutherland bloc to strike down the so-called Guffey Coal Act, upon the ground that mining coal was a local matter under the control of the states and the attempt to regulate labor in the industry rendered the Act unconstitutional.[79] The Chief Justice took the middle ground of holding that, since Congress had expressly provided that the market provisions of the Act should be separable from the labor provisions, the Act should be sustained as to the marketing in interstate commerce.[80] Justice Cardozo agreed with the Chief Justice about the separability and validity of the marketing provisions and maintained that the labor provisions did not call for adjudication at that time. As to those, he said: "What the code will provide as to wages and hours of labor, or whether it will provide anything, is still in the domain of prophecy. . . . To adopt a homely form of words, the complainants have been crying before they are really hurt."[81] Brandeis and Stone agreed. The Chief Justice "explained" this decision later.

Roberts joined the McReynolds bloc in striking down the Municipal Bankruptcy Act of 1934.[82] The Act had been designed to permit local governmental units to adjust their affairs under the National Bankruptcy Act. The majority denied the congressional power. The Chief Justice joined with the liberals in dissent.

The Court undertook to curb the inevitable administrative agencies' tendency to become dictatorial when fifty suits were instituted to restrain enforcement of an order of the Secretary of Agriculture fixing maximum rates to be charged by market agencies for buying and selling livestock at the Kansas City stockyards. The secretary had initiated an inquiry, and an examiner had taken the testimony. The plaintiffs claimed that the secretary had fixed the rates without having heard or read any of the evidence and without hearing oral argument or reading the briefs. The Court held that "the officer who makes the determination must consider and appraise the evidence which justifies them."[83]

Subsequently, the case came back to the Court.[84] It now appeared that the

[77] *Ibid.*, 32.
[78] *Ibid.*, 33.
[79] Carter v. Carter Coal Co., 298 U.S. 298 (1936).
[80] *Ibid.*, 323–24.
[81] *Ibid.*, 341.
[82] Ashton v. Cameron County, 298 U.S. 513 (1936).
[83] Morgan v. United States, 298 U.S. 468, 482 (1936).
[84] Morgan v. United States, 304 U.S. 1 (1938).

evidence received at the first hearing was resubmitted, and this was supplemented by additional testimony and exhibits. Again the appellants contended that they had not had a fair hearing. And now the Court held, over the dissent of Justice Black, that they had not had an opportunity to learn the government's contentions, nor an opportunity to answer them. Chief Justice Hughes said:

> The maintenance of proper standards on the part of administrative agencies in the performance of their quasi-judicial functions is of the highest importance and in no way cripples or embarrasses the exercise of their appropriate authority. . . . if these multiplying agencies deemed to be necessary in our complex society are to serve the purpose for which they are created and endowed with vast powers, they must accredit themselves by acting in accordance with the cherished judicial tradition embodying the basic concepts of fair play.[85]

Later, another phase of the case came to the Court, and finally, after eleven years of litigation, the order was sustained. The over-all score for the 1935 term showed that of sixteen decisions during the term, Roberts voted conservative in all but one. Four of these conservative decisions were by a five-to-four vote, Roberts making the fifth. In his one liberal opinion, he also made the fifth. All the other decisions were by six-to-three vote, but one, and that by a six-to-two vote. The Chief Justice invariably made the sixth, with the result that, of the sixteen decisions, the Chief Justice joined the conservatives eleven times and the liberals five.

[85] *Ibid.*, 22.

CHAPTER X

The Roosevelt Era—2

WHEN THE 1936–37 TERM OPENED, it was no longer necessary to speculate where Roberts stood. And one could understand the doubts expressed about the august Chief Justice.

Nothing had disturbed the calm of the Court while the electorate was being importuned to re-elect Franklin Roosevelt as President of the United States and did so, giving him an overwhelming mandate represented by 515 out of a total of 523 electoral votes, only Maine and Vermont being unconvinced. Though the President had made no overt attempt to make the Supreme Court and its reactionary attitude an issue in the campaign, it was an issue nevertheless. And the President was not one to take the Court's veto of his New Deal policies lying down. Following his re-election, however, the atmosphere of the Court changed.

During the term the Court unanimously approved six New Deal enactments,[1] approved three more by five-to-four votes,[2] another by a seven-to-two vote,[3] four gold clause cases (akin to those previously approved) by five-to-four votes,[4] and three state enactments, two by five-to-four votes[5] and the third by a seven-to-two vote.[6] In each case the Chief Justice and Roberts voted with the liberals, where needed, to constitute a majority.

The West Coast decision was handed down on March 29, 1937. Mean-

[1] United States v. Hudson, 299 U.S. 498 (1937); Aetna Life Ins. Co. v. Haworth, 300 U.S. 227 (1937); Wright v. Mountain Trust Bank, 300 U.S. 440 (1937); Sonzinsky v. United States; 300 U.S. 506, 514 (1937); Virginian R.R. v. Federation 300 U.S. 515 (1937); Highland Farms Dairy v. Agnew, 300 U.S. 608, 617 (1937).

[2] NLRB v. Jones & Laughlin Steel Corp., 301 U.S. 1 (1937); Associated Press v. NLRB; Tribune Co. v. Associated Press; Associated Press v. United States, 301 U.S. 103 (1937); Steward Mach. Co. v. Davis, 301 U.S. 548 (1937).

[3] Helvering v. Davis, 301 U.S. 619 (1937).

[4] Holyoke Water Power Co. v. American Writ. Paper Co., 300 U.S. 324 (1937); Guaranty Trust Co. v. Henwood; Chemical Bank & Trust Co. v. Henwood, 307 U.S. 247 (139); Bethlehem Steel Co. v. Zurich Ins. Co., 307 U.S. 265 (1939).

[5] Senn v. Tile Layers Union, 301 U.S. 468 (1937); Carmichael v. Southern Coal & Coke Co., 301 U.S. 495 (1937).

[6] Henneford v. Silas Mason Co., 300 U.S. 577, 588 (1937).

while, on February 5, 1937, the President had sent a message to Congress, proposing an increase of membership of the Court, giving as a euphemistic Rooseveltian reason the need for more justices to expedite the work of the Court and lessen its burden.

Since the West Coast decision had been under consideration for six weeks preceding the President's message to Congress, it was possible that, as the Chief Justice claimed, the latter had had no effect on the Court's attitude.[7] However, it is conceivable that Mr. Justice Roberts' about-face justified Mr. Dooley's conclusion that "th' Supreme Court follows th' iliction returns" (although Justice Frankfurter characterized this as "the wit of cynicism, not the demand of principle"), or perhaps, as Thomas Reed Powell put it: "A switch in time saved nine."

The President's message had not been the only reaction to the Court's attitude toward the New Deal legislation. Following the re-election of the President, Senator Burton K. Wheeler introduced a resolution proposing to amend the Constitution to permit Congress, by a two-thirds vote, to override a Supreme Court ruling of unconstitutionality (a proposal Theodore Roosevelt had advocated as the recall of judicial decisions). Senator O'Mahoney introduced a resolution to require a two-thirds vote of the Court for a finding of unconstitutionality. So there were plenty of straws to indicate to Justice Roberts and his associates just how the opposition winds were blowing.

Whatever the reason, Roberts, the erstwhile liberal turned conservative, now moved back to the liberal front, and his change of heart in the West Coast case marked the beginning of the era of his liberal dominance of his conservative associates.

While the fires of controversy raged over the President's court-packing plan, the Court continued to mend its fences. In the second of two Social Security cases approved by a seven-to-two vote, Justice Cardozo said in his inimitable style:

> Congress may spend money in aid of the "general welfare." . . . There have been great statesmen in our history who have stood for other views. We will not resurrect the contest. It is now settled by decision. . . . Yet difficulties are left when the power is conceded. The line must still be drawn between one welfare and another, between particular and general. . . . The discretion belongs to Congress, unless the choice is clearly wrong. . . .[8]
>
> The purge of nation-wide calamity that began in 1929 has taught us many lessons. Not the least is the solidarity of interests that may once have seemed to be divided. Unemployment spreads from state to state, the hinterland now

---

[7] Merlo J. Pusey, *Charles Evans Hughes* (2 vols., New York, The Macmillan Company, 1952), II, 757.

[8] Helvering v. Davis, 301 U.S. 619, 640 (1937).

settled that in pioneer days gave an avenue of escape. . . . But the ill is all one, or at least not greatly different, whether men are thrown out of work because there is no longer work to do or because the disabilities of age make them incapable of doing it. Rescue becomes necessary irrespective of the cause. The hope behind this statute is to save men and women from the rigors of the poorhouse as well as from the haunting fear that such a lot awaits them when journey's end is near.

Congress did not improvise a judgment when it found that the award of old age benefits would be conducive to the general welfare. . . .[9]

Whether wisdom or unwisdom resides in the scheme of benefits . . . it is not for us to say. The answer to such inquiries must come from Congress, not the courts. Our concern here, as often, is with power, not with wisdom. . . .[10]

When money is spent to promote the general welfare, the concept of welfare or the opposite is shaped by Congress, not the states. So the concept be not arbitrary, the locality must yield.[11]

During March, 1937, the President's proposal to pack the Court had come before the Senate Judiciary Committee, to which Chief Justice Hughes had written a letter which largely disposed of the President's arguments favoring the bill. Even more effectively, the events within the Court revealed by the decisions handed down on March 29 and thereafter effectively cooled the ardor of the proponents of the bill, with the result that on May 18 it was voted down by the Senate Judiciary Committee, whose report characterized the bill as "needless, futile and utterly dangerous."[12]

The final blow to the President's plan came when Justice Van Devanter decided to retire at the end of the term and the bill itself was killed by action of the Senate after the Court had recessed for the summer.

The record of dissent from the earlier terms and that of the 1936 term exhibited an increase of dissents by the members of the Sutherland group and a corresponding decrease in the dissents registered by the members of the liberal group, now including the Chief Justice and Roberts.[13] Thus was reflected the Court's shift of majority that countered the court-packing plan under the aegis of Roberts, with the aid of the vote of the Chief Justice. Incidentally, indicative of bloc voting, more than a third of the dissents during the 1936 term were by five-to-four votes.[14]

The 1937–38 term opened with Hugo Black, a liberal who had been a senator from Alabama, replacing Justice Van Devanter. Justice Black came to the bench under the cloud of being charged with membership in the Ku

[9] Ibid., 641.
[10] Ibid., 644.
[11] Ibid., 645.
[12] United States Senate Report 711, 75th Cong., 1st Sess., 23.
[13] C. Herman Pritchett, The Roosevelt Court (New York, The Macmillan Co., 1948), 32–34.
[14] Ibid., 25.

Klux Klan and with having been one of the President's supporters in his court-packing plan. Too, he had opposed the confirmation of the Chief Justice in 1930.

By the retirement of Justice Van Devanter, the conservative bloc had been reduced to three, and the following January, when Justice Sutherland retired and Stanley Reed, formerly solicitor general, was appointed in his place, a new day had dawned.

The time was ripe for a lagging court to catch up with the trend of the times, for adherence to the policies expressed by Holmes's and Brandeis' dissents in the days of the White and Taft courts, especially those rejecting dependence on equal protection and due process under the Fourteenth Amendment to create a superlegislature of the high court. Now the Court was ready for a renascence of the Waite policy of judicial restraint.

But this change, as effected, was accompanied by a startling increase of dissent, dissent from the decisions of the past and dissent from the decisions of the present. C. Herman Pritchett, in his study of the Roosevelt court, computed the dissents from 1930 to 1946 and found that the high for the 1930–36 period was 19 per cent and that, beginning with the 1937 term, they increased almost steadily to a maximum of 64 per cent in 1946–47.[15]

The erosion of the Sutherland bloc ended Roberts' period of dominance, and the interment of the court-packing plan left Roberts free to be himself. For a diversity of reasons which have been the subject of subsequent professorial rumination and speculation, the 1937 term marked the beginning of a housecleaning which, according to Justice Douglas,[16] resulted in twenty-six decisions expressly overruling precedents, of which nineteen were in constitutional cases. Of course, as examination of decisions demonstrates, Justice Douglas' statement is sober understatement, for the fact of the matter is that the Court went on a rampage as dissent produced a plethora of "limiting," "explaining," and "distinguishing" decisions, often when objection to "overruling" might jeopardize alliances. And the fact that the decisions "limited," "explained," "distinguished," or "overruled" happened to be of recent vintage did not matter. For they were decanted and, with the older vintages, poured into the newly fashioned bottles.

In six cases, all of which were decided by a divided court, fourteen cases were distinguished, four were limited, and one was explained.[17] In one of

[15] Ibid.

[16] William O. Douglas, We the Judges (Garden City, N.Y., Doubleday & Co., 1956), 431.

[17] James v. Dravo Contracting Co., 302 U.S. 134 (1937); Baltimore & Ohio R.R. v. United States, 264 U.S. 258 (1924); Frost v. Corporation Commission, 278 U.S. 515 (1929); Railroad Commission v. Pacific Gas Co., 302 U.S. 388 (1938); Indiana ex rel. Anderson v. Brand, 303 U.S. 95 (1938); Santa Cruz Co. v. NLRB, 303 U.S. 453 (1938); United States v. Bekins, 304 U.S. 27 (1938); Webster Elec. Co. v. Splitdorf Elec. Co., 264 U.S. 463 (1924). Helvering v. Gerhardt; Helvering v. Wilson; Helvering v. Mulcahy, 304 U.S. 405 (1938).

these Roberts dissented, saying that "the judgment seems to me to overrule, *sub silentio,* a century of precedents."[18]

When the Court sent a rate case back to the district court with instructions to determine reproduction value,[19] freshman Justice Black, who was to demonstrate that he had come to the Court with some strong preconceived notions, surprised with the unusual step of dissenting from a per curiam opinion. He said, with justice, that the particular rate proceeding had commenced in 1931, that it was now 1937, and that after the second trial that had been ordered by the Court the case would be back again, probably in 1943, so that the trial court, in fixing reproduction values, would have to guess what price levels would be *in futuro,* in coming to its conclusion.[20]

The point of Justice Black's sound objection was disclosed when he said: "For the first hundred years of this Nation's history, federal courts did not interfere with state legislation fixing maximum rates for public services performed within the respective states." He then quoted Chief Justice Waite in Munn v. Illinois: " '. . . against abuses by legislatures, the people must resort to the polls, not to the courts.' "[21] And, he continued, when in 1890 "a divided court finally repudiated its earlier constitutional interpretation and declared that due process of law requires judicial invalidation of legislative rates which the courts believe confiscatory, the dissenting justices adhered to the long existing principle that regulation of public utilities was a 'legislative prerogative and not a judicial one.' "[22]

Further illustration of the Dickensian longevity and complications of litigation: a suit involving the basic question of the market value of natural gas called for this opening statement by Justice Jackson, writing for a majority during a subsequent term, over the dissent of the Chief Justice and Justice Reed: "This litigation, begun a decade ago, has been terminated by a summary judgment, and whether rightly so is the issue. The suit has weathered four adjudications, including two trials, in District Court and four decisions by the Court of Appeals."[23] And then the high court reversed the judgment below and the case went back for further litigation.

Seven members of the Court struck down a taxing statute of California which undertook to tax receipts received in Connecticut on reinsurance contracts with California insurance companies, as transgressing the due process clause of the Fourteenth Amendment. Justice Black startled the Court by contending that the due process clause in the Fourteenth Amendment was

---

18 James v. Dravo Contracting Co., 302 U.S. 134, 161 (1937).
19 McCart v. Indianapolis Water Co., 302 U.S. 419 (1938).
20 *Ibid.,* 423 *et seq.*
21 *Ibid.,* 427.
22 *Ibid.,* 428.
23 Sartor v. Arkansas Nat. Gas Corp., 321 U.S. 620 (1944).

restricted to "persons" and that "persons," as so employed, did not include corporations. He said, "I believe this Court should now overrule previous decisions which interpreted the Fourteenth Amendment to include corporations."[24]

No member of the Court was moved. Later, after William O. Douglas was appointed to the bench, he was persuaded to join with Black in dissenting on the basis of this view,[25] despite a long line of cases to the contrary.

While Justice Black was thus willing to disregard the rule of stare decisis when a favored theory was involved, elsewhere Justice Roberts was available to rally to its support. Here, in a tax case, the issue was the rule of stare decisis. Justice Frankfurter, writing for the majority, concerning interpretation of the statute, which had previously been construed and with which construction the Court no longer agreed, said:

> . . . stare decisis embodies an important social policy. It represents an element of continuity in law, and is rooted in the psychologic need to satisfy reasonable expectations. But stare decisis is the principle of policy and not a mechanical formula of adherence to the latest decision, however recent and questionable, when such adherence involves collision with a prior doctrine more embracing in its scope, intrinsically sounder, and verified by experience. . . .
>
> Nor does want of specific congressional repudiations [of the former interpretation] serve as an implied instruction by Congress to us not to reconsider, in the light of new experience.[26]

Justice Roberts, dissenting, pointed out that Congress had "three times re-enacted the law." He said that "the settled doctrine, that re-enactment of a statute so construed, without alteration, renders such construction a part of the statute itself."[27] He went on, "To nullify more than fifty decisions, five of them by this court, some of which have stood for a decade, in order to change a mere rule of statutory construction, seems to me an altogether unwise and unjustified exertion of power."[28] Justice McReynolds joined in Roberts' dissent.

According to Pritchett, Justice Black dissented fifteen times during the term, eleven of the dissents being sole. The two remaining members of the diminished rearguard, Justices McReynolds and Butler, kept the flag flying, McReynolds having twenty-eight dissents and Butler twenty-two. Obviously, the conservatives no longer held the helm. The percentage of dissents during the term was twenty-seven.

[24] Connecticut Gen. Life Ins. Co. v. Johnson, 303 U.S. 77 (1938).
[25] Wheeling Steel Corp. v. Glander, 337 U.S. 562, 576 (1949).
[26] Helvering v. Hallock; Helvering v. Squire; Rothensies v. Huston; Bryant v. Helvering, 309 U.S. 106, 119 (1940).
[27] Ibid., 123.
[28] Ibid., 129–30.

As a result of the death of Justice Cardozo in July, the 1938–39 term opened with eight justices, the same number that had functioned because of the illness of Justice Cardozo, after the retirement of Justice Sutherland and the appointment of Justice Reed. Felix Frankfurter, Harvard professor of law, who had been a New Deal activist from its beginning, survived the Senate committee hearings and finally took the seat vacated by Cardozo on January 30, 1939. Then, Justice Brandeis having retired in February, William O. Douglas, chairman of the Securities and Exchange Commission, was appointed in his place. The pattern of the prior term stressing dissent continued.[29]

During the term a noteworthy case was heard which arose from the fact that in June, 1924, Congress proposed an amendment to the Constitution, known as the Child Labor Amendment. In January, 1925, the Kansas legislature rejected the proposed amendment. In 1937 a resolution was introduced in the Kansas senate, which consisted of forty members, to ratify the proposed amendment. When the resolution came up for consideration, the vote was twenty to twenty, and the Lieutenant Governor, the presiding officer, voted in favor. The lower house also adopted the resolution. Thereupon the twenty senators who had voted against the resolution and three members of the house, instituted a mandamus proceeding to compel the secretary of the senate to certify that the amendment had not been adopted, upon the ground that the Lieutenant Governor was not qualified to vote. The state court denied the writ, and the supreme court of the state affirmed. On appeal, the high court, finding that it had jurisdiction, affirmed.[30] Justice Black wrote a concurring opinion, in which Justices Roberts, Frankfurter, and Douglas joined. Black believed, for reasons stated by Justice Frankfurter, that the Court lacked jurisdiction, but that since a majority had held otherwise, they would go along, on the ground that, "since Congress has sole and complete control over the amending process, subject to no judicial review, the views of any court upon this process cannot be binding upon Congress. . . ."[31] Justice Frankfurter said, "One who is merely the self-constituted spokesman of a constitutional point of view cannot ask us to pass on it."[32] However, Justice Butler wrote in dissent, Justice McReynolds joining him.

During the 1938 term three prior cases were expressly and two impliedly overruled, one was disapproved, two were limited and eleven were distinguished. Four New Deal acts were found valid, two unanimously. The government was sustained in three tax cases. Six state statutes were sustained. Negroes were upheld in two civil rights cases. However, the NLRB did not

[29] Pritchett, *The Roosevelt Court*, 35–37.
[30] Coleman v. Miller, 307 U.S. 433 (1939).
[31] *Ibid.*, 459.
[32] *Ibid.*, 467.

fare too well at the hands of the Court in four cases. Accompanying a rise in dissents to 34 per cent,[33] there were many concurring opinions.

Roberts' swing to the right was evidenced by his alliance with Butler and McReynolds in eleven of his thirteen dissents. The latter continued to sing their swan songs with thirty-two and thirty-four dissents respectively. Of the rest, Black was the principal dissenter, with seven dissents by himself of a total of seventeen.[34]

The 1939–40 term was marked by the death of Justice Butler on November 16, 1939, and the entry of the superliberal Frank Murphy of Michigan on February 5, 1940. Thus the conservative ranks were denuded and the superliberal New Deal ranks augmented. With the appointment of Murphy, the President had packed the Court with his own majority. While the liberal activists thus became powerful, their inability or unwillingness to compromise, their lack of experience in leading and consolidating, and their intransigence and personal obduracy fabricated opposition. Thus the Chief Justice, who had prided himself on his liberality, who had dissented twice during the 1936 term and had not dissented at all during the 1937 term, dissented fourteen times during the 1939 term and, in his last year of service, registered twenty-four dissents, of which nineteen were with Roberts and eight with McReynolds, the archconservative, who himself dissented only nine times. Roberts, conservative by inclination, was encouraged by liberal intransigence to register twenty-three dissents, while McReynolds was leading with thirty-two.[35] Thus it was evidenced that the liberals were in control, as it was made clear that no one could control the liberals. The "distinguishing technique" was remarked by Justice Roberts when Justice Stone, writing for six members, distinguished two prior decisions; and Roberts, dissenting, while relying on the distinguished cases, said: ". . . it is apparent that, under the guise of distinguishing the earlier case, the court in fact overrules it."[36]

The 1940–41 term was marked by the retirement of the last of the Four Horsemen: Justice McReynolds retired on February 1, 1941. He had dissented to the last. His successor was not appointed until too late in the term to function; hence, from the time of his resignation, the Court again consisted of eight members.

The pattern of the previous term continued: dissent, notably from previous decisions and a continuation of the Roberts and Hughes embracery of the antiliberalism engendered by their free-wheeling associates. As to the former, the Court overruled four prior decisions, two of them being on constitutional

---

[33] Pritchett, *The Roosevelt Court*, 37.
[34] *Ibid.*, 36.
[35] *Ibid.*, 37.
[36] Deitrick v. Greaney, 309 U.S. 190, 206 (1940).

rulings, distinguished six, and explained three. In nine cases Justice Roberts and the Chief Justice dissented on questions of interpretation.[37]

In a one-hundred page opinion Justice Douglas, writing for a unanimous court, affirmed convictions under an indictment charging violations of the Sherman Anti-Trust Act.[38] The Court followed one prior decision[39] and distinguished seven others.[40]

In twenty-one of twenty-eight cases[41] involving taxes, there were dissents. In the twenty-eight cases nine prior cases were distinguished and three were overruled.

While the liberals on the Court tended to deify personal rights and to denigrate property rights, the areas of civil rights and the rights of labor did not escape the blight of disagreement. Of ten cases affecting labor,[42] only one was unanimous while five previous cases were being distinguished.

So the Court, in an opinion by the Chief Justice, had to overcome the dissent of McReynolds and Butler, to hold that the equal protection clause of the Fourteenth Amendment was violated, when a Negro was refused admission

[37] Maguire v. Commissioner, 313 U.S. 1 (1941): Helvering v. Gambrill, 313 U.S. 11 (1941); Helvering v. Campbell; Helvering v. Knox; Helvering v. Rogers, 313 U.S. 15 (1941); Helvering v. Reynolds, 313 U.S. 428 (1941); Cary v. Commissioner; Flagler v. Commissioner; Est. of Flagler v. Commissioner; Matthews v. Commissioner, 313 U.S. 441 (1941).

[38] United States v. Socony-Vacuum Oil Co.; Socony-Vacuum Oil Co. v. United States, 310 U.S. 150 (1940).

[39] United States v. Trenton Potteries, 273 U.S. 392 (1927).

[40] Standard Oil Co. v. United States, 221 U.S. 1 (1911); United States v. American Tobacco Co., 221 U.S. 106 (1911); Chicago Board of Trade v. United States, 246 U.S. 231 (1918); Maple Flooring Mfrs. Assoc. v. United States, 268 U.S. 563 (1925); Cement Mfrs. Assoc. v. United States, 268 U.S. 588 (1925); Sugar Inst. v. United States, 297 U.S. 553 (1936); Appalachian Coals v. United States, 288 U.S. 344 (1933).

[41] White v. United States, 305 U.S. 281 (1938); Helvering v. Chester N. Weaver Co., 305 U.S. 293 (1938); Cooney v. Mountain States Tel. Co., 294 U.S. 384 (1935); Ozark Pipe Line v. Monier, 266 U.S. 555 (1925); Puget Sound Co. v. Tax Commission, 302 U.S. 90 (1937); Western Live Stock v. Bureau of Revenue, 303 U.S. 250 (1938); Welch v. Henry, 305 U.S. 134 (1938); Curry v. McCanless, 307 U.S. 357 (1939); Graves v. Elliott, 307 U.S. 383 (1939); McGoldrick v. Berwind-White Co., 309 U.S. 33 (1940); McGoldrick v. DuGrenier; McGoldrick v. Felt & T. Mfg. Co., 309 U.S. 70 (1940); Robbins v. Shelby County Tax Dist., 120 U.S. 489 (1887); McGoldrick v. Compagnie Gen. Trans., 309 U.S. 430 (1940); Helvering v. Leonard, 310 U.S. 80 (1940); Helvering v. Fuller, 310 U.S. 69 (1940); Ford Motor Co. v. Beauchamp, 308 U. S. 331 (1939); Buckstaff Bath House Co. v. McKinley, 308 U.S. 358 (1939); Deputy v. du Pont, 308 U.S. 488 (1940); Colgate v. Harvey, 296 U.S. 404 (1935); Helvering v. Fitch, 309 U.S. 149 (1940); McCarroll v. Dixie Lines, 309 U.S. 176 (1940); Helvering v. Hallock, 309 U.S. 106 (1940); Whitney v. Tax Commission, 309 U.S. 530 (1940); Connecticut Gen. Life Ins. Co. v. Johnson, 303 U.S. 77 (1938); Wisconsin v. Minnesota M. & M. Co., 311 U.S. 452 (1940); Helvering v. Horst, 311 U.S. 112 (1940); Helvering v. Eubank, 311 U.S. 122 (1940).

[42] Milk Wagon Drivers v. Meadowmoor Dairies, 312 U.S. 287 (1941); A. F. of L. v. Swing, 312 U.S. 321 (1941); NLRB v. Express Pub. Co., 312 U.S. 426 (1941); NLRB v. Fansteel Metal Corp., 306 U.S. 240 (1939); NLRB v. Columbian Co., 306 U.S. 292 (1939); NLRB v. Sands Mfg. Co., 306 U.S. 332 (1939); Pacific Ins. Co. v. Industrial Accident Commission, 306 U.S. 493 (1939); Apex Hosiery Co. v. Leader, 310 U.S. 469 (1940); Thornhill v. Alabama, 310 U.S. 88 (1940); Carlson v. California, 310 U.S. 106 (1940).

196

to the law school of the University of Missouri.[43] It held that a provision for the state to pay the Negro's tuition at the university of any adjacent state was insufficient to avoid a finding of discrimination. Though the state contended that it intended to establish a law school for Negroes, the Chief Justice did not undertake to pass on the question of whether that would satisfy the Amendment. Instead, he concluded that the petitioner was entitled to be admitted to the law school of the state university in the absence of other and proper provision for his legal training within the state, thus not departing from the doctrine of the Plessy case.

Characteristically, Justice McReynolds said in dissent:

> For a long time Missouri has acted upon the view that the best interests of her people demands separation of whites and Negroes in schools. Under the opinion just announced, I presume she may abandon her law school and thereby disadvantage her white citizens without improving petitioner's opportunities for legal instruction; or she may break down the settled practice concerning separate schools and thereby, as indicated by experience, damnify both races.[44]

A majority of six, over the dissent of Butler and McReynolds, held that the Fifteenth Amendment prohibited "sophisticated as well as simple-minded modes of discrimination" in registration for voting, as well as "onerous procedural requirements which effectively handicap exercise of the franchise by the colored race, although the abstract right to vote may remain unrestricted as to race."[45] Accordingly, the Court held that a Negro unlawfully prevented from registration might maintain an action for damages under the Civil Rights Act. Justice Douglas did not sit. The Court distinguished a prior decision.[46]

The growing power of the CIO, the national labor organization, clashed with the dying power of Frank ("I am the Law") Hague, mayor of Jersey City, New Jersey, whose claim of dictatorship founded his pseudonym. Hague attempted to keep the CIO out of Jersey City through the medium of an ordinance that required a permit, issued at the discretion of the director of public safety, for any public assembly in or upon the public streets, highways, parks, or public buildings of the city. An injunction against the enforcement of the ordinance issued by the district court was modified by the high court when it held the ordinance void.[47]

Justice Butler announced a splintered court in these terms:

The judgment of the Court in this case is that the decree is modified and as

[43] Missouri *ex rel.* Gaines v. Canada, 305 U.S. 337 (1938).
[44] *Ibid.,* 353.
[45] Lane v. Wilson, 307 U.S. 268, 275 (1939).
[46] Giles v. Harris, 189 U.S. 475 (1903).
[47] Hague v. CIO, 307 U.S. 496 (1939).

modified affirmed. Mr. Justice Frankfurter and Mr. Justice Douglas took no part in the consideration or decision of the case. Mr. Justice Roberts has an opinion in which Mr. Justice Black concurs, and Mr. Justice Stone an opinion in which Mr. Justice Reed concurs. The Chief Justice concurs in an opinion. Mr. Justice McReynolds and Mr. Justice Butler dissent for reasons stated in opinions by them respectively.[48]

Justice Roberts' opinion held that the ordinance violated the privileges and immunities clause of the Fourteenth Amendment. Justice Stone saw no need for such a finding, pointing out that of "fifty or more cases which have been brought to this Court since the adoption of the Fourteenth Amendment . . . in only a single case was a statute held to infringe" that clause.[49] He did not see why the due process clause of the Fourteenth Amendment, as held in the Gitlow case, did not suffice to void the ordinance.[50] The Chief Justice concurred, saying he agreed with Justice Roberts that the CIO's rights in the premises constituted a privilege as a citizen of the United States, but he agreed with Justice Stone that the record was deficient in that respect. Justice McReynolds thought the bill for the injunction should have been dismissed, and Justice Butler thought the ordinance was constitutional. Of the seven sitting Justices, only Reed and Black did not take up their pens. Justice Roberts distinguished a prior decision[51] on which, naturally, Justice Butler relied.

A Minnesota statute defining "psychopathic personalities" and authorizing proceedings against them was held valid despite a Fourteenth Amendment objection.[52] The definition was held sufficiently definite. It read:

The existence in any person of such conditions of emotional instability, or impulsiveness of behavior or lack of customary standards of good judgment, or failure to appreciate the consequences of his acts, or a combination of any such conditions, as to render such person irresponsible for his conduct with respect to sexual matters and thereby dangerous to other persons.[53]

Later, during the 1966 term, the Court had occasion to pass upon the same definition in connection with the deportation of a homosexual alien, pursuant to a provision in the Immigration Act of 1952 excluding aliens "afflicted with psychopathic personality." Six members of the Court sustained the deportation order. Justices Brennan, Douglas, and Fortas dissented, contending that the definition was constitutionally vague.[54] The case gave Justice Douglas op-

[48] *Ibid.* 500.
[49] *Ibid.,* 520 n.1.
[50] *Ibid.,* 519.
[51] Davis v. Massachusetts, 167 U.S. 43 (1897).
[52] Minnesota v. Probate Court, 309 U.S. 270 (1940).
[53] *Ibid.,* 272.

portunity to indulge in favored extracurricular roving in the bypaths of psychiatry and elsewhere.

As the Chief Justice and Justice Roberts emulated Achates and Aeneas in dissenting during the term, so an affinity sprang up between Justices Douglas and Black, who joined in fifteen dissents and in other common votes in a variety of issues and cases, while neither dissented with any other Justice without the other.[55] Thus we find them joining forces with Roberts to dissent from a tax opinion of Justice Murphy's for a majority of six.[56]

Again they joined with Justices Frankfurter and Murphy in opposing a five-man majority holding that Congress had the power to require a plaintiff in a negligence suit to submit to a mental or physical examination, despite what Justice Frankfurter termed an invasion of privacy.[57] They joined with Justice Reed in opposing a finding that the Federal Trade Commission lacked authority to prevent the use of unfair methods of competition in interstate commerce.[58] Justice Frankfurter, writing for the majority, distinguished a prior case[59] upon which the dissenters relied. The Douglas and Black minds also met in a dissent in two inheritance tax cases.[60]

An opinion by Justice Frankfurter affirming the power of the NLRB to denominate as an unfair labor practice the refusal of an employer to hire employees solely because of their affiliations with a labor union resulted in a remand to the Board for consideration of two matters out of six considered.[61] Justice Murphy wrote, disapproving the modification, with the concurrence of Justices Black and Douglas. The Chief Justice and Justice Stone also disagreed concerning two other rulings of the majority. Justice Roberts did not participate. A companion case went the same way.[62]

Justices Black and Douglas joined with Justice Murphy in dissenting from a ruling that a federal court might award interest upon a contractual obligation to the United States as damages for delay in payment, at a rate prevailing in the state where the obligation was to be performed.[63]

To the ruling of a majority of six that the federal Criminal Code justified the indictment of election officers in Louisiana who conspired to falsify the

---

[54] Boutilier v. Immigration Service, 387 U.S. 118 (1967).

[55] Pritchett, *The Roosevelt Court*, 38.

[56] Neuberger v. Commissioner, 311 U.S. 83 (1940).

[57] Sibbach v. Wilson, 312 U.S. 1 (1941).

[58] Federal Trade Commission v. Bunte Bros., 312 U.S. 349 (1941).

[59] Houston & Texas R.R., Texas & Pac. R.R. v. United States, 234 U.S. 342 (1914).

[60] Maass v. Higgins; Estate of Abendroth v. Commissioner; Estate of Blacque v. Commissioner, 312 U.S. 443 (1941).

[61] Phelps Dodge v. NLRB, 313 U.S. 177 (1941).

[62] Continental Oil Co. v. NLRB, 313 U.S. 212 (1941).

[63] Royal Indemnity v. United States, 313 U.S. 289 (1941).

result of a primary to select congressional candidates, Justices Douglas, Black, and Murphy dissented.[64]

Basic to its conclusion, the majority found that the Constitution protected voters in a primary as well as in a general congressional election which, in effect, overruled the prior Newberry case. Justice Douglas, writing for the dissenters, expressly stated his disagreement with this facet of the Newberry case, while disagreeing that the statute under which the indictment was found provided for criminal penalties.

To a five-man finding that the Union Pacific Railroad had violated the Elkins Act, Justices Black and Douglas joined Justice Roberts in dissent.[65]

Black and Douglas joined in a majority opinion written by Justice Mc-Reynolds, in which Justices Murphy and Roberts joined to make a majority. When Justice Frankfurter wrote, concurring, Black and Douglas joined in that too. Then Justice Stone wrote, dissenting, joined by the Chief Justice and Justice Reed. The issue involved affirmance by the majority of a dismissal of a bill for an injunction to prevent a railroad from extending its line to a market operated by competitors of the plaintiff.[66]

Black and Douglas voted together in disapproving the Pennsylvania Alien Registration Act upon the ground that Congress had preempted the subject. The Chief Justice and Justices Stone and McReynolds dissented.[67]

The Black-Douglas team pulled together in four unanimous decisions worthy of mention:

(1) In affirming the conviction of Earl R. Browder, head of the United States Communist party, for using a passport obtained by false statements designed to facilitate re-entry into the country.[68] The decision distinguished a prior decision.[69]

(2) In giving the Jehovah's Witnesses' cause a setback when the Court affirmed the conviction of five Witnesses who, with sixty-three others, attempted to conduct an "information march" without a permit to parade, as required by a New Hampshire statute.[70]

(3) In approving the separate but equal doctrine laid down by the Plessy case while reversing the dismissal of a Negro congressman's complaint to the Interstate Commerce Commission that he was denied Pullman accommodations on a train from Chicago to Little Rock, Arkansas.[71]

[64] United States v. Classic, 313 U.S. 299 (1941).
[65] Union Pac. R.R. v. United States, 313 U.S. 450 (1941).
[66] Singer v. Union Pac. R.R.; Kansas City v. Singer, 311 U.S. 295 (1940).
[67] Hines v. Davidowitz, 312 U.S. 52 (1941).
[68] Browder v. United States, 312 U.S. 335 (1941).
[69] United States v. Murdock, 290 U.S. 389 (1933).
[70] Cox v. New Hampshire, 312 U.S. 569 (1941).
[71] Mitchell v. United States, 313 U.S. 80 (1941).

(4) In finally disposing of the eleven-year-old Morgan case on its fourth trip to the Court, over the dissent of Justice Roberts, by approving an order of the Secretary of Agriculture fixing the same rates as he fixed in the invalid order of June 1933.[72]

However, one of the rare occasions on which Black and Douglas differed was, of all things, on a civil liberties question during the later 1943 term. In a prosecution under the Espionage Act of 1917, the first such in the course of World War II, the Court was confronted with the question of whether defendant's pamphlets willfully obstructed the recruiting and enlistment service of the United States. Justice Murphy, writing for a majority and referring to Justice Holmes's dissent in the Abrams case, found the charge not proved.[73] Justice Reed wrote, dissenting, supported by Justices Frankfurter, Douglas, and Jackson, maintaining that there was sufficient evidence to justify the jury's verdict and referred to Justice Holmes's opinion for the Court in the Schenck case. Interestingly enough, Justice Roberts played his former role of being the fifth and anchor man to determine what the majority decision should be.

The conclusion of the 1940 term marked the conclusion of the services of the Chief Justice; his resignation took effect shortly thereafter.

[72] United States v. Morgan, 313 U.S. 409 (1941).
[73] *Ex parte* Endo, 323 U.S. 283 (1944).

CHAPTER XI

The Post-New Deal Court

IN 1937, WHEN THE COURT WAS CALLED UPON to consider the first of the Jehovah's Witnesses cases to come before it, it found itself enmeshed in a series of cases with intertwined free speech and practice of religion problems that were to plague communities well into the forties.

The first of the cases, involving the distribution of pamphlets and magazines in the nature of religious tracts setting forth the gospel of the Kingdom of Jehovah, came to the Court as a result of the conviction of Alma Lovell for violation of a city ordinance of the city of Griffin, Georgia. The ordinance forbade distribution of literature without written permission from the city manager. The defendant did not apply for a permit, since she regarded herself as "sent by Jehovah to do his work."[1]

A unanimous Court, in an opinion by the Chief Justice, held that the Gitlow case was authority for the inclusion in the protections of the Fourteenth Amendment, including freedom of speech and freedom of the press; hence it held the ordinance violated the Fourteenth Amendment.

Thereafter, as its last decision of the 1939 term, Justice Frankfurter rendered an opinion for seven members, with which Justice McReynolds concurred and from which only Justice Stone dissented, in a case which involved the difficult and delicate issue of whether the requirement of participation by pupils in public schools in the ceremony of saluting the national flag did not, in the case of a pupil who refused to participate on sincere religious grounds, infringe, without due process of law, upon the liberty guaranteed by the Fourteenth Amendment. The Gobitis children had been expelled from the public schools of Minersville, Pennsylvania, for refusing to salute the national flag as part of a daily school exercise. They had been brought up by their parents, members of Jehovah's Witnesses, to believe that saluting the flag was forbidden by the Scriptures. Justice Frankfurter said the issue lay between "the conflicting claims of liberty and authority." But, after discussing these and a diversity of related matters, he concluded, by falling back on

[1] Lovell v. City of Griffin, 303 U.S. 444 (1938).

Justice Waite's early precept, that "to the legislature no less than to courts is committed the guardianship of deeply-cherished liberties."[2]

When eight members of the Court held with "authority" vis-à-vis "liberty," as determined by the legislature, Justice Stone, alone, laid the foundation in a dissent for the 1943 overruling of the decision of the majority.[3]

Justice Stone wrote:

> The guaranties of civil liberty are but guaranties of freedom of the human mind and spirit and of reasonable freedom and opportunity to express them. They presuppose the right of the individual to hold such opinions as he will and to give them reasonably free expression. . . . If these guaranties are to have any meaning they must, I think, be deemed to withhold from the state any authority to compel belief or the expression of it where that expression violates religious convictions, whatever may be the legislative view of the desirability of such compulsion.
>
> History teaches us that there have been but few infringements of personal liberty by the state which have not been justified, as they are here, in the name of righteousness and the public good, and few which have not been directed, as they are now, at politically helpless minorities. . . .[4] The Constitution may well elicit expressions of loyalty to it and to the government which it created, but it does not command such expressions. . . . And while such expressions of loyalty, when voluntarily given, may promote national unity, it is quite another matter to say that their compulsory expression by children in violation of their own and their parents' religious convictions can be regarded as playing so important a part in our national unity . . . despite the constitutional guarantee of freedom of religion. . . .[5]
>
> The Constitution expresses more than the conviction of the people that democratic processes must be preserved at all costs. It is also an expression of faith and command that freedom of mind and spirit must be preserved.[6]

Meanwhile and later, situations similar to that presented by the Lovell case had arisen and called for similar disposition. A group of four cases[7] brought to the Court ordinances from towns in New Jersey, California, Wisconsin, and Massachusetts, each of which sought to restrict the distribution of literature. The California conviction had stemmed from distribution of notices of a meeting of Friends of the Lincoln Brigade, presumably a leftist group, the Wisconsin literature pertained to a labor dispute, the New Jersey material was from Jehovah's Witnesses, the Massachusetts leaflets concerned a protest

[2] Minersville School Dist v. Gobitis, 310 U.S. 586, 600 (1940).
[3] West Virginia Board of Education v. Barnette, 319 U.S. 624 (1943).
[4] Minersville School Dist. v. Gobitis, 310 U.S. 586, 604 (1940).
[5] *Ibid.*, 605.
[6] *Ibid.*, 606.
[7] Schneider v. Irvington; Young v. California; Snyder v. Milwaukee; Nichols v. Massachusetts, 308 U.S. 147 (1939).

in connection with the administration of state unemployment insurance. The Court applied the rule of the Lovell case and held the ordinances void under the Fourteenth Amendment.

A later case[8] struck down a Connecticut statute that left it to the secretary of the public welfare council to determine whether solicitation for any alleged religious, charitable, or philanthropic cause was bona fide. It reversed the conviction of members of the Jehovah's Witnesses sect who, having received permission to do so, played a phonograph record attacking Roman Catholicism.

Then followed the affirmance of the conviction of a Mr. Cox and a Mr. Chaplinsky, who had participated in what the Court considered a "parade" without obtaining a permit as required by a local ordinance and the subsequent and second conviction of Chaplinsky for distributing Jehovah's Witnesses' literature and denouncing complainant as a racketeer and a fascist.[9]

Meanwhile, the Jehovah's Witnesses had also suffered the Gobitis setback and now a man named Jones appealed from a conviction in a state court of Arizona. The majority opinion affirming the conviction was written by Justice Reed and held that a licensing ordinance applied to transient agents, dealers, or distributors of books also required payment of a license fee by Jehovah's Witnesses for distribution of books setting forth their views in return for a contribution of twenty-five cents a book.[10] If a person was unable to contribute, the contribution in some instances was waived. The majority held the sale of the books sufficiently commercial to warrant the imposition of the license fee.

The Chief Justice, writing in dissent, held that the ordinance prohibited the free exercise of religion. He was joined by Justices Black, Douglas, and Murphy; in turn, all four joined in an opinion by Murphy, who said the distributors were ordained ministers "evangelizing their faith."[11] Then Justices Black, Douglas, and Murphy subscribed to another dissenting opinion, in which they said:

> This is but another step in the direction which Minersville School District v. Gobitis . . . took against the same religious minority and is a logical extension of the principles upon which that decision rested. Since we joined in the opinion in the Gobitis case, we think this is an appropriate occasion to state that we now believe that it was also wrongly decided.[12]

Then the Court granted reargument, and the case was argued with a group

[8] Cantwell v. Connecticut, 310 U.S. 296 (1940).
[9] Cox v. New Hampshire, 312 U.S. 569 (1941); Chaplinsky v. New Hampshire, 315 U.S. 568 (1942).
[10] Jones v. Opelika; Jobin v. Arizona, 316 U.S. 584 (1942).
[11] *Ibid.*, 612.
[12] *Ibid.*, 623–24.

of other cases. Meanwhile, the Court had voided one municipal ordinance forbidding distribution of handbills on city streets at the instance of a member of Jehovah's Witnesses,[13] and had voided another making it unlawful for any person to solicit orders or to sell books or merchandise without a permit issued only after the mayor deemed it advisable.[14]

On reargument, the Court vacated the judgments and convictions in three cases[15] for the reasons stated in a companion case,[16] in which it managed to obtain a five-man majority by the accession of the newcomer Rutledge, who was to prove an ardent liberal, replacing the conservative Byrnes. In this case, the Court held an ordinance imposing a license fee for the privilege of canvassing or soliciting within a municipality, when applied to religious disseminators selling their books or pamphlets, an unconstitutional invasion of the rights of freedom of religion, speech, and press.

In addition to Justice Rutledge, the majority was composed of the Chief Justice, the solitary dissenter in the Gobitis case, and the recanting trio, Justices Black, Douglas, and Murphy, who had confessed fault publicly in the Jones case. Of the dissenters, Justices Reed and Frankfurter wrote while Justice Jackson, who wrote in a companion case, had that opinion stand as a dissent in the present case.

For the majority, Justice Douglas said: "... an itinerant evangelist, however misguided or intolerant he may be, does not become a mere book agent by selling the Bible or religious tracts to help defray his expenses or to sustain him. Freedom of speech, freedom of the press, freedom of religion are available to all, not merely to those who can pay their own way."[17]

Justice Reed based his dissent on the fact that the "plan of national distribution by the Watch Tower Bible & Tract Society . . . justifies the characterization of the transaction as a sale by all the state courts."[18] He added, "The rites which are protected by the First Amendment are in essence spiritual—prayer, mass, sermons, sacrament—not sales of religious goods."[19]

Justice Frankfurter's supplement said in addition:

A tax can be a means for raising revenue, or a device for regulating conduct, or both. . . . Their [the Witnesses'] claim is that no tax, no matter how trifling, can constitutionally be laid upon the activity of distributing religious literature. . . . [20]

---

[13] Jamison v. Texas, 318 U.S. 413 (1943).
[14] Largent v. Texas, 318 U.S. 418 (1943).
[15] Jones v. Opelika; Jobin v. Arizona; Bowden v. Fort Smith, 319 U.S. 103 (1943).
[16] Murdock v. Pennsylvania, 319 U.S. 105 (1943).
[17] *Ibid.*, 111.
[18] *Ibid.*, 119.
[19] *Ibid.*, 132.
[20] *Ibid.*, 134.

It cannot be said that the petitioners are constitutionally exempt from taxation merely because they may be engaged in religious activities.... It will hardly be contended, for example, that a tax upon the income of a clergyman would violate the Bill of Rights, even though the tax is ultimately borne by the members of his church....[21]

There is no doubt that these petitioners, like all who use the streets, have received the benefits of government. . . . To secure them costs money and a state's source of money is its taxing power. There is nothing in the Constitution which exempts persons engaged in religious activities from sharing equally in the costs of benefits to all, including themselves, provided by government.[22]

Simultaneously, the Court struck down an ordinance of an Ohio town forbidding anyone to ring doorbells for the purpose of distributing literature, upon the ground that it failed to distinguish between householders who were willing to receive the literature and those who were not.[23] Justice Murphy wrote, concurring. Justices Reed, Roberts, and Jackson dissented. Justice Frankfurter wrote, indicating that he was not quite certain what the scope of the majority holding was and left his own conclusions in equal ambiguity.

Another Jehovah's Witnesses decision handed down the same day held that a court should not enjoin criminal prosecution of Witnesses violating an allegedly void licensing statute. The Chief Justice, writing for the majority, indicated that the statute was unconstitutional and would be so found by the criminal court.[24]

Justice Jackson wrote, concurring in this case, but dissenting in the two previous cases.[25] He recited in detail the methods and practices of the Witnesses and the content of the distributed literature and said, "I dissent—a disagreement induced in no small part by the facts recited."

He said further:

The stubborn persistence of the officials of smaller communities in their efforts to regulate this conduct indicates a strongly held conviction that the Court's many decisions in this field are at odds with the realities of life in these communities. . . .[26]

Doubtless there exist fellow spirits who welcome these callers, but the issue here is what are the rights of those who do not and what is the right of the community to protect them in the exercise of their own faith in peace. . . .[27]

21 *Ibid.*, 135.
22 *Ibid.*, 140.
23 Martin v. Struthers, 319 U.S. 141 (1943).
24 Douglas v. Jeanette, 319 U.S. 157, 165 (1943).
25 *Ibid.*, 166 *et seq.*
26 *Ibid.*, 174.
27 *Ibid.*, 177.

The real question is where do their rights end and the rights of others begin. . . .[28]

The First Amendment grew out of an experience which taught that society cannot trust the conscience of a majority to keep its religious zeal within the limits that a free society can tolerate. . . . Civil government cannot let any group ride roughshod over others simply because their "consciences" tell them to do so. . . .[29]

This Court is forever adding new stories to the temples of constitutional law, and the temples have a way of collapsing when one story too many is added. So it was with liberty of contract, which was discredited by being overdone. . . .[30]

. . . Civil liberties had their origin and must find their ultimate guaranty in the faith of the people. If that faith should be lost, five or nine men in Washington could not supply its want. Therefore we must do our utmost to make clear and easily understandable the reasons for deciding these cases as we do. Forthright observance of rights presupposes their forthright definition.[31]

Completing the Jehovah's Witnesses turnabout and, incidentally, justifying the dissent of the Chief Justice in the Gobitis case, an opinion by Justice Jackson, concurred in by Justices Black and Douglas, over the dissent of Justices Reed, Roberts, and Frankfurter, overruled the Gobitis case and held that a requirement that public school pupils salute the flag and recite a pledge of allegiance under penalty transcends constitutional limitations of the First and Fourteenth amendments.[32]

Justice Jackson, writing for four members, pointed out that the objection to the salute by the Jehovah's Witnesses sect was based upon their belief that the flag was an "image" which they were forbidden to worship by Exodus 20: 4–5. He said that the "sole conflict is between authority and the rights of the individual."[33] He continued:

There is no doubt that, in connection with the pledges, the flag salute is a form of utterance. Symbolism is a primitive but effective way of communicating ideas. The use of an emblem or flag to symbolize some system, idea, institution or personality, is a short cut from mind to mind. Causes and nations, political parties, lodges and ecclesiastical groups seek to knit the loyalty of their followings to a flag or banner. . . . A person gets from a symbol the meaning he puts into it, and what is one man's comfort and inspiration is another's jest and scorn. . . .[34]

[28] *Ibid.*, 178.
[29] *Ibid.*, 179.
[30] *Ibid.*, 181.
[31] *Ibid.*, 182.
[32] West Virginia Board of Education v. Barnette, 319 U.S. 624 (1943).
[33] *Ibid.* 629–30.
[34] *Ibid.*, 632–33.

It is now a commonplace that censorship or suppression of opinion is tolerated by our Constitution only when the expression presents a clear and present danger of action of a kind the State is empowered to prevent and punish. It would seem that involuntary affirmation could be commanded only on even more immediate and urgent grounds than silence. . . . To sustain the compulsory flag salute we are required to say that a Bill of Rights which guards the individual's right to speak his own mind, left it open to public authorities to compel him to utter what is not in his mind. . . .[35]

Those who begin coercive elimination of dissent soon find themselves exterminating dissenters. Compulsory unification of opinion achieves only the unanimity of the graveyard. . . .

We set up government by consent of the governed, and the Bill of Rights denies those in power any legal opportunity to coerce that consent. Authority here is to be controlled by public opinion, not public opinion by authority.

The case is made difficult not because the principles of its decision are obscure but because the flag involved is our own. . . .[36]

But freedom to differ is not limited to things that do not matter much. . . . The test of its substance is the right to differ as to things that touch the heart of the existing order.

If there is any fixed star in our constitutional constellation, it is that no official, high or petty, can prescribe what shall be orthodox in politics, nationalism, religion, or other matters of opinion or force citizens to confess by word or act their faith therein.[37]

Dissenting, Justice Frankfurter said that he could not bring himself to believe that the

"liberty" secured by the Due Process Clause gives this Court authority to deny to the State of West Virginia the attainment of that which we all recognize as a legitimate legislative end, namely, the promotion of good citizenship, by employment of the means here chosen. . . .[38]

The validity of secular laws cannot be measured by their conformity to religious doctrines. It is only in a theocratic state that ecclesiastical doctrines measure legal right or wrong. . . .[39]

That claims are pressed on behalf of sincere religious convictions does not of itself establish their constitutional validity. Nor does waving the banner of religious freedom relieve us from examining into the power we are asked to deny the states. Otherwise the doctrine of separation of church and state. . . .

[35] *Ibid.*, 633–34.
[36] *Ibid.*, 641.
[37] *Ibid.*, 642.
[38] *Ibid.*, 647.
[39] *Ibid.*, 654.

would mean not the disestablishment of a state church but the establishment of all churches and of all religious groups.[40]

The following term another facet of the problems posed by the Jehovah's Witnesses came to the Court when it undertook to review the conviction of a parent who was convicted of violating the Massachusetts child labor laws when she permitted her nine-year-old daughter to hawk religious literature on the streets. Justice Rutledge, writing for a majority, held that such legislation was paramount to a parent's claim of control of the child or a claim that religious scruples transcend the statutes.[41]

Justice Rutledge wrote:

> . . . the family itself is not beyond regulation in the public interest, as against a claim of religious liberty. . . . And neither rights of religion nor rights of parenthood are beyond limitation. Acting to guard the general interest in youth's well being, the state as *parens patriae* may restrict the parent's control . . . in many . . . ways. Its authority is not nullified merely because the parent grounds his claim to control the child's course of conduct on religion or conscience. . . .[42]
>
> A democratic society rests, for its continuance, upon the healthy, well-rounded growth of young people into full maturity as citizens. . . . It may secure this against impending restraints and dangers. Among evils most appropriate for such action are the crippling effects of child employment.[43]

Justice Murphy dissented. Justice Jackson found the grounds stated by the Court inconsistent with the Murdock case but concurred in the result and was joined by Justices Roberts and Frankfurter.

Later, during the 1945 term, the Court held that the management of a company-owned town could not prevent the distribution of religious literature by the Witnesses on the streets of the town.[44] Justice Jackson did not participate, Justice Frankfurter concurred, and the Chief Justice and Justices Reed and Burton dissented.

Non–Jehovah's Witnesses cases also bore upon their doctrines. Thus, when the Ballard family claimed supernatural healing powers and promoted a so-called "I Am" movement of religious doctrines and beliefs, they were indicted and convicted for using the mails to defraud in the distribution of literature and solicitation of funds. The trial judge submitted to the jury only the question of whether the defendants honestly and in good faith believed what they

---

[40] *Ibid.*, 655.
[41] Prince v. Massachusetts, 321 U.S. 158 (1944).
[42] *Ibid.*, 166.
[43] *Ibid.*, 168.
[44] Marsh v. Alabama, 326 U.S. 501 (1946).

were representing. He expressly excluded the truth of defendants' religious beliefs. The majority, in an opinion by Justice Douglas, agreed with the trial judge while resubmitting other claims of error to the lower court.[45] The Chief Justice and Justices Roberts, Frankfurter, and Jackson dissented. Justice Jackson said:

> I should say the defendants have done just that for which they are indicted. If I might agree to their conviction without creating a precedent, I cheerfully would do so. I can see in their teachings nothing but humbug, untainted by any trace of truth. But that does not dispose of the constitutional question whether misrepresentation of religious experience or belief is prosecutable. . . .
>
> I do not see how we can separate an issue as to what is believed from considerations as to what is believable. . . . How can the Government prove these persons knew something to be false which it cannot prove to be false? If we try religious sincerity severed from religious verity, we isolate the dispute from the very considerations which in common experience provide its most reliable answer. . . .[46]
>
> I do not know what degree of skepticism or disbelief in a religious representation amounts to actionable fraud. . . . Belief in what may demonstrate to the senses is not faith. All schools of religious thought make enormous assumptions, generally on the basis of revelations authenticated by some sign or miracle. . . . Some who profess belief in the Bible read literally what others read as allegory or metaphor, as they read Aesop's fables. Religious symbolism is even used by some with the same mental reservations one has in teaching of Santa Claus or Uncle Sam or Easter bunnies or dispassionate judges. . . .
>
> If the members of the sect get comfort from the celestial guidance of their "Saint Germain," however doubtful it seems to me, it is hard to say that they do not get what they pay for. Scores of sects flourish in this country by teaching what to me are queer notions. It is plain that there is wide variety in American religious taste. The Ballards are not alone in catering to it with a pretty dubious product.
>
> The chief wrong which false prophets do their following is not financial. . . . individual payments are not ruinous. I doubt if the vigilance of the law is equal to making money stick by overcredulous people. . . . The wrong of these things, as I see it, is not in the money the victims part with half so much as in the mental and spiritual poison they get. But that is precisely the thing the Constitution put beyond the reach of the prosecutor, for the price of freedom of religion or of speech or of the press is that we must put up with, and even pay for, a good deal of rubbish.
>
> Prosecutions of this character easily could degenerate into religious persecution. . . .

45 United States v. Ballard, 322 U.S. 78 (1944).
46 Ibid., 92–93.

I would dismiss the indictment and have done with this business of judicially examining other people's faith.[47]

When the case came to the Court again, Justice Douglas, writing for four members of the Court, held that the systematic exclusion of women from the panel of grand and petit jurors vitiated the convictions which had been affirmed by the Circuit Court.[48] He said that

the two sexes are not fungible; a community made up exclusively of one is different from a community composed of both; the subtle interplay of influence one on the other is among the imponderables. To insulate the courtroom from either may not in a given case make an iota of difference. Yet a flavor, a distinct quality, is lost if either sex is excluded. The exclusion of one may indeed make the jury less representative of the community than would be true if an economic or racial group were excluded.[49]

Justice Jackson concurred in the dismissal upon the grounds stated in his previous dissent.

Chief Justice Vinson (who had succeeded Chief Justice Stone) and Justices Jackson and Burton joined in an opinion by Justice Frankfurter, saying that the Court should proceed to determine the constitutional question involved in the case and not let the Court's decision rest on the jury question alone, since that would only result in another indictment and further litigation. Justice Burton dissented from the conclusion that women had to be included in jury lists. He concluded that the convictions should be affirmed, and the Chief Justice and Justice Frankfurter joined in his dissent, as did Justice Jackson, except as to affirmance of the convictions—all of which indicated that the accession of a new Chief Justice was not going to produce the harmony lacking under Chief Justice Stone; indeed, the rate of dissent during the term moved up to 64 per cent.[50]

The meaning of the language of the First Amendment prohibiting any "law respecting the establishment of religion" and its application came to the Court for the first time. A New Jersey statute authorized its local school districts to make rules and contracts for the transportation of children to and from schools. A township board of education authorized reimbursement to parents of money expended by them for the bus transportation of their children. Such reimbursement was challenged in the case of some children attend-

[47] Ibid., 93–95.
[48] Ballard v. United States, 329 U.S. 187 (1946).
[49] Ibid., 193–94.
[50] C. Herman Pritchett, The Roosevelt Court, (New York, The Macmillan Co., 1948), 25.

ing Roman Catholic parochial schools, upon the ground that it violated the First Amendment. Justice Black delivered the opinion of the Court for five members, holding the Amendment was not violated. Justice Jackson wrote in dissent, with the concurrence of Justice Frankfurter. Justice Rutledge also delivered a dissenting opinion, in which Justices Frankfurter, Jackson, and Burton joined.[51]

Justice Black said:

> The establishment of religion clause of the First Amendment means at least this: Neither a state nor the Federal Government can set up a church. Neither can pass laws which aid one religion, aid all religions, or prefer one religion over another. Neither can force nor influence a person to go to or to remain away from church against his will or force him to profess a belief or disbelief in any religion. No person can be punished for entertaining or professing religious beliefs or disbeliefs, for church attendance or nonattendance. No tax in any amount, large or small, can be levied to support any religious activities or institutions, whatever they may be called, or whatever form they may adopt to teach or practice religion. Neither a state nor the Federal Government can, openly or secretly, participate in the affairs of any religious organizations or groups and vice versa. In the words of Jefferson, the clause against establishment of religion by law was intended to erect "a wall of separation between Church and State."[52]

The majority concluded that the benefits under the statute were of a nature which the state might extend to all its citizens without regard to their religious beliefs.

Justice Jackson pointed out that the reimbursement was restricted to attendance at either public schools or Catholic Church schools. Hence, he said,

> . . . the basic fallacy in the Court's reasoning . . . is in ignoring the essentially religious test by which beneficiaries of this expenditure are selected. A policeman protects a Catholic, of course—but not because he is a Catholic; it is because he is a man and a member of our society. The fireman protects the Church school; it is because it is property, part of the assets of our society. Neither the fireman nor the policeman has to ask before he renders aid, "Is this man or building identified with the Catholic Church?" But before these school authorities draw a check to reimburse for a student's fare they must ask just that question, and if the school is a Catholic one, they may render aid because it is such, while if it is of any other faith or is run for profit, the help must be withheld. . . .[53]

[51] Everson v. Board of Education, 330 U.S. 1 (1947).
[52] Ibid., 15–16.
[53] Ibid., 25.

It was intended not only to keep the states' hands out of religion, but to keep religion's hands off the state, and, above all, to keep bitter religious controversy out of public life by denying to every denomination any advantage from getting control of public policy or the public purse. . . .[54]

If the state may aid these religious schools, it may therefore regulate them. Many groups have sought aid from tax funds only to find that it carried political controls with it. . . .[55]

Justice Rutledge said:

. . . the object was broader than separating church and state in this narrow sense. It was to create a complete and permanent separation of the spheres of religious activity and civil authority by comprehensively forbidding every form of public aid or support for religion. . . .[56]

. . . the Amendment forbids any appropriation, large or small, from public funds to aid or support any and all religious exercises. . . .[57]

The great condition of religious liberty is that it be maintained free from sustenance, as also from other interferences, by the state. . . . Public money devoted to payment of religious costs, educational or other, brings the quest for more. It brings too the struggle of sect against sect for the larger share or for any. Here one by numbers alone will benefit most, there another.[58]

The following term, the Court held invalid an arrangement whereby pupils who desired to do so could receive religious instruction during regular hours in the school building from outside teachers, while other pupils continued their secular studies.[59] Justice Black wrote, saying that the arrangement violated the First Amendment, made applicable by the Fourteenth. He was joined by Justices Rutledge and Burton. Justice Frankfurter, joined by Jackson, Rutledge, and Burton, wrote, concurring. Justice Jackson also wrote separately, concurring, but expressing reservations. Justice Reed dissented.

Justice Black declared: "This is beyond all question a utilization of the tax-established and tax-supported public school system to aid religious groups to spread their faith. . . ."[60] Neither a state nor the Federal Government can, openly or secretly, participate in the affairs of any religious organizations or groups and vice versa."[61]

Justice Frankfurter said: "Separation means separation, not something less.

[54] *Ibid.*, 26–27.
[55] *Ibid.*, 27–28.
[56] *Ibid.*, 31–32.
[57] *Ibid.*, 41.
[58] *Ibid.*, 53.
[59] McCollum v. Board of Education, 333 U.S. 203 (1948).
[60] *Ibid.*, 210.
[61] *Ibid.*, 211.

... In no activity of the State is it more vital to keep out divisive forces than in its schools. . . .[62] If nowhere else, in the relation between Church and State, 'good fences make good neighbors.' "[63]

Later the Court found valid a New York City program that permitted students, upon request, one free hour a week to obtain religious instruction outside the school building.[64] Justices Black, Jackson, and Frankfurter dissented. Justice Douglas, writing for the majority, distinguished the McCollum case, pointing out that this "released time" involved neither instruction in the classrooms nor the expenditure of public funds. He said that, despite the Amendment, the state and religion were not required to be "aliens to each other—hostile, suspicious, and even unfriendly." He added that

> prayers in our legislative halls; the appeals to the Almighty in the messages of the Chief Executive; the proclamation making Thanksgiving Day a holiday; "so help me God" in our courtroom oaths—these and all other references to the Almighty that run through our laws, our public rituals, our ceremonies would be flouting the First Amendment. A fastidious atheist or agnostic could even object to the supplication with which the Court opens each session: "God save the United States and this Honorable Court.". . .[65]
>
> We are a religious people whose institutions presuppose a Supreme Being. . . . When the state encourages religious instruction or cooperates with religious authorities by adjusting the schedule of public events to sectarian needs, it follows the best of our traditions. For it then respects the religious nature of our people and accommodates the public service to their spiritual needs. To hold that it may not would be to find in the Constitution a requirement that the government show a callous indifference to religious groups. That would be preferring those who believe in no religion over those who do believe.[66]

Justice Black maintained that New York was "manipulating its compulsory education laws to help religious sects get pupils."[67]

Justice Jackson, dissenting, contended that the government was employing coercion, since, without release of school time, pupils were free to obtain religious instruction and that the release of school time was a means of inducement to accept religious instruction. As to those who do not take the released time, he said, schooling "serves as a temporary jail."[68]

He added:

[62] *Ibid.*, 231.
[63] *Ibid.*, 232.
[64] Zorach v. Clauson, 343 U.S. 306 (1952).
[65] *Ibid.*, 312–13.
[66] *Ibid.*, 313–14.
[67] *Ibid.*, 318.
[68] *Ibid.*, 324.

My evangelistic brethren confuse an objection to compulsion with an objection to religion. It is possible to hold a faith with enough confidence to believe that what should be rendered to God does not need to be decided and collected by Caesar.

The day that this country ceases to be free for irreligion it will cease to be free for religion—except for the sect that can win political power. . . .

Today's judgment will be more interesting to students of psychology and of the judicial processes than to students of constitutional law.[69]

During the 1967 term the Court ruled constitutional a New York statute that required public school systems to lend textbooks to students in private and parochial schools. Justice White, writing for six judges, held that the benefits flowed to the children, not to the schools. Justices Douglas, Black and Fortas, dissenting, maintained that the fact that the private and parochial schools chose the books rather than that the books were regular textbooks used by the public schools vitiated the statute.[70]

Simultaneously, the Court overruled a previous decision[71] to hold that a taxpayer may bring suit to challenge federal spending programs, thus permitting individuals to seek to strike down further inroads on the religious separation of school and state. Justice Harlan dissented.[72]

During the 1961 term, the Court considered the so-called school-prayer cases. A New York Board of Education had directed the school principal to cause the following prayer to be said aloud by each class in the presence of a teacher at the beginning of each school day: "Almighty God, we acknowledge our dependence upon Thee, and we beg Thy blessings upon us, our parents, our teachers and our Country."

The prayer had been composed and recommended by state officials. Parents challenged the constitutionality of the state law authorizing the school district to direct the recitation of the prayer, upon the ground that the First Amendment was thereby violated. The lower courts found adversely to the plaintiffs' contention. Justice Black, writing for five members of the Court, reversed. Justice Douglas concurred; Justice Stewart dissented. Justices Frankfurter and White did not participate.[73]

Justice Black said:

We think that by using its public school system to encourage recitation of the Regents' prayer, the State of New York has adopted a practice wholly incon-

[69] *Ibid.*, 324–25.

[70] Board of Education v. Allen, 392 U.S. 236 (1968).

[71] Massachusetts v. Mellon; Frothingham v. Mellon, 262 U.S. 447 (1923).

[72] Flast v. Cohen, 392 U.S. 83 (1968).

[73] Engel v. Vitale, 370 U.S. 421 (1962).

sistent with the Establishment Clause. There can, of course, be no doubt that New York's program . . . is a religious activity. It is a solemn avowal of divine faith and supplication for the blessings of the Almighty. The nature of such a prayer has always been religious. . . .[74]

. . . we think that the constitutional prohibition against laws respecting an establishment of religion must at least mean that in this country it is no part of the business of government to compose official prayers for any group of the American people to recite as a part of a religious program carried on by government.[75]

The First Amendment was added to the Constitution to stand as a guarantee that neither the power nor the prestige of the Federal Government would control, support or influence the kinds of prayer the American people can say. . . .[76]

Neither the fact that the prayer may be denominationally neutral nor the fact that its observance on the part of the students is voluntary can serve to free it from the limitations of the Establishment Clause, as it might from the Free Exercise Clause of the First Amendment, both of which are operative against the States by virtue of the Fourteenth Amendment. Although these two clauses may in certain instances overlap, they forbid two quite different kinds of governmental encroachment upon religious freedom. The Establishment Clause, unlike the Free Exercise Clause, does not depend upon any showing of direct governmental compulsion. . . .[77]

When the power, prestige and financial support of government is placed behind a particular religious belief, the indirect coercive pressure upon religious minorities to conform to the prevailing officially approved religion is plain. But the purposes underlying the Establishment Clause go much further than that. Its first and most immediate purpose rested on the belief that a union of government and religion tends to destroy government and to degrade religion. . . .[78]

The New York laws officially prescribing the Regents' prayer are inconsistent both with the purposes of the Establishment Clause and with the Establishment Clause itself.[79]

Justice Douglas, concurring, remarked:

. . . the only one who need utter the prayer is the teacher; and no teacher is complaining of it. Students can stand mute or even leave the classroom, if they desire. . . .[80]

There is . . . no effort at indoctrination and no attempt at exposition. . . .

[74] *Ibid.*, 424–25.
[75] *Ibid.*, 425.
[76] *Ibid.*, 429–30.
[77] *Ibid.*, 430.
[78] *Ibid.*, 431.
[79] *Ibid.*, 433.
[80] *Ibid.*, 438.

New York's prayer is of a character that does not involve any element of proselytizing. . . .

The question presented . . . is whether New York oversteps the bounds when it finances a religious exercise. . . .[81]

. . . the person praying is a public official on the public payroll, performing a religious exercise in a governmental institution. . . .

I cannot say that to authorize this prayer is to establish a religion in the strictly historic meaning of those words. . . . Yet once government finances a religious exercise it inserts a divisive influence in our communities. . . .[82]

The First Amendment leaves the Government in a position not of hostility to religion but of neutrality. The philosophy is that the atheist or agnostic— the nonbeliever—is entitled to go his own way. The philosophy is that if government interferes in matters spiritual, it will be a divisive force.[83]

Justice Stewart, dissenting, declared:

I think this decision is wrong. . . .

I think the Court has misapplied a great constitutional principle. I cannot see how an "official religion" is established by letting those who want to say a prayer say it. . . .

. . . we deal here not with the establishment of a state church . . . but with whether school children who want to begin their day by joining in prayer must be prohibited from doing so. . . . What is relevant to the issue here is not the history of an established church in sixteenth century England or in eighteenth century America, but the history of the religious traditions of our people, reflected in countless practices of the institutions and officials of government.

At the opening of each day's Session of this Court we stand, while one of our officials invokes the protection of God. . . . Both the Senate and the House of Representatives open their daily Sessions with prayer. Each of our Presidents, from George Washington to John F. Kennedy, has upon assuming his office asked the protection and help of God. . . . One of the stanzas of "The Star-Spangled Banner," made our National Anthem by Act of Congress in 1931, contains these verses:

> "Blest with victory and peace, may the heav'n rescued land
> Praise the Pow'r that hath made and preserved us a nation!
> Then conquer we must, when our cause it is just,
> And this be our motto in God is our Trust."

In 1954 Congress added a phrase in the Pledge of Allegiance to the Flag so that it now contains the words "one Nation under God indivisible, with liberty and justice for all." In 1952 Congress enacted legislation calling upon

[81] *Ibid.*, 439.
[82] *Ibid.*, 441–42.
[83] *Ibid.*, 443.

the President each year to proclaim a National Day of Prayer. Since 1865 the words "IN GOD WE TRUST" have been impressed on our coins.[84]

Countless similar examples could be listed here but there is no need to belabor the obvious. It was all summed up by this Court just ten years ago in a single sentence: "We are a religious people whose institutions presuppose a Supreme Being." . . .

I do not believe that this Court, or the Congress, or the President has by the actions and practices I have mentioned established an "official religion" in violation of the Constitution. And I do not believe the State of New York has done so in this case. What each has done has been to recognize and to follow the deeply entrenched and highly cherished spiritual traditions of our Nation— traditions which come down to us from those who almost two hundred years ago avowed their "firm Reliance on the Protection of divine Providence" when they proclaimed the freedom and independence of this brave new world.[85]

In footnotes Justice Stewart quoted appositely from statements of Presidents Washington, John Adams, Madison, Lincoln, Cleveland, Wilson, Franklin D. Roosevelt, and Eisenhower. He also said: "My brother Douglas says that the only question before us is whether government 'can constitutionally finance a religious exercise.' The official chaplains of Congress are paid with public money. So are military chaplains. So are state and federal prison chaplains."[86]

Referring to the "Court's unsupported *ipse dixit* that these official expressions of religious faith in and reliance upon a Supreme Being 'bear no true resemblance to the unquestioned religious exercise that the State of New York has sponsored in this instance,' " Justice Stewart said: "I can hardly think that this Court means to say that the First Amendment imposes a lesser restriction upon the Federal Government than does the Fourteenth Amendment upon the States. Or is the Court suggesting that the Constitution permits judges and Congressmen and Presidents to join in prayer, but prohibits school children from doing so?"[87]

During the next term three cases involving the religious issue came to the Court. Two were particularly apposite with the New York school prayer case since they involved school prayers in Maryland and Pennsylvania schools.[88] In the first of these, members of the Schempp family sought an adjudication of invalidity of a Pennsylvania statute requiring that "at least ten verses from the Holy Bible shall be read, without comment, at the opening of each public school on each school day. Any child shall be excused from such Bible read-

---

[84] *Ibid.*, 445–46, 449.
[85] *Ibid.*, 450.
[86] *Ibid.*, 449 n.4.
[87] *Ibid.*, 450 n.9.
[88] School Dist. v. Schempp; Murray v. Curlett, 374 U.S. 203 (1963).

ing, or attending such Bible reading upon the written request of his parent or guardian."[89]

In the second case the Board of School Commissioners of Baltimore had adopted a rule, pursuant to a provision of the Maryland code, that provided for the holding "of opening exercises in the schools of the city, consisting primarily of the 'reading,' without comment, of a chapter in the Holy Bible and/or the use of the Lord's Prayer."[90] The petitioners, atheists, claimed their rights to freedom of religion, although the son had been excused from the exercise on request of the parent. Justice Clark wrote for five members of the Court. Justices Douglas, Brennan, and Goldberg each wrote, concurring. Justice Stewart dissented.

Holding "the practices at issue and the Laws requiring them . . . unconstitutional" under the First Amendment applicable to the states by the Fourteenth,[91] Justice Clark said:

> The fact that the Founding Fathers believed devotedly that there was a God and that the inalienable rights of man were rooted in Him is clearly evidenced in their writings, from the Mayflower Compact to the Constitution itself. This background is evidenced today in our public life through the continuance in our oaths of office from the Presidency to the Alderman of the final supplication, "So help me God." Likewise each House of the Congress provides through its Chaplain an opening prayer, and the sessions of this Court are declared open by the crier in a short ceremony, the final phrase of which invokes the grace of God. . . .[92]
>
> This is not to say, however, that religion has been so identified with our history and government that religious freedom is not likewise as strongly imbedded in our public and private life.[93]
>
> The wholesome "neutrality" of which this Court's cases speak . . . stems from a recognition of the teachings of history that powerful sects or groups might bring about a fusion of governmental and religious functions or a concert or dependency of one upon the other to the end that official support of the State or Federal Government would be placed behind the tenets of one or of all orthodoxies. This the Establishment Clause prohibits. And a further reason for neutrality is found in the Free Exercise Clause, which recognizes the value of religious training, teaching and observance and, more particularly, the right of every person to freely choose his own course with reference thereto, free of any compulsion from the state. This the Free Exercise Clause guarantees. . . .[94]
>
> . . . such an opening exercise is a religious ceremony and was intended by

[89] *Ibid.*, 205.
[90] *Ibid.*, 211.
[91] *Ibid.*, 205.
[92] *Ibid.*, 213.
[93] *Ibid.*, 214.
[94] *Ibid.*, 222.

the State to be so. . . . Given that finding the exercises and the law requiring them are in violation of the Establishment Clause. . . .[95]

It certainly may be said that the Bible is worthy of study for its literary and historic qualities. Nothing we have said here indicates that such study of the Bible or of religion, when presented objectively as part of a secular program of education, may not be effected consistently with the First Amendment.[96]

Justice Stewart, dissenting, maintained that:

. . . permission of such exercises for those who want them is necessary if the schools are truly to be neutral in the matter of religion. And a refusal to permit religious exercises thus is seen, not as the realization of state neutrality, but rather as the establishment of a religion of secularism, or at the least, as government support of the beliefs of those who think that religious exercises should be conducted only in private. . . .[97]

. . . religious exercises are not constitutionally invalid if they simply reflect differences which exist in the society from which the school draws its pupils. They become constitutionally invalid only if their administration places the sanction of secular authority behind one or more particular religious or irreligious beliefs. . . .[98]

Viewed in this light, it seems to me clear that the records in both of the cases before us are wholly inadequate to support an informed or responsible decision. Both cases involve provisions which explicitly permit any student who wishes, to be excused from participation in the exercises. There is no evidence in either case as to whether there would exist any coercion of any kind upon a student who did not want to participate. . . .

What our Constitution indispensably protects in the freedom of each of us, be he Jew or Agnostic, Christian or Atheist, Buddhist or Freethinker, to believe or disbelieve, to worship or not worship, to pray or keep silent, according to his own conscience, uncoerced and unrestrained by government. . . . It is conceivable that these school boards, or even all school boards, might eventually find it impossible to administer a system of religious exercises during school hours in such a way as to meet this constitutional standard.[99]

[95] *Ibid.*, 223.
[96] *Ibid.*, 225.
[97] *Ibid.*, 313.
[98] *Ibid.*, 317–18.
[99] *Ibid.*, 319–20.

CHAPTER XII

The Era of the Wild Horses—1

JAMES F. BYRNES OF SOUTH CAROLINA and Robert H. Jackson of New York joined the Court at the beginning of the 1941 term, replacing Justice McReynolds and Chief Justice Hughes. Justice Byrnes resigned at the beginning of the 1942 term and was replaced by Wiley Rutledge of Iowa the following February. Meanwhile, the Court functioned with eight members.

During the 1941 term, dissents mounted to 36 per cent, an all-time high that was shortly to seem surprisingly low. Again, dissents were accompanied by concurrences and bred overruling and "distinguishing" and other similar limitations. The new Chief Justice, mild-mannered and tolerant Harlan F. Stone, found his colleagues "wild horses."[1] As time went on, they proved to be rude, short-tempered, and, on occasion, unusually frank in criticism. Of this they frequently gave public evidence; what went on behind the public scene was largely left for Washington rumor and gossip until the feud between Justices Jackson and Black burst into the open.

Douglas led the dissenters during this term with twenty-eight dissents, of which twenty-one were with Black, all of whose twenty-one dissents were with Douglas. Surprisingly enough, surrounded by liberals, the former liberal Stone found it necessary to dissent twenty-one times, of which twelve were with no less a conservative than Roberts; twelve of his dissents were with Frankfurter. As might be expected, Roberts dissented no less than nineteen times, but the extremely liberal Murphy found it necessary to dissent eighteen times, thirteen of his dissents being with Black and fifteen with Douglas. The low men were Jackson with ten dissents, Byrnes with twelve and Reed with fourteen.[2] Anyone trying to outguess the Court had an obviously impossible task, and that would seem to include members of the Court itself. On one occasion, as the story goes, that was Justice Jackson's expressed conclusion, when, addressing a floundering lawyer, he suggested that the lawyer's diffi-

[1] Alpheus T. Mason, *Harlan Fiske Stone: Pillar of the Law* (New York, The Viking Press, 1956), 580.

[2] C. Herman Pritchett, *The Roosevelt Court* (New York, The MacMillan Co., 1948), 39.

culty lay in trying to fit his argument to various members of the Court in accord with his opinion of what they were thinking.

Dissents again mounted to a new high during the 1942 term—44 per cent.[3] Roberts led with thirty-one dissents, nine sole, fourteen with Frankfurter, and ten each with Reed and the Chief Justice. Considering the fact that the Court was a liberal one, with a majority appointed by a New Deal President still in office, it was surprising that, aside from Roberts, the three outstanding liberals, Black, Douglas, and Murphy, should be leading dissenters. Of Black's twenty-four dissents, three were sole and twenty were joint with Douglas. Sixteen were cast with Murphy, who dissented with Douglas sixteen times. The Chief Justice was low man this term, with fifteen dissents, and Jackson and Reed each had seventeen.[4] The dissents revealed that Black, Douglas, and Murphy constituted an extreme liberal bloc and that the Chief Justice, Jackson, Reed, and Frankfurter might have been rated as moderate, with Frankfurter tending to be conservative with Roberts.

The differences of opinion manifested by increasing dissents undoubtedly took their toll of the mutual tolerance one might expect to find among members of the Court, or at least of the usual show of it. Yet when Chief Justice Stone, who considered himself skilled in the patent art, wrote the first opinion handed down in the 1943–44 term, he was shocked by the nature of the dissent it aroused on the part of Justice Frankfurter, who was joined by Roberts. Justice Rutledge also dissented in part.[5] The suit involved claimed infringements of radio patents, particularly those granted to Marconi, which patents the Chief Justice found invalid.

Justice Rutledge said:

> Until now law has united with almost universal repute in acknowledging Marconi as the first to establish wireless telegraphy on a commercial basis. Before his invention, now in issue, etherborne communication traveled some eighty miles. He lengthened the arc to 6,000. Whether or not this was "inventive" legally, it was a great and beneficial achievement. Today, forty years after the event, the Court's decision reduces it to an electrical mechanic's application of mere skill in the art. . . .
>
> By present knowledge, it would be no more. School boys and mechanics now could perform what Marconi did in 1900. But before then wizards had tried and failed. . . .[6]
>
> The invention was, so to speak, hovering in the general climate of science, momentarily awaiting birth. But just the right releasing touch had not been found. Marconi added it.[7]

[3] *Ibid.*, 25.
[4] *Ibid.*, 41.
[5] Marconi Wireless Co. v. United States, 320 U.S. 1 (1943).
[6] *Ibid.*, 64–65.

But it was Justice Frankfurter who administered the Brutus-like stab when he wrote:

> It is an old observation that the training of Anglo-American judges ill fits them to discharge the duties cast upon them by patent legislation. . . . consciousness of their limitations should make them vigilant against importing their own notions of the nature of the creative process into congressional legislation. . . . Above all, judges must avoid the subtle temptation of taking scientific phenomena out of their contemporaneous setting and reading them with a retrospective eye. . . .
>
> Seldom indeed has a great discoverer or inventor wandered lonely as a cloud. Great inventions have always been parts of an evolution, the culmination at a particular moment of an antecedent process. . . .[8]
>
> To find in 1943 that what Marconi did really did not promote the progress of science because it had been anticipated is more than a mirage of hindsight. . . . And yet, because a judge of unusual capacity for understanding scientific matters is able to demonstrate by a process of intricate ratiocination that anyone could have drawn precisely the inferences that Marconi drew . . . the Court finds that Marconi's patent was invalid.[9]

Again, in approving rate-fixing by the Federal Power Commission under the Natural Gas Act, Justice Douglas, writing for the majority,[10] disapproved a prior decision.[11] Justices Reed, Frankfurter, and Jackson each wrote in dissent. Justice Roberts did not participate.

Justice Frankfurter wrote, approving Justice Jackson's analysis of "the economic and social aspects of natural gas."[12] He went on to say: "Congressional acquiescence to date in the doctrine of Chicago, M. & St. P. Ry. v. Minnesota may fairly be claimed. But in any event that issue is not here in controversy."[13]

While this statement bound none of the other justices, the clash of personalities on the Court that had increasingly resulted in dissent and disagreement led Justices Murphy and Black to a wholly gratuitous and unnecessary opinion in which they said: "We agree with the Court's opinion and would add nothing to what has been said but for what is patently a wholly gratuitous assertion as to Constitutional law in the dissent of Mr. Justice Frankfurter. We refer to the statement that 'Congressional acquiescence' . . . may fairly be

[7] *Ibid.,* 66.
[8] *Ibid.,* 60–62.
[9] *Ibid.,* 63.
[10] Federal Power Commission v. Hope Nat. Gas Co., 320 U.S. 591 (1944).
[11] United Railways v. West, 280 U.S. 234 (1930).
[12] Federal Power Commission v. Hope Nat. Gas Co., 320 U.S. 591, 624–25. (1944).
[13] *Ibid.,* 625.

claimed. The present case does not afford a proper occasion to discuss the soundness of that doctrine."[14]

In a following case handed down the same day, the same acerbity was manifested when Justice Black said: "Although I entirely agree with the Court's judgments and the grounds on which they rest, I find it necessary to add a few remarks in order that silence may not be understood as acquiescence in the views expressed in the dissenting opinion of Mr. Justice Frankfurter." Justice Murphy went along.[15]

These outbursts were symptomatic of a tension borne of disagreement, publicly revealed by a new high of 58 per cent of dissent,[16] and by the content of decisions handed down on January 3, 1944, the occasion of these diatribes. Of fourteen decisions so handed down, only two were unanimous, nine bore dissents, with a total of twenty-two dissents and eight concurrences. Murphy registered five dissents. Jackson, Reed, and Frankfurter dissented together in three cases.

A decision in an admiralty case [17] overruled a prior decision.[18] The nullification of the case aroused Justice Roberts to say:

> The evil resulting from overruling earlier considered decisions must be evident. . . . the law becomes not a chart to govern conduct but a game of chance; instead of settling rights it unsettles them. . . . Respect for tribunals must fall when the bar and the public come to understand that nothing that has been said in prior adjudication has force in a current controversy. . . .
>
> The tendency to disregard precedents in the decision of cases like the present has become so strong in this court of late as, in my view, to shake confidence in the consistency of decision and leave the courts below on an uncharted sea of doubt and difficulty without any confidence that what was said yesterday will hold good tomorrow.[19]

Justice Frankfurter agreed.

Later in the term, when a five-man majority held that shareholders of a bank holding company were liable for assessments on stock of an insolvent bank subsidiary, Justice Jackson, with the support of Justices Roberts, Reed, and Frankfurter, wrote in dissent:

> If to legislate were the province of this Court, we would be at liberty candidly to exercise discretion toward the undoing of the holding company. . . .

14 *Ibid.*, 619–20.
15 Mercoid Corp. v. Mid-Continent Inv. Co., 320 U.S. 661 (1944).
16 Pritchett, *The Roosevelt Court*, 25.
17 Mahnich v. Southern S. S. Co., 321 U.S. 96 (1944).
18 Palmals v. Pinar Del Rio, 277 U.S. 151 (1928).
19 Mahnich v. Southern S. S. Co., 321 U.S. 96, 113 (1944).

But we are of one opinion that no such latitude is confided to judges as here is exercised. We are dealing with a variety of liability without fault. The Court is professing to impose it, not as a matter of judge-made law, but as a matter of legislative policy, and it cannot cite so much as a statutory hint of such a policy. The Court is not enforcing a policy of Congress; it is competing with Congress. . . .[20]

The Court admits the judgment is "harsh." Why is it so if it is according to any law that was known or knowable at the time of the transactions? . . . This decision is made harsh by the element of surprise. Its only harshness is that which comes of the Court's doing with backwards effect what Congress has not seen fit to do with forward effect.[21]

A question of whether the Fair Labor Standards Act called for underground miners to be paid while traveling from the mine portal to the working face resulted in an affirmative answer by a majority, but drew from Justice Roberts, dissenting, the statement:

The question for decision in this case should be approached not on the basis of any broad humanitarian prepossessions we may all entertain, not with a desire to construe legislation so as to accomplish what we deem worthy objects, but in the traditional and, if we are to have a government of laws, the essential attitude of ascertaining what Congress has enacted rather than what we wish it had enacted.[22]

Later the same question arose respecting portal-to-face travel in bituminous coal mines, and a majority followed the Tennessee decision, over the dissent of the Chief Justice and Justices Jackson, Frankfurter, and Roberts, who maintained that Congress had not intended to supersede the agreements of the parties which called for no such result.[23]

The demise of Grovey v. Townsend and of Newberry v. United States, which had been foretold, if not effected, by United States v. Classic, was consummated when, over the protest of Justice Roberts, the Court held that the Constitution protected voting rights in a Texas primary election, despite a legislative attempt to make restrictions against Negroes flow from action of the members, rather than from action of the state.[24]

Justice Roberts inveighed against the

intolerance for what those who have composed this court in the past have conscientiously and deliberately concluded, and involves an assumption that

[20] Anderson v. Abbott, 321 U.S. 349, 379–80 (1944).

[21] Ibid., 382–83.

[22] Tennessee Coal Co. v. Muscoda Local No. 123; Sloss-Sheffield S. & I. Co. v. Sloss Red Ore Local; Republic Steel v. Raimund Local, 321 U.S. 590 (1944).

[23] Jewell Ridge Coal Corp. v. Local No. 6167, 325 U.S. 161 (1945).

[24] Smith v. Allwright, 321 U.S. 649 (1944).

knowledge and wisdom reside in us which was denied to our predecessors. . . .[25]

The reason for my concern is that the instant decision, overruling that announced about nine years ago, tends to bring adjudications of this tribunal into the same class as a restricted railroad ticket, good for this day and this train only. I have no assurance, in view of current decisions, that the opinion announced today may not be shortly repudiated and overruled by justices who deem they have new light on the subject. In the present term the court has overruled three cases. . . .[26]

It is regrettable that in an era marked by doubt and confusion, an era whose greatest need is steadfastness of thought and purpose, this court, which has been looked to as exhibiting consistency in adjudication, and a steadiness which would hold the balance even in the face of temporary ebbs and flows of opinion, should now itself become the breeder of fresh doubt and confusion in the public mind as to the stability of our institutions.[27]

Lacking the restraint that might have been furnished by the absent Justices Jackson and Roberts, and over the dissent of the Chief Justice, six members of the Court construed the federal Anti-Racketeering Act of 1934, concluding that it was intended to apply to gangsters of the then prominent Dillinger types and not as between bona fide employees and bona fide employers in the guise of wages. The case arose when members of a labor union lay in wait for trucks passing from New Jersey to New York, forced their ways on to the trucks and, by beating or threats of beating the drivers, compelled them or their employers to pay a sum of money for each truck, said to be the equivalent of the union wage scale for a day's work.[28] The Chief Justice, in a dissent, expressed the anger that the Court's decision engendered in the public and in Congress. He said: "When the Anti-Racketeering Act was under consideration by Congress, no member of Congress and no labor leader had the temerity to suggest that such payments, made only to secure immunity from violence and intentionally compelled by assault and battery, could be regarded as the payment of 'wages by a bona fide employer!' "[29]

Following this decision, Congress amended the Act by passing the so-called Hobbs Act,[30] which the Court construed in a subsequent 1956 case.[31] There the Court held that "the legislative history makes clear that the New Act was meant to eliminate any grounds for future judicial conclusion that Congress did not intend to cover the employer-employee relationship."[32]

[25] *Ibid.*, 666.
[26] *Ibid.*, 669.
[27] *Ibid.*, 670.
[28] Local No. 807, v. United States, 315 U.S. 521 (1942).
[29] *Ibid.*, 541.
[30] 18 U.S. Judicial Code, Sec. 1951.
[31] United States v. Green, 350 U.S. 415 (1956).
[32] *Ibid.*, 419.

The Court held that there was nothing in any statute "that indicates any protection for unions or their officials in attempts to get personal property through threats of force or violence. Those are not legitimate means for improving labor conditions. . . . The Hobbs Act was meant to stop just such conduct."[33] There was a dissent on technical grounds by Justices Douglas and Black. It may be noted that the Court was passing on an indictment and remarked that it was framed in the words of the statute and did not disclose the acts that actuated it.

Several years later, in 1960, the Court reversed a conviction for a variance between proof and indictment. But it held that a union official who had extorted some $31,000 from a manufacturer by threats of causing labor disputes and thereby holding up interstate shipments of sand which the manufacturer needed to produce concrete to satisfy an existing contract, was guilty of a violation of the Hobbs Act.[34]

Over the dissent of Justice Murphy, the Court took the unusual step of finding against a union charged with aiding and abetting businessmen in committing acts prohibited by the Sherman Anti-Trust Act.[35] Then, on the same day, a majority held a labor union guiltless of violating the Sherman Act when it refused to admit to membership the employees of a trucking company doing an interstate business and withholding the services of its members from this company, thereby putting the company out of business.[36] The Chief Justice and Justices Roberts, Frankfurter, and Jackson dissented. Justice Roberts said:

> The union determined to punish petitioners. . . . There is no suggestion in the record that they did so because of any labor conditions or considerations. . . . They intended to drive petitioners out of business . . . and they succeeded in so doing. . . .
> The union compelled A & P, their principal patron, to break its contract with them. . . . The union frustrated efforts of petitioners to obtain contracts with other shippers. . . .
> The conspiracy, therefore, was clearly within the denunciation of the Sherman Act, as one intended and effective, to lessen competition in commerce, and not within any immunity conferred by the Clayton Act.[37]

Justice Jackson added:

> It is hard to see how this union is excused from the terms of the Act when

[33] Ibid., 420.
[34] Stirone v. United States, 361 U.S. 212 (1960).
[35] Allen Bradley Co. v. Local No. 3, 325 U.S. 797 (1945).
[36] Hunt v. Crumboch, 325 U.S. 821 (1945).
[37] Ibid., 827–28.

in the Allen-Bradley Co. case we hold that labor unions even though further-ing their members' interests as wage earners violate the Act when they com-bine with business to do the things prohibited by the Act. . . .[38]

With this decision, the labor movement has come full circle. The working man has struggled long, the fight has been filled with hatred, and conflict has been dangerous, but now workers may not be deprived of their livelihood merely because their employers oppose and they favor unions. Labor has won other rights as well. . . . This Court now sustains the claim of a union to the right to deny participation in the economic world to an employer simply be-cause the union dislikes him. This Court permits to employees the same arbi-trary dominance over the economic sphere which they control that labor has so long, so bitterly and so rightly asserted should belong to no man.[39]

The Court divided five-to-four in upholding the right of a labor organ-izer to speak and solicit members without registering as required by a Texas statute.[40] The organizer had spoken to a meeting of workers and had solicited members despite an injunction issued by a Texas court and previously served upon him. He was adjudged in contempt and took an appeal from a decision of the Texas Supreme Court denying his application for a writ of habeas corpus.

Justice Rutledge, writing for the majority, held to the Holmes-Brandeis rule, saying that

any attempt to restrict those liberties [secured by the First Amendment] must be justified by clear public interest, threatened not doubtfully or remotely, but by clear and present danger. The rational connection between the remedy pro-vided and the evil to be curbed, which in other contexts might support legis-lation against attack on due process grounds, will not suffice. These rights rest on firmer foundation. . . . Only the gravest abuses, endangering paramount interests, give occasion for permissible limitation. It is therefore in our tradi-tion to allow the widest room for discussion, the narrowest range for its re-striction, particularly when this right is exercised in conjunction with peaceable assembly.[41]

Justice Jackson, concurring, said:

The modern state owes and attempts to perform a duty to protect the public from those who seek for one purpose or another to obtain its money. When one does so through the practice of a calling, the state may have an interest in shield-ing the public against the untrustworthy, the incompetent, or the irresponsible, or

[38] *Ibid.*, 828.
[39] *Ibid.*, 830–31.
[40] Thomas v. Collins, 323 U.S. 516 (1945).
[41] *Ibid.*, 530.

against unauthorized representation of agency. A usual method of performing this function is through a licensing system.

But it cannot be the duty, because it is not the right, of the state to protect the public against false doctrine. . . . In this field every person must be his own watchman for truth, because the forefathers did not trust any government to separate the true from the false for us. . . .

. . . this liberty was protected because they knew of no other way by which free men could conduct representative democracy. . . .[42]

But I must admit that we are applying to Thomas a rule the benefit of which in all its breadth and vigor this Court denies to employers in National Labor Relations cases.[43]

Dissenting, Justice Roberts, supported by the Chief Justice and Justices Reed and Frankfurter, maintained that the statute was valid since it was intended only to serve the purpose of identification, that the labor union was a business association, and that the transaction was in essence a business one.

This five-to-four decision and the consequent division respecting the right to disregard an injunction was not settled, for twenty-five years later, in 1967, a similar division in the Court high-lighted an inability to find agreement on the question. Here, a group of Negro ministers, headed by the respected Nobel Peace Prize winner Martin Luther King, undertook to parade in the streets of Birmingham, where Police Commissioner Eugene Connor, yclept "Bull," said to be a notorious racist and one of those who stimulated Congress to pass civil rights legislation, was commissioner of safety. The authorities obtained an injunction which the paraders ignored, intending to challenge its First Amendment constitutionality in subsequent contempt proceedings. They did so, but the Alabama Supreme Court and a five-man majority of the high court invoked a fifty-year-old case[44] to affirm the conviction.[45] The Chief Justice and Justices Douglas, Brennan, and Fortas, the die-hard liberals, dissented. Justice Black abandoned their cause to vote with Justice Stewart, who wrote for the conservatives. In dissent, Justice Warren likened the anti-Negro injunction to those issued and subsequently legislated against in labor cases.

However, in one case at least the Norris–La Guardia Act forbidding labor injunctions proved unavailing.

While the United States was in possession of and operating the major portion of the country's bituminous coal mines, in violation of a restraining order, the United Mine Workers struck the mines. Thereafter the union and John L. Lewis, its president, were adjudged in criminal contempt and Lewis

[42] *Ibid.*, 545–46.
[43] *Ibid.*, 548.
[44] Howat v. Kansas, 258 U.S. 181 (1922).
[45] Walker v. Birmingham, 388 U.S. 307 (1967).

was fined $10,000 and the union $3,500,000. On appeal the Court held that the Norris–La Guardia Act's anti-injunction provisions had no application to the government and, reducing the union's fine to $700,000 conditionally, affirmed the lower court.[46] Justices Jackson and Frankfurter concurred. The latter said: "In our country law is not a body of technicalities in the keeping of specialists or in the service of any special interest. There can be no free society without law administered through an independent judiciary. If one man can be allowed to determine for himself what is law, every man can. That means first chaos, then tyranny."[47] Justices Black and Douglas dissented as to the fines. Justices Murphy and Rutledge also dissented.

The Court held that, under the Norris–La Guardia Act, an organization or its members participating in or interested in a labor dispute were not liable for the unlawful acts of individual members, officers or agents except upon clear proof of participation or authorization after knowledge.[48] Justice Frankfurter, supported by the Chief Justice and Justice Burton (Justice Jackson not participating), said:

> Practically speaking, the interpretation given by the Court . . . serves to immunize unions, especially the more alert and powerful, as well as corporations involved in labor disputes, from Sherman Law liability. . . . for those entrusted with the enforcement of the Sherman Law there may be found in the opinion words of promise to the ear, but the decision breaks the promise to the hope.[49]

By a vote of six to two the Court vacated the conviction of one Glasser, charged, while an assistant federal attorney, with conspiring to solicit bribes to avoid prosecution for liquor violations.[50] Glasser claimed he had not been independently represented by counsel.

Justice Frankfurter wrote for himself and the Chief Justice, saying in dissent:

> . . . the perspective of the living trial is lost in the search for error in a dead record. To set aside the conviction of Glasser (a lawyer who served as an Assistant United States Attorney for more than four years) after a trial lasting longer than a month on the ground that he was denied the basic constitutional right "to have the assistance of counsel for his defence" is to give fresh point to this regrettably familiar phenomenon.

[46] United States v. United Mine Workers; United States v. Lewis; United Mine Workers v. United States; Lewis v. United States, 330 U.S. 258 (1947).

[47] Ibid., 312.

[48] United Brotherhood of Carpenters v. United States; Bay Counties v. United States; Lumber Products Assoc. v. United States; Almeda County v. United States; Boorman Lumber Co. v. United States, 330 U.S. 395 (1947).

[49] Ibid., 422.

[50] Glasser v. United States; Kretske v. United States; Roth v. United States, 315 U.S. 60 (1942).

For Glasser himself made no such claim at any of the critical occasions throughout the proceedings. . . . Not until . . . fifteen weeks after the trial had ended, did Glasser discover that he had been deprived of his constitutional rights. This was obviously a lawyer's afterthought.[51]

In another case a stockbroker, who had studied law and had previously conducted litigation against the New York Stock Exchange, was indicted for using the mails to defraud and insisted on representing himself. He waived trial by jury by an instrument in writing. He conducted his own trial, and to advise him after conviction, retained counsel, who contended he had waived his constitutional rights. A majority of the Court voted to dismiss the writ.[52]

Justice Douglas wrote in dissent, saying that even the fact "that a defendant ordinarily may dispense with a trial by admitting his guilt is no reason for accepting this layman's waiver of a jury trial."[53] He was supported by Justices Black and Murphy, the latter of whom wrote separately saying that he did not "concede that the right to a jury trial can be waived in criminal proceedings in the federal court."[54]

Defendant Betts, a farm hand, out of a job and on relief, was indicted in a Maryland state court on a charge of robbery. He was too poor to hire a lawyer. His request for counsel was denied by the Court. After trial and conviction, he appealed to the Supreme Court. A majority, over the dissent of Justices Black, Douglas, and Murphy, affirmed the conviction.[55]

Justice Roberts, writing for the majority, said:

The Sixth Amendment of the national Constitution applies only to trials in federal courts. The due process clause of the Fourteenth Amendment does not incorporate, as such, the specific guarantees found in the Sixth Amendment, although a denial by a state of rights or privileges specifically embodied in that and others of the first eight amendments may, in certain circumstances, or in connection with other elements, operate, in a given case, to deprive a litigant of due process of law in violation of the Fourteenth. Due process of law is secured against invasion by the Federal Government by the Fifth Amendment and is safeguarded against state action in identical words by the Fourteenth. The phrase formulates a concept less rigid and more fluid than those envisaged in other specific and particular provisions of the Bill of Rights. Its application is less a matter of rule. Asserted denial is to be tested by an appraisal of the totality of facts in a given case. That which may, in one setting, constitute a denial of fundamental fairness, shocking to the universal sense of justice,

[51] *Ibid.*, 88–89.
[52] Adams v. United States, 317 U.S. 269 (1942).
[53] *Ibid.*, 285.
[54] *Ibid.*, 286.
[55] Betts v. Brady, 316 U.S. 455 (1942).

may, in other circumstances, and in the light of other considerations, fall short of such denial.[56]

He quoted from a previous case:[57]

"All that it is necessary now to decide, as we do decide, is that, in a capital case, where the defendant is unable to employ counsel, and is incapable adequately of making his own defense because of ignorance, feeble-mindedness, illiteracy, or the like, it is the duty of the Court, whether requested or not, to assign counsel for him as a necessary requisite of due process of law"[58]

Justice Black wrote in dissent:

. . . I believe that the Fourteenth Amendment makes the Sixth applicable to the states. But this view, although often used in dissents, has never been accepted by a majority of this Court and is not accepted today.[59]

A practice cannot be reconciled with "common and fundamental ideas of fairness and right," which subjects innocent men to increased dangers of conviction merely because of their poverty. . . . Denial to the poor of the request for counsel in proceedings based on charges of serious crime has long been regarded as shocking to the "universal sense of justice" throughout this country.[60]

Later the Court refused to hold the Sixth Amendment applicable to the states through the medium of the Fourteenth Amendment where the Court failed to provide counsel.[61] Justices Black and Rutledge wrote in dissent, with Justices Douglas and Murphy in support. Another such case found Frankfurter writing for himself, the Chief Justice and Justices Reed and Jackson, with Justice Burton concurring, with the same four dissenters.[62]

On the same day the Court refused to hold the Fourteenth Amendment inclusive of the Sixth and Seventh amendments in denying a plea that a "blue-ribbon" jury constituted a denial of due process.[63] The same four dissented. Another case involving the same issue went the same way, with the same four dissenters.[64]

But subsequent cases are of academic interest, for during the 1962 term the Court passed upon the plea made by Abe Fortas, later to be appointed one

56 *Ibid.*, 461–62.
57 Powell v. Alabama, 287 U.S. 45 (1932).
58 Betts v. Brady, 316 U.S. 455 (1942) 463–64.
59 *Ibid.*, 474–75.
60 *Ibid.*, 476.
61 Foster v. Illinois, 332 U.S. 134 (1947).
62 Gayes v. New York, 332 U.S. 145 (1947).
63 Fay v. New York, 332 U.S. 261 (1947).
64 Moore v. New York, 333 U.S. 565 (1948).

of its justices, on behalf of a Mr. Gideon, convicted of misdemeanor called a felony in a Florida state court. It appeared that Gideon had sought the appointment of counsel and that the Court had refused upon the ground that Gideon was not charged with a capital offense. The Court undertook to pass upon the question and the Court's holding in the prior Betts case.[65] It held that the circumstances of the two cases were "so nearly indistinguishable" that Gideon's plea would have to be denied or the Betts case overruled. Whereupon, they did the latter.

Justice Black, for a majority of seven, proceeded, in a dignified way, to crow. (Later, in a lecture at the Columbia Law School, he said, apropos of the foregoing, "While I didn't get the whole pie, I got a large piece of it.") Now he could say that "made immune from state invasion by the Fourteenth [Amendment] or some part of it, are the First Amendment's freedom of speech, press, religion, assembly, association, and petition for redress of grievances." (He was citing nine cases.)[66] "For the same reason," he continued, "though not always in precisely the same terminology, the Court has made obligatory on the States the Fifth Amendment's command that private property shall not be taken for public use without just compensation,"[67] "the Fourth's prohibition of unreasonable searches and seizures,"[68] and "the Eighth's ban on cruel and unusual punishment."[69]

Concurring, Justice Douglas said that, since the adoption of the Fourteenth Amendment, "ten Justices have felt that it protects from infringement by the States the privileges, protections, and safeguards granted by the Bill of Rights."

He referred to Justice Field, the first Justice Harlan, and probably Justice Brewer in O'Neil v. Vermont, 144 U.S. 323, 362–63, 360–71; to himself, Justices Black, Murphy, and Rutledge in Adamson v. California, 332 U.S. 46, 71–72, 124; to the dissenting opinion in Poe v. Ullman, 367 U.S. 497, 515–22; and to Justices Bradley and Swayne in the Slaughter House Cases, 16 Wall. 36, 118–19, 122 "and seemingly . . . by Justice Clifford when he dissented with

[65] Gideon v. Wainwright, 372 U.S. 335, 338 (1963).

[66] Gitlow v. New York, 268 U.S. 652, 666 (1925) (speech and press); Lovell v. City of Griffin, 303 U.S. 444, 450 (1938) (speech and press); Staub v. City of Baxley, 355 U.S. 313, 321 (1958) (speech); Grosjean v. American Press Co., 297 U.S. 233, 244 (1936) (press); Cantwell v. Connecticut, 310 U.S. 296, 303 (1940) (religion); De Jonge v. Oregon, 299 U.S. 353, 364 (1937) (assembly); Shelton v. Tucker, 364 U.S. 479, 486, 488 (1960) (association); Louisiana ex rel. Gremillion v. NAACP, 366 U.S. 293, 296 (1961) (association); Edwards v. South Carolina, 372 U.S. 229 (1963) (speech, assembly, petition for redress of grievances).

[67] Chicago, B. & Q. R.R. v. Chicago, 166 U.S. 226 (1897); Smyth v. Ames, 169 U.S. 466 (1898).

[68] Wolf v. Colorado, 338 U.S. 25, 27–28 (1949); Elkins v. United States, 364 U.S. 206, 213 (1960); Mapp v. Ohio, 367 U.S. 643, 655 (1961).

[69] Gideon v. Wainwright, 372 U.S. 335, 341–42 (1963); Robinson v. California, 370 U.S. 660, 666 (1962).

Justice Field in Walker v. Sauvinet, 92 U.S. 90, 92." "Unfortunately," he added, "it has never commanded a Court. Yet, happily, all constitutional questions are always open."[70]

Justice Clark, concurring, said that the decision did no more than "to erase a distinction which has no basis in logic and an increasingly eroded basis in authority."[71] He concluded that "the Constitution makes no distinction between capital and noncapital cases."[72]

Justice Harlan, also concurring, said wryly: "I agree that Betts v. Brady should be overruled, but consider it entitled to a more respectful burial."[73] He added, "In what is done today I do not understand the Court to depart from the principles laid down in Palko v. Connecticut, 302 U.S. 319, or to embrace the concept that the Fourteenth Amendment 'incorporates' the Sixth Amendment as such."[74]

Later, during the 1966 term, the denial of a writ of certiorari resulted in a dissent by Justice Stewart, who argued that the Court should "clarify the scope of Gideon v. Wainwright" and determine whether its application should "depend upon artificial labels of 'felony' or 'misdemeanor' attached to criminal offenses by 50 different States." He maintained that "it is at least our duty to see to it that a vital guarantee of the United States Constitution is accorded with an even hand in all the States."[75] Justice Black also dissented.

Still later in the term Justice Stewart, joined by Justices Black and Douglas, dissented from a denial of certiorari, saying, "This case illustrates, in even more compelling terms than Winters v. Beck, . . . the need for this Court to make clear the meaning of Gideon v. Wainwright."[76]

In this case the petitioner had been charged in a Connecticut court with criminal nonsupport, a misdemeanor. The Court refused his request for counsel upon the ground of his indigency, since the alleged crime was only a misdemeanor. Justice Stewart pointed out that in another Connecticut case the district judge had set aside a conviction on the same charge because counsel had not been assigned, though the defendant, ignorant of his rights, had not requested such appointment.

Later, during the 1967 term, a unanimous Court holding that a defendant released on probation had a right to counsel in proceedings to revoke his probation, or to require him to serve a sentence previously suspended, also

70 Gideon v. Wainwright, 372 U.S. 335, 345–46 (1963).
71 *Ibid.*, 348.
72 *Ibid.*, 349.
73 *Ibid.*
74 *Ibid.*, 352.
75 Winters v. Beck, 385 U.S. 907 (1966).
76 DeJoseph v. Connecticut, 385 U.S. 982 (1966).

held that, under such circumstances, the state was required to appoint counsel for an indigent.[77]

In a per curiam decision, over the dissent of Justice Black, the Court reversed a conviction upon the ground that "the trial court should have explored the possibility that petitioner could afford only partial payment for the services of trial counsel and that counsel be appointed on that basis,"[78] although the circuit court had affirmed the conviction after granting leave to appeal in forma pauperis and assigning counsel.

However, the Court refused to grant certiorari to a conscientious objector sentenced to a two-year jail term for refusing to report to a hospital for civilian duty, who claimed the right to have counsel in his appearance before the local draft board.[79]

Following the Gideon decision, the Court dealt with a defendant's right of confrontation of witnesses, in a case where on a preliminary hearing of a robbery charge against the defendant, the complaining witness testified, but was not cross-examined, since the defendant had no counsel. At defendant's subsequent trial, the complaining witness having left the state, the transcript of the previous testimony was introduced in evidence over defendant's objection. The high court reversed the conviction, Justice Black writing for six members of the Court. Justices Harlan, Stewart, and Goldberg concurred.[80]

Justice Black held that the defendant's right of confrontation of the witness under the Sixth Amendment had been violated by the introduction of the transcript of the previous testimony without the presence of the witness for cross-examination, since, he maintained, the Sixth Amendment was applicable to the states through the Fourteenth Amendment, the thesis he had expounded throughout his career in insisting that the Fourteenth Amendment was "shorthand" for the Bill of Rights. Justices Harlan and Stewart dissented from this conclusion, saying that the situation was amply covered by the due process clause of the Fourteenth Amendment, since "a right of confrontation is 'implicit in the concept of ordered liberty,' Palko v. Connecticut . . . , reflected in the Due Process Clause of the Fourteenth Amendment independently of the Sixth." He characterized Justice Black's decision as "another step in the onward march of the long-since discredited 'incorporation' doctrine."[81] Justice Goldberg subscribed to Justice Black's theory.[82]

The Pointer decision (above) was followed in a decision the same day where

---

[77] Mempa v. Rhay; Walkling v. Washington State Board, 389 U.S. 128 (1967).
[78] Wood v. United States, 389 U.S. 20, 21 (1967).
[79] Mientke v. United States, 390 U.S. 1011 (1968).
[80] Pointer v. Texas, 380 U.S. 400 (1965). See also Barber v. Page, 390 U.S. 719 (1968).
[81] Ibid., 408.
[82] Ibid., 410.

the confession of an accomplice was read to the jury with no opportunity to the defendant to cross-examine the accomplice. Justice Brennan wrote for seven members, vacating the conviction. Justices Harlan and Stewart concurred, but differed with the majority on the same ground as in the Pointer case respecting the Sixth and Fourteenth amendments.[83]

Then, during the 1966 term, the Court held that "the right to a speedy trial is as fundamental as any of the rights secured by the Sixth Amendment."[84] Chief Justice Warren, writing for seven members of the Court, quoted from the Pointer decision: " 'In the light of Gideon, Malloy, and other cases cited in those opinions holding various provisions of the Bill of Rights applicable to the States by virtue of the Fourteenth Amendment, the statements made in West and similar cases generally declaring that the Sixth Amendment does not apply to the States can no longer be regarded as the law.' "[85]

Justices Stewart and Harlan concurred in the result. Justice Harlan wrote:

> I am unable to subscribe to the constitutional premises upon which that result is based—quite evidently the viewpoint that the Fourteenth Amendment 'incorporates' or 'absorbs' *as such* all of some of the specific provisions of the Bill of Rights. . . . See my opinion concurring in the result in Pointer v. Texas.[86]

In a 1968 case the Court, holding that the right of confrontation under the Sixth Amendment included the right of cross-examination to a point where a witness having admitted that the name he had been using was a false one was required to answer questions about his true name and where he lived. With the concurrence of Justices White and Marshall and over the dissent of Justice Harlan, who maintained the error harmless or of disingenuous constitutionality, the Court reversed a conviction where the presiding judge had sustained an objection to such questions.[87]

Previous to the Gideon decision, a failure of Illinois to furnish indigent convicted criminals with transcripts of the record was held by four members of the Court, in an opinion by Justice Black, to violate the due process and equal protection clauses of the Fourteenth Amendment. Justice Frankfurter concurred; Justices Burton, Minton, Reed, and Harlan dissented.[88] Justice Black said:

> Providing equal justice for poor and rich, weak and powerful alike is an age-old problem. People have never ceased to hope and strive to move closer to that

83 Douglas v. Alabama, 380 U.S. 415 (1965).
84 Klopfer v. North Carolina, 386 U.S. 213, 223 (1967).
85 *Ibid.*, 222.
86 *Ibid.*, 226.
87 Smith v. Illinois, 390 U.S. 129 (1968).
88 Griffin v. Illinois, 351 U.S. 12 (1956).

goal.[89] . . . our own constitutional guaranties of due process and equal protection both called for procedures in criminal trials which allow no invidious discriminations between persons. . . . all people charged with crime must, so far as the law is concerned, "stand on an equality before the bar of justice in every American court." . . . In criminal trials a State can no more discriminate on account of poverty than on account of religion, race or color.[90]

Justice Frankfurter, concurring in the result, said:

The admonition of de Tocqueville not to confuse the familiar with the necessary has vivid application to appeals in criminal cases. The right to an appeal from a conviction for crime is today so established that this leads to the easy assumption that it is fundamental to the protection of life and liberty and therefore a necessary ingredient of due process of law. "Due process" is, perhaps, the least frozen concept of our law. . . . It is significant that no appeals from convictions in the federal courts were afforded (with roundabout exceptions negligible for present purposes) for nearly a hundred years; and, despite the civilized standards of criminal justice in modern England, there was no appeal from convictions (again with exceptions not now pertinent) until 1907. Thus, it is now settled that due process of law does not require a State to afford review of criminal judgments. . . .[91]

Of course a State need not equalize economic conditions. A man of means may be able to afford the retention of an expensive, able counsel not within reach of a poor man's purse. Those are contingencies of life which are hardly within the power, let alone the duty, of a State to correct or cushion. But when a State deems it wise and just that convictions be susceptible to review by an appellate court, it cannot by force of its exactions draw a line which precludes convicted indigent persons, forsooth erroneously convicted, from securing such a review merely by disabling them from bringing to the notice of an appellate tribunal errors of the trial court which would upset the conviction were practical opportunity for review not foreclosed.

To sanction such a ruthless consequence . . . would justify a latter-day Anatole France to add one more item to his ironic comments on the "majestic equality" of the law. "The law, in its majestic equality, forbids the rich as well as the poor to sleep under bridges, to beg in the streets, and to steal bread" (John Cournos, *A Modern Plutarch*, p. 27).

A state is not free to produce such a squalid discrimination.[92]

Justice Burton, writing for the dissenters, said:

Illinois, as the majority admit, could . . . deny an appeal altogether in a crimi-

[89] *Ibid.*, 16.
[90] *Ibid.*, 17.
[91] *Ibid.*, 20–21.
[92] *Ibid.*, 23–24.

nal case without denying due process of law. McKane v. Durston, 153 U.S. 684. . . . To allow an appeal at all, but with some difference among convicted persons . . . does not deny due process. It may present a question of equal protection. . . .

. . . The whole practice of criminal law teaches that there are valid distinctions between the ways in which criminal cases may be looked upon and treated without violating the Constitution. . . . There is something pretty final about a death sentence.

If the actual practice of law recognizes this distinction between capital and non-capital cases, we see no reason why the legislature of a State may not extend the full benefit of appeal to those convicted of capital offenses and deny it to those convicted of lesser offenses. . . .[93]

Illinois is not bound to make the defendants economically equal before its bar of justice. For a State to do so may be a desirable social policy, but what may be a good legislative policy for a State is not necessarily required by the Constitution of the United States. . . .

The Constitution requires the equal protection of the law, but it does not require the States to provide equal financial means for all defendants to avail themselves of such laws.[94]

Justice Harlan, also dissenting, said: "Much as I would prefer to see free transcripts furnished to indigent defendants in all felony cases, I find myself unable to join in the Court's holding that the Fourteenth Amendment requires a State to do so or to furnish indigents with equivalent means of exercising a right to appeal."[95]

Six members of the Court held that an indigent Washington state prisoner, denied a free transcript of his trial record, was entitled to habeas corpus on the authority of the Griffin case.[96] Justices Harlan and Whittaker dissented, saying the Griffin case, decided in 1956, was not applicable, since the petitioner was convicted in 1935. Justice Frankfurter did not participate.

On the same day that the Gideon decision was handed down, two indigent defendants, tried jointly and convicted of thirteen felonies, sought the assistance of counsel on an appeal. The Court examined the record and determined that the appointment of counsel would not be "of advantage to the defendant or helpful to the appellate court."

Justice Douglas, writing for six members of the Court, found that the evil in this, as in the Griffin case, was "the same: discrimination against the indigent." He held that "when an indigent is forced to run this gantlet of a pre-

[93] *Ibid.*, 27–28.
[94] *Ibid.*, 28–29.
[95] *Ibid.*, 29.
[96] Eskridge v. Washington State Board, 357 U.S. 214 (1958).

liminary showing of merit, the right to appeal does not comport with fair procedure."[97]

Justice Clark, dissenting, held that the Griffin case was not applicable:

> With this new fetish for indigency the Court piles an intolerable burden on the State's judicial machinery. Indeed, if the Court is correct it may be that we should first clean up our own house. We have afforded indigent litigants much less protection than has California. Last term we received over 1,200 *in forma pauperis* applications in none of which had we appointed attorneys or required a record. Some were appeals of right. Still we denied the petitions or dismissed the appeals on the moving papers alone.[98]

Justice Harlan, joined by Justice Stewart, also wrote in dissent. He said that

> laws such as these do not deny equal protection to the less fortunate for one essential reason: The Equal Protection Clause does not impose on the States "an affirmative duty to lift the handicaps flowing from differences in economic circumstances." To so construe it would be to read into the Constitution a philosophy of leveling that would be foreign to many of our basic concepts of the proper relations between government and society. The State may have moral obligation to eliminate the evils of poverty, but it is not required by the Equal Protection Clause to give to some whatever others can afford.[99]

Pursuant to the high court's direction, New Jersey furnished transcripts of the record to indigent prisoners taking an appeal but provided, by statute, that the cost of the transcript should be repaid out of the inmate's prison earnings. The Court held that this provision violated the equal protection clause of the Fourteenth Amendment since released prisoners were not compelled to reimburse the state.[100] Justice Harlan dissented, saying the New Jersey legislature might rationally conclude it was not worth while to attempt to obtain reimbursement from released prisoners.

A per curiam decision during the 1966 term held that, when a defendant whose indigency and desire to appeal are manifest does not have the services of his trial counsel on appeal, a knowing waiver cannot be inferred from his failure specifically to request appointment of appellate counsel.[101] Another judgment was vacated, and the case remanded for further consideration, the Court citing the case last mentioned, Eskridge v. Washington, 357 U.S. 214 and Tehan v. Shott, 382 U.S. 406, 16.[102]

[97] Douglas v. California, 372 U.S. 353, 357 (1963).
[98] *Ibid.*, 358–59.
[99] *Ibid.*, 362.
[100] Rinaldi v. Yeager, 384 U.S. 305 (1966).
[101] Swenson v. Bosler, 386 U.S. 258 (1967).
[102] Hester v. Swenson, 386 U.S. 261 (1967).

Again, on the same day that the Douglas case was decided, a unanimous Court vacated the conviction of a prisoner convicted of murder and sentenced to death. The Court held that Indiana had denied the defendant due process in foreclosing him from appealing "at the unreviewable discretion of a Public Defender by whom . . . the indigent has been represented at the trial. It ignores the human equation not to recognize the possibility that a Public Defender so circumstanced may decide not to appeal questions which a lawyer who has had no previous connection with the case might consider worthy of appellate review."[103]

In still another indigent case decided on the same day, Justice Goldberg, writing for five members of the Court, found that the conclusion of the trial judge that indigents' appeal was frivolous was an inadequate substitute for a full appellate review when the effect of that finding was to prevent defendants from having stenographic support or its equivalent for presentation of each of their separate contentions to the appellate tribunal.[104]

Justice White, supported by Justices Clark, Harlan, and Stewart, dissented, saying, "In my judgment petitioners were afforded an adequate appellate review upon a satisfactory record." He called attention to the fact that the Court had "carefully" avoided requiring the state "to supply an indigent with a stenographic transcript of proceedings in every case." (He was citing the Griffin case; Eskridge v. Washington St. Bd.; Johnson v. United States, 352 U.S. 565; and Coppedge v. United States, 369 U.S. 438, 446.)[105]

A prisoner, convicted and sentenced to death by a California court in 1948, who became notorious by reason of the many years he was able to delay his execution, defended himself at his trial. About a month after the conclusion of the trial, the official court stenographer died, having at that time completed the dictation into a recording machine of what later turned out to be 646 of 1,810 pages of the trial transcript. A court reporter was employed in 1948 to transcribe the uncompleted portion of the original notes, and the completed transcript, approved by the trial judge, was made available to the defendant, who suggested some two hundred corrections and asked for a hearing to determine the reporter's ability to transcribe the notes. The motion was denied. The trial judge allowed some eighty of the defendant's corrections and though he held hearings thereon, defendant was not represented.

The record was approved and the conviction affirmed by the California Supreme Court. Thereafter, in 1955, the high court remanded to the district court defendant's application for a writ of habeas corpus, after, on five previous occasions, denying defendant's petitions for certiorari.[106] The district

103 Lane v. Brown, 372 U.S. 477, 485–86 (1963).
104 Draper v. Washington, 372 U.S. 487 (1963).
105 *Ibid.*, 500.
106 Chessman v. Teets, 350 U.S. 3 (1955).

court denied the application, and the circuit court affirmed. In the hearing before the district court, it appeared that the substitute reporter was related to the deputy district attorney in charge of the case and worked in close collaboration with the prosecutor and police officers who testified at the trial and that he had destroyed his first "rough draft" of his transcription which defendant had fruitlessly sought.

Five members of the Court held that the defendant was entitled to be represented at the settlement of the record and that the failure to permit him to do so was a violation of due process. Justices Douglas, Burton, and Clark dissented, maintaining that the defendant had been accorded due process. The Chief Justice did not participate.[107]

During the 1966 term, following Smith v. Bennett, 365 U.S. 708 and Lane v. Brown 372 U.S. 477, the Court, per curiam, reversed a judgment because Iowa had not furnished a convicted defendant a copy of the transcript for use on an appeal.[108]

Then, in Anders v. California,[109] judgment was reversed when court-appointed appellate counsel decided that there was no merit to the indigent's appeal and the court refused to appoint another attorney. Justice Stewart, joined by Justices Black and Harlan, dissented. He said: "The fundamental error in the Court's opinion, it seems to me, is its implicit assertion that there can be but a single inflexible answer to the difficult problem of how to accord equal protection to indigent appellants in each of the 50 States."[110]

In a case decided the same day, court-appointed counsel, apparently believing that the indigent defendant's appeal from his forgery conviction lacked merit, failed to file the entire record.[111] Justice Clark, who wrote for six members in the preceding Anders case, again did so, while Justices Stewart, Black, and Harlan concurred, but excepted to Justice Clark's conclusion that the case presented a problem similar to that involved in the Anders case.

At the August, 1967, meeting of the American Bar Association in Honolulu, a study group recommended that free legal counsel be provided for indigent defendants in all cases where the accused stands to be put in jail if convicted, whether the charge is a felony or a misdemeanor.[112]

107 Chessman v. Teets, 354 U.S. 156 (1957); see also Roberts v. La Vallee, 389 U.S. 40 (1967).
108 Long v. Iowa, 385 U.S. 192 (1966).
109 386 U.S. 738 (1967).
110 Ibid., 747.
111 Entsminger v. Iowa, 386 U.S. 748 (1967).
112 New York Times, August 13, 1967.

CHAPTER XIII

The Era of the Wild Horses—2

THE COURT, UNDER THE AEGIS OF CHIEF JUSTICE STONE, by the use of the commerce clause, made nationalization by prior courts pale. Here the Court showed as little respect for past decisions as it did for other branches of the law.

Following approval of the Fair Labor Standards Act of 1938 in a prior case,[1] the Court held employees of a building where tenants manufactured ladies' garments shipped in interstate commerce subject to the provisions of the Act, as being engaged in interstate commerce. Justice Frankfurter, writing for the majority, said: "To search for a dependable touchstone by which to determine whether employees are 'engaged in commerce or in the production of goods for commerce' is as rewarding as an attempt to square the circle."[2] Thereupon he held that engineers, firemen, electricians, elevator operators, watchmen, carpenters, and porters employed in the building were all persons who came within the Act. Justice Roberts, dissenting, thought that congressional power did not reach so far and that Congress had not intended that it should.[3]

At the next term the same question was raised concerning a member of an independent contractor's crew drilling for oil, and the Court held, as it did in the previous Kirschbaum case, that, since the oil was destined for interstate shipment, the crew member came under the Fair Labor Standards Act.[4] Justice Roberts dissented, as he did in the Kirschbaum case, and for the same reason.

Also at the next term the Court demonstrated that the periphery of the commerce clause knew no bounds when it concluded that an Ohio farmer who harvested 239 bushels of wheat in excess of his allotted quota, was subject to a penalty of $117.11 under the terms of the AAA Act of 1938.[5] Justice Jackson, writing for the Court, said that even home-consumed wheat

---

[1] United States v. Darby, 312 U.S. 100 (1941).
[2] Kirschbaum v. Walling, 316 U.S. 517, 520 (1942).
[3] *Ibid.*, 527.
[4] Warren-Bradshaw Drill. Co. v. Hall, 317 U.S. 88 (1942).
[5] Wickard v. Filburn, 317 U.S. 111 (1942).

would have a substantial influence on price and market conditions . . . because being in marketable condition such wheat overhangs the market and checks price increases. But if we assume that it is never marketed, it supplied a need of the man who grew it which would otherwise be reflected by purchases in the open market. Home-grown wheat in this sense competes with wheat in commerce.[6] . . . with the wisdom, workability, or fairness of the plan of regulation we have nothing to do.[7]

This was nationalization with a vengeance.

Also in the following term the Court held that persons engaged "in maintaining or operating a toll road and a drawbridge over a navigable waterway, which together constitute a medium for the interstate movement of goods" are persons engaged in commerce within the meaning of the Act.[8] Here there were two dissents: from Justices Roberts and Jackson.

But a five-to-four vote held that a cook employed by a contractor to prepare and serve meals to maintenance-of-way employees of an interstate railroad in a car running on the railroad's tracks was not engaged in commerce under the Fair Labor Standards Act.[9]

For the first time the Court was required to decide whether Congress had the power, under the commerce clause, to regulate insurance transactions crossing state lines, as the result of an indictment of an underwriters' association for violation of the Sherman Act.[10] With Justices Roberts and Reed absent, four Justices held that Congress had such power, overruling an early decision to the contrary,[11] which had been followed consistently for seventy-five years. The Chief Justice, supported by Justice Frankfurter, wrote in dissent, relying on the overruled case and those following it.[12] Justice Frankfurter said that he was satisfied Congress had not intended to include the insurance business when it passed the Sherman Act.[13]

Justice Jackson maintained that, since insurance had always been the subject of state, not of national regulation,

the orderly way to nationalize, if it be desirable, is not by court decision but through legislation. . . .

A judgment, as to when the evil of a decisional error exceeds the evil of an innovation must be based on very practical and in part upon policy considerations. When, as in this problem, such practical and political judgments can

[6] *Ibid.*, 128.
[7] *Ibid.*, 129.
[8] Overstreet v. North Shore Corp., 318 U.S. 125 (1943).
[9] McLeod v. Threlkeld, 319 U.S. 491 (1943).
[10] United States v. South-Eastern Underwriters, 322 U.S. 533 (1944).
[11] Paul v. Virginia, 8 Wall. 168 (1869).
[12] United States v. South-Eastern Underwriters, 322 U.S. 533, 578 (1944).
[13] *Ibid.*, 583–84.

be made by the political branches of the Government, it is the part of wisdom and self-restraint and good government for courts to leave the initiative to Congress.

Moreover, this is the method of responsible democratic government. To force the hand of Congress is no more the proper function of the judiciary than to tie the hands of Congress. To use my office, at a time like this, and with so little justification in necessity, to dislocate the functions and revenues of the states and to catapult Congress into immediate and undivided responsibility for supervision of the nation's insurance business is more than I can reconcile with my view of the function of this Court in our society.[14]

The perennial issue of whether taxes by states and their subdivisions constituted burdens on interstate commerce called upon the Court periodically. In holding that a state sales tax, in view of the commerce clause, may not be imposed on sales which are consummated by acceptance of orders in and shipment of goods from another state, the Court distinguished two prior cases,[15] over the dissent of Justices Black, Douglas, Murphy, and Rutledge.[16] Justice Douglas maintained that the decision was "squarely opposed" to another decision,[17] which, he said, "should be overruled if the present decision goes down."[18]

The Court struck down a municipal ordinance imposing upon solicitors of orders for goods a license tax upon the ground that it constituted a burden upon interstate commerce, explaining and distinguishing a prior case[19] which was relied on by Justice Douglas, with whom Justice Murphy concurred. Justice Black dissented.[20]

In holding invalid as a burden on interstate commerce an Indiana gross income tax, when applied to the receipt by one domiciled in the state of the proceeds of a sale of securities sent out of the state to be sold,[21] the Court distinguished three prior cases.[22] Justice Frankfurter wrote for the Court. Justice Rutledge concurred, saying[23] that he could not determine from the opinion "whether the Court now intends simply to qualify or to repudiate entirely,

[14] Ibid., 593–95.

[15] McGoldrick v. Berwind-White Co., 309 U.S. 33 (1940); Wisconsin v. J. C. Penney Co., 311 U.S. 435 (1940).

[16] McLeod v. Dilworth Co., 322 U.S. 327 (1944); see also National Bellas Hess v. Dept. of Revenue, 386 U.S. 753 (1967).

[17] McGoldrick v. DuGrenier; McGoldrick v. Felt & Co., 309 U.S. 70 (1940).

[18] McLeod v. Dilworth Co., 322 U.S. 327, 332 (1944).

[19] McGoldrick v. Berwind-White Co., 309 U.S. 33 (1940).

[20] Nippert v. Richmond, 327 U.S. 416 (1946).

[21] Freeman v. Hewit, 329 U.S. 249 (1946).

[22] McGoldrick v. Berwind-White Co., 309 U.S. 33 (1940); American Mfg. Co. v. St. Louis, 250 U.S. 459 (1919); International Harvester Co. v. Dept. of Treasury, 322 U.S. 340 (1944).

[23] Freeman v. Hewit, 329 U.S. 249, 250 (1946)

except in result" a prior case.[24] Justices Black and Douglas dissented, Justice Murphy concurring with Douglas, who relied on the distinguished cases.

The Court held valid a municipal ordinance which prohibited peddlers or canvassers from calling upon the occupants of private residences without having been requested or invited to do so.[25] The Chief Justice, supported by Justice Douglas, dissented upon the ground that the ordinance discriminated against interstate commerce in favor of local merchants. Justice Black dissented upon the ground that as respects canvassers for magazines, the ordinance violated the guaranty of freedom of the press.

The consequence of the broad application of the commerce clause to industry enabled the Court to find constitutional the National Labor Relations Act of 1935 and to affirm jurisdiction in the NLRB to denominate "unfair labor practices" so as to require a party guilty of them to cease and desist.[26] Thus there arose a myriad of cases, where the Board so acted.

As a consequence, the Labor Board, over the years, has passed upon thousands of cases involving claims of unfair labor practices, which gave it jurisdiction under the commerce clause. There was an early case involving an out-of-state employer who was found subject to the Act because he was engaged in receiving materials from a New York customer which he processed and returned in finished form.[27]

The widespread application of the commerce clause had equally widespread consequences and even sports were not overlooked. In an opinion by Chief Justice Warren, the Court held that professional boxing was interstate business and, as such, was subject to the Sherman Anti-Trust Act.[28] The opinion refused to follow the previous Toolson baseball case, which had held the contrary regarding baseball.[29] The Court pointed out that the baseball case merely followed a previous case[30] "without re-examination of the underlying issues" as a result of the Court's conclusion that Congress had no intention of including the business of baseball within the scope of the federal antitrust laws. Hence, the Chief Justice concluded, since there existed no precedent respecting boxing, the Court was free to examine the facts, which indicated that "over 25 per cent of the revenue from championship boxing was derived from interstate operations through the sale of radio, television, and motion picture rights."[31] Justices Burton and Reed concurred, basing their concurrence on

24 Adams Mfg. Co. v. Storen, 304 U.S. 307 (1938).

25 Breard v. Alexandria, 341 U.S. 622 (1951).

26 NLRB v. Jones & Laughlin Steel Corp., 301 U.S. 1 (1937).

27 NLRB v. Fainblatt, 306 U.S. 601 (1939).

28 United States v. International Boxing Club, 348 U.S. 236 (1955).

29 Toolson v. New York Yankees; Kowalski v. Chandler; Corbett v. Chandler, 346 U.S. 356 (1953).

30 Federal Baseball Club v. National League, 259 U.S. 200 (1922).

31 United States v. International Boxing Club, 348 U.S. 236, 241 (1955).

the views expressed in their dissents in the Toolson case. Justices Frankfurter and Minton, expressing the view that there was no difference between baseball and boxing, dissented, relying on the previous baseball cases. Justice Minton also expressed the view that boxing was not trade or commerce.

Justice Frankfurter said:

It would baffle the subtlest ingenuity to find a single differentiating factor between other sporting exhibitions, whether boxing or football or tennis, and baseball insofar as the conduct of the sport is relevant to the criteria or considerations by which the Sherman Law becomes applicable to a "trade or commerce" . . . Indeed, the interstate aspects of baseball and the extent of the exploitation of baseball through mass media are far more extensive than is true of boxing. . . .[32]

Whatever unsavory elements there be in boxing contests is quite beside the mark.[33]

Justice Minton said:

When boxers travel from State to State, carrying their shorts and fancy dressing robes in a ditty bag in order to participate in a boxing bout, which is wholly intrastate, it is now held by this Court that the boxing bout becomes interstate commerce. What this Court held in the Federal Baseball Case to be incident to the exhibition now becomes more important than the exhibition. This is as fine an example of the tail wagging the dog as can be conjured up. . . .[34]

Of course, there was at the time (1949) only one champion, Joe Louis. He had a monopoly on that, and while he got it by competition, he did not get it in trade or commerce. I do not suppose that Joe Louis had to go back into the ring and be walloped to a knockout or a decision before he could surrender his championship. . . .

What does a boxer or athlete have for sale but "personal effort not related to production," which, as Justice Holmes said, is not commerce? . . .

If there is a conspiracy, it is not one to control commerce between the States.[35]

Later William Radovich, a professional football player, sued the National Football League, claiming he was blacklisted as a result of a conspiracy among the defendants, which violated the Sherman Anti-Trust Act. The lower courts felt bound by the previous baseball cases and dismissed the complaint. Six members of the high court voted for reversal, upon the grounds stated in the International Boxing Club case, saying that they were not bound by the

[32] *Ibid.*, 248–49
[33] *Ibid.*, 251.
[34] *Ibid.*
[35] *Ibid.*, 252–53.

baseball cases.[36] Justice Clark, writing for the majority, recognized the incongruity, saying:

> If this ruling is unrealistic, inconsistent, or illogical, it is sufficient to answer, aside from the distinctions between the businesses, that were we considering the question of baseball for the first time upon a clean slate we would have no doubts. But Federal Baseball held the business of baseball outside the scope of the Act. No other business claiming the coverage of those cases has such an adjudication.[37]

Justices Frankfurter, Harlan, and Brennan dissented, pleading the compulsion of stare decisis. The former said:

> ... conscious as I am of my limited competence in matters athletic, I have yet to hear of any consideration that led this Court to hold that "the business of providing baseball games for profit between clubs of professional baseball players was not within the scope of the federal antitrust laws," ... that is not equally applicable to football.[38]

In 1964 Congress passed a civil rights law, Title II of which prohibited racial discrimination in places of public accommodation serving interstate travelers. When its constitutionality was challenged, Justice Clark wrote for the Court, while Justices Black, Goldberg, and Douglas concurred, finding the act constitutional.[39]

The issue concerned a 216-room Georgia motel available to transient guests, which solicited patronage from outside the state through national advertising media. It appeared that approximately 75 per cent of its registered guests were from out of state. It refused to rent to Negroes and sought a declaratory judgment denying the constitutionality of the Act forbidding it to do so.

Justice Clark distinguished the Civil Rights Cases[40] which declared provisions of the Civil Rights Act of 1875 unconstitutional; the commerce clause was not then considered as the source of the congressional power.[41] He said the evidence was "overwhelming ... that discrimination by hotels and motels impedes interstate travel.[42] He listed the fields in which Congress had legislated because of interstate transportation of people and goods[43] and added:

---

[36] Radovich v. National Football League, 352 U.S. 445 (1957).

[37] *Ibid.*, 452.

[38] *Ibid.*, 455.

[39] Heart of Atlanta Motel v. United States, 379 U.S. 241 (1964).

[40] 109 U.S. 3 (1883).

[41] Heart of Atlanta Motel v. United States, 379 U.S. 241, 250–52 (1964).

[42] *Ibid.*, 253.

[43] *Ibid.*, 257, citing "to gambling, Lottery Case, 188 U.S. 321 (1903); to criminal enterprises, Brooks v. United States, 267 U.S. 432 (1925); to deceptive practices in the sale of products,

"That Congress was legislating against moral wrongs in many of these areas rendered its enactments no less valid."

In a companion case the Court found "Ollie's Barbecue, a family-owned restaurant in Birmingham, Alabama," which purchased 46 per cent of its meat from a local supplier who bought it outside the state, under the statutory prohibition.[44]

The overruling tendencies of the Stone court found manifestation respecting a matrimonial case that had withstood several decades, when O. B. Williams, who had been married and had lived with his wife in North Carolina, and Lillie Shaver Hendrix, who had been married and had lived with her husband in that state, left their respective spouses, went to Nevada, where they obtained divorces, and married. On their return to North Carolina they lived together and were indicted and convicted for bigamous cohabitation. Over the dissent of Justice Jackson the Court held that despite the lack of service upon or appearance by the defendants in the Nevada divorce proceedings, residence for six weeks in Nevada, in accordance with the Nevada law, sufficed to give its courts jurisdiction to grant divorce and the full faith and credit clause of the Constitution required North Carolina to recognize the validity of the divorce, since Nevada's finding of domicile was not questioned.[45] In so holding, the Court overruled the prior Haddock case.[46]

After the Court's reversal of the judgment of the North Carolina court, the defendants were again tried before judge and jury. The state had not previously challenged Nevada's finding of domicile on the previous appeal, since it had rested on the precedent of the previous Haddock case, which had since been overruled. Now it challenged the Nevada finding of domicile, and a jury again convicted the defendants, finding that defendants' alleged domicile in Nevada was not a bona fide one. A majority of the high court affirmed the conviction in an opinion by Justice Frankfurter.[47] Justice Murphy concurred. Justice Black, with the support of Justice Douglas, who wrote the earlier opinion, dissented. He said:

Federal Trade Commission v. Mandel Bros., 359 U.S. 385 (1959); to fraudulent security transactions, Securities and Exchange Commission v. Ralston Purina Co., 346 U.S. 119 (1953); to misbranding of drugs, Weeks v. United States, 245 U.S. 618 (1918); to wages and hours, United States v. Darby, 312 U.S. 100 (1941); to members of labor unions, NLRB v. Jones and Laughlin Steel Corp., 301 U.S. 1 (1937); to crop control, Wickard v. Filburn, 317 U.S. 111 (1942); to discrimination against shippers, United States v. Baltimore and Ohio R.R. Co., 333 U.S. 169 (1948); to resale price maintenance, Hudson Distributors, Inc. v. Eli Lilly & Co., 377 U.S. 386 (1964), Schwegmann v. Calvert Distillers, 341 U.S. 384 (1951); to professional football, Radovich v. National Football League, 352 U.S. 445 (1957); and to racial discrimination by owners and managers of terminal restaurants, Boynton v. Virginia, 364 U.S. 454 (1960)."

44 Katzenbach v. McClung, 379 U.S. 294 (1964).
45 Williams v. North Carolina, 317 U.S. 287 (1942).
46 Haddock v. Haddock, 201 U.S. 562 (1906).
47 Williams v. North Carolina, 325 U.S. 226 (1945).

...the petitioners are being deprived of their freedom because the State of Nevada, through its legislature and courts, follows a liberal policy in granting divorces.... without holding the decrees invalid under Nevada law, this Court affirms a conviction of petitioners for living together as husband and wife.[48]

The same day the Court affirmed a finding by a Pennsylvania court that a husband who had obtained a Nevada divorce had not acquired a domicile there and that, in consequence, his liability to his wife under an agreement for her support remained unimpaired.[49] Justice Douglas concurred saying that a difference should be recognized between holding a subsequent marriage bigamous and requiring a husband to continue support. Justices Black and Rutledge joined in the opinion.

Later the Court held that a Florida divorce granted a wife in a suit in which Sherrer, the husband, appeared and the Florida court found the wife living in Florida, though the parties had been domiciled in Massachusetts, was entitled to full faith and credit in Massachusetts. Justices Frankfurter and Murphy dissented.[50] Again, the Court overruled a prior case.[51] A similar result followed in Coe, a companion case.[52]

Thereafter the Court held a decree of divorce obtained by a husband in a state in which he had become domiciled against an absent wife who did not appear in the suit but was notified by constructive service entitled to full faith and credit in New York.[53] The Court divided on a question of alimony under a previous New York separation decree. Justice Frankfurter dissented. Justice Jackson, dissenting, wrote:

> If there is one thing that the people are entitled to expect from their lawmakers, it is rules of law that will enable individuals to tell whether they are married and, if so, to whom. Today . . . the most learned lawyer cannot advise them with any confidence.... In a society as mobile and nomadic as ours, such uncertainties affect large numbers of people and create a social problem of some magnitude.[54]

A companion case went the same way.[55]

Later the Court held that a wife not personally served and who did not appear in a Nevada divorce proceeding could, in a Connecticut court, chal-

[48] Ibid., 262.
[49] Esenwein v. Pennsylvania, 325 U.S. 279 (1945).
[50] Sherrer v. Sherrer, 334 U.S. 343 (1948).
[51] Andrews v. Andrews, 188 U.S. 14 (1903).
[52] Coe v. Coe, 334 U.S. 378 (1948).
[53] Estin v. Estin, 334 U.S. 541 (1948).
[54] Ibid., 553.
[55] Kreiger v. Kreiger, 334 U.S. 555 (1948).

lenge the alleged acquisition of a Nevada domicile by the husband.[56] Now it distinguished the Sherrer and Coe cases.

In a subsequent case the wife maintained in a suit brought in Vermont to annul her marriage that a decree she obtained in Florida was fraudulently obtained since she had no intention of establishing a domicile there. The majority, reversing the Vermont Supreme Court which granted a judgment of annulment, found the record insufficient to disclose the facts but held that if the Florida judgment was procured without the appearance or consent of the husband it would not be entitled to full faith and credit,[57] citing a previous case.[58] Justice Frankfurter dissented, maintaining that the record disclosed the fact that the husband had neither appeared in nor consented to the Florida jurisdiction.

In a 1956 case the wife had left the residence of her husband in Florida and had gone to Ohio. Thereupon, employing constructive service, the husband obtained a divorce decree in Florida which, he maintained, denied alimony to the wife. In a later suit for divorce brought by the wife in Ohio, the Court held itself bound by the Florida decree as to divorce, but granted the wife alimony. Writing for four members of the Court, Justice Minton found that the Florida court had not passed on the alimony question; hence Ohio was free to act.[59] Justice Frankfurter, concurring, joined in Justice Minton's opinion. The Chief Justice and Justices Black, Douglas, and Clark also concurred, but with an opinion by Justice Black, in the course of which he found that the Florida court had denied alimony and that therefore the constitutional question whether the Ohio court was justified in denying full faith and credit to the Florida decree was before the Court. On that score, he said:

> We believe that Ohio was not compelled to give full faith and credit to the Florida decree denying alimony to Mrs. Armstrong. Our view is based on the absence of power in the Florida court to render a personal judgment against Mrs. Armstrong depriving her of all right to alimony although she was a nonresident of Florida, had not been personally served with process in that State, and had not appeared as a party.[60]

He maintained further that a prior case[61] "stands alone in the United States Reports in supporting the proposition that a valid ex parte divorce in one State cuts off alimony rights in another . . . and should no longer be considered to be the law."[62]

[56] Rice v. Rice, 336 U.S. 674 (1949).
[57] Cook v. Cook, 342 U.S. 126 (1951).
[58] Johnson v. Muelberger, 340 U.S. 581 (1951); see also Sutton v. Leib, 342 U.S. 402 (1952).
[59] Armstrong v. Armstrong, 350 U.S. 568 (1956).
[60] Ibid., 576.
[61] Thompson v. Thompson, 226 U.S. 551 (1913).

Six members of the Court held that a Nevada decree of divorce obtained by the husband without service upon or appearance by the wife was entitled to full faith and credit in New York but that the Nevada court, having no personal jurisdiction over the wife, could not extinguish her rights under New York law to seek and obtain alimony.[63] Justice Frankfurter concurred with the full-faith-and-credit holding but dissented from the holding that New York had jurisdiction to award alimony. Justice Harlan dissented on the ground that domicile might affect the result and said that that fact was not clearly disclosed. The Chief Justice did not participate.

Analysis of the 58 per cent of dissents during the 1943 term found Roberts dissenting by himself thirteen out of a total of thirty-nine times while his net of twenty-six with others was a maximum, with a minimum of sixteen by the Chief Justice and Rutledge. The exceptions to everyone dissenting from everyone else were principally Douglas and Black in unison fifteen times and Roberts and Frankfurter a like number. Murphy, Douglas, Black, and Rutledge formed the liberal bloc; Roberts, Frankfurter, Reed, and Jackson, and the Chief Justice, the moderates.[64]

During the 1944 term dissents equaled the previous term record of 58 per cent representing 94 of 163 opinions, carrying 245 votes. Of the dissents, thirty, almost one-third, were by five-to-four votes.

Roberts dissented fifty-seven times, of which twenty-one dissents were sole. The Chief Justice led the others with thirty-one dissents, of which twenty-six were cast with Roberts, fifteen with Frankfurter and eleven with Reed. Frankfurter teamed with Roberts twenty-two times of a total of twenty-four dissents. Jackson with seventeen cast eleven with Roberts.[65]

On the other side of the Court, we find Black teamed with Douglas in sixteen of his thirty dissents, with Rutledge seventeen times and with Murphy fourteen.[66] The liberal pattern was obvious, as was the difficulty of the moderates going as far as it stretched.

Justice Jackson was named American prosecutor at the Nuremberg War Crime Trials and, in consequence, was absent during the 1945 term. This left a court of eight members even before the death of the Chief Justice, and since division was so prevalent, it required delay in determination of cases where an equal division prevailed. Justice Roberts resigned before the beginning of the term and was replaced by Harold H. Burton of Ohio. Chief Justice Stone died on April 22, 1946, and was not replaced until after the term had ended.

[62] Armstrong v. Armstrong, 350 U.S. 568, 581 (1956).
[63] Vanderbilt v. Vanderbilt, 354 U.S. 416 (1957).
[64] C. Herman Pritchett, *The Roosevelt Court* (New York, The Macmillan Co., 1948), 41–42.
[65] *Ibid.*, 42.
[66] *Ibid.*, 42–43.

During the 1945 term dissents, with Justice Jackson absent, remained at the high level of 56 per cent. Justice Frankfurter was the leading dissenter, with thirty dissents, of which five were sole, eleven were with the liberal Rutledge, and nine were with the conservative Burton. Burton dissented twenty-one times. Reed and the Chief Justice (to the time of his death), each cast fifteen dissents. Of the liberals, Rutledge led with twenty-two dissents, four being sole and eleven, as noted, with the mercurial Frankfurter. Douglas also dissented twenty-two times, with seven sole and only nine with Black. Black dissented eighteen times, with no affiliation of substance other than with Douglas. Murphy with three dissents confined his dissents in association with the other three liberals, excepting only three with Frankfurter.[67] The dissent record revealed the lack of unanimity affecting the entire membership of the Court.

The wake of World War II washed up its detritus, just and unjust, on the judicial shores. Injustices were engendered, as might have been expected, when the fear of Japanese sabotage on the West Coast moved Congress, on March 21, 1942, to enact a statute making it a misdemeanor knowingly to disregard restrictions imposed by the military authorities pursuant to presidential order. The first of such cases to reach the Court involved a senior of Japanese parentage in the University of Washington, who had failed to register for evacuation, as directed, because, he contended, such order was violative of his rights as an American citizen. A unanimous Court affirmed the defendant's conviction, the Chief Justice writing for the Court and Justices Douglas, Rutledge, and Murphy concurring in apologetic opinions.[68]

In upholding a military curfew, which the defendant had violated, the Chief Justice said,

> Distinctions between citizens solely because of their ancestry are by their very nature odious to a free people whose institutions are founded upon the doctrine of equality. For that reason, legislative classification or discrimination based on race alone has often been held to be a denial of equal protection. . . . We may assume that these considerations would be controlling here were it not for the fact that the danger of espionage and sabotage, in time of war and of threatened invasion, calls upon the military authorities to scrutinize every relevant fact bearing on the loyalty of populations in the danger areas.[69]

Justice Douglas, concurring, said: ". . . we are dealing here with a problem of loyalty not assimilation. Loyalty is a matter of mind and of heart not of

[67] *Ibid.*, 25.
[68] Hirabayshi v. United States, 320 U.S. 81 (1943).
[69] *Ibid.*, 100.

face. That indeed is the history of America."[70] A companion case went the same way.[71]

Later, when the invasion fears had dimmed, the Court considered the case of Fred Korematsu, an American citizen of Japanese descent, who was convicted of violating an order excluding all persons of Japanese ancestry from certain areas. The Court, in an opinion by Justice Black, upheld the exclusion order and the conviction upon the ground that it could not "now say that at the time these actions were unjustified."[72]

Justice Frankfurter concurred. Justice Roberts wrote, dissenting, saying the case differed from the previous Hirabayshi case in that it involved

convicting a citizen as a punishment for not submitting to imprisonment in a concentration camp, based on his ancestry, without evidence or inquiry concerning his loyalty and good disposition towards the United States. If this be a correct statement . . . I need hardly labor the conclusion that constitutional rights have been violated.[73]

Justices Murphy and Jackson also wrote in dissent, with Justice Jackson saying:

. . . if any fundamental assumption underlies our system, it is that guilt is personal and not inheritable. . . . here is an attempt to make an otherwise innocent act a crime merely because this prisoner is the son of parents as to whom he had no choice, and belongs to a race from which there is no way to resign. . . .[74]

I cannot say, from any evidence before me, that the orders of General De Witt were not reasonably expedient military precautions, nor could I say that they were. But even if they were permissible military procedures, I deny that it follows that they are constitutional. . . .

In the very nature of things military decisions are not susceptible of intelligent judicial appraisal. They do not pretend to rest on evidence. . . .[75]

A military order, however unconstitutional, is not apt to last longer than the military emergency. . . . But once a judicial opinion . . . rationalizes the Constitution to show that the Constitution sanctions such an order, the Court for all time has validated the principle of racial discrimination in criminal procedure and of transplanting American citizens. The principle then lies about like a loaded weapon ready for the hand of any authority that can bring forward a plausible claim of an urgent need. . . . All who observe the work of the courts

[70] *Ibid.*, 107.
[71] Yasui v. United States, 320 U.S. 115 (1943).
[72] Korematsu v. United States, 323 U.S. 214, 224 (1944).
[73] *Ibid.*, 226.
[74] *Ibid.*, 243.
[75] *Ibid.*, 245.

are familiar with what Judge Cardozo described as "the tendency of a principle to expand itself to the limit of its logic." A military commander may overstep the bounds of constitutionality, and it is an incident. But if we review and approve, that passing incident becomes the doctrine of the Constitution. There it has a generative power of its own, and all that it creates will be in its own image. Nothing better illustrates this danger than does the Court's opinion in this case.

It argues that we are bound to uphold the conviction of Korematsu because we upheld one in Hirabayshi. . . . Now the principle of racial discrimination is pushed from support of mild measures to very harsh ones. . . . Because we said that these citizens could be made to stay in their homes during the hours of dark, it is said we must require them to leave home entirely. . . .[76]

If the people ever let command of the war power fall into irresponsible and unscrupulous hands, the courts wield no power equal to its restraint.[77]

Justice Cardozo's estimate of the generative force of a principle and Justice Jackson's application of the estimate were promptly borne out when the Court was asked to free a woman of Japanese ancestry, admittedly a loyal citizen, from the strictures of the rules and the grasp of the Civil War Relocation Authority, which succeeded to the control of the centers in which those evacuated had been lodged. The Court ordered her release upon the ground her detention was unauthorized.[78]

Justices Murphy and Roberts wrote, concurring. The latter attacked the basis of Justice Douglas' opinion for the majority, saying it was hiding one's head in the sand in asserting that "the detention of the relator resulted from an excess of authority by subordinate officials." He concluded: "An admittedly loyal citizen has been deprived of her liberty for a period of years. Under the Constitution she should be free to come and go as she pleases."[79]

In another case the Court was charged with the duty of supplementing the military when seven Germans, six concededly German citizens, all of whom had lived in the United States, had returned to Germany and received training as saboteurs and then, wearing German uniforms and carrying explosives, were brought back to the United States by submarines. Three landed on Long Island, New York; four landed in Florida; each buried his uniform and donned civilian clothes. All were apprehended and charged with violation of the laws of war and other offenses. They were convicted and sentenced to death by a military commission. They sought habeas corpus, maintaining that the President lacked authority to order them tried by military author-

---

[76] *Ibid.*, 246, 247.
[77] *Ibid.*, 248.
[78] *Ex parte* Endo, 323 U.S. 283 (1944).
[79] *Ibid.*, 309, 310.

ities. A unanimous Court held the contrary, explaining and distinguishing *ex parte* Milligan.[80]

Thereafter the Court considered the conviction of Anthony Cramer, a German by birth, who had been naturalized. His prosecution resulted from his association with Thiel and Kerling, two of the German saboteurs involved in the Quirin case (above), as a result of his former association and friendship with Thiel. His conviction for treason was reversed in an opinion by Justice Jackson, for a majority of the Court, holding that treason was not proved as required by the Constitution. Justice Jackson said:

> The innovations made by the forefathers in the law of treason were conceived in a faith such as Paine put in the maxim that "He that would make his own liberty secure must guard even his enemy from oppression; for if he violates this duty he establishes a precedent that will reach himself." We still put trust in it.[81]

Justice Douglas wrote in dissent, with the support of the Chief Justice and Justices Black and Reed. He charged that the majority had ignored the facts in the record and had decided the case on an "untenable but . . . also unnecessary" interpretation of the Constitution.

By a five-to-four vote the conviction of members of the German-American Bund for conspiracy to counsel evasion of military service was set aside for lack of proof. The Chief Justice and Justices Reed, Douglas, and Jackson dissented.[82] Previously, a majority of the Court had held that George Sylvester Viereck, a notorious German propagandist, was not required, under a congressional statute, to disclose propagandist activities in which he engaged on his own behalf, and accordingly his conviction for failure to make such disclosure was reversed.[83] Justices Black and Douglas dissented; Justices Jackson and Rutledge did not participate.

The commanding general of the Japanese Army in the Philippine Islands sought writs of habeas corpus and certiorari to review an order of the Supreme Court of the Philippines. He had been tried by a military commission on a charge of violation of the laws of war, had been convicted and sentenced to be hanged. Over the dissent of Justices Murphy and Rutledge the Court affirmed the action of the commission.[84] In substance the majority held that, as long as a military commission was properly convened and authorized to act, its determinations were for the military, not the civilian courts, to review.

[80] *Ex parte* Quirin, Haupt, Kerling, Burger, Heinck, Thiel, Neubauer; United States *ex rel.* Quirin v. Cox, 317 U.S. 1 (1942).
[81] Cramer v. United States, 325 U.S. 1, 48 (1945).
[82] Keegan v. United States; Kunze v. United States, 325 U.S. 478 (1945).
[83] Viereck v. United States, 318 U.S. 236 (1943).
[84] *In re* Hamashita, 327 U.S. 1 (1946).

Justice Murphy contended that the Japanese general was entitled to invoke the Constitution and that he was entitled to due process, since these rights "belong to every person in the world, victor or vanquished, whatever may be his race, color or beliefs. They survive," he contended, "any popular passion or frenzy of the moment."[85] Justice Rutledge struck the same note; both dissenters maintained that the defendant had not had a fair trial. The same result followed in the case of General Homma, over the same dissent.[86]

Illustrative of a splintered court was the affirmance of convictions of draftees who had absented themselves from a civilian public service camp to which they had been sent by a draft board. Four members joined in an opinion by Justice Reed; Justice Frankfurter concurred; Justices Black and Douglas dissented on one ground, and Justices Rutledge and Murphy dissented on another.[87]

Provisions of a California statute forbidding ownership of agricultural lands by aliens ineligible to citizenship were held to violate the Fourteenth Amendment in a case where a Japanese father caused lands to be deeded to his son, a citizen by birth.[88] Justice Black wrote, concurring, with the support of Justice Douglas, saying he preferred to find the basic provisions of the act violative on broader grounds. Justice Murphy, joined by Justice Rutledge, held the act unconstitutional as discriminating against the Japanese.

Later the Court struck down a California statute forbidding the issuance of commercial fishing licenses to aliens ineligible to citizenship as violative of equal protection.[89] Justice Murphy, joined by Rutledge, said the statute was racially discriminatory. Justices Reed and Jackson dissented.

The Court denied habeas corpus to German nationals, taken in custody in China by the United States Army after the Japanese surrender and convicted of war crimes by a military commission.[90] Justice Jackson, writing for six justices, called attention to a similar result in previous war crime cases. Justices Black, Douglas, and Burton dissented.

Recurrently the dissension in the Court manifested itself. For example, Justice Jackson, writing for the Court, held invalid an Ohio tax statute upon intangibles, such as receivables, owned by foreign corporations and owing from out-of-state debtors, while identical property owned by its residents and domestic corporations was exempted, as denying protection under the Fourteenth Amendment.[91] He supplemented his opinion for the Court with an-

[85] *Ibid.*, 26.

[86] Homma v. Patterson, 327 U.S. 759 (1946).

[87] Cox v. United States; Thompson v. United States; Roisum v. United States, 332 U.S. 442 (1947).

[88] Oyama v. California, 332 U.S. 633 (1948).

[89] Takahashi v. Fish & Game Commission, 334 U.S. 410 (1948).

[90] Johnson v. Eisentrager, 339 U.S. 763 (1950).

other, an acerbic one, in reply to a dissenting opinion by Justice Douglas, supported by Justice Black, maintaining that the Court had held a corporation entitled to the benefits of the equal protection afforded a "person" under the Fourteenth Amendment without ever having really considered the question.

Also illustrative of the splintered court was a case in which five members of the Court found valid a congressional statute extending the diversity juris-diction of the district courts to citizens of the District of Columbia.[92] Three members of the majority found the act valid for one reason; two, for another. Six justices disagreed with the reason advanced by the three of the majority; seven disagreed with the reason advanced by the two of the majority. Justice Frankfurter wrote in dissent, with the support of Justice Reed; the Chief Justice, dissenting, wrote, with the support of Justice Douglas. A five-to-four admiralty decision,[93] overruled a previous and recent decision.[94]

A conflict between federal and state authorities claiming the right to regu-late rates of a public utility was decided by a majority of the Court which relied heavily on legislative history. Justice Jackson concurred, saying, "I should concur in this result more readily if the Court could reach it by analysis of the statute instead of by psychoanalysis of Congress. . . . Never having been a Congressman, I am handicapped in that weird endeavor. That process seems to me not interpretation of a statute but creation of a statute."[95]

Whereupon, Justice Frankfurter, concurring, said:

The light shed by Mr. Justice Jackson on the underpinning of the Court's opinion makes me unwilling to share responsibility for a decision resting on such underpinning. . . .

Preoccupation with other matters pending before the Court precludes an independent pursuit by me of all the tributaries in search of legislative purpose that the Court has followed. I am therefore constrained to leave the decision of this case to those who have no doubts about the matter.[96]

The practice of overruling also continued. The first decision of the 1941 term overruled two cases[97] in upholding, by a unanimous Court, a state tax collectible from a seller of materials bought by a contractor having a cost-plus contract with the Government, to which, as a result, the tax was ultimately charged.[98]

[91] Wheeling Steel Corp. v. Glander; National Dist. Prod. Corp. v. Glander, 337 U.S. 562 (1949).
[92] National Mutual Ins. Co. v. Tidewater Trans. Co., 337 U.S. 582 (1949).
[93] Cosmopolitan Ship Co. v. McAllister, 337 U.S. 783 (1949).
[94] Hust v. Moore-McCormack Lines, 328 U.S. 707 (1946).
[95] United States v. Public Utilities Commission, 345 U.S. 295, 319 (1953).
[96] Ibid., 321.
[97] Panhandle Oil Co. v. Mississippi, 277 U.S. 218 (1928); Graves v. Texas Co., 298 U.S. 393 (1936).
[98] Alabama v. King & Boozer, 314 U.S. 1 (1941).

Later the federal authorities were successful in inducing a majority of the Court to deny the right of the state to levy a sales tax on a purchase by contractors of tractors to be used in constructing a Navy depot. This too involved a cost-plus contract with the contractor, but the Navy Department had provided that the purchase was made by the government, and the Court held the contractor an agent of the government.[99] The Chief Justice and Justices Black and Douglas dissented.

In another state tax case the Court construed the Atomic Energy Act to prohibit taxation of private contractors for materials used in performing contracts for the Atomic Energy Commission and denied the states' right to tax.[100] Here again we find the result of a desire to increase the national collection of taxes at the expense of the states, a philosophy under a growing and justified challenge.

By a vote of seven to two over the dissent of Justices Jackson and Roberts, the Court held[101] that a state might impose a transfer tax on shares of a domestic corporation owned by a nonresident decedent and overruled a previous case.[102]

A majority of five held that a trust agreement which reserved a life income in the trust property to the settlor was taxable as part of his estate,[103] overruling a prior decision.[104] Justice Jackson concurred; Justices Reed and Frankfurter dissented, saying that the prior decision should not be overruled. Justice Burton also dissented. A companion case found the same result where the settlor provided that income should go to children and grandchildren, but failed to make provision for distribution of corpus in the event he survived all his children and grandchildren.[105] A majority of five subscribed to an opinion by Justice Black; Justice Reed concurred and Justices Burton, Frankfurter, and Jackson dissented.

The Court held valid Oklahoma taxing statutes affecting mineral rights in allotted and restricted Indian lands,[106] overruling prior decisions.[107] Thus the Court wended a tortuous and bickering way through precedents, past and present.

---

99 Kern Limerick v. Scurlock, 347 U.S. 110 (1954).

100 Carson v. Roane-Anderson Co., 342 U.S. 232 (1952).

101 Tax Commission v. Aldrich, 316 U.S. 174 (1942).

102 First National Bank v. Maine, 284 U.S. 312 (1932).

103 Commissioner v. Church, 335 U.S. 632 (1949).

104 May v. Heiner, 281 U.S. 238 (1930).

105 Spiegel v. Commissioner of Int. Rev., 335 U.S. 701 (1949).

106 Oklahoma Tax Commission v. Texas Co.; Oklahoma Tax Commission v. Magnolia Petroleum Co., 336 U.S. 342 (1949).

107 Howard v. Gipsy Oil Co., 247 U.S. 503 (1918); Large Oil Co. v. Howard, 248 U.S. 549 (1919); Oklahoma v. Barnsdall Refineries, 296 U.S. 521 (1936); Choctaw & Gulf R.R. v. Harrison, 235 U.S. 292 (1914); Indian Territory Oil Co. v. Oklahoma, 240 U.S. 522 (1916).

CHAPTER XIV

The Years of the Witch-Hunt—I

FRED M. VINSON OF KENTUCKY, who had had previous judicial service and had also been secretary of the treasury, replaced Chief Justice Stone. Justice Jackson rejoined the Court, and there were no other changes in personnel during the 1946 term. Justices Murphy and Rutledge died following the close of the 1948 term and were replaced by Tom C. Clark of Texas and Sherman Minton of Indiana. With the Chief Justice, Justices Burton, Clark, and Minton constituted a conservative bloc on the Court. Justice Jackson, a Roman Catholic, had had an anti-Communist innoculation at Nuremberg. Justices Frankfurter and Reed were essentially conservative; both had testified for Alger Hiss, convicted of giving information to the Russians, and were necessarily defensive on the Communist issue. In consequence, Communists and alleged Communists did not fare as well as they otherwise might have.

Congress, of course, reflected public opinion, which was strongly anti-Communist and which became rabidly so when inflamed by Senator Joseph McCarthy and the Korean War. Congress had passed the Smith Act as far back as 1940 and during the fifties supplemented it with such enactments as the McCarran Internal Security Law, the Subversive Activities Control Act, and the Labor-Management Reporting and Disclosure Act. The Taft-Hartley Law also contained provisions directed at Communists in the labor movement. President Truman yielded to the furor by requiring loyalty checks, though he had vetoed the McCarran and Hartley acts, which Congress had passed over his veto. The notorious un-American Activities Committee of the House, which still continues its disputable existence, then headed by the since discredited Congressmen Dies and Parnell, hunted headlines as they hunted subversives. On one occasion the committee denounced three government employees and caused a bill to be enacted by Congress providing for cessation of payment of their salaries. Nevertheless, they continued in their employment and sued for their salaries. The court of claims found for them; the high court affirmed, holding the act of Congress unconstitutional as constituting a bill of attainder.[1] Justices Frankfurter and Reed concurred, saying the plaintiffs were entitled to recover without recourse to the question of constitutionality.

Similar attacks upon government employees became a favored means of persecution, supplementing requirements for loyalty oaths. A government employee occupying a nonsensitive position was charged with association with Communists and was summarily dismissed under the Summary Suspension Act of 1950. A majority of six held that that summary discharge authorized by the Act had reference only to activities affecting the nation's safety. Justices Clark, Reed, and Minton dissented, interpreting the congressional purpose as authorizing summary dismissal of employees whose retention would be inimical to the national interest regardless of the sensitivity of their positions.[2]

Construing the 1951 loyalty and security regulations of the Department of State, the Court vitiated the discharge of a high-ranking foreign service officer in the Department of State upon the ground that the Secretary of State had not made an independent determination that there was reasonable doubt about the employee's loyalty.[3] Justice Clark did not participate.

Six members of the Court sustained the discharge of a Pennsylvania school teacher for "incompetency" because of his refusal to answer a school superintendent's questions respecting his Communist affiliations.[4] The Chief Justice and Justices Black and Douglas dissented, maintaining that his refusal to answer by reason of his Fifth Amendment privilege was involved in his discharge, which thus violated due process. Justice Brennan dissented on the ground that the discharge was for disloyalty, of which there was no proof.

On the same day Justice Harlan, writing for five members of the Court, sustained the discharge of a subway conductor by his employer after he had claimed the privilege of the Fifth Amendment when asked concerning his Communist party membership, upon the ground that his refusal to answer had created doubt about his reliability, thus justifying his discharge.[5] The Chief Justice and Justices Douglas, Black, and Brennan dissented.

The petitioner, an officer of a private corporation engaged in government work, had been given security clearance by the government. It was revoked by a proceeding in which he had no opportunity to confront or examine witnesses, in consequence of which he lost his job. He sued for a declaratory judgment and an injunction. The lower courts found against him. Writing for five members of the Court, the Chief Justice reversed, holding that revocation of security clearance in such fashion had not been authorized. Justices Frank-

---

[1] United States v. Lovett; United States v. Watson; United States v. Dodd, 328 U.S. 303 (1946).
[2] Cole v. Young, 351 U.S. 536 (1956).
[3] Service v. Dulles, 354 U.S. 363 (1957).
[4] Beilan v. Board of Pub. Educ. 357 U.S. 399 (1958).
[5] Lerner v. Casey, 357 U.S. 468 (1958).

260

furter, Harlan, and Whittaker concurred. Justice Clark, dissenting, maintained the action taken had been authorized.[6]

Later, a short-order cook at a cafeteria operated by her employer on the premises of the naval gun factory at Washington, which required identification badges and security clearance for access, was required to turn in her badge because of the security officer's determination that she had failed to meet security requirements. The commander of the base denied her a hearing. The lower court dismissed her complaint. Five members of the Court held that the responsibility and authority of the commanding officer was absolute and that due process was not violated by a denial of information and a hearing.[7] Justices Black, Douglas, and Brennan and the Chief Justice dissented.

The acting director of a government agency issued a press release containing information on the basis of which he was suspending two officers of the agency. They sued for libel, and the lower courts found in their favor. The high court reversed and remanded the case for further proceedings.[8] The lower court reaffirmed the judgment. Justice Harlan, writing for four members, held the statements in the release were privileged, and, with the concurrence of Justice Black, the judgment was vacated.[9] The Chief Justice and Justices Brennan and Douglas dissented, holding that the defendant, as a government official of rank, should have only a qualified privilege respecting public statements. Justice Stewart also dissented, maintaining that the defendant had acted beyond the call of his duty.

In a companion case a majority of the Court held that the commander of the Boston Naval Shipyard had an absolute privilege to include defamatory matter in a missive to his superiors and that the publication of the matter to Congress was in the discharge of his duties. Justice Black concurred. The Chief Justice maintained that the officer was not required to report to Congress. Justice Brennan also dissented, maintaining that the defendant's privilege was only a qualified one.[10]

A permanent employee and a temporary employee of the county of Los Angeles were discharged for insubordination when they took their Fifth Amendment privileges before a congressional committee. Five members of the Court held that, since the discharge was on the ground of "insubordination," it was to be sustained.[11] Justices Black and Douglas dissented upon the ground that the county was penalizing the exercise of the privilege. Justice Brennan made the same contention respecting the permanent employee.

[6] Greene v. McElroy, 360 U.S. 474 (1959).
[7] Cafeteria & Restaurant Workers Union v. McElroy, 367 U.S. 886 (1961).
[8] Barr v. Matteo, 355 U.S. 171 (1957).
[9] Barr v. Matteo, 360 U.S. 564 (1959).
[10] Howard v. Lyons, 360 U.S. 593 (1959).
[11] Nelson v. Los Angeles, 362 U.S. 1 (1960).

Revocation of naturalization became one form of attack upon individual Communists. An action was brought to cancel the naturalization of a William Schneiderman upon the ground that he had represented himself to be "attached to the principles of the Constitution" when such was not the case. A majority of the Court held that the charge was not established by mere proof that, at the time of applying for naturalization, he was a member of and subscribed to the principles of the Communist party and was active therein.[12] The Chief Justice and Justices Roberts and Frankfurter dissented.

Justice Murphy wrote for the majority:

> . . . it is safe to say that nowhere in the world today is the right of citizenship of greater worth to an individual than it is in this country. . . . such a right once conferred should not be taken away without the clearest sort of justification and proof. . . . we believe the facts and the law should be construed as far as is reasonably possible in favor of the citizen. . . . the burden of proof is on the Government. . . . this burden must be met with evidence of a clear and convincing character. . . .[13]
>
> . . . under our traditions beliefs are personal and not a matter of mere association, and . . . men in adhering to a political party or other organization notoriously do not subscribe unqualifiedly to all of its platforms or asserted principles.[14]

He concluded that the government had not proved that the Communist party advocated a change of government by force and violence, and he quoted Holmes's dissent in the Schwimmer case respecting criticism of and a desire to improve the Constitution. Justice Douglas concurred and maintained that, in the absence of a showing of fraud, the decree awarding naturalization was final. Justice Rutledge concurred similarly.

Dissenting, Chief Justice Stone, with the support of Justices Frankfurter and Roberts, maintained that the lower courts had found that the defendant had not been attached to the principles of the Constitution, that such findings had been sustained by the evidence, and that, since Congress had made such attachment a condition of obtaining citizenship, it should be revoked.

Later in the term, the Court followed the Schneiderman decision by reversing a decision setting aside a certificate of naturalization issued to one who had strongly expressed opinions of the superiority of the German people and of German virtues, including those of Hitler and his movement.[15] Justice Murphy wrote, concurring, and was joined by Justices Black, Douglas, and Rutledge.

[12] Schneiderman v. United States, 320 U.S. 118 (1943).
[13] Ibid., 122–23.
[14] Ibid., 136.
[15] Baumgartner v. United States, 322 U.S. 665 (1944).

Subsequently, finding fraud proved, the Court denaturalized a Bund member, over the dissent of Justices Rutledge and Murphy.[16]

By a five-to-four vote the Court affirmed a conviction for contempt found against a woman, against whom denaturalization proceedings were pending, who took the stand in her own behalf but refused to tell whether or not she was still a Communist, invoking the privilege against self-incrimination. The majority held that the rule in criminal cases of a waiver of the privilege by taking the stand applied equally in civil proceedings.[17] The Chief Justice and Justices Black, Douglas, and Brennan dissented.

In two denaturalization cases directed against alleged Communists, six members of the Court reversed judgments favorable to the government upon the ground that it had not met its burden of proof.[18] Justices Burton, Clark, and Whittaker dissented. Subsequently, in holding that citizenship cannot be taken away, the majority opinion called attention to the fact that, "as the Chief Justice said in his dissent, 356 U.S. at 66 . . . naturalization unlawfully procured can be set aside," pointing to the cases discussed above.[19]

Akin to efforts to denaturalize alleged Communists were proceedings, with congressional sanction, to deport them. The Court found valid a section of the Internal Security Act of 1950 empowering the Attorney General in his discretion to continue in custody or to release under bond an alien, pending final determination of his deportability. It held the Attorney General might hold without bail aliens solely on the ground that they were members of the Communist party and active in Communist work, even though no specific acts of sabotage or incitement to subversive action were shown.[20] Justice Reed wrote for five members of the Court; Justices Black, Frankfurter, Burton, and Douglas dissented.

Justice Black said:

Today the Court holds that law-abiding persons, neither charged with nor convicted of any crime, can be held in jail indefinitely, without bail, if a subordinate Washington bureau agent believes they are members of the Communist party, and therefore dangerous to the nation because of the possibility of their "indoctrination of others."[21]

. . . denial of bail may well be the equivalent of a life sentence, at least for Zydok, 56 years old, and Carlisle, whose health is bad. Such has become the fate of ordinary family people selected and classified, on secret information, as "dangerous" by Washington bureau agents.

[16] Knauer v. United States, 328 U.S. 654 (1946).
[17] Brown v. United States, 356 U.S. 148 (1958).
[18] Nowak v. United States, 356 U.S. 660 (1958); Maisenberg v. United States, 356 U.S. 670 (1958).
[19] Afroyim v. Rusk, 387 U.S. 253, 267 n.23 (1967).
[20] Carlson v. Landon, 342 U.S. 524 (1952).
[21] Ibid., 547–48.

. . . Zydok's case illustrates what is happening. He has lived in this country 39 years, owns his home, has violated no law, is "not likely to engage in any subversive activities," has a wife, two sons, a daughter and five grandchildren, all born in the United States. Both sons served in the armed services in World War II. Zydok himself, then a waiter, sold about $50,000 worth of U. S. war bonds and "donated blood on seven occasions to the Red Cross for the United States Army." This jailing of Zydok, despite a patriotic record of which many citizens could well be proud, is typical of what actually happens when public feelings run high against an unpopular minority.[22]

Justice Frankfurter added: ". . . in the case of Carlisle and Stevenson the Government had no evidence of activity or membership in the Communist Party more recent than the 1930's."[23]

Concurrently, six members of the Court joined in an opinion of Justice Jackson upholding a provision of the Alien Registration Act requiring deportation of any alien who was at the time of entering the United States or had been thereafter a member of an organization advocating the overthrow of the government.[24] Justices Douglas and Black dissented; Justice Clark did not participate.

The deportation orders involved Harisiades, a Greek national, who at the age of thirteen had accompanied his father to the United States in 1916 and whose wife and two children were citizens; Mascitti, an Italian, who came to the United States in 1920 at the age of sixteen, had married, and had one American-born child; and Mrs. Coleman, a Russian, who had come to the United States in 1914 at the age of thirteen, had married an American citizen, and had three children, citizens by birth.

Justice Jackson said: "That aliens remain vulnerable to expulsion after long residence is a practice that bristles with severities. But it is a weapon of defense and reprisal confirmed by international law as a power inherent in every sovereign state."[25]

Justice Frankfurter, concurring, declared:

It is not for this Court to reshape a world order based on politically sovereign States. . . . Ever since national States have come into being, the right of people to enjoy the hospitality of a State of which they are not citizens has been a matter of political determination by each State. . . .

This Court . . . has recognized that the determination of a selective and exclusionary immigration policy was for the Congress and not for the Judiciary. . . .[26]

---

[22] Ibid., 549.
[23] Ibid., 567.
[24] Harisiades v. Shaughnessy; Mascitti v. McGrath; Coleman v. McGrath, 342 U.S. 580 (1952).
[25] Ibid., 587–88.
[26] Ibid., 596.

... whether immigration laws have been crude and cruel, whether they may have reflected xenophobia in general or anti-Semitism or anti-Catholicism, the responsibility belongs to Congress. . . .

In recognizing this power and this responsibility of Congress one does not in the remotest degree align oneself with fears unworthy of the American spirit or with hostility to the bracing air of the free spirit. One merely recognizes that the place to resist unwise or cruel legislation touching aliens is the Congress, not this Court.[27]

Justice Douglas, dissenting, said that "the view that the power of Congress to deport aliens is absolute and may be exercised for any reason which Congress deems appropriate rests" upon a prior case decided in 1893 by a six-to-three vote.[28] "The decision," he said, "seems to me to be inconsistent with the philosophy of constitutional law which we have developed for the protection of resident aliens...."[29] And he quoted Justice Brewer's dissent in the prior case.

Later Justice Douglas wrote for five members of the Court upholding a provision of the Immigration Act of 1917 which made it a felony for an alien against whom a deportation order was outstanding willfully to fail or refuse to make timely application in good faith for travel and other documents necessary to his departure.[30] Justices Black, Jackson, and Frankfurter dissented. Justice Clark did not participate.

Justice Douglas pointed out that the decision rested solely on the lack of definiteness and certainty of the statute; Justice Black dissented from that finding. Justice Jackson maintained that the statute was unconstitutional but the majority refused to consider the constitutional question since it had not been put in issue.

A later decision sustained the deportation of an alien upon the ground that he had been a member of the Communist party from 1944 to 1946.[31] Justice Frankfurter wrote for six members of the Court; Justice Reed concurred, while Justices Black and Douglas dissented. The majority held it was not necessary for the government to prove that the defendant was aware of the party's advocacy of violence.

An alien, ordered deported because he had been a member of the Communist party from 1935 to 1940, was denied a suspension of the order on the basis of undisclosed confidential information in the possession of the immigration authorities. Five members of the Court supported the denial upon the ground that Congress had authorized the use of such information by the

27 *Ibid.*, 597–98.
28 Fong Yue Ting v. United States; Wong Quan v. United States; Lee Joe v. United States, 149 U.S. 698 (1893).
29 Harisiades v. Shaughnessy, 342 U.S. 580, 598 (1952).
30 United States v. Spector, 343 U.S. 169 (1952).
31 Galvan v. Press, 347 U.S. 522 (1954).

Attorney General. The Chief Justice and Justices Black, Frankfurter, and Douglas dissented.[32]

The Chief Justice, dissenting, wrote:

> In the interest of humanity, the Congress, in order to relieve some of the harshness of the immigration laws, gave the Attorney General discretion to relieve hardship in deportation cases. . . .
>
> . . . on the basis of such "confidential" information, after more than 40 years of residence here, we are tearing petitioner from his relatives and friends and from the country he fought to sustain. (Petitioner's only absence from this country since his original entry in 1914 was during World War I to serve in the Armed Forces of our neighbor and ally, the Dominion of Canada. . . . I am unwilling to write such a departure from American standards into the judicial or administrative process or to impute to Congress an intention to do so.[33]

Justice Black said:

> This is a strange case in a country dedicated by its founders to the maintenance of liberty under law. The petitioner, Cecil Reginald Jay, is being banished because he was a member of the Communist party from 1935 to 1940. His Communist Party membership at that time did not violate any law. The Party was recognized then as a political organization and had candidates in many state elections. Jay's Communist Party membership ended 10 years before such membership was made a ground for deportation by Congress. . . .
>
> He is entitled to suspension "in the discretion" of the Attorney General if he "proves" that during the preceding 10 years he has been a person of good moral character and if deportation would result in exceptional and unusual hardship. . . . Jay proved his case. . . .[34]
>
> Jay is now 65 years of age. . . .[35]
>
> What is meant by "confidential information?" No nation can remain true to the ideal of liberty under law and at the same time permit people to have their homes destroyed and their lives blasted by the slurs of unseen and unsworn informers; there is no possible way to contest the truthfulness of anonymous accusations. The supposed accuser can neither be identified nor interrogated. He may be the most worthless and irresponsible character in the community. What he said may be wholly malicious, untrue, unreliable, or inaccurately reported. In a court of law the triers of fact could not even listen to such gossip, much less decide the most trifling issue on it. . . .[36]
>
> Unfortunately, this case is not the first one in recent years where arbitrary

[32] Jay v. Boyd, 351 U.S. 345 (1956).
[33] *Ibid.*, 361–62.
[34] *Ibid.*, 362–63.
[35] *Ibid.*, 364.
[36] *Ibid.*, 365.

power has been approved and where anonymous information has been used to take away vital rights and privileges of people. . . .[37]

Unfortunately this condemnation of Jay on anonymous information is not unusual—it manifests the popular fashion in these days of fear. . . .[38]

Justice Douglas asserted:

The statement that President Eisenhower made in 1953 on the American code of fair play is more than interesting Americana. As my Brother Frankfurter says, it is Americana that is highly relevant to our present problem. The President said: "In this country, if someone dislikes you, or accuses you, he must come up in front. He cannot hide behind the shadow. He cannot assassinate you or your character from behind, without suffering the penalties an outraged citizenry will impose."[39]

Six members of the Court approved dismissal of an indictment of an alien against whom a final order of deportation had been outstanding, for refusal to answer questions, as provided by the Immigration and Nationality Act. The majority held that the statute required answers only to questions reasonably designed to keep the Attorney General advised regarding the continued availability for departure of aliens whose deportation was overdue.[40] Justices Clark and Burton dissented. Justice Whittaker did not participate.

The Court, with the concurrence of Justices Frankfurter, Clark, and Harlan, held that a refusal to admit petitioner to practice as a lawyer because he had had a Communist affiliation fifteen years before was a violation of due process.[41] Justice Whittaker did not participate. Justice Black held that the petitioner's use of aliases so that he could secure a job in businesses which discriminated against Jews twenty years before did not impugn his present good character.

Five members of the Court held, in an opinion by Justice Frankfurter, that an old man, who had lived in this country for forty years, was not to be deported because "the dominating impulse of his 'affiliation' with the Communist Party may well have been wholly devoid of any 'political' implications"[42] and though he had been a salesman in a Communist book store. Justice Harlan, joined by Justices Burton, Clark, and Whittaker, dissenting, said: "I regret my inability to join the Court's opinion, for its effort to find a way out from the rigors of a severe statute has alluring appeal."[43]

[37] *Ibid.*, 366.
[38] *Ibid.*, 368.
[39] *Ibid.*, 374.
[40] United States v. Witkovich, 353 U.S. 194 (1957).
[41] Schware v. Board of Bar Exam., 353 U.S. 232 (1957).
[42] Rowoldt v. Petfetto, 355 U.S. 115 (1957).
[43] *Ibid.*, 121.

In two cases a majority of five members held that Chinese who were admitted to this country on parole could not claim the benefits accorded aliens "within the country."[44] The Chief Justice and Justices Black, Douglas, and Brennan dissented, maintaining that the statute permitting withholding of deportation when the Attorney General is of the opinion that it may subject the alien to physical persecution, should be construed liberally.

Five members of the Court affirmed a judgment of a district judge who found that an alien facing deportation had perjured himself in denying membership in the Communist party.[45] The Chief Justice and Justices Black, Douglas, and Brennan dissented, maintaining the evidence insufficient to sustain the finding. Justice Douglas pointed out that the "petitioner was born in Finland in 1908, and came here when he was less than a year old and has resided here ever since. He is married to a native-born citizen; he served honorably in our Army; and he has no criminal record of any kind except for a petty offense, back in 1930."[46]

In another deportation case the same majority held that an alien seeking suspension of deportation had the burden of proving that he was not a member of the Communist party and that his refusal to answer questions concerning such membership because of the Fifth Amendment did not relieve him of that burden.[47] Justice Douglas, speaking for the Chief Justice and Justice Black, dissenting, said:

> It has become much the fashion to impute wrongdoing to or to impose punishment on a person for invoking his constitutional rights. Lloyd Barenblatt has served a jail sentence for invoking his First Amendment rights. . . . As this is written, Dr. Willard Uphaus, as a consequence of our decision . . . is in jail in New Hampshire for invoking rights guaranteed to him by the First and Fourteenth Amendments. So is the mathematician, Horace Chandler Davis, who invoked the First Amendment against the House Un-American Activities Committee. Today, we allow invocation of the Fifth Amendment to serve, in effect though not in terms, as proof that an alien lacks the "good moral character" which he must have . . . to become eligible for the dispensing powers entrusted to the Attorney General.
>
> The import of what we do is underlined by the fact that there is not a shred of evidence of bad character in the record against this alien. . . . He entered as a student in 1928 and pursued his studies until 1938. . . . Since 1938 he has been continuously employed in gainful occupations. That is the sole basis of his deportability. . . . His employment since 1938 has been as manager of a produce company, as chemist, as foundry worker, and as a member of OSS during the

44 Leng May Ma v. Barber, 357 U.S. 185 (1958); Rogers v. Quan, 357 U.S. 193 (1958).
45 Niukkanen v. Alexander, 362 U.S. 390 (1960).
46 Ibid., 391.
47 Kimm v. Rosenberg, 363 U.S. 405 (1960).

latter part of World War II. . . . No one came forward to testify that he was a Communist. . . . The only thing that stands in his way . . . is his invocation of the Fifth Amendment.[48]

An alien who became eligible for old-age social security benefits in 1955 was deported in 1956 for membership in the Communist party. Under the provisions of the Social Security Act, his wife, who had remained in this country, was given notice of the termination of his social security benefits. He sued, challenging the constitutionality of such deprivation. Five members of the Court found the statute constitutional. Justices Black, Douglas, Brennan, and the Chief Justice dissented.[49]

Justice Harlan, writing for the majority, said:

The "right" to Social Security benefits is in one sense "earned" for the entire scheme rests on the legislative judgment that those who in their productive years were functioning members of the economy may justly call upon that economy, in their later years, for protection from "the rigors of the poorhouse as well as from the haunting fear that such a lot awaits them when journey's end is near." . . .

To engraft upon the Social Security system a concept of "accrued property rights" would deprive it of the flexibility and boldness in adjustment to ever-changing conditions which it demands. . . . It was doubtless out of an awareness of the need for such flexibility that Congress included in the original Act and has since retained, a clause expressly reserving to it "(t)he right to alter, amend, or repeal any provision" of the Act. . . .

We must conclude that a person covered by the Act has not such a right in benefit payments (as) would make every defeasance of "accrued" interests violative of the Due Process Clause of the Fifth Amendment. . . .

This is not to say, however, that Congress may exercise its power to modify the statutory scheme free of all constitutional restraint. . . .[50]

The fact of a beneficiary's residence abroad—in the case of a deportee, a presumably permanent residence—can be of obvious relevance to the question of eligibility.[51]

Justice Black, dissenting, said:

. . . I agree with the District Court that the United States is depriving appellee . . . of his statutory right to old-age benefits in violation of the United States Constitution.

Nestor came to this country from Bulgaria in 1913 and lived here contin-

[48] *Ibid.*, 408–10.
[49] Flemming v. Nestor, 363 U.S. 603 (1960).
[50] *Ibid.*, 610–11.
[51] *Ibid.*, 612.

uously for 43 years, until July, 1956. He was then deported from this country for having been a Communist from 1933 to 1939. At that time membership in the Communist Party was not even a statutory ground for deportation. From December, 1936, to January, 1955, Nestor and his employers made regular payments to the Government under the Federal Insurance Contributions Act. . . . These funds went to a special federal old-age and survivors insurance trust fund, in return for which Nestor, like millions of others, expected to receive payments when he reached the statutory age. In 1954, 15 years after Nestor had last been a Communist, and 18 years after he began to make payments into the old-age security fund, Congress passed a law providing, among other things, that any person who had been deported because of past Communist membership . . . should be wholly cut off from any benefits of the fund to which he had contributed under the law. . . . This action, it seems to me, takes Nestor's insurance without just compensation and in violation of the Due Process Clause of the Fifth Amendment. Moreover, it imposes an ex post facto law and bill of attainder by stamping him, without a court trial, as unworthy to receive that for which he has paid and which the Government promised to pay him. The fact that the Court is sustaining this action indicates the extent to which people are willing to go these days to overlook violations of the Constitution perpetrated against anyone who has ever even innocently belonged to the Communist Party.

Justice Black quoted Senator George, the chairman of the Finance Committee when the Social Security Act was passed: " 'Social Security is not a handout; it is not charity; it is not relief. It is an earned right based upon the contributions and earnings of the individual.' " He continued:

People who pay premiums for insurance usually think they are paying for insurance, not for "flexibility and boldness." . . .[52]

A basic constitutional infirmity of this Act, in my judgment, is that it is a part of a pattern of laws all of which violate the First Amendment out of fear that this country is in grave danger if it lets a handful of Communist fanatics or some other extremist group make their arguments and discuss their ideas. . . . It is an unworthy fear in a country that has a Bill of Rights containing provisions for fair trials, freedom of speech, press and religion, and other specific safeguards designed to keep men free.[53]

Five members of the Court held that the government had failed to establish that a proposed deportee's association with the Communist party was "meaningful" and vacated the deportation order.[54] Justices Harlan, Clark, Stewart, and White dissented, holding that there was sufficient evidence for

[52] *Ibid.*, 621, 624.
[53] *Ibid.*, 628.
[54] Gastelum-Quinones v. Kennedy, 374 U.S. 469 (1963).

the Board's contrary conclusion below and that the high court was not the place to evaluate evidence.

A majority of the Court construed a section of the Immigration Act to prevent deportation of aliens having familial relationships here who had been admitted by misrepresentation for the purpose of evading quota restrictions. Justice Stewart, joined by Justices Harlan and White, dissented, saying: "There is nothing to indicate that Congress enacted this legislation to allow whole-sale evasion of the Immigration and Nationality Act or as a general reward for fraud."[55]

A majority of the Court held that it is incumbent upon the government in deportation proceedings "to establish the facts supporting deportability by clear, unequivocal and convincing evidence."[56] Justice Stewart, writing for the majority, said: "In denaturalization cases the Court has required the Government to establish its allegations by clear, unequivocal, and convincing evidence. The same burden has been imposed in expatriation cases. That standard of proof is no stranger to the civil law."[57]

Justice Clark, joined by Justice Harlan, dissented, saying:

> The Court, by placing a higher standard of proof on the Government, in de-portation cases, has usurped the legislative function of the Congress and has in one fell swoop repealed the long-established "reasonable, substantial, and probative" burden of proof placed on the Government by specific Act of the Congress. . . . This is but another case in a long line in which the Court has tightened the noose around the Government's neck in immigration cases.[58]

Another facet of prosecution of Communists involved charges of criminal conspiracy. One such produced the much-publicized trial of eleven leaders of the Communist party on charges of conspiring to teach and advocate the overthrow of the government by force or violence. The trial dragged on for nine months and was marked by controversy between the trial judge and the Communist lawyers, which left neither free from justified criticism.

Following the conviction of the defendants, four members of the Court joined in an opinion by the Chief Justice upholding the convictions; Justices Frankfurter and Jackson concurred, Justices Black and Douglas dissented, and Justice Clark did not participate.[59]

Justice Black said:

> These petitioners were not charged with overt acts of any kind designed to

[55] Immigration Service v. Errico, 385 U.S. 214, 230 (1966).
[56] Woodby v. Immigration Service, 385 U.S. 276, 277 (1966).
[57] *Ibid.*, 285
[58] *Ibid.*, 287.
[59] Dennis v. United States, 341 U.S. 494 (1951).

overthrow the Government. They were not even charged with saying anything or writing anything designed to overthrow the Government. The charge was that they agreed to assemble and to talk and publish certain ideas at a later date. The indictment is that they conspired to organize the Communist Party and to use speech or newspapers and other publications in the future to teach and advocate the forcible overthrow of the Government. No matter how it is worded, this is a virulent form of prior censorship of speech and press, which I believe the First Amendment forbids. . . .

. . . the only way to affirm these convictions is to repudiate directly or indirectly the established "clear and present danger" rule. . . . The opinions for affirmance indicate that the chief reason for jettisoning the rule is the expressed fear that advocacy of Communist doctrine endangers the safety of the Republic.[60]

Justice Douglas, dissenting, maintained:

If we are to take judicial notice of the threat of Communists within the nation, it should not be difficult to conclude that *as a political party* they are of little consequence. Communists in this country have never made a respectable or serious showing in any election. I would doubt that there is a village, let alone a city or county or state, which the Communists could carry. Communism in the world scene is no bogey-man; but Communists as a political faction or party in this country plainly is. . . . Free speech has destroyed it as an effective political party. . . .

How it can be said that there is a clear and present danger that this advocacy will succeed is, therefore, a mystery.[61]

The aftermath of the trial and conviction of the eleven leaders of the party was the conviction of their lawyers for contempt of court.[62] Five members of the Court affirmed; Justices Black, Frankfurter, and Douglas dissented; Justice Clark did not participate.

Other consequences were the disbarment of Isserman and Sacher, two of the Communists' lawyers. Isserman was disbarred by the New Jersey court where he had been admitted to practice. Automatically, this was followed by proceedings to disbar him from practice in the United States Supreme Court. This application was granted by a divided court, the Chief Justice, joined by Justices Reed, Burton, and Minton favoring disbarment, Justices Jackson, Black, Frankfurter, and Douglas opposed.[63]

Sacher, the other lawyer, whose contempt conviction had resulted in his serving a sentence of six months, was disbarred by the federal Court. He

[60] *Ibid.,* 579–80.
[61] *Ibid.,* 588.
[62] Sacher v. United States, 343 U.S. 1 (1952).
[63] *In re* Isserman, 345 U.S. 286 (1953).

appealed to the high court which, feeling that disbarment was too severe an added penalty, reversed the lower courts.[64] Justices Reed and Burton dissented; Justice Clark did not participate.

Later, Sacher was again convicted of contempt for refusing to answer questions before a congressional committee. The high court vacated the judgment and remanded the case for further proceedings compatible with the Watkins case.[65] Again he was convicted. Then six members of the Court held that the questions which he had refused to answer were not pertinent to the subject the committee was authorized to pursue and vacated the conviction.[66] Justice Harlan concurred. Justices Clark and Whittaker dissented. Justice Burton did not participate.

Green and Winston, two of the eleven Communist leaders who had been convicted, failed to surrender when their convictions were affirmed. They remained in hiding for some four years; thereafter they were convicted of criminal contempt for their failure to surrender and were sentenced therefor. Five members of the Court, in an opinion by Justice Harlan, affirmed.[67] Justice Frankfurter concurred. Justices Black, Douglas, and the Chief Justice dissented, holding that defendants were entitled to a trial by jury after indictment. Brennan dissented on the ground that the evidence did not establish the defendants' knowledge of the surrender order, and Black and Douglas also supported that view. (Later, Governor Barnett of Mississippi was to make a similar contention.)

The conviction under the Pennsylvania Sedition Act of Steve Nelson, a prominent Communist leader, was reversed by a six-man majority upon the ground that Congress, by the federal Smith and other acts, had pre-empted the field of sedition.[68] Justices Reed, Burton, and Minton dissented.

Subsequently the Court voted, in an opinion by Justice Harlan, to vacate convictions of Communists charged with conspiring, in violation of the Smith Act, to advocate and teach the forcible overthrow of the government and to organize a society of persons to so advocate and teach.[69] Justice Clark dissented on the first count; Justices Clark and Burton on the second. Justices Brennan and Whittaker did not participate.

Five members of the Court struck down an Arkansas statute that required teachers in a state-supported school or college to file an affidavit each year listing their organizational affiliations upon the ground of its "unlimited

[64] Sacher v. New York Bar Assoc., 347 U.S. 388 (1954).
[65] Sacher v. United States, 354 U.S. 930 (1957).
[66] Sacher v. United States, 356 U.S. 576 (1958).
[67] Green v. United States, 356 U.S. 165 (1958).
[68] Pennsylvania v. Nelson, 350 U.S. 497 (1956).
[69] Yates v. United States; Schneiderman v. United States; Richmond v. United States, 354 U.S. 298 (1957).

and indiscriminate sweep." The majority found that "the statute's comprehensive interference with associational freedom goes far beyond what might be justified in the exercise of the State's legitimate inquiry into the fitness and competency of its teachers."[70]

Justices Frankfurter, Harlan, Clark, and Whittaker dissented. Justice Frankfurter said:

> As one who has strong views against crude intrusions by the state into the atmosphere of creative freedom in which alone the spirit and mind of a teacher can fruitfully function, I may find displeasure with the Arkansas legislation now under review. But in maintaining the distinction between private views and constitutional restrictions, I am constrained to find that it does not exceed the permissible range of state action limited by the Fourteenth Amendment.[71]

The usual division of the Court prevailed when a majority of five upheld the Subversive Activities Control Act and the action of the control board thereunder requiring the Communist party of the United States to register under Section 7 of the Act.[72] Justice Frankfurter wrote for the majority; each of the four dissenters also wrote. All four dissenters maintained that the registration requirement violated the self-incrimination privilege of the Fifth Amendment, while Justice Black regarded the Act as a bill of attainder, and the other three maintained that it violated the freedom of expression and of association protected by the First Amendment.

When, on June 29, 1959, the Court ordered reargument of the appeal of Julius Irving Scales, Justice Clark dissented, saying: "Much has been said of late of the law's delay and criticism has been heaped on the courts for it. This case affords a likely Exhibit A. It looks as if Scales' case, like Jarndyce v. Jarndyce, will go on forever."[73]

When on February 5, 1959, the Court set the case for argument on October 10, 1960, Justice Clark again dissented. However, it was argued at that time and was decided with the Communist registration case. The usual five members of the Court, over the dissent of the usual four liberal members, affirmed Scales's conviction for violation of the membership clause of the Smith Act, which made a felony the acquisition or holding of knowing "membership" in an organization which advocated the overthrow of the government by force or violence.[74]

The majority found the Dennis and the Yates cases controlling. Justice Black maintained that the conviction violated the First Amendment and also

[70] Shelton v. Tucker, 364 U.S. 479, 490 (1960).
[71] *Ibid.*
[72] Communist Party v. SACB, 367 U.S. 1 (1961).
[73] Scales v. United States, 360 U.S. 924 (1959).
[74] Scales v. United States, 367 U.S. 203 (1961).

that the law was unconstitutionally vague and ex post facto. Justice Douglas quoted Mark Twain: " 'It is by the goodness of God that in our country we have those three unspeakably precious things: freedom of speech, freedom of conscience, and the prudence never to practice either of them.' "[75] Douglas added: "Even the Alien and Sedition Laws . . . never went so far as we go today. . . .[76] What we lose by majority vote today may be reclaimed at a future time when the fear of advocacy, dissent and nonconformity no longer cast a shadow over us."[77]

The companion case of John Francis Noto, which involved a similar conviction in the New York Federal Court, found the five members who had affirmed Scales's conviction vacating that of Noto, upon the ground that the evidence "fails to establish that the Communist Party was an organization which presently advocated violent overthrow of the Government now or in the future."[78] Justices Black and Douglas concurred, saying that the First Amendment required vacation of the conviction. Justice Brennan and the Chief Justice advocated dismissal of the indictment since they believed that the prosecution was barred by Section 4(f) of the Internal Security Act.[79]

Later, in a per curiam opinion, a majority of the Court remanded to the Subversive Activities Control Board the issue of whether an organization was a "Communist-front," upon the ground that the Board's decision rested on the activities of the organization's executive secretary, who had since died, rather than on the activities of the organization itself subsequent to his death.[80] Justices Black, Douglas, and Harlan dissented. Justice White did not participate.

In his dissent Justice Black wrote:

I have additional reasons for objecting to the remand. . . . I think that among other things the Act is a bill of attainder; that it imposes cruel, unusual and savage punishments for thought, speech, writing, petition and assembly; and that it stigmatizes people for their beliefs, associations and views about politics, law and government. The Act has borrowed the worst features of old laws intended to put shackles on the minds and bodies of men, to make them confess to crime, to make them miserable while in this country, and to make it a crime even to attempt to get out of it. It is difficult to find laws more thought-stifling than this one even in countries considered the most benighted. Previous efforts to have this Court pass on the constitutionality of the various provisions of this freedom-crushing law have met with frustration on one excuse or another.

[75] Ibid., 262–63.
[76] Ibid., 263.
[77] Ibid., 275.
[78] Noto v. United States, 367 U.S. 290, 298 (1961).
[79] Ibid., 300–302.
[80] American Committee v. SACB, 380 U.S. 503 (1965).

I protest against following this course again. My vote is to hear the case now and hold the law to be what I think it is—a wholesale denial of what I believe to be the constitutional heritage of every freedom-loving American.[81]

Simultaneously, in a companion case, the Court found the Board's order based almost exclusively on events before 1950, and very largely on events before 1940. It found that the hearings had been concluded ten years before and said that "on so stale a record we do not think it is either necessary or appropriate that we decide the serious constitutional questions raised by the order." The majority returned the case to the Board for further proceedings.[82]

Justice Douglas, dissenting, with the support of Justices Black and Harlan, said: "None of the parties before us has suggested that the record is stale or incomplete. . . . None of the parties before us has suggested that we need to know more about the Brigade since the Board's decision in 1955. We are told by counsel that what the Brigade once was, it still is. . . . I think it is indefensible not to decide the important constitutional questions tendered here and now."[83]

Five members of the Court joined in an opinion by the Chief Justice to hold that a section of the Labor-Management Reporting and Disclosure Act of 1959, which made it a crime for one who belonged to the Communist party or had been a member during the past five years willfully to serve as a member of the executive board of a labor organization, constituted a bill of attainder in that it inflicted punishment without a trial.[84]

The Chief Justice said:

We do not hold today that Congress cannot weed dangerous persons out of the labor movement. . . . Rather, we make . . . the point . . . that Congress must accomplish such results by rules of general application. It cannot specify the people upon whom the sanction it prescribes is to be levied. Under our Constitution, Congress possesses full legislative authority, but the task of adjudication must be left to other tribunals.[85]

Justice White, joined by Justices Clark, Harlan, and Stewart, wrote in dissent. He maintained that the statute was not punitive but regulatory and that it was Congress' purpose to prevent political strikes and the means were reasonable to that end.

Despite the order of the Subversive Activities Control Board, the Communist party failed to register with the Attorney General. It failed to file a

81 *Ibid.,* 511–12.
82 Veterans v. SACB, 380 U.S. 513 (1965).
83 *Ibid.,* 516, 517.
84 United States v. Brown, 381 U.S. 437 (1965).
85 *Ibid.,* 461.

membership list, which would be followed, under the statute, by required registration of members. Hence the Attorney General, as permitted by the statute, petitioned the Board for an order requiring certain persons to register, and the Board made orders accordingly. The alleged members appealed, and the high court reversed.[86] The Court held that the petitioners were faced with the choice of registering or subjecting themselves to serious punishment, that the information called for in registering might be used as evidence in a criminal prosecution, and that the Act's immunity provision did not suffice to answer the petitioners' claim of privilege under the Fifth Amendment.

These decisions, in effect, made the Subversive Activities Control Board concededly inactive, although it previously and thereafter, during its seventeen-year existence, controlled no subversives. Nevertheless, its members stayed on the payroll, a not unusual political practice, and this gave rise to a minor scandal when, in 1967, with no business on its books, and $5,000,000 spent on doing nothing, the President appointed as a new member of the five-man defunct Board, at a salary of $26,000 a year, a young man who had married one of the President's secretaries, and a complaisant and co-operating senator "kissed" senatorial approval of the appointment through an empty Senate chamber. Senators, irked by the fact that the bridegroom was sworn in before they learned of the appointment, undertook to abolish the unneeded Board as a means of vitiating the appointment, and similar bills were introduced in the House.

However, the unwillingness of politicians to abolish jobs held by politicians, and the added unwillingness of congressmen to be recorded as opposed to anticommunism, resulted in a congressional watering down of the Board's functions in an effort to enable it to survive, and then, almost simultaneously, the Court breathed life into the congressional corpse by holding that the lower federal courts of the District of Columbia had properly refused to bar the Board from conducting hearings to determine whether the well-known W. E. B. DuBois Clubs of America were a Communist-front organization, with Justices Douglas and Black dissenting.[87] At the same time the Court severed another limb of the Board by declaring unconstitutional the section of the 1950 act that made it a crime for a member of the Communist party to take a job in a defense facility. Justices Harlan and White dissented.[88]

Thereafter, on January 16, 1968, a unanimous Court struck down screening procedure under the Magnuson Act of 1950, as empowered by President Truman, to enable the Coast Guard to keep subversives from getting jobs on United States merchant ships. The plaintiff was denied a license upon the

[86] Albertson v. SACB, 382 U.S. 70 (1965).
[87] Du Bois Clubs v. Clark, 389 U.S. 309 (1967).
[88] United States v. Robel, 389 U.S. 258 (1967).

ground of his previous Communist membership. Justice Douglas said that it could not be assumed that Congress had given the government the right to inquire into seamen's political beliefs without saying so, and four members of the Court said that, had Congress undertaken to do so, the act would have been unconstitutional.[89]

A group of alleged Communists were indicted for conspiracy, charged with filing false affidavits in order to qualify their union as bargaining representative under the National Labor Relations Act. Their convictions were reversed upon the ground that they should have been granted permission to inspect the grand jury minutes.[90] Justices Black and Douglas dissented in part, maintaining that the defendants were entitled to attack the constitutionality of the act as a bill of attainder.

A woman lawyer, engaged in defending Communists, in a public speech made while the trial was pending, impeached the proceedings, in consequence of which she was suspended from practice. Five judges concurred in reversing. Justices Frankfurter, Clark, Harlan, and Whittaker dissented.[91]

Justice Brennan said he voted to reverse because the petitioner had not impugned the judge's impartiality and fairness in connection with the trial and thus had not reflected upon his integrity. He said: "Lawyers are free to criticize the state of the law. . . . And, needless to say, a lawyer may criticize the law-enforcement agencies of the government, and the prosecution, even to the extent of suggesting wrongdoing on their part."[92]

Justice Frankfurter maintained that the "evidence establishes more than that Mrs. Sawyer was attacking the conduct of the Honolulu trial at large. It clearly reflects on the judge who was permitting or participating in these 'shocking and horrible' things."[93]

Justice Clark said:

> . . . this broad brush leaves the whitewash too thin. For not only Mrs. Sawyer's testimony but also the statement of her own lawyer stand clear and unanswerable. At the initial hearing in Hawaii, Mrs. Sawyer's then counsel said that hers "was a talk about what was going on in the Smith Act trial here in Honolulu. Now let's not fool ourselves about that." Her present counsel has talked the Court into doing just that and in so doing has also made a fool of our judicial processes.
>
> To say that there is no reasonable support in the evidence for Hawaii's conclusion, as disclosed by a fair reading of the record some six and a half years later and some 5,000 miles away, is only to say that the 12 concurring officials,

[89] Schneider v. Smith, 390 U.S. 17 (1968); *see also* McBride v. Smith, 390 U.S. 411 (1968).
[90] Dennis v. United States, 384 U.S. 855 (1966).
[91] *In re* Sawyer, 360 U.S. 622 (1959).
[92] *Ibid.*, 631–32.
[93] *Ibid.*, 659.

all of whom are trained in the law and who under oath made and passed upon these findings at trial and on appeal, arrived at a conclusion no reasonable man could reach.[94]

[94] *Ibid.*, 670–71.

CHAPTER XV

The Years of the Witch-Hunt—2

EXPOSURE OF PINKISH ACTIVITIES often served the purposes of the anti-Communist headline-hunting investigators, and refusals to testify resulting in contempt citations further served their purposes.

An alleged Communist, found in contempt for refusal to testify, challenged the constitutionality of the Immunity Act of 1954. Seven members of the Court found the immunity provided by the Act sufficient to avoid the privilege of self-incrimination and held that Congress was empowered to grant immunity from federal and state prosecution. Justices Douglas and Black, dissenting, felt that the Act would not protect a Communist from various disabilities and said that no immunity act could supplant the Fifth Amendment.[1]

Five members of the Court held that a congressional committee, which was inquiring about the past Communist affiliations of a labor union officer, must, upon objection of the witness, state for the record the subject under inquiry and the manner in which questions sought to be answered are pertinent thereto. Justice Frankfurter concurred; Justice Clark dissented; Justices Burton and Whittaker did not participate.[2]

On the same day the Court held that a state violated the due process clause in punishing for contempt the refusal of Sweezy, a witness in an investigation by the New Hampshire attorney general concerning subversive activities to answer questions with respect to lectures given by the witness at a state university and with respect to his knowledge of the Progressive party and its adherents. It said the inquiry violated academic freedom and freedom of political expression.[3] The Chief Justice wrote for the Court, joined by Justices Black, Douglas, and Brennan; Justices Frankfurter and Harlan concurred; Justices Clark and Burton dissented; Justice Whittaker did not participate.

The Attorney General also sought from a defendant, Uphaus, a list of

[1] Ulmann v. United States, 350 U.S. 422 (1956).
[2] Watkins v. United States, 354 U.S. 178 (1957).
[3] Sweezy v. New Hampshire, 354 U.S. 234 (1957).

persons who were guests at a New Hampshire camp operated by the witness as executive director of a corporation. Upon the defendant's refusal to produce the list, he was adjudged in contempt. The high court vacated the judgment and remanded the case to the state court for further action in accordance with the previous Sweezy case. The New Hampshire court reaffirmed the adjudication, and, on appeal, five members of the Court affirmed the conviction.[4] Justices Brennan, Black, and Douglas and the Chief Justice dissented.

Justice Clark, writing for the majority, denied that the federal Smith Act proscribed state prosecutions. He said:

> . . . the governmental interest in self-preservation is sufficiently compelling to subordinate the interest in associational privacy of persons who, at least to the extent of the guest registration statute, made public at the inception the association they now wish to keep private. In the light of such a record we conclude that the State's interest has not been "pressed, in this instance, to a point where it has come into fatal collision with the overriding" constitutionally protected rights of appellant and those he may represent.[5]

Justice Brennan wrote in dissent:

> I do not agree that a showing of any requisite legislative purpose or other state interest that constitutionally can subordinate appellant's rights is to be found in this record. Exposure purely for the sake of exposure is not such a valid subordinating purpose. . . .[6]
>
> . . . in an era of mass communications and mass opinion, and of international tensions and domestic anxiety, exposure and group identification by the state of those holding unpopular and dissident views are fraught with such serious consequences for the individual as inevitably to inhibit seriously the expression of views which the Constitution intended to make free. . . .[7]
>
> . . . there was some sort of assemblage at the camp that was oriented toward the discussion of political and other public matters. The activities going on were those of private citizens. The views expounded obviously were minority views. But the assemblage was, on its face, for purposes to which the First and Fourteenth Amendments give constitutional protection against incursion by the powers of government. . . .[8]
>
> . . . the entire report (of the Attorney General) is on individual guilt, individual near-guilt, and individual questionable behavior. Its flavor and tone, regardless of its introductory disclaimers, cannot help but stimulate readers to attach a "badge of infamy" to the persons named in it. . . .[9]

[4] Uphaus v. Wyman, 360 U.S. 72 (1959).
[5] Ibid., 81.
[6] Ibid., 82.
[7] Ibid., 84.
[8] Ibid., 86–87.
[9] Ibid., 93–94.

The investigation, as revealed by the report, was overwhelmingly and predominantly a roving, self-contained investigation of individual and group behavior, and behavior in a constitutionally protected area. Its whole approach was to name names, disclose information about those named, and observe that "facts are facts."[10]

Later the Legislature having amended the statute under which the Attorney General had acted by omitting the provision for determining whether subversives were present in New Hampshire, Uphaus sought review of his contempt conviction. The state court reaffirmed its former decision. On appeal the high court held that no federal question was involved. The Chief Justice and Justices Black and Douglas dissented; Justice Brennan concurred.[11]

Decided the same day as the Uphaus case was an affirmance of the conviction of Barenblatt, a former college teacher, who refused to answer questions respecting his Communist affiliations propounded by the House Committee on Un-American Activities. His former conviction had been vacated by the high court and the case remanded.[12] The conviction was reaffirmed, and five members of the Court affirmed. Justice Black, supported by Justice Douglas and the Chief Justice, dissented, holding that the Committee had violated the rights of the witness under the First and Fifth amendments. Justice Brennan, dissenting, held that "an investigation in which the processes of law-making and law-evaluating are submerged entirely in exposure of individual behavior —in adjudication, of a sort, through the exposure process—is outside the constitutional pale of inquiry."[13]

Later, in deciding Gibson v. Florida Legislative Comm., the Court distinguished the Uphaus and Barenblatt cases.

Similar convictions of witnesses claiming self-incrimination privileges before an Ohio Un-American Activities Commission were vacated and remanded for reconsideration.[14] On reaffirmation of the convictions by the state court, eight members of the high court reversed the convictions of all but one of the defendants upon the ground that they had been told by the chairman of the commission that the privilege of refusal because of self-incrimination was available to them. Justice Stewart did not participate.[15] A divided Court affirmed the conviction of the remaining witness, to whom such assurance had not been given. Justices Clark, Frankfurter, Harlan, and Whittaker voted for affirmance; the Chief Justice, and Justices Brennan, Douglas, and Black voted to reverse.

10 *Ibid.*, 100.
11 Uphaus v. Wyman, 364 U.S. 388 (1960).
12 Barenblatt v. United States, 354 U.S. 930 (1957).
13 Barenblatt v. United States, 360 U.S. 109, 166 (1959).
14 Raley, Stern, Brown, Morgan v. Ohio, 354 U.S. 929 (1957).
15 Raley, Stern, Brown, Morgan v. Ohio, 360 U.S. 423 (1959).

A defendant, subpoenaed to produce records of a "Civil Rights Congress" before the House Un-American Committee, refused to do so and claimed privilege under the Fifth Amendment. Five members of the Court affirmed his conviction, since he made no claim that he was not in possession of the subpoenaed material.[16] The Chief Justice and Justices Black, Douglas, and Brennan dissented, maintaining that the defendant was presumed to be innocent in the absence of proof that he was in possession of the records.

Five members of the Court affirmed the conviction of a witness before the House Un-American Committee, who refused to answer a question concerning his membership in the Communist party, on the ground that the Barenblatt case controlled. The same four dissenters upheld the defendant's claim that he had been subpoenaed by the committee solely because of his outspoken criticism of it, and Justice Brennan stressed his conclusion that "the dominant purpose of these questions was . . . to harass the petitioner and expose him for the sake of exposure."[17]

In a companion case, with the same division, five members upheld a contempt conviction of a witness who refused to answer questions before the committee, especially about his membership in the Communist party, when he signed a letter opposing certain bills in Congress. Writing in dissent, Justice Black admitted that the Barenblatt case constituted "ample authority" for the conviction.[18]

Five members of the Court vacated convictions for contempt for failure to answer pertinent questions before a congressional committee upon the ground that the indictment was defective in not identifying the subject under inquiry. Justices Harlan and Clark dissented upon the ground that it was unnecessary for the indictment to so state. Justice Douglas concurred upon the ground that the committee was investigating Communist infiltration into the press and that, therefore, the investigation was unconstitutional. Justices Frankfurter and White did not participate.[19]

The same majority, over the same dissent, invalidated a contempt conviction for failure to answer questions by a congressional subcommittee, upon the same ground of a faulty indictment.[20]

At a subsequent term the Court reversed the conviction of one Gojack, who refused to answer questions asked by a subcommittee of the House Committee on Un-American Activities on the ground that the subject of the inquiry by the subcommittee was not specified or authorized by the committee, as

16 McPhaul v. United States, 364 U.S. 372 (1960).

17 Wilkinson v. United States, 365 U.S. 399, 429 (1961).

18 Braden v. United States, 365 U.S. 431, 440–41 (1961).

19 Russell, Shelton, Whitman, Liveright, Price, Gojack v. United States, 369 U.S. 749 (1962).

20 Silber v. United States, 370 U.S. 717 (1962).

required by its own rules.[21] In an opinion by Justice Fortas, it was held that an authorization of a major investigation by the House Un-American Activities Committee must occur during the term of Congress in which the investigation takes place, since neither the House or its committees are continuing bodies.

On appeal by witnesses before an Ohio Un-American Activities Committee adjudged in contempt for refusal to answer questions, the Court unanimously reversed convictions for failure to answer questions which the witnesses were not specifically directed to answer, and affirmed, by an equally divided vote, the convictions of witnesses for failure to answer questions which they were specifically directed to answer.[22]

Five members of the Court reversed convictions of witnesses before a congressional subcommittee upon the ground that the subcommittee had been authorized to investigate Communist infiltration in the Albany, New York, area, while the questions asked had related to Cornell University at Ithaca, New York.[23] Justices Harlan, Frankfurter, Whittaker, and Clark dissented, maintaining that the questions were pertinent to the subcommittee's functions.

A witness summoned to appear before the House Un-American Activities Committee, convicted of contempt for refusal to answer questions, had previously asked to be permitted to testify in executive session pursuant to the committee's Rule IV. The request had been denied by counsel for the committee. A majority of the Court reversed the conviction, holding that the committee's failure to give consideration to the defendant's request violated its own rule and justified defendant's refusal to answer.[24] Justices White, Clark, Harlan, and Stewart dissented.

Finding the conduct of Louisiana officials such as to irreparably injure the First Amendment rights of petitioners, who were also indicted under Louisiana's Subversive Activities Law, which they alleged to be unconstitutional, a majority of the Court directed the district court to enjoin prosecution under the statute, which the high court found unconstitutional, and to direct the return of petitioners' papers and records, improperly seized.[25]

Writing for five members of the Court, Justice Brennan found the statutory definition of subversion substantially identical with the Washington statute found unduly vague, uncertain, and broad in a previous case, thus creating a "danger zone within which protected expression may be inhibited."[26]

Justice Harlan, with the support of Justice Clark, wrote in dissent. He said:

21 Gojack v. United States, 384 U.S. 702 (1966).
22 Slagle v. Ohio, 366 U.S. 259 (1961).
23 Deutch v. United States, 367 U.S. 456 (1961).
24 Yellin v. United States, 374 U.S. 109 (1963).
25 Dombrowski v. Pfister, 380 U.S. 479 (1965).
26 Ibid., 494.

The basic holding in this case marks a significant departure from a wise procedural principle designed to spare our federal system from premature federal judicial interference with state statutes or proceedings challenged on federal constitutional grounds. This decision abolishes the doctrine of federal judicial abstention in all suits attacking state criminal statutes for vagueness on First–Fourteenth Amendment grounds.[27]

Justices Stewart and Black did not participate.

Subsequently Dombrowski sued Senator Eastland, chairman, and Sourwine, counsel, of the Senate subcommittee who, he alleged, had tortiously entered into a conspiracy with the Louisiana committee to unlawfully seize his records. The Court affirmed dismissal against the Senator upon the ground of his legislative privilege, but reversed the dismissal as against Sourwine and remanded the claim against him for further proceedings upon the ground that his privilege was not absolute.[28]

Six justices, evidently tired of the New Hampshire subversive investigation which had jailed Dr. Uphaus, reversed a contempt conviction of a witness who testified that he had not been involved with the Communist party since 1957 and refused to answer questions respecting a prior period, holding the basis of the investigation and the subject matter had become stale and of historical rather than current interest.[29] Justice Douglas' opinion said that the witness' First Amendment rights took priority over any need of exposure of his past affiliations and that the record was devoid of any evidence of any Communist movement in New Hampshire. Justices Harlan, Stewart, and White dissented.

A miscellany of other problems posed by reaction to communism reached the Court. The most notorious—a case destined to take its place with the Sacco-Vanzetti case and other *causes célèbres* in the disputed annals of the law—was that which involved the conviction of Julius Rosenberg and Ethel, his wife, charged with a conspiracy to violate the Espionage Act by communicating atomic secrets to Russia in time of war. The trial court imposed the death sentence, and the court of appeals affirmed. The Supreme Court denied certiorari. Justice Frankfurter explained, in a memorandum opinion, that four members of the Court did not find sufficient grounds to consider an appeal. Justice Black noted that he favored taking the case.[30]

Thereafter, while the Court was in vacation, Justice Douglas granted a stay of execution after the Court had refused to hear oral argument and had denied a stay. Thereupon the Court was convened in special session, heard

[27] *Ibid.*, 498.
[28] Dombrowski v. Eastland, 387 U.S. 82 (1967).
[29] DeGregory v. Attorney General, 383 U.S. 825 (1966).
[30] Rosenberg v. United States, 344 U.S. 838 (1952).

argument, and after consideration, vacated the stay, since the Court did not "entertain the serious doubts" which led Justice Douglas to grant the stay. Justices Black, Douglas, and Frankfurter dissented.[31] Following the vacation of the stay, executive clemency was denied, and the defendants were executed.

Justice Frankfurter, who felt that an opportunity should be afforded to make a more adequate presentation of the issues involved, wrote this requiem:

> To be writing an opinion in a case affecting two lives after the curtain has been rung down upon them has the appearance of pathetic futility. But history also has its claims. . . .
>
> American criminal procedure has its defects, though its essentials have behind them the vindication of long history. But all systems of law, however wise, are administered through men and therefore may occasionally disclose the frailties of men. Perfection may not be demanded of law, but the capacity to counteract inevitable, though rare, frailties is the mark of a civilized legal mechanism.[32]

The Rosenbergs were convicted partly because of the testimony of David Greenglass, a brother of Mrs. Rosenberg, who was also charged as a coconspirator. Greenglass, in consideration of his services for the government, received a fifteen-year sentence and after the lapse of some years was released on parole.

Applications for issuance of passports raised questions of Communist affiliations and purposes. Five members of the Court ruled that existing acts did not authorize the Secretary of State to withhold passports because of refusal of applicants to file affidavits concerning Communist party membership.[33] Justices Clark, Burton, Harlan, and Whittaker dissented, contending that the Secretary had statutory authority to withhold passports for the stated reason.

In a companion case the same majority, over the same dissent, ruled that findings of Communist affiliations did not justify the Secretary in refusing to issue passports.[34] Later, the Court held unconstitutional Section 6 of the Subversive Activities Control Act of 1950, which provided that when a Communist organization is registered or finally ordered so to do, it shall be unlawful for any member with knowledge or notice thereof to apply for a passport.[35] The petitioners, citizens, and members of the party, having been denied passports, sued seeking relief. The majority opinion by Justice Goldberg was written for five members of the Court, including Justice Douglas; Justice Black concurred; Justices Clark, Harlan, and White dissented.

31 Rosenberg v. United States, 346 U.S. 273 (1953).
32 Ibid., 310.
33 Kent v. Dulles, 357 U.S. 116 (1958).
34 Dayton v. Dulles, 357 U.S. 144 (1958).
35 Aptheker v. Secretary of State, 378 U.S. 500 (1964).

Justice Goldberg cited the holding in Kent v. Dulles, declaring that the right to travel abroad is "an important aspect of the citizen's 'liberty' guaranteed in the Due Process Clause of the Fifth Amendment."[36] He said that it had been held that a member of an organization did not necessarily subscribe to all its policies, that such a person may desire to go abroad for an innocent purpose, and that the Act was unnecessarily broad and restrictive in curtailing constitutional rights.

Justice Clark, writing in dissent, maintained that the particular complainants before the Court were the heads of the Communist party, that there was no possible question respecting their subscription to Communist aims, and therefore that there was no question before the Court of application to "unknowing" persons. He maintained also that the regulation complained of was related to the national security.

"The right to travel," he said, "is not absolute. Congress had ample evidence that use of passports by Americans belonging to the world Communist movement is a threat to our national security. Passports were denied to Communists from the time of the Soviet Revolution until the early 30's and then again later in the 40's. . . . evidence afforded the Congress a rational basis upon which to place the denial of passports to members of the Communist Party in the United States. . . ."[37]

Six members of the Court held that the Secretary of State had authority to refuse to validate passports for travel to Cuba under the terms of the Passport Act of 1926. In distinguishing the case from the previous one, the Chief Justice found that the Secretary's refusal was based on policy considerations affecting all citizens, while the previous decision turned on the applicant's political beliefs or associations.[38] Justice Black, dissenting, maintained that while Congress had power to enact legislation regulating the issuance and use of passports to travel abroad, he denied that the Passport Act of 1926 had delegated such power to the President or Secretary of State, saying that if it did, it would, in the words of Justice Cardozo, be "delegation running riot," that it would violate the constitutional command that "all" legislative power be vested in the Congress.[39]

Justice Douglas, dissenting, said:

. . . the only so-called danger here is the Communist regime in Cuba. The world, however, is filled with Communist thought; and Communist regimes are on more than one continent. They are part of the world spectrum; and if we are to know them and understand them, we must mingle with them, as

[36] *Ibid.*, 505.
[37] *Ibid.*, 526–27.
[38] Zemel v. Rusk, 381 U.S. 1 (1965).
[39] *Ibid.*, 21, 23.

Pope John said. Keeping alive intellectual intercourse between opposing groups has always been important and perhaps never more important than now.[40]

The First Amendment presupposes a mature people, not afraid of ideas. The First Amendment leaves no room for the official, whether truculent or benign, to say nay or yea because the ideas offend or please him or because he believes some political objective is served by keeping the citizen at home or letting him go. Yet that is just what the Court's decision today allows to happen. . . . we have only the claim that Congress has painted with such a "broad brush" that the State Department can ban travel to Cuba simply because it is pleased to do so. . . .

. . . the right to travel is at the periphery of the First Amendment, rather than its core, largely because travel is, of course, more than speech: it is speech brigaded with conduct. . . . Restrictions on the right to travel in times of peace should be so particularized that a First Amendment right is not precluded unless some clear countervailing national interest stands in the way of its assertion.[41]

Justice Goldberg, dissenting, said he did not believe that the Executive had inherent authority to impose area restrictions in time of peace.[42] Nor did he believe that Congress meant the 1926 Act to authorize the Executive to do so.[43]

Although the Court had thus sustained the statutory power of the Secretary of State to refuse to validate passports for travel to Cuba,[44] it held in two cases[45] that "the right to travel is a part of the 'liberty' of which the citizen cannot be deprived without due process of law . . ."[46] and that the Immigration and Nationality Act of 1952 did not authorize the conviction of a citizen holding a valid passport for ignoring area restrictions imposed by the Secretary of State.

The Vietnam "war" resulted in an attempt to punish Americans who visited North Vietnam, despite the fact that it was one of five countries placed "off limits" by the State Department. However, following the philosophy previously expressed by the Supreme Court respecting freedom of travel, the Court of Appeals of the District of Columbia held that, while the Secretary of State had authority to control the lawful passage of a passport, he had no control of the person holding it; hence a citizen who visited or intended to visit an off-limits country might not be denied a passport, provided he promised not to take it with him into an off-limits country but to leave it in another country that was not off limits.[47]

[40] *Ibid.*, 25.
[41] *Ibid.*, 26.
[42] *Ibid.*, 28.
[43] *Ibid.*, 39–40.
[44] *Ibid.*
[45] United States v. Laub, 385 U.S. 475 (1967); Travis v. United States, 385 U.S. 491 (1967).
[46] United States v. Laub, 385 U.S. 475, 481 (1967), citing Kent v. Dulles, 357 U.S. 116, 125 (1958).
[47] Lynd v. Rusk, 389 F.2d 940 (1967).

A miscellany of cases involved communism in one aspect or another. The conviction of a member of the Communist party for contempt of Congress was challenged because employees of the government were, by a statute of the District of Columbia, qualified to serve as jurors. A majority of five affirmed the conviction, with Justices Douglas and Clark not sitting. Justices Black and Frankfurter dissented.[48]

Four members of the majority held that the fact that Dennis was a Communist and thus opposed to the government did not prevent the application of the rule that government employees were not disqualified from jury service, as held in previous cases.[49] Justice Reed concurred, as did Justice Jackson. Justice Black dissented upon the ground that disqualifying bias had been shown; Justice Frankfurter dissented upon the ground that where the prosecution concerned national security, disqualification of government employees should follow.

Later, the Attorney General included three organizations, ostensibly of a charitable nature, in a list of groups designated by him as Communist. This list was distributed for use in considering the loyalty of government employees. From dismissal of their complaints seeking deletion of their names from the lists, the organizations appealed to the high court. Five members of the Court agreed that the organizations were entitled to their day in court, though two, Burton and Douglas, based their conclusion on one ground and Justices Black, Frankfurter, and Jackson, each on a separate ground, Justices Reed and Minton, with the Chief Justice, dissented. Justice Clark did not participate.[50]

Eight members of the Court, with the concurrence of Justice Black, reversed a finding of the New York courts that the Communist Control Act of 1954 required the cancellation of the Communist party's status as an employer under the New York unemployment compensation system.[51]

Perhaps worthy of mention in connection with the anti-Communist aura was the furore caused by charges that Hollywood writers were "pinks," if not Communists, and were propagandizing in connection with motion pictures for which they were writing. In consequence, they were called before the ubiquitous House Un-American Activities Committee and then, when having taken their Fifth Amendment privileges, found themselves banned by producers fearing public reaction. Their suit in the California state court to avoid the alleged blacklisting was dismissed, and the high court affirmed upon the ground that no federal question was involved. Justice Douglas dissented, saying that since California gave remedies for interference with right to work

---

[48] Dennis v. United States, 339 U.S. 162 (1950).

[49] United States v. Wood, 299 U.S. 123 (1936); Frazier v. United States, 335 U.S. 497 (1948).

[50] Joint Anti-Fascist Committee; National Council; International Workers Order; Drayton v McGrath, 341 U.S. 123 (1950).

[51] Communist Party v. Catherwood, 367 U.S. 389 (1961).

on the score of race, it violated the equal protection clause by permitting a denial of the right to work because plaintiffs had exercised a constitutional privilege.[52]

An unusual situation brought out legislative anti-Communist bias: when dissidents declared their independence of the mother Russian Orthodox Church, a contest ensued for possession of the Church property. The New York legislature, during the anti-Communist era, enacted a statute giving recognition to the separatists. The Court held that the statute violated the First Amendment. Six members of the Court joined in an opinion by Justice Reed; Justices Frankfurter, Black, and Douglas concurred; Justice Jackson dissented.[53]

Five members of the Court found procedure of the Post Office, under a provision of the Postal Service Act of 1962, violative of the First Amendment in detaining and delivering only upon the addressee's request unsealed foreign mailings of Communist political propaganda.[54] Justices Brennan, Goldberg, and Harlan concurred; Justice White did not participate.

Justice Brennan said:

It is true that the First Amendment contains no specific guarantee of access to publications. However, the protection of the Bill of Rights goes beyond the specific guarantees to protect from congressional abridgment those equally fundamental personal rights necessary to make the express guarantees fully meaningful. . . . I think the right to receive publications is such a fundamental right. The dissemination of ideas can accomplish nothing if otherwise willing addressees are not free to receive and consider them. It would be a barren marketplace of ideas that had only sellers and no buyers.[55]

In addition to denaturalization for fraud in obtaining naturalization, the Court had occasion to consider the loss of citizenship on other grounds prescribed by Congress. Thus, the Court held invalid the provision of the Immigration and Nationality Act of 1952 providing that a naturalized citizen should lose citizenship by continuously residing abroad for three years in a foreign state of which he was formerly a national or in which he was born.[56]

Justice Douglas, writing for the majority, said:

This statute proceeds on the impermissible assumption that naturalized citizens as a class are less reliable and bear less allegiance to this country than do the native born. . . .[57] Living abroad, whether the citizen be naturalized or native

[52] Wilson v. Loews, 355 U.S. 597, 599 (1958).
[53] Kedroff v. St. Nicholas Cathedral, 344 U.S. 94 (1952).
[54] Lamont v. Postmaster General, 381 U.S. 301 (1965).
[55] Ibid., 308.
[56] Schneider v. Rusk, 377 U.S. 163 (1964).

born, is no badge of lack of allegiance and in no way evidences a voluntary renunciation of nationality and allegiance.[58]

Justice Clark wrote in dissent, with the support of Justices Harlan and White. He said: ". . . appellant has been away from the country for ten years, has married a foreign citizen, has continuously lived with him in her native land for eight years, has borne four sons who are German nationals, and admits she has no intention to return to this country."[59]

Five members of the Court held it was within the power of Congress to adopt a provision of the Nationality Act of 1940 taking away the citizenship of a native-born citizen who votes in a foreign election.[60] The Chief Justice, with the support of Justices Black and Douglas, dissented, maintaining that the government was powerless to take away citizenship and that the act of voting in a foreign election is not an abandonment of citizenship. Justice Whittaker dissented on the latter ground.

On the same day five members of the Court held unconstitutional another provision of the Nationality Act providing that a court-martial conviction and dishonorable discharge for wartime desertion resulted in loss of citizenship.[61] The Chief Justice, with the concurrence of Justices Black, Douglas, and Whittaker held that the government had no power to divest citizenship and that the use of such power would be a punishment barred by the Eighth Amendment. Justice Brennan joined in denying the power of Congress. Justices Frankfurter, Burton, Clark, and Harlan, who, with Justice Brennan, had constituted the majority in the previous case, dissented. Later a majority of the Court found another provision of the Act unconstitutional.

Again, on the same day, the Chief Justice wrote for five members of the Court, reversing a lower-court finding that a native-born American, who also had Japanese nationality under Japanese law, had lost his American citizenship by induction into the Japanese armed services, upon the ground that the government had not proved he had served Japan voluntarily.[62] Justices Frankfurter and Burton concurred; Justices Harlan and Clark dissented, saying the burden of proof was not on the government.

In a denaturalization proceeding affecting an alleged Communist, six members of the Court joined in vacating a judgment unfavorable to the petitioner upon the ground that it was not supported by the evidence. Justices Clark, Whittaker, and Stewart maintained the contrary.[63]

[57] *Ibid.*, 168.
[58] *Ibid.*, 169.
[59] *Ibid.*
[60] Perez v. Brownell, 356 U.S. 44 (1958).
[61] Trop v. Dulles, 356 U.S. 86 (1958).
[62] Nishikawa v. Dulles, 356 U.S. 129 (1958).
[63] Chaunt v. United States, 364 U.S. 350 (1960).

Six members of the Court upheld the denaturalization of Frank Costello, who admitted that he had been a "bootlegger," upon the ground that, in seeking naturalization, he had misrepresented his occupation.[64] Justices Douglas and Black dissented. Justice Harlan did not participate. Justice Douglas wrote, saying that "real estate," which was the answer Costello had given to the question of his occupation, was one of his occupations and that the form did not ask for all his occupations. Respecting his bootlegging, Justice Douglas said:

> I do not think "bootlegging" per se would have been a ground for denying naturalization to an alien in the 1920's. If it were, it would be an act of hypocrisy unparalleled in American life. For the "bootlegger" in those days came into being because of the demand of the great bulk of people in our communities— including lawyers, prosecutors, and judges—for his products.[65]

A majority of the Court held that the provisions of the Nationality Act of 1940 and of the Immigration and Nationality Act of 1952 purporting to deprive an American of his citizenship automatically, and without any prior judicial or administrative proceedings, for "departing from or remaining outside of the jurisdiction of the United States in time of war or . . . national emergency for the purpose of evading or avoiding training and service" was unconstitutional because they would inflict severe punishment without due process of law and without the safeguards which must attend a criminal prosecution under the Fifth and Sixth amendments.[66] Justices Douglas and Black joined the opinion of the Court while pointing out that, as they had held in a dissent in a prior case,[67] Congress lacked power to deprive a native-born person of citizenship. Justice Brennan concurred, calling attention to a prior case where American nationality was lost by deserters from the armed forces in time of war.[68] Justices Harlan, joined by Justice Clark, and Justice Stewart, joined by Justice White, dissented.

Justice Goldberg, writing for the majority, said: "The Constitution is silent about the permissibility of involuntary forfeiture of citizenship rights. While it confirms citizenship rights, plainly there are imperative obligations of citizenship. . . . One of the most important of these is to serve the country in time of war."[69]

Justice Stewart, dissenting, maintained that the statute was not punitive and that Congress was exercising its war powers by "removing a corrosive

[64] Costello v. United States, 365 U.S. 265 (1961).
[65] Ibid., 288.
[66] Kennedy v. Mendoza-Martinez; Rusk v. Cort, 372 U.S. 144 (1963).
[67] Ibid., 186, citing Perez v. Brownell, 356 U.S. 44 (1958).
[68] Ibid., 188, citing Trop v. Dulles, 356 U.S. 86 (1958).
[69] Ibid., 159.

influence upon the morals of a nation at war."[70] Hence, he concluded, the Fifth and Sixth amendments were inapplicable.

During the 1966 term, in an opinion by Justice Black for five members of the Court, it was held that Section 401(e) of the Nationality Act of 1940, providing that a citizen lost his citizenship if he voted in a political election in a foreign state was unconstitutional.[71] Justices Harlan, Clark, Stewart, and White dissented.

Justice Black said: "In our country the people are sovereign and the Government cannot sever its relationship to the people by taking away their citizenship.... The Constitution, of course, grants Congress no express power to strip people of their citizenship."[72]

Citing the words of the Fourteenth Amendment, " 'All persons born or naturalized in the United States . . . are citizens of the United States . . . ,' " Justice Black went on to say: "There is no indication in these words of a fleeting citizenship, good at the moment it is acquired but subject to destruction by the Government at any time. Rather the Amendment can most reasonably be read as defining a citizenship which a citizen keeps unless he voluntarily relinquishes it."[73]

Justice Harlan, dissenting, wrote:

I can find nothing in this extraordinary series of circumventions which permits, still less compels, the imposition of this constitutional constraint upon the authority of Congress....

There is no need here to rehearse Mr. Justice Frankfurter's opinion for the Court in Perez; it then proved and still proves to my satisfaction that Section 401e is within the power of Congress....[74]

The Citizenship Clause . . . neither denies nor provides to Congress any power of expatriation. . . . The construction now placed on the Citizenship Clause rests, in the last analysis, simply on the Court's *ipse dixit,* evincing little more, it is quite apparent, than the present majority's own distaste for the expatriation power.[75]

[70] *Ibid.,* 213.
[71] Afroyim v. Rusk, 387 U.S. 253 (1967).
[72] *Ibid.,* 257.
[73] *Ibid.,* 262.
[74] *Ibid.,* 270.
[75] *Ibid.,* 292.

PART TWO

The Last Decade

PART TWO

CHAPTER XVI

The Fourth Amendment

IN 1886 THE COURT HELD that a subpoena requiring the production before a federal grand jury of papers previously seized in violation of the Fourth Amendment would not be enforced.[1] Thereafter, in 1904, when the Court was asked to reverse a conviction obtained after admitting in evidence papers seized in violation of the Fourth Amendment, it unanimously refused to do so, saying that the common-law rule did not require the trial court to consider how the evidence was obtained.[2]

Subsequently, the Court, by Justice Day, who had written the previous decision, held that, since in the instant case Weeks, the defendant, had moved for the return of the illegally seized evidence before his trial in the federal court, his motion should have been granted. Consequently, the evidence seized was inadmissible.[3]

The rationale adopted by Justice Day to avoid overruling his own decision and the common-law rule were ignored thereafter in the federal courts; the Weeks case stood and stands as the landmark for refusing, upon a trial in a federal court, to admit evidence seized in violation of the Fourth Amendment.

In 1926 the question was presented to the New York Court of Appeals[4] when a Mr. Defore was improperly arrested for a misdemeanor and a search of his room revealed a blackjack, for the possession of which he was indicted and convicted. The blackjack was received in evidence at his trial, although, under the New York Civil Rights Law, the equivalent of the Fourth Amendment, he had moved to suppress the evidence before his trial. Justice Cardozo, writing the opinion, summed up for the opponents of the rule. He wrote:

> The question is not a new one. It was put to us more than twenty years ago in People v. Adams . . . and there deliberately answered. . . . On appeal to the Supreme Court, the judgment was affirmed.[5]

[1] Boyd v. United States, 116 U.S. 616 (1886).
[2] Adams v. New York, 192 U.S. 585 (1904).
[3] Weeks v. United States, 232 U.S. 383 (1914).
[4] People v. Defore, 242 N.Y. 13 (1926).
[5] *Ibid.*, 19–20.

The ruling thus broadly made is decisive, while it stands, of the case before us now. It is at variance, however, with later judgments of the Supreme Court of the United States. Those judgments do not bind us, for they construe provisions of the Federal Constitution, the Fourth and Fifth Amendments, not applicable to the States. Even though they are not binding, they merit our attentive scrutiny.[6]

. . . The Supreme Court has overruled its own judgment in Adams v. New York, for the facts were undisputed there. The procedural condition of a preliminary motion has been substantially abandoned, or, if now enforced at all, is an exceptional requirement. There has been no blinking the consequences. The criminal is to go free because the constable has blundered . . . .[7]

The truth is that the statute says nothing about consequences. It does no more than deny a privilege. Denying this, it stops. Intrusion without privilege has certain liabilities and penalties. The statute does not assume to alter or increase them. No scrutiny of its text can ever evoke additional consequences by a mere process of construction . . . . We scan the statute in vain for any token of intention that search by intruders wearing a badge of office shall have any different consequence in respect of the law of evidence than search by intruders generally. . . .[8]

Evidence is not excluded because the private litigant has gathered it by lawless force. By the same token, the State, when prosecuting an offender . . . incurs no heavier liability. . . .[9]

We are confirmed in this conclusion when we reflect how far-reaching in its effect upon society the new consequences would be. The pettiest peace officer would have it in his power through overzeal or indiscretion to confer immunity upon an offender for crimes the most flagitious. . . .[10] The privacy of the home has been infringed and the murderer goes free. . . .

We are not unmindful of the argument that unless the evidence is excluded, the statute becomes a form and its protection an illusion. This has a strange sound when the immunity is viewed in the light of its origin and history. The rule now embodied in the statute was received into English law as the outcome of the prosecution of Wilkes and Entick. . . . Wilkes sued the messengers who had ransacked his papers, and recovered a verdict of £ 4000 against one and £ 1000 against the other. Entick too had a substantial verdict.

No doubt the protection of the statute would be greater from the point of view of the individual whose privacy had been invaded if the government were required to ignore what it had learned through the invasion. The question is whether protection for the individual would not be gained at a disproportionate loss of protection for society. On the one side is the social need that crime shall be repressed. On the other, the social need that law shall not be

[6] *Ibid.,* 20.
[7] *Ibid.,* 20–21.
[8] *Ibid.,* 23.
[9] *Ibid.,* 22.
[10] *Ibid.,* 23.

flouted by the insolence of office. There are dangers in any choice. The rule of the Adams case strikes a balance between opposing interests. We must hold it to be the law until those organs of government by which a change of policy is normally effected, shall give notice to the Courts that the change has come to pass.[11]

With the law as laid down in the Weeks case in 1948, the Court was asked by a Mr. Wolf to hold that the due process clause of the Fourteenth Amendment required that the federal rule be declared applicable to trials in the state courts. A majority said "no"; Justices Rutledge, Murphy, and Douglas dissented.[12]

Justice Frankfurter, writing for the majority, again rejected the argument that the Fourteenth Amendment was "shorthand" for the Bill of Rights and repeated the doctrine of the Palko case, saying: "Due process of law thus conveys neither formal nor fixed nor narrow requirements. It is the compendious expression for all those rights which the courts must enforce because they are basic to our free society."[13] He reaffirmed, too, "the Court's insight when first called upon to consider the problem" in the early Davidson case, holding that application of the due process clause must rest upon the "gradual and empiric process of 'inclusion and exclusion.' " He held that the protection of the Fourth Amendment was available through the Fourteenth against the states. But, he said, the admission of evidence was a way of enforcement: "The immediate question is whether the basic right to protection against arbitrary intrusion by the police demands the exclusion of logically relevant evidence obtained by an unreasonable search and seizure because, in a federal prosecution for a federal crime, it would be excluded."[14]

In regard to this as Justice Frankfurter demonstrated, many jurisdictions had given different answers.

As of today 30 States rejected the Weeks doctrine, 17 States are in agreement with it. . . . Of 10 jurisdictions within the United Kingdom and the British Commonwealth of Nations which have passed on the question, none has held evidence obtained by illegal search and seizure inadmissible.[15]

Indeed, the exclusion of evidence is a remedy which directly serves only to protect those upon whose person or premises something incriminating has been found. We cannot, therefore, regard it as a departure from basic standards to remand such persons, together with those who emerge scatheless from a search, to the remedies of private action and such protection as the internal

---

11 *Ibid.*, 24–25.
12 Wolf v. Colorado, 338 U.S. 25 (1949).
13 *Ibid.*, 27.
14 *Ibid.*, 28.
15 *Ibid.*, 29–30.

discipline of the police, under the eyes of an alert public opinion, may afford. Granting that in practice the exclusion of evidence may be an effective way of deterring unreasonable searches, it is not for this Court to condemn as falling below the minimal standards assured by the Due Process Clause a State's reliance upon other methods which, if consistently enforced, would be equally effective. . . .

Weighty testimony against such an insistence on our own view is furnished by the opinion of Mr. Justice, then Judge, Cardozo in People v. Defore,[16] and though we have interpreted the Fourth Amendment to forbid the admission of such evidence, a different question would be presented if Congress under its legislative powers were to pass a statute purporting to negate the Weeks doctrine. We would then be faced with the problem of the respect to be accorded the legislative judgment on an issue as to which, in default of that judgment, we have been forced to depend upon our own.[17]

Justice Black, concurring, said:

I should be for reversal of this case if I thought the Fourth Amendment not only prohibited "unreasonable searches and seizure," but also, of itself, barred the use of evidence so unlawfully obtained. But I agree with what appears to be a plain implication of the Court's opinion that the federal exclusionary rule is not a command of the Fourth Amendment but is a judicially created rule of evidence which Congress might negate.[18]

Justice Douglas, dissenting, thought that the Fourth Amendment, as such, was applicable to the states, and he said that "in [the] absence of that rule of evidence the Amendment would have no effective sanction."[19]

Justice Murphy added: "The conclusion is inescapable that but one remedy exists to deter violations of the search and seizure clause. That is the rule that excludes illegally obtained evidence. Only by exclusion can we impress upon the zealous prosecutor that violation of the Constitution will do him no good."[20]

Justice Rutledge, with the support of Justice Murphy, wrote, insisting that inadmissibility of evidence was a command of the Constitution, not a rule of evidence subject to the Congressional will.[21]

Meanwhile, the so-called "silver platter" doctrine was in effect. It had originated from an "unobstrusive" but nonetheless definite statement in the Weeks case permitting the introduction of evidence improperly seized, provided fed-

[16] *Ibid.*, 30–31.
[17] *Ibid.*, 33.
[18] *Ibid.*, 39–40.
[19] *Ibid.*, 40.
[20] *Ibid.*, 44.
[21] *Ibid.*, 48.

eral officers had not "participated in the illegal search." The doctrine got its name from a statement by Justice Frankfurter in a 1948 decision referring to "evidence secured by state authorities . . . turned over to the federal authorities on a silver platter."[22]

While the silver platter rule was in existence, the judges busied themselves, on numerous occasions, with determining the often undeterminable question of whether a federal agent "participated" in the unlawful search made by state officers, instead of concerning themselves with what they considered the less important question of the guilt or innocence of the defendant.

Typical of such cases was the one which gave the silver platter doctrine its name and which was decided simultaneously with the Wolf case. Here the Secret Service received telephone calls indicating that counterfeiting was going on in a hotel room. Greene, a federal agent, went to the hotel, looked through a keyhole, but saw no evidence of counterfeiting, though he was satisfied from what he saw and heard that "something was going on." He so reported to the state police, who obtained a warrant to arrest the occupants of the room for failure to register with the police, since they were known criminals. Greene remained at police headquarters while the police gained entrance to the defendants' hotel room because he was "curious to see what they would find." On finding evidence, the police sent for Greene, "who came . . . and examined the evidence."

Justice Frankfurter made a fifth to reverse the conviction because he felt Greene joined the search before it "was concluded." Four judges dissented, saying that Greene did not participate in the search and seizure.[23]

However, some ten years later, two defendants indicted and convicted in the Oregon Federal Court for intercepting and divulging telephone communications, contended that evidence unlawfully seized by state officers had been admitted at their trial. The court of appeals affirmed, saying that the federal silver platter rule permitted the introduction of evidence unlawfully seized by state officers as long as federal officers did not participate in the seizure. Writing for five members of the Court, Justice Stewart vacated the conviction, saying that the majority had concluded that the silver platter doctrine "can no longer be accepted."[24]

Justices Frankfurter, Clark, Harlan, and Whittaker dissented, the opinions by Justice Frankfurter and Harlan appearing in a companion case. In discussing the majority's proposal to extend the rule that excluded evidence obtained by unlawful search and seizure, Justice Stewart said:

> The exclusionary rule has for decades been the subject of ardent controversy.

[22] Lustig v. United States, 338 U.S. 74, 79 (1949).
[23] *Ibid.,* 78, 81.
[24] Elkins v. United States, 364 U.S. 206, 208 (1960).

The arguments of its antagonists and of its proponents have been so many times marshalled as to require no lengthy elaboration here. Most of what has been said in opposition to the rule was distilled in a single Cardozo sentence— "The criminal is to go free because the constable has blundered." . . . The same point was made at somewhat greater length in the often quoted words of Professor Wigmore: "Titus, you have been found guilty of conducting a lottery; Flavius, you have confessedly violated the constitution. Titus ought to suffer imprisonment for crime, and Flavius for contempt. But no! We shall let you *both* go free. We shall not punish Flavius directly, but shall do so by reversing Titus' conviction. This is our way of teaching people like Flavius to behave, and of teaching people like Titus to behave, and incidentally of securing respect for the Constitution. Our way of upholding the Constitution is not to strike at the man who breaks it, but to let off somebody else who broke something else. . . ."

The rule is calculated to prevent, not to repair. Its purpose is to deter—to compel respect for the constitutional guaranty in the only effectively available way—by removing the incentive to disregard it.[25]

Shortly thereafter the Court had occasion to consider the case of Dollree Mapp, who had been convicted in the Ohio courts of the crime of possessing obscene literature. On her trial evidence procured by what may have been an unlawful search and seizure was received by the court. On appeal the Ohio Supreme Court expressed doubt of the validity of the search and seizure but said the Ohio law permitted the introduction of such evidence though it had been illegally obtained. It also noted that, in the opinion of a majority of the Court of less than six members, the obscenity statute that the defendant had violated was unconstitutional but that under the law of Ohio this vote was not sufficient for such a determination.

Disregarding this invitation to strike down the obscenity statute and thus reverse the conviction, the high court undertook to re-examine and overrule the prior Wolf case, to hold that the Fourth Amendment was applicable to the states and to reverse the conviction on that ground. Five members of the Court, in an opinion by Justice Clark, so held; Justices Harlan, Stewart, Frankfurter, and Whittaker dissented.[26]

Justice Clark said:

There are those who say, as did Justice (then Judge) Cardozo, that under our constitutional exclusionary doctrine "(t)he criminal is to go free because the constable has blundered." . . . In some cases this will undoubtedly be the result. But . . . "there is another consideration—the imperative of judicial integrity. . . . The criminal goes free, if he must, but it is the law that sets him free. . . ."[27]

[25] *Ibid.*, 216–17.
[26] Mapp v. Ohio, 367 U.S. 643 (1961).
[27] *Ibid.*, 659.

Justice Black, concurring, said:

I agree with what appears to be a plain implication of the Court's opinion that the federal exclusionary rule is not a command of the Fourth Amendment, but is a judicially created rule of evidence which Congress might negate.

I am still not persuaded that the Fourth Amendment, standing alone, would be enough to bar the introduction into evidence against an accused of papers and effects seized from him in violation of its commands. . . . Reflection on the problem . . . has led me to conclude that when the Fourth Amendment's ban . . . is considered together with the Fifth Amendment's ban against compelled self-incrimination, a constitutional basis emerges which not only justifies but actually requires the exclusionary rule.[28]

Justice Harlan, dissenting, with the support of Justices Frankfurter and Whittaker, said:

I . . . believe the Wolf rule represents sounder Constitutional doctrine than the new rule. . . .[29]

. . . five members of this Court have simply "reached out" to overrule Wolf. . . .[30]

The reasons given by the majority for now suddenly turning its back on Wolf seem to me notably unconvincing. . . . a recent survey indicates that at present one-half of the States still adhere to the common-law non-exclusionary rule, and one, Maryland, retains the rule as to felonies. . . . Our concern here . . . is not with the desirability of that rule but only with the question whether the States are Constitutionally free to follow or not as they may themselves determine. . . .[31]

For us the question remains, as it has always been, one of state power, not one of passing judgment on the wisdom of one state course or another. In my view this Court should continue to forbear from fettering the States with an adamant rule which may embarrass them in coping with their own peculiar problems in criminal law enforcement. . . .[32]

I do not see how it can be said that a trial becomes unfair simply because a State determines that evidence may be considered by the trier of fact, regardless of how it was obtained, if it is relevant to the one issue with which the trial is concerned, the guilt or innocence of the accused. . . .[33]

I regret that I find so unwise in principle and so inexpedient in policy a decision motivated by the high purpose of increasing respect for Constitutional rights. But in the last analysis I think this Court can increase respect for the

28 *Ibid.*, 661–62.
29 *Ibid.*, 672.
30 *Ibid.*, 674.
31 *Ibid.*, 680.
32 *Ibid.*, 681.
33 *Ibid.*, 683.

Constitution only if it rigidly respects the limitations which the Constitution places upon it, and respects as well the principles inherent in its own processes. In the present case, I think we exceed both, and that our voice becomes only a voice of power, not of reason.[34]

Justice Stewart said he would reverse on the unconstitutionality of the Ohio obscenity statute.

Following the Mapp decision, a ruling promising repercussions reversed a four-to-three holding of the Pennsylvania Superior Court.[35] State liquor control board officers had stopped and searched an automobile and found liquor not bearing state seals. Lacking a search warrant, the district judge found the search unauthorized and held that the automobile could not be forfeited. The supreme court of the state reversed, holding the Mapp decision had no application to civil proceedings. The high court reversed.

Thereafter, in consequence of the ruling, a New Jersey judge ruled that the Mapp case applied equally to evidence illegally obtained in a civil divorce suit[36] although the New York Court of Appeals had held the contrary in a five-to-two decision.[37]

The effort to "punish" federal and state arresting officers by freeing admittedly guilty criminals has found reflection in some contradictory judicial bylaw, to say nothing of what may perhaps be considered by many to be untoward consequences.

Relying on a previous decision[38] holding that "search warrants must be procured when 'practicable' even in a case of search incident to arrest," the court of appeals had reversed the conviction of a stamp-dealer charged with the possession of stamps bearing forged overprints upon the ground that the evidence had been obtained by a search of the premises without a warrant at the time of the arrest. Overruling the previous decision, the high court reinstated the conviction.[39] In so doing, it held that a search of the defendant's one-room office, open to the public, and under the control of the defendant, accompanying his lawful arrest, was reasonable and it relied on previous decisions.[40] It distinguished other previous decisions[41] where the Court con-

---

[34] Ibid., 686.

[35] One 1958 Plymouth Sedan v. Pennsylvania, 380 U.S. 693 (1965).

[36] New York Times, October 8, 1966.

[37] Sackler v. Sackler, 15 N.Y. 2d 40 (1964).

[38] Trupiano v. United States, 334 U.S. 699 (1948).

[39] United States v. Rabinowitz, 339 U.S. 56 (1950).

[40] Agnello v. United States, 269 U.S. 20 (1925); Carroll v. United States, 267 U.S. 132 (1925); Marron v. United States, 275 U.S. 192 (1927); Harris v. United States, 331 U.S. 145 (1947).

[41] Go-Bart Importing Co. v. United States, 282 U.S. 344 (1931); United States v. Lefkowitz, 285 U.S. 452 (1932).

demned "general exploratory searches," which, the Court said, could not be conducted with or without a warrant.[42]

Justice Douglas did not participate. Justices Black, Frankfurter, and Jackson dissented, Justice Frankfurter maintained that to overrule the Trupiano case involved overruling "the underlying principle of a whole series of recent cases."[43]

A man named Breithaupt was convicted of manslaughter because of an automobile collision involving a car which he was driving while intoxicated. A physician took a sample of his blood while he was unconscious, and the result was put in evidence at the trial. The defendant contended his Fourth Amendment rights were violated under the due process clause of the Fourteenth Amendment.[44] Six members of the Court, in an opinion by Justice Clark, held the contrary. The Chief Justice, with the concurrence of Justices Douglas and Black, dissented, saying that a prior case governed.[45] That case involved an unlawful breaking into the defendant's room by three deputy sheriffs, who found the defendant in bed, with two morphine capsules on a night stand alongside his bed. These the defendant swallowed despite efforts of the deputies to prevent him from doing so. Thereupon the deputies took him to a hospital where they had his stomach pumped. The result was the subject of evidence at the trial. Reversing the conviction, the Court held the action of the deputies violated the due process clause of the Fourteenth Amendment.

Later, in an opinion by Justice Brennan for four members of the Court, it was held that, following the Breithaupt decision, the withdrawal of blood from the body of one arrested for driving an automobile, while intoxicated, over his objection, did not violate defendant's rights under the Fourth, Fifth, or Sixth amendments.[46] Justices Harlan and Stewart concurred. Justices Douglas and Black and the Chief Justice dissented, standing on their previous dissents in the Breithaupt case.

During the 1959 term a defendant convicted of unlawfully possessing three cartons of radios stolen from an interstate shipment appealed to the Court. FBI agents, investigating a theft of whisky from an interstate shipment, had been told that one Pierotti had been implicated in interstate shipments. They saw Pierotti and the defendant load cartons into a car. They stopped the car and took the defendant and Pierotti, with the cartons, to the FBI office, where they held them for two hours, when they found that the cartons contained stolen radios. They then arrested the men.

[42] United States v. Rabinowitz, 339 U.S. 56, 62 (1950).
[43] Citing United States v. Di Re, 332 U.S. 581 (1948); Johnson v. United States, 333 U.S. 10 (1948); McDonald v. United States, 335 U.S. 451 (1948).
[44] Breithaupt v. Abram, 352 U.S. 432 (1957).
[45] Rochin v. California, 342 U.S. 165 (1952).
[46] Schmerber v. United States, 384 U.S. 757 (1966).

The defendant contended that he was arrested when the agents stopped the car and contended that, at that time, the officers, having no warrant, had no probable cause to arrest him. Consequently, he claimed the subsequent search and seizure was unwarranted under the Fourth Amendment. Justice Douglas, writing for six members of the Court, agreed and vacated the conviction.[47]

Justice Clark, supported by the Chief Justice, dissented. He maintained that the previous information received by the agents and their observance of defendant's actions justified the stopping of the car; that the defendant's lies, recognized by the agents to be such, and the sight of the cartons in the car, justified the arrest, search, and seizure since the agents had reasonable cause to believe an offense was being committed. "It is only by such alertness," he said, "that crime is discovered, interrupted, prevented, and punished. We should not place additional burdens on law enforcement agencies."[48]

An important search and seizure case decided during the same term was that which involved a notorious Russian spy, Abel. The FBI had been suspicious of Abel's activities but did not have enough information upon which to base an application for a search warrant. However, Abel had failed to notify the Attorney General of his whereabouts, as required by law, with the consequence that the immigration department was able to issue a warrant for his administrative arrest as a preliminary to his deportation. FBI agents accompanied the immigration officers to Abel's hotel where it was arranged that the FBI men should question Abel and that, should he prove unco-operative, they would signal the immigration officers, who would then proceed with their warrant for his arrest. This was done and the immigration agents searched the room. After Abel was taken from the room, the FBI agents also searched it.

When Abel was tried for espionage, some of the items found in the various searches were offered and received in evidence over the defendant's objection that the searches had been illegal. Abel was convicted; the high court affirmed the conviction by a vote of five to four.[49] The Chief Justice and Justices Brennan, Black, and Douglas dissented.

Justice Frankfurter, writing for the majority, held that the arrest was valid and, in consequence, the searches and seizures were authorized. Justice Douglas, dissenting, maintained that the government had acted in bad faith; that the FBI had evaded the Fourth Amendment by "wearing the masks of immigration officials while in fact they are preparing a case for criminal prosecution."

Justice Brennan, dissenting, said:

47 Henry v. United States, 361 U.S. 98 (1959).
48 Ibid., 106.
49 Abel v. United States, 362 U.S. 217 (1960).

... we must take care to enforce the Constitution without regard to the nature of the crime or the nature of the criminal. . . . The Amendment's protection is made effective for everyone only by upholding it when invoked by the worst of men. . . .

It does not follow that Congress may strip aliens of the protections of the Fourth Amendment and authorize unreasonable searches of their premises. . . .[50]

In Rios, a companion case[51] to that of Elkins, Los Angeles police officers, on duty in a "narcotics activity" neighborhood, observed the defendant acting suspiciously. When he entered a taxicab, they followed and stopped it. One went to one side of the cab; one to another. One identified himself as a policeman.

In the next minute there occurred a rapid succession of events. The cab door was opened; the petitioner dropped a recognizable package of narcotics to the floor of the vehicle; one of the officers grabbed the petitioner as he alighted from the cab; the other officer retrieved the package; and the first officer drew his revolver.

The precise chronology of all that happened is not clear in the record. In their original arrest report the police stated that the petitioner dropped the package only after one of the officers had opened the cab door. In testifying later, this officer said that he saw the defendant drop the package before the door was opened. The taxi driver gave a substantially different version.[52]

At the trial the seized narcotics were put in evidence. The defendant urged that the officers had no probable cause to make an arrest; hence the seizure was unlawful under the Fourth Amendment. Justice Stewart, writing for five members of the Court, vacated the conviction and remanded the case to the lower court for a determination of when the arrest occurred. He held that if the defendant dropped the package to the floor and the police saw it before they opened the door, the arrest was lawful and the seizure proper; that if they undertook to open the door before the defendant dropped the package, that act constituted an arrest, and since they had not yet seen the package, the arrest was without probable cause and the seizure unlawful. Justices Frankfurter, Clark, Harlan, and Whittaker dissented.

The Rios case also involved the rejection of the silver platter doctrine; hence the dissenters addressed themselves solely to that major issue. Justice Frankfurter pointed out that the Court was overruling the basic Weeks rule, announced in 1914, and argued that the new rule found no justification "either

[50] *Ibid.*, 248, 250.
[51] Rios v. United States, 364 U.S. 253 (1960).
[52] *Ibid.*, 256–57.

by the demands of new experience . . . or by new insight into the undesirable consequences of the old rule."[53]

Another such Tweedledee-Tweedledum factual situation engaged the attention of the Court in a Massachusetts case.[54] Here, on a dismissal of a writ because of an insufficient record, the basic factual question on which the validity of a search rested, according to the dissenters, involved the question of whether a paper bag containing guns, thrown by the defendant from the window, "had been abandoned and whether the bag was searched before or after the guns were observed."[55]

Justice Fortas, concurring in the dismissal, characterized the dissent thus: "He [Justice White] would remand the case for a purpose which seems to me to be unreal; that is, to hold an inquiry, almost ten years after the event. . . . This inquiry—at this late date—is as elusive as an attempt to capture last night's moonbeam."[56]

A continuing cause of judicial dissension arose when five members of the Court affirmed the conviction of a Baltimore householder who refused to permit a health inspector, who had evidence of rodent infestation, to inspect his premises without a search warrant. The refusal violated provisions of the Baltimore City Code. Justice Frankfurter, writing for the majority, held that

> giving the fullest scope to this constitutional right to privacy, its protection cannot be here invoked. The attempted inspection . . . is merely to determine whether conditions exist which the Baltimore Health Code proscribes. . . .[57]
>
> . . . the system of inspection here under attack, having its beginning in Maryland's colonial history, has been an integral part of Baltimore's health laws for more than a century and a half. The legal significance of such a long and consistent history of state practice has been illuminated for us by Mr. Justice Holmes: "The Fourteenth Amendment . . . did not destroy history for the States. . . . If a thing has been practised for two hundred years by common consent, it will need a strong case for the Fourteenth Amendment to affect it."[58]

Justice Whittaker concurred, saying he understood the Court's opinion to adhere fully to the principle that "the core of the Fourth Amendment prohibiting unreasonable searches applies to the Due Process Clause of the Fourteenth Amendment."[59]

Justice Douglas said: "The decision today greatly dilutes the right of

[53] Ibid., 234, 261–62.
[54] Massachusetts v. Painten, 389 U.S. 560 (1968).
[55] Ibid., 567.
[56] Ibid., 562.
[57] Frank v. Maryland, 359 U.S. 360, 366 (1959).
[58] Ibid., 370.
[59] Ibid., 373.

privacy which every homeowner had the right to believe was part of our American heritage. We witness indeed an inquest over a substantial part of the Fourth Amendment."[60]

Another case, involving the same state of facts, came to the Court from Ohio on an application for a writ of certiorari respecting a similar conviction. Justice Stewart did not participate. However, those who had dissented in the Frank case voted "probable jurisdiction," whereupon, contrary to custom, four of the justices who constituted the majority in the Frank case wrote in protest at considering an issue just disposed of.[61] Nevertheless, four justices having voted to accept the case, it came on for argument during the next term. At that time, by an equal division, with Justice Stewart, who had voted with the majority in the Frank case, not participating, the Frank case was followed, and the conviction was affirmed.[62]

Then Justice Brennan, saying that the affirming justices had violated tradition in expressing opinions on the application for certiorari, found the usual practice not applicable and for himself and his coadjutors, the Chief Justice and Justices Black and Douglas, wrote at length maintaining that the Frank decision should be overruled upon the ground that the ordinances were unconstitutional.[63]

Later, in 1967, six members of the Court held that a householder had a constitutional right to insist that building inspectors obtain a search warrant and overruled the Frank case.[64] Justices Clark, Harlan, and Stewart dissented. Justice White wrote for the majority and tempered the probable cause rule applicable to the issuance of a warrant:

> There is unanimous agreement among those most familiar with this field that the only effective way to seek universal compliance with the minimum standards required by municipal codes is through routine periodic inspections of all structures. . . .[65]
>
> Having concluded that the area inspection is a "reasonable" search of private property within the meaning of the Fourth Amendment, it is obvious that "probable cause" to issue a warrant to inspect must exist if reasonable legislative or administrative standards for conducting an area inspection are satisfied with respect to a particular dwelling. . . . The warrant procedure is designed to guarantee that a decision to search private property is justified by a reasonable governmental interest. . . . If a valid public interest justified the intrusion con-

---

[60] Ibid., 374.

[61] Eaton v. Price, 360 U.S. 246 (1959).

[62] Ohio v. Price, 364 U.S. 263 (1960).

[63] Ibid., 263 et seq.

[64] Camara v. Municipal Court, 387 U.S. 523 (1967).

[65] Ibid., 535–36.

templated, then there is probable cause to issue a suitable restricted search warrant. . . .[66]

. . . nothing we say today is intended to foreclose prompt inspections, even without a warrant, that the law has traditionally upheld in emergency situations. . . . it seems likely that warrants should normally be sought only after entry is refused unless there has been a citizen complaint or there is other satisfactory reason for securing immediate entry.[67]

In a companion case[68] the same majority reversed the conviction of a defendant for refusal to permit a member of the Seattle Fire Department to inspect his locked commercial warehouse without a warrant. Again the three dissenters expressed the view that no warrant was required for inspections under municipal fire, health, and housing inspection programs.

Justice Clark, dissenting, wrote in both cases, saying that the Court

renders this municipal experience, which dates back to Colonial days, for naught . . . by striking down hundreds of city ordinances throughout the country and jeopardizing thereby the health, welfare, and safety of literally millions of people.

But this is not all. It prostitutes the command of the Fourth Amendment that "no Warrants shall issue, but upon probable cause" and sets up in the health and safety codes area inspection a newfangled "warrant" system that is entirely foreign to Fourth Amendment standards. It is regrettable that the Court wipes out such a long and widely accepted practice and creates in its place such enormous confusion in all of our towns and metropolitan cities in one fell swoop.[69]

Justice Clark predicted (undoubtedly truly) that this "boxcar warrant" would be "printed up in pads of a thousand or more—with space for the street number to be inserted—and issued by magistrates in broadcast fashion as a matter of course."[70]

However, the Court upheld seizures in two cases where, lacking a warrant, policemen "stopped and frisked" suspects under circumstances which the Court held gave them objective grounds for suspicion that the suspect was a source of immediate danger, though short of probable cause for an arrest.[71] Justice Douglas dissented. The Court held that each such case would have to rest upon its particular circumstances; hence the search was justified in the one case, when it disclosed a loaded revolver, in the other, burglar tools. How-

[66] *Ibid.*, 538–39.
[67] *Ibid.*, 539–40.
[68] See v. Seattle, 387 U.S. 541 (1967).
[69] *Ibid.*, 547.
[70] *Ibid.*, 554.
[71] Terry v. Ohio, 392 U.S. 1 (1968); Peters v. New York, 392 U.S. 40 (1968); *see also* Wainwright v. New Orleans, 392 U.S. 598 (1968).

ever, the Court held that the search was to be limited to a "patting-down" of the suspect's clothes. In a third case,[72] where the police were searching for narcotics, the Court held that these could not be deemed a source of immediate danger; hence it vacated the conviction.

A decision that prompted an indignant article in the American Bar Association *Journal* (September 1964) by Kingsley A. Taft, chief justice of the Supreme Court of Ohio, followed after Preston and two companions were arrested at four o'clock in the morning on a charge of vagrancy. They had been sitting in a parked car in downtown Newport, Kentucky, since ten o'clock the previous night. They were taken to the police station and booked and their car taken to a garage. There, lacking a search warrant, the police searched the car and found revolvers and other accessories of the burglar's trade.

Later Preston was charged with and convicted of conspiring to rob a bank, and the seized articles were received in evidence. On appeal the Supreme Court held that, though the arrest was lawful, the search of the car was too remote in point of time to be said to accompany the arrest and reversed the conviction.[73]

Later, during the 1966 term, Justice Black, who had written for a unanimous court in the Preston case, wrote for himself and Justices Harlan, Stewart, Clark, and White, holding that evidence found in the defendant's car a week after his arrest was admissible and that the California court which had held the contrary had misconstrued the decision in the Preston case, which he proceeded to attempt to distinguish.[74] Justice Douglas, writing for the four dissenting liberals, properly said that the case was on all fours with the Preston case, which he found was being overruled sub silentio.[75] He noted the criticism of the Preston case which, one might conclude, like Mr. Dooley's comment concerning the election returns, may have influenced the majority's change of mind.

Subsequently, on an application for certiorari, a per curiam opinion expressing the views of seven members of the Court (Justice Marshall not participating) rejected the petitioner's contention that the automobile registration card belonging to the victim of a robbery found in the petitioner's automobile could not be lawfully placed in evidence, since it "was in plain view and its discovery was not the result of a search, but of a measure taken to protect the car while it was in police custody."[76] This somewhat sophistic distinction vis-à-vis the Preston case enabled Justice Douglas, concurring, to say that,

[72] Sibron v. New York, 392 U.S. 40 (1968).
[73] Preston v. United States, 376 U.S. 364 (1964).
[74] Cooper v. California, 386 U.S. 58 (1967).
[75] *Ibid.*, 65.
[76] Harris v. United States, 390 U.S. 234 (1968).

"although Preston . . . was not mentioned in the court's opinion, he assumed that it survived."[77]

Thereafter the Court agreed with Justice Douglas that the Preston case had survived the last-mentioned case when it held that an air rifle found in the defendants' car was not admissible in evidence since "whether or not a car may constitutionally be searched 'incident' to arrest for a traffic offense, the search here did not take place until petitioners were in custody inside the courthouse and the car was parked on the street outside. Preston . . . holds that under such circumstances a search is 'too remote in time or place to (be) incidental to the arrest.' "[78]

Concurrently with the Preston decision, the Court reversed the conviction of one Stoner, whose room had been searched in his absence and a revolver found, after the police, with probable cause to suspect him of robbery of a food market, had gone to his hotel to apprehend him. Since he was not arrested at the time of the search, the Court held the revolver improperly admitted in evidence at his trial. It held, too, that the situation was not helped by the fact that the hotel clerk had admitted the police to the room. Justice Harlan dissented, maintaining that the case should be remanded to the California court to determine whether the admission of the revolver in evidence constituted "harmless error."[79]

In a previous case[80] the Connecticut Supreme Court had found that admission of evidence illegally seized from the car of a defendant convicted of painting swastikas on a synagogue was "harmless error." Nevertheless, five members of the high court, disagreeing with the finding, reversed the conviction. Justices Harlan, Clark, Stewart, and White dissented.

Later, during the 1966 term, the Court held that it had jurisdiction to formulate a harmless-error rule and that before a constitutional error could be held to be harmless, the court must be able to declare its belief that it was harmless beyond a reasonable doubt. Justice Stewart maintained that no constitutional error could be harmless.[81]

Another decision that awakened widespread criticism came about when

about January 1, 1960, Officers Strickland and Rogers from the narcotics division of the Houston Police Department received reliable information from a credible person that petitioner Aguilar had heroin and other narcotic drugs and narcotic paraphernalia in his possession at his residence, 509 Pinckney Street, Houston,

77 Ibid., 236–37.
78 Dyke v. Taylor Implement Co., 391 U.S. 216, 220 (1968).
79 Stoner v. California, 376 U.S. 483 (1964).
80 Fahy v. Connecticut, 375 U.S. 85 (1963).
81 Chapman v. California, 386 U.S. 18, 42 (1967); see also Anderson v. Nelson, 390 U.S. 523 (1968); Fontaine v. California, 390 U.S. 593 (1968).

Texas; after receiving this information the officers, the record indicates, kept the premises of the petitioner under surveillance for about a week.

On January 8, 1960, the two officers applied for a search warrant and executed an affidavit before a justice of the peace in which they alleged under oath that petitioner's residence at 509 Pinckney Street "is a place where we each have reason to believe and do believe that (Aguilar) . . . has in his possession therein narcotic drugs . . . for the purpose of the unlawful sale thereof, and where such narcotic drugs are unlawfully sold." In addition and in support of their belief, the officers included in the affidavit the further allegation that they "have reliable information from a credible person and do believe that heroin . . . and other narcotics and narcotic paraphernalia are being kept at . . . (petitioner's) premises for the purposes of sale and use contrary to the provisions of law."[82]

The officers executing the search warrant entered the house, pursued Aguilar, who ran into a bathroom and threw a packet of heroin into the commode, which an officer retrieved.

On his trial, the defendant objected to the admission of the heroin on the ground that the warrant had been issued on an affidavit insufficient to justify its issuance and that, therefore, the search and seizure violated the Fourth Amendment. In an opinion by Justice Goldberg for five members of the Court, it was held that a magistrate issuing a warrant must be informed of some of the underlying circumstances relied on by the person providing the information to the officers and some of the underlying circumstances from which the officer concluded that the informant was creditable or his information reliable. In consequence, the conviction was voided.

Justice Clark, writing for himself and Justices Black and Stewart, reviewed the prior cases and concluded: "Believing that the Court has substituted a rigid, academic formula for the unrigid standards of reasonableness and 'probable cause' laid down by the Fourth Amendment itself—a substitution of technicality for practicality—and believing that the Court's holding will tend to obstruct the administration of criminal justice throughout the country, I respectfully dissent."[83] Justice Harlan concurred, feeling bound by a prior decision.[84]

The Aguilar decision followed a number of others where the "informer issue" had met varying results, and it was followed by a 1966 term decision where a majority upheld a conviction based on the use of hearsay from an informer.

In a prior case, where a paid informer notified a federal narcotics agent that one Draper had gone to Chicago to replenish his stock of narcotics and

[82] Aguilar v. Texas, 378 U.S. 108, 117 (1964).
[83] Ibid., 122.
[84] Ibid., 116.

that he would return by train at a given time, the agent, armed with a description of the man, made the arrest and found the narcotics Draper was carrying.

The informer died following the arrest and was not available to give testimony. The narcotics were admitted in evidence, and Draper was convicted. On appeal he contended that the hearsay furnished by the absent informer had not constituted probable cause for his arrest and that the search, without a warrant, was unlawful. Six of the sitting Justices affirmed the conviction; Justice Douglas dissented.[85]

Justice Whittaker, writing for the majority, quoted a previous decision which said: "In dealing with probable cause . . . as the very name implies, we deal with probabilities. These are not technical; they are the factual and practical considerations on which reasonable and prudent men, not legal technicians, act."[86]

In a 1964 case a warrant was issued based on an undisclosed informant's statements that he had seen furs in petitioner's home and had been told they had been stolen.[87] Five judges held that there was sufficient probable cause for the issuance of the warrant without passing on the issue of disclosure of the identity of the informer. Justices Brennan, Douglas, and Goldberg and the Chief Justice dissented, maintaining that the informer should have been named.

In another and earlier narcotics case[88] an officer obtained a search warrant upon his affidavit that he had been given information by one unnamed that petitioner and another were involved in the illicit narcotic traffic and kept a ready supply of heroin on hand in the apartment. The defendant claimed the affidavit insufficient, relying on a previous decision[89] holding that a mere statement of belief was insufficient. Over the dissent of Justice Douglas, Justice Frankfurter, writing for the majority, said that an affidavit could rely upon information received through an informant "so long as the informant's statement is reasonably corroborated by other matters within the officer's knowledge."[90]

In still another early narcotics case, six members of the Court held a complaint for a warrant insufficient since it contained "no affirmative allegation that the affiant spoke with personal knowledge." Justice Clark, writing for himself and Justices Burton and Whittaker, said: "Such purblindness may set petitioner free but it shackles law enforcement."[91]

85 Draper v. United States, 358 U.S. 307 (1959).
86 Brinegar v. United States, 338 U.S. 160, 175 (1949).
87 Rugendorf v. United States, 376 U.S. 528 (1964).
88 Jones v. United States, 362 U.S. 257 (1960).
89 Nathanson v. United States, 290 U.S. 41 (1933).
90 Jones v. United States, 362 U.S. 257, 269 (1960).
91 Giordenello v. United States, 357 U.S. 480, 492 (1958).

In a case following Aguilar, Justice Goldberg, who wrote the decision for the majority striking down Aguilar's conviction, joined six other Justices in sustaining a warrant. He repeated Justice Frankfurter's statement in the Jones case, that hearsay in an affidavit will be considered evidence of probable cause so long "as there . . . (is) a substantial basis for crediting the hearsay." He also said the affidavit must be read in a "common sense way."[92]

On an application for certiorari, five members of the Court granted the writ and summarily reversed a judgment of conviction upon the ground that evidence had been received which was inadmissible under the Fourth Amendment, citing a prior case.[93] Justice Clark, with the support of Justices Black, Harlan, and Stewart, wrote in dissent, saying that an apartment was searched as the result of a warrant issued upon "the recital in the affidavit of 'personal observation of the premises' by Officer Stover, the affiant, and 'information from sources believed by the police department to be reliable.' "

Justice Clark said also:

The Supreme Court of Appeals of Virginia found that Officer Stover had the apartment building . . . under his personal surveillance in December, 1962, and January, 1963. During those months he saw the petitioner Riggan "come and go" from the building. Riggan was known to the police, having been arrested in November, 1962, on a charge of assault. That arrest was made at apartment 604C (the one watched) by Officer Hartel, who noticed telephones cut from their wires and placed in a closet, along with other suspicious circumstances. . . . In addition to receiving this report, Officer Stover learned from two fellow police officers and two other informants, whom he believed to be reliable, that a lottery was being conducted from apartment 604C.[94]

In a footnote[95] Justice Clark noted the approval of a similar affidavit by the Virginia court in a previous case from which the high court denied certiorari. He commented: "It is stranger still that the Court now grants and reverses this case summarily without giving Virginia a chance to argue the legality of its affidavit, which it had every reason to think was sufficient."

Writing for six members of the Court, Justice Stewart reversed the conviction of an Ohio gambler on the ground that the police had no probable cause to arrest him and that, in consequence, gambling slips found in a search of his car and admitted in evidence on his trial were inadmissible under the Fourth Amendment, as applied to the states by the Fourteenth.[96]

It appeared that police officers accosted the defendant while he was driving

[92] United States v. Ventresca, 380 U.S. 102, 108 (1965).
[93] Riggan v. Virginia, 384 U.S. 152 (1966).
[94] Ibid., 153.
[95] Ibid., 152n.
[96] Beck v. Ohio, 379 U.S. 89 (1964).

in downtown Cleveland and placed him under arrest, although they had no warrant. The police justified the arrest by the fact that the arresting officer "had a police picture" of the defendant "and knew what he looked like" and that he knew that the defendant had "a record" in connection with gambling. He said also he had had "information" or "reports" concerning the defendant, without disclosing a source.

The majority said the record was too scant to justify the Ohio court's finding of "probable cause" to make the arrest; hence the search was illegal and the evidence inadmissible, and the conviction based thereon could not stand.

Justice Clark, joined by Justice Black, said that the Ohio court had determined the following facts in the case:

> The Cleveland police had good reason to believe that defendant was regularly engaged in carrying on a scheme of chance involving clearinghouse slips. There was testimony that he had previously been convicted on that score. Information was given to the police by an informer that the defendant would be in a certain locality at a certain time pursuing his unlawful activities. He was found in the locality, as predicted, driving an automobile. Police officers stopped the car and searched it, without result. Defendant was then arrested and taken to a police station and his clothing was examined, resulting in the discovery and seizure of the illegal clearinghouse slips, which formed the basis of the charge against him and his subsequent conviction.[97]

He added:

> The Court ignores these findings entirely. Where the highest Court of a State after detailed and earnest consideration determines the facts and they are reasonably supportable, I would let them stand.... Otherwise, this Court will be continually disputing with state and federal courts over the minutiae of facts in every search and seizure case. Especially is this true if the Court disputes the findings *sua sponte* where, as here, no attack is levelled at them.

Justice Harlan, also dissenting, said: "I regard . . . as the crucial point in the case, . . . if the informant did give the police . . . information, the fact of its occurrence would sufficiently indicate the informant's reliability to provide a basis for petitioner's arrest."[98]

Later, during the 1966 term, a five-man majority, including Justice Black, held that a state court was not obligated to disclose the identity of an informer at a pretrial hearing to determine probable cause to make an arrest where the informer was known to the police to be reliable and they had made the arrest

[97] *Ibid.*, 97–98.
[98] *Ibid.*, 99.

on information he had supplied.[99] The Chief Justice and Justices Douglas, Brennan, and Fortas dissented.

A unanimous court reversed the conviction of a defendant charged with the unlawful possession of narcotics upon the ground that, though the police had probable cause to arrest the defendant, the narcotics seized and placed in evidence were found after an intensive search at the defendant's home two blocks from the scene of the arrest.[100]

Chief Justice Warren wrote for the majority, affirming a conviction of a seller of narcotics to a federal agent, who, misrepresenting his identity, was invited by the defendant to his home where the sale and purchase occurred.[101] He distinguished a previous case[102] in holding that there had been no violation of the Fourth Amendment. In answer to the defendant's contention that he had not waived his right to keep his home inviolate because of the deception practiced by the agent, the Chief Justice said:

> Both petitioner and the Government recognize the necessity for some under-cover police activity and both concede that the particular circumstances of each case govern the admissibility of evidence obtained by stratagem or deception. Indeed, it has long been acknowledged by the decisions of this Court . . . that, in the detection of many types of crime, the Government is entitled to use decoys and to conceal the identity of its agents. The various protections of the Bill of Rights, of course, provide checks upon such official deception for the protection of the individual. . . .[103]
>
> Without question, the home is accorded the full range of Fourth Amendment protections. . . . But when, as here, the home is converted into a commercial center to which outsiders are invited for purposes of transacting unlawful business, that business is entitled to no greater sanctity than if it were carried on in a store, a garage, a car, or on the street.[104]

Justices Brennan and Fortas concurred, and Justice Brennan said:

> I affirm solely on the reasoning on which the Court ultimately relies, namely that petitioner's apartment was not an area protected by the Fourth Amendment as related to the transactions in the present case. . . .
>
> There was . . . no intrusion upon the "sanctity" of petitioner's home or the "privacies of life."[105]

In his dissent in the later Osborn case Justice Douglas included a dissent in

[99] McCray v. Illinois, 386 U.S. 300 (1967).
[100] James v. Louisiana, 382 U.S. 36 (1965).
[101] Lewis v. United States, 385 U.S. 206 (1966).
[102] Gouled v. United States, 255 U.S. 298 (1921).
[103] Lewis v. United States, 385 U.S. 206, 208–209 (1966).
[104] Ibid., 213.
[105] Ibid.

the Lewis case (above). He maintained that "privacy, though not expressly mentioned in the Constitution, is essential to the other rights guaranteed by it."[106]

Referring specifically to the Lewis case, he said: "Entering another's house in disguise to obtain evidence is a 'search' that should bring into play all the protective features of the Fourth Amendment. When the agent in Lewis had reason for believing that petitioner possessed narcotics, a search warrant should have been obtained."[107]

And he declared: "A home is still a sanctuary, however the owner may use it. . . . We downgrade the Fourth Amendment when we forgive noncompliance with its mandate and allow these easier methods of the police to thrive."[108]

In the previous Gouled case, which had been so frequently cited and followed, an army private, attached to the intelligence department, acting under instructions of a superior officer, pretended to make a friendly call upon one Gouled, an acquaintance suspected of defrauding the government, searched his office in his absence, and abstracted documents therefrom. One of these papers was admitted in evidence over objection at the subsequent trial of Gouled, who was convicted. The Supreme Court reversed, holding that an admission "obtained by stealth" is the equivalent of one obtained "by force or coercion."[109]

The Court's recantation respecting Fourth Amendment rules continued when a search accompanying the arrest of a robber resulted in finding weapons and clothing that were introduced at his trial and resulted in his conviction. In affirming the conviction, Justice Brennan, writing for a majority, noted that "the distinction made by some of our cases between seizure of items of evidential value only and seizure of instrumentalities, fruits or contraband has been criticized by courts and commentators." And he noted the validity of the criticism when he added: "We today reject the distinction as based on premises no longer accepted as rules governing the application of the Fourth Amendment."[110]

The majority overruled the Gouled case, holding that "the premise in Gouled that Government may not seize evidence simply for the purpose of proving crime has . . . been discredited,"[111] as a result of the recognition that "the principal object of the Fourth Amendment is the protection of privacy rather than property."[112] Justice Black concurred, as did Justice Fortas and

[106] Osborn v. United States, 385 U.S. 323, 340, 341 (1966).
[107] *Ibid.*, 345.
[108] *Ibid.*, 346.
[109] Gouled v. United States, 255 U.S. 298 (1921).
[110] Warden v. Hayden, 387 U.S. 294, 300–301 (1967).
[111] *Ibid.*, 306.
[112] *Ibid.*, 304.

the Chief Justice, but not in the "repudiation of the so-called 'mere evidence' rule."[113] Justice Douglas dissented, saying, *inter alia,* that "which is taken from a person without his consent and used as testimonial evidence violates the Fifth Amendment," while admitting that the Court had held otherwise in the Schmerber case.[114]

Previously, one Sandoval had been denied certiorari to review a conviction for possession of heroin. Justice Douglas dissented, saying that a police officer who answered the telephone while in the house of a possessor of narcotics and had a conversation that led to the arrest of the petitioner "was engaged in a general, exploratory search to obtain evidence and leads incriminating anyone of any possible crime,"[115] and that such extension of the bounds of search was impermissible.

A case that attracted nation-wide attention was that involving James R. Hoffa, president of the Teamsters Union.[116] Hoffa was charged with and convicted of the crime of attempting to bribe a juror. Relevant evidence was furnished by Partin, an associate of Hoffa, of admissions and other incriminating statements by Hoffa made to Partin and in his presence, in Hoffa's hotel room and elsewhere. Hoffa maintained that Partin's testimony violated his Fourth, Fifth, and Sixth Amendment rights. As to the Fourth Amendment, Justice Stewart, writing for a majority, said:

> In the present case . . . it is evident that no interest legitimately protected by the Fourth Amendment is involved. . . . The petitioner, in a word, was not relying on the security of the hotel room; he was relying upon his misplaced confidence that Partin would not reveal his wrongdoing. . . .
> Neither this Court nor any member of it has ever expressed the view that the Fourth Amendment protects a wrongdoer's misplaced belief that a person to whom he voluntarily confides his wrongdoing will not reveal it. Indeed, the Court unanimously rejected that very contention less than four years ago in Lopez v. United States.[117]

Justice Stewart said that the Fifth Amendment furnished no ground for objection since "no claim has been or could be made that the petitioner's incriminating statements were the product of any sort of coercion, legal or factual."[118]

He further disclaimed validity of any objection under the Sixth Amendment for the reason that none of the petitioner's incriminating statements

---

113 *Ibid.,* 310.
114 *Ibid.,* 320.
115 Sandoval v. California, 386 U.S. 948, 950 (1967).
116 Hoffa, Parks, Campbell, King v. United States, 385 U.S. 293 (1966).
117 *Ibid.,* 302.
118 *Ibid.,* 304.

were made in the presence of counsel, even though Partin may have been present at conversations between petitioner and his counsel. Finally he found that "the use of secret informers is not *per se* unconstitutional."[119]

Justice Clark, supported by Justice Douglas, held, since two lower courts had found that the government had not deceptively placed Partin in the counsels of Hoffa, the writ of certiorari to review the conviction should not have been granted and the appeal should therefore be dismissed. Justices Fortas and White did not participate. The Chief Justice dissented, maintaining that "Partin was acting as a paid federal informer" and that "an invasion of basic rights made possible by prevailing upon friendship with the victim is no less proscribed than an invasion accomplished by force."[120]

He added: "one of the important duties of this Court is to give careful scrutiny to practices of government agents when they are challenged in cases before us, in order to insure that the protections of the Constitution are respected and to maintain the integrity of federal law enforcement."[121] Finding that Partin was a "type of informer and the uses to which he was put . . . evidence a serious potential for undermining the integrity of the truth-finding process in the federal courts . . . ,"[122] the Chief Justice would have reversed the conviction.

Simultaneously, the Court affirmed the conviction of Osborn, one of Hoffa's lawyers in a previous trial, for endeavoring to bribe a juror.[123] Osborn had retained Vick, a policeman, to investigate persons on the panel from which a jury to try Hoffa would be drawn. Unknown to Osborn, Vick had agreed to report to the government any illegal activities he might observe.

Vick reported to Osborn that Elliott, one of the prospective jurors, was his cousin, whereupon Osborn authorized Vick to pay Elliott $10,000 if he should become a juror in the case. Upon Vick's reporting this to the government, he was furnished with a recording device to record conversations with Osborn, which were admitted at the trial to substantiate Vick's testimony. The use of the concealed recorder had been authorized by two of the judges of the federal district court.

Justice Stewart, writing for a majority, said that the use of the recorder and the recorded testimony was not only justified by the majority opinion in Lopez v. United States, but also under the strictures of the minority opinion,[124] since it was the judges who sought verification in "a testimonial contest between the only two people in the world who knew the truth—one an informer, the

---

119 *Ibid.*, 311.
120 *Ibid.*, 314.
121 *Ibid.*, 315.
122 *Ibid.*, 320.
123 Osborn v. United States, 385 U.S. 323 (1966).
124 *Ibid.*, 325–26, 328, 330.

other a lawyer of previous good repute. There could hardly be a clearer example of 'the procedure of antecedent justification before a magistrate that is central to the Fourth Amendment' as 'a precondition of lawful electronic surveillance,' " said Justice Stewart.

Dissenting, Justice Douglas said, "I would . . . bar the use of all testimonial evidence obtained by wiretapping or by an electronic device."[125] Justice White did not participate.

If a reading of the pros and cons on these various Fourth Amendment cases leaves one with some measure of doubt and confusion, he may find consolation in the words of Justice Harlan in a late case where, writing for six members of the Court, he said: "Since search-and-seizure claims depend heavily upon their individual facts (see e.g., United States v. Rabinowitz, 339 U.S. 56, 63) and since the law of search and seizure is in a state of flux (e.g., compare Warden v. Hayden, 387 U.S. 294 with Gouled v. United States, 255 U.S. 298; compare Camara v. Municipal Court, 387 U.S. 523 with Frank v. Maryland, 359 U.S. 360), the incidence of such marginal cases cannot be said to be negligible."[126]

In that case Justice Harlan, writing for six members of the Court, Justices Black and White dissenting and Justice Marshall not participating, explained the reversal of the conviction of a man named Garrett, indicted and convicted for bank robbery. Part of the evidence introduced by the government, was a suitcase seized by FBI agents, acting without a warrant, in the house of the mother of another alleged coconspirator. The suitcase contained a gun holster, a sack similar to the one used in the robbery, and several coin cards and bill wrappers from the bank which had been robbed.

Prior to his trial, Garrett moved to suppress the use of the suitcase as evidence. In order to establish his standing so to move, he testified that, although he could not identify the suitcase as his with certainty, it was similar to one he had owned and that he was the owner of the clothing found inside the suitcase. The district court denied the motion to suppress, and Garrett's testimony at the suppression hearing was admitted at his subsequent trial. On appeal Garrett contended that the admission of his previous testimony violated his Fourth Amendment rights, since he could give that testimony only by assuming the risk that the testimony would later be admitted against him at his trial.

After saying that "at one time, a defendant who wished to assert a Fourth Amendment objection was required to show that he was the owner or possessor of the seized property or that he had a possessory interest in the searched

[125] *Ibid.*, 352.

[126] Simmons v. United States, 390 U.S. 377, 393 (1968); *see also* Jones v. United States, 362 U.S. 257 (1960).

premises (see, e.g., Jones v. United States, 362 U.S. 257, at 262,"[127] Justice Harlan went on to say that the Jones case relaxed the rule in two alternative ways:

First, we held that when, as in Jones, possession of the seized evidence is itself an essential element of the offense with which the defendant is charged, the Government is precluded from denying that the defendant has the requisite possessory interest to challenge the admission of the evidence. Second, we held alternatively that the defendant need have no possessory interest in the searched premises in order to have standing; it is sufficient that he be legitimately on those premises when the search occurs. . . .[128]

The only, or at least the most natural way in which he [Garrett] could be found standing to object to the admission of the suitcase was to testify that he was its owner. . . . Under the rule laid down by the courts below, he could give that testimony only by assuming the risk that the testimony would later be admitted against him at trial. . . .[129]

The dilemma faced by defendants like Garrett is most extreme in prosecutions for possessory crimes, for then the testimony required for standing itself proves an element of the offense. We eliminated that Hobson's choice in Jones v. United States . . . by relaxing the standing requirements. This Court has never considered squarely the question whether defendants charged with nonpossessory crimes, like Garrett, are entitled to be relieved of their dilemma entirely. In Jones, the only reference to the subject was a statement that "(The defendant) has been faced . . . with the chance that the allegations made on the motion to suppress may be used against him at the trial, although that they may is by no means an inevitable holding. . . ."

It seems obvious that a defendant who knows that his testimony may be admissible against him at trial will sometimes be deterred from presenting the testimonial proof of standing necessary to assert a Fourth Amendment claim.[131]

At this point, Justice Harlan concluded that the law is so confused that

a defendant with a substantial claim for the exclusion of evidence may conclude that the admission of the evidence, together with the Government's proof linking it to him, is preferable to risking the admission of his own testimony connecting himself with the seized evidence. . . .[132]

. . . in this case Garrett was obliged either to give up what he believed, with advice of counsel, to be a valid Fourth Amendment claim or, in legal effect, to waive his Fifth Amendment privilege against self-incrimination. In these circumstances, we find it intolerable that one constitutional right should have to

[127] Simmons v. United States, 390 U.S. 377, 389–90 (1968).
[128] Ibid., 390.
[129] Ibid., 391.
[130] Ibid., 391–92.
[131] Ibid., 392–93.
[132] Ibid., 393.

be surrendered in order to assert another. We therefore hold that when a defendant testifies in support of a motion to suppress evidence on Fourth Amendment grounds, his testimony may not thereafter be admitted against him at trial on the issue of guilt unless he makes no objection.[133]

Justice Black's added words in a prior discussion of this case may well be given here. Dissenting, he concluded:

> There is certainly no language in the Fourth Amendment which gives support to any such device to hobble law enforcement in this country.... that governmental charter holds out no promises to stultify justice by erecting barriers to the admissibility of relevant evidence voluntarily given in a court of justice. Under the first principles of ethics and morality a defendant who secures a court order by telling the truth should not be allowed to seek a court advantage later based on a premise directly opposite to his prior solemn judicial oath. This Court should not lend the prestige of its high name to such a justice-defeating stratagem.[134]

Over the dissents of Justices Black and White, the Court vacated the conviction of a defendant because a rifle found in the house of his grandmother had been admitted in evidence. The officers had obtained the woman's consent to make the search when they told her they had a search warrant, but no search warrant was produced at the trial. The Court held the grandmother's consent invalid.[135] Justice Black charged that the Court had gone too far in voiding convictions under the Fourth Amendment.[136]

Justice Black's statement in the last-mentioned case was documented by his dissent in a later case.[137] In a prior case[138] the Court had given "ungrudging application" to Section 3109 of the United States Judicial Code, which requires a police officer to give prior notice of his authority and purpose before breaking into premises for the purpose of searching pursuant to a warrant. In that (the prior case), the Court had voided a conviction because the notice was given by the officer "in a low voice" and might not have been heard by the suspect. In the later case over Justice Black's dissent, the Court "enlarged" its "ungrudging application" of the statute by extending its requirement of "breaking" to "the opening of an unlocked door," thus voiding a conviction. It may well be that this sort of decision has produced a three-to-two public disfavor of the Court, as reported by a Gallup poll mentioned in *The New York Times* of July 10, 1968.

[133] *Ibid.*, 394.
[134] *Ibid.*, 398–99.
[135] Bumper v. North Carolina, 391 U.S. 543, 560–61 (1968).
[136] *Ibid.*
[137] Sabbath v. United States, 391 U.S. 585 (1968).
[138] Miller v. United States, 357 U.S. 301 (1958).

CHAPTER XVII

The Negro Racial Issue—I

DURING THE PAST SEVERAL DECADES the Court has been striving, as has Congress, to undo the strictures placed upon Negroes as a result of the prior courts' niggardly constructions of the Fourteenth and Fifteenth Amendments and the civil rights acts passed in the late sixties and seventies.

The efforts of southern states to maintain segregation resulted in most of the cases brought to the Court. Before the Plessy doctrine was overruled, the Court had invalidated a railroad arrangement for ten tables in a dining car for whites and one for Negroes, divided by a curtain.[1] Before that, writing for three members of the Court, Justice Reed held that a Virginia statute which, in providing for the segregation of white and Negro bus passengers, required passengers, under a penalty, to change seats from time to time to increase the seats available to one race or the other was invalid as an undue burden on interstate commerce and as occupying a field in which natural uniformity of regulation was desirable.[2]

Justices Rutledge, Black and Frankfurter concurred. Justice Burton dissented. Justice Black expressed his dissent from the policy of the Court in nullifying state legislation upon the ground that it created an "undue burden" on commerce, saying it was for Congress, not the Court, to legislate on questions of policy. However, he concurred because bound by the Court's policy. Justice Burton maintained that congressional inaction in the face of the fact that eighteen states had prohibited in some degree racial separation in public carriers indicated its opinion of the lack of need for national uniformity.

Over the years the pressures for recognition of personal rights and privileges did not evade the members of the Negro race. Nor did the Court lack cognizance of the trend, as it strikingly evidenced when it rejected the equal but separate doctrine enunciated by the Plessy decision and undertook to desegregate the public schools.

The Court had previously sought to enforce equality of treatment in grad-

[1] Henderson v. United States, 339 U.S. 816 (1950).
[2] Morgan v. Virginia, 328 U.S. 373 (1946).

uate schools without affirming or disaffirming the Plessy doctrine.[3] But in 1954, for the first time, the Chief Justice, writing for a unanimous Court in four cases,[4] held that school segregation by race violated the equal protection guaranteed by the Fourteenth Amendment. He said that "any language in Plessy v. Ferguson contrary to this finding is rejected,"[5] but he failed to mention the elder Justice Harlan's prior rejection in his dissent in that case with the stirring words: "Our Constitution is color-blind, and neither knows or tolerates classes among citizens."

The Chief Justice added:

Today, education is perhaps the most important function of state and local governments. . . . It is the very foundation of good citizenship. . . . where the state has undertaken to provide it, (it) is a right which must be made available to all on equal terms. . . .

Does segregation of children in public schools solely on the basis of race, even though the physical facilities and other "tangible" factors may be equal, deprive the children of the minority group of equal educational opportunities? We believe it does. . . .[6]

To separate them from others of similar age and qualifications solely because of their race generates a feeling of inferiority as to their status in the community that may affect their hearts and minds in a way unlikely ever to be undone. . . .[7]

We conclude that in the field of public education the doctrine of "separate but equal" has no place. Separate educational facilities are inherently unequal.[8]

Having invited discussion respecting the enforcement of its decision, the Court, in an opinion by the Chief Justice, remanded the cases to the lower courts with instructions to enforce the decision of the high court by requiring the defendants to "make a prompt and reasonable start toward full compliance." And to make "such orders and decrees consistent with this opinion as are necessary and proper to admit to public schools on a racially nondiscriminatory basis with all deliberate speed the parties to these cases."[9]

Supplementing the Brown decision, the Court held, in a companion case,

[3] Sweatt v. Painter, 339 U.S. 629 (1950); McLaurin v. Oklahoma Regents, 339 U.S. 637 (1950).

[4] Brown v. Board of Education; Briggs v. Elliott; Davis v. School Board; Gebhart v. Belton. 347 U.S. 483 (1954).

[5] Ibid., 494–95.

[6] Ibid., 493.

[7] Ibid., 494.

[8] Ibid., 495.

[9] Brown v. Board of Education; Briggs v. Elliott; Davis v. School Board; Bolling v. Sharpe; Gebhart v. Belton, 349 U.S. 294, 300, 301 (1955).

that as to the District of Columbia public schools, the due process clause of the Fifth Amendment compelled the same conclusion.[10]

Later, to avoid the effect of the Court's decision in one of the four cases decided with Brown, the school authorities of Prince Edward County, Virginia, closed the public schools but contributed to the support of private segregated white schools substituted for them.[11] Thereupon the Court affirmed, in an opinion by Justice Black, the district court's finding that the closing of the county public schools denied the plaintiffs equal protection of the laws and that it (the district court) had power to enjoin the county officials from contributing to the maintenance of the private segregated schools while the public schools remained closed and also to order the reopening of the public schools.[12] Justices Clark and Harlan concurred, but dissented from the holding that the district court could order the reopening of the public schools.

The resistance of Governor Faubus and the legislature of Arkansas to the enforcement of the Court's decision in the Brown case necessitated the intervention of troops and caused the Little Rock School Board to seek a suspension of the enforcement of the Court's decree until there had been a final determination of efforts to nullify the Brown decision. The district court granted the application; the circuit court reversed, and, in an opinion subscribed by each member of the high court, it affirmed the decision of the circuit court refusing to suspend enforcement.[13]

The Court construed the situation as involving

a claim by the Governor and Legislature of a State that there is no duty on state officials to obey federal court orders resting on this Court's considered interpretation of the United States Constitution. Specifically it involves actions by the Governor and Legislature of Arkansas upon the premises that they are not bound by our holding in Brown. . . . That holding was that the Fourteenth Amendment forbids States to use their governmental powers to bar children on racial grounds from attending schools where there is state participation through any arrangement, management, funds or property. . . .[14]

The constitutional rights of respondents are not to be sacrificed or yielded to the violence and disorder which have followed upon the actions of the Governor and Legislature. . . . law and order are not here to be preserved by depriving the negro children of their constitutional rights. . . .[15]

. . . the constitutional rights of children . . . can neither be nullified openly and directly by state legislators or state executive or judicial officers, nor nulli-

10 Bolling v. Sharpe, 347 U.S. 497 (1954).
11 Davis v. School Board, 347 U.S. 483 (1954).
12 Griffin v. School Board, 377 U.S. 218 (1964).
13 Cooper v. Aaron, 358 U.S. 1 (1958).
14 *Ibid.*, 4.
15 *Ibid.*, 16.

fied indirectly by them through evasive schemes for segregation whether attempted 'ingeniously or ingenuously." . . .[16]

... the interpretation of the Fourteenth Amendment enunciated by this Court in the Brown Case is the supreme law of the land. . . .

No state legislator or executive or judicial officer can war against the Constitution without violating his undertaking to support it.[17]

Justice Frankfurter, concurring, said:

... the power of the State was used not to sustain law but as an instrument for thwarting law. . . . while Arkansas is not a formal party in these proceedings ... it is legally and morally before the Court. . . .

We are now asked to hold that the illegal, forcible interference by the State of Arkansas . . . should be recognized as justification for undoing what the School Board had formulated. . . . No explanation . . . can obscure the inescapable meaning that law should bow to force. To yield to such a claim would be to enthrone official lawlessness, and lawlessness if not checked is the precursor of anarchy. . . . Violent resistance to law cannot be made a legal reason for its suspension. . . . For those in authority thus to defy the law of the land is profoundly subversive not only of our constitutional system but of the presuppositions of a democratic society. . . .[18]

Local customs, however hardened by time, are not decreed in heaven. Habits and feelings they engender may be counteracted and moderated. . . .

Deep emotions have, no doubt, been stirred. They will not be calmed by letting violence loose—violence and defiance employed and encouraged by those upon whom the duty of law observance should have the strongest claim. . . .[19]

The responsibility of those who exercise power in a democratic government is not to reflect inflamed public feeling but to help form its understanding.[20]

Following the Brown decision, a unanimous Court ordered the admission of two Negro women to the University of Alabama.[21]

Later, over the dissent of Justice Harlan, the Court held that students suing to avoid segregation in an Illinois school did not have to exhaust state remedies before appealing to the federal courts, since the right they were asserting was a federal one.[22]

The well-publicized effort of James Meredith, a Negro, to attend the University of Mississippi resulted in an injunction directed to Mississippi's Governor Barnett and its Lieutenant Governor forbidding them to interfere with

[16] *Ibid.,* 17.
[17] *Ibid.,* 18.
[18] *Ibid.,* 22.
[19] *Ibid.,* 25.
[20] *Ibid.,* 26.
[21] Lucy v. Adams, 350 U.S. 1 (1955).
[22] McNeese v. Board of Education, 373 U.S. 668 (1963).

Meredith's admission. Thereafter, they were charged with contempt for violation of the injunction and sought a jury trial. The Court in a majority-of-five decision denied the application.[23] Justice Goldberg, supported by the Chief Justice and Justices Black and Douglas, held that the respondents had a statutory right to a jury trial.

When, during the 1962 term, Negro residents of Memphis, Tennessee, sued to require the city to immediately desegregate public parks and other recreational facilities, the city pleaded that it had already partially desegregated and urged the need and wisdom of proceeding slowly. In unanimously holding that "constitutional rights are to be promptly vindicated,"[24] the Court took occasion to say that "the nature of the ultimate resolution effected in the second Brown decision largely reflected no more than a recognition of the unusual and particular problems inherent in desegregating large numbers of schools throughout the country."[25]

During the same term the Court struck down a provision in a school segregation plan that would have permitted any student, upon request, solely on the basis of his own race and the racial composition of the school to which he was assigned by virtue of rezoning, to transfer from such school, where he would be in a racial minority, back to his former segregated school, where his race would be in the majority. The Court held that "the transfer plans promote discrimination and are therefore invalid."[26]

Again the Court took occasion to utter a warning to recalcitrants:

> In reaching this result we are not unmindful of the deep-rooted problems involved. Indeed, it was consideration for the multifarious local difficulties and "variety of obstacles" which might arise in this transition that led this Court eight years ago to frame its mandate in Brown in such language as "good faith compliance at the earliest practicable date" and "all deliberate speed." ... Now, however, eight years after this decree was rendered and over nine years after the first Brown decision, the context in which we must interpret and apply this language to plans for desegregation has been significantly altered.[27]

During the 1965 term, the Court handed down two apposite school decisions. In the first case the Court required a district court which had approved desegregation plans to grant a full evidentiary hearing upon objectants' contention that faculty allocation on an alleged racial basis invalidated the plans. Here the Court said: "... more than a decade has passed since we directed

23 United States v. Barnett, 376 U.S. 681 (1964).

24 Watson v. Memphis, 373 U.S. 526, 539 (1963).

25 Ibid., 531.

26 Goss v. Board of Education, 373 U.S. 683, 688 (1963).

27 Ibid., 689.

desegregation of public school facilities 'with all deliberate speed.' ...Delays in desegregating school systems are no longer tolerable."[28]

In the second case five members of the Court held that Negro high school students whose class had not yet been desegregated could insist upon immediate transfer to a white school offering better educational facilities. The Court said, "We have emphasized that 'delays in desegregating school systems are no longer tolerable.' "[29] Justices Clark, Harlan, White, and Fortas would have set the case down for argument and plenary consideration.

While refusing to declare "freedom of choice" school plans adopted by many southern states unconstitutional, the Court held, in a unanimous opinion, that such plans must give way to other plans if they do not effect desegregation as quickly as other available plans would.[30] Justice Brennan, writing for the Court, said: "The burden is on a school board today to come forward with a plan that promises realistically to work, and promises realistically to work now."[31]

It appeared that, while under "freedom of choice" plans some Negro children had elected to transfer to white schools, few, if any whites had chosen to transfer to Negro schools, with the result that the latter schools, in fact, remained segregated.

During the 1967 term the Court affirmed a lower court holding which struck down as unconstitutional certain Alabama statutes which required segregation of the races in prisons and jails and which established a schedule for desegregation of the institutions.[32]

Justices Harlan, Stewart, and Black, concurring, held that "prison authorities have the right, acting in good faith and in particularized circumstances, to take into account racial tensions in maintaining security, discipline, and good order in prisons and jails."[33]

The refusal of Negroes to respect state and local segregation requirements in restaurants and motels and the denial of congressional power to justify it have been considered. The efforts to enforce segregation in restaurants, on golf courses, in parks, and elsewhere, which resulted in arrests and convictions under state statutes forbidding trespass and defining breach of the peace, were widespread in the South. With many of these the Court dealt with varying results and, during recent years, largely depending on the view taken by Justice Black.

[28] Bradley v. School Board, 382 U.S. 103, 105 (1965).

[29] Rogers v. Paul, 382 U.S. 198 (1965).

[30] Green v. School Board; Raney v. Board of Education; Monroe v. Board of Commissioners, 391 U.S. 430 (1968).

[31] *Ibid.*, 439.

[32] Lee v. Washington, 390 U.S. 333 (1968).

[33] *Ibid.*, 334.

Unable to agree on the state of the record, the Court refused to review a conviction for trespass on a golf course, where a state court jury, properly instructed, had found the defendants had not been barred from the course.[34]

At the next term seven members of the Court reversed the conviction of a Negro law student who refused to leave the white section of a restaurant in a bus terminal at which the interstate bus on which he was a passenger had stopped. The majority held that, even though the bus carrier did not own, control, or operate the restaurant, the Negro, as an interstate passenger, had a federal right under the Interstate Commerce Act to remain in the white portion of the restaurant, where the terminal and restaurant operated as an integral part of the bus carrier's transportation service for interstate passengers. Justices Clark and Whittaker dissented. Justice Whittaker, writing, based his dissent on the lack of ownership or control of the restaurant by the bus company, maintaining that the ICC Act made that the decisive factor and that the Commission had so determined.[35]

In a later case five members of the Court reversed a Delaware judgment holding that a private corporation leasing premises operated as a restaurant in an automobile parking building owned and operated by a state agency might exclude Negroes.[36] The high court held that Fourteenth Amendment protections were to be read into such a lease. Justice Stewart concurred; Justices Frankfurter, Harlan, and Whittaker dissented, saying that the case should be remanded to the state courts for its interpretation of a Delaware statute permitting segregation. Justice Stewart found the statute unconstitutional.

The first of the Negro cases during the 1961 term involved the conviction of persons for violation of a Louisiana statute which defined "breach of the peace" as conduct "unreasonably and foreseeably" disturbing the public, in that "they refused to move from a cafe counter seat . . . after having been ordered to do so." Reversing the convictions, the Chief Justice wrote for six members of the Court. Justices Douglas, Frankfurter, and Harlan concurred.[37]

The Chief Justice said:

> . . . we must look to Louisiana for guidance in the meaning of the phrase "forseeably disturb or alarm the public." . . . it is evident from the court's prior treatment of them that they were not intended to embrace peaceful conduct. On the contrary, it is plain that under the court's application of the statute these words encompass only conduct which is violent or boisterous in itself, or which is provocative in the sense that it induces a forseeable physical disturbance. . . .[38]

[34] Wolfe v. North Carolina, 364 U.S. 177 (1960).
[35] Boynton v. Virginia, 364 U.S. 454, 469 (1960).
[36] Burton v. Wilmington Parking Authority, 365 U.S. 715 (1961).
[37] Garner, Briscoe, Hoston v. Louisiana, 368 U.S. 157 (1961).
[38] Ibid., 166–67.

We are willing to assume. . . . that the Louisiana courts might construe the statute more broadly to encompass the traditional common-law concept of disturbing the peace. Thus construed, it might permit the police to prevent an imminent public commotion even though caused by peaceful and orderly conduct on the part of the accused. . . .[39]

The undisputed evidence shows that the police were left with nothing to support their actions except their own opinions that it was a breach of the peace for the petitioners to sit peacefully in a place where custom decreed they should not sit. Such activity, in the circumstances of these cases, is not evidence of any crime. . . .[40]

Justice Douglas, concurring, said:

Restaurants, whether in a drug store, department store, or bus terminal, are a part of the public life of most of our communities. Though they are private enterprises, they are public facilities in which the states may not enforce a policy of racial segregation. . . .

State policy violative of the Fourteenth Amendment may be expressed in *legislative* enactments that permit or require segregation of the races in public places or public facilities. . . .

It may be expressed through *executive* action, as where the police or other law enforcement officials act pursuant to or under the color of, state law. . . .

It may be expressed through the administrative action of state agencies in leasing public facilities. . . .

It may result from judicial action. . . .

. . . Mr. Justice Bradley suggested . . . that state policy may be as effectively expressed in customs as in formal legislative, executive, or judicial action. . . .

There is a deep-seated pattern of segregation of the races in Louisiana. . . . It was restated in 1960 . . . by Act. No. 630 . . .[41]

Segregation is basic to the structure of Louisiana as a community, the custom that maintains it is at least as powerful as any law. . . . where the segregation policy is the policy of a state, it matters not that the agency to enforce it is a private enterprise. . . .

It is my view that a State may not constitutionally enforce a policy of segregation in restaurant facilities. . . .[42]

Under Louisiana law, restaurants are a form of private property affected with a public interest. . . .[43]

Justice Harlan, concurring in the result, said:

[39] *Ibid.*, 169.
[40] *Ibid.*, 174.
[41] *Ibid.*, 177–79.
[42] *Ibid.*, 181.
[43] *Ibid.*, 183.

I agree that these convictions are unconstitutional, but not for the reasons given by the Court. . . . I believe the convictions are vulnerable under the Fourteenth Amendment on other grounds: (1) the kind of conduct revealed . . . could not be punished under a generalized breach of the peace provision. . . . (2) [the statute] . . . is unconstitutionally vague and uncertain.[44]

In an action brought by Negroes to enjoin interference with their rights to nonsegregated service in interstate and intrastate transportation, the Court, in a per curiam opinion, said, "We have settled beyond question that no State may require racial segregation of interstate or intrastate transportation facilities" and directed the district court to dispose expeditiously of the appellants' claim of right to such service.[45]

Another per curiam opinion held that a municipal airport restaurant operated under a lease from the city could not enforce segregation and directed the district court to issue an injunction accordingly.[46]

Again a per curiam opinion vacated a conviction under the Louisiana breach-of-the-peace statute for using a bus terminal waiting room reserved for whites.[47] Justice Harlan suggested argument; Justice Frankfurter did not participate.

At the 1962 term the Court considered the conviction of a group of 187 Negro students who convened at the Southern Carolina state house grounds to protest the condition of discriminatory actions against Negroes. The convocation was peaceful, and neither pedestrian nor vehicular traffic within the state house grounds was obstructed. The police ordered the Negroes to disperse; instead they sang and listened to speakers. Thereupon they were arrested and convicted of breach of the peace. A majority of the Court vacated the convictions.[48] Justice Clark dissented.

Thereafter, during the term, the Court passed on a considerable number of similar convictions. A group of five racial discrimination cases came to the Court. Four arose out of sit-in demonstrations by Negro students and involved convictions for violations of criminal trespass laws or similar statutes in South Carolina,[49] in Louisiana,[50] in Alabama,[51] and in North Carolina,[52] respectively. The fifth case involved the conviction of two Negro ministers for inciting, aiding, or abetting criminal trespasses in Alabama.[53] Another

[44] *Ibid.,* 185–86.
[45] Bailey v. Patterson, 369 U.S. 31, 33, 34 (1962).
[46] Turner v. Memphis, 369 U.S. 350 (1962).
[47] Taylor v. Louisiana, 370 U.S. 154 (1962).
[48] Edwards v. South Carolina, 372 U.S. 229 (1963).
[49] Peterson v. Greenville, 373 U.S. 244 (1963).
[50] Lombard v. Louisiana, 373 U.S. 267 (1963).
[51] Gober v. Birmingham, 373 U.S. 374 (1963).
[52] Avent v. North Carolina, 373 U.S. 375 (1963).
[53] Shuttlesworth v. Birmingham, 373 U.S. 262 (1963).

case involved six young Negroes convicted of breach of the peace for peacefully playing basketball in a public park in Savannah, Georgia, customarily used only by white people, and not dispersing when ordered to do so by the police.[54]

The Chief Justice wrote in the South Carolina case:

> It cannot be denied that . . . the City of Greenville, an agency of the State, has provided by its ordinance that the decision as to whether a restaurant facility is to be operated on a desegregated basis is to be reserved to it. When the State has commanded a particular result, it has saved to itself the power to determine that result and thereby "to a significant extent" has "become involved" in it, and, in fact, has removed that decision from the sphere of private choice. It has thus effectively determined that a person owning, managing or controlling an eating place is left with no choice of his own but must segregate his white and Negro patrons.[55]

In the Lombard case the Chief Justice said:

> . . . unlike a number of cases this day decided, no state statute or city ordinance here forbids desegregation of the races in all restaurant facilities. Nevertheless, we conclude that this case is governed by the principles announced in Peterson . . . and that the convictions for this reason must be reversed. . . .[56]
>
> The . . . evidence all tended to indicate that the store officials' actions were coerced by the city. But the evidence of coercion was not fully developed because the trial judge forbade petitioners to ask questions directed to that very issue. . . .
>
> As we interpret the New Orleans city officials' statements, they here determined that the city could not permit Negroes to seek desegregated service in restaurants. Consequently, the city must be treated exactly as if it had an ordinance prohibiting such conduct.[57]

The conviction in the lunch-counter sit-in in the South Carolina case was vacated, with Justice Harlan concurring. The Louisiana convictions, which were vacated, also involved a lunch-counter sit-in, with Justice Douglas concurring and Justice Harlan voting to vacate the judgment and to remand the case for a new trial to determine whether state action denying equal protection was involved, in the absence of which, he would have affirmed the convictions. In the Alabama case, which concerned sit-ins at five different department stores, the convictions were vacated, Justice Harlan maintaining that the case should be remanded for further consideration. In the North Carolina case the judgment was vacated and the case remanded.

[54] Wright v. Georgia, 373 U.S. 284 (1963).
[55] Peterson v. Greenville, 373 U.S. 244, 248 (1963).
[56] Lombard v. Louisiana, 373 U.S. 267, 268 (1963).
[57] *Ibid.*, 273.

The Court also held that, since the Alabama convictions had been set aside, the Shuttlesworth clerical defendants could not be convicted for aiding and abetting what had been adjudicated an innocent act. Justice Harlan dissented, saying "I cannot say that it was constitutionally impermissible for the State to find that Shuttlesworth had urged the volunteers to demonstrate on privately owned premises despite any objections by their owners, and thus to engage in criminal trespass."[58]

Later in the term the Court reversed a contempt conviction of a Negro who refused to move from a section of a Virginia courtroom reserved for whites into a section reserved for Negroes.[59]

During the 1963 term the Court also reversed a number of convictions of Negroes for breach of peace and for trespass. Unanimously it freed demonstrators who had assembled peacefully and were singing without violence to protest segregation at a city hall.[60]

Negroes picketing a privately owned Maryland amusement park to protest segregation who refused to leave the park were convicted of criminal trespass. Six members of the Court joined in reversing the conviction. Justice Clark concurred. Justices Harlan, Black, and White dissented,[61] for the reasons stated by Justice Black in the Bell case.

In the Bell case, Negro sit-in demonstrators refused to leave a Baltimore restaurant, which refused service because of their race and were convicted of criminal trespass.[62] Later Maryland passed a public accommodations law which, had it been in effect previously, would have nullified the convictions. The high court, by a majority, vacated the convictions and remanded the cases to the state court for further consideration. Justice Douglas dissented from the remand and said the indictments should have been dismissed. Justice Goldberg concurred, maintaining that Negroes were entitled to equal treatment, with which the Chief Justice and Justice Douglas agreed. Justice Black, joined by Justices Harlan and White in dissent, contended that the Fourteenth Amendment, standing alone, did not prohibit privately owned restaurants from choosing their own customers, that the Maryland trespass law was constitutional, and that the convictions should be affirmed.

A companion case involved conviction under South Carolina's criminal trespass law for a sit-in in a drugstore, which resulted from a new construction given by the state supreme court to the statute. A majority of the Court held this was retroactive construction violative of the due process clause of the Fourteenth Amendment.[63] Justice Goldberg concurred, as did Justice Douglas.

[58] Peterson v. Greenville, 373 U.S. 244, 260 (1963).
[59] Johnson v. Virginia, 373 U.S. 61 (1963).
[60] Henry v. Rock Hill, 376 U.S. 776 (1964).
[61] Griffin v. Maryland, 378 U.S. 130 (1964).
[62] Bell v. Maryland, 378 U.S. 226 (1964).

334

Justice Black, with the support of Justices Harlan and White, wrote in dissent, saying the defendants deliberately violated a valid antitrespass law.

For the reasons given in the last-mentioned case, the Court reversed convictions of five Negro college students for criminal trespass for sit-in demonstrations at a drugstore lunch counter and reversed breach-of-peace convictions upon the ground that they were not supported by evidence.[64] Eight members of the Court joined in an opinion by Justice Black, reversing the breach-of-peace convictions; the criminal trespass convictions were reversed in a per curiam opinion; Justices Douglas and Goldberg and the Chief Justice concurred, while Justice Black, joined by Justices Harlan and White, dissented from the reversal of the trespass convictions on the grounds stated in their separate opinions in the last-mentioned cases.

The Court also reversed Florida convictions for a restaurant sit-in, Justice Black, writing for seven members, saying that the convictions violated the equal protection clause of the Fourteenth Amendment since the state had promulgated regulations requiring separate facilities for Negroes and whites in a restaurant.[65] Justice Douglas concurred; Justice Harlan acquiesced, saying he was bound by a prior decision.[66]

Convictions for violations of state trespass statutes for participating in sit-ins at lunch counters prior to the adoption of the Civil Rights Act of 1964 which were under review from affirmances by the state courts were reversed on the ground that the Act created federal rights which took priority over conflicting state laws.[67] Justice Clark wrote for three members of the Court. Justices Douglas and Goldberg concurred. Justices Black, Harlan, Stewart, and White dissented.

Justice Douglas, with the support of Justice Goldberg, said he had no difficulty with the case because, as Justice Goldberg had pointed out in his concurring opinion in the Heart of Atlanta Motel case, the fact was that Congress had passed the Civil Rights Act to enforce the Fourteenth Amendment as well as the commerce clause.[68]

Differing with Justice Douglas, Justice Black, dissenting, said he could not find that congressional intent to prevent discrimination also gave "persons who are unlawfully refused service a 'right' to take the law into their own hands by sitting down and occupying the premises for as long as they choose to stay." He maintained also that there was no basis for finding that Congress

---

[63] Bouie v. Columbia, 378 U.S. 347 (1964).
[64] Barr v. Columbia, 378 U.S. 146 (1964).
[65] Robinson v. Florida, 378 U.S. 153 (1964).
[66] Peterson v. Greenville, 373 U.S. 244, 249 (1963).
[67] Hamm v. Rock Hill; Lupper v. Arkansas, 379 U.S. 306 (1964).
[68] *Ibid.*, 317.

"also meant to compel States to abate convictions . . . for lawless conduct occurring before the Act was passed."[69]

Following the Hamm decision affecting prior sit-ins, five members of the Court joined in a per curiam decision, vacating the convictions of Negroes who refused to leave premises outside a restaurant that refused Negroes service; this, too, occurred prior to the enactment of the Civil Rights Act.[70] Justices Black, Harlan, and White dissented, as they had in the Hamm case. Justice Stewart voted to vacate the convictions and remand the case, as he had advocated in the Hamm case.

Another five-to-four decision reversed the conviction of the leader of a civil rights demonstration in which two thousand Negro students protested segregation and previous arrests of Negroes by assembling a few blocks from a courthouse and marching toward and reassembling opposite it where they displayed signs, made speeches, and sung.[71]

Justice Goldberg wrote for a six-man majority, holding the arrest violated the petitioner's rights of free speech and free assembly under the previous Edwards case, and because the statute defining "breach of the peace" was too vague to be enforceable. Justices Black, White, and Clark concurred.

In a companion case a majority reversed a second conviction under a statute prohibiting picketing "near" a courthouse with intent to obstruct justice.[72] Justices Black, White, and Clark dissented. The majority held that the demonstrators were given permission to demonstrate where they did; hence they were within their rights.

Justice Black dissented because he felt that the purpose of the "picketing" of the courthouse was to influence the Court, which the statute expressly forbade.[73]

> The very purpose of a court system is to adjudicate controversies, both criminal and civil, in the calmness and solemnity of the courtroom according to legal procedures. Justice cannot be rightly administered, nor are the lives and safety of prisoners secure, where throngs of people clamor against the processes of justice right outside the courthouse or jailhouse doors. The streets are not now and never have been the proper place to administer justice.[74]

Justice Clark, dissenting, added: "Indeed, one judge was obliged to leave

[69] *Ibid.*, 318, 319.
[70] Blow v. North Carolina, 379 U.S. 684 (1965).
[71] Cox v. Louisiana, 379 U.S. 536 (1965).
[72] Cox v. Louisiana, 379 U.S. 559 (1965).
[73] *Ibid.*, 582.
[74] *Ibid.*, 583.

the building.["75] Justice White, supported by Justice Harlan, dissented because of the "obstruction of public passages.["76]

Later, an unusual dissent was filed from a refusal to grant certiorari when five persons sought to appeal Maryland convictions for disorderly conduct.[77] Chief Justice Warren, supported by Justice Douglas, dissenting from the denial of certiorari, said that two Negroes and three whites went to an amusement park in Baltimore County, where, "ironically, All Nations Day" was being celebrated.[78] They stood peacefully by themselves. A park guard told them they would have to leave. They refused. The police arrested them, whereupon they joined arms, and the three men dropped to the ground and assumed a prostrate position. The police handcuffed one of the women and led both women from the park. The men were carried out. The park was "a place of public resort and amusement."

Four of the five were found guilty of disorderly conduct, which was defined as "the doing or saying, or both, of that which offends, disturbs, incites, or tends to incite, a number of people gathered in the same area."

Previously, the high court had vacated the judgments and remanded the case to the court of appeals for consideration in the light of Griffin v. Maryland and Bell v. Maryland. The court of appeals had reaffirmed the judgments, with one dissent. The Chief Justice said it seemed to him apparent that "petitioners' conduct is protected under the Civil Rights Act . . . and under our decision in Hamm v. City of Rock Hill . . . and Lupper v. Arkansas. . . . the passage of the Act must be deemed to have abated the convictions.["79]

The federal district court dismissed a suit to enjoin enforcement of a Mississippi antipicketing statute. The high court vacated the judgment and remanded the case for action in accordance with a per curiam opinion.[80] The issue involved was the state's power to make it an offense for people to obstruct public streets and highways and to block ingress and egress to and from its public buildings and properties; also whether, having passed such a law, the United States courts had power to enjoin prosecutions thereunder on the ground of unconstitutionality, without first determining the constitutionality of the statute.

Justice Black, with the support of Justices Harlan and Stewart, dissented:

> Cryptic, uninformative *per curiam* order is no way, I think, for this Court to decide a case involving what this one does. . . .
> Every person who has the slightest information about what is going on in

[75] *Ibid.*, 586.
[76] *Ibid.*, 591.
[77] Drews v. Maryland, 381 U.S. 421 (1965).
[78] *Ibid.*, 421.
[79] *Ibid.*, 423–24.
[80] Cameron v. Johnson, 381 U.S. 741 (1965).

this country can understand the importance of these issues.... There are many earnest, honest, good people in this Nation who are entitled to know exactly how far they have a constitutional right to go in using the public streets to advocate causes they consider just. State officials are also entitled to the same information. The Court has already waited entirely too long, in my judgment, to perform its duty of clarifying these constitutional issues.[81]

Justice White also dissented.

A Negro who was standing on a street corner and refused to move on when directed to do so by a policeman was charged with and convicted of a breach of the peace. The Court reversed the conviction, holding that the ordinance was so broad in its terms as to violate the due process clause of the Fourteenth Amendment.[82] Justices Douglas and Fortas, concurring, found that there was no factual basis for the charge.

Five Negroes, who in order to protest segregation, refused to leave a library operated on a segregated basis, were indicted and convicted of a breach of the peace under a Louisiana statute. Justice Fortas, writing for himself, the Chief Justice, and Justice Douglas, held there was no factual basis for such a charge and that the petitioners were within their rights in peacefully protesting segregation. Justice Brennan concurred, holding that the statute was so broad as to violate due process, and Justice White concurred upon the ground that the petitioners had not remained overlong in the library.[83]

The Court held, in an opinion by Justice Stewart, that Negroes charged with violating a Georgia antitrespass statute for a refusal to leave restaurant facilities of public accommodation, when ordered to do so solely for racial reasons, were entitled to remove their cases to the federal court, since the Hamm case made it clear that the Civil Rights Act of 1964 protects them not only from conviction but also from prosecution in the state courts.[84]

However, simultaneously, again in an opinion by Justice Stewart, a majority held that while the Civil Rights Act protected persons, as in the preceding case, against prosecutions for trespass, for any act under color of authority derived from any federal law providing for civil rights, it was restricted to federal officers or agents and those authorized to act with or for them.[85]

Justice Stewart said:

... no federal law confers an absolute right on private citizens—on civil rights advocates, on Negroes, or on anybody else—to obstruct a public street, to contribute to the delinquency of a minor, to drive an automobile without a license,

---

81 *Ibid.*, 742–43.
82 Shuttlesworth v. Birmingham, 382 U.S. 87 (1965).
83 Brown v. Louisiana, 383 U.S. 131 (1966).
84 Georgia v. Rachel, 384 U.S. 780 (1966).
85 Greenwood v. Peacock, 384 U.S. 808 (1966).

or to bite a policeman. . . . no federal law confers immunity from state prosecution on such charges. . . .[86]

The civil rights removal statute does not require and does not permit the judges of the federal courts to put their brethren of the state judiciary on trial.[87]

Justice Douglas, dissenting, with the support of the Chief Justice and Justices Brennan and Fortas, said that the petitioners were members of various civil rights groups who, while peacefully picketing, were arrested on various charges for the sole purpose of harassing them and of punishing them for exercising their constitutional rights to protest the conditions of racial discrimination and segregation. He said that "the federal regime was designed from the beginning to afford some protection against local passions and prejudices by the important pretrial federal remedy of removal and that the civil rights legislation with which we deal supports the mandates of the Court of Appeals,"[88] which upheld removal.

The issue between the majority and the minority was one of statutory interpretation. Justice Douglas characterized that of the majority as "a narrow, cramped meaning."[89]

Five judges joined in an opinion written by Justice Black, which affirmed a conviction for trespass of thirty-two students who demonstrated on the premises of a jail protesting the arrest of schoolmates and perhaps segregation.[90] Justice Black held that the Florida trespass statute was not unconstitutionally vague as were the statutes in Edwards v. South Carolina and Cox v. Louisiana. The majority opinion also distinguished Hamm v. City of Rock Hill, where the charge had abated by reason of the subsequent passage of the civil rights statute.

He pointed out that in the Edwards case the charge was one of violating a vague breach of the peace statute by demonstrating on the state capitol grounds, which were open to the public, while here the trespass was upon premises of a jail, built for security.

Justice Douglas, joined by Justices Brennan and Fortas and the Chief Justice, wrote in dissent, maintaining that the students had assembled to petition for redress of grievances and their conviction violated their rights to do so under the First Amendment.

By a vote of seven to two, a majority, including Justice Marshall, held constitutional a 1964 Mississippi statute which forbade unreasonable interference "with free ingress or egress" to and from courthouses, jails, and other

[86] *Ibid.*, 826–27.
[87] *Ibid.*, 828.
[88] *Ibid.*, 836.
[89] *Ibid.*, 854.
[90] Adderley v. Florida, 385 U.S. 39 (1966).

public buildings. Justice Fortas, joined by Justice Douglas, found the proof of obstruction so deficient that he felt the lower court should have barred the prosecutions of some fifty Negro demonstrators who had picketed a courthouse to protest racial discrimination in voting.[91]

[91] Cameron v. Johnson, 390 U.S. 611 (1968).

CHAPTER XVIII

The Negro Racial Issue—2

Efforts to enforce the privileges and sanctions of the Civil Rights Act met with surreptitious retaliation by die-hard zealots who committed arson and murder in Ku Klux Klan fashion in order to terrorize southern Negroes. Efforts to bring these law violators to justice were almost invariably rendered futile by sympathetic local law enforcement officers or the unbridled prejudices of jurors selected in state courts to try the offenders, on the rare occasions they were apprehended, which resulted in rubber-stamp acquittals. The fervid state of anti-Negro public opinion could also be gauged by the not infrequent re-election of racist public officers, including some under civil rights indictment, as well as by the attitudes of many of the local judges.

Thus we find a district judge dismissing indictments of six persons charged with conspiring to deprive Negro citizens of the free exercise of their rights of accommodation in motion picture theaters, restaurants, and other places of public accommodation, under provisions of the Civil Rights Act of 1964. The Court held the indictment defective, *inter alia,* for its failure to ascribe race as the motive of the discrimination.

Justice Stewart, writing for himself and Justice White, stressed that in this, as in the subsequent Price case, the issue was one of statutory construction and not one of constitutional power.[1] He distinguished the two cases in that the Price case involved rights under the due process clause of the Fourteenth Amendment, while the instant case involved the equal protection clause.[2] He reversed the judgment below, holding that if a specific intent to interfere with a federal right is proved, "then, whether or not motivated by racial discrimination, the conspiracy becomes a proper object of the federal law."[3]

Justice Clark, joined by Justices Black and Fortas, concurred; Justice Harlan concurred in part and dissented in part. The key to his dissent appears in the following words: "If I have succeeded in showing anything in this

[1] United States v. Guest, 383 U.S. 745 (1966).
[2] *Ibid.*, 753.
[3] *Ibid.*, 760.

341

constitutional exercise, it is that until today there was no federal right to be free from private interference with interstate transit, and very little reason for creating one."[4] Justice Brennan, joined by the Chief Justice and Justice Douglas, also dissented in part and concurred in part. He disagreed with the Court's construction of one of the sections of the law involved.

In a subsequent case three Mississippi law enforcement officials and fifteen others were indicted for conspiracy to deprive three men of their rights under the Fourteenth Amendment. The source of the statute involved was the ancient Civil Rights Act of 1866 designed to protect Negroes in their newly won rights. A divided court had enabled the statute to survive a claim of unconstitutionality at the hands of a Georgia sheriff who had wantonly killed a Negro and whom the government sought to prosecute under the statute in a federal court. Three dissenting judges had said that the statute "was never designed for the use to which it has now been fashioned. The Government admits that it is appropriate to leave the punishment of such crimes as this to local authorities."[5] Later the Court upheld a conviction under the Act of a special police officer, acting in his official capacity, who used force and violence to extract a confession.[6]

The indictments under consideration arose out of the shocking murder of three civil rights workers who were detained and jailed by Price, a deputy sheriff, and then released in the dark of the night. It was alleged that the deputy sheriff then proceeded to intercept the automobile in which the three were riding, to remove them, place them in an official automobile of the sheriff's office, and then transport them to an unpaved road where they were shot and killed and their bodies hidden. The defendants were indicted under provisions of the federal Criminal Code. The disappearance of the three men and the search for their bodies became matters of national concern, as did the later arrest and indictment of those alleged to have committed this unspeakable crime.

Two indictments were returned, one charging conspiracy and the other charging a deprivation of rights protected by the Constitution. The lower court dismissed the second indictment against the private defendants, holding that, since they were not officers, they were not acting, as the statute required, "under color of law."[7] In an opinion by Justice Fortas, with the concurrence of Justice Black, the Court reversed, holding that the statute was satisfied as to the private parties since they acted in concert with officials and thus were acting under "color of law" and that, as to dismissal of all defendants, it based its reversal on the fact that the statute encompassed violations of the Fourteenth

[4] *Ibid.*, 773.
[5] Screws v. United States, 325 U.S. 91, 161 (1945).
[6] Williams v. United States, 341 U.S. 97 (1951).
[7] Price v. United States, 384 U.S. 933 (1966).

Amendment, and again, since state officials participated, the action was state action.

Subsequently a group of defendants were brought to trial in the state court; the result was a landmark conviction of seven, two of whom, one the reputed leader of the Ku Klux Klan, received maximum sentences of ten years.[8]

A 1968 per curiam decision (Justice Marshall not participating) held that, in a class action brought under the public accommodations part of the Civil Rights Act of 1964 to enjoin racial discrimination at defendants' drive-in restaurants and sandwich shop, the district court should assess reasonable counsel fees as part of the costs to be required to be paid by the defendants.[9]

Over the years the Court had sought to void convictions of Negroes when Negroes had been deliberately excluded from jury service. However, the conviction of a Negro for rape was affirmed when he failed to prove that there had been racial discrimination in the selection of jurors or in the exercise of peremptory challenges.[10] Justice White wrote for members of the Court; Justices Harlan and Black concurred; Justices Goldberg and Douglas and the Chief Justice dissented.

Justice White said:

Venires drawn from the jury box . . . contained a smaller proportion of the Negro community than of the white community. But a defendant in a criminal case is not constitutionally entitled to demand a proportionate number of his race on the jury. . . . Neither the jury roll nor the venire need be a perfect mirror of the community or accurately reflect the proportionate strength of every identifiable group. . . .[11]

We cannot say that purposeful discrimination based on race alone is satisfactorily proved by showing that an identifiable group in a community is underrepresented by as much as 10% . . . an imperfect system is not equivalent to purposeful discrimination based on race. . . .[12]

The essential nature of the peremptory challenge is that it is one exercised without a reason stated, without inquiry and without being subject to the court's control. . . . the peremptory [challenge] permits rejection for a real or imagined partiality. . . .[13]

. . . we cannot hold that the striking of Negroes in a particular case is a denial of equal protection of the laws. In the quest for an impartial and qualified jury, Negro and white, Protestant and Catholic, are alike subject to being chal-

[8] New York Times, December 30, 1967.
[9] Newman v. Piggie Park Enterprises, 390 U.S. 400 (1968).
[10] Swain v. Alabama, 380 U.S. 202 (1965).
[11] Ibid., 208.
[12] Ibid., 208–209.
[13] Ibid., 220.

lenged without cause. To subject the prosecutor's challenge in any particular case to the demands and traditional standards of the Equal Protection Clause would entail a radical change in the nature and operation of the challenge. The challenge, *pro tanto,* would no longer be peremptory....

... we cannot hold that the Constitution requires an examination of the prosecutor's reasons for the exercise of his challenges in any given case. The presumption in any particular case must be that the prosecutor is using the State's challenges to obtain a fair and impartial jury.... The presumption is not overcome ... by allegations that in the case at hand all Negroes were removed from the jury or that they were removed because they were Negroes....[14]

... when the prosecutor in a county, in case after case, whatever the circumstances, whatever the crime and whoever the defendant or the victim may be, is responsible for the removal of Negroes who have been selected as qualified jurors by the jury commissioners and who have survived challenges for cause, with the result that no Negroes ever serve on petit juries, the Fourteenth Amendment claim takes on added significance.... In these circumstances, giving even the widest leeway to the operation of irrational but trial-related suspicions and antagonisms, it would appear that the purposes of the peremptory challenge are being perverted. If the State has not seen fit to leave a single Negro on any jury in a criminal case, the presumption protecting the prosecutor may well be overcome.[15]

The majority felt the record was not sufficient to show the discrimination necessary for reversal; the minority, with Justice Goldberg writing, maintained the contrary.

In a later case[16] the Court held that, while the burden of proof of discrimination in the selection of jurors was upon the defendant,[17] once the defendant had made out a prima facie case, the burden shifted to the prosecution.

Hence the Court reversed a conviction for failure of the prosecution to prove nondiscrimination. Previously the Court had remanded the case to the lower court for a hearing on the question of discrimination.[18]

Justice Clark, writing for the Court, said:

For over fourscore years it has been federal statutory law, 18 Stat. 336 (1875), 18 U.S.C. Sec. 243, and the law of this Court as applied to the States through the Equal Protection Clause of the Fourteenth Amendment, that a conviction

[14] *Ibid.,* 221–22.

[15] *Ibid.,* 223–24.

[16] Whitus v. Georgia, 385 U.S. 545 (1967); *see also* Sims v. Georgia, 389 U.S. 404 (1967); Coleman v. Alabama, 389 U.S. 22 (1967); Jones v. Georgia, 389 U.S. 24 (1967).

[17] Whitus v. Georgia, 385 U.S. 545, 550 (1967), citing Tarrance v. Florida, 188 U.S. 519 (1903).

[18] Whitus v. Balkcom, 370 U.S. 728 (1962).

cannot stand if it is based on an indictment of a grand jury or the verdict of a petit jury from which Negroes were excluded by reason of their race.[19]

The Court also struck down miscegenation laws. Writing for six members of the Court, Justice White held that a Florida criminal statute prohibiting an unmarried interracial couple from habitually living in and occupying the same room in the nighttime was invalid under the equal protection clause of the Fourteenth Amendment. He said that "no couple other than a Negro and a white person can be convicted" under the statute.[20] Justices Harlan, Stewart, and Douglas concurred.

Justice Stewart, joined by Justice Douglas, said:

> ...the Court implies that a criminal law of the kind here involved might be constitutionally valid if a State could show "some overriding statutory purpose." This is an implication in which I cannot join, because I cannot conceive of a valid legislative purpose under our Constitution for a state law which makes the color of a person's skin the test of whether his conduct is a criminal offense. ...I think it is simply not possible for a state law to be valid under our Constitution which makes the criminality of an act depend upon the race of the actor.[21]

Then, during the 1966 term, Chief Justice Warren wrote for eight members of the Court, reversing the conviction of husband and wife who had violated the Virginia antimiscegenation statutes, which he held violated the equal protection and due process clauses of the Fourteenth Amendment.

Loving, a white man, and his wife, a Negro, both Virginia residents, had married in the District of Columbia and had returned to live in Virginia. Charged with violation of the statutes, they pleaded guilty and were sentenced to one year in jail. The trial judge suspended the sentence for a period of twenty-five years on the condition that they leave the state and not return to Virginia together for twenty-five years, saying that "Almighty God created the races...and he placed them on separate continents.... The fact that he separated the races shows that he did not intend for the races to mix."[22]

The Lovings left the state but instituted an action to declare the statutes unconstitutional. The Virginia court of appeals denied the plea; the high court reversed—demonstrating the truth of the old saw that "love will find

---

[19] Whitus v. Georgia, 385 U.S. 545, 549–50 (1967), citing Strauder v. West Virginia, 10 Otto (100 U.S.) 303 (1880); Pierre v. Louisiana, 306 U.S. 354 (1939); Avery v. Georgia, 345 U.S. 559 (1953); Williams v. Georgia, 349 U.S. 375 (1955); Cassell v. Texas, 339 U.S. 282 (1950).

[20] McLaughlin v. Florida, 379 U.S. 184, 188 (1964).

[21] *Ibid.,* 198.

[22] Loving v. Virginia, 388 U.S. 1, 3 (1967).

a way." Justice Stewart concurred, calling attention to the last sentence in his opinion in the case last mentioned above.[23]

The Chief Justice said, *inter alia:*

> Marriage is one of the "basic civil rights of man, fundamental to our very existence and survival.... To deny this fundamental freedom on so unsupportable a basis as the racial classifications so directly subversive to the principle of equality at the heart of the Fourteenth Amendment, is surely to deprive all the State's citizens of liberty without due process of law."[24]

The effort of Congress to end discrimination against Negro voting, which had been the subject of previous decisions by the Court, through the passage of the Civil Rights Act of 1957, providing for registration of voters regardless of race, color, or previous condition of servitude, was held valid by the Court, which sustained suits brought by the Attorney General to enforce it.[25]

Later in the term seven members of the Court found valid rules of procedure adopted by the Federal Commission on Civil Rights (appointed pursuant to the Civil Rights Act), over the dissents of Justices Black and Douglas, who held the rules violated due process.[26]

The first decision of the following term struck down a gerrymandering Alabama statute as violating the Fifteenth Amendment in denying Negroes their votes. Justice Whittaker, concurring, thought it was the equal protection clause of the Fourteenth Amendment that was being violated.[27] Later a unanimous Court vitiated a statute requiring the designation of the race of a candidate for office, upon the ground that it operated as a discrimination-inducing expression of racial prejudice at the polls, violating the equal protection clause of the Fourteenth Amendment.[28]

Again a unanimous Court upheld a complaint filed by the government against the state of Mississippi, alleging that the state, its election commissioners, and its voting registrars were destroying the right of Mississippi Negroes to vote and reversed an adverse judgment below. Justice Harlan concurred, saying he felt that "constitutional conclusions reached in this opinion can properly be based only on the provisions of the Fifteenth Amendment."[29]

Simultaneously the Court held, with like concurrence by Justice Harlan, that a Louisiana statute requiring voting registration tests of applicants' inter-

---

23 *Ibid.,* 13.
24 *Ibid.,* 12, citing Skinner v. Oklahoma, 316 U.S. 535 (1942); Maynard v. Hill, 125 U.S. 190 (1888).
25 United States v. Raines, 362 U.S. 17 (1960).
26 Hannah v. Larche; Hannah v. Lawson, 363 U.S. 420 (1960).
27 Gobillion v. Lightfoot, 364 U.S. 339 (1960).
28 Anderson v. Martin, 375 U.S. 399 (1964).
29 United States v. Mississippi, 380 U.S. 128, 144 (1965).

preting federal and state constitutions to the satisfaction of voting registrars were unconstitutional under the Fourteenth and Fifteenth amendments.[30]

Later South Carolina sought an adjudication that certain provisions of the Voting Rights Act of 1965 were unconstitutional and asked for an injunction against their enforcement.[31] The Chief Justice, writing for eight members of the Court, ordered dismissal of the complaint. He said:

> The Voting Rights Act was designed by Congress to banish the blight of racial discrimination in voting, which has infected the electoral process in parts of our country for nearly a century....[32]
>
> The course of . . . Fifteenth Amendment litigation in this Court demonstrates the variety and persistence of . . . institutions designed to deprive Negroes of the right to vote....[33]
>
> Discriminatory administration of voting qualifications has been found in all eight Alabama cases, in all nine Louisiana cases, and in all nine Mississippi cases which have gone to final judgment. Moreover, in almost all of these cases, the courts have held that the discrimination was pursuant to a widespread "pattern or practice."...[34]
>
> Despite the earnest efforts of the Justice Department and of many federal judges,... new laws have done little to cure the problem of voting discrimination....[35]
>
> The heart of the Act is a complex scheme of stringent remedies aimed at areas where voting discrimination has been most flagrant....[36]
>
> As against the reserved powers of the States, Congress may use any rational means to effectuate the constitutional prohibition of racial discrimination in voting....[37]
>
> Section 1 of the Fifteenth Amendment declares that "the right of citizens of the United States to vote shall not be denied or abridged by the United States or by any State on account of race, color, or previous condition of servitude." This declaration has always been treated as self-executing....the Fifteenth Amendment supersedes contrary exertions of state power....[38]
>
> After enduring nearly a century of widespread resistance to the Fifteenth Amendment, Congress has marshalled an array of potent weapons against the evil....Hopefully, millions of non-white Americans will now be able to participate for the first time on an equal basis in the government under which they live.[39]

[30] Louisiana v. United States, 380 U.S. 145 (1965).
[31] South Carolina v. Katzenbach, 383 U.S. 301 (1966).
[32] *Ibid.*, 308.
[33] *Ibid.*, 311.
[34] *Ibid.*, 312.
[35] *Ibid.*, 313.
[36] *Ibid.*, 315.
[37] *Ibid.*, 324.
[38] *Ibid.*, 325.
[39] *Ibid.*, 337.

347

Justice Black, while concurring in large part, dissented from the "holding that every part of Sec. 5 is constitutional," in particular the provision that a state, to amend its constitution or laws relating to voting, must first "persuade the Attorney General . . . or the District Court of the District of Columbia that the new proposed laws do not have the purpose and will not have the effect of denying the right to vote" on account of race or color.[40] He maintained that this violated the provision for a republican form of government contained in the Constitution.[41]

Another medium of Negro racial discrimination involved the disenfranchisement of the Negro through the requirement that a poll tax be paid as a condition of voting. In avoidance, the states adopted the Twenty-fourth Amendment to the Constitution, abolishing the poll tax with respect to federal elections.

With the concurrence of Justice Harlan, the Court held the Amendment constitutional and struck down a Virginia statute that attempted to require a certificate of residence six months before a federal election from those who did not pay a poll tax as repugnant to the Amendment.[42]

However, Virginia attempted to retain the poll tax respecting state elections, and in a suit to declare it unconstitutional, over the dissent of Justices Black, Harlan, and Stewart, six members of the Court joined in an opinion by Justice Douglas holding it unconstitutional.[43] Justice Douglas, writing for the Court, said:

> While the right to vote in federal elections is conferred by Art. 1, Sec. 2, of the Constitution . . . the right to vote in state elections is nowhere expressly mentioned. It is argued that it may not constitutionally be conditional upon the payment of a tax or fee. . . . it is enough to say that once the franchise is granted to the electorate, lines may not be drawn which are inconsistent with the Equal Protection Clause of the Fourteenth Amendment. . . .[44]
>
> We conclude that a State violates the Equal Protection Clause whenever it makes the affluence of the voter or payment of any fee an electoral standard. Voter qualifications have no relation to wealth nor to paying or not paying this or any other tax.[45]
>
> The principle that denies the State the right to dilute a citizen's vote on account of his economic status or other such factors by analogy bars a system which excludes those unable to pay a fee to vote or who fail to pay. . . .
>
> Wealth, like race, creed, or color is not germane to one's ability to participate intelligently in the electoral process. Lines drawn on the basis of wealth or

[40] Ibid., 356.
[41] Ibid., 359.
[42] Harman v. Forssenius, 380 U.S. 528 (1965).
[43] Harper v. Virginia Board of Elections; Butts v. Harrison, 383 U.S. 663 (1966).
[44] Ibid., 665.
[45] Ibid., 666.

property, like those of race...are traditionally disfavored...To introduce wealth or payment of a fee as a measure of a voter's qualifications is to introduce a capricious or irrelevant factor....

Notions of what constitutes equal treatment for purposes of the Equal Protection Clause *do* change.[46]

Justice Black, ordinarily in agreement with Justice Douglas, maintained, in dissent, that the Court had previously approved a Georgia poll tax and that there had been no finding that Virginia's purpose in retaining it was as a device or mechanism to deny Negroes voting rights. He maintained that voting laws draw distinctions without violating the equal protection clause when he said: "Although I join the Court in disliking the policy of the poll tax, this is not in my judgment a justifiable reason for holding this poll tax law unconstitutional...."[47]

He added comments of more general application:

The Court's justification for consulting its own notions rather than following the original meaning of the Constitution, as I would, apparently is based on the belief of the majority of the Court that for this Court to be bound by the original meaning of the Constitution is an intolerable and debilitating evil; that our Constitution should not be "shackled to the political theory of a particular era," and that to save the country from the original Constitution the Court must have constant power to renew it and keep it abreast with this Court's more enlightened theories of what is best for our society....[48]

It seems to me that this is an attack not only on the great value of our Constitution itself but also on the concept of a written constitution which is to survive through the years as originally written unless changed through the amendment process which the Framers wisely provided. Moreover, when a "political theory" embodied in our Constitution becomes outdated, it seems to me that a majority of the nine members of this Court are not only without constitutional power but are far less qualified to choose a new constitutional political theory than the people of this country proceeding in the manner provided by Article V....[49]

Moreover, the people, in Sec. 5 of the Fourteenth Amendment, designated the governmental tribunal they wanted to provide additional rules to enforce the guarantees of that Amendment. The branch of Government they chose was not the Judicial Branch but the Legislative.[50]

Justice Harlan, joined by Justice Stewart, dissenting, said:

[46] *Ibid.*, 668–69.
[47] *Ibid.*, 674–75.
[48] *Ibid.*, 677.
[49] *Ibid.*, 678.
[50] *Ibid.*, 678–79.

The final demise of state poll taxes, already totally proscribed by the Twenty-fourth Amendment with respect to federal elections and abolished by the States themselves in all but four States with respect to state elections, is perhaps in itself not of great moment. But the fact that the *coup de grace* has been administered by this Court instead of being left to the affected States or to the federal political process should be a matter of continuing concern to all interested in maintaining the proper role of this tribunal under our scheme of government.[51]

My disagreement with the present decision is that in holding the Virginia poll tax violative of the Equal Protection Clause the Court has departed from long-established standards governing the application of that clause.

The Equal Protection Clause prevents States from arbitrarily treating people differently under their laws. Whether any such differing treatment is to be deemed arbitrary depends on whether or not it reflects an appropriate differentiating classification among those affected.... The test ... is whether such a classification can be deemed to be founded on some rational and otherwise constitutionally permissible state policy.... This standard reduces to a minimum the likelihood that the federal judiciary will judge state policies in terms of the individual notions and predilections of its own members....[52]

Reynolds v. Sims, among its other breaks with the past, also marked a departure from these traditional and wise principles. Unless its "one man, one vote" thesis of state legislative apportionment is to be attributed to the unsupportable proposition that "Equal Protection" simply means indiscriminate equality, it seems inescapable that what Reynolds really reflected was but this Court's own views of how modern American representative government should be run....[53]

Property qualifications and poll taxes have been a traditional part of our political structure....[54]

Property and poll-tax qualifications, very simply, are not in accord with current egalitarian notions of how a modern democracy should be organized. It is of course entirely fitting that legislatures should modify the law to reflect such changes in popular attitudes. However, it is all wrong, in my view, for the Court to adopt the political doctrines popularly accepted at a particular moment of our history and to declare all others to be irrational and invidious, barring them from the range of choice by reasonably minded people acting through the political process. It was not too long ago that Mr. Justice Holmes felt impelled to remind the Court that the Due Process Clause of the Fourteenth Amendment does not enact the *laissez-faire* theory of society.... The times have changed, and perhaps it is appropriate to observe that neither does the Equal Protection Clause of that Amendment rigidly impose upon Americans an ideology of unrestrained egalitarianism.[55]

51 *Ibid.*, 680–81.
52 *Ibid.*, 681–82.
53 *Ibid.*, 682.
54 *Ibid.*, 684.

With the concurrence of Justices Douglas, Brennan, and Harlan, the Court held flagrantly violative of the First Amendment an Alabama statute making it a crime for a newspaper editor to publish an editorial on election day urging people to vote in a particular way, because it tended to curb free discussion of governmental affairs.[56]

Alabama contended that since the defendant had not yet been convicted in the state court and might be freed by a jury, the appeal to the high court was premature; the Court maintained, however, that since the editor admitted he had no defense, and since the state court had held the statute valid, and since the effect of the prosecution had been to stifle newspaper comment on election day, it would take jurisdiction.

Then, during the 1966 term, when the judge of a Georgia court initiated a grand jury investigation of Negro sale of votes in the midst of a political campaign, the sheriff of the county issued public statements denouncing the judge's action as attempted political intimidation and race agitation. The sheriff was convicted of contempt, but five members of the Court reversed the finding, holding that he had exercised his rights of free speech. Justices Clark and Harlan dissented; Justices Frankfurter and White did not participate.[57]

The question of open housing has long been a troublesome one. As far back as 1917, the Court struck down a local ordinance that prohibited the purchase of land by Negroes in certain areas.[58]

A decision during the 1947 term involved the invalidation of judicial action for the enforcement of racial restrictions affecting the ownership or occupancy of real property. Writing for six members of the Court, with Justices Reed, Jackson, and Rutledge not participating, Chief Justice Vinson held that judicial action constituted state action that required the Court to invoke the equal protection clause of the Fourteenth Amendment.[59] The Court distinguished prior cases.[60]

In a later case,[61] following the Shelley case (above), six members of the Court held that a restrictive covenant could not be enforced at law by a suit for damages against one who broke the covenant. Chief Justice Vinson dissented, saying that the situation was to be distinguished from the Shelley case because no non-Caucasian had been or could be injured if the covenant was enforced by the state court. Justices Reed and Jackson did not participate.

---

[55] *Ibid.,* 686.

[56] Mills v. Alabama, 384 U.S. 214 (1966).

[57] Wood v. Georgia, 370 U.S. 375 (1962).

[58] Buchanan v. Warley, 245 U.S. 60 (1917).

[59] Shelley v. Kraemer; McGhee v. Sipes, 334 U.S. 1 (1948).

[60] Corrigan v. Buckley, 271 U.S. 323 (1926); Hansberry v. Lee, 311 U.S. 32 (1940).

[61] Barrows v. Jackson, 346 U.S. 249 (1953).

Later the problem was presented to the Court in its broadest aspects when, after the California legislature had enacted a number of statutes restricting the right of private landowners to discriminate on the basis of such factors as race in the sale or rental of property, in 1964 the California electorate adopted a constitutional amendment denying the state, or any subdivision or agency, the right to restrict the discretion of any person in the sale, leasing, or rental of property. Justice White, writing for four members of the Court, found the amendment violative of the Fourteenth Amendment. Justice Douglas concurred. Justice Harlan, supported by Justices Clark, Black, and Stewart, wrote in dissent.[62]

While admitting that he could quote no apposite authority, Justice White concluded that the amendment made "the right to discriminate one of the basic policies of the State" and would "significantly encourage and involve the State in private discriminations," as found by the California court, which had voided the amendment.[63]

Justice Douglas, concurring, held that "urban housing, like restaurants, inns, and carriers . . . or like telephone companies, drugstores, or hospitals, is affected with a public interest."[64]

Justice Harlan wrote in dissent:

> I consider that this decision, which cuts deeply into state political processes, is supported neither by anything "found" by the Supreme Court of California nor by any of our past cases. . . . In my view today's holding, salutary as its result may seem at first blush, may in the long run actually serve to handicap progress in the extremely difficult field of racial concerns. . . .
>
> The Equal Protection Clause . . . does not undertake to control purely personal prejudices and predilections, and individuals acting on their own are left free to discriminate on racial grounds if they are so minded. . . . By the same token, the Fourteenth Amendment does not require of States the passage of laws preventing such private discrimination, although it does not of course disable them from enacting such legislation if they wish.
>
> In the case at hand California . . . has decided to remain "neutral" in the realm of private discrimination affecting the sale or rental of private residential property. . . . This runs no more afoul of the Fourteenth Amendment than would have California's failure to pass any such antidiscrimination statutes in the first instance.[65]

It is to be noted that Congress, moved by the pressure of public opinion following the deplorable assassination of the Reverend Martin Luther King,

[62] Reitman v. Mulkey, 387 U.S. 369 (1967).
[63] *Ibid.*, 376.
[64] *Ibid.*, 385–86.
[65] *Ibid.*, 387.

the leader of the movement for improvement of the lot of the Negro by the use of nonviolent protest and action, passed, in April, 1968, a strengthened Civil Rights Act which, *inter alia,* bars racial discrimination in the sale or rental of a considerable percentage of housing, a subject that has been controversial throughout the country.

Finally, at the end of the 1967 term, over the dissent of Justices Harlan and White, a seven-man majority resurrected the Civil Rights Act of 1866 and the Thirteenth Amendment, to hold that there may not be discrimination in the sale or rental of property.[66] The decision respecting the Amendment was in direct opposition to the holding of the Court in the Civil Rights Cases which restricted the Thirteenth Amendment by saying it had only "to do with slavery and its incidents," over the dissent of the elder Justice Harlan.[67] The dissenters would have had the Court avoid a decision since Congress had dealt with the subject only recently and, as a compromise, had excepted small units from the operation of the statute.

Concurrently the Court rejected a holding of the Virginia courts that a private community swimming club could reject a Negro for membership on racial grounds and remanded the case for further consideration in the light of its simultaneous holding.[68]

Attacks on Negro organizations were not unusual. Alabama sought to prevent the NAACP from continuing its activities in the state, claiming it had not complied with statutory requirements for foreign corporations by not producing its membership lists. Adjudged in contempt, it appealed, and a unanimous Court held it immune from such production under its members' right of free association.[69] Thereupon the case was remanded to the state court for further proceedings in accordance with the high court's opinion.

Thereafter the Alabama Supreme Court reaffirmed the contempt conviction, saying that the high court had been mistaken in the assumptions upon which it had based its decision. Thereupon the latter held that "the Alabama Supreme Court is foreclosed from re-examining the grounds of our disposition. 'Whatever was before the Court, and is disposed of, is considered as finally settled.' "

The Court refused to issue a mandamus, as requested by the petitioner, saying it assumed that the state supreme court, "thus advised, will not fail to proceed promptly with the disposition of the matters left open under our mandate."[70] Justice Stewart did not participate.

With the concurrence of Justices Black and Douglas, the Court struck down

---

[66] Jones v. Mayer Co., 392 U.S. 409 (1968).
[67] Civil Rights Cases, 109 U.S. 3 (1883).
[68] Sullivan v. Little Hunting Park, Inc., 392 U.S. 657 (1968).
[69] NAACP v. Alabama *ex rel.* Patterson, 357 U.S. 449 (1958).
[70] NAACP v. Alabama *ex rel.* Patterson and Livingston, 360 U.S. 240, 244 (1959).

Arkansas ordinances requiring the furnishing of membership lists of the NAACP as violative of freedom of association protected by the due process clause of the Fourteenth Amendment.[71]

Thereafter the NAACP sued to enjoin enforcement of a Virginia statute that forbid the improper solicitation of any legal or professional business, under which, it was contended by Virginia authorities, the practices of the association in furnishing lawyers and legal advice to Negroes in civil rights cases was proscribed. The NAACP contended the statute violated its rights under the Fourteenth Amendment, making applicable the First Amendment. The Court held "that the activities of the NAACP, its affiliates and legal staff . . . are modes of expression and association" so protected.[72] Justice Douglas concurred; Justice White concurred in part and dissented in part, holding that in his opinion "neither the practice of law by such an organization nor its management of the litigation of its members or others is constitutionally protected. Both practices are well within the regulatory power of the State."[73]

Justice Harlan, dissenting, joined by Justices Clark and Stewart, said:

> . . . I believe that the striking down of this Virginia statute cannot be squared with accepted constitutional doctrine in the domain of state regulatory power of the legal profession. . . .[74]
>
> Freedom of expression embraces more than the right of an individual to speak his mind. It includes also his right to advocate and his right to join with his fellows in an effort to make that advocacy effective. . . .[75]
>
> . . . it must include the right to join together for purposes of obtaining judicial redress. . . . Litigation is often the desirable and orderly way of resolving disputes of broad public significance, and of obtaining vindication of fundamental rights. This is particularly so in the sensitive area of racial relationships.
>
> But to declare that litigation is a form of conduct that may be associated with political expression does not resolve this case. . . . Neither the First Amendment nor the Fourteenth constitutes an absolute bar to government regulation in the fields of free expression and association. . . . The problem in each such case is to weigh the legitimate interest of the State against the effect of the regulation on individual rights. . . .[76]
>
> . . . as we move away from speech alone and into the sphere of conduct . . . the area of legitimate governmental interest expands. . . .
>
> . . . litigation, whether or not associated with the attempt to vindicate constitutional rights, is *conduct*; it is speech *plus*. . . . the State may impose reason-

[71] Bates v. Little Rock, 361 U.S. 516 (1960).
[72] NAACP v. Button, 371 U.S. 415 (1963).
[73] *Ibid.*, 447.
[74] *Ibid.*, 448.
[75] *Ibid.*, 452.
[76] *Ibid.*, 453.

able regulations limiting the permissible form of litigation and the manner of legal representation within its borders. . . .[77]

The regulation before us has its origins in the long-standing common-law prohibitions of champerty, barratry, and maintenance, the closely related prohibitions in the Canons of Ethics against solicitation and intervention by a lay intermediary, and statutory provisions forbidding the unauthorized practice of law. . . .[78]

. . . a State's felt need for regulation of professional conduct may reasonably extend beyond mere "ambulance chasing.". . .[79]

Petitioner is merely one of a variety of organizations that may come within the scope of the long-standing prohibitions against solicitation and unauthorized practice.[80]

Subsequently the Court approved a plan whereby workers were advised to consult specific attorneys, but the decision did not extend to protect plans involving an explicit hiring of such attorneys by the union.[81] Later the Illinois Supreme Court held that the Trainman decision did not protect a plan under which the attorneys recommended to members were actually paid by the union. However, Justice Black, writing for eight members of the Court, over the dissent of Justice Harlan, held that "the freedom of speech, assembly, and petition guaranteed by the First and Fourteenth Amendments" gave "petitioner the right to hire attorneys on a salary basis to assist its members in the assertion of their legal rights." Hence, the Court sustained the right of a union to hire a lawyer to represent workers claiming injury or death benefits under the Illinois workmen's compensation law. He suggested that many kinds of citizens' groups could offer legal services to their members, provided the organization did not interfere with the lawyers' legal judgments and that the members were free to engage other counsel. Justice Harlan argued as he had in the previous NAACP v. Button case.[82]

In holding that the Florida legislature's committee investigating infiltration of communism into various organizations could not require the president of the Miami branch of the NAACP to divulge information contained in the membership lists of the Association under the protections of the First and Fourteenth amendments,[83] the Court distinguished prior cases.[84]

Justice Goldberg, writing for the majority, said that

[77] *Ibid.*, 454–55.
[78] *Ibid.*, 456.
[79] *Ibid.*, 457.
[80] *Ibid.*, 470.
[81] Railroad Trainmen v. Virginia Bar, 377 U.S. 1 (1964).
[82] United Mine Workers v. Illinois Bar Assoc., 389 U.S. 217 (1967).
[83] Gibson v. Florida Legislative Comm., 372 U.S. 539 (1963).
[84] Barenblatt v. United States, 360 U.S. 109 (1959); Wilkinson v. United States, 365 U.S. 399 (1961); Braden v. United States, 365 U.S. 431 (1961); Uphaus v. Wyman, 360 U.S. 72 (1959).

there was no claim made . . . that the NAACP or its Miami branch was engaged in any subversive activities or that its legitimate activities have been dominated or influenced by Communists. . . .

The respondent committee has laid no adequate foundation for its direct demands upon the officers and records of a wholly legitimate organization for disclosure of its membership.[85]

Justices Black and Douglas concurred; Justice Harlan, supported by Justices Clark, Stewart, and White, wrote in dissent:

The Court's reasoning is difficult to grasp. I read its opinion as basically proceeding on the premise that the governmental interest in investigating Communist infiltration into admittedly nonsubversive organizations, as distinguished from investigating organizations themselves suspected of subversive activities, is not sufficient to overcome the countervailing right to freedom of association. . . .

Until today, I had never supposed that any of our decisions relating to state or federal power to investigate in the field of Communist subversion could possibly be taken as suggesting any difference in the degree of governmental investigatory interest as between Communist infiltration of organizations and Communist activity *by* organizations. . . .

(He cited the distinguished cases.)[86]

Justice White, dissenting, said: "In my view, the opinion of the Court represents a serious limitation upon the Court's previous cases dealing with this subject matter and upon the right of the legislature to investigate the Communist Party and its activities."[87]

A situation akin to that presented by the Girard case arose in connection with a park in Macon, Georgia. As a result, five members of the Court joined in an opinion by Justice Douglas holding that though the park had been devised for the pleasure of whites only and the city had appointed trustees and managers thereof for a number of years, the substitution of individual trustees not controlled by the city would not operate to keep the park segregated.[88] Justice White concurred; Justices Black, Harlan, and Stewart dissented.

Justice Douglas said:

There are two complementary principles to be reconciled in this case. One is the right of the individual to pick his own associates so as to express his preferences and dislikes, and to fashion his private life by joining such clubs and groups as he chooses. The other is the constitutional ban in the Equal Protection

85 Gibson v. Florida Legislative Comm., 372 U.S. 539, 555 (1963).
86 *Ibid.*, 579.
87 *Ibid.*, 583.
88 Evans v. Newton, 382 U.S. 296 (1966).

Clause of the Fourteenth Amendment against state-sponsored racial inequality.[89]

What is "private" action and what is "state action" is not always easy to determine. . . . Conduct that is formally "private" may become so entwined with governmental policies or so impregnated with a governmental character as to become subject to the constitutional limitations placed upon state action. . . .[90]

If a testator wanted to leave a school or center for the use of one race only and in no way implicated the State. . . . we assume *arguendo* that no constitutional difficulty would be encountered.[91]

This park, however, is in a different posture. For years it was an integral part of the City of Macon's activities. . . . we assume it was swept, manicured, watered, patrolled and maintained by the city as a public facility for whites only, as well as granted tax exemption. . . . The momentum it acquired as a public facility is certainly not dissipated *ipso facto* by the appointment of "private" trustees. . . . Whether these public characteristics will in time be dissipated is wholly conjectural. If the municipality remains entwined in the management or control of the park, it remains subject to the restraints of the Fourteenth Amendment. . . . We only hold that where the tradition of municipal control had become firmly established, we cannot take judicial notice that the mere substitution of trustees instantly transferred this park from the public to the private sector.[92]

Justice White, concurring, agreed with the result for a different reason.

I would . . . hold that the racial condition in the trust may not be given effect by the new trustees because, in my view, it is incurably tainted by discriminatory state legislation validating such a condition under state law. . . .[93]

This case must accordingly be viewed as one where the State has forbidden all private discrimination except racial discrimination. As a result, "the State through its regulations has become involved to such a significant extent" in bringing about the discriminatory provision in Senator Bacon's trust that the racial restriction "must be held to reflect . . . state policy and therefore to violate the Fourteenth Amendment."[94]

The dissenters maintained that no constitutional question was involved; that the Georgia courts had done nothing but permit the substitution of trustees and had not considered the powers of the substituted trustees. However, Justice Harlan, with the support of Justice Stewart, said, respecting the constitutional question:

[89] *Ibid.*, 298.
[90] *Ibid.*, 299.
[91] *Ibid.*, 300.
[92] *Ibid.*, 301.
[93] *Ibid.*, 305.
[94] *Ibid.*, 311.

From all that now appears, this is a case of "private discrimination."[95]

The first ground for the majority's state action holding rests on nothing but an assumption and a conjecture. The assumption is that the city itself maintained Baconsfield in the past. The conjecture is that it will continue to be connected with the administration of the park in the future. . . .[96]

. . . the majority advances another which ultimately emerges as the real holding. This ground derives from what is asserted to be the "public character" of Baconsfield and the "municipal" nature of its services. . . .

Except for one case which will be found to be a shaky precedent, the cases cited by the majority do not support this novel state action theory. . . .[97]

More serious than the absence of any firm doctrinal support for this theory of state action are its potentialities for the future. . . .[98]

I find it difficult . . . to avoid the conclusion that this decision opens the door to reversal of these basic constitutional concepts, and, at least in logic, jeopardizes the existence of denominationally restricted schools while making of every college entrance rejection letter a potential Fourteenth Amendment question. . . .

While this process of analogy might be spun out to reach privately owned orphanages, libraries, garbage collection companies, detective agencies, and a host of other functions commonly regarded as nongovernmental though paralleling fields of governmental activity, the examples of schools is, I think, sufficient to indicate the pervasive potentialities of this "Public function" theory of state action. . . . And it carries the seeds of transferring to federal authority vast areas of concern whose regulation has wisely been left by the Constitution to the States.[99]

Though the issue did not involve a racial question but arose in connection with picketing by a labor union outside a supermarket in a privately owned shopping center, six judges joined in holding that the area was essentially a public one since it was freely accessible and open to the people, and hence the union was free to picket. Justices Black, White, and Harlan dissented,[100] Justice Black maintaining that shopping centers are private property and "whether this Court likes it or not the Constitution recognizes the concept of private ownership of property."[101]

[95] *Ibid.,* 316.
[96] *Ibid.,* 318.
[97] *Ibid.,* 319.
[98] *Ibid.,* 321.
[99] *Ibid.,* 322.
[100] Amalgamated Union v. Logan Valley Plaza, 391 U.S. 308 (1968).
[101] *Ibid.,* 330.

CHAPTER XIX

Crime and the Criminal Law: Confessions and Counsel—1

THE NATIONALIZATION PROMOTED BY THE HIGH COURT has had no greater mani-festation than in the area of the criminal law and its administration by the states. The first inroads were by application of the sanctions of the First Amendment in the Gitlow case. Then, yielding to the persuasions of Justices Black and Douglas, the Court extended the proscriptions laid down by the Palko case by applying directly the restrictions of the Fourth Amendment, the self-incrimination privileges of the Fifth and the fair trial provisions of the Sixth. The consequences have been further, and there have been im-portant rendings of the principle of separation of the functions of the national and state governments in the field of the criminal law and its administration.

One of the sore spots in the administration of the criminal law has been convictions obtained after admissions of confessions by defendants. Lurking in the background of such convictions has always been the general suspicion that unorthodox and unfair methods have been used by the police to extract confessions. The term "third degree" found a common place in the popular vocabulary. Hence the high court became more and more alert to the need of obtaining assurance that a confession was voluntary and not coerced in the eyes of the law.

During the 1962 term the Court considered the case of a man named Noia, who, with two codefendants, had been convicted in a New York state court of murder committed during a robbery. Each was sentenced to life imprison-ment. The sole evidence against each of them was his confession. Noia did not appeal, but his codefendants did. Their appeals were unsuccessful. However, subsequent proceedings resulted in their release upon the ground that their confessions had been coerced and hence their convictions violated the Four-teenth Amendment. After an unsuccessful attempt to review his case in the state court, Noia sought a writ of habeas corpus in the federal court. The high court affirmed the court of appeals' decision that he should be released.[1]

Justice Clark and Justice Harlan, with the support of Justice Stewart, dissented. Justice Clark said:

[1] Fay v. Noia 372 U.S. 391 (1963).

Beyond question the federal courts until today have had no power to release a prisoner in respondent Noia's predicament, there being no basis for such power in either the Constitution or the statute. But the Court today in releasing Noia makes an "abrupt break" not only with the Constitution and the statute but also with its past decisions, disrupting the delicate balance of federalism so foremost in the minds of the Founding Fathers and so uniquely important in the field of law enforcement. The short of it is that Noia's incarceration rests entirely on an adequate and independent state ground—namely, that he knowingly failed to perfect any appeal from his conviction of murder. While it may be that the Court's "decision today swings open no prison gates," the Court must admit in all candor that it effectively swings closed the doors of justice in the face of the State, since it certainly cannot prove its case 20 years after the fact....[2]

... the effective administration of criminal justice in state courts receives a staggering blow. Habeas corpus is in effect substituted for appeal, seriously disturbing the orderly disposition of state prosecutions and jeopardizing the finality of state convictions.... After today state judgments will be relegated to a judicial limbo, subject to federal collateral attack—as here—a score of years later despite a defendant's wilful failure to appeal.[3]

In a footnote Justice Clark showed the increase of habeas corpus applications filed in the federal district courts by state prisoners from 127 in 1941 to 1,232 in 1962.

Justice Harlan characterized the decision and its "consequences for the future" as "one of the most disquieting that the Court has rendered in a long time." He called attention to Section 2241 of the Judicial Code restricting power to grant a writ to a prisoner "in custody in violation of the Constitution" and maintained that Noia was in custody "pursuant to a conviction whose validity rests upon an adequate and independent state ground which the federal courts are required to respect." He maintained that "today the Court has turned its back on history and struck a heavy blow at the foundations of our federal system."[4]

He concluded:

I recognize that Noia's predicament may well be thought one that strongly calls for correction. But the proper course to that end lies with the New York Governor's powers of executive clemency, not with the federal courts. (At the oral argument the State District Attorney advised us that his office would support an application for clemency once the case had been disposed of in this Court.)[5]

[2] *Ibid.*, 445.
[3] *Ibid.*, 446.
[4] *Ibid.*, 448, 449.
[5] *Ibid.*, 476.

After the New York Court of Appeals had affirmed a conviction for murder and the Supreme Court had denied certiorari, the petitioner sought a writ of habeas corpus, asserting his conviction invalid because the trial court followed the New York procedure in admitting his confession. Five members of the Court reversed and remanded the case to the district court for a determination of whether the confession was voluntary, holding violative of the Fourteenth Amendment the New York practice of excluding the confession only if the trial court found that in no circumstances could it be found voluntary, and, not so finding, leaving it to the jury to determine its voluntariness as well as its truthfulness.[6]

Justice White, for the majority, overruled a prior and contrary decision,[7] and held that the judge could not submit the confession to the jury until he had found it voluntary. Justices Black, Clark, Harlan, and Stewart dissented, each maintaining the procedure did not violate the Fourteenth Amendment. They also disagreed with the finding that a jury could not be assumed to have reliably found a confession voluntary where it also determines its truthfulness. Justice Black also contended that the evidence showed the confession coerced.

Later, a unanimous Court, following the above rule, reversed a Georgia conviction for rape where, under the Georgia rule, the Court had left the question of voluntariness of a confession to the jury without first itself finding it voluntary,[8] and during the same term the Court reversed a conviction based on a confession the Court found was not voluntary.[9]

However, the Court later affirmed a conviction where defense counsel had said he had no objection to a determination by the Court, in the presence of the jury, of the voluntariness of defendant's confession, since the confession had been found voluntary and had thereupon been received in evidence. Incidentally, the per curiam opinion said that "this Court has never ruled that all voluntariness hearings must be held outside the presence of the jury, regardless of the circumstances."[10]

In holding that the confession of one defendant could not be introduced in a trial involving a codefendant, Justice Brennan, writing for the Court, referred to the prior case of Jackson v. Denno, which required the Court to pass upon the voluntariness of a confession and determine it voluntary before disclosure to a jury, as "expressly rejecting the proposition that a jury, when determining the confessor's guilt, could be relied on to ignore his confession

---

[6] Jackson v. Denno, 378 U.S. 368 (1964).

[7] Stein, Wissner, Cooper v. New York, 346 U.S. 156 (1953).

[8] Sims v. Georgia, 385 U.S. 538 (1966).

[9] Clewis v. Texas, 386 U.S. 707 (1967); *see also* Brooks v. Florida, 389 U.S. 413 (1967); Beecher v. Alabama, 389 U.S. 35 (1967); Greenwald v. Wisconsin, 390 U.S. 519 (1968).

[10] Pinto v. Pierce, 389 U.S. 31, 32 (1967).

of guilt should they find the confession involuntary," (citing the Jackson case at 388–89).[11] He added: "Significantly, we supported that conclusion in part by reliance upon the dissenting opinion of Mr. Justice Frankfurter for the four Justices who dissented in Delli Paoli. . . .[12] That dissent challenged the basic premise of Delli Paoli that a properly instructed jury would ignore the confessor's inculpation of the nonconfessor in determining the latter's guilt."[13]

"Besides," concluded Justice Brennan:

> not only are such incriminations devastating to the defendant but their credibility is inevitably suspect, a fact recognized when accomplices do take the stand and the jury is instructed to weigh their testimony carefully given the recognized motivation to shift blame onto others. The unreliability of such evidence is intolerably compounded when the alleged accomplice, as here, does not testify and cannot be tested by cross-examination. . . .[14]
>
> We cannot accept limiting instructions as an adequate substitute for petitioner's constitutional right of cross-examination. The effect is the same as if there had been no instruction at all.[15]

Justice White, dissenting, said:

> I dissent from this excessively rigid rule. There is nothing in this record to suggest that the jury did not follow the trial judge's instructions. There has been no new learning since Delli Paoli indicating that juries are less reliable than they were considered in that case to be. There is nothing in the prior decisions of this Court which supports this new constitutional rule. . . .[16]
>
> I persist in believing that the reversal of Delli Paoli unnecessarily burdens the already difficult task of conducting criminal trials. . . .[17]

Justice Harlan joined in Justice White's opinion without abandoning his original disagreement with the Jackson decision. Justices Black and Stewart concurred in the result, the latter saying, "Although I did not agree with the decision in Jackson v. Denno . . . I accept its holding and share the Court's conclusion that it compels the overruling of Delli Paoli. . . ."[18] Justice Marshall did not participate. This was one of five cases overruling prior decisions on criminal procedure handed down on a single day. Later, over the dissents of Justices Harlan and White, the Court held the decision retroactive.[19]

[11] Bruton v. United States, 391 U.S. 123 (1968).
[12] Ibid., 129.
[13] Ibid.
[14] Ibid., 136.
[15] Ibid., 137.
[16] Ibid., 139.
[17] Ibid., 144.
[18] Ibid., 137.
[19] Roberts v. Russell, 392 U.S. 293 (1968); see also Williams v. Florida, 392 U.S. 306 (1968).

Of course, the difficulties attendant upon determining whether or not a confession was voluntary would be avoided if the defendant had counsel present when he made his statement. So we find the Court embracing this apparently simple expedient in the case of a defendant accused of narcotics activities who retained a lawyer and was released on bail. While he was free, he made incriminating statements to an alleged confederate while in the latter's automobile. The confederate had placed a radio transmitter in the car without the defendant's knowledge, whereby federal agents were able to overhear the conversation. The Court held the statements inadmissible as being made in the absence of counsel.[20] Justice White, with the support of Justices Clark and Harlan, wrote in dissent:

> The current incidence of serious violations of the law represents not only an appalling waste of the potentially happy and useful lives of those who engage in such conduct but also an overhanging, dangerous threat to those unidentified and innocent people who will be the victims of crime today and tomorrow. This is a festering problem for which no adequate cures have yet been devised. At the very least there is much room for discontent with remedial measures so far undertaken....
>
> In my view, a civilized society must maintain its capacity to discover transgressions of the law and to identify those who flout it....
>
> It is therefore a rather portentous occasion when a constitutional rule is established barring the use of evidence which is relevant, reliable and highly probative of the issue which the trial court has before it—whether the accused committed the act with which he is charged. Without the evidence, the quest for truth may be seriously impeded and in many cases the trial court, although aware of proof of defendant's guilt, must nevertheless release him because the crucial evidence is inadmissible. This result is entirely justified in some circumstances because exclusion serves other policies of overriding importance, as where evidence seized in an illegal search is excluded, not because of the quality of the proof, but to secure meaningful enforcement of the Fourth Amendment.[21]
>
> It is only a sterile syllogism—an unsound one, besides, to say that because Massiah had a right to counsel's aid before and during the trial, his out-of-court conversations and admissions must be excluded if obtained without counsel's consent or presence. The right to counsel has never meant as much before ...and its extension in this case requires some further explanation, so far unarticulated by the Court....[22]
>
> Under the prior law, announced in countless cases in this Court, the defendant's pretrial statements were admissible evidence if voluntarily made; inadmissible if not the product of his free will.... The Court presents no

[20] Massiah v. United States, 377 U.S. 201 (1964).
[21] Ibid., 207–208.
[22] Ibid., 209.

facts, no objective evidence, no reasons to warrant scrapping the voluntary-involuntary test for admissibility in this area.[23]

Following this decision came two landmark discussions that have aroused controversy and concurrent criticism of the Court.

Danny Escobedo, a twenty-two-year-old man of Mexican extraction was arrested and interrogated in connection with the fatal shooting of his brother-in-law. He had been arrested previously immediately after the shooting, but had been released after his lawyer obtained a writ of habeas corpus from a state court. Arrested a second time during the further police investigation, he made several requests to see his lawyer, who, though in the building, was refused access to his client.

Escobedo was not advised by the police of his right to remain silent and, after persistent questioning by the police, made a damaging statement to an assistant state's attorney, which was admitted in evidence at his trial.

Following his conviction, in an opinion by Justice Goldberg for five members of the Court, the conviction was reversed. Justices Harlan, White, Clark, and Stewart dissented. Justice Goldberg said:

> ... the purpose of the interrogation was to "get him" to confess his guilt despite his constitutional right not to do so. ... .[24]
> The "guiding hand of counsel" was essential to advise petitioner of his rights in this delicate situation. ... This was the "stage when legal aid and advice" were most critical to petitioner. ... .[25]
> It is argued that if the right to counsel is afforded prior to indictment, the number of confessions obtained by the police will diminish significantly, because most confessions are obtained during the period between arrest and indictment, and "any lawyer worth his salt will tell the suspect in no uncertain terms to make no statement to police under any circumstances." This argument, of course, cuts two ways. The fact that many confessions are obtained during this period points up its critical nature as a "stage when legal aid and advice" are surely needed. ... The right to counsel would indeed be hollow if it began at a period when few confessions were obtained. ... .[26]
> No system worth preserving should have to *fear* that if an accused is permitted to consult with a lawyer, he will become aware of, and exercise, these rights. If the exercise of constitutional rights will thwart the effectiveness of a system of law enforcement, then there is something very wrong with that system.
> We hold, therefore, that where, as here, the investigation is no longer a general inquiry into an unsolved crime but has begun to focus on a particular

[23] *Ibid.,* 210.
[24] Escobedo v. Illinois, 378 U.S. 478, 485 (1964).
[25] *Ibid.,* 486.
[26] *Ibid.,* 488.

suspect, the suspect has been taken into police custody, the police carry out a process of interrogations that lends itself to eliciting incriminating statements, the suspect has requested and been denied an opportunity to consult with his lawyers, and the police have not effectively warned him of his absolute constitutional right to remain silent, the accused has been denied "the Assistance of Counsel" in violation of the Sixth Amendment to the Constitution as "made obligatory upon the States by the Fourteenth Amendment,"...and that no statement elicited by the police during the interrogation may be used against him at a criminal trial.[27]

The opinion distinguished two prior cases.[28] Justices Harlan and Stewart, dissenting, said that the instant case was controlled directly by the latter of the two distinguished cases. Justice Harlan said that he thought "the rule announced today is most ill-conceived and that it seriously and unjustifiably fetters perfectly legitimate methods of criminal law enforcement."[29]

Justice Stewart wrote:

> Under our system of criminal justice the institution of formal, meaningful judicial proceedings, by way of indictment, information, or arraignment, marks the point at which a criminal investigation has ended and adversary proceedings have commenced. It is at this point that the constitutional guarantees attach which pertain to a criminal trial. Among these guarantees...is the guarantee of the assistance of counsel....
>
> The Court says that what happened during this investigation "affected" the trial. I had always supposed that the whole purpose of a police investigation of a murder was to "affect" the trial of the murderer, and that it would be only an incompetent, unsuccessful, or corrupt investigation which would not do so. The Court further says that the Illinois police officers did not advise the petitioner of his "constitutional rights" before he confessed to the murder. This Court has never held that the Constitution requires the police to give any "advice" under circumstances such as these.
>
> Supported by no stronger authority than its own rhetoric, the Court today converts a routine police investigation of an unsolved murder into a distorted analogue of a judicial trial. It imports into this investigation constitutional concepts historically applicable only after the onset of formal prosecutorial proceedings. But doing so, I think the Court perverts those previous constitutional guarantees, and frustrates the vital interests of society in preserving the legitimate and proper function of honest and purposeful police investigation....
> I cannot escape the logic of my Brother White's conclusions as to the extraordinary implications which emanate from the Court's opinion in this case, and I share their views as to the untold and highly unfortunate impact today's

[27] *Ibid.,* 490–91.
[28] Crooker v. California, 357 U.S. 433 (1958); Cicenia v. Lagay, 357 U.S. 504 (1958).
[29] Escobedo v. Illinois, 378 U.S. 478, 493 (1964).

decision may have upon the fair administration of criminal justice. I can only hope we have completely misunderstood what the Court has said.[30]

Justice White stated:

The decision is ... another major step in the direction of the goal which the Court seemingly has in mind—to bar from evidence all admissions obtained from an individual suspected of crime, whether involuntarily made or not. ...[31]

... the Court seems driven by the notion that it is uncivilized law enforcement to use an accused's own admissions against him at his trial. ... The right to counsel ... stands as an unpenetrable barrier to any interrogation once the accused has become a suspect. From that very moment apparently his right to counsel attaches, a rule wholly unworkable and impossible to administer unless police cars are equipped with public defenders and undercover agents and police informants have defense counsel at their side. ...[32]

Under this new approach one might as well argue that a potential defendant is constitutionally entitled to a lawyer before, not after, he commits a crime, since it is then that crucial incriminating evidence is put within the reach of the Government by the would-be accused. ...

The Court chooses ... to rely on the virtues and morality of a system of criminal law enforcement which does not depend on the "confession." No such judgment is to be found in the Constitution. ... The only "inquisitions" the Constitution forbids are those which compel incrimination. Escobedo's statements were not compelled and the Court does not hold that they were. ...[33]

... law enforcement ... will be crippled and its task made a great deal more difficult, all in my opinion, for unsound, unstated reasons, which can find no home in any of the provisions of the Constitution.[34]

Later, in four cases considered together,[35] three convictions were reversed by the high court and a reversal by the California court affirmed, in an opinion by the Chief Justice for five members of the Court. Justice Clark concurred in the affirmance of the fourth case and dissented in the reversal of the other three. Justices Harlan, Stewart, and White dissented in all four.

The occasion for the review of police practices in these cases stemmed from the Court's expansion of its power of the administration of the criminal law in the states arising from its holding in the prior Malloy case. In that case, the Court held that the Fifth Amendment, awarding the privilege of avoiding self-incrimination, was applicable to the states under the due process clause

---

[30] *Ibid.,* 493–95.
[31] *Ibid.,* 495.
[32] *Ibid.,* 496.
[33] *Ibid.,* 497–98.
[34] *Ibid.,* 499.
[35] Miranda v. Arizona; Vignera v. New York; Westover v. United States; California v. Stewart, 384 U.S. 436 (1966).

of the Fourteenth Amendment, as the Court had expanded its supervision over state criminal processes by holding the Fourth Amendment similarly applicable in its Mapp decision. Hence, as the Chief Justice said:

the substantive and procedural safeguards surrounding admissibility of confessions in state cases had become exceedingly exacting, reflecting all the policies embedded in the privilege. . . . The voluntariness doctrine in the state cases . . . encompasses all interrogation practices which are likely to exert pressure upon an individual as to disable him from making a free and rational choice. The implications of this proposition were elaborated in our decision in Escobedo. . . .

Our holding there stressed the fact that the police had not advised the defendant of his constitutional privilege to remain silent at the outset of the interrogation. . . . The entire thrust of police interrogation there, as in all the cases today, was to put the defendant in such an emotional state as to impair his capacity for rational judgment. The abdication of the constitutional—the choice on his part to speak to the police—was not made knowingly or competently because of the failure to apprise him of his rights; the compelling atmosphere of the in-custody interrogation, and not an independent decision on his part, caused the defendant to speak.

A different phase of the Escobedo decision was significant in its attention to the absence of counsel during the questioning. There, as in the cases today, we sought a protective device to dispel the compelling atmosphere of the interrogation.[36] . . . The presence of counsel, in all the cases before us today, would be the adequate protective device necessary to make the process of police interrogation conform to the dictates of the privilege. His presence would insure that statements made in the government-established atmosphere are not the product of compulsion. . . . That counsel is present when statements are taken from an individual during interrogation obviously enhances the integrity of the fact-finding processes in court. The presence of an attorney, and the warnings delivered to the individual, enable the defendant under otherwise compelling circumstances to tell his story without fear, effectively, and in a way that eliminates the evils in the interrogation process. . . .[37]

Today, then, there can be no doubt that the Fifth Amendment privilege is available outside of criminal court proceedings and serves to protect persons in all settings in which their freedom of action is curtailed from being compelled to incriminate themselves. . . .

We cannot say that the Constitution necessarily requires adherence to any particular solution for the inherent compulsions of the interrogation process as it is presently conducted. Our decision in no way creates a constitutional straitjacket which will handicap sound efforts at reform. . . . We encourage Congress and the States to continue their laudable search for increasingly effective ways of protecting the rights of the individual while promoting efficient enforcement of

[36] *Ibid.*, 464–65.
[37] *Ibid.*, 466.

our criminal laws. However, unless we are shown other procedures which are at least as effective in apprising accused persons of their right of silence and in assuring a continuous opportunity to exercise it, the following safeguards must be observed....[38]

The warning of the right to remain silent must be accompanied by the explanation that anything said can and will be used against the individual in court....

The right to have counsel present at the interrogation is indispensable.... A mere warning given by the interrogators is not alone sufficient....the need for counsel to protect the Fifth Amendment privilege comprehends not merely a right to consult with counsel prior to questioning, if the defendant so desires.

His failure to ask for a lawyer does not constitute a waiver. No effective waiver of the right to counsel during interrogation can be recognized unless specifically made after the warnings we have here delineated have been given.[39]

An individual held for interrogation must be clearly informed that he has the right to consult with a lawyer and to have the lawyer with him during interrogation....this warning is an absolute prerequisite to interrogation....[40]

The need for counsel in order to protect the privilege exists for the indigent as the affluent....[41]

In order fully to apprise a person interrogated of the extent of his rights under this system then, it is necessary to warn him not only that he has the right to consult with an attorney, but also that if he is indigent a lawyer will be appointed to represent him....[42]

Once warnings have been given, the subsequent procedure is clear. If the individual indicates in any manner, at any time prior to or during questioning, that he wishes to remain silent, the interrogation must cease....If the individual states that he wants an attorney, the interrogation must cease until an attorney is present. At that time, the individual must have an opportunity to confer with the attorney....[43]

A valid waiver will not be presumed simply from the silence of the accused after warnings are given or simply from the fact that a confession was in fact eventually obtained....there is no room for the contention that the privilege is waived if the individual answers some questions or gives some information on his own prior to invoking his right to remain silent....

...the fact of lengthy interrogation or incommunicado incarceration before a statement is made is strong evidence that the accused was threatened, tricked, or cajoled into a waiver will, of course, show that the defendant did not voluntarily waive his privilege....[44]

Statements merely intended to be exculpatory by the defendant are often

[38] *Ibid.*, 467.
[39] *Ibid.*, 469–70.
[40] *Ibid.*, 471.
[41] *Ibid.*, 472.
[42] *Ibid.*, 473.
[43] *Ibid.*, 473–74.
[44] *Ibid.*, 475–76.

used to impeach his testimony at trial or demonstrate untruths in the statement given under the interrogation and thus to prove guilt by implication. These statements are incriminating ... and may not be used without the full warnings and effective waiver required for any other statement. ...

Our decision is not intended to hamper the traditional function of police officers in investigating crime. ... General on-the-scene questioning as to facts surrounding a crime or other general questioning of citizens in the fact-finding process is not affected by our holding. ... [45]

There is no requirement that police stop a person who enters a police station and states that he wishes to confess to a crime. ... Volunteered statements of any kind are not barred by the Fifth Amendment. ... [46]

A recurrent argument made in these cases is that society's need for interrogation outweighs the privilege. This argument is not unfamiliar to this Court. [47]

In announcing these principles, we are not unmindful of the burdens which law enforcement officials must bear. . . . Although confessions may play an important role in some convictions, the cases before us present graphic examples of the overstatement of the "need" for confessions. In each case authorities conducted interrogations ranging up to five days in duration despite the presence, through standard investigating practices, of considerable evidence against each defendant. ... [48]

Over the years the Federal Bureau of Investigation has compiled an exemplary record of effective law enforcement while advising any suspect or arrested person, at the outset of an interview, that he is not required to make a statement, that any statements may be used against him in court, that the individual may obtain the services of an attorney of his own choice and, more recently, that he has a right to free counsel if he is unable to pay. [49]

Justice Clark, dissenting, said:

I am unable to join the majority because its opinion goes too far on too little, while my dissenting brethren do not go quite far enough. . . . the examples of police brutality mentioned by the Court are rare exceptions to the thousands of cases that appear every day in the law reports. ...

The Court has added more to the requirements. ... Such a strict constitutional specific inserted at the nerve center of crime detection may well kill the patient. ... [50]

Custodial interrogation has long been recognized as "undoubtedly an essential tool in effective law enforcement.". ... Recognition of this fact should put us on our guard against the promulgation of doctrinaire rules. Especially is this

[45] *Ibid.*, 477.
[46] *Ibid.*, 478.
[47] *Ibid.*, 479.
[48] *Ibid.*, 481.
[49] *Ibid.*, 483.
[50] *Ibid.*, 499–500.

true where the Court finds that "the Constitution has prescribed" its holding and where the light of our past cases ... are to the contrary. Indeed, even in *Escobedo* the Court never hinted that an affirmative "waiver" was a prerequisite to questioning; that the burden of proof as to waiver was on the prosecution; that the presence of counsel—absent a waiver—during interrogation was required; that a waiver can be withdrawn at the will of the accused; that counsel must be furnished during an accusatory stage to those unable to pay; nor that admissions and exculpatory statements are "confessions." To require all those things at one gulp should cause the Court to choke over more cases than Crooker v. State of California ... and Cicenia v. La Gay ... which it expressly overrules today.[51]

Rather than employing the arbitrary Fifth Amendment rule which the Court lays down, I would follow the more pliable dictates of Due Process Clauses of the Fifth and Fourteenth Amendments which we are accustomed to administering and which we know from our cases are effective instruments in protecting persons in police custody. In this way we would not be acting in the dark nor in one full sweep changing the traditional rules of custodial interrogation which this Court has for so long recognized as a justifiable and proper tool in balancing individual rights against the rights of society.[52]

Justice Harlan, joined by Justices White and Stewart, made the statement:

I believe the decision of the Court represents poor constitutional law and entails harmful consequences for the country at large. How serious these consequences may prove to be only time can tell. But the basic flaws in the Court's justification seem to be readily apparent now once all sides of the problem are considered.[53]

While the fine points of this scheme are far less clear than the Court admits, the tenor is quite apparent. The new rules are not designed to guard against police brutality or other unmistakably banned forms of coercion. Those who use third-degree tactics and deny them in court are equally able and destined to lie as skillfully about warnings and waivers. Rather, the thrust of the new rules is to negate all pressures, to reinforce the nervous or ignorant suspect, and ultimately to discourage any confession at all. The aim in short is toward "voluntariness" in a utopian sense, or to view it from a different angle, voluntariness with a vengeance.

To incorporate this notion into the Constitution requires a strained reading of history and precedent and a disregard of the very pragmatic concerns that alone may on occasion justify such strains....[54]

There are several relevant lessons to be drawn from this constitutional history. The first is that with over 25 years of precedent the Court has developed an elaborate, sophisticated, and sensitive approach to admissibility of confessions.

[51] *Ibid.*, 501–502.
[52] *Ibid.*, 503.
[53] *Ibid.*, 504.
[54] *Ibid.*, 505.

It is "judicial" in its treatment of one case at a time ... flexible in its ability to respond to the endless mutations of fact presented. . . .[55]

... in practice and from time to time in principle, the Court has given ample recognition to society's interest in suspect questioning as an instrument of law enforcement. . . . Of course the limitations imposed today were rejected by necessary implication in case after case, the right to warnings having been explicitly rebuffed in this Court many years ago. . . . recently . . . the Court openly acknowledged that questioning of witnesses and suspects "is undoubtedly an essential tool in effective law enforcement." . . .[56]

The Court's opinion in my view reveals no adequate basis for extending the Fifth Amendment's privilege against self-incrimination to the police station. Far more important, it fails to show that the Court's new rules are well supported, let alone compelled by Fifth Amendment precedents. Instead, the new rules actually derive from quotation and analogy drawn from precedents under the Sixth Amendment, which should properly have no bearing on police interrogation. . . .[57]

. . . the Court's unspoken assumption that *any* pressure violates the privilege is not supported by the precedents. . . .

The Court appears similarly wrong in thinking that precise knowledge of one's rights is a settled prerequisite under the Fifth Amendment to the loss of its protections. . . . No Fifth Amendment precedent is cited for the Court's contrary view . . .

While the Court finds no pertinent difference between judicial proceedings and police interrogation, I believe the differences are so vast as to disqualify wholly the Sixth Amendment precedents as suitable analogies in the present cases. . . .

The sound reason why this right [of counsel] is so freely extended for a criminal trial is the severe injustice risked by confronting an untrained defendant with a range of technical points of law, evidence, and tactics familiar to the prosecutor but not to himself. This danger shrinks markedly in the police station where indeed the lawyer in fulfilling his professional responsibilities of necessity may become an obstacle to truth-finding. . . .[58]

Examined as an expression of public policy, the Court's new regime proves so dubious that there can be no due compensation for its weakness in constitutional law. . . . the Court has not and cannot make the powerful showing that its new rules are plainly desirable in the context of our society, something which is surely demanded before those rules are engrafted onto the Constitution and imposed on every State and county in the land. . . .

A confession is wholly and incontestably voluntary only if a guilty person gives himself up to the law and becomes his own accuser. . . . Until today, the

[55] *Ibid.*, 508.
[56] *Ibid.*, 509.
[57] *Ibid.*, 510.
[58] *Ibid.*, 513–14.

role of the Constitution has been only to sift out *undue* pressure, not to assure spontaneous confessions. . . .[59]

The rules work for reliability in confessions almost only in the Pickwickian sense that they can prevent some from being given at all. . . .

What the Court largely ignores is that its rules impair, if they will not eventually serve wholly to frustrate, an instrument of law enforcement that has long and quite reasonably been thought worth the price paid for it. . . . to suggest or provide counsel for the suspect simply invites the end of the interrogation. . . . (quoting Jackson, J.: "[A]ny lawyer worth his salt will tell the suspect in no uncertain terms to make no statement to police under any circumstances.)"

How much harm this decision will inflict on law enforcement cannot fairly be predicted with accuracy. . . . the Court is taking a real risk with society's welfare in imposing its new regime on the country. The social costs of crime are too great to call the new rules anything but a hazardous experimentation. . . . Society has always paid a stiff price for law and order, and peaceful interrogation is not one of the dark moments of the law.

This brief statement of the competing considerations seems to me ample proof that the Court's preference is highly debatable at best and therefore not to be read into the Constitution. However, it may make the analysis more graphic to consider the actual facts of one of the four cases reversed by the Court. Miranda v. Arizona serves best, being neither the hardest nor easiest of the four under the Court's standards.

On March 3, 1963, an 18-year-old girl was kidnapped and forcibly raped near Phoenix, Arizona. Ten days later, on the morning of March 13th, petitioner Miranda was arrested and taken to the police station. At this time Miranda was 23 years old, indigent, and educated to the extent of completing half of the ninth grade. He had "an emotional illness" of the schizophrenic type, according to the doctor who eventually examined him; the doctor's report also stated that Miranda was "alert and oriented as to time, place, and person," intelligent within normal limits, competent to stand trial, and sane within the legal definition. At the police station, the victim picked Miranda out of a line-up, and two officers then took him into a separate room to interrogate him, starting about 11:30 a.m. Though at first denying his guilt, within a short time Miranda gave a detailed oral confession and then wrote out in his own hand and signed a brief statement admitting and describing the crime. All this was accomplished in two hours or less without any force, threats or promises and—I will assume this though the record is uncertain . . .—without any effective warnings at all.

Miranda's oral and written confessions are now held inadmissible under the Court's new rules. One is entitled to feel astonished that the Constitution can be read to produce this result. . . . There was, in sum, a legitimate purpose, no perceptible unfairness, and certainly little risk of injustice in the interrogation. Yet the resulting confessions, and the responsible course of police practice they represent, are to be sacrificed to the Court's own finespun conception

[59] *Ibid.*, 514–15.

of fairness which I seriously doubt is shared by many thinking citizens in this country....[60]

No state in the country has urged this Court to impose the newly announced rules, nor has any State chosen to go nearly so far on its own.[61]

Justice White also wrote, saying that

the proposition that the privilege against self-incrimination forbids in-custody interrogation without the warning specified in the majority opinion and without a clear waiver of counsel has no significant support in the history of the privilege or in the language of the Fifth Amendment....[62]

... the Court has not discovered or found the law in making today's decision, nor has it derived it from some irrefutable sources; what it has done is to make new law and new public policy in much the same way that it has in the course of interpreting other great clauses of the Constitution. This is what the Court historically has done. Indeed, it is what it must do and will continue to do until and unless there is some fundamental change in the constitutional distribution of governmental powers.

But if the Court is here and now to announce new and fundamental policy to govern certain aspects of our affairs, it is wholly legitimate to examine the mode of this or any other constitutional decision in this Court and to inquire into the advisability of its end product in terms of the long-range interest of the country. At the very least, the Court's text and reasoning should withstand analysis and be a fair exposition of the constitutional provision which its opinion interprets. Decisions like these cannot rest alone on syllogism, metaphysics or some ill-defined notions of natural justice, although each will perhaps play its part. . . . the Court should not proceed to formulate fundamental policies based on speculation alone....

The Court does not point to any sudden inrush of new knowledge requiring the rejection of 70 years experience.... Insofar as it appears from the Court's opinion, it has not examined a single transcript of any police interrogation, let alone the interrogation that took place in any one of these cases which it decides today....[63]

In sum, for all the Court's expounding on the menacing atmosphere of police interrogation procedures, it has failed to supply any foundation for the conclusions it draws or the measures it adopts....

The Court's duty to assess the consequences of its action is not satisfied by the utterance of the truth that a value of our system of criminal justice is "to respect the inviolability of the human personality" and to require government to produce the evidence against the accused by its own independent labors.... More than the human dignity of the accused is involved: the human personality

[60] *Ibid.*, 516–19.
[61] *Ibid.*, 521.
[62] *Ibid.*, 526.
[63] *Ibid.*, 531–33.

of others in the society must also be preserved. . . . society's interest in the general security is of equal weight. . . .

As the Court all but admonishes the lawyer to advise the accused to remain silent, the result adds up to a judicial judgment that evidence from the accused should not be used against him in any way, whether compelled or not. This is the not so subtle overtone of the opinion—that it is inherently wrong for the police to gather evidence from the accused himself. And this is precisely the nub of this dissent. . . .

The most basic function of any government is to provide for the security of the individual and of his property. . . . These ends of society are served by the criminal laws which for the most part are aimed at the prevention of crime. Without the reasonably effective performance of the task of preventing private violence and retaliation, it is idle to talk about human dignity and civilized values. . . .[64]

In some unknown number of cases the Court's rule will return a killer, a rapist or other criminal to the streets and to the environment which produced him, to repeat his crime whenever it pleases him. As a consequence, there will not be a gain, but a loss, in human dignity. The real concern is . . . the impact on those who rely on the public authority for protection . . . There is, of course, a saving factor; the next victims are uncertain, unnamed and unrepresented in this case. . . .

The easier it is to get away with rape and murder, the less the deterrent effect on those who are inclined to attempt it.[65]

Another dissent was registered when Congress, following the assassination of Senator Robert F. Kennedy, passed a "Crime Bill" which provided, *inter alia,* that the Miranda rule rendering invalid voluntary confessions unless the defendant was first warned of his rights be overturned. Though the congressional challenge may well be ruled unconstitutional, it put the Court on notice of the temper of the times.

A *New York Times* article of December 22, 1966, marked Justice White as a minor prophet when it reported:

> When Criminal Court Judge Joseph L. Carter agreed to George McChan's release from prison he remarked that recent court decisions left him no choice but to "foist a professional holdup man on the public."
>
> Five days ago the 34-year-old convict, who has served 10 sentences in the last 18 years, was freed from the Maryland penitentiary.
>
> Today he was arrested and charged with the killing of a Baltimore tavern manager. . . .
>
> McChan left prison last Friday. . . .
>
> . . . In October a 40-year sentence he had been serving for assault with a deadly weapon was dissolved. . . .

[64] *Ibid.,* 537–39.　　　　[65] *Ibid.,* 542–43.

McChan had won a new trial. . . .

The prosecution decided it lacked evidence to carry out a second trial . . . when a Supreme Court ruling invalidated a statement obtained from McChan by two policemen who first questioned him. . . .

Justice Carter, in granting the state's motion to drop the assault charges, declared: "Because of the recent (Maryland C)ourt of Appeals and (Supreme Court) decisions, there is nothing we can do about it."

As Justice White noted in his Miranda dissent, subsequent victims, here Albert Poland and Viola Forrester, received no consideration at the hands of the majority when decreeing the Miranda rule to return killers to the streets.

It might also be noted that, as headlined by *The New York Times* of August 4, 1967, Justice White, at the American Bar Association meeting at Honolulu, "Defends High Court for Criminal Law Rulings He Criticized in Dissents," thus, as in the case of corporate directors, justifying them, however wrong they may be, since in good faith they exercised their best judgment.

Also, Justice Black took note of the criticism of the Miranda decision and defended it in a later five-to-three decision[66] in which the majority, which had been responsible for that decision, extended the requirement of its protection by voiding the conviction of one Mathis who had been convicted of income tax frauds. Justice Black held that Mathis-made statements to a revenue agent visiting him in the Florida State Penitentiary where he was doing time on a bad-check charge were inadmissible for lack of warnings called for by the Miranda decision. Justice White, dissenting, with Justices Harlan and Stewart (the three who dissented in the Miranda case), maintained that the decision might well require Miranda warnings in civil tax investigations, as well as in the other fields which frequently lead to criminal inquiries,[67] since Justice Black defined while in custody "to anyone deprived of his freedom by the authorities in any significant way and is subjected to questioning."

The strictures placed upon procedure resulting in confession were extended to arraignment when the Court reversed the conviction of a nineteen-year-old youth of limited intelligence charged with rape. The Court held that his confession, introduced in evidence at his trial, was obtained after questioning during a delay in arraigning him, in violation of the Federal Rules of Criminal Procedure, which called for the "officer making an arrest" . . . to "take the arrested person without unnecessary delay before the nearest available commissioner. . . ."[68]

The Court said:

[66] Mathis v. United States, 391 U.S. 1 (1968).
[67] *Ibid.*, 7.
[68] Mallory v. United States, 354 U.S. 449, 451 (1957).

We cannot sanction this extended delay, resulting in confession, without subordinating the general rule of prompt arraignment to the discretion of arresting officers. . . . Presumably, whomever the police arrest they must arrest on "probable cause." It is not the function of the police to arrest, as it were, at large and to use an interrogating process at police headquarters in order to determine whom they should charge before a committing magistrate on "probable cause."[69]

It is to be noted that a bill was passed by Congress in 1967 which extended the prearraignment questioning period in the District of Columbia to three hours.[70] This was signed by the President who, in 1966, had vetoed a bill extending the time to ten hours. However, the "Crime Bill" passed by Congress following the assassination of Senator Robert F. Kennedy extended the time between arrest and arraignment to six hours.

Largely at the instance of Justice Fortas, the Court extended procedural protections to the juvenile courts. In the first case five members of the Court joined in an opinion by Justice Fortas holding that the District of Columbia Juvenile Court should not have waived jurisdiction of a sixteen-year-old boy charged with housebreaking, robbery, and rape and remanded the case for a full investigation of whether the waiver was appropriate. They also directed vacation of the conviction if the waiver was found inappropriate.[71]

While not accepting "the invitation to rule that constitutional guaranties which would be applicable to adults . . . must be applied in juvenile court proceedings concerned with allegations of law violation," the majority opinion said: "There is evidence, in fact that there may be grounds for concern that the child receives the worst of both worlds: that he gets neither the protections accorded to adults nor the solicitous care and regenerative treatment postulated for children."[72]

The majority opinion indicated the need for improvement and criticized both the district court and the court of appeals for failure to "review" the case adequately. Justices Stewart, Black, Harlan, and White dissented, saying that the case should be remanded to the court of appeals for reconsideration in the light of subsequent decisions.[73]

Following the Kent case last mentioned came the Miranda case, so that when the Court was called upon to review the conviction of fifteen-year-old Gerald Gault for making lewd telephone calls and his sentence by an Arizona juvenile court judge to the State Industrial School as a juvenile delinquent,

[69] Ibid., 455–56.
[70] New York Times, December 14, 1967.
[71] Kent v. United States, 383 U.S. 541 (1966).
[72] Ibid., 556.
[73] Ibid., 568.

the majority, in a manner of speaking, was loaded for bear. In an opinion of fifty-eight pages, Justice Fortas, writing for five members of the Court, abandoned the restraint he exercised in the Kent case and held that in juvenile court proceedings, due process required adequate written notice to the child and his parents, the right to counsel, to be appointed, if necessary, and the constitutional privileges of criminal trials against self-incrimination, respecting admissions and confessions and the rights of confrontation and cross-examination of witnesses.[74]

Justice Black, concurring, said that he would have preferred not to "pass on all these issues until they are more squarely presented. But since," he added, "the majority of the Court chooses to decide all these questions, I must either do the same or leave my views unexpressed."[75] Whereupon, in pursuance of his reiterated view, he said that "the Constitution requires that he [Gault] be tried in accordance with the guarantees of all the provisions of the Bill of Rights made applicable to the States by the Fourteenth Amendment."[76]

Justice White, concurring, joined the Court's opinion but took exception to the Court's Fifth Amendment conclusion, saying: "I have previously recorded my views with respect to what I have deemed unsound applications of the Fifth Amendment."[77]

Justice Harlan concurred in part and dissented in part, adhering to his views that it was the requirements of the due process clause of the Fourteenth Amendment, not the provisions of the Bill of Rights that should prevail and that

> measured by these criteria, only three procedural requirements should . . . now be deemed required of state juvenile courts. . . . first, timely notice to parents and children . . . second, unequivocal and timely notice must be given that counsel may appear . . . and third, the court must maintain a written record, or its equivalent, adequate to permit effective review on appeal.[78]

The high court's insistence on affording the opportunity to obtain counsel has produced in lower judicial regions ripples, like those of a stone cast into the middle of a lake. This is so often the case when lower court judges find a penumbra of permissiveness about high court opinions. These Supreme Court liberal departures from previous rulings become assumed mandates for liberal lower court judges to further liberalization. Thus a federal district judge, newly appointed in the Southern District of New York, enjoined school officials

[74] In re Gault, 387 U.S. 1 (1967).
[75] Ibid., 60.
[76] Ibid., 61.
[77] Ibid., 65.
[78] Ibid., 72.

377

from holding a "guidance conference" to determine whether a principal's suspension of a student should stand, unless the latter was represented by counsel. The circuit court properly reversed the lower court decision and dismissed the student's complaint,[79] and the Supreme Court thereafter denied certiorari.

Another New York civil court judge followed suit in holding that a high school student charged with cheating could not have Regents privileges revoked without a hearing with the aid of counsel.[80]

Then an Illinois court held that to prove a juvenile charged with murder delinquent, in addition to the requirements of the Gault decision, the prosecution would have to prove the crime by criminal standards, *i.e.*, beyond a reasonable doubt.[81] A District of Columbia judge differed.[82]

Previously, a less liberally activated Court had held that witnesses called to give testimony at a fire marshal's investigation under an Ohio statute had no constitutional right under the due process clause of the Fourteenth Amendment to the assistance of counsel.[83] Justice Reed wrote for three members of the Court, while Justices Harlan and Frankfurter concurred. Justices Black, Douglas, Brennan, and the Chief Justice, who came to dominate the later Court, dissented.

Conformably, conducting an "ambulance chasing" investigation, a judge presiding at a special term excluded lawyers for witnesses from the hearing room, although he instructed witnesses that he would permit them to consult counsel outside the room when they so requested. Two private investigators refused to answer questions in the absence of counsel and were held in contempt. Five members of the Court affirmed, holding due process was not violated.[84] Justices Brennan, Douglas, and Black dissented, as they had in the previous case.

In cases decided during the 1966 term, the Court held that a defendant charged as a sex offender was entitled, under the due process clause, to procedure common to criminal trials,[85] including counsel, distinguishing a previous case.[86]

The parting words of the 1966 term on the subject of crime were delivered after two bank employees observed a lineup of the defendant, accused of robbing the bank, and five or six others, in which those in the lineup were required, like the robber, to wear strips of tape on their faces and to say, "Put the

79 Madera v. Board of Education, 267 F. Supp. 356 (1967); rev'd 386 F. 2d 778 (1967).
80 *In re* Goldwyn v. Allen, 54 Misc. 2d (N.Y.) 94 (1967).
81 *In re* Urbasek, 232 N.E.2d 716 (1967).
82 *In re* Wylie, 231 A. 81 (1967).
83 *In re* Groban, 352 U.S. 330 (1957).
84 Anonymous v. Baker, 360 U.S. 287 (1959).
85 Specht v. Patterson, 386 U.S. 605 (1967).
86 Williams v. New York, 337 U.S. 241 (1949).

money in the bag." Justice Brennan delivered the opinion of the Court, for five members. He remanded the case for a further hearing, holding that (1) the defendant's Fifth Amendment privilege was not violated by the lineup; (2) the Court must determine whether counsel's presence was necessary at any pretrial confrontation; (3) the Sixth Amendment does not afford defendant the right to counsel at analyses of his fingerprints, blood sample, clothing, hair and other identification; (4) under the Sixth Amendment the defendant was entitled to have counsel at the lineup; and (5) the courtroom identification was proper if based on observation other than at the lineup.

Justice Black concurred in items 2, 3, and 4 and dissented in 1 and 5. Justice White, joined by Justices Harlan and Stewart, concurred in 1 and 3, but dissented in 2, 4, and 5. Justice Fortas, joined by the Chief Justice and Justice Douglas, dissented from 1, holding that the defendant's Fifth Amendment rights had been violated by requiring him to utter the words spoken by the robber.[87]

In a companion case, in which the robber had used a handwritten note, the police took writing examples from the defendant, seized photographs without a warrant to do so, and had him appear in a lineup without notice to his appointed counsel.[88] Writing for five members of the Court, Justice Brennan held that (1) taking of handwriting samples did not violate the accused's Fifth or Sixth Amendment rights; (2) admission of an accomplice's pretrial statement was harmless error, as found by the California court; (3) factual data in the record did not permit the Court to pass upon the claims of improper seizure; but (4) the denial of counsel at the lineup made inadmissible identifications then or thereafter made, since the latter were not free from the lineup taint.

Justice Douglas and the Chief Justice joined the Court's opinion except on item 3. Justice Black, concurring in part, said that the accused's Fifth and Sixth Amendment privileges were violated by taking his handwriting sample without the presence of counsel and by requiring him to participate in the lineup, but that the identifications in court were admissible. Justice Douglas added that he would reverse and remand for a new trial on the search and seizure claim. Justice White, joined by Justices Harlan and Stewart, concurred in items 1, 2, and 3, but dissented from 4; while Justice Fortas, joined by the Chief Justice, concurring in part, dissented on the ground that the accused was entitled to have counsel in connection with the handwriting sample.

The "Crime Bill" enacted by Congress following the assassination of Senator Robert F. Kennedy vetoed the Court's requirement that a suspect's identi-

[87] United States v. Wade, 388 U.S. 218 (1967).
[88] Gilbert v. California, 388 U.S. 263 (1967).

fication fell in the absence of recognition of his right to have counsel present at a lineup.

In a later case the defendant "looked to the foregoing lineup decisions in which this Court first departed from the rule that the manner of an extra-judicial identification affects only the weight, not the admissibility, of identification testimony at trial. The rationale of those cases was that an accused is entitled to counsel at any 'critical stage of the prosecution,' and that a post-indictment lineup is such a critical stage."[89]

However, the defendant did not plead lack of counsel but that the identification procedure was unduly prejudicial in that the police showed only his picture, and not that of others, to the prospective witnesses. The Court expressed its unwillingness to declare that practice constitutionally impermissible and said each case must rest on its own facts.[90]

All the foregoing testifies not only to a splintered court but also to the fact that Gilbert and Sullivan were right when they said a policeman's lot was not a happy one.

[89] Simmons v. United States, 390 U.S. 377, 382–83 (1968); *see also* Biggers v. Tennessee, 390 U.S. 404 (1968).
[90] *Ibid.*, 384.

CHAPTER XX

Crime and the Criminal Law—2

EXCESSIVE PUBLICITY HAS SERVED to vitiate convictions. An outstanding example was the voiding of the conviction of Dr. Samuel Sheppard, whose trial on a charge of wife murder attracted nation-wide attention. Convicted in 1954, with the Court denying certiorari in 1956, Dr. Sheppard served ten years in jail before a differently constituted Court held that he had not had a fair trial because of the attendant and excessive publicity.[1] The Court found that the trial judge had failed to "protect Sheppard sufficiently from the massive, pervasive and prejudicial publicity that attended his prosecution . . . consistent with the Due Process Clause of the Fourteenth Amendment."[2] Upon a retrial Sheppard was acquitted.

Another noted case, which brought television to the Court, was that involving the once high-flying and the later bankrupt financier, Billie Sol Estes. Over the dissent of Justices Stewart, Black, Brennan, and White, in an opinion by Justice Clark, the Court held that the televising, over defendant's objection, of the courtroom proceedings of his criminal trial, in which there was widespread public interest, was inherently invalid as infringing the fundamental right to a fair trial guaranteed by the due process clause of the Fourteenth Amendment.[3] The opinion of Justice Clark stated:

> The free press has been a mighty catalyst in awakening public interest in governmental affairs . . . and generally informing the citizenry of public events and occurrences, including court proceedings. While maximum freedom must be allowed the press in carrying on this important function in a democratic society its exercise must necessarily be subject to the maintenance of absolute fairness in the judicial process. . . .[4]
>
> . . . the chief function of our judicial machinery is to ascertain the truth. The use of television, however, cannot be said to contribute materially to this objec-

[1] Sheppard v. Maxwell, 384 U.S. 333 (1966).
[2] *Ibid.,* 335.
[3] Estes v. Texas, 381 U.S. 532 (1965).
[4] *Ibid.,* 439.

tive. Rather its use amounts to the injection of an irrelevant factor into court proceedings. . . .[5]

The Chief Justice wrote, concurring, with the support of Justices Douglas and Goldberg:

I believe that it violates the Sixth Amendment for federal courts and the Fourteenth Amendment for state courts to allow criminal trials to be televised. . . .
. . . the criminal trial has one well-defined purpose—to provide a fair and reliable determination of guilt. . . . How much more harmful is a procedure which not only offers the temptation to judges to use the bench as a vehicle for their own ends, but offers the same temptation to every participant in the trial, be he defense counsel, prosecutor, witness or juror. . . .[6]
. . . television is one of the great inventions of all time and can perform a large and useful role in society. But the television camera, like other technological innovations, is not entitled to pervade the lives of everyone in disregard of constitutionally protected rights. The television industry, like other institutions, has a proper area of activities and limitations beyond which it cannot go with its cameras. That area does not extend into an American courtroom. On entering that hallowed sanctuary, where the lives, liberty and property of people are in jeopardy, television representatives have only the rights of the general public, namely, to be present, to observe the proceedings, and thereafter, if they choose, to report them.[7]

Justice Harlan, also concurring, wrote:

No constitutional provision guarantees a right to televise trials. The "public trial" guarantee of the Sixth Amendment . . . certainly does not require that television be admitted to the courtroom. . . . Essentially, the public-trial guarantee embodies a view of human nature, true as a general rule, that judges, lawyers, witnesses, and jurors will perform their respective functions more responsibly in an open court than in secret proceedings. . . . A fair trial is the objective, and "public trial" is an institutional safeguard for attaining it. . . .[8]

In dissent, Justice Stewart wrote:

. . . I think that the introduction of television into a courtroom is, at least in the present state of the art, an extremely unwise policy. It invites many constitutional risks, and it detracts from the inherent dignity of a courtroom. But I am unable to escalate this personal view into a *per se* constitutional rule. And I am unable to find, on the specific record of the case, that the circumstances

[5] *Ibid.*, 544.
[6] *Ibid.*, 565.
[7] *Ibid.*, 585–86.
[8] *Ibid.*, 588.

attending the limited televising of the petitioner's trial, resulted in the denial of any right guaranteed to him by the United States Constitution....[9]

... as the Court rightly says, the problem before us is not one of choosing between the conflicting guidelines reflected in ... *Canons of Judicial Ethics*. It is a problem rooted in the Due Process Clause....[10]

... we do not deal here with mob domination of a courtroom, with a kangaroo trial, with a prejudiced judge or jury inflamed with bias....the sole question...concerns only the regulated presence of television...at the trial.[11]

... In the courtroom itself, there is nothing to show that the trial proceeded in any way other than it would have proceeded if cameras and television had not been present...

... this was not a trial where the judge was harassed or confused or lacking in command of the proceedings....[12]

What ultimately emerges...is one bald question—whether the Fourteenth Amendment...prohibits all television cameras from a state courtroom whenever a criminal trial is in progress....I can find no such prohibition.[13]

Justice White, dissenting, with the support of Justice Brennan, wrote:

I agree with Mr. Justice Stewart that a finding of constitutional prejudice on this record entails erecting a flat ban on the use of cameras in the courtroom and believe that it is premature to promulgate such a broad constitutional principle at the present time....[14]

... our experience is inadequate and our judgment correspondingly infirm.[15]

And Justice Brennan declared:

I write merely to emphasize that only four of the five Justices voting to reverse rest on the proposition that televised criminal trials are constitutionally infirm, whatever the circumstances. Although the opinion announced by my Brother Clark purports to be an "opinion of the Court," my Brother Harlan subscribes to a significantly less sweeping proposition. He states:

"The Estes trial was a heavily publicized and highly sensational affair. I therefore put aside all other types of cases.... The resolution of those further questions should await an appropriate case; the Court should proceed only step by step in this unplowed field. The opinion of the Court necessarily goes no farther, for only the four members of the majority who unreservedly join the Court's opinion would resolve those questions now."...

[9] *Ibid.*, 601–602.
[10] *Ibid.*, 603.
[11] *Ibid.*, 611.
[12] *Ibid.*, 613.
[13] *Ibid.*, 614.
[14] *Ibid.*, 615.
[15] *Ibid.*, 616.

Thus today's decision is *not* a blanket constitutional prohibition against the televising of state criminal trials.[16]

During the 1962 term the Court reversed the conviction of a defendant charged with murder who had been denied a change of venue after a motion picture film with a sound track had been made of an interview in the jail between defendant and the sheriff, in the course of which the defendant had confessed the killing, and the interview had been broadcast over the local television station.[17]

Justice Clark, supported by Justice Harlan, dissented. He said that defendant's contention that he did not have counsel present at the interview with the sheriff was answered by previous cases. He also held that the three jurors who testified to having seen the film said they would not be influenced by it and that the defendant had not shown the contrary.

The consequence of the high court's attitude concerning prejudicial pretrial and trial publicity has been to cause lower court judges to make stringent rules respecting press coverage and district attorneys to restrict their press releases. A panel of the American Bar Association's advisory committee on fair trial and free press, headed by Justice Paul C. Reardon of the Supreme Judicial Court of Massachusetts, recommended new rules of conduct for lawyers and prosecutors designed to limit the release of crime news to news media, in an effort to lessen publicity that might make it more difficult for defendants to obtain fair trials. The rules were assailed as "a revolutionary reversal of our free press traditions" by newspaper editors and district attorneys, whereupon the association appointed a new committee to consider the matter.[18]

In its effort to see that defendants get a fair trial, as assured by the due process clause of the Fourteenth Amendment and the Sixth Amendment, the Court has found a variety of other reasons for reversing convictions.

Three of the five cases concerning criminal procedure which, on a single day, overruled prior decisions, involved the right of trial by jury assured by the Sixth Amendment. The first,[19] vacated the conviction for battery of a Negro boy, based on the testimony of white boys that he had "slapped" one of them; the Negro boys present testified that the defendant "had merely touched" the complainant. The trial judge found the defendant guilty beyond a reasonable doubt and sentenced him to serve sixty days in prison and pay a fine of $150.

The Court, over the dissents of Justices Harlan and Stewart, finding the Louisiana statute prescribing a penalty for battery of as much as two years,

---

16 *Ibid.*, 617.
17 Rideau v. Louisiana, 373 U.S. 723 (1963).
18 *New York Times,* August 5, 1967; February 22, 1968; March 15 and 29, 1968.
19 Duncan v. Louisiana, 391 U.S. 145 (1968).

held, that while "there is a category of petty crimes or offenses which is not subject to the Sixth Amendment jury trial provision,"[20] as crimes carrying penalties up to six months,[21] "a crime punishable by two years in prison is . . . a serious crime and not a petty offense."[22]

The Court distinguished prior cases,[23] saying that in Maxwell, which had held that no provision of the Bill of Rights applied to the states—"a position long since repudiated"—the Court had permitted a jury of fewer than twelve, but that in no prior case had there been "no jury at all . . . provided."[24]

Justices Black and Douglas concurred, the former writing to lock horns with Justice Harlan, joined by Justice Stewart, dissenting, respecting his (Justice Black's) dissent in the prior Adamson case, in which he had maintained that the Fourteenth Amendment made the Bill of Rights applicable to the states. Once more, Justice Black dwelled on his Fourteenth Amendment successes, i.e., "the right against compelled self-incrimination, the right to counsel, the right to compulsory process for witnesses, the right to confront witnesses, the right to a speedy and public trial, and the right to be free from unreasonable searches and seizures."[25]

Justice Harlan characterized the Court's approach to this case as "an uneasy and illogical compromise among the views of various Justices on how the Due Process Clause should be interpreted. . . .[26] With all respect," he said, "the Court's approach and its reading of history are altogether topsy-turvy."[27] He concluded: "In sum, there is a wide range of views on the desirability of trial by jury, and on the ways to make it most effective when it is used; there is also considerable variation from State to State in local conditions such as the size of the criminal case load, the ease or difficulty of summoning jurors, and other trial conditions bearing on fairness."[28]

A June 1, 1968, article in *The New York Times* promptly attested the validity of some of Justice Harlan's rhetoric when it said:

When does a crime stop being petty and become serious?

The question is being asked eagerly by defense lawyers, cautiously by prosecutors and apprehensively by judges. The answer could cost New York City millions of dollars for several new courthouses, thousands of additional

[20] *Ibid.*, 159.

[21] *Ibid.*, citing Cheff v. Schnackenberg, 384 U.S. 373 (1966).

[22] *Ibid.*, 162.

[23] Maxwell v. Dow, 176 U.S. 581 (1900); Palko v. Connecticut, 302 U.S. 319 (1937); Snyder v. Massachusetts, 201 U.S. 97 (1934).

[24] Duncan v. Louisiana, 391 U.S. 145, 155 (1968).

[25] *Ibid.*, 164.

[26] *Ibid.*, 172.

[27] *Ibid.*, 173.

[28] *Ibid.*, 193.

jurors, dozens more judges, assistant district attorneys, court clerks and stenographers—and create chaos in court in the process. . . .

In New York City, people accused of felonies—all of which carry sentences of a year or more—receive a trial by jury.

But those accused of class "A" misdemeanors do not. . . . These include such crimes as assault in the third degree, petty larceny, possession of narcotics, possession of stolen property or gambling. All of them carry sentences of up to a year's imprisonment, which exceeds the Federal guide line. . . .

District Attorney Frank S. Hogan of New York County . . . wrote that . . . "the prospect of cramming jury trials into these facilities is little short of a nightmare."

The second 1968 case of the trilogy involving trial by jury involved a conviction for criminal contempt, followed by a sentence of a two-year prison term.[29] Justice White, writing for the Court, over the dissent of Justices Harlan and Stewart, said:

By deciding to treat criminal contempt like other crimes insofar as the right to jury trial is concerned, we similarly place it under the rule that petty crimes need not be tried to [sic] a jury.[30]

Under Illinois law no maximum punishment is provided for convictions for criminal contempt. . . . In Duncan we have said that we need not settle "the exact location of the line between petty offenses and serious crimes" but that "a crime punishable by two years in prison is . . . a serious crime."[31]

Thus, in vacating the conviction, the Court overruled prior cases.[32]

Justice Harlan wrote briefly in dissent, saying:

The Court now . . . imposes on the States a related rule that, as recently as Cheff v. Schnackenberg, the Court declined to find in the Bill of Rights. That the words of Mr. Justice Holmes inveighing against a century of "unconstitutional assumption of (state) powers by the courts of the United States," in derogation of the central premise of the Constitution, should be invoked to support the Court's action here can only be put down to the vagaries of the times.[33]

The third of these three decisions also involved a conviction for criminal contempt for which the Court imposed the maximum authorized sentence, 10 days in jail and a fine of $50.[34] Since the sentence authorized was less than

29 Bloom v. Illinois, 391 U.S. 194 (1968).

30 Ibid., 210.

31 Ibid., 211.

32 Ibid., 196n., and cases there collected, including Green v. United States, 356 U.S. 165 (1958).

33 Ibid., 215.

34 Dyke v. Taylor Implement Co., 391 U.S. 216 (1968).

six months, Justice White, citing the previous decision, held that there was no constitutional right to a jury trial.[35]

However, Justice Black dissented, saying, "I am not as sure as the Court seems to be that this classification should be used to deprive a criminal defendant of a jury trial. . . . The word 'petty' has no exact meaning, and until it is given a better definition than that which the Court gives it today, I do not desire to condemn the right of trial by jury to such an uncertain fate."[36]

In one case that came to the Court, two deputy sheriffs, who were the principal prosecution witnesses, were put in custody of the jury and their association continued for three days. The defendant was convicted of murder. The state court affirmed, though disapproving the practice, and said no prejudice had been shown. The Supreme Court reversed eight to one, Clark dissenting, holding that this deprived petitioner of the right to trial by an impartial jury which the due process clause of the Fourteenth Amendment required.[37]

Justice Stewart said a three-day association could not but foster the jurors' confidence in those who were their official guardians through the entire period of the trial. And Turner's fate depended upon how much confidence the jury placed in those two witnesses.[38] Justice Clark dissented on the grounds stated by the state court, i.e., that no prejudice to the defendant had been shown.

In a per curiam opinion, over the dissent of Justices Clark and Harlan, the Court reversed a conviction on one count of an indictment upon the ground that when the jury sent a note to the trial judge advising that it was unable to arrive at a verdict "on both counts because of insufficient evidence," the judge told the jury that it had to reach a decision. The majority construed this as coercion.[39]

Later, during the 1966 term, the Court reversed a conviction for second degree murder because it appeared that a court bailiff "assigned to shepherd the sequestered jury which sat for eight days, stated to one of the jurors in the presence of others while the jury was out walking on a public sidewalk: 'Oh that wicked fellow [petitioner], he is guilty'; and on another occasion said to another juror under similar circumstances, 'If there is anything wrong [in finding petitioner guilty] the Supreme Court will correct it.' Both statements were overheard by at least one regular juror or an alternate."[40] The per curiam opinion cited the Turner case last mentioned.

Justice Harlan dissented, reciting the background of the proceeding. It

[35] *Ibid.,* 219–20.
[36] *Ibid.,* 223.
[37] Turner v. Louisiana, 379 U.S. 466 (1965).
[38] *Ibid.,* 474.
[39] Jenkins v. United States, 380 U.S. 445 (1965).
[40] Parker v. Gladden, 385 U.S. 363, 364 (1966).

appeared that two years after his conviction, the defendant's wife acquired a jury list and invited two regular jurors and an alternate who had been most sympathetic to her husband to her house to discuss the case. Aside from his unwillingness to "accede to the view that the Sixth Amendment is directly applicable to the States through the Fourteenth,"[41] Justice Harlan found the occurrences "inconsequential . . . in light of the eight-day trial and twenty-six hour jury deliberation."[42] He added: "The potentialities of today's decision may go far beyond what, I am sure, the Court intends. Certainly the Court does not wish to encourage convicted felons to 'intimidate, beset and harass' . . . a discharged jury in an effort to establish possible grounds for a new trial. Our courts have always been alert to protect the sanctity of the jury process."[43]

Chief Justice Warren referred to the preceding decision and the Turner case it mentioned in concurring in an opinion written by Justice Douglas, for six members of the Court, over the dissent of Justices Harlan, Black and White. He held that in a Texas trial under its recidivist statute, it was reversible error to permit the jury to be informed of prior convictions in cases in which the defendant had not been represented by counsel, even though the Court had instructed the jury to disregard the testimony concerning the prior convictions but without giving "the jurors . . . the slightest clue as to why matters which consumed so much time at trial were suddenly being removed from their consideration."[44] The dissenters relied on the previous Spencer case,[45] which had approved the Texas practice of introducing proof of prior convictions in a recidivist trial, to which decision Chief Justice Warren and others voting to reverse in the instant case had taken violent exception.

A 1967 per curiam decision reversed a conviction, holding that the arbitrary revocation of bail and remission of a defendant to custody in a jail forty miles distant from the courtroom during defendant's trial constituted "an unwarranted burden upon defendant and his counsel in the conduct of the case."[46]

Before the Malloy case made the Fifth Amendment applicable to the states, a defendant, convicted of robbery in a state court, after having been acquitted of the same charge in a federal court, maintained he had been placed in double jeopardy. Five members of the Court held that the double jeopardy provision of the Fifth Amendment was not applicable to the states

41 *Ibid.,* 366–67.
42 *Ibid.,* 368.
43 *Ibid.,* 369.
44 Burgett v. Texas, 389 U.S. 109, 119 (1967).
45 Spencer v. Texas, 385 U.S. 554 (1967); *see also* Wilson v. Wiman, 390 U.S. 1042 (1968).
46 Bitter v. United States, 389 U.S. 15, 17 (1967).

and affirmed the conviction.[47] Justices Black, Douglas, and the Chief Justice dissented, contending that the Fifth Amendment, of itself and through the Fourteenth, applied. Justice Brennan dissented, maintaining that the Fifth Amendment applied because of the co-operation in the state court prosecution of federal officers.

In another case, after conviction of a conspiracy to dynamite facilities of a telephone company in violation of an Illinois statute, defendants were convicted in the federal district court of Mississippi for violating a federal statute, on the same state of facts. Six members of the Court overruled their double jeopardy plea under the Fifth Amendment.[48] Justices Black and Douglas and the Chief Justice dissented.

In a previous case seven members of the Court had held that a witness granted immunity by a state against state prosecution could be compelled to testify in a state proceeding though he might be liable to federal prosecution.[49] The Chief Justice and Justices Black and Douglas had dissented, voting to remand the petitioner's contempt conviction back to the state court for further consideration.

Thereafter the Court upheld contempt convictions of witnesses who refused to testify, claiming their privilege under the Fifth Amendment, despite a grant of statutory immunity from state prosecution. Following the last-mentioned Knapp decision, Justices Black and Douglas and the Chief Justice dissented,[50] maintaining that evidence of federal collaboration in the state proceedings justified the exercise of the Fifth Amendment privilege and that the rule in a previous case[51] permitting use in a federal prosecution of testimony compelled in state proceedings should be overruled.

In another case five members of the Court held that a defendant was not subjected to double jeopardy when given a second trial, after the first trial judge declared a mistrial of his own motion without approval or objection by defendant's counsel.[52] The Chief Justice and Justices Black, Douglas, and Brennan dissented. Justice Warren, writing in dissent, said that the double jeopardy clause must be strictly enforced.

A defendant convicted of robbing a bank just missed obtaining absolution when Justice Stewart failed to join a four-man minority consisting of the Chief Justice and Justices Black, Douglas, and Brennan. The bank robber contended, among other things, that he had not been afforded an opportunity to speak in his own behalf before sentence was pronounced. All the judges

[47] Bartkus v. Illinois, 359 U.S. 121 (1959).
[48] Abbate v. United States, 359 U.S. 187 (1959).
[49] Knapp v. Schweitzer, 357 U.S. 371 (1958).
[50] Mills v. Louisiana, 360 U.S. 230 (1959).
[51] Feldman v. United States, 322 U.S. 487 (1944).
[52] Gori v. United States, 367 U.S. 364 (1961).

agreed that the rule required that a defendant should have such an opportunity. However, four judges agreed that the defendant had not shown he was denied such an opportunity, while the Chief Justice and Justices Black, Douglas, and Brennan held the contrary. However, Justice Stewart did not find the rule inflexible and voted to affirm.[53]

Justice Frankfurter, writing for affirmance, said:

> ... we do not read the record before us to have denied the defendant the opportunity to which Rule 32a entitled him. The single pertinent sentence— the trial judge's question "Did you want to say something?" may well have been directed to the defendant and not to his counsel. A record, certainly this record, unlike a play, is unaccompanied with stage directions which may tell the significant case of the eye or the nod of the head. ... the defendant has raised this claim seven years after the occurrence. ... Hereafter trial judges should leave no room for doubt that the defendant has been issued a personal invitation to speak prior to sentencing.[54]

Justice Black quoted Justice Frankfurter, who said: "The most persuasive counsel may not be able to speak for a defendant as the defendant might, with halting eloquence, speak for himself."[55]

Under the common law rule retained by Georgia, a defendant in a criminal case was incompetent to testify under oath in his own behalf at his trial but could make an unsworn statement which was not treated as evidence. Under those circumstances the Court held that due process was violated by the refusal of the trial judge to permit defendant's counsel to question him in order to elicit his unsworn statement.[56] Justices Frankfurter and Clark would have had the Court hold the incompetency statute invalid.

In its insistence upon granting a defendant a fair trial, the Court held, during the 1956 term, in an opinion by Justice Brennan, that a defendant, an officer of a labor union charged with falsely swearing concerning Communist affiliations, was entitled to inspect reports made to the FBI by two government witnesses regarding events and activities to which they had testified at the trial.[57] He cited a prior case[58] as holding that "for production purposes, it need only appear that the evidence is relevant, competent, and outside of any exclusionary rule."

Justice Brennan held that

[53] Green v. United States, 365 U.S. 301 (1961).
[54] Ibid., 304–305.
[55] Ibid., 311.
[56] Ferguson v. Georgia, 365 U.S. 570 (1961).
[57] Jencks v. United States, 353 U.S. 657 (1957).
[58] Gordon v. United States, 344 U.S. 414, 420 (1953).

the defense must initially be entitled to see them [the reports] to determine what use may be made of them. Justice requires no less.

The practice of producing government documents to the trial judge for his determination of relevancy and materiality without hearing the accused, is disapproved.[59]

Justice Brennan added:

It is unquestionably true that the protection of vital national interests may militate against public disclosure of documents in the Government's possession.

But this Court has noticed the holdings of the Court of Appeals for the Second Circuit that in criminal causes ... "the Government can invoke its evidentiary privileges only at the price of letting the defendant go free" ... it is unconscionable to allow it to undertake prosecution and then invoke its governmental privileges to deprive the accused of anything that might be material to his defense.[60]

Citing a prior case, Justice Brennan added: "The burden is the Government's not to be shifted to the trial judge, to decide whether the public prejudice of allowing the crime to go unpunished is greater than that attendant upon the possible disclosure of state secrets and other confidential information in the Government's possession."[61]

Justice Frankfurter joined the opinion of the Court but agreed with Justices Burton and Harlan, concurring in the result, that the trial judge should determine relevancy as well as the applicability of the privilege claimed by the government. Justice Clark dissented from the ruling that dismissal should follow refusal to produce the records for inspection by the defendant. Justice Whittaker did not participate.

Later, after the Court had remanded a case for further proceedings to determine whether defendant's motion to require the government to produce pretrial statements of a government witness had been erroneously denied in a trial for robbery of a bank,[62] the district court conducted hearings and concluded that the statement should be produced. The court of appeals reversed. A majority of the high court reversed the court of appeals and vacated the judgments of conviction.[63]

Justice Clark, supported by Justices Harlan and Stewart, wrote in dissent:

In this case an FBI agent, John F. Toomey, Jr., conducted a 30-minute interview

[59] Jencks v. United States, 353 U.S. 657, 669 (1957).
[60] Ibid., 670, citing United States v. Reynolds, 345 U.S. 1 (1953).
[61] Ibid., 672, citing Roviero v. United States, 353 U.S. 53, 60–61 (1957).
[62] Campbell v. United States, 365 U.S. 85 (1961).
[63] Campbell v. United States, 373 U.S. 487 (1963).

of Dominic Staula, a witness to the bank robbery involved. The Special Agent asked Staula some questions and while they were being answered jotted down notes. Upon completion of the interview the Special Agent orally recited to Staula the substance of the interview, refreshing his memory from his notes as he did so. He then asked Staula if the recitation was correct and received an affirmative reply. This was at noon. About nine o'clock that night the Special Agent transcribed the report on a dictating machine for subsequent typing, using the notes, as well as his memory, for the dictation. After the report was typed by a secretary, working entirely from the transcription, he checked its accuracy and then destroyed the notes.

The Court holds the "oral recitation" to be a written statement made by said witness.... It reaches this result via a construction reminiscent of the Rube Goldberg cartoons....

The Court thus transmutes the interview report into a written statement made by Staula...and strikes down the conviction because the interview report was not produced at the trial at the request of the defense....[64]

Extension of the statute to include such reports can only result in mischief, permitting a skillful defense lawyer to repudiate and destroy a witness and obstruct the administration of justice.[65]

The right of confrontation guaranteed by the Sixth Amendment through the due process clause of the Fourteenth was held by the Court, in order to ensure a fair trial, to require that a defendant's constitutional right to plead "not guilty" and to have a trial where he could confront and cross-examine adversary witnesses could not be waived by his counsel without his consent.[66]

In a later case, during the 1966 term, Chief Justice Warren, writing for eight members of the Court, said: "We hold that the petitioner in this case was denied his right to have compulsory process for obtaining witnesses in his favor because the State arbitrarily denied him the right to put on the stand a witness who was physically and mentally capable of testifying to events that he had personally observed, and whose testimony would have been relevant and material to the defense."[67]

The facts disclosed that petitioner and Fuller, another boy, had been in front of a house with a shotgun; that one or the other had fired the gun and killed a third boy; that Fuller had been tried and convicted of the crime and sentenced to prison; and that Texas statutes provided that coparticipants in a crime could not testify for one another, for which reason the Court denied petitioner's application to call Fuller as a witness.

Justice Harlan concurred in the result but maintained, as he had previously,

[64] *Ibid.*, 497–98.
[65] *Ibid.*, 502.
[66] Brookhart v. Janis, 384 U.S. 1 (1966).
[67] Washington v. Texas, 388 U.S. 14 (1967).

that the Sixth Amendment was not incorporated by the due process clause of the Fourteenth; that the latter sufficed under the Palko rule.[68]

During the 1966 term the Court found that a crucial element of the circumstantial evidence against a defendant tried and convicted of rape-murder was a pair of underwear shorts, allegedly bearing bloodstains of the defendant's blood type. In subsequent proceedings, chemical analysis revealed that the stains were not blood, but paint, and that the prosecution knew of the paint stains at the time of the trial. Justice Stewart, writing for a unanimous court, reversed the judgment below and remanded the case for further proceedings,[69] following prior cases.[70]

It is to be noted that, at the same term, in another case where there had been a conviction of two boys charged with rape, the Court vacated the judgment and remanded the case for further proceedings when it appeared that the prosecution had suppressed evidence of the girl's unchastity and her contradictory statements which appeared in an unproduced police report.[71] Here, Justices Harlan, Black, Clark, and Stewart dissented.

Following the Court's remand, the two defendants were released on bail, and then, when they were called for retrial, the state dropped the charges against them and they were freed.[72]

That in defining and punishing crime the Court has begun to question earlier definitions of what constitutes crime is made evident by two recent cases. In one, five members of the Court joined in an opinion by Justice Stewart, reversing the conviction of a defendant of the criminal offense of being addicted to the use of narcotics.[73] While recognizing the power of a state to regulate the narcotic drugs traffic within its borders, Justice Stewart found that the California courts had construed the statute as justifying the conviction of an addict without proof that he had used narcotics within the state's jurisdiction. He found also that the statute did not purport to provide or require medical treatment but made the "status" of narcotics addiction a criminal offense. He said:

> It is unlikely that any State at this moment in history would attempt to make it a criminal offense for a person to be mentally ill, or a leper, or to be afflicted with a venereal disease. A State might determine that the general health and welfare require that the victims of these and other human afflictions be dealt with by compulsory treatment, involving quarantine, confinement, or

[68] *Ibid.,* 23 *et seq.*
[69] Miller v. Pate, 386 U.S. 1 (1967).
[70] *Ibid.,* 7, citing Mooney v. Holohan, 294 U.S. 103 (1935); Napue v. Illinois, 360 U.S. 264 (1959); Pyle v. Kansas, 317 U.S. 213 (1942); *cf.* Alcorta v. Texas, 355 U.S. 28 (1957). *See also* dissent in Nash v. Illinois, 389 U.S. 906 (1967).
[71] Giles v. Maryland, 386 U.S. 66 (1967).
[72] *New York Times,* November 1, 1967.
[73] Robinson v. California, 370 U.S. 660 (1962).

393

sequestration. But, in the light of contemporary human knowledge, a law which made a criminal offense of such a disease would doubtless be universally thought to be an infliction of cruel and unusual punishment in violation of the Eighth and Fourteenth Amendments. . . . We cannot but consider the statute before us as of the same category. In this Court counsel for the State recognized that narcotic addiction is an illness. Indeed, it is apparently an illness which may be contracted innocently or involuntarily. . . . Even one day in prison would be a cruel and unusual punishment for the "crime" of having a common cold.[74]

Justice Douglas, concurring, pointed out that, though in sixteenth-century England one prescription for insanity was to beat "the subject 'until he had regained his reason,' "[75] insanity is today treated as a disease. But he said, "Those living in a world of black and white put the addict in the category of those who could, if they would forsake their evil ways,"[76] although "the addict is under compulsions not capable of management without outside help."[77] He maintained that cruel and unusual punishment results not from confinement, but from convicting the addict of a crime."[78]

Justice Harlan, concurring, said that he was not prepared to hold "on the present state of medical knowledge [that] it is completely irrational and hence unconstitutional for a State to conclude that narcotics addiction is something other than an illness, nor that it amounts to cruel and unusual punishment for the State to subject narcotics addicts to its criminal law."[79] However, he held that without proof of use within the State, the defendant was being convicted for having "a bare desire to commit a criminal act."[80]

Justices Clark and White dissented, the former arguing that the statute provided for treatment and not for punishment, the latter maintaining that the jury's verdict involved a finding that the appellant "had frequently used narcotics in the recent past."[81] Justice Frankfurter did not participate.

During the subsequent 1966 term Justice Fortas, dissenting from denial of a writ of certiorari[82] argued that the writ should have been granted to review a conviction under a California statute providing for the conviction of a person "found in any public place under the influence of intoxicating liquor . . . in such a condition that he is unable to exercise care for his own safety or that

74 *Ibid.*, 666–67.
75 *Ibid.*, 668.
76 *Ibid.*, 669–70.
77 *Ibid.*, 671.
78 *Ibid.*, 676.
79 *Ibid.*, 678.
80 *Ibid.*, 679.
81 *Ibid.*, 656.
82 Budd v. California, 385 U.S. 909 (1966).

of others." Citing the previous Robinson case, Justice Fortas maintained that chronic alcoholism, like narcotic addiction, was a disease that should be treated as such and that a criminal conviction therefore involved the infliction of cruel and unusual punishment. Justice Douglas joined in the dissent upon the grounds stated by him in his concurrence in the Robinson case.

Justice Fortas proved consistent when the question of arresting and jailing chronic alcoholics for public drunkenness came to the Court. However, a five-man majority held that such arrest and jailing did not violate the alcoholic's constitutional rights and did not constitute cruel and unusual punishment. Justice Fortas, supported by Justices Douglas, Brennan, and Stewart dissented.[83]

The tendency of the Court to overrule precedents necessarily brought to the fore the issue of retroactivity. That question becomes especially important when, in criminal cases, jailhouse lawyers eagerly await the opportunity to seek writs of certiorari to upset stale convictions.

When Tompkins sued the Erie Railroad, he was proceeding on the basis of a rule which had been accepted for more than a century, but, for him and subsequent suitors, the rule was no more from the date of his adverse decision. But the thousands who had taken advantage of the rule before him retained their advantages and their respective opponents their losses, as Justice Jackson pointed out.

Yet when the high court announces that confession and conviction obtained without affording a defendant the presence of counsel are void, thousands of prison lawyers sharpen their pencils, to prepare applications for writs of certiorari to the Court and have visions of cell doors swinging outward.[84]

Thus, when after so many years the liberals succeeded in persuading Justice Clark to join their cause and hold that the Fourteenth Amendment made the Fourth applicable to the states, Justice Clark began to envisage the possible retroactive consequences of his decision. As a result, when the Court was asked to apply the new Mapp rule retroactively, Justice Clark joined in a majority to hold that it did not apply to convictions which had become final before its rendition.[85] He wrote:

While to some it may seem "academic" it might be helpful to others for us to briefly outline the history and theory of the problem presented.

At common law there was no authority for the proposition that judicial decisions made law only for the future. Blackstone stated the rule that the

---

[83] Powell v. Texas, 392 U.S. 514 (1968).

[84] Indeed, a federal court at Atlanta, Georgia, struck down penitentiary rules that prevented a convicted bank robber from helping fellow inmates prepare legal documents (*New York Times*, November 23, 1967).

[85] Linkletter v. Walker, 381 U.S. 618 (1965).

duty of the Court was not to "pronounce a new law, but to maintain and expound the old one" .... This Court followed that rule in Norton v. Shelby County, 118 U.S. 425 (1886), holding that unconstitutional action "confers no rights; it imposes no duties; it affords no protection; it creates no office; it is, in legal contemplation, as inoperative as though it had never been passed." At 442. The judge rather than being the creator of the law was but its discoverer. ...

On the other hand, Austin maintained that judges do in fact do something more than discover law; they make it interstitially by filling in with judicial interpretation the vague, indefinite, or generic statutory or common-law terms that alone are but the empty crevices of the law. Implicit in such an approach is the admission when a case is overruled that the earlier decision was wrongly decided. However, rather than being erased by the later overruling decision, it is considered as an existing juridical fact until overruled, and intermediate cases finally decided under it are not to be disturbed. ... [86]

... we believe that the Constitution neither prohibits nor requires retrospective effect. ...

Once the premise is accepted ... we must then weigh the merits and demerits in each case by looking to the prior history of the rule in question, its purpose and effect, and whether retrospective operation will further or retard its operation. ... [87]

We believe that the existence of the Wolf doctrine prior to Mapp is "an operative fact and may have consequences which cannot justly be ignored. The past cannot always be erased by a new judicial declaration."—Chicot County Drainage Dist. v. Baxter State Bank. ... The thousands of cases that were finally decided on Wolf cannot be obliterated. ... [88]

To make a rule of Mapp retrospective would tax the administration of justice to the utmost. ... To thus legitimatize such an extraordinary procedural weapon that has no bearing on guilt would seriously disrupt the administration of justice. [89]

Justice Black, dissenting, said:

This different treatment of Miss Mapp and Linkletter points up at once the arbitrary and discriminatory nature of the judicial contrivance utilized here to break the promise of Mapp by keeping all people in jail who are unfortunate enough to have had their unconstitutional convictions affirmed before June 19, 1961. ... [90]

I think those now in prison under convictions resting on the use of uncon-

86 *Ibid.,* 622–24.
87 *Ibid.,* 629.
88 *Ibid.,* 636.
89 *Ibid.,* 637.
90 *Ibid.,* 641.

stitutionally seized evidence should have their convictions set aside and be granted new trials conducted in conformity with the Constitution....[91]

One reason—perhaps a basic one—put forward by the Court for its refusal to give Linkletter the benefit of the search and seizure exclusionary rule is the repeated statement that the purpose of that rule is to deter sheriffs, policemen, and other law officers from making unlawful searches and seizures. The inference I gather from these repeated statements is that the rule is not a right or privilege accorded to defendants charged with crime but is a sort of punishment against officers in order to keep them from depriving people of their constitutional rights. In passing I would say that if that is the sole purpose, reason, object and effect of the rule, the Court's action in adopting it sounds more like lawmaking than construing the Constitution. Compare Mapp v. Ohio, 367 U.S. 643, 661 (concurring opinion). Both the majority and the concurring members of the Body Court seemed to believe they were construing the Constitution. Quite aside from that aspect, however, the undoubted implication of today's opinion that the rule is not a safeguard for defendants but is a mere punishing rod to be applied to law enforcement officers is a rather startling departure from many past opinions, and even from Mapp itself....[92]

If the exclusionary rule has the high place in our constitutional plan . . . what possible valid reason can justify keeping people in jail under convictions obtained by wanton disregard of a constitutional protection.[93]

In a companion case[94] seven members of the Court held, as they had in the prior case, that the Mapp rule would not be retroactive upon cases finally decided preceding the Mapp decision, even though federal agents had participated in the search and seizure. Justices Black and Douglas subscribed to their dissent in the prior case.

Later the Chief Justice must have contemplated the criticism which would follow the holocaust caused by retroactive application of the already criticized Miranda decision, for a week after the decision had been handed down, he delivered an opinion for the Court holding that the Escobedo and Miranda decisions were to be applied prospectively, applicable only to persons whose trials began after June 22, 1964, the date on which Escobedo was decided, and not retroactively. In the cases before the Court, where the Escobedo rule was sought to be applied to Johnson and Cassidy, convicted of murder in the first degree and sentenced to death, their convictions had become final six years before.[95] Justices Clark, Harlan, Stewart, and White concurred, while restating the dissents they had recorded in the Miranda case. Justices Black and

[91] *Ibid.,* 645.
[92] *Ibid.,* 648–49.
[93] *Ibid.,* 650.
[94] Angelet v. Fay, 381 U.S. 654 (1965).
[95] Johnson v. New Jersey, 384 U.S. 719 (1966).

Douglas dissented, maintaining that the petitioners were entitled to "the full protections of the Fifth and Sixth Amendments as this Court has construed them in Escobedo . . . and Miranda . . . for substantially the same reasons stated in their dissenting opinion in Linkletter."[96]

The Chief Justice defended the failure to make Escobedo and Miranda retroactive by saying their application "would seriously disrupt the administration of our criminal laws. It would require the retrial or release of numerous prisoners found guilty by trustworthy evidence in conformity with previously announced constitutional standards. . . .[97] Future defendants will benefit fully from our new standards. . . . while past defendants may still avail themselves of the voluntariness test."[98]

Following the Linkletter case the Court held that it would not apply retroactively the doctrine of a previous case, which held that the self-incrimination privilege of the Fifth Amendment prevented adverse comment on a defendant's failure to take the stand in a state trial despite the state provision permitting it.[99]

Simultaneously, upon the ground that his confession was coerced, the Court reversed the conviction of an impoverished Negro with a third- or fourth-grade education who had escaped from a state prison camp and who had been interrogated repeatedly over a period of sixteen days but had not been advised of his rights until after he had confessed orally to rape and murder, of which he was convicted.[100] The Chief Justice, writing for the Court, said that, while Miranda was not applicable, this was an example of the protection afforded by the voluntariness doctrine, as pointed out in the Johnson case, above.

Justice Black concurred; Justice Clark, with the support of Justice Harlan, dissented. Justice Clark maintained that the defendant had a long criminal record, that "his intelligence was far above that of a fourth grader," that he was not held incommunicado, that he was not "grilled" or questioned unduly; in short, Clark denied that the confession was coerced.

Later, during the 1966 term, the Court held that conviction after comment concerning the defendant's failure to take the stand under the California constitution could not stand in view of the previous case of Griffin v. California,[101] and the Court subsequently remanded one case[102] and twenty-one companion cases on the basis of the holding in the last-mentioned case.

[96] Ibid., 736.
[97] Ibid., 731.
[98] Ibid., 732.
[99] Tehan v. United States, 382 U.S. 406 (1966).
[100] Davis v. North Carolina, 384 U.S. 737 (1966).
[101] Chapman v. California, 386 U.S. 18 (1967).
[102] Hollis v. California, 386 U.S. 262 (1967).

After his rape conviction had been vacated, Miranda applied for a writ of habeas corpus to vacate an earlier robbery conviction, which had resulted in a twenty- to twenty-five-year sentence. Ironically, the state supreme court rejected his petition since the United States Supreme Court had not made the rule of his rape case retroactive.[103]

At the close of the 1967 term the Court held that it would not reverse state convictions for failure to grant jury trials where trials began prior to May 20, 1968, the date of the Court's decisions in Duncan v. Louisiana and Bloom v. Illinois. Justices Douglas and Black dissented.[104]

The Court's disposition to liberalize rules of criminal procedure was evidenced on that date (May 20), when it handed down no less than five decisions that benefited defendants and, in the course of so doing, overruled or distinguished prior decisions. Two such cases involved the right to maintain habeas corpus proceedings in the federal courts. In one[105] the Court held that a state prisoner whose term had expired could still pursue such proceedings instituted while he was in custody, despite a previous ruling to the contrary.[106] Justice Fortas contended that following conviction for a felony, the defendant, though his imprisonment had ceased, still suffer disabilities or burdens flowing from the conviction; hence, he held, the issue was not moot and the federal habeas corpus statute, which required that the applicant be "in custody" was satisfied when the application for the writ was filed, and, once federal jurisdiction attached, it was not defeated by the subsequent release of the prisoner.[107]

Justices Harlan and Stewart, concurring, said that, though they had joined in the per curiam decision which was being overruled, they were "now persuaded that what the Court there decided was wrong."[108] Justice Marshall did not participate.

In the second case, which also involved the writ of habeas corpus,[109] the Chief Justice wrote for a unanimous court, holding that a prisoner in state custody under consecutive sentences could challenge the validity of the sentence he had not yet commenced to serve, by instituting habeas corpus proceedings in the federal courts, again despite a prior ruling to the contrary,[110] which the Court proceeded to overrule.[111]

[103] *New York Times*, December 13, 1967.
[104] DeStefano v. Woods; Carcerano v. Gladden, 392 U.S. 631 (1968).
[105] Carafas v. La Vallee, 391 U.S. 234 (1968).
[106] Parker v. Ellis, 362 U.S. 574 (1960).
[107] Carafas v. La Vallee, 391 U.S. 234, 237–39 (1968).
[108] *Ibid.*, 242.
[109] Peyton v. Rowe, 391 U.S. 54 (1968).
[110] McNally v. Hill, 293 U.S. 131 (1934).
[111] Peyton v. Rowe, 391 U.S. 54, 67 (1968).

CHAPTER XXI

Censorship and Obscenity

IN THE 1920'S THE COURT DID NOT HESITATE to condemn prior restraints upon and censorship of the press even under wartime conditions. Still less have the later Courts had any difficulty in expressing their distaste for attempted prior censorship of motion pictures.

Thus the Vinson court overruled a prior decision[1] in holding that motion pictures were entitled to the protection of the First Amendment and, accordingly, striking down state censorship of a film as "sacrilegious."[2] Justices Reed, Frankfurter, Jackson, and Burton concurred, the last three finding the term "sacrilegious" constitutionally vague.

Thereafter the Court held that the constitutional guarantee of free speech and press was violated by a state's vesting in an official the power to refuse to license the showing of motion pictures found by the official to be "immoral," "harmful," or "tending to corrupt morals."[3] Justices Douglas and Black concurred, maintaining that the government could not establish censorship over motion pictures.

Without dissent, the Court struck down a Texas ordinance permitting a board of censors to deny a license for a picture when the board was of the opinion that it was "of such character as to be prejudicial to the best interests of the people" of the city.[4]

A later case involved a motion picture made from the controversial book by D. H. Lawrence, *Lady Chatterley's Lover*. The New York Court of Appeals upheld the board of regents, which had denied a license for the exhibition of the film on the ground that its subject matter was adultery. Five members of the Court, in an opinion by Justice Stewart, reversed the New York court, holding that the New York statute was invalid under the Fourteenth Amendment incorporation of the First Amendment.[5] Justices Black

[1] Mutual Film Corp. v. Ohio Industrial Comm., 236 U.S. 230 (1915).

[2] Burstyn v. Wilson, 343 U.S. 495 (1952).

[3] Superior Films v. Dept. of Education; Commercial Pictures Corp. v. Regents, 346 U.S. 587 (1954).

[4] Gelling v. Texas, 343 U.S. 960 (1952).

and Douglas concurred as did Justice Frankfurter, holding that the film was not barred by the statute. Justice Clark concurred, finding the statute vague. Justice Harlan also concurred in the result but dissented from the majority finding of unconstitutionality, with the support of Justice Frankfurter.

Justice Stewart concluded that the New York board had barred the picture "because that picture advocates an idea—that adultery under certain circumstances may be proper behavior."[6] He added:

> This argument misconceives what it is that the Constitution protects. Its guarantee is not confined to the expression of ideas that are conventional or shared by a majority. It protects advocacy of the opinion that adultery may sometimes be proper, no less than advocacy of socialism or the single tax. And in the realm of ideas it protects expression which is eloquent no less than that which is unconvincing.[7]

Justice Black said:

> My view is that stated by Mr. Justice Douglas, that prior censorship of moving pictures like prior censorship of newspapers and books, violates the First and Fourteenth Amendments. If despite the Constitution, however, this Nation is to embark on the dangerous road of censorship, my belief is that this Court is about the most inappropriate Supreme Board of Censors that could be found. So far as I know, judges possess no special expertise providing exceptional competency to set standards and to supervise the private morals of the Nation.[8]

Justice Frankfurter added these words:

> As one whose taste in art and literature hardly qualifies him for the avant-garde, I am more than surprised, after viewing the picture, that the New York authorities should have banned *Lady Chatterley's Lover*. To assume that this motion picture would have offended Victorian moral sensibilities is to rely only on the stuffiest of Victorian conventions.[9]

Later five members of the Court held that a municipal ordinance requiring, as a prerequisite of public exhibition, the production of a motion picture at the office of a censor for examination does not, upon its face, violate the freedom of speech guaranteed by the First and Fourteenth amendments.[10]

Justice Clark, writing for the majority, said that he could not agree with

[5] Kingsley Pictures Corp. v. Regents, 360 U.S. 684 (1959).
[6] *Ibid.*, 688.
[7] *Ibid.*, 689.
[8] *Ibid.*, 690.
[9] *Ibid.*, 691.
[10] Times Film Corp. v. Chicago, 365 U.S. 43 (1961).

the petitioner's argument that previous restraint cannot be justified.[11] He added: "Certainly petitioner's broadside attack does not warrant, nor could it justify on the record here, our saying that—aside from any consideration of the other 'exceptional cases' mentioned in our decisions—the State is stripped of all constitutional power to prevent, in the most effective fashion, the utterance of this class of speech." The Chief Justice and Justices Black, Douglas, and Brennan dissented. The Chief Justice said that the "case clearly presents the question of our approval of unlimited censorship of motion pictures before exhibition through a system of administrative licensing."[12]

Justice Douglas said that his "view that censorship is unconstitutional because it is a prior restraint and violative of the First Amendment has been expressed on prior occasions."[13]

Later the Court supplemented its last-mentioned Times Film decision by holding that a statute requiring prior submission of a film to a censor must provide procedural safeguards designed to eliminate the dangers of censorship. In particular, the censor must have the burden of proving that the film is expression unprotected by the Constitution; any restraint prior to judicial review must be limited to preservation of the status quo and for the shortest period compatible with sound judicial procedure and a prompt final judicial determination of obscenity must be assured. For the lack of such safeguards, the Court struck down a Maryland statute.[14] Justices Douglas and Black concurred.

In a per curiam opinion, representing the views of seven justices, the Court followed the last-mentioned case and reversed a decision enjoining defendants from showing a motion picture upon the ground that the ordinance was unconstitutional in that it did not assure that the censor would, within a specific brief period, either issue a license or go to court to restrain a showing of the film, nor did it assure a prompt final judicial decision.[15] Justices Black, Douglas, and Stewart concurred on the basis of the prior Redrup case, which had engendered much controversy.

However, cases involving obscenity in literature have given the Court more trouble. On the last day of the 1956 term the Court handed down decisions in three obscenity cases. Two were considered together.[16] In the Roth case the defendant was convicted of violating a federal statute which provided that obscene, lewd, lascivious, filthy, or indecent material may not be mailed, under criminal penalties. In the Alberts case the defendant was convicted

[11] *Ibid.*, 49.
[12] *Ibid.*, 50–51.
[13] *Ibid.*, 78.
[14] Freedman v. Maryland, 380 U.S. 51 (1965).
[15] Teitel Film Corp. v. Cusack, 390 U.S. 139 (1968).
[16] Roth v. United States; Alberts v. California, 354 U.S. 476 (1957).

under a California statute that proscribed the production or advertising of lewd, obscene, or indecent material.

Justice Brennan wrote for five members of the Court, holding that obscenity was not protected by the First or Fourteenth amendments. He also held that the statutes were not vague and that the federal postal laws did not prevent the states from legislating concerning the mailing of obscene matter. The Chief Justice concurred in the result. Justice Harlan concurred in the Alberts case but dissented respecting Roth on the ground that the regulation of obscenity embodied in the federal statute was beyond federal power. Justices Black and Douglas maintained that the statutes were unconstitutional as violating the First Amendment.

Justice Brennan said:"... sex and obscenity are not synonymous. Obscene material is material which deals with sex in a manner appealing to prurient interest." He quoted with approval from the charge of the trial judge in Roth: " 'The test in each case is the effect of the book, picture or publication considered as a whole, not upon any particular class, but upon all those whom it is likely to reach ... the average person in the community.' "[17]

The Chief Justice said:

The line dividing the salacious or pornographic from literature or science is not straight or unwavering. Present laws depend largely upon the effect that the materials may have upon those who receive them. . . . But there is more to these cases. It is not the book that is on trial; it is the person. The conduct of the defendant is the central issue, not the obscenity of a book or picture. The nature of the materials is, of course, relevant as an attribute of the defendant's conduct, but the materials are thus placed in context from which they draw color and character. A wholly different result might be reached in a different setting. . . .

The defendants in both these cases were engaged in the business of purveying sexual or graphic matter openly advertised to appeal to the erotic interest of their customers. They were plainly engaged in the commercial exploitation of the morbid and shameful craving for materials with prurient effect.[18]

Justice Harlan stated:

I do not understand how the Court can resolve the constitutional problems now before it without making its own independent judgment upon the character of the material upon which these convictions were based.[19]

... the Court compounds confusion when it superimposes on these two statutory definitions a third, drawn from the American Law Institute's Model Code, Tentative Draft No. 6. . . .[20]

[17] *Ibid.*, 487, 490.
[19] *Ibid.*, 498.

[18] *Ibid.*, 495.
[20] *Ibid.*, 499.

...we deal here with an area where knowledge is small, data are insufficient and experts are divided. Since the domain of sexual morality is pre-eminently a matter of state concern, this Court should be slow to interfere with state legislation calculated to protect that morality.[21]

In the Roth case Justice Harlan said that he did not believe that the federal statute affected anything but "hard-core" pornography.

Justice Douglas wrote, with the support of Justice Black:

When we sustain these convictions, we make the legality of a publication turn on the purity of thought which a book or tract instills in the mind of the reader. I do not think we can approve that standard and be faithful to the command of the First Amendment, which by its terms is a restraint on Congress and which by the Fourteenth is a restraint on the States....[22]

...punishment is inflicted for thoughts provoked, not for overt acts nor antisocial conduct. This test cannot be squared with our decisions under the First Amendment.... This issue cannot be avoided by saying that obscenity is not protected by the First Amendment. The question remains, what is the constitutional test of obscenity?

...the arousing of sexual thoughts and desires happens every day in normal life in dozens of ways. Nearly 30 years ago a questionnaire sent to college and normal school women graduates asked what things were most stimulating sexually. Of 409 replies, 9 said "music"; 18 said "pictures"; 29 said "dancing"; 40 said "drama"; 95 said "books"; and 218 said "man." ...[23]

The absence of dependable information on the effect of obscene literature on human conduct should make us wary....[24]

Any test that turns on what is offensive to the community's standards is too loose, too capricious, too destructive of freedom of expression to be squared with the First Amendment. Under that test, juries can censor, suppress, and punish what they don't like, provided the matter relates to "sexual impurity" or has a tendency "to excite lustful thoughts." This is community censorship in one of its worst forms....

Government should be concerned with antisocial conduct, not with utterances.... literature should not be suppressed merely because it offends the moral code of the censor....[25]

I would give the broad sweep of the First Amendment full support. I have the same confidence in the ability of our people to reject noxious literature as I have in their capacity to sort out the true from the false in theology, economics, politics, or any other field.[26]

[21] Ibid., 502.
[22] ibid., 508.
[23] Ibid., 509.
[24] Ibid., 511.
[25] Ibid., 512–13.
[26] Ibid., 514.

On the same day, in the third case, a majority of five upheld a New York statute permitting the municipality to sue to enjoin the sale or distribution of obscene written and printed matter and charging a seller or distributor with knowledge of content once an action had been brought.[27] The Chief Justice dissented, finding the statute imposing an invalid prior restraint. Justice Brennan dissented on the ground that the statute did not award the defendant a jury trial. Justices Black and Douglas dissented on the ground that the provision for an injunction pending a trial constituted censorship and that the procedure violated the First Amendment.

Justice Frankfurter, writing for the majority, relied on the Alberts case just decided. He held that the method of dealing with obscenity was for the state to determine.

Justice Harlan said:

> Unlike the criminal cases decided today, this New York law places the book on trial. There is totally lacking any standard in the statute for judging the book in context. The personal element basic to the criminal laws is entirely absent. . . .
>
> It is the conduct of the individual that should be judged, not the quality of art or literature. To do otherwise is to impose a prior restraint and hence to violate the Constitution. . . .

Justice Douglas declared: "We tread here on First Amendment grounds. And nothing is more devastating to the rights that it guarantees than the power to restrain publication before even a hearing is held. This is prior restraint and censorship at its worst."[28]

The Post Office Department barred from the mails magazines which it found obscene. The magazines consisted "largely of photographs of nude, or near-nude, male models" and gave "the names of each model and photographer, together with the address of the latter." They also "contained a number of advertisements offering nudist photographs for sale." The record indicated that the magazines were composed primarily, if not exclusively, for homosexuals and had no literary, scientific or other merit and would appeal to the "prurient interest" of such sexual deviates. The Court reversed the dismissal of the publisher's complaint seeking to enjoin the Postmaster.[29]

Justice Harlan, joined by Justice Stewart, held that the magazines were not obscene and that proof was lacking that they gave information where obscene matter could be obtained. Justice Brennan, joined by the Chief Justice and Justice Douglas, concurred upon the ground that the statute did not

[27] Kingsley Books v. Brown, 354 U.S. 436 (1957).
[28] *Ibid.*, 446.
[29] Manual Enterprises v. Day, 370 U.S. 478 (1962).

authorize the Postmaster General to exclude matter from the mails on his own determination of obscenity; Justice Black also concurred, while Justice Clark dissented on the ground that the magazines gave information where obscene matter could be obtained and that the Postmaster General had authority to reject such matter.

Justice Harlan said:

These magazines cannot be deemed so offensive on their face as to affront current community standards of decency—a quality that we shall hereafter refer to as "patent offensiveness" or "indecency." Lacking that quality, the magazines cannot be deemed legally "obscene" ....[30]

Obscenity under the federal statute . . . requires proof of two distinct elements: (1) patent offensiveness; and (2) "prurient interest" appeal. Both must conjoin before challenged material can be found "obscene" ....[31]

... neither with respect to the advertisements nor the magazines themselves, do we understand the Government to suggest that the "advertising" provisions of Sec. 1461 are violated if the mailed material merely "gives the leer that promises the customers some obscene pictures" ....[32]

Justice Clark, dissenting, said:

While those in the majority like ancient Gaul are split into three parts, the ultimate holding of the Court today, despite the clear congressional mandate found in Sec. 1461, requires the United States Post Office to be the world's largest disseminator of smut and Grand Informer of the names and places where obscene material may be obtained. The Judicial Officer of the Post Office Department, the District Court, and the Court of Appeals have all found the magazines in issue to be nonmailable on the alternative grounds that they are obscene and that they contain information on where obscene material may be obtained. The Court, however, says that these magazines must go through the mails ....[33]

How one can fail to see the obvious in this record is beyond my comprehension. In the words of Milton: "O dark, dark, dark amid the blaze of noon."[34]

Writing for five members of the Court, Justice Brennan held that a Rhode Island commission practice to notify distributors of books or magazines that the commission had reviewed the literature and found it objectionable for sale, distribution or display to youths under eighteen years of age, and stating that it was the commission's duty to recommend prosecution of purveyors of

30 *Ibid.,* 482.
31 *Ibid.,* 486.
32 *Ibid.,* 491.
33 *Ibid.,* 519.
34 *Ibid.,* 528.

obscenity, constituted intimidation violating the Fourteenth Amendment.[35]

Justice Brennan found this a "system of prior restraints of expression" that "fall far short of the constitutional requirements of governmental regulation of obscenity," a "system of informal censorship" . . . which "violates the Fourteenth Amendment."[36]

Justices Black, Douglas, and Clark concurred, Justice Douglas said, "The evils of unreviewable administrative action of this character are as ancient as dictators."[37]

Justice Clark said: "As I read the opinion of the Court, it does much fine talking about freedom of expression . . . but, as if shearing a hog, comes up with little wool. In short, it creates the proverbial tempest in a teapot over a number of notices sent out by the Commission."[38]

Justice Harlan, dissenting, said:

> This Rhode Island Commission was formed for the laudable purpose of combatting juvenile delinquency. . . .
>
> Rhode Island's approach to the problem is not without respectable support . . . The States should have a wide range of choice in dealing with such problems. . . .
>
> I can find nothing in this record that justifies the view that Rhode Island has attempted to deal with this problem in an irresponsible way. I agree with the Court that the tenor of some of the Commission's letters and reports is subject to serious criticism. . . .[39]
>
> Any affected distributor or publisher wishing to stand his ground may test the Commission's views. . . .[40]
>
> The Constitution requires no more.[41]

Over the dissent of Justice Harlan the Court held, in an opinion by Justice Marshall, with a concurring opinion by Justice Douglas in which Justice Black joined, that a Dallas ordinance which gave a board the power to declare films unsuitable for persons under sixteen years of age was vague and hence unconstitutional. The ordinance provided that if the motion picture was so brutal that it might incite such children to crime or if it depicted nudity and sex in such a way as to encourage sexual promiscuity among the young it might be declared unsuitable.[42]

However, simultaneously, over the dissent of Justices Black, Douglas, and

[35] Bantam Books v. Sullivan, 372 U.S. 58 (1963).
[36] Ibid., 71.
[37] Ibid., 73
[38] Ibid., 74.
[39] Ibid., 76–77.
[40] Ibid., 78.
[41] Ibid., 79.
[42] Interstate Circuit v. Dallas; United Artists Corp. v. Dallas, 390 U.S. 676 (1968).

Fortas, a majority approved a New York statute forbidding the sale to minors under seventeen of "girlie" magazines depicting nudity, sexual excitement, sexual conduct, and sadomasochistic abuse and affirmed the conviction of a newsdealer who sold such magazines to a sixteen-year-old boy,[43] although, under a previous ruling, the Court had said the magazines were not obscene for adults.[44]

Justice Brennan, writing for the Court, doubted that such publications were harmful to children but said that a legislature might find otherwise.[45] Justice Fortas, dissenting, said that the Court had not defined obscenity for children, nor had it found the particular magazines sold obscene.[46]

The Court's confusion respecting obscenity was illustrated when Justice Brennan and Justice Goldberg wrote, reversing a conviction of an Ohio theater manager for showing a French film entitled *The Lovers* upon the ground that the film violated the Ohio antiobscenity statute.[47] Justice Black wrote, concurring, with the support of Justice Douglas, saying that the conviction violated the First Amendment made applicable to the states by the Fourteenth. Justice Stewart concurred, saying the film was not "hard-core pornography." Justice White also concurred. Justice Warren, supported by Justice Clark, dissented, as did Justice Harlan.

Justice Brennan said:

> Application of an obscenity law to suppress a motion picture ... requires ascertainment of the "dim and uncertain line" that often separates obscenity from constitutionally protected expression....[48]
>
> Nor can we understand why the Court's performance of its constitutional and judicial function in this sort of case should be denigrated by such epithets as "censor" or "supercensor" ... Use of an opprobrious label can neither obscure nor impugn the Court's performance of its obligation to test challenged judgments against the guarantee of the First and Fourteenth Amendments and, in doing so, to delineate the scope of constitutionally protected speech....
>
> Material dealing with sex in a manner that advocates ideas ... or that has literary or scientific or artistic value or other form of social importance, may not be branded as obscenity and denied the constitutional protection. Nor may the constitutional status of the material be made to turn on a "weighing" of its social importance against its prurient appeal, for a work cannot be proscribed unless it is "utterly" without social importance....[49]
>
> It is true that local communities throughout the land are in fact diverse,

43 Ginsberg v. New York, 390 U.S. 629 (1968).
44 *Ibid.*, 634, citing Redrup v. New York, 386 U.S. 767 (1967).
45 *Ibid.*, 641.
46 *Ibid.*, 674–75.
47 Jacobellis v. Ohio, 378 U.S. 184 (1964).
48 *Ibid.*, 187.
49 *Ibid.*, 191.

and that in cases such as this one the Court is confronted with the task of reconciling the rights of such communities with the rights of individuals. Communities vary, however, in many respects other than their toleration of alleged obscenity, and such variances have never been considered to require or justify a varying standard for application of the Federal Constitution....[50]

The constitutional status of an alleged obscene work must be determined on the basis of a national standard....[51]

Justice Stewart wrote:

I have reached the conclusion ... that under the First and Fourteenth Amendments criminal laws in this area are constitutionally limited to hard-core pornography. I shall not today attempt further to define the kinds of material I understand to be embraced within that shorthand description; and perhaps I could never succeed in intelligibly doing so. But I know it when I see it, and the motion picture involved in this case is not that.[52]

The Chief Justice, dissenting, wrote:

. . . neither courts nor legislatures have been able to evolve a truly satisfactory definition of obscenity. . . . The obscenity problem . . . is aggravated by the fact that it involves the area of public expression, an area in which a broad range of freedom is vital to our society and is constitutionally protected.

Recently this Court put its hand to the task of defining the term "obscenity" in Roth v. United States. The definition enunciated in that case has generated much legal speculation as well as further judicial interpretation by state and federal courts. It has also been relied upon by legislatures. Yet obscenity cases continue to come to this Court, and it becomes increasingly apparent that we must settle as well as we can the question of what constitutes "obscenity" . . . .

It is my belief that when the Court said in Roth that obscenity is to be defined by reference to "community standards," it meant community standards —not a national standard. . . . I believe that there is no provable "national standard," and perhaps there should be none. At all events, this Court has not been able to enunciate one, and it would be unreasonable to expect local courts to divine one....[53]

... who can define "hard-core pornography" with any greater clarity than "obscenity?"

In my opinion, the use to which various materials are put—not just the words and pictures themselves—must be considered in determining whether or not the materials are obscene. A technical or legal treatise on pornography

[50] Ibid., 194.
[51] Ibid., 195.
[52] Ibid., 197.
[53] Ibid., 199–200.

may well be inoffensive under most circumstances but, at the same time, "obscene" in the extreme when sold or displayed to children....[54]

... I would reiterate my acceptance of the rule of the Roth case: ... I would commit the enforcement of this rule to the appropriate state and federal courts, and I would accept their judgment ... limiting myself to a consideration only of whether there is sufficient evidence in the record upon which a finding of obscenity could be made.... the effective administration of justice require(s) that this Court not establish itself as an ultimate censor, ... making an independent *de novo* judgment on the question of obscenity....

This is the only reasonable way I can see to obviate the necessity of this Court's sitting as the Super Censor of all the obscenity purveyed throughout the Nation.[55]

Justice Harlan remarked in dissent:

The more I see of these obscenity cases the more convinced I become that in permitting the States wide, but not federally unrestricted, scope in this field, while holding the Federal Government with a tight rein, lies the best promise for achieving a sensible accommodation between the public interest sought to be served by obscenity laws ... and protection of genuine rights of free expression.[56]

In passing upon the obscenity of *Memoirs of a Woman of Pleasure (Fanny Hill)* (long read surreptitiously between pages of textbooks by teen-age schoolboys), Justice Brennan, joined by the Chief Justice and Justice Fortas, said that, under the test of a previous case, to be found obscene a book must satisfy three requirements: (1) the dominant theme must appeal to a prurient interest in sex, (2) it must be patently offensive to contemporary community standards, and (3) it must be without redeeming social value. Hence, holding that the first and second standards were satisfied but that the state court had found that book had a modicum of social value, the fact that it had not found that the book was *utterly* without social value, precluded a finding of obscenity and required reversal of the judgment below.[57] Justices Black and Stewart concurred upon the grounds stated in their respective opinions in two cases.[58] Justice Douglas also concurred. Justices Clark and Harlan dissented.

Justice Douglas, saying that the majority had based its decision on the finding that the book had "some minimal literary value," went on to declare:

I do not believe that the Court should decide this case on so disingenuous a

54 *Ibid.*, 201.

55 *Ibid.*, 202–203.

56 *Ibid.*, 203–204.

57 *Memoirs* v. Massachusetts, 383 U.S. 413 (1966).

58 Ginzburg v. United States, 383 U.S. 463 (1966); Mishkin v. New York, 383 U.S. 502 (1966).

basis as this. I base my vote to reverse on my view that the First Amendment does not permit the censorship of expression not brigaded with illegal action. ... The defense ... introduced considerable and impressive testimony to the effect that this was a work of literary, historical, and social importance.

We are judges, not literary experts or historians or philosophers. We are not competent to render an independent judgment as to the worth of this or any other book, except in our capacity as private citizens. I would pair my Brother Clark on *Fanny Hill* with the Universalist minister I quote in the appendix.[59]

Justice Clark considered that

... the public should know of the continuous flow of pornographic material reaching this Court.... *Memoirs of a Woman of Pleasure,* the book involved here, is typical. I have "stomached" past cases for almost ten years without much outcry. Though I am not known to be a purist—or a shrinking violet—this book is too much even for me.[60]

In his dissent Justice Harlan said:

The central development that emerges from the aftermath of Roth v. United States ... is that no stable approach to the obscenity problem has yet been devised by this Court. Two Justices believe that the First and Fourteenth Amendments absolutely protect obscene and non-obscene material alike. Another Justice believes that neither the States nor the Federal Government may suppress any material save for "hard-core pornography" ....[61]

As Roth has been expounded in this case, in Ginzburg ... and Mishkin ... it has undergone significant transformation. The concept of "pandering," ... now emerges as an uncertain gloss ... and the further requisite of "patent offensiveness" has been made explicit.... Given this tangled state of affairs, I feel free to adhere to the principles first set forth in my separate opinion in Roth....

My premise is that in the area of obscenity the Constitution does not bind the States and the Federal Government in precisely the same fashion.[62]

Federal suppression of allegedly obscene matter should, in my view, be constitutionally limited to that often described as "hard-core pornography." ... I would characterize as "hard-core" that prurient material that is patently offensive or whose indecency is self-demonstrating and I would describe it substantially as does Mr. Justice Stewart's opinion in Ginzburg....[63]

State obscenity laws present problems of quite a different order. The vary-

[59] *Memoirs* v. Massachusetts, 383 U.S. 413, 426–27 (1966).
[60] *Ibid.,* 441.
[61] *Ibid.,* 455
[62] *Ibid.,* 456.
[63] *Ibid.,* 457.

ing conditions across the country, the range of views on the need and reasons for curbing obscenity, and the traditions of local self-government in matters of public welfare all favor a more flexible attitude in defining the bounds for the States. . . . The latitude which I believe the States deserve cautions against any federally imposed formula. . . .[64]

I think it more satisfactory to acknowledge that on this record the book has been shown to have some quantum of social value, that it may at the same time be deemed offensive and salacious, and that the State's decision to weigh these elements and to ban this particular work does not exceed constitutional limits.[65]

Justice White thought that

it should be remembered that if the publication and sale of *Fanny Hill* and like books are proscribed, it is not the Constitution that imposes the ban. Censure stems from a legislative act, and legislatures are constitutionally free to embrace such books whenever they wish to do so. But if a State insists on treating *Fanny Hill* as obscene and forbidding its sale, the First Amendment does not prevent it from doing so.[66]

On the same day, by a vote of five to four, the Court affirmed the conviction of Ralph Ginzburg, sentenced to five years for publication of magazines found obscene.[67] Justices Black, Douglas, Harlan, and Stewart dissented. The prosecution charged and the Court found that, while the publications themselves might not be obscene, their production, sale, and publicity would be an aid in determining the question of obscenity.

The Court found that

each of the accused publications was originated or sold as stock in trade of the sordid business of pandering—"the business of purveying textual or graphic matter openly advertised to appeal to the erotic interest of their customers"; [that mailing privileges were sought from the] postmasters of Intercourse and Blue Ball, Pennsylvania . . . that these hamlets were chosen only for the value their names would have in furthering petitioners' efforts to sell their publications on the basis of salacious appeal. . . .[68]

Justice Brennan said:

The "leer of the sensualist" also permeates the advertising for the three publications. The circulars . . . stressed the sexual candor of the respective publi-

---

[64] *Ibid.*, 458.
[65] *Ibid.*, 459.
[66] *Ibid.*, 462.
[67] Ginzburg v. United States, 383 U.S. 463 (1966).
[68] *Ibid.*, 467.

cations and openly boasted that the publishers would take full advantage of what they regarded as an unrestricted license allowed by law in the expression of sex and sexual matters....[69]

This evidence, in our view, was relevant in determining the ultimate question of obscenity and . . . serves to resolve all ambiguity and doubt. The deliberate representation of petitioners' publications as erotically arousing, for example, stimulated the reader to accept them as prurient; he looks for titillation, not for saving intellectual content....[70]

We perceive no threat to First Amendment guarantees in thus holding that in close cases evidence of pandering may be probative with respect to the nature of the material in question and thus satisfy the Roth test.[71]

Justice Black, dissenting, repeated his assertion that the First Amendment prevented the government from putting "any type of burden on speech and expression of ideas of any kind (as distinguished from conduct)."[72]
He said too:

It is obvious that the effect of the Court's decisions in the three obscenity cases handed down today is to make it exceedingly dangerous for people to discuss either orally or in writing anything about sex. Sex is a fact of life. Its pervasive influence is felt throughout the world and it cannot be ignored. Like all other facts of life it can lead to difficulty and trouble and sorrow and pain. But while it may lead to abuses, and has in many instances, no words need be spoken in order for people to know that the subject is one pleasantly interwoven in all human activities and involves the very substance of the creation of life itself. It is a subject which people are bound to consider and discuss whatever laws are passed by any government to try to suppress it.... For myself, I would follow the course which I believe is required by the First Amendment, that is, recognize that sex at least as much as any other aspect of life is so much a part of our society that its discussion should not be made a crime.[73]

In the words of Justice Douglas:

This new exception condemns an advertising technique as old as history. The advertisements of our best magazines are chock-full of thighs, ankles, calves, bosoms, eyes, and hair, to draw the potential buyer's attention to lotions, tires, food, liquor, clothing, autos, and even insurance policies. The sexy advertisement neither adds to nor detracts from the quality of the merchandise being offered for sale. And I do not see how it adds to or detracts one whit from the legality of the book being distributed. A book should stand on its own, irre-

[69] *Ibid.*, 468.
[70] *Ibid.*, 470.
[71] *Ibid.*, 474.
[72] *Ibid.*, 476.
[73] *Ibid.*, 481–82.

spective of the reasons why it was written or the wiles used in selling it. I cannot imagine any promotional effort that would make chapters 7 and 8 of the Song of Solomon any the less or any more worthy of First Amendment protection than does its unostentatious inclusion in the average edition of the Bible.[74]

Justice Harlan said that the Court was adding to the federal statute a pandering supplement; that, in effect, it was writing a new statute other than the one under which the defendants had been tried and that "if there is anything to this new pandering dimension to the mailing statute, the Court should return the case for a new trial."[75]

Justice Stewart maintained that only "hard-core pornography" should be banned and undertook to define it.[76] He said he knew of no statute that made "commercial exploitation" or "pandering" or "titillation" a criminal offense. Nor did he see where the Court got the power to punish Ginzburg for his "sordid business."[77]

Over the dissent of Justices Black, Douglas, and Stewart the Court affirmed a conviction of a bookseller for knowingly publishing and selling obscene literature in violation of the provisions of the New York Penal Law.[78] Justice Brennan, writing for the Court, said that the New York courts had interpreted "obscenity" as "hard-core pornography."[79] Justice Harlan concurred. Justice Stewart disagreed with the New York court's finding that the books were "hard-core pornography."[80]

The aftermath of what one guilty of lese majesty might call "palaver" was that practically nothing was to be found "obscene." So, during the 1966 term obscenity convictions were reversed in three cases[81] and, without opinion, an Oklahoma obscenity statute was held unconstitutional.[82]

Illustrating the consequent dissension and confusion, we find in Volume 388 of the Official Reports, commencing at page 440, writs of certiorari granted and obscenity judgments below reversed in thirteen cases in the light of the Redrup case. In the first two Justice Harlan voted to affirm on the basis of his opinions in the Roth and *Memoirs* cases;[83] in the next two he was joined by the Chief Justice and Justices Clark and Brennan;[84] and in the next the Chief

[74] *Ibid.*, 482–83.
[75] *Ibid.*, 495–96.
[76] *Ibid.*, 499 n.3.
[77] *Ibid.*, 500–501.
[78] Mishkin v. New York, 383 U.S. 502 (1966).
[79] *Ibid.*, 508.
[80] *Ibid.*, 518.
[81] Redrup v. New York; Austin v. Kentucky; Gent v. Arkansas, 386 U.S. 767 (1967).
[82] Holding v. Blankenship, 387 U.S. 94 (1967); Blankenship v. Holding, 387 U.S. 95 (1967).
[83] 388 U.S. 440–41.
[84] *Ibid.*, 442–43.

Justice and Justice Clark relied on the Mishkin case.[85] Of the remaining seven cases Justice Harlan voted to reverse in two, while Justice Clark voted to affirm. In the first of these the Chief Justice and Justice Brennan voted to vacate the judgment and remand, and in the second the Chief Justice wanted argument. In four of the remaining five Justice Harlan voted to affirm, and in the fifth he sought argument. The Chief Justice voted for argument in four and for affirmance in the fifth. Justice Clark voted to affirm in three and voted for argument in the fourth.

An article in *The New York Times* of August 28, 1967, reported that

> In a discussion of censorship, the liberties union said it would back a proposal that the Departments of Justice and of Health, Education and Welfare were exploring for "a scientific study to determine the effects, if any, of obscenity on the mind."
>
> It reported that a poll of 934 psychologists and psychiatrists by the New Jersey Committee for the Right to Read had found 95.3 per cent reporting no normal patients had been provoked to antisocial acts by sexually stimulating literature.
>
> The poll, the liberties union said, found "66.8 per cent replied affirmatively to the question of whether sexually geared materials might serve as a vicarious outlet for some individuals and thus minimize the chances of antisocial behavior."

[85] *Ibid.*, 444–46.

CHAPTER XXII

Reapportionment and Literacy in Voting

In 1949 Justice Frankfurter elaborated the terse statement of principle which had been enunciated by John Marshall and followed by the Court for well over one hundred years: "It is not for us to depart from the beaten track prescribed for us, and to tread the devious and intricate path of politics."[1]

The occasion to repeat Marshall's injunction came when Justice Frankfurter announced the judgment of the Court, in an opinion in which Justices Reed and Burton concurred, affirming a dismissal of the complaint of Illinois voters who sued to restrain an election on the ground that congressional districts lacked "compactness of territory and approximate equality of population."[2] Justice Frankfurter held that the question had been disposed of in a previous case,[3] which had found that the federal Reapportionment Act of 1929 did not require "compactness," "contiguity," or "equality of population of districts."[4]

Justice Frankfurter said:

We are of opinion that the petitioners ask of this Court what is beyond its competence to grant. This is one of those demands on judicial power which cannot be met by verbal fencing about "jurisdiction." It must be resolved by considerations on the basis of which this Court, from time to time, has refused to intervene in controversies. It has refused to do so because due regard for the effective working of our government revealed this issue to be of a peculiarly political nature and therefore not meet for judicial determination. . . .[5]

From the determination of such issues this Court has traditionally held aloof. It is hostile to a democratic system to involve the judiciary in the politics of the people. And it is not less pernicious if such judicial intervention in an essentially political contest be dressed up in the abstract phrases of the law.

The petitioners urge with great zeal that the conditions of which they com-

[1] The Nereide, 9 Cranch 388, 422–23 (1815).
[2] Colegrove v. Green, 328 U.S. 549 (1946).
[3] Wood v. Broom, 287 U.S. 1 (1932).
[4] Colegrove v. Green, 328 U.S. 549, 551 (1946).
[5] Ibid., 552.

416

plain are grave evils and offend public morality. The Constitution of the United States gives ample power to provide against these evils. But due regard for the Constitution as a viable system precludes judicial correction. Authority for dealing with such problems resides elsewhere. Article 1, Sec. 4 of the Constitution provides that "The Times, Places and Manner of holding Elections for ... Representatives, shall be prescribed in each State by the Legislature thereof; but the Congress may at any time by Law make or alter such Regulations...." The short of it is that the Constitution has conferred upon Congress exclusive authority to secure fair representation by the States in the popular House and left to that House determination whether States have fulfilled their responsibility. If Congress failed in exercising its powers, whereby standards of fairness are offended the remedy ultimately lies with the people.... An aspect of government from which the judiciary, in view of what is involved, has been excluded by the clear intention of the Constitution cannot be entered by the federal courts because Congress may have been in default in exacting from States obedience to its mandate.

The one stark fact that emerges from a study of the history of Congressional apportionment is its embroilment in politics, in the sense of party contests and party interests....[6]

Justice Rutledge concurred, saying that but for a previous case,[7] he would have thought the constitutional provisions cited by Justice Frankfurter would have made the case a nonjusticiable one. However, he thought that for the Court to interfere, "the cure sought may be worse than the disease." Accordingly he felt the Court should decline jurisdiction.[8]

Justice Black, supported by Justices Douglas and Murphy, stated:

The Equal Protection Clause of the Fourteenth Amendment forbids such discrimination. It does not permit the states to pick out certain qualified citizens or groups of citizens and deny them the right to vote at all.... The probable effect ... will be that certain citizens ... will in some instances have votes only one-ninth as effective ... as the votes of other citizens.... Such discriminatory legislation seems to me exactly the kind that the Equal Protection Clause was intended to prohibit....[9]

While the Constitution contains no express provision requiring that congressional election districts established by the states must contain approximately equal populations, the constitutionally guaranteed right to vote and the right to have one's vote counted clearly imply the policy that state election systems, no matter what their form, should be designed to give approximately equal weight to each vote cast. To some extent this implication of Article I is expressly

[6] Ibid., 554.
[7] Smiley v. Holm, 285 U.S. 355 (1932).
[8] Colegrove v. Green, 328 U.S. 549, 566 (1946).
[9] Ibid., 569.

stated by Sec. 2 of the Fourteenth Amendment which provides that "Representatives shall be apportioned among the several States according to their
respective numbers...." The purpose of this requirement is obvious: It is to
make the votes of the citizens of the several States equally effective in the
selection of members of Congress....[10]

It is argued ... that the Court is entering the area of "political questions."
I cannot agree with that argument....

It is true that voting is a part of elections and that elections are "political." But
... it is a mere "play on words" to refer to a controversy such as this as "political"
in the sense that courts have nothing to do with protecting and vindicating the
right of a voter to cast an effective ballot.[11]

Justice Jackson did not participate; the Chief Justice died before the decision came down. However, with the Warren court's disposition to rush in
where Congress fears or fails to tread, a majority of seven members of the Court
set at naught the century-long abstention of the Court in the field of legislative
apportionment when plaintiffs sued to obtain a declaratory judgment that the
Tennessee Apportionment Act of 1901 was unconstitutional and to enjoin
further elections thereunder. The district court held it had no jurisdiction.
Justice Brennan wrote for the Court, holding that it had jurisdiction and
remanded the case for further action. Justices Douglas, Clark, and Stewart
concurred. Justices Frankfurter and Harlan dissented. Justice Whittaker did
not participate.[12]

Justice Stewart, concurring, said:

The separate writings of my dissenting and concurring Brothers stray so far
from the subject of today's decision as to convey, I think, a distressingly in-
accurate impression of what the Court decides. For that reason, I think it
appropriate, in joining the opinion of the Court, to emphasize in a few words
what the opinion does and does not say.

The Court today decides three things and no more: "(a) that the court
possessed jurisdiction of the subject matter; (b) that a justiciable cause of
action is stated upon which appellants would be entitled to appropriate relief;
and (c) ... that the appellants have standing to challenge the Tennessee apportionment statutes" ....[13]

Speaking for the Court, Justice Brennan stated:

It is clear that the cause of action is one which "arises under the Federal Constitution. The complaint alleges that the 1901 statute effects an apportionment

[10] Ibid., 570.
[11] Ibid., 572–73.
[12] Baker v. Carr, 369 U.S. 186 (1962).
[13] Ibid., 265.

that deprives the appellants of the equal protection of the laws in violation of the Fourteenth Amendment....[14]

Since the complaint plainly sets forth a case arising under the Constitution, the subject matter is within the federal judicial power defined in Art. 3 Sec. 2, and so within the power of Congress to assign to the jurisdiction of the District Courts. Congress has exercised that power....[15]

An unbroken line of our precedents sustains the federal courts' jurisdiction of the subject matter of federal constitutional claims of this nature....[16]

We hold that the appellants do have standing to maintain this suit. Our decisions plainly support this conclusion. Many of the cases have assumed rather than articulated the premise in deciding the merits of similar claims....[17]

It would not be necessary to decide whether appellants' allegations of impairment of their votes by the 1901 apportionment will, ultimately, entitle them to any relief, in order to hold that they have standing to seek it....[18]

...the mere fact that the suit seeks protection of a political right does not mean it presents a political question. Such an objection "is little more than a play upon words"....

We hold that the claim pleaded here neither rests upon nor implicates the Guaranty Clause [of a Republican Form of Government: Art. 4 Sec. 4] and that its justiciability is therefore not foreclosed by our decisions of cases involving that clause.... Appellants' claim that they are being denied equal protection is justiciable....

The nonjusticiability of a political question is primarily a function of the separation of powers....[19]

Deciding whether a matter has in any measure been committed by the Constitution to another branch of government, or whether the action of that branch exceeds whatever authority has been committed, is itself a delicate exercise in constitutional interpretation, and is a responsibility of this Court as ultimate interpreter of the Constitution....[20]

The question here is the consistency of state action with the Federal Constitution. We have no question decided, or to be decided by a political branch of government coequal with this Court....

This case does, in one sense, involve the allocation of political power within a State, and the appellants might conceivably have added a claim under the Guaranty Clause. Of course, as we have seen, any reliance on that clause would be futile. But because any reliance on the Guaranty Clause could not have succeeded it does not follow that appellants may not be heard on the equal protection claim which in fact they tender. True, it must be clear that the Fourteenth Amendment claim is not so enmeshed with those political question

[14] *Ibid.*, 199.
[15] *Ibid.*, 200.
[16] *Ibid.*, 201.
[17] *Ibid.*, 206.
[18] *Ibid.*, 208.
[19] *Ibid.*, 209–10.
[20] *Ibid.*, 211.

elements which render Guaranty Clause claims nonjusticiable as actually to present a political question itself. But we have found that not to be the case here....[21]

We conclude then that the nonjusticiability of claims resting on the Guaranty Clause which arises from their embodiment of questions that were thought "political," can have no bearing upon the justiciability of the equal protection claim presented in this case....[22]

... the equal protection claim tendered in this case does not require decision of any political question....[23]

The right asserted is within the reach of judicial protection under the Fourteenth Amendment.[24]

Justice Douglas, concurring, declared:

I put to one side the problems of "political" questions involving the distribution of power between this Court, the Congress and the Chief Executive.... the question is the extent to which a State may weight one person's vote more heavily than it does another's....[25]

The power of Congress to prescribe the qualifications for voters and thus override state law is not in issue here. It is, however, clear that by reason of the commands of the Constitution there are several qualifications that a State may not require.

Race, color, or previous condition of servitude is an impermissible standard. Sex is another impermissible standard....

There is a third barrier ... and that is the Equal Protection Clause of the Fourteenth Amendment.... And so the question is, may a State weight the vote of one county or one district more heavily than it weights the vote in another.[26]

... We are told that a single vote in Moore County, Tennessee, is worth 19 votes in Hamilton County.... The opportunity to prove that an "invidious discrimination" exists should therefore be given the appellants....[27]

With the exceptions of Colegrove v. Green ... MacDougall v. Green ... South v. Peters ... and the decisions they spawned, the Court has never thought that protection of voting rights was beyond judicial cognizance. Today's treatment of those cases removes the only impediment to judicial cognizance of the claims stated in the present complaint.[28]

Also concurring, Justice Clark said:

[21] *Ibid.*, 226–27.
[22] *Ibid.*, 228–29.
[23] *Ibid.*, 232.
[24] *Ibid.*, 237.
[25] *Ibid.*, 241–42.
[26] *Ibid.*, 244.
[27] *Ibid.*, 245.
[28] *Ibid.*, 250.

420

Although I find the Tennessee apportionment statute offends the Equal Protection Clause, I would not consider intervention by this Court so delicate a field if there were any other relief available to the people of Tennessee. But the majority of the people of Tennessee have no "practical opportunities for exerting their political weight at the polls" to correct the existing "invidious discrimination" . . . .[29]

It is said that there is recourse in Congress and perhaps that may be, but from a practical standpoint this is without substance. To date Congress has never undertaken such a task in any State. We therefore must conclude that the people of Tennessee are stymied and without judicial intervention will be saddled with the present discrimination. . . .[30]

It is well for this Court to practice self-restraint and discipline in constitutional adjudication, but never in its history have those principles received sanction where the national rights of so many have been so clearly infringed for so long a time. . . . In my view the ultimate decision today is in the greatest tradition of this Court.[31]

On the other hand, Justice Frankfurter said in dissent:

The Court today reverses a uniform course of decision established by a dozen cases, including one by which the very claim now sustained was unanimously rejected only five years ago. The impressive body of rulings thus cast aside reflected the equally uniform course of our political history regarding the relationship between population and legislative representation. . . . Such a massive repudiation of the experience of our whole past in asserting destructively novel judicial power demands a detailed analysis of the role of this Court in our constitutional scheme. Disregard of inherent limits in the effective exercise of the Court's "judicial power" not only presages the futility of judicial intervention in the essentially political conflict of forces by which the relation between population and representation has time out of mind been and now is determined. It may well impair the Court's position as the ultimate organ of "the supreme Law of the Land" in that vast range of legal problems, often strongly entangled in popular feeling, on which this Court must pronounce. The Court's authority—possessed of neither the purse nor the sword—ultimately rests on sustained public confidence in its moral sanction. Such feeling must be nourished by the Court's complete detachment, in fact and in appearance, from political entanglements and by abstention from injecting itself into the clash of political forces in political settlements. . . .[32]

To charge courts with the task of accommodating the incommensurable factors of policy that underlie these mathematical puzzles is to attribute, however flatteringly, omnicompetence to judges. The Framers of the Constitution

[29] *Ibid.*, 258–59.
[30] *Ibid.*, 259.
[31] *Ibid.*, 262.
[32] *Ibid.*, 266–67.

persistently rejected a proposal that embodied this assumption and Thomas Jefferson never entertained it. . . .[33]

In effect, today's decision empowers the courts of the country to devise what should constitute the proper composition of the legislatures of the fifty States. . . .

We were soothingly told at the bar of this Court that . . . legislatures would heed the Court's admonition. This is not only a euphoric hope. It implies a sorry confession of judicial impotence in place of a frank acknowledgment that there is not under our Constitution a judicial remedy for every political mischief for every undesirable exercise of legislative power. The Framers carefully and with deliberate forethought refused so to enthrone the judiciary. In this situation, as in others of like nature, appeal for relief does not belong here. Appeal must be to an informed, civically militant electorate. In a democratic society like ours, relief must come through an aroused popular conscience that sears the conscience of the people's representatives. . . .[34]

The Colegrove doctrine . . . was not an innovation. It represents long judicial thought and experience. From its earliest opinions this Court has consistently recognized a class of controversies which do not lend themselves to judicial standards and judicial remedies. To classify the various instances as "political questions" is rather a form of stating this conclusion than revealing of analysis.[35]

A controlling factor in such cases is that decision respecting these kinds of complex matters of policy being traditionally committed not to courts but to the political agencies of government for determination by criteria of political expediency, there exists no standard ascertainable by settled judicial experience or process by reference to which a political decision affecting the question at issue between the parties can be judged. . . . where its determination is the sole function to be served by the exercise of the judicial power, the Court will not entertain the action. . . .[36]

The Court has been particularly unwilling to intervene in matters concerning the structure and organization of the political institutions of the States. . . .[37]

The present case involves all of the elements that have made the Guarantee Clause cases non-justiciable. It is, in effect, a Guarantee Clause claim masquerading under a different label. But it cannot make the case more fit for judicial action that appellants invoke the Fourteenth Amendment rather than Art. 4 Sec. 4, where, in fact, the gist of their complaint is the same. . . . Art. 4 Sec. 4 is not committed by express constitutional terms to Congress. It is the nature of the controversies arising under it, nothing else, which has made it judicially unenforceable. . . . where judicial competence is wanting, it cannot be created by invoking one clause of the Constitution rather than another. . . .[38]

A federal court is not a forum for political debate. . . .[39]

33 *Ibid.*, 268.
34 *Ibid.*, 269–70.
35 *Ibid.*, 280–81.
36 *Ibid.*, 282.
37 *Ibid.*, 284.
38 *Ibid.*, 297.
39 *Ibid.*, 298.

Appellants . . . would make the Equal Protection Clause the charter of adjudication, asserting that the equality which it guarantees comports, if not the assurance of equal weight to every voter's vote, at least the basic conception that representation ought to be proportionate to population, a standard by reference to which the reasonableness of apportionment plans may be judged.

To find such a political conception legally enforceable in the broad and unspecific guarantee of equal protection is to rewrite the Constitution.[40]

And Justice Harlan also said in dissent that, in his opinion,

appellants' allegations, accepting all of them as true, do not, parsed down or as a whole, show an infringement by Tennessee of any rights assured by the Fourteenth Amendment....

The issue here relates ... solely to the right of a State to fix the basis of representation in its *own* legislature....[41]

In the last analysis, what lies at the core of this controversy is a difference of opinion as to the function of representative government.... The federal courts have not been empowered by the Equal Protection Clause to judge whether ... resolution of the State's internal political conflict is desirable or undesirable, wise or unwise....

The Federal Constitution imposes no limitation on the form which a state government may take other than generally committing to the United States the duty to guarantee to every State "a Republican Form of Government."[42]

In short, there is nothing in the Federal Constitution to prevent a State, acting not irrationally, from choosing any electoral legislative structure it thinks best suited to the interests, temper, and customs of its people....[43]

The fact that the appellants have been unable to obtain political redress of their asserted grievances appears to be regarded as a matter which should lead the Court to stretch to find some basis for judicial intervention. While the Equal Protection Clause is invoked, the opinion for the Court notably eschews explaining how, consonant with past decisions, the undisputed facts in this case can be considered to show a violation of that constitutional provision.... what the Court is doing reflects more an adventure in judicial experimentation than a solid piece of constitutional adjudication....

It is appropriate to say that one need not agree, as a citizen, with what Tennessee has done or failed to do, in order to deprecate, as a judge, what the majority is doing today. Those observers of the Court who see it primarily as the last refuge for the correction of all inequality or injustice, no matter what its nature or source, will no doubt applaud this decision and its break with the past. Those who consider that continuing national respect for the Court's author-

---

[40] *Ibid.*, 300.
[41] *Ibid.*, 331.
[42] *Ibid.*, 333.
[43] *Ibid.*, 334.

ity depends in large measure upon its wise exercise of self-restraint and discipline in constitutional adjudication, will view the decision with deep concern.[44]

Thereafter, a qualified voter of the state of Georgia sued the chairman and secretary of the Georgia State Democratic Executive Committee and the Secretary of State of Georgia to restrain them from using Georgia's county unit system as a basis for counting votes in a Democratic primary for the nomination of a United States senator and statewide officers. The plaintiff contended that the use of the county unit system violated the equal protection clause and the due process clause of the Fourteenth Amendment and the Seventeenth Amendment. The district court, as a result of Baker v. Carr, enjoined the conduct of an election under a county unit system that did not meet the requirements specified by the Court.

On appeal, writing for six members of the Court, Justice Douglas held that all that was involved in the case was "voting." He said that while Georgia gave every qualified voter one vote in a statewide election, under the county unit system, it weighted the rural vote more heavily than the urban vote and weighted some small rural counties heavier than other larger rural counties. Hence, he said:

> Once the geographical unit for which a representative is to be chosen is designated, all who participate in the election are to have an equal vote—whatever their race, whatever their sex, whatever their occupation, whatever their income, and wherever their home may be in that geographical unit. This is required by the Equal Protection Clause of the Fourteenth Amendment....[45]
>
> The conception of political equality from the Declaration of Independence, to Lincoln's Gettysburg Address, to the Fifteenth, Seventeenth, and Nineteenth Amendments can mean only one thing—one person, one vote.[46]

Justice Stewart, joined by Justice Clark, concurred, saying: "We do not deal here with 'the basic ground rules implementing Baker v. Carr.' . . . Within a given constituency, there can be room for but a single constitutional rule—one voter, one vote."[47]

Justice Harlan dissented:

> When Baker v. Carr ... was argued at the last term we were assured that if this Court would only remove the roadblocks of Colegrove v. Green . . . and its predecessors to judicial review in "electoral" cases, this Court in all likelihood would never have to get deeper into such matters. State legislatures, it

[44] Ibid., 339–40.
[45] Gray v. Sanders, 372 U.S. 368, 379 (1963).
[46] Ibid., 381.
[47] Ibid., 382.

was predicted, would be prodded into taking satisfactory action by the mere prospect of legal proceedings.

These predictions have not proved true. . . .[48]

Preliminarily, it is symptomatic of the swift pace of current constitutional adjudication that the majority opinion should have failed to mention any of the four occasions on which Georgia's County Unit System has previously but unsuccessfully been challenged in this Court. . . .[49]

This estimate of the earlier situation is highlighted by the dissenting opinion of Justices Black and Douglas in South v. Peters, supra, at 277, in which they unsuccessfully espoused the very views which now become the law. Presumably my two Brothers also reflected these same views in noting their dissents in the Cox and Hartsfield cases. . . .[50]

The Court's holding surely flies in the face of history. For, as impressively shown by the opinion of Frankfurter, J. in Baker v. Carr[51] . . . "one person, one vote" has never been the universally accepted political philosophy in England, the American Colonies, or in the United States. . . .

But, independently of other reasons . . . any such distinction finds persuasive refutation in the Federal Electoral College whereby the President of the United States is chosen on principles wholly opposed to those now held constitutionally required in the electoral process for statewide office. . . .[52]

Indeed this Court itself some 15 years ago rejected, in a comparable situation, the notion of political equality now pronounced. . . . In disallowing this claim, the Court said[53]

"To assume that political power is a function exclusively of numbers is to disregard the practicalities of government. . . . It would be strange indeed, and doctrinaire, for this Court, applying such broad constitutional concepts as due process and equal protection of the laws, to deny a State the power to assure a proper diffusion of political initiative as between its thickly populated counties and those having concentrated masses, in view of the fact that the latter have practical opportunities for exerting their political weight at the polls not available to the former. The Constitution—a practical instrument of government—makes no such demands on the States."[54]

Certainly no support for this equal protection doctrine can be drawn from the Fifteenth, Seventeenth, or Nineteenth Amendment. The Fifteenth Amendment simply assures that the right to vote shall not be impaired "on account of race, color or previous condition of servitude." The Seventeenth Amendment provides that Senators shall be "elected by the people," with no indication

---

[48] Ibid.

[49] Ibid., 383, citing Cook v. Fortson; Turman v. Duckworth, 329 U.S. 675 (1946); South v. Peters, 339 U.S. 276 (1950); Cox v. Peters, 342 U.S. 936 (1952); Hartsfield v. Sloan, 357 U.S. 916 (1958).

[50] Gray v. Sanders, 372 U.S. 368, 383 (1963).

[51] Ibid., 384, citing Baker v. Carr, 369 U.S. 186, 301–24 (1962).

[52] Gray v. Sanders, 372 U.S. 368, 384 (1963).

[53] Ibid., 385, citing MacDougall v. Green, 334 U.S. 281 (1948).

[54] MacDougall v. Green, 334 U.S. 281, 283–84 (1948).

that all people must be accorded a vote of equal weight. The Nineteenth Amendment merely gives the vote to women....[55]

The disproportions in the Georgia County Unit System are indeed not greatly out of line with those existing under the Electoral College count for the Presidency ....

It was of course imponderables like these that lay at the root of the Court's steadfast pre-Baker v. Carr refusal "to enter [the] political thicket." ... Having turned its back on this wise chapter in its history, the Court, in my view, can no longer escape the necessity of coming to grips with the thorny problems it so studiously strove to avoid in Baker v. Carr.[56]

They appeared shortly thereafter in Georgia's gubernatorial election.

As Justice Harlan noted in his dissent in the Tennessee case previously discussed, the high court's decision empowered the courts of the country to compose the legislatures of fifty states and objectors in many of those states were not slow to put grievances before the courts. So, respecting New York,[57] the Court found the provisions of the New York State Constitution violated the Fourteenth Amendment and set afoot a course in litigation that later found reflection in the proceedings of a constitutional convention.

Later the Court struck down a Georgia apportionment statute, holding that the constitutional requirement in Article 1, Section 2, that representatives be chosen "by the People of the several States" means that, as nearly as is practicable, one person's vote in a congressional election is to be worth as much as another's.[58] Justice Black, writing for six members of the Court, said:

> In urging the people to adopt the Constitution, Madison said in No. 57 of *The Federalist:*
> "Who are to be the electors of the Federal Representatives? Not the rich more than the poor; not the learned more than the ignorant; not the haughty heirs of distinguished names, more than the humble sons of obscure and unpropitious fortune. The electors are to be the great body of the people of the United States...."
> Readers surely could have fairly taken this to mean "one person, one vote."[59]

Justice Clark, concurring in part and dissenting in part, said: "... in my view, Brother Harlan has clearly demonstrated that both the historical background and language preclude a finding that Art. 1, Sec. 2, lays down the *ipse dixit* 'one person, one vote' in congressional elections."[60]

[55] Gray v. Sanders, 372 U.S. 368, 385–86 (1963).
[56] *Ibid.,* 388.
[57] WMCA v. Lomenzo, 377 U.S. 633 (1964).
[58] Wesberry v. Sanders, 376 U.S. 1 (1964); *see also* Lucas v. Rhodes, 389 U.S. 212 (1967); Rockefeller v. Wells, 389 U.S. 421 (1967).
[59] Wesberry v. Sanders, 376 U.S. 1, 18 (1964).

Justice Stewart, dissenting in part, agreed, and Justice Harlan, also dissenting, said:

> I had not expected to witness the day when the Supreme Court of the United States would render a decision which casts grave doubt on the constitutionality of the composition of the House of Representatives. . . .[61]
>
> . . . today's decision impugns the validity of the election of 398 Representatives from 37 States. . . .
>
> Only a demonstration which could not be avoided would justify this Court in rendering a decision the effect of which . . . is to declare constitutionally defective the very composition of a coordinate branch of the Federal Government. The Court's opinion not only fails to make such a demonstration, it is unsound logically on its face and demonstrably unsound historically.[62]
>
> . . . it is beyond the province of this Court to decide whether equally populated districts is the preferable method for electing Representatives, whether state legislatures would have acted more fairly or wisely had they adopted such a method, or whether Congress had been derelict in not requiring state legislatures to follow that course. Once it is clear that there is no *constitutional* right at stake, that ends the case.[63]
>
> . . . the Court's talk about "debasement" and "dilution" of the vote is a model of circular reasoning, in which the premises of the argument feed on the conclusion. . . .[64]
>
> The constitutional scheme vests in the States plenary power to regulate the conduct of elections for Representatives, and, in order to protect the Federal Government, provides for congressional supervision of the States' exercise of their power.[65]
>
> The claim for judicial relief in this case strikes at one of the fundamental doctrines of our system of government, the separation of powers. In upholding that claim, the Court attempts to effect reforms in a field which the Constitution, as plainly as can be, has committed exclusively to the political process. . . .
>
> The Constitution does not confer on the Court blanket authority to step into every situation where the political branch may be thought to have fallen short. . . .
>
> What is done today saps the political process. The promise of judicial intervention in matters of this sort cannot but encourage popular inertia in efforts for political reform through the political process, with the inevitable result that the process is itself weakened.[66]

[60] *Ibid.*
[61] *Ibid.*, 20.
[62] *Ibid.*, 21–22.
[63] *Ibid.*, 24.
[64] *Ibid.*, 25.
[65] *Ibid.*, 42.
[66] *Ibid.*, 48.

Thereafter the Court held that the equal protection clause of the Fourteenth Amendment required substantially equal legislative representation for all citizens in a state regardless of where they reside, since legislators represent people, not areas, and found invalid apportionment plans adopted by the Alabama legislature.[67] The Chief Justice wrote for six members of the Court. Justices Clark and Stewart concurred. Justice Harlan dissented in this and six other companion cases.[68] He said:

> These decisions, with Wesberry v. Sanders... and Gray v. Sanders... have the effect of placing basic aspects of state political systems under the pervasive overlordship of the federal judiciary. Once again, I must register my protest.[69]
>
> Today's holding is that the Equal Protection Clause of the Fourteenth Amendment requires every State to structure its legislature so that all the members of each house represent substantially the same number of people.... Whatever may be thought of this holding as a piece of political ideology... I think it demonstrable that the Fourteenth Amendment does not impose this political tenet on the States or authorize this Court to do so....
>
> Had the Court paused to probe more deeply into the matter, it would have found that the Equal Protection Clause was never intended to inhibit the States in choosing any democratic method they pleased for the apportionment of their legislatures....[70]
>
> Mention should be made finally of the decisions of this Court which are disregarded or, more accurately, silently overruled today.[71]
>
> Between 1947 and 1957, four cases raising issues precisely the same as those decided today were presented to the Court. Three were dismissed because the issues presented were thought insubstantial and in the fourth the lower court's dismissal was affirmed....[72]
>
> The Court's elaboration of its new "constitutional" doctrine indicates how far—and how unwisely—it has strayed from the appropriate bounds of its authority. The consequence of today's decision is that in all but the handful of States which may already satisfy the new requirements, the local District Court or, it may be the state courts, are given blanket authority and the constitutional duty to supervise apportionment of the State Legislatures. It is difficult to imagine a more intolerable and inappropriate interference by the judiciary with the independent legislatures of the States....[73]
>
> ... no thinking person can fail to recognize that the aftermath of these

[67] Reynolds v. Sims; Vann v. Baggett; McConnell v. Baggett, 377 U.S. 533 (1964).
[68] WMCA v. Lomenzo, 377 U.S. 633 (1964); Maryland Comm. v. Tawes, 377 U.S. 656 (1964); Davis v. Mann, 377 U.S. 678 (1964); Roman v. Sincock, 337 U.S. 695 (1964); Lucas v. Colorado Gen. Assembly, 377 U.S. 713 (1964).
[69] Reynolds v. Sims, 377 U.S. 533, 589 (1964).
[70] Ibid., 590–91.
[71] Ibid., 612.
[72] Ibid., 614.
[73] Ibid., 615.

cases ... will have been achieved at the cost of a radical alteration in the relationship between the States and the Federal Government, more particularly the Federal Judiciary. . . .

Finally, these decisions give support to a current mistaken view of the Constitution and the constitutional function of this Court. This view, in a nutshell, is that every major social ill in this country can find its cure in some constitutional "principle," and that this Court should "take the lead" in promoting reform when other branches of government fail to act. The Constitution is not a panacea for every blot upon the public welfare, nor should this Court, ordained as a judicial body, be thought of as a general haven for reform movements. . . . This Court ... does not serve its high purpose when it exceeds its authority, even to satisfy justified impatience with the slow workings of the political process. For when, in the name of constitutional interpretation, the Court *adds* something to the Constitution that was deliberately excluded from it, the Court in reality substitutes its view of what should be so for the amending process.[74]

Justice Stewart wrote in dissent, with the support of Clark, in one of the subsequent cases,[75] saying that

the question is to what degree, if at all, the Equal Protection Clause of the Fourteenth Amendment limits each sovereign State's freedom to establish appropriate electoral constituencies from which representatives of the State's bicameral legislative assembly are to be chosen. The Court's answer is a blunt one, and, I think, woefully wrong. . . .

First, says the Court, it is "established that the fundamental principle of representative government in this country is one of equal representation for equal numbers of people. . . ." With all respect, I think that this is not correct, simply as a matter of fact. . . .[76]

To put the matter plainly, there is nothing in all the history of this Court's decisions which supports this constitutional rule. The Court's Draconian pronouncement, which makes unconstitutional the legislatures of most of the 50 States, finds no support in the words of the Constitution, in any prior decision of this Court, or in the 175-year political history of our Federal Union. With all respect, I am convinced these decisions mark a long step backward into that unhappy era when a majority of the members of this Court were thought by many to have convinced themselves and each other that the demands of the Constitution were to be measured not by what it says, but by their own notions of wise political theory. . . .[77]

What the Court has done is to convert a particular political philosophy into a constitutional rule ... binding upon each of the 50 States, from Maine to Hawaii, from Alaska to Texas, without regard and without respect for the

---

[74] *Ibid.,* 624–25.
[75] Lucas v. Colorado Gen. Assembly, 377 U.S. 713 (1964).
[76] *Ibid.,* 745.
[77] *Ibid.,* 746–48.

many individualized and differentiated characteristics of each State ... even if it were thought that the rule announced today by the Court is, as a matter of political theory, the most desirable general rule which can be devised as a basis for the make-up of the representative assembly of a typical State, I could not join in the fabrication of a constitutional mandate which imports and forever freezes one theory of political thought into our Constitution, and forever denies to every State any opportunity for enlightened and progressive innovation in the design of its democratic institutions....[78]

The fact is, of course, that population factors must often to some degree be subordinate in devising a legislative apportionment plan which is to achieve the important goal of ensuring a fair, effective, and balanced representation of the regional, social and economic interests within a State. And the further fact is that throughout our history the apportionments of State Legislatures have reflected the strongly felt American tradition that the public interest is composed of many diverse interests, and that in the long run it can better be expressed by a medley of component voices than the majority's monolithic command ....

I think that the Equal Protection Clause demands but two basic attributes of any plan of state legislative apportionment. First, it demands that, in the light of the State's own characteristics and needs, the plan must be a rational one. Secondly, it demands that the plan must be such as not to permit the systematic frustration of the will of a majority of the electorate of the State.[79]

In a per curiam opinion, the Court affirmed a decree of the district court holding the senatorial apportionment of California invalid.[80] Justices Harlan, Clark, and Stewart concurred. Justice Harlan, writing for the three, said:

Prior to 1926 the California Constitution ... provided that both houses of the legislature would be apportioned on the basis of population. In 1926 an initiative measure ... was submitted to the voters which deleted the requirement that the Senate be apportioned on a strict population basis....[81] [It] was approved ... and the following year the legislature adopted apportionment statutes to effect the constitutional amendment. This legislation was submitted to the people ... and approved.[82]

Since the adoption of these changes, various initiative measures have been submitted to the voters on more than one occasion in an attempt to change this apportionment system for the Senate. In 1948 such a proposition was defeated. ... In 1960 such a proposition was defeated.... And in 1962 another such proposition was defeated....

Were I able to detect ... the slightest basis for optimism that the Court might consider last Term's reapportionment pronouncements to leave room for

[78] *Ibid.*, 748.
[79] *Ibid.*, 751, 753–54.
[80] Jordan v. Silver, 381 U.S. 415 (1965).
[81] *Ibid.*, 415–16.
[82] *Ibid.*, 416–18.

the people of a State to choose for themselves the kind of legislative structure they wish to have—at least when the democratic processes employed are as straightforward and flexible as those of California—I would vote to "Note" and hear this case. Finding, however, that the judgment of the District Court is squarely required by Lucas v. Forty-fourth General Assembly . . . I reluctantly acquiesce in the Court's summary affirmance.[83]

During the 1963 term the Court had reversed a judgment of a three-judge district court upholding the then-current legislative apportionment in Florida and remanding the case for further proceedings, consistent with the Court's opinion in the Sims and companion cases. Thereafter the legislature reapportioned the state but the district court found the reapportionment invalid. However, it permitted it to stand until sixty days after the adjournment of the 1967 session of the legislature. Thereupon the high court reversed the judgment and directed the adoption of a valid plan effective for the 1966 elections.[84] The legislature then adopted a new plan which the district court approved. But the Supreme Court reversed[85] "for the failure of the State to present or the District Court to articulate acceptable reasons for the variations among the populations of the various legislative districts with respect to both the Senate and the House of Representatives."[86]

Justice Harlan, joined by Justice Stewart, dissented, holding that the plan was "in substantial compliance" with the requirements of the Sims case. On the same day the Court remanded an Indiana reapportionment plan to the district court, with a similarly divided Court.[87]

Later a divided Court rejected a Texas reapportionment, with Justice Douglas concurring and Justices Clark, Harlan, and Stewart voting to affirm; the latter two "on the basis of the reasoning contained in Justice Harlan's dissenting opinion in Swann v. Adams."[88]

When no gubernatorial candidate received a majority vote in the Georgia election of 1966, a three-judge federal district court enjoined the Georgia legislature from selecting a governor from among the two candidates receiving the highest number of votes, as provided by the Georgia Constitution, upon the ground that the Supreme Court had held in Gray v. Sanders (above) and Toombs v. Fortson[89] that the Georgia legislature was elected as a result of a denial of equal protection of the law in violation of the Fourteenth Amendment. However, in an opinion by Justice Black, in which four other members

---

[83] *Ibid.*, 419–20.
[84] Swann v. Adams, 383 U.S. 210 (1966).
[85] Swann v. Adams, 385 U.S. 440 (1967).
[86] *Ibid.*, 443–44.
[87] Duddleston v. Grills, 385 U.S. 455 (1967).
[88] Kilgarlin v. Hill, 386 U.S. 120 (1967).
[89] 384 U.S. 210 (1966).

of the Court joined, it was held that since the Court had permitted the Georgia legislature to continue to function until May 1, 1968, it was not disqualified from electing a governor.[90] The Chief Justice and Justices Douglas, Brennan, and Fortas dissented. Justice Douglas argued that "the substitution of the Georgia Legislature for a runoff vote is an unconstitutional weighting of votes, having all the vices of the county unit system that we invalidated in Gray v. Sanders."[91]

Justice Fortas, dissenting, said: "It is no less a denial of equal protection of the laws for the result of an election to be determined not by the voters, but by the legislature on a basis which is not related to the votes cast."[92]

Respecting Justice Black's statement that the legislature was qualified to act until May 1, 1968, as a reason for justifying its selection of a governor, Justice Fortas wrote:

> This is indeed a weak reed for so monumental a conclusion. The use of a malapportioned legislature to select a Governor is to perpetuate the electoral vices which this Court decreed that the Equal Protection Clause of the Fourteenth Amendment forbade a State to incorporate in its election procedures. ... To a reader of Gray v. Sanders, Fortson v. Toombs, and Toombs v. Fortson, it must seem inconceivable that the Court would permit this malapportioned legislature to select Georgia's Governor in these circumstances.[93]

Subsequently the Court limited its reapportionment jurisdiction, holding that the federal jurisdiction was not applicable where the state statute under attack was one of limited application,[94] that it was inapplicable to a county school board where no election was required,[95] and that it had no application where a city consolidation plan embodied a charter which was local only and not of state-wide effect.[96]

Thereafter, over the dissents of Justices Harlan, Stewart, and Fortas (Justice Marshall not participating), five members of the Court joined in an opinion by Justice White following Reynolds v. Sims, holding that the Constitution permits no substantial variation from equal population in drawing districts for units of local government having general governmental powers over the entire geographic area served by the body.[97] He added that "the Sailors and Dusch cases demonstrate that the Constitution and this Court are

---

[90] Fortson v. Morris, 385 U.S. 231, 235 (1966).
[91] Ibid., 241.
[92] Ibid., 243.
[93] Ibid., 245.
[94] Moody v. Flowers; Board of Supervisors v. Bianchi, 387 U.S. 97 (1967).
[95] Sailors v. Board of Education, 387 U.S. 105 (1967).
[96] Dusch v. Davis, 387 U.S. 112 (1967).
[97] Avery v. Midland County, 390 U.S. 474 (1968).

not roadblocks in the path of innovation, experiment, and development among units of local government."[98]

Justice Harlan said in his dissent:

I consider this decision, which extends the state apportionment rule of Reynolds v. Sims ... to an estimated 80,000 units of local government throughout the land, both unjustifiable and ill-advised....[99]

I am not foreclosed ... from remonstrating against the extension of that decision to new areas of government. At the present juncture I content myself with stating two propositions which, in my view, stand strongly against what is done today.

The first is that the "practical necessities" which have been thought to some to justify the profound break with history that was made in 1962 by this Court's decision in Baker v. Carr ... are not present here. The second is that notwithstanding Reynolds the "one-man, one-vote" ideology does not provide an acceptable formula for structuring local government units.[100]

Justice Fortas, dissenting, stated:

Dusch and Sailors were wisely and prudently decided....[101] I know of no reason why we should insist that there is and can be only one role for voters in local governmental units—that districts for units of local government must be drawn solely on the basis of population.[102] It is our duty to insist upon due regard for the value of the individual vote but not to ignore realities....[103]

In 1963 population estimates relied upon in this case show that the City of Midland with 67,906 people has one representative, and the three rural districts, each of which has its own representative, have 852, 814 and 828 people respectively.

While it may be that this cannot be regarded as satisfying the equal protection clause, under any view, I suggest that applying the Court's formula merely errs in the opposite direction. Only the city population will be represented and the rural areas will be eliminated from a voice in the county government to which they must look for essential services. With all respect, I submit that this is a destructive result. It kills the very value which it purports to serve.[104]

The decisions of the Court stirred congressional objection and resulted in the introduction and partial passage of a number of bills; however, only a bill

[98] *Ibid.*, 485.
[99] *Ibid.*, 487.
[100] *Ibid.*, 488.
[101] *Ibid.*, 496.
[102] *Ibid.*, 497.
[103] *Ibid.*, 509.
[104] *New York Times*, August 11, 1967.

barring at-large elections for the House in all states except Hawaii and New Mexico secured final approval of both houses.

A noteworthy, if somewhat ridiculous, consequence of judicial supervision of elections found a federal judge who had found districting in New Haven unconstitutional ordering the city to elect all its aldermen in an at-large poll, which would call upon voters to select thirty candidates from a sixty-name ballot, a model of discriminating selection.[105]

Once the reapportionment bars were down, the Court was free to roam at will in intrastate voting pastures. So a provision in a Texas law denying a serviceman's right to vote on the sole ground of his status as a serviceman was held to violate the equal protection clause by seven members of the Court. Justice Harlan dissented on the ground that the equal protection clause was not intended to include state electoral matters and differences in voting eligibility between Texans and servicemen ordered to Texas by military authority were valid distinctions.[106]

The petitioner had been domiciled in Texas since 1962; he owned a residence in El Paso, where he lived with his wife and children. He also owned a business there. He commuted regularly to New Mexico, where he was posted. He paid property taxes in Texas and had an automobile registered there.

Justice Harlan said the Court ignored, as it did in the reapportionment cases, all the history of the Fourteenth Amendment and the course of judicial decisions which together show plainly that the equal protection clause was not intended to touch state electoral matters. He referred to his opinion in Reynolds v. Sims when he said:

> While I cannot express surprise over today's decision in the reapportionment cases, which though bound to follow, I continue to believe are constitutionally indefensible, and ... record my protest against this further extension of federal judicial power into political affairs of the States. Reapportionment cases do not require this extension. They were concerned with methods of constituting state legislatures; this case involves a state voter qualification.[107]

> The question here is simply whether the differentiation in voting eligibility is founded on rational classification.

> Essentially, the Texas statute establishes a rule that servicemen from other states stationed at Texas bases are to be treated as transients for voting purposes. No one disputes that in the vast majority of cases Texas' view of things accords with fact.[108]

In an opinion by Justice Brennan, the Court held valid a provision of the

[105] Carrington v. Rash, 380 U.S. 89 (1965).
[106] Ibid., 97–98.
[107] Ibid., 99.
[108] Katzenbach v. Morgan; New York City Board of Elections v. Morgan, 384 U.S. 641 (1966).

Voting Rights Act of 1965 precluding denial of registration to one successfully completing the sixth primary grade of an accredited Puerto Rican school, despite his inability to read or write English.[109]

Holding that the provision was appropriate under the equal protection clause, Justice Brennan said it might be viewed as "a measure to secure for the Puerto Rican community residing in New York nondiscriminatory treatment by government—both in the imposition of voting qualifications and the provision for administration of governmental services, such as public schools, public housing, and law enforcement." Hence he found that "the practical effect of Sec. 4 (e) is to prohibit New York from denying the right to vote to large segments of its Puerto Rican community. . . . This enhanced political power," he said,

> will be helpful in gaining nondiscriminatory treatment in public services for the entire Puerto Rican community [and] thereby enables the Puerto Rican minority better to obtain "perfect equality of civil rights and equal protection of the laws." It was well within congressional authority to say that this need of the Puerto Rican minority for the vote warranted federal intrusion upon any state interests served by the English literacy requirement. . . . It is not for us to review the congressional resolution. . . . It is enough that we perceive a basis upon which the Congress might resolve the conflict as it did. . . .[110]
>
> We are told that New York's English literacy requirement originated in the desire to provide an incentive for non-English speaking immigrants to learn the English language and in order to assure the intelligent exercise of the franchise. Yet Congress might well have questioned, in light of the many exemptions provided, and some evidence suggesting that prejudice played a prominent role in the enactment of the requirement, whether these were actually the interests being served.[111]

Justice Douglas concurred in the result. Justice Harlan, supported by Justice Stewart, dissented in this and in the following case, in which the Court affirmed a denial of relief to a prospective voter who maintained that the New York literacy requirement violated the federal Constitution, upon the ground that her complaint did not show she came within the provisions of the Voting Rights Act by having completed successfully the sixth grade of a Puerto Rican accredited school.[112] Justice Douglas, with the support of Justice Fortas, dissented thus:

> I doubt that literacy is a wise prerequisite for exercise of the franchise. Literacy

[109] *Ibid.*, 652–53.
[110] *Ibid.*, 654.
[111] Cardona v. Power, 384 U.S. 672 (1966).
[112] *Ibid.*, 675.

435

and intelligence are not synonymous. The experience of nations, like India, where illiterate persons have returned to office responsible governments over and again, emphasizes that the ability to read and write is not necessary for an intelligent use of the ballot....[113]

I cannot say that it is an unconstitutional exercise for that [state] power to condition the use of the ballot on the ability to read and write.... But we are a multiracial and multi-linguistic nation; and there are groups in this country as versatile in Spanish, French, Japanese and Chinese, for example, as others in English. Many of them constitute communities in which there were widespread organs of public communication in one of these tongues.... Such is the case in New York City where Spanish-language newspapers and periodicals flourish.... And so our equal protection question is whether intelligent use of the ballot should not be as much presumed where one is versatile in the Spanish language as it is where English is the medium....

A Spanish-speaking person is offered no literacy test in Spanish.... The heavier burden which New York has placed on the Spanish-speaking American cannot in my view be sustained, under the Equal Protection Clause of the Fourteenth Amendment....

Our philosophy that removal of unwise laws must be left to the ballot, not to the courts, requires that recourse to the ballot not be restricted as New York has attempted.[114]

In dissenting in this and the preceding case, with the support of Justice Stewart, Justice Harlan declared:

The issue in this case is whether New York has shown that its English-language literacy test is reasonably designed to serve a legitimate state purpose. I think that it does.

In 1959...a North Carolina English literacy test was challenged. We held that there was "wide scope" for State qualifications of this sort.... Dealing with literacy tests generally, the Court there held:

"The ability to read and write . . . has some relation to standards designed to promote intelligent use of the ballot. . . . in our society where newspapers, periodicals, books, and other printed matter canvass and debate campaign issues, a State might conclude that only those who are literate should exercise the franchise.... We do not sit in judgment on the wisdom of that policy. We cannot say, however, that it is not an allowable one measured by constitutional standards...."[115]

Although ... there is a difference between a totally illiterate person and one who is literate in a foreign tongue, I do not believe that this added factor vitiates the constitutionality of the New York statute.... it is ... true that the range

[113] *Ibid.*
[114] *Ibid.*, 675–77.
[115] Katzenbach v. Morgan, 384 U.S. 641, 661 (1966), quoting Lassiter v. Northampton Election Board, 360 U.S. 45, 51, (1959).

of material available to a resident of New York literate only in Spanish is much more limited than what is available to an English-speaking resident, that the business of national, state, and local government is conducted in English, and that propositions, amendments, and offices for which candidates are running listed on the ballot are likewise in English. It is also true that most candidates, certainly those campaigning on a national or state-wide level, make their speeches in English. New York may justifiably want its voters to be able to understand candidates directly rather than through possibly imprecise translations or summaries reported in a limited number of Spanish news media. It is noteworthy that the Federal Government requires literacy in English as a prerequisite to naturalization ... attesting to the national view of its importance as a prerequisite to full integration into the American political community. Relevant too is the fact that the New York English test is not complex, that it is fairly administered, and that New York maintains free adult education classes which appellant and members of her class are encouraged to attend. Given the State's legitimate concern with promoting and safeguarding the intelligent use of the ballot, and given also New York's long experience with the process of integrating non-English speaking residents into the mainstream of American life, I do not see how it can be said that this qualification for suffrage is unconstitutional....[116]

The pivotal question in this instance is what effect the added factor of a congressional enactment has on the straight equal protection argument dealt with above....[117]

Section 4(e), however, presents a significantly different type of congressional enactment. The question here is not whether the statute is appropriate remedial legislation to cure an established violation of a constitutional command, but whether there has in fact been an infringement of that constitutional command, that is, whether a particular state practice or, as here, a statute is so arbitrary or irrational as to offend the command of the Equal Protection Clause of the Fourteenth Amendment. That question is one for the judicial branch ultimately to determine. Were the rule otherwise, Congress would be able to qualify this Court's constitutional decisions under the Fourteenth and Fifteenth Amendments let alone those under other provisions of the Constitution by resorting to congressional power under the Necessary and Proper Clause. In view of this Court's holding in Lassiter, *supra,* that an English literacy test is a permissible exercise of state supervision over its franchise, I do not think it is open to Congress to limit the effect of that decision as it has undertaken to do by Section 4(e)....[118]

There is simply no legislative record supporting hypothesized discrimination of the sort we have hitherto insisted upon when congressional power is brought to bear on constitutionally reserved state concerns....

Thus, we have here not a matter of giving deference to a congressional

---

[116] Katzenbach v. Morgan, 384 U.S. 641, 662–64 (1966).
[117] *Ibid.,* 665.
[118] *Ibid.,* 667–68.

DISSENT IN THE SUPREME COURT

estimate, based on its determination of legislative facts, bearing upon the validity . . . of a statute, but rather what can at most be called a legislative announcement that Congress believes a state law to entail an unconstitutional deprivation of equal protection. Although this kind of declaration is entitled to the most respectful consideration . . . I do not believe it lessens our responsibility to decide the fundamental issue of whether in fact the state enactment violates federal constitutional rights. . . .[119]

To hold, on this record, that Section 4(e) overrides the New York literacy requirement seems to me tantamount to allowing the Fourteenth Amendment to swallow the State's constitutionally ordained primary authority in this field.[120]

[119] *Ibid.*, 669–70.
[120] *Ibid.*, 671.

CHAPTER XXIII

The First Amendment

ISSUES ARISING UNDER THE FIRST AMENDMENT have occupied the attention of the Court in a variety of guises. A five-man majority found that arbitrary restriction of the use of amplifying devices on the streets and in public places was invalid under the First Amendment.[1] Justices Frankfurter, Reed, Burton, and Jackson dissented.

Justice Frankfurter wrote:

The native power of human speech can interfere little with the self-protection of those who do not wish to listen. They may easily move beyond earshot, just as those who do not choose to read need not have their attention bludgeoned by undesired reading matter.... But modern devices for amplifying the range and volume of the voice, or its recording, afford easy, too easy, opportunities for aural aggression. If uncontrolled, the result is intrusion into cherished privacy.

Municipalities have conscientiously sought to deal with the new problems ... to make city life endurable.... Surely there is not a constitutional right to force unwilling people to listen.[2]

Justice Jackson said:

I dissent from this decision, which seems to me neither judicious nor sound and to endanger the great right of free speech by making it ridiculous and obnoxious. . . .[3]

It is astonishing news to me if the Constitution prohibits a municipality from policing, controlling or forbidding erection of such equipment [for amplification] by a private party in a public park....[4]

To my mind this is not a free speech issue. Lockport has in no way denied or restricted the free use, even in its park, of all of the facilities for speech with

---

[1] Saia v. New York, 334 U.S. 558 (1948).

[2] *Ibid.*, 563.

[3] *Ibid.*, 566.

[4] *Ibid.*, 567.

which nature has endowed the appellant.... But can it be that society has no control of apparatus which, when put to unregulated proselytizing, propaganda and commercial uses, can render life unbearable?

But the Court points out that propagation of his religion is the avowed and only purpose of appellant.... Only a few weeks ago we held that the Constitution prohibits a state or municipality from using tax-supported property "to aid religious groups to spread their faith," Illinois *ex rel*. McCullum v. Board of Education.... Today we say it compels them to let it be used for that purpose....[5]

The Court expresses great concern lest the loudspeakers of political candidates be controlled if Jehovah's Witnesses can be. That does not worry me. Even political candidates ought not to be allowed irresponsibly to set up sound equipment in all sorts of public places, and few of them would regard it as tactful campaigning to thrust themselves upon picnicking families who do not want to hear their messages.[6]

Later the Court upheld a city ordinance that prohibited the operation upon the streets of sound amplifiers which emitted loud and raucous noises.[7] Three members of the Court dissented from affirmance of the conviction upon the ground that there was no proof that the sound truck had emitted "loud and raucous noises." However, the dissenters and the rest of the Court, except Justice Murphy, agreed that such amplification was subject to regulation, and Justices Frankfurter and Jackson held that the use of sound trucks in the streets might be prohibited. Justice Murphy dissented without opinion.

Writing for five members of the Court, Justice Douglas held that an ordinance which provided that persons making any improper noise, riot, disturbance, breach of the peace, or diversion tending to a breach of the peace, was violative of the right of free speech of a street orator whose speech at a public meeting resulted in a public disturbance requiring police intervention.[8] The Chief Justice and Justices Frankfurter, Jackson, and Burton dissented on technical grounds. Justice Jackson wrote, denying that the conviction infringed constitutional rights.

Justice Douglas said:

... the statutory words, "breach of the peace" were defined in instructions to the jury to include speech which "stirs the public to anger, invites dispute, brings about a condition of unrest, or creates a disturbance" ....

The vitality of civil and political institutions in our society depends on free discussion....

A function of free speech under our system of government is to invite dis-

[5] *Ibid.*, 568–69.
[6] *Ibid.*, 571.
[7] Kovacs v. Cooper, 336 U.S. 77 (1949).
[8] Terminiello v. Chicago, 337 U.S. 1 (1949).

pute. It may indeed best serve its high purpose when it induces a condition of unrest, creates dissatisfaction with conditions as they are, or even stirs people to anger. Speech is often provocative and challenging. It may strike at prejudices and preconceptions and have profound unsettling effects as it presses for acceptance of an idea....[9]

The ordinance as construed by the trial court seriously invaded this province. ... A conviction resting on any of those grounds may not stand.[10]

In his dissent Justice Jackson wrote:

The Court reverses this conviction by reiterating generalized approbations of freedom of speech with which, in the abstract, no one will disagree. Doubts as to their applicability are lulled by avoidance of more than passing reference to the circumstances of Terminiello's speech and judging it as if he had spoken to persons as dispassionate as empty benches, or like a modern Demosthenes practicing his Philippics on a lonely seashore.

But the local court that tried Terminiello was not indulging in theory. It was dealing with a riot and with a speech that provoked a hostile mob and incited a friendly one, and threatened violence between the two....

Underneath a little issue of Terminiello and his hundred-dollar fine lurk some of the most far-reaching constitutional questions that can confront a people who value both liberty and order. This Court seems to regard these as enemies of each other and to be of the view that we must forego order to achieve liberty. So it fixes its eyes on a conception of freedom of speech so rigid as to tolerate no concession to society's need for public order.

An old proverb warns us to take heed lest we "walk into a well from looking at the stars."[11]

...recent decisions have almost completely immunized this battle for the streets from any form of control.[12]

...no serious outbreak of mob violence, race rioting, lynching or public disorder is likely to get going without help of some speech-making to some mass of people.... Unity of purpose, passion and hatred, which merges the many minds of a crowd into the mindlessness of a mob, almost invariably is supplied by speeches. It is naive, or worse, to teach that oratory with this object or effect is a service to liberty. No mob has ever protected any liberty, even its own....

The law is more tolerant of discussion than are most individuals or communities....[13]

The crowd mind is never tolerant of any idea which does not conform to its herd opinion. It does not want a tolerant effort at meeting of minds. It does

[9] *Ibid.*, 4.
[10] *Ibid.*, 5.
[11] *Ibid.*, 13–14.
[12] *Ibid.*, 30.
[13] *Ibid.*, 32.

441

not know the futility of trying to mob an idea. . . . mobs endanger liberty as well as order. The authorities must control them and they are entitled to place some checks upon those whose behavior or speech calls such mobs into being. When the right of society to freedom from probable violence should prevail over the right of an individual to defy opposing opinion, presents a problem that always tests wisdom and often calls for immediate and vigorous action to preserve public order and safety. . . .[14]

The Terminiello case was followed by three cases decided the same day. The first involved the conviction of Jehovah's Witnesses charged with disorderly conduct for speaking in a public park without a permit. A permit had been denied not because of a statute or an ordinance but because of a local practice not defining any standards or limitations. There was no issue of disorder. Seven members of the Court joined in an opinion by the Chief Justice, holding the practice of requiring such a permit violated the First Amendment and the refusal was a denial of equal protection.[15] Justices Black and Frankfurter concurred.

Later the Court held that a Jehovah's Witness who conducted a religious service in a public park after he had been denied a license was properly convicted since he had not exhausted his civil remedies to compel the issuance of a license.[16] Justices Black and Douglas dissented upon the ground that the ordinance was invalid as violative of free speech.

The second case was that of Kunz, a Baptist minister convicted of holding a religious meeting on a public street without a permit, in violation of a city ordinance.[17] The permit had been refused because the speaker's remarks had previously stirred strife and threatened violence. The Court reversed the conviction on the ground that the ordinance was invalid as a previous restraint on the rights of free speech since the ordinance contained no standards to guide the action of the authorities. Justices Black and Frankfurter concurred; Justice Jackson dissented, saying:

. . . to blanket hateful and hate-stirring attacks on races and faiths under the protections for freedom of speech may be a noble innovation. On the other hand, it may be a quixotic tilt at windmills which belittles great principles of liberty. Only time can tell. But I incline to the latter view. . . .[18]

Equally inciting and more clearly "fighting words," when thrown at Catholics and Jews who are rightfully on the streets of New York, are statements that "The Pope is the anti-Christ" and the Jews are "Christ-killers." These terse

[14] Ibid., 33–34.
[15] Niemotko v. Maryland; Kelley v. Maryland, 340 U.S. 268 (1951).
[16] Poulos v. New Hampshire, 345 U.S. 395 (1953).
[17] Kunz v. New York, 340 U.S. 290 (1951).
[18] Ibid., 295.

442

epithets come down to our generation weighted with hatreds accumulated through centuries of bloodshed. They are recognized words of art in the profession of defamation. They are not the kind of insult that men bandy and laugh off when the spirits are high and the flagons are low.... Of course, people might pass this speaker by as a mental case, and so they might file out of a theatre in good order at the cry of "fire." But in both cases there is genuine likelihood that someone will get hurt.[19]

The Kunz case was followed by another, in which a student addressing a crowd, including Negroes, made derogatory remarks concerning public officials and indicated that Negroes should rise up in arms and fight for equal rights.[20] In view of the excitement engendered by his speech, the police requested him to stop speaking, but he ignored these requests and was arrested and charged with disorderly conduct. Five members of the Court joined in an opinion by the Chief Justice sustaining the conviction; Justice Frankfurter concurred; Justices Black, Douglas, and Minton dissented.

A later case affirmed a conviction for distributing libelous leaflets attacking the Negro race.[21] Justice Frankfurter wrote for a majority of five; Justices Jackson, Black, Reed, and Douglas dissented. While Justices Reed, Black, and Douglas maintained that the Fourteenth Amendment made the First Amendment available, Justice Jackson held the contrary, but the majority did not pass on that issue.

Justice Frankfurter said that "wilful purveyors of falsehood concerning racial and religious groups promote strife and tend powerfully to obstruct the manifold adjustments required for the free, ordered life in a metropolitan, polyglot community."[22] He concluded that such attacks transgressed the protections of free speech.

Justice Black, dissenting, argued that the defendant was entitled, under the First Amendment, to urge the segregation of white and Negro persons; that he and his followers were exercising their right to petition their elected representatives. He charged that the Court was merely acting "on the bland assumption that the First Amendment is wholly irrelevant."[23]

Justice Jackson wrote: "The history of criminal libel in America convinces me that the Fourteenth Amendment did not 'incorporate' the First, that the powers of Congress and of the States over this subject are not of the same dimensions, and that because Congress probably could not enact this law, it does not follow that the States may not."[24]

[19] Ibid., 299.
[20] Feiner v. New York, 340 U.S. 315 (1951).
[21] Beauharnais v. Illinois, 343 U.S. 250 (1952).
[22] Ibid., 259.
[23] Ibid., 268.
[24] Ibid., 288.

In a landmark decision concerning the law of libel, the Court held that a public official may not recover damages for defamatory falsehood relating to his official conduct unless he proves actual malice.[25] Justice Black concurred; Justice Goldberg, with the support of Justice Douglas, concurred in the result.

The grievance alleged by the plaintiff, one of three elected commissioners of the city of Montgomery, Alabama, was that he had been libeled by statements in a full-page advertisement in *The New York Times* signed by sixty-four persons. Concededly, a number of the statements in the advertisement did not describe accurately some of the events referred to.

Justice Brennan, writing for the Court, stated:

> That the *Times* was paid for publishing the advertisement is as immaterial . . . as is the fact that newspapers and books are sold. . . .[26]
>
> Like insurrection, contempt, advocacy of unlawful acts, breach of the peace, obscenity, solicitation of legal business, and the various other formulae for the repression of expression that have been challenged in this Court, libel can claim no talismanic immunity from constitutional limitations. It must be measured by standards that satisfy the First Amendment.
>
> The general proposition that freedom of expression upon public questions is secured by the First Amendment has long been settled by our decisions. . . .[27]
>
> The constitutional guarantees require, we think, a federal rule that prohibits a public official from recovering damages for a defamatory falsehood relating to his official conduct unless he proves that the statement was made with "actual malice."[28]

Following *The New York Times* decision, the Court had occasion to pass on a libel judgment obtained in a New Hampshire court by a Mr. Baer, who managed the financial affairs of a ski recreation center owned and operated by a county, against an unpaid local newspaper columnist who wrote implying dishonest manipulation in the handling of finances for the center. A majority of the Court remanded the case for consideration by the trial court, in the first instance, of whether the plaintiff was a public official subject to *The New York Times* rule. Justices Clark, Stewart, and Douglas concurred. Justice Harlan concurred in part and dissented in part. Justice Black, joined by Justice Douglas, concurred and dissented. Justice Fortas dissented.[29]

Justice Douglas remarked:

> We now have the question as to how far its [*The New York Times* decision]

25 *New York Times* Co. v. Sullivan; Abernathy v. Sullivan, 376 U.S. 254 (1964); *see also* St. Amant v. Thompson, 390 U.S. 727 (1968).

26 *New York Times* Co. v. Sullivan, 376 U.S. 254, 266 (1964).

27 *Ibid.*, 269.

28 *Ibid.*, 279–80.

29 Rosenblatt v. Baer, 383 U.S. 75 (1966).

444

principles extend or how far down the hierarchy we should go.

The problems presented are considerable ones. Maybe the key man in a hierarchy is the night watchman responsible for thefts of state secrets....[30]

Yet if free discussion of public issues is the guide, I see no way to draw lines that exclude the night watchman, the file clerk, the typist, or, for that matter, anyone on the public payroll....[31]

If the term "public official" were a constitutional term, we would be stuck with it and have to give it content. But the term is our own; and so long as we are fashioning a rule of free discussion of public issues, I cannot relate it only to those who, by the Court's standard, are deemed to hold public office.[32]

Justice Black repeated what he had said in *The New York Times* case, that he felt that the First Amendment barred all such libel suits against public officials, malice or no malice. Justice Harlan maintained that "if the article in question is read by the jury as an accusation of wrongdoing by Baer, he has a good cause of action in libel. I see no reason," he added, "why that cause of action should fail if the jury finds that the article was read as accusing the three Commissioners along with Baer...."[33] Justice Fortas complained of the insufficiency of the record to present a *New York Times* question.

A unanimous Court reversed the conviction of Garrison, a Louisiana district attorney, under a criminal defamation statute for charging judges with laziness and inefficiency and of hampering his efforts to enforce the vice laws, saying the trial judge had misconstrued the high court's decision in *The New York Times* case.[34]

Writing for the Court, Justice Brennan stated:

The reasonable-belief standard applied by the trial judge is not the same as the reckless-disregard-of-truth standards. According to the trial court's opinion, a reasonable belief is one which "an ordinarily prudent man might be able to assign a just and fair reason for"; the suggestion is that under this test the immunity from criminal responsibility in the absence of ill-will disappears on proof that the exercise of ordinary care would have revealed that the statement was false. The test which we laid down in New York Times is not keyed to ordinary care; defeasance of the privilege is conditioned, not on mere negligence, but on reckless disregard for the truth.

Justice Black, concurring, said:

I believe that the First Amendment ... protects every person from having a

[30] *Ibid.,* 88.
[31] *Ibid.,* 89.
[32] *Ibid.,* 90.
[33] *Ibid.,* 100.
[34] Garrison v. Louisiana, 379 U.S. 64 (1964).

State or the Federal Government fine, imprison, or assess damages against him when he has been guilty of no conduct ... other than expressing an opinion, even though others may believe that his views are unwholesome, unpatriotic, stupid or dangerous ... Fining men or sending them to jail for criticizing public officials not only jeopardizes the free, open discussion which our Constitution guarantees, but can wholly stifle it.[35]

Justice Douglas, who joined with Justice Black, said:

I am in hearty agreement with the conclusion that this prosecution for a seditious libel was unconstitutional. Yet I feel that the gloss which the Court has put on "the freedom of speech" in the First Amendment to reach that result ... makes that basic guarantee almost unrecognizable....[36]

I think little need be added to what Mr. Justice Holmes said nearly a half century ago:

"I wholly disagree with the argument of the Government that the First Amendment left the common law as to seditious libel in force...."

The philosophy of the Sedition Act of 1798 which punished "false, scandalous and malicious" writings ... is today allowed to be applied to the States. Yet Irving Brant has shown that seditious libel was "entirely the creation of the Star Chamber." It is disquieting to know that one of its instruments of destruction is abroad in the land today.[37]

Judgments obtained by a county attorney and a chief of police in suits for libel brought against a man who had been arrested on a charge of disturbing the peace and who had charged the officials with "a diabolical plot" were vacated by a per curiam opinion following the Garrison case (above).[38]

A defendant who went to Kentucky to appeal for food, clothing, and aid for unemployed miners issued a pamphlet attacking public officials. He was prosecuted for criminal libel, which was defined as a writing calculated to create disturbances of the peace. The Court held the statute too vague for enforcement and violative of the First Amendment.[39] Justice Harlan concurred.

With the concurrence of Justices Black and Douglas, Justice Brennan, writing for the Court, expanded *The New York Times* rule to hold that "the constitutional protections for speech and press" do not permit recovery for "false reports of matters of public interest in the absence of proof that the defendant published the report with knowledge of falsity or in reckless disregard of the truth." He said that "the guarantees for speech and press are not the preserve of political expression or comment upon public affairs, essen-

35 *Ibid.*, 79–80.
36 *Ibid.*, 80.
37 *Ibid.*, 82–83.
38 Henry v. Collins, 380 U.S. 356 (1965).
39 Ashton v. Kentucky, 384 U.S. 195 (1966).

tial as those are to healthy government.... Exposure of the self to others in varying degrees is a concomitant of life in a civilized community. The risk of this exposure is an essential incident of life in a society which places a primary value on freedom of speech and of press."[40] He added that "the constitutional guarantees can tolerate sanctions against *calculated* falsehood without significant impairment of their essential function."[41]

The case involved an article in *Life* magazine commenting on a play *The Desperate Hours,* made from a novel of the same name, which *Life* mirrored as an experience of the Hill family, which had been held hostage in their Pennsylvania home by three escaped convicts. The New York Court of Appeals had held the defendant liable for invasion of the privacy of the Hill family under the New York statute on the theory that the article was published not to disseminate news but as a fictionalized version of the Hill episode for the purpose of advertising the play or of increasing the magazine's circulation.

Justices Black and Douglas concurred, while maintaining that even the restrictions of the *Times* decision improperly narrowed the ambit of the First Amendment. Justice Harlan concurred but maintained that negligence alone would justify a recovery. Justice Fortas, joined by the Chief Justice and Justice Clark, dissented, arguing that the Court's instructions sufficed to bring the jury's verdict within the scope of what the Court was now holding.

During the 1966 term the Court considered two libel cases. In the first, the *Saturday Evening Post* had published an article charging Wally Butts, former athletic director of the University of Georgia, with conspiring to "fix" a football game between his college and the University of Alabama. In the second case the Associated Press had published a dispatch about a riot on the campus of the University of Mississippi which accompanied the enrollment of James Meredith, a Negro, and the participation therein of Edwin A. Walker, a former army general who had resigned to engage in political activity.[42]

Justice Harlan wrote in both cases for four members of the Court. He held that in the case of Walker, the evidence having been found insufficient to support more than a finding of even ordinary negligence, *The New York Times* rule prevented any recovery. General Walker was, as stated by the Chief Justice,[43] "a public man in whose public conduct society and the press had a legitimate and substantial interest." Justices White, Brennan, Black, and Douglas also concurred.

In the case of Butts Justice Harlan held that a "public figure" who is not a

[40] *Time,* Inc. v. Hill, 385 U.S. 374, 387–88 (1967); *see also* Beckley Newspaper Corp. v. Hanks, 389 U.S. 81 (1967).

[41] *Time,* Inc. v. Hill, 385 U.S. 374, 389 (1967).

[42] Curtis Publishing Co. v. Butts; Associated Press v. Walker, 388 U.S. 130 (1967).

[43] *Ibid.,* 165.

"public official" may recover damages on a showing of highly unreasonable conduct short of the *Times* rule, and hence was entitled to an affirmance of the award below, which had been reduced to $460,000 for compensatory and punitive damages. The Chief Justice concurred in the result, though he contended that the *Times* rule applied both to "public figures" and to "public officials" but felt that the verdict below satisfied the rule. Justices Black, Brennan, and White also found themselves in agreement with the Chief Justice's views respecting the application of an undiminished *Times* rule.

By the vote of five members of the Court a radio-television station was held free from liability for defamatory statements of candidates for public office awarded equal time under federal acts, since under the Federal Communications Act it had no power of censorship. Justice Frankfurter, supported by Justices Harlan, Whittaker, and Stewart, dissented, holding that though the station had no power of censorship, the federal statute contained no grant of immunity from liability for libel.[44]

In two cases the Court followed *The New York Times* decision by holding that teachers may not be punished for criticizing public school officials, even though some of the charges are false, as long as they are not made recklessly or deliberately.[45]

As the Court has been called upon to mediate between the claims of free speech and the promotion of strife between religious and racial adherents, so it has been faced with religious issues under the First Amendment in connection, not only with school prayers, but also with Sunday-closing laws and their enforcement.[46]

In the first case (McGowan) six members of the Court joined in an opinion by the Chief Justice holding that a Maryland statute requiring Sunday closings, with specified exemptions, did not violate the equal protection clause or the First Amendment and that it was designed not to further religious practices but to enforce Sunday as a day for rest and recreation. Justices Frankfurter and Harlan concurred. Justice Douglas dissented on the ground that the statute violated the First Amendment.[47]

Concerning the exemptions and the equal protection challenge, the Chief Justice said:

> The constitutional safeguard is offended only if the classification rests on grounds wholly irrelevant to the achievement of the State's objective....

[44] Farmers Union v. WDAY, 360 U.S. 525 (1959).

[45] Pickering v. Board of Education, 391 U.S. 163 (1968); Watts v. Seward School Board, 391 U.S. 592 (1968).

[46] McGowan v. Maryland, 366 U.S. 420 (1961); Two Guys v. McGinley, 366 U.S. 582 (1961); Braunfeld v. Brown, 366 U.S. 599 (1961); Gallagher v. Crown Kosher Market, 366 U.S. 617 (1961).

[47] McGowan v. Maryland, 366 U.S. 420 (1961).

448

It would seem that a legislature could reasonably find that the Sunday sale of the exempted commodities was necessary either for the health of the populace or for the enhancement of the recreational atmosphere of the day—that a family which takes a Sunday ride into the country will need gasoline for the automobile and may find pleasant a soft drink or fresh fruit; that those who go to the beach may wish ice cream or some other item normally sold there; that some people will prefer alcoholic beverages or games of chance to add to their relaxation; that newspapers and drug products should always be available to the public....[48]

The essence of appellants' "establishment" argument is that Sunday is the Sabbath day of the predominant Christian sects; that the purpose of the enforced stoppage of labor on that day is to facilitate and encourage church attendance; that the purpose of setting Sunday as a day of universal rest is to induce people with no religion or people with marginal religious beliefs to join the predominant Christian sects; that the purpose of the atmosphere of tranquility created by Sunday closing is to aid the conduct of church services and religious observance of the sacred day.... There is no dispute that the original laws which deal with Sunday labor were motivated by religious forms. But what we must decide is whether present Sunday legislation, having undergone extensive changes from the earliest forms, still retains its religious character....[49]

... despite the strongly religious origin of these laws, beginning before the eighteenth century, nonreligious arguments began to be heard more distinctly and the statutes began to lose some of their totally religious flavor. In the middle 1700's, Blackstone wrote, "(T)he keeping one day in the seven holy, as a time of relaxation and refreshment as well as for public worship, is of admirable service to a state considered merely as a civil institution. It humanizes by the help of conversation and society, the manners of the lower classes, which would otherwise degenerate into a sordid ferocity and savage selfishness of spirit; it enables the industrious workman to pursue his occupation in the ensuing week with health and cheerfulness."[50]

The proponents of Sunday closing legislation are no longer exclusively representatives of religious interests....

Almost every State in our country presently has some type of Sunday regulation....[51]

... it is common knowledge that the first day of the week has come to have special significance as a rest day in this country.... The cause is irrelevant; the fact exists.... For these reasons, we hold that the Maryland statutes are not laws respecting an establishment of religion....[52]

We do not hold that Sunday legislation may not be a violation of the

---

[48] *Ibid.*, 425–26.
[49] *Ibid.*, 431.
[50] *Ibid.*, 433–44.
[51] *Ibid.*, 435.
[52] *Ibid.*, 451–52.

"Establishment" Clause if it can be demonstrated that its purpose . . . is to use the State's coercive power to aid religion. . . .[53]

Justice Frankfurter, concurring, said:

Individual opinions in constitutional controversies have been the practice throughout the Court's history. Such expression of differences in view or even in emphasis converging toward the same result makes for the clarity of candor and thereby enhances the authority of the judicial process. . . .[54]

Cultural history establishes not a few practices and prohibitions religious in origin which are retained as secular institutions and ways long after their religious sanctions and justifications are gone. . . .[55]

A provision for one day's closing per week, at the option of every particular enterpriser, might be disruptive of families whose members are employed by different enterprises . . . More important, one-day-a-week laws do not accomplish all that is accomplished by Sunday laws. They provide only a periodic physical rest, not that atmosphere of entire community repose which Sunday has traditionally brought. . . .[56]

The will of a majority of the community, reflected in the legislative process during scores of years, presumably prefers to take its leisure on Sunday. . . . At all events, Maryland, Massachusetts and Pennsylvania, like thirty-one other States with similar regulations, could reasonably so find. . . .

The question before the Court in these cases is not a new one. During a hundred and fifty years Sunday laws have been attacked in state and federal courts. . . . Every other appellate court that has considered the question has found the statutes supportable as civil regulations. . . .[57]

Appellees in the Gallagher Case . . . contend that, as applied to them, Orthodox Jewish retailers and their Orthodox Jewish customers, the Massachusetts Lord's day statute and the Pennsylvania Sunday retail sales act violate the Due Process Clause of the Fourteenth Amendment because, in effect, the statutes deter the exercise and observance of their religion. The argument runs that by compelling the Sunday closing of retail stores and thus making unavailable for business and shopping uses one-seventh part of the week, these statutes force them either to give up the Sabbath observance—an essential part of their faith—or to forego advantages enjoyed by the non-Sabbatarian majority of the community. . . .[58]

. . . the Gallagher appellees . . . point to such exceptions in twenty-one of the thirty-four jurisdictions which have statutes banning labor or employment or the selling of goods on Sunday. . . .[59]

[53] *Ibid.*, 453.
[54] *Ibid.*, 459.
[55] *Ibid.*, 503–504.
[56] *Ibid.*, 506.
[57] *Ibid.*, 507–508.
[58] *Ibid.*, 512.
[59] *Ibid.*, 514.

There are tenable reasons why a legislature might choose not to make such an exception. To whatever extent persons who come within the exception are present in a community, their activity would disturb the atmosphere of general repose, and reintroduce into Sunday the business tempo of the week. Administration would be more difficult, with violations less. . . .[60]

. . . the Sabbatarian, in proportion as he is less numerous, and hence the competition less severe, might incur through the exception a competitive advantage over the non-Sabbatarian, who would then be in a position, presumably, to complain of discrimination against *his* religion. Employers who wished to avail themselves of the exception would have to employ only their co-religionists, and there might be introduced into private employment practices an element of religious differentiation which a legislature could regard as undesirable. . . .

Administration of such a provision may require judicial inquiry into religious belief. . . . there would be nothing to prevent an enterpriser from closing on his slowest business day, to take advantage of the whole of the profitable week-end trade, thereby converting the Sunday labor ban, in effect, into a day-of-rest-in-seven statute, with choice of the day left to the individual. . . .[61]

In view of the importance of the community interests which must be weighed in the balance, is the disadvantage wrought by the nonexempting Sunday statutes an impermissible imposition upon the Sabbatarian's religious freedom? Every court which has considered the question during a century and a half has concluded that it is not. . . .[62]

In his dissent, Justice Douglas said:

The question is not whether Sunday can by force of custom and habit be retained as a day of rest. The question is whether a State can impose criminal sanctions on those who, unlike the Christian majority that makes up our society, worship on a different day or do not share the religious scruples of the majority. . . .[63]

I do not see how a State can make protesting citizens refrain from doing innocent acts on Sunday because the doing of those acts offends sentiments of their Christian neighbors. . . .[64]

It seems to me plain that by these laws, the States compel one, under sanction of law, to refrain from work or recreation on Sunday because of the majority's religious views about that day. The State by law makes Sunday a symbol of respect or adherence. . . . By what authority can government compel it? . . .[65]

A legislature of Christians can no more make minorities conform to their weekly regime than a legislature of Moslems, or a legislature of Hindus. . . .[66]

[60] *Ibid.*, 515.
[61] *Ibid.*, 516–17.
[62] *Ibid.*, 522.
[63] *Ibid.*, 561.
[64] *Ibid.*, 562.
[65] *Ibid.*, 573.
[66] *Ibid.*, 575.

451

The State can, of course, require one day of rest a week; one day when every shop or factory is closed. . . . The "day of rest" becomes purely and simply a health measure. But the Sunday laws operate differently. They force minorities to obey the majority's religious feelings of what is due and proper for a Christian community. . . .

There is an "establishment" of religion in the constitutional sense if any practice of any religious group has the sanction of law behind it. . . .[67]

When . . . the State uses its coercive powers . . . to compel minorities to observe a second Sabbath, not their own, the State undertakes to aid and "prefer one religion over another"—contrary to the command of the Constitution. . . .[68]

"Why should my faith be favored by the State over any other man's faith?" . . . None of the opinions filed today has answered that question.[69]

In the second case (Two Guys), involving a Pennsylvania statute, the Chief Justice, writing for the Court, said that the case was "essentially" the same as the McGowan case, the major differences between the Maryland and Pennsylvania statutes being the exemptions. Again the majority held the statute's purpose and effect nonreligious.[70]

In the companion case (Braunfeld) the action was brought by Orthodox Jewish merchants who closed their establishments from sundown on Friday until sundown on Saturday. The Chief Justice wrote for four members of the Court, holding the Pennsylvania statute constitutional. Justices Frankfurter and Harlan concurred; Justice Douglas dissented; Justices Brennan and Stewart dissented in part.

The Chief Justice said that all questions but one had been answered in the two previous decisions, leaving for discussion only the question of whether "the statute interferes with the free exercise of appellants' religion."[71] On that score, he said:

> The Sunday law simply regulates a secular activity and, as applied to appellants, operates so as to make the practice of their religious beliefs more expensive. Furthermore, the law's effect does not inconvenience all members of the Orthodox Jewish faith but only those who believe it necessary to work on Sunday. . . .
>
> To strike down . . . legislation which imposes only an indirect burden on the exercise of religion . . . would radically restrict the operating latitude of the legislature. . . .[72]

If the State regulates conduct by enacting a general law within its power,

[67] *Ibid.*, 576.
[68] *Ibid.*, 577.
[69] *Ibid.*, 581.
[70] Two Guys v. McGinley, 366 U.S. 582, 598 (1961).
[71] Braunfeld v. Brown, 366 U.S. 599, 600 (1961).
[72] *Ibid.*, 605–606.

the purpose and effect of which is to advance the State's secular goals, the statute is valid despite its indirect burden on religious observance unless the State may accomplish its purpose by means which do not impose such a burden.[73]

Justice Brennan, supported by Justice Stewart, maintained that

... the issue in this case ... is whether a State may put an individual to a choice between his business and his religion. The Court today holds that it may. But I dissent, believing that such a law prohibits the free exercise of religion....[74]

In this case the Court seems to say, without so much as a deferential nod towards that high place which we have accorded religious freedom in the past, that any substantial state interest will justify encroachments on religious practice, at least if these encroachments are cloaked in the guise of some non-religious public purpose....

... the laws do not say that appellants must work on Saturday. But their effect is that appellants may not simultaneously practice their religion and their trade, without being hampered by a substantial competitive disadvantage.... This clog upon the exercise of religion, this state-imposed burden on Orthodox Judaism, has exactly the same economic effect as a tax levied upon the sale of religious literature....

What then, is the compelling state interest ... to impede appellants' freedom of worship? ... It is the mere convenience of having everyone rest on the same day....

It is true, I suppose, that the granting of such an exemption would make Sundays a little noisier and the task of police and prosecutor a little more difficult. It is also true that a majority—21—of the 34 States which have general Sunday regulations have exemptions of this kind. We are not told that those States are significantly noisier, or that their police are significantly more burdened, than Pennsylvania's....[75]

The Court, in my view, has exalted administrative convenience to a constitutional level high enough to justify making one religion economically disadvantageous. The Court would justify this result on the ground that the effect on religion, though substantial, is indirect. The Court forgets, I think, a warning uttered during the congressional discussion of the First Amendment itself: "the rights of conscience are, in their nature, of peculiar delicacy, and will little bear the gentlest touch of governmental hand."[76]

Justice Stewart, agreeing with Justice Brennan, added:

Pennsylvania has passed a law which compels an Orthodox Jew to choose between his religious faith and his economic survival. That is a cruel choice. It is

[73] *Ibid.*, 607.
[74] *Ibid.*, 611.
[75] *Ibid.*, 613–15.
[76] *Ibid.*, 616.

a choice which I think no State can constitutionally demand. For me this is not something that can be swept under the rug and forgotten in the interest of enforced Sunday togetherness. I think the impact of this law upon these appellants grossly violates their constitutional right to the free exercise of their religion.[77]

In the fourth of the above cases (Gallagher) the plaintiff was a corporation operating a kosher market and owned by Orthodox Jews. Again the Chief Justice wrote for four members of the Court, Justices Frankfurter and Harlan concurred in upholding the Massachusetts statute, and Justices Douglas, Stewart, and Brennan dissented.[78]

Another novel and interesting case involving religion came to the Court when a member of the Seventh-Day Adventists, whose religion would not permit her to work on Saturday, the Sabbath of her faith, was discharged from her employment and could not find another job, as a result of which she sought unemployment insurance. The state commission denied her application upon the ground that she would not accept suitable work when offered. The Court, with Justice Brennan writing for six members, held the South Carolina statute, which so provided, violated the petitioner's rights under the First and Fourteenth amendments.[79] Justice Stewart concurred; Justices Harlan and White dissented.

Justice Stewart said:

I think that the guarantee of religious liberty embodied in the Free Exercise Clause affirmatively requires government to create an atmosphere of hospitality and accommodation to individual belief or disbelief. In short, I think our Constitution commands the positive protection by government of religious freedom —not only for a minority, however small—not only for the majority, however large—but for each of us. . . . the Court . . . holds that the State must prefer a religious over a secular ground for being unavailable for work—that state financial support of the appellant's religion is constitutionally required to carry out "the governmental obligation of neutrality in the face of religious differences" . . . .

. . . so long as the resounding but fallacious fundamentalist rhetoric of some of our Establishment Clause opinions remains on our books, to be disregarded at will as in the present case, or to be indiscriminatingly invoked as in the Schempp case, so long will the possibility of consistent and perceptive decision in this most difficult and delicate area of constitutional law be impeded and impaired. . . .[80]

[77] Ibid.
[78] Gallagher v. Crown Kosher Market, 366 U.S. 617 (1961).
[79] Sherbert v. Verner, 374 U.S. 398 (1963).
[80] Ibid., 415–17.

It is clear to me that in order to reach this conclusion the Court must explicitly reject the reasoning of Braunfeld v. Brown. I think the Braunfeld case was wrongly decided and should be overruled. . . .[81]

Justice Harlan, dissenting, said:

In the present case all that the state court has done is to apply . . . accepted principles. Since virtually all of the mills . . . were operating on a six-day week, the appellant was "unavailable for work," and thus ineligible for benefits, when personal considerations prevented her from accepting employment on a full-time basis. . . . The fact that these personal considerations sprang from her religious convictions was wholly without relevance to the state court's application of the law. Thus in no proper sense can it be said that the State discriminated against the appellant on the basis of her religious beliefs or that she was denied benefits *because* she was a Seventh-day Adventist. She was denied benefits who was not "available for work" for personal reasons. . . .

What the Court is holding is that if the State chooses to condition unemployment compensation on the applicant's availability for work, it is constitutionally compelled to *carve out an exception*—and to provide benefits—for those whose unavailability is due to their religious convictions.[82]

Seven members of the Court joined in an opinion holding that a provision in the Maryland Constitution requiring a state officeholder to declare a "belief in the existence of God" was contrary to Article 6 of the federal Constitution and violated the First and Fourteenth amendments.[83] Justices Frankfurter and Harlan concurred.

Justice Black said: "We repeat and again reaffirm that neither a State nor the Federal Government can constitutionally force a person 'to profess a belief or disbelief in any religion.' "[84]

The Court held that three conscientious objectors met the test of the statute in which Congress used the expression "Supreme Being" rather than the designation "God" as intending to indicate a "belief that is sincere and meaningful . . . parallel to that filled by the orthodox belief in God."[85] Justice Douglas concurred.

Although as a matter of strict legal rule, refusal by the high court to grant certiorari is not to be deemed the equivalence of affirmance, it may be noted that the Court refused certiorari, over the dissent of Justice Douglas, to an atheist who complained that the maintenance supported by private donations

81 *Ibid.*, 418.
82 *Ibid.*, 419–20.
83 Torcaso v. Watkins, 367 U.S. 488 (1961).
84 *Ibid.*, 495.
85 United States v. Seeger; United States v. Jakobson; Peter v. United States, 380 U.S. 163 (1965).

of a large cross on the Dade County, Miami, Florida, Courthouse at Christmas time, violated First Amendment rights.[86]

A number of other First Amendment cases may be considered worthy of mention. Seven members of the Court struck down an ordinance requiring persons seeking to solicit members for any organization requiring payment of dues to obtain a permit which the authorities might refuse if they did not approve of the applicant or of his organization or of the latter's effect on the general welfare of the citizens of the city.[87] The majority held the statute violated freedom of speech. Justices Frankfurter and Clark dissented on a nonconstitutional ground.

The Court struck down a Los Angeles ordinance prohibiting the distribution of any anonymous handbill as violating freedom of speech and press.[88] The opinion of the Court excluded consideration of a limited ordinance. Justice Harlan concurred; Justices Clark, Frankfurter, and Whittaker dissented.

The Court held valid the Hatch Act, which made it unlawful for employees in the executive branch of the federal government to take any active part in political management or in political campaigns out of, as well as in, working hours.[89] Justice Frankfurter concurred; Justices Murphy and Jackson did not participate. Justice Black dissented; Justice Douglas dissented in part. Justice Black maintained that

> our political system, different from many others, rests on the foundation of a belief in rule by the people—not some, but all the people. . . . In a country whose people elect their leaders and decide great public issues, the voice of none should be suppressed—at least such is the assumption of the First Amendment. That Amendment, unless I misunderstand its meaning, includes a command that the Government must, in order to promote its own interest, leave the people at liberty to speak their own thoughts about government, advocate their own favored governmental causes and work for their own political candidates and parties.[90]

A unanimous Court subscribed to an opinion by the Chief Justice reversing the finding of a three-judge district court that the exclusion by the Georgia House of Representatives of Julian Bond, a Negro duly elected, did not violate his constitutional rights.[91]

Bond had made statements at variance with government policy concerning the Vietnam war and the operation of the draft in connection therewith that

---

[86] Paul v. Dade County, 390 U.S. 1041 (1968).
[87] Staub v. City of Baxley, 355 U.S. 313 (1958).
[88] Talley v. California, 362 U.S. 60 (1960).
[89] United Public Workers v. Mitchell, 330 U.S. 75 (1947).
[90] *Ibid.*, 114.
[91] Bond v. Floyd, 385 U.S. 116 (1966).

the Georgia legislature maintained were at variance with the obligations of one taking the constitutional oath required of an elected legislator. A special committee of the House reported that Bond "does not and will not support the Constitutions of the United States and of Georgia."[92] Georgia argued that the legislature might determine "whether a given Representative may take the oath with sincerity" in determining whether or not such a representative meets the qualification prescribed by the Georgia Constitution.[93]

Writing for a unanimous Court, Chief Justice Warren held that Bond's statements were protected by the First Amendment; that the requirement for an oath did not permit limitation of a legislator's capacity to discuss his views of local or national policy and that the rationale of *The New York Times* case protected those utterances.

Worthy of mention is the Griswold decision that unnecessarily struck down the obsolete and repealed statute that made it a criminal offense for married persons to use contraceptives.[94] In 1965, after previous futile attempts to invoke the Court's jurisdiction by seeking declaratory judgments,[95] the Court was able, in passing on convictions under the statute, to take jurisdiction and by a vote of six to three, to strike down the statute.

Justice Douglas wrote for four members of the Court. Justice Goldberg, supported by the Chief Justice and Justice Brennan, joined in the opinion, and the latter two joined in a concurring opinion by Goldberg. Justices Harlan and White concurred in the result. Justices Black and Stewart dissented.

Finding the statute unconstitutional as a violation of constitutionally guaranteed privacy, Justice Douglas wrote:

> The First Amendment has a penumbra where privacy is respected from governmental intrusion. . . .[96]
>
> . . . specific guaranties in the Bill of Rights have penumbras, formed by emanations from those guarantees that help give them life and substances. . . . Various guarantees create zones of privacy. . . .[97]
>
> We deal with a right of privacy older than the Bill of Rights—older than our political parties, older than our school system. Marriage is a coming together for better or for worse, hopefully enduring and intimate to the degree of being sacred. It is an association that promotes a way of life, not causes; a harmony in living, not political faiths; a bilateral loyalty, not commercial or social projects. Yet it is an association for as noble a purpose as any involved in our prior decisions.[98]

[92] *Ibid.*, 125.
[93] *Ibid.*, 130.
[94] Griswold v. Connecticut, 381 U.S. 479 (1965).
[95] Tileston v. Ullman, 318 U.S. 44 (1943); Poe, Doe, Buxton v. Ullman, 367 U.S. 497 (1961).
[96] Griswold v. Connecticut, 381 U.S. 479, 483 (1965).
[97] *Ibid.*, 484.
[98] *Ibid.*, 486.

Justice Goldberg, concurring, wrote:

This Court ... has held that the Fourteenth Amendment absorbs and applies to the States those specifics of the first eight amendments which express fundamental personal rights.[99]

To hold that a right so basic and fundamental and so deep-rooted in our society as the right of privacy in marriage may be infringed because that right is not guaranteed in so many words by the first eight amendments to the Constitution is to ignore the Ninth Amendment and to give it no effect whatever....[100]

I do not take the position of my Brother Black in his dissent in Adamson v. California ... that the entire Bill of Rights is incorporated in the Fourteenth Amendment....[101]

The entire fabric of the Constitution and the purposes that clearly underlie its specific guarantees demonstrate that the rights to marital privacy and to marry and raise a family are of similar order and magnitude as the fundamental rights specifically protected.[102]

Justice Harlan, concurring, said that, in his view,

the proper constitutional inquiry in this case is whether this Connecticut statute infringes the Due Process Clause of the Fourteenth Amendment because the enactment violates basic values "implicit in the concept of ordered liberty" [quoting Palko v. Connecticut]....I believe that it does....[103]

Judicial self-restraint will not, I suggest, be brought about in the "due process" area by the historically unfounded incorporation formula long advanced by my Brother Black, and now in part espoused by my Brother Stewart.[104]

Justice White, also concurring, declared: "In my view this Connecticut law as applied to married couples deprives them of 'liberty' without due process of law.... There is a 'realm of family life which the state cannot enter' without substantial justification." (He was citing Prince v. Massachusetts.)[105]

Justice Black said in his dissent:

The Court talks about a constitutional "right of privacy" as though there is some constitutional provision or provisions forbidding any law ever to be passed which might abridge the "privacy" of individuals. But there is not. There are, of course, guarantees in certain specific constitutional provisions which are designed in part to protect privacy at certain times and places with respect to

[99] *Ibid.*, 488.
[100] *Ibid.*, 491.
[101] *Ibid.*, 492.
[102] *Ibid.*, 495.
[103] *Ibid.*, 500.
[104] *Ibid.*, 501.
[105] *Ibid.*, 502.

certain activities. Such, for example, is the Fourth Amendment's guarantee against "unreasonable searches and seizures"....[106]

While I completely subscribe to the holding in Marbury v. Madison...I do not believe that we are granted power by the Due Process Clause or any other constitutional provision or provisions to measure constitutionality by our belief that legislation is arbitrary, capricious or unreasonable....Such an appraisal of the wisdom of legislation is an attribute of the power to make laws, not of the power to interpret them....[107]

I realize that many good and able men have eloquently spoken and written, sometimes in rhapsodical strains about the duty of this Court to keep the Constitution in tune with the times. The idea is that the Constitution must be changed from time to time and that this Court is charged with a duty to make those changes. For myself, I must with all deference reject that philosophy. The Constitution makers knew the need for change and provided for it....That method of change was good for our Fathers, and being somewhat old-fashioned I must add it is good enough for me.[108]

Justice Stewart, dissenting, elaborated further:

...to say that the Ninth Amendment has anything to do with this case is to turn somersaults with history. The Ninth Amendment, like its companion, the Tenth, which this Court held "states but a truism that all is retained which has not been surrendered," United States v. Darby, was framed by James Madison and adopted by the States simply to make clear that the adoption of the Bill of Rights did not alter the plan that the *Federal* Government was to be a government of express and limited powers, and that all rights and powers not delegated to it were retained by the people and the individual States. Until today no member of this Court has ever suggested that the Ninth Amendment meant anything else....

With all deference, I can find no such general right of privacy in the Bill of Rights, in any other part of the Constitution, or in any case ever before decided by this Court....[109]

If the law before us does not reflect the standards of the people of Connecticut, the people of Connecticut can freely exercise their true Ninth and Tenth Amendment rights to persuade their elected representatives to repeal it. That is the constitutional way to take this law off the books.[110]

It is again to be noted that, pending the litigation, Justice Stewart's suggestion had been anticipated: the law had been repealed.

Later Justice Douglas and the rest of the Court refused to extend the um-

---

[106] *Ibid.*, 508–509.
[107] *Ibid.*, 513.
[108] *Ibid.*, 522.
[109] *Ibid.*, 529–30.
[110] *Ibid.*, 531.

brella of the right of privacy over a contention that a New York State law authorizing the sale of records of car registrations to the highest bidder (who presumably would use them for purposes of solicitation) was unconstitutional as violating citizens' right of privacy, by denying review of a lower court determination.[111]

[111] Lamont v. Commissioner of Motor Vehicles, 391 U.S. 915 (1968).

Labor

THE GROWTH OF THE LABOR MOVEMENT and the removal of restrictions upon its use of political power have flooded the courts with labor controversies. While the National Labor Relations Act diverted the bulk of these to the National Labor Relations Board, the high court has been called upon, with considerable frequency, to consider issues of moment. Some of these cases merit mention.

Holding that an injunction may issue against peaceful picketing by a union for the purpose of coercing a wholesale distributor of ice to agree to refrain from selling ice to peddlers not members of the union,[1] the Court distinguished prior cases.[2]

Five members of the Court sustained an injunction against picketing of a self-employer's place of business for the purpose of compelling him to adopt a union shop,[3] distinguishing prior cases.[4] Justice Clark concurred; Justices Black, Minton, and Reed dissented; Justice Douglas did not participate.

Justice Frankfurter, writing for himself and for Justices Jackson and Burton and the Chief Justice, said: "While picketing has an ingredient of communication it cannot dogmatically be equated with the constitutionally protected freedom of speech."[5] Justices Minton and Reed relied on the distinguished cases.

A majority of six members held that a state court could enjoin violence, intimidation, and threats by strikers but could not enjoin peaceful picketing.[6] The Chief Justice and Justices Black and Douglas dissented, maintaining that the NLRB had exclusive jurisdiction of the controversy.

[1] Giboney v. Empire Storage Co., 336 U.S. 490 (1949).
[2] Thornhill v. Alabama, 310 U.S. 88 (1940); Allen Bradley Co. v. Local No. 3, 325 U.S. 797 (1945); Carlson v. California, 310 U.S. 106 (1940); Carpenters Union v. Ritter's Cafe, 315 U.S. 722 (1942); Bakery Drivers Local v. Wohl, 315 U.S. 769 (1942).
[3] Teamsters Union v. Hanke; Automobile Drivers v. Cline, 339 U.S. 470 (1950).
[4] A.F. of L. v. Swing, 312 U.S. 321 (1941); Bakery Drivers Local v. Wohl, 315 U.S. 769 (1942); Cafeteria Employees v. Angelos, 320 U.S. 293 (1943).
[5] Teamsters Union v. Hanke, 339 U.S. 470, 474 (1950).
[6] Youngdahl v. Rainfair, 355 U.S. 131 (1957).

Right-to-work laws posed and still pose controversial questions. The Court upheld the Virginia courts, which had enjoined picketing by a labor union because some of the subcontractors employed nonunion help, as violative of the Virginia right-to-work law. Justices Black and Douglas dissented.[7]

The Court upheld right-to-work laws in North Carolina and Nebraska.[8] Justice Black, writing for six members of the Court, said that such laws do not violate the guarantees of free speech and peaceable assembly, the contract clause, or the equal protection and due process clauses of the Constitution. Justices Frankfurter, Murphy, and Rutledge concurred, with varying reservations. Justice Black, writing for the majority, said that

what these state laws do is to forbid employers acting alone or in concert with labor organizations deliberately to restrict employment to none but union members....[9]

There cannot be wrung from a constitutional right of workers to assemble to discuss improvement of their own working standards, a further constitutional right to drive from remunerative employment all other persons who will not or cannot, participate in union assemblies....[10]

This Court, beginning at least as early as 1934 ... has steadily rejected the due process philosophy enunciated in the Adair-Coppage line of cases. In doing so it has consciously returned closer and closer to the earlier constitutional principle that states have power to legislate against what are found to be injurious practices in their internal commercial and business affairs.... Under this constitutional doctrine the Due Process Clause is no longer to be so broadly construed that the Congress and state legislatures are put in a straitjacket when they attempt to suppress business and industrial conditions which they regard as offensive to the public welfare.

Appellants now ask us to return, at least in part, to the due process philosophy that has been deliberately discarded. Claiming that the Federal Constitution itself affords protection for union members against discrimination, they nevertheless assert that the same Constitution forbids a state from providing the same protection for non-union members. Just as we have held that the Due Process Clause erects no obstacle to block legislative protection of union members, we now hold that legislative protection can be afforded non-union workers.[11]

Justices Frankfurter and Rutledge each wrote, concurring; Justice Murphy joined with Rutledge.

A companion case[12] involved a right-to-work amendment to the Arizona

---

7 Local Union No. 10 v. Graham, 345 U.S. 192 (1953).
8 Lincoln Union v. Northwestern Co.; Whitaker v. North Carolina, 335 U.S. 525 (1949).
9 Ibid., 530.
10 Ibid., 531.
11 Ibid., 536–37.
12 A.F. of L. v. American Sash Co., 335 U.S. 538 (1949).

Constitution. Justice Black wrote for six members upholding the constitution-ality of the provision. Justices Frankfurter and Rutledge concurred with opinions applicable to this and the former case. Justice Murphy dissented.

Justice Frankfurter stated:

> Unions are powers within the State. Like the power of industrial and financial aggregations, the power of organized labor springs from a group which is only a fraction of the whole that Mr. Justice Holmes referred to as "the one club to which we all belong"....[13]
>
> If concern for the individual justifies incorporating in the Constitution itself devices to curb public authority, a legislative judgment that his protection requires the regulation of the private power of unions cannot be dismissed as insupportable. A union is no more than a medium through which individuals are able to act together; union power was begotten of individual helplessness. But that power can come into being only when, and continue to exist only so long as, individual aims are seen to be shared in common with the other mem-bers of the group.... It is an easy transition to thinking of the union as an entity having rights and purposes of its own....
>
> At the point where the mutual advantage of association demands too much individual disadvantage, a compromise must be struck....[14]
>
> Mr. Justice Brandeis ... before he came to this Court, had been a staunch promoter of unionism....[15]
>
> Yet at the same time he believed that "The objections, legal, economic and social, against the closed shop are so strong, and the ideas of the closed shop so antagonistic to the American spirit, that the insistence upon it has been a serious obstacle to union progress" ... On another occasion he wrote: "But the American people should not, and will not, accept unionism if it involves the closed shop. They will not consent to the exchange of the tyranny of the employer for the tyranny of the employee." ... In summing up his views on unionism, he said: "... a nucleus of unorganized labor will check oppression by the union as the union checks oppression by the employer."[16]

With the concurrence of Justice Frankfurter, a unanimous Court upheld the permission of the Railway Labor Act to make union-shop agreements, despite the right-to-work provisions of the Nebraska Constitution, over a claim of violation of the First and Fifth amendments.[17]

Justice Douglas, writing for the Court, remarked:

> The choice by the Congress of the union shop as a stabilizing force seems to us to be an allowable one. Much might be said pro and con if the policy issue

[13] *Ibid.*, 544.
[14] *Ibid.*, 545–46.
[15] *Ibid.*, 550.
[16] *Ibid.*, 551–52.
[17] Railway Employees' Dept. v. Hanson, 351 U.S. 225 (1956).

were before us. . . . But the question is one of policy with which the judiciary has no concern. . . .[18]

On the present record, there is no more an infringement or impairment of First Amendment rights than there would be in the case of a lawyer who by state law is required to be a member of an integrated bar. It is argued that compulsory membership will be used to impair freedom of expression. But that problem is not presented by this record . . . if the exaction of dues, initiation fees, or assessments is used as a cover for forcing ideological conformity or other action in contravention of the First Amendment, this judgment will not prejudice the decision in that case.[19]

Justice Frankfurter, concurring, said: "The Court has put to one side situations not now before us for which the protection of the First Amendment was earnestly urged at the bar. I, too, leave them to one side."[20]

Strikes affecting the national interest still engage the attention of the President and the Congress. In 1952, to avoid a strike in the steel industry which would affect the prosecution of the Korean War, President Truman, without statutory authority, ordered the Secretary of Commerce to take possession of and operate most of the steel mills throughout the country, in order to avoid a national catastrophe, since a work stoppage would immediately imperil the national defense at a time when American armed forces were fighting in Korea. Justice Black wrote for the Court, maintaining that the President lacked power to seize private property, despite the emergency. Justices Frankfurter, Douglas, Jackson, and Burton concurred, each writing a separate opinion, as did Justice Clark. The Chief Justice, supported by Justices Reed and Minton, dissented.[21]

Later the Supreme Court of Missouri held valid statutes authorizing the Governor to seize a strike-bound public utility and enjoin the strike, though the injunction previously issued had expired. Six members of the high court voted to vacate the judgment, holding the controversy moot.[22] The Chief Justice and Justices Black and Brennan dissented, maintaining that since the statute imposed penalties on the union, its constitutionality should be determined, meanwhile contending that the statute was unconstitutional under a prior decision. Previously, efforts to prevent public hardship arising from strikes of public utility employees had met with rebuffs from the Court.

By a vote of six to three the Court struck down a Wisconsin statute that prohibited strikes against public utilities and provided for compulsory arbitration for labor disputes after an impasse in collective bargaining had been

18 *Ibid.*, 233–34.
19 *Ibid.*, 238.
20 *Ibid.*, 242.
21 Youngstown Co. v. Sawyer, 343 U.S. 579 (1952).
22 Local Nos. 8–6 v. Missouri, 361 U.S. 363 (1960).

reached, upon the ground that it conflicted with the federal statutes governing the subject.[23]

Justice Frankfurter, dissenting, said that "the states are not precluded from enacting laws on labor relations merely because Congress had—to use the conventional phrase—entered the field." And, construing the Taft-Hartley Act, he added: "Congress decided no more than that it did not wish to subject local utilities to the control of the Federal Government."[24] "A stoppage in utility service," he said, "clearly involves the needs of a community as to evoke instinctively the power of government," and "...the principle of hands-off collective bargaining is no more absolute than the right to strike."[25]

Citing a previous case,[26] the Court held that a Missouri statute making a strike against a utility company unlawful was violative of the provisions of the National Labor Relations Act. The Court said: "It is hardly necessary to add that nothing we have said even remotely affects the right of a State to own or operate a public utility or any other business, nor the right or duty of the chief executive or legislature of a State to deal with emergency conditions of public danger, violence, or disaster."[27]

The obvious need of restraining the political power of the unions, with their own paucity of democratic control, met with favor at the hands of an earlier conservative court, while a later one gave the unions an out.

Thus six members of the Court upheld an indictment of a labor organization under a federal statute for making a contribution or expenditure in connection with an election for federal office by using union dues to sponsor commercial television broadcasts to influence the selection of candidates. The Chief Justice and Justices Black and Douglas dissented.[28]

Justice Frankfurter, writing for the majority, said:

> ... what is involved here is the integrity of our electoral process. ...
>
> The concentration of wealth consequent upon the industrial expansion in the post-Civil War era had profound implications for American life.... "The nation was fabulously rich but its wealth was gravitating rapidly into the hands of a small portion of the population, and the power of wealth threatened to undermine the political integrity of the Republic." ...
>
> In the 90's many States passed laws requiring candidates for office and their political committees to make public the sources and amounts of contributions to their campaign funds and the recipients and amounts of their cam-

---

[23] Amalgamated Assoc., United Workers v. Wisconsin Board, 340 U.S. 383 (1951).

[24] Ibid., 403.

[25] Ibid., 405.

[26] Ibid.

[27] Amalgamated Assoc. v. Missouri, 374 U.S. 74, 83 (1963).

[28] United States v. International Union, 352 U.S. 567 (1957).

paign expenditures. . . . But these state publicity laws either became dead letters or were found to be futile. . . .[29]

This Act of 1907 was merely the first concrete manifestation of a continuing congressional concern for elections "free from the power of money" . . .[30]

The need for unprecedented economic mobilization propelled by World War II enormously stimulated the power of organized labor and soon aroused consciousness of its power outside its ranks. . . . the belief grew that, just as the great corporations had made high political contributions to influence governmental action or inaction, whether consciously or unconsciously, the powerful unions were pursuing a similar course, and with the same untoward consequences for the democratic process. . . .[31]

The 1945 Report of the House Special Committee to Investigate Campaign Expenditures expressed concern over the vast amounts that some labor organizations were devoting to politics.[32]

Referring to the Act in question, prohibiting corporations and labor organizations from making contributions or expenditures in connection with federal elections (18 U. S. C., Sec. 610), Justice Frankfurter held that the indictment stated an offense under the statute. He distinguished a prior decision[33] where the political recommendation was distributed only to union members or to purchasers of the *CIO News,* and not to the public at large. He directed the prosecution to proceed and therefore found it unnecessary to pass on the constitutional question, which, however, became the subject of the dissent.

Dissenting, Justice Douglas wrote:

> We deal here with a problem that is fundamental to the electoral process. . . . It is whether a union can express its views on the issues of an election and on the merits of the candidates, unrestrained and unfettered by the Congress. The principle at stake is not peculiar to unions. It is applicable as well to associations of manufacturers, retail and wholesale trade groups, consumers' leagues, farmers' unions, religious groups and every other association representing a segment of American life and taking an active part in our political campaigns and discussion. . . .
>
> It is important—vitally important—that all channels of communication be open to them during every election, that no point of view be restrained or barred, and that the people have access to the views of every group in the community. . . .
>
> Making a speech endorsing a candidate for office does not . . . deserve to be identified with anti-social conduct. Until today political speech has never been considered a crime. . . . It usually costs money to communicate an idea to a

[29] *Ibid.,* 570–71.
[30] *Ibid.,* 575.
[31] *Ibid.,* 578.
[32] *Ibid.,* 580.
[33] United States v. CIO, 335 U.S. 106 (1948); United States v. International Union, 352 U.S. 567 (1957).

large audience.... Yet this statute ... makes criminal any "expenditure" by a union for the purpose of expressing its views on the issues of an election and the candidates.... The principle applied today would make equally criminal the use by a union of funds to print pamphlets for general distribution or to distribute political literature at large....[34]

... the size of the audience has heretofore been deemed wholly irrelevant to First Amendment issues. One has a right to freedom of speech whether he talks to one person or to one thousand....[35]

... the Court asks whether the broadcast was "paid for out of the general dues of the union membership".... Behind this question is the idea that there may be a minority of union members who are of a different political school than their leaders.... All union expenditures for political discourse are banned because a minority might object....[36]

If minorities need protection against the use of union funds for political speech-making, there are ways of reaching that and without denying the majority their First Amendment rights....

Some may think that one group or another should not express its views in an election because it is too powerful, because it advocates unpopular ideas, or because it has a record of lawless action. But these are not justifications for withholding First Amendment rights from any group—labor or corporate.[37]

Later, union members sued to enjoin enforcement of a union-shop agreement, which resulted in a holding that a provision of the Railway Labor Act was unconstitutional because it permitted union use of funds for political purposes. The Court reversed the judgment below.[38] Justice Brennan wrote for four members of the Court, saying it was unnecessary to pass on the constitutionality of the provision since it denied authority to a union, over a member's objection, to spend his money for political purposes. The opinion suggested possible means of meeting the objections. Justice Douglas concurred; Justice Whittaker also concurred but dissented from the suggestions for remedies. Justice Black dissented, maintaining that the provision violated the First Amendment. Justices Frankfurter and Harlan dissented.

Justice Brennan maintained that:

appellees' grievance stems from the spending of their funds for purposes not authorized by the Act in the face of their objection.... If their money were used for purposes contemplated by Section 2, Eleventh, the appellees would have no grievance at all....[39]

[34] *Ibid.*, 593–94.
[35] *Ibid.*, 595.
[36] *Ibid.*, 596.
[37] *Ibid.*, 597.
[38] International Machinists v. Street, 367 U.S. 740 (1961).
[39] *Ibid.*, 771.

Whatever may be the powers of Congress or the States to forbid unions altogether to make various types of political expenditures, as to which we express no opinion here. . . .

. . . an injunction would work a restraint on the expression of political ideas which might be offensive to the First Amendment. For the majority also has an interest in stating its views without being silenced by the dissenters. . . .[40]

One remedy would be an injunction against expenditures for political causes opposed by each complaining employee of a sum from those moneys to be spent by the union for political purposes.[41]

Justice Douglas observed:

The collection of dues for paying the costs of collective bargaining of which each member is a beneficiary is one thing. If, however, dues are used, or assessments are made, to promote or oppose birth control, to repeal or increase the taxes on cosmetics, to promote or oppose the admission of Red China into the United Nations, and the like, then the group compels an individual to support with his money causes beyond what gave rise to the need for group action.[42]

I think the same must be said when union dues or assessments are used to elect a Governor, a Congressman, a Senator or a President. It might be said that election of a Franklin D. Roosevelt rather than a Calvin Coolidge might be the best possible way to serve the cause of collective bargaining. But even such a selective use of union funds for political purposes subordinates the individual's First Amendment rights to the views of the majority. I do not see how that can be done, even though the objector retains his rights to campaign, to speak, to vote as he chooses. For when union funds are used for that purpose, the individual is required to finance political projects against which he may be in rebellion. The furtherance of the common cause leaves some leeway for the leadership of the group. As long as they act to promote the cause which justified bringing the group together, the individual cannot withdraw his financial support merely because he disagrees with the group's strategy. . . . But since the funds here in issue are used for causes other than defraying the costs of collective bargaining, I would affirm the judgment below with modifications. . . . there is the practical problem of mustering five Justices for a judgment in this case. So I have concluded *dubitante* to agree to the one suggested by Mr. Justice Brennan.[43]

Justice Black said in dissent:

The Supreme Court of Georgia affirmed, holding that "(o)ne who is compelled to contribute the fruits of his labor to support or promote political or

[40] *Ibid.*, 773.
[41] *Ibid.*, 774–75.
[42] *Ibid.*, 777.
[43] *Ibid.*, 778–79.

economic programs or support candidates for public office is just as much deprived of his freedom of speech as if he were compelled to give his vocal support to doctrines he opposes." I fully agree with this holding....[44]

... Congress with its eyes wide open passed that section, knowing that its broad language would permit the use of union dues to advocate causes, doctrines, laws, candidates and parties, whether individual members objected or not....[45]

There is, of course, no constitutional reason why a union or other private group may not spend its funds for political or ideological causes if its members voluntarily join it and can voluntarily get out of it....[46]

But a different situation arises when a federal law steps in and authorizes such a group to carry on activities at the expense of persons who do not choose to be members of the group as well as those who do....

And it makes no difference if, as is urged, political and legislative activities are helpful adjuncts of collective bargaining. Doubtless employers could make the same arguments in favor of compulsory contributions to an association of employers for use in political and economic programs calculated to help collective bargaining on their side. But the argument is equally unappealing whoever makes it. The stark fact is that this Act of Congress is being used as a means to exact money from these employees to help get votes to win elections for parties and candidates and to support doctrines they are against. If this is constitutional the First Amendment is not the charter of political and religious liberty its sponsors believed it to be.[47]

Concurrently the same issue was presented when the Court passed on the dismissal of an action brought by a Wisconsin lawyer to recover dues he paid to the integrated Wisconsin State Bar, claiming that the compulsion to join and pay violated his Fourteenth Amendment rights. Justice Brennan announced the affirmance of the judgment below in an opinion in which the Chief Justice and Justices Clark and Stewart joined, supported by an opinion by Justice Harlan, who was joined by Justice Frankfurter, all agreeing that it was constitutional for a state to require membership in an integrated bar association as a condition of practicing law. Justice Douglas dissented.[48]

Justice Brennan's opinion held that the issue whether plaintiff's rights under the First Amendment were infringed by the use of his money for causes he opposed did not require determination. Justice Harlan maintained that the requirement was constitutional. Justice Whittaker concurred in the result. Justice Black, dissenting, maintained that the compulsion to pay dues violated the First Amendment.

[44] *Ibid.*, 783–84.
[45] *Ibid.*, 784–85.
[46] *Ibid.*, 788.
[47] *Ibid.*, 789–90.
[48] Lathrop v. Donahue, 367 U.S. 820 (1961).

It was admitted that the state bar engaged in political activities, although it seemed "plain that legislative activity" was "not the major activity of the State Bar. The activities without apparent political coloration are many."[49]

Justice Brennan found that the claim of impingement upon freedom of association was no different from that overruled in the previous Hanson case. He refused to consider the constitutional question as the Court had refused in the preceding International Machinist case. Justice Harlan, agreeing with Justice Black that "the Constitutional issue is inescapably before us," said he felt that the previous Hanson case disposed of the issue.

Justice Black declared:

I do not believe that either the bench, the bar or the litigants will know what has been decided in this case—certainly I do not.... the only proposition in this case for which there is a majority is that the constitutional question is properly here, and the five members of the Court who make up that majority express their views on this constitutional question. Yet a minority of four refuses to pass on the question and it is therefore left completely up in the air— the Court decided nothing....[50]

On the merits, the question posed in this case is, in my judgment, identical to that posed to but avoided by the Court in the Street Case. Thus, the same reasons that led me to conclude that it violates the First Amendment for a union to use dues compelled under a union-shop agreement to advocate views contrary to those advocated by the workers paying the dues under protest led me to the conclusion that an integrated bar cannot take the money of protesting lawyers and use it to support causes they are against....[51]

... I can think of few plainer, more direct abridgments of the freedoms of the First Amendment than to compel persons to support candidates, parties, ideologies or causes that they are against.... I do not subscribe to the theory that abridgments of First Amendment freedoms can ever be permitted on a "balancing" basis....[52]

At stake here is the interest of the individual lawyers of Wisconsin in having full freedom to think their own thoughts, speak their own minds, support their own causes and wholeheartedly fight whatever they are against, as well as the interest of the people of Wisconsin and, to a lesser extent, the people of the entire country in maintaining the political independence of Wisconsin lawyers.[53]

Justice Douglas said:

Once we approve this measure, we sanction a device where men and women in

49 *Ibid.*, 839.
50 *Ibid.*, 865–66.
51 *Ibid.*, 871.
52 *Ibid.*, 873.
53 *Ibid.*, 874.

almost any profession or calling can be at least partially regimented behind causes which they oppose. I look on the Hanson case as a narrow exception to be closely confined. Unless we so treat it, we practically give carte blanche to any legislature to put at least professional people into goose-stepping brigades. Those brigades are not compatible with the First Amendment. . . . the First Amendment applies strictures designed to keep our society from becoming moulded into patterns of conformity which satisfy the majority.[54]

Subsequently, following the Street decision, Justice Brennan, writing for six members of the Court, held that dissenting employees were entitled to a refund of a proportionate amount of moneys exacted from them representing the amount which the union expended for political purposes bore to its total budget, taking into consideration a division of political expenditures from "those germane to collective bargaining."[55] Justice Black concurred; Justice Harlan dissented, saying that the Street case required dissenters to give particular information respecting their dissent. Justice Goldberg did not participate.

The Court's tenderness, or its blindness, respecting labor unions and their devious political activities is illustrated by recent news items. On March 7, 1968, the *Wall Street Journal* headlined: "Supreme Court Clears the Way for Unions to Try to Organize Insurance Salesmen." In the following article it pointed out that

since 1947, individuals who work largely on their own had been thought, at least by many labor-law experts, to be beyond the reach of the National Labor Relations Act. The law, originally passed in 1935, gives "employees" the right to organize. . . . Congress in 1947 amended the law with the Taft-Hartley Act, which placed various limits on unions' rights, including a provision that the term "employees" wasn't to include "independent contractors." The provision was a direct response to an earlier Supreme Court decision that had widened the meaning of "employees."

An attempt by the Insurance Workers International Union to organize the so-called debit agents of United Insurance Co. of America offered the High Court its first, clear-cut opportunity to define the meaning of "independent contractors."

The Court said, in effect, that honest men may disagree over whether independent contractors are employees but that the NLRB had decided insurance agents are employees and the board's reasoning was good enough. The Court reversed the Court of Appeals, which had refused to go along with the Board's view, saying "As we said in Universal Camera Corp. v NLRB, 340 U.S. 474," at page 488, that even as to matters not requiring expertise, a court may not "displace the Board's choice between two fairly conflicting views, even though

[54] *Ibid.*, 884–85.
[55] Brotherhood of Railway Clerks v. Allen, 373 U.S. 113 (1963).

471

the court would justifiably have made a different choice had the matter been before it de nova."[56]

The *Wall Street Journal* article quoted the board as saying that the Court's ruling would affect "'countless other individuals who work on their own—traveling salesmen, collection agents, newsboys and milkmen,' for instance."

The Court's support of the superiority of the views of the NLRB, manifested over the years by decisions too numerous to discuss, becomes trenchant in the face of another *Wall Street Journal* article (March 29, 1968), headed "NLRB Under Fire: Businessmen Complain National Labor Board Shows Pro-Union Bias: Firms Charge Undue Backing for Organizers; Unions, Agency Dispute Allegations; Democrats Dominate Panel." The article says, *inter alia,* "Many employers and their attorneys maintain the NLRB has exhibited a pronounced pro-union bias in the seven years since President Kennedy's first appointment gave the five-member panel a Democratic majority."

Conclusions from a chain of circumstance are heightened by two further news items. On May 2, 1968, the *Wall Street Journal* said that "the Justice Department is worried about Lawrence Callanan—not so much because he's an ex-convict holding union office but because a proposed exposure of his doings might harm the Democratic Party."

The article goes on to point out that the *Journal* had previously reported the local political influence of Callanan, "business manager and boss of Steamfitters Local 562 in St. Louis" and adds that, "on the national level, Mr. Callanan has been the beneficiary of an eyebrow-raising tax decision by the Internal Revenue Service and the grateful recipient of a presidential commutation enabling him to resume activity in 1964 following a six-year prison term for extortion." The article continues:

> Federal prosecutors would like to send him back to jail. They have presented to a grand jury in St. Louis evidence seeking to show that he has converted union dues money to political purposes, including $60,000 contributed to the Democrats six months after the Presidential commutation. If he's brought to trial, the courtroom disclosures might impel the Government to investigate how other unions, local and national, raise money to help underwrite the Democratic Party's campaign expenses. So far, however, the prosecutors' efforts to try Mr. Callanan have been blocked by higher-ranking Justice Department officials.
>
> Besides drying up or scaring away millions of dollars in campaign cash, putting Mr. Callanan on trial could also expose law avoidance by certain of the party's leading fundraisers.
>
> It's known, for example, that Mr. Callanan met with two Democratic money men in October, 1964, to receive instructions on how to divide the prearranged

56 NLRB v. United Ins. Co., 390 U.S. 254 (1968).

$60,000 campaign gift. Specifically, he was told to send one check for $25,000 directly to Doyle Dane Bernbach, Inc., the New York advertising agency that handled LBJ's 1964 campaign. In this way the fund-raisers ducked the law requiring national political committees to disclose the sources of all their income.

One Government man (notes) that few beneficiaries of Mr. Callanan's $300,000-a-year political fund care to be identified with him. Accordingly, the White House is known to be interested in the case, and the Justice Department is handling it with particular care.

In recent months, Justice Department attorneys Brian Conboy and Edgar Brown have twice urged prosecution. Each time they have had the approval of Henry Peterson, chief of the department's organized crime section, and Robert Rosthal, chief of the election fraud unit. But each time higher-ups overruled the recommendations. From 97 counts the draft indictment has been progressively pared to one. And even this third abbreviated draft, dated March 1st, seems in danger of being sidetracked. Top Justice Department officials refuse comment on any aspect of the Callanan matter beyond saying it's still under investigation.

Between last October 16th and February 2nd, a special 23-man grand jury in St. Louis spent 18 days . . . taking testimony from more than 60 witnesses. These included many members of Local 562 who pay 50 cents a day (outsiders working temporarily in the local jurisdiction pay $2) into a "voluntary political fund" controlled by Mr. Callanan.

The witnesses' statements raised doubts that these political collections are truly voluntary, as required by law. . . .

. . . for reasons that haven't been explained, the Government failed to follow up with a recommendation either to indict or to ignore the mass of testimony. Indeed, there hasn't been a peep from Washington in three months. . . .

New members of Local 562 arriving on the job routinely receive political fund check-off cards. . . . Somehow, nearly every man becomes a voluntary contributor. Almost automatically, the job steward collects from the rank-and-file, the area foreman collects from the job steward, the general foreman collects from the area foreman and then it all goes into the local political fund.

Steamfitters from Kansas, Illinois and other neighboring states working temporarily in Local 562's area have been similarly trained to contribute. Some simply regard the political payments as a cost of working in Mr. Callanan's bailiwick.

Significantly, a week after the publication of the foregoing article, *The New York Times* of May 10, 1968, reported that on the day before, Callanan, the union and two others of its officers were indicted by the grand jury, charging that they conspired to use "a supposedly 'voluntary' fund . . . to collect money regularly from union members and pass it on to political candidates."

Forty-five contributions totaling a $105,000 fund were listed in the indictment, although that amount represents only a small fraction of a total of a million dollars contributed to candidates for federal, state and local offices from 1963 to 1967, according to the *Wall Street Journal* of May 10, 1968.

(It might be noted that "voluntary" meets the unrealistic standards which, as construed by the Court, represents the congressional intent in the Street and other political contribution cases.)

Another consequence of congressional and court tolerance was disclosed by a May 6, 1968 article in *The New York Times,* which says: "Occasionally Senator Frank Lausche votes the way of organized labor, but that is coincidental.... That is why unions are directing their heaviest thrust in years at Mr. Lausche in the Democratic (Ohio) primary on Tuesday."

After listing details of labor's "computer approach to campaigning" directed by AFL-CIO President George Meany, the article says: "To finance all this, the state body last winter doubled per capita payments.... The unions cannot legally give any of this dues money to a candidate for Federal office, but they believe they are on safe legal ground in spending it to elect a candidate so long as they confine their operations to their own members."

Following the defeat of Senator Lausche in the Democratic primary, *The New York Times* reported (May 6, 1968) that the AF of L had claimed the defeat of Senator Lausche was due to its efforts. However, in Indiana, where labor organizations supported the Governor, candidate of the Democratic political organization, which exacts from its officeholders a percentage of their salaries, neither organization was successful. About this effort, which necessarily involved the use of union funds, *The New York Times* commented editorially:

> The oddest performance of all in this curious primary was turned in by the Committee on Political Education, the political arm of the AFL-CIO. It actively sought votes for Governor Branigin, no friend of liberal causes, as a way of advancing Vice President Humphrey's fortunes and retarding those of Senators McCarthy and Kennedy. Since both Senators have liberal, pro-labor voting records, it is hard to see what legitimate interest of the working man was served by investing funds to defeat either of them. The pro-Branigin activity makes sense only as a way of promoting the hawkish views on Vietnam of AFL-CIO President George Meany and other union leaders. For the rank-and-file Indiana unionists, as perhaps for all the rival candidates, it was strictly a no-win primary.

And in a final relevant news item, *The New York Times* of May 25, 1968, reporting the New York legislative session, said concerning the lobbying activities of Shanker, president of the New York teachers' union, who had recently served a jail term for contempt in connection with his activities respecting the illegal teachers' strike:

474

Mr. Shanker—very visible in Albany today huddling with aides in corridors, remonstrating with legislative officials in their offices, talking intently on hallway pay phones—has threatened to use funds of his 55,000-member union to defeat legislators who vote against the union's position.

The labor leader is believed to control a sizable bloc of city Democratic votes, particularly in the Assembly.

This morning, the legislative leaders bowed to the Shanker demands and introduced a second bill, amending the first.

The same newspaper said, on May 27, 1968, "Mr. Shanker also estimated that his union had spent from $125,000 to $250,000 in its campaign to defeat broad decentralization of the city schools by the Legislature, but he asserted that the union had been 'outspent 20 to 1' by advocates of radical decentralization."

The Court's devotion to the cause of individual liberty has, on occasion, permitted it to afford protection to individual union members as against entrenched union management. Thus the Court held that a union representing white trainmen could not bargain, under the authority of the Railway Labor Act, to abolish jobs of Negro workers though they were represented by their own union.[57] Writing for six members of the Court, Justice Black found the situation akin to a previous case which had held similarly.[58] The Chief Justice and Justices Minton and Reed dissented. Later, the Court held that Negro employees of a railroad, members of a union, were entitled to be represented by their bargaining agent, without discrimination as regards race or color.[59]

Six members of the Court held that a state court had jurisdiction to entertain an action brought by a labor union member, alleging that he had been unlawfully expelled from membership in the union and seeking damages.[60] The Chief Justice and Justice Douglas dissented on the ground that the federal Labor Relations Act afforded an adequate remedy. Justice Black did not participate.

On the same day the same members of the Court affirmed a recovery by an employee against a union engaged in picketing and making threats which denied him access to his place of work.[61] The Chief Justice and Justice Douglas dissented on the same ground, and Justice Black did not participate.

Thereafter, the Court refused to disturb a finding below that a picketing union member who won his claim of right so to do in Court was entitled to recover his legal costs.[62]

[57] Brotherhood of Trainmen v. Howard, 343 U.S. 768 (1952).
[58] Steele v. Louisville & Nashville R.R., 323 U.S. 192 (1944).
[59] Conley v. Gibson, 355 U.S. 41 (1957).
[60] International Machinists v. Gonzales, 356 U.S. 617 (1958).
[61] International Union v. Russell, 356 U.S. 634 (1958).
[62] Soloner v. Gartner, 390 U.S. 1040 (1968).

On the other hand, construing the National Labor Relations Act, four members of the Court, in an opinion by Justice Brennan, held that a union may fine members who crossed picket lines and worked during a lawfully called strike.[63] Justice White, concurring, split the conservative camp to make the fifth, while the liberal bloc split as Justices Black and Douglas joined Justices Harlan and Stewart in dissent. Justice Black wrote for the dissenters, holding that Section 7 of the Act gave workers the right to "refrain from engaging in such 'concerted activities,'" while Section 8 (b) (1) (A) of the Act made "it an unfair labor practice for a union to 'restrain or coerce' employees in their exercise of their Section 7 rights."[64]
He said:

> The real reason for the Court's decision is its political judgment that unions, especially weak ones, need the power to impose fines on strikebreakers.... It is not enough, says the Court, that the unions have the power to expel those members who refuse to participate in a strike or who fail to pay fines imposed on them ...; it is essential that weak unions have the choice between expulsion and court-enforced fines, simply because the latter are more effective in the sense of being more punitive.[65]

It might be said that, since a worker must join a union to get a job where an employer has been compelled to agree to maintain a union shop, the Court, in its attention to a doubtful question of statutory construction, might well have given some thought to the protection of individual liberties by not adding to the prior coercions the withdrawal of the worker's right independently to make up his mind about the justice of the union's course of action, without the threat of union punishment.

Seven members of the Court, with Justices Stewart and Goldberg not participating, held that it was not an unfair labor practice for an employer to close his entire business, even if it is due to antiunion animus,[66] although closing part of a business with the intent of discouraging unionism in the remainder is an unfair labor practice.

Although Justice Goldberg, an ardent labor man, and the Chief Justice concurred in the result reached by six members of the Court, with Justice Brennan writing the opinion, Justice White dissented from a holding that employer members of a multiemployer bargaining group might properly lock out employees when a whipsaw strike was conducted against one member of the group, without being guilty of an unfair labor practice.[67] Justice Goldberg

[63] NLRB v. Allis-Chalmers Co., 388 U.S. 175 (1967).
[64] Ibid., 199.
[65] Ibid., 201–202.
[66] Textile Workers Union v. Darlington Co.; NLRB v. Darlington Co., 380 U.S. 263 (1965).
[67] NLRB v. Brown, 380 U.S. 278 (1965).

476

pointed out that the temporary replacements hired by the employers during the strike were, in turn, replaced by the union men once the strike was settled.

With the concurrence of Justices Goldberg, White, and the Chief Justice, the Court held that an employer does not commit an unfair labor practice when, after an impasse has been reached in negotiations, he temporarily shuts down his plant and lays off his employees for the sole purpose of applying economic pressure in support of his legitimate bargaining position.[68]

In the first of two sets of late cases[69] five members of the Court, in an opinion by Justice Brennan, construed the National Labor Relations Act to permit a product boycott under the provisions of a collective bargaining contract between a union and a general contractors association. The majority relied upon what Justice Brennan, citing an early case,[70] said was the "familiar rule, that a thing may be within the letter of the statute and yet not within the statute, because not within its spirit, nor within the intention of its makers." He distinguished a prior case.[71] Justice Stewart, joined by Justices Black, Douglas, and Clark, wrote in dissent, saying: "The Union's boycott of the prefitted doors clearly falls within the express terms of the federal labor law. ...And the collective bargaining provision that authorizes such a boycott likewise stands condemned by the law's prohibition."[72] The companion cases went the same way for the same reasons.[73]

In an earlier case Justice White wrote for six members of the Court, holding the United Mine Workers subject to the antitrust laws when they agreed with the larger coal companies that they might dump coal at such low prices as to force small competitors, who could not compete, out of business.[74] Justices Douglas, Black, and Clark concurred. Justice Goldberg, joined by Justices Harlan and Stewart, concurred in the result but dissented on another point. Justice Douglas, concurring, said: "The only architect of our economic system is Congress. We are right in adhering to its philosophy of the free enterprise system as expressed in the anti-trust laws . . . until the Congress delegates to big business and big labor the power to remold our economy in the manner charged here."[75]

Justice Goldberg maintained that the union's agreement and purpose was to achieve high wages, fringe benefits, and good working conditions for its

[68] American Ship Bldg. Co. v. NLRB, 380 U.S. 300 (1965).
[69] National Woodwork Mfrs. Assoc. v. NLRB; NLRB v. National Woodwork Mfrs. Assoc., 386 U.S. 612 (1967); Houston Contractors v. NLRB; NLRB v. Houston Contractors, 386 U.S. 664 (1967).
[70] Holy Trinity Church v. United States, 143 U.S. 457 (1892).
[71] Allen Bradley Co. v. Local Union No. 3, 325 U.S. 797 (1945).
[72] National Woodwork Mfrs. Assoc. v. NLRB, 386 U.S. 612, 650 (1967).
[73] Houston Contractors v. NLRB; NLRB v. Houston Contractors, 386 U.S. 664 (1967).
[74] United Mine Workers v. Pennington, 381 U.S. 657 (1965).
[75] Ibid., 675.

members in exchange for accepting the burdens and consequences of automation and that the existence of marginal operators who could not afford such standards of wages and other benefits, does not serve the interests of the miners since the union espouses high wages for fewer men rather than low wages for a greater number. He contended that Congress had not attempted to bar such objectives.[76]

In a companion case Justice White, joined by the Chief Justice and Justice Brennan, held that a multiemployer and multiunion agreement fixing marketing hours did not violate the Sherman Act.[77] Justice Goldberg, joined by Justices Harlan and Stewart, concurred in the result. Justice Douglas, supported by Justices Black and Clark, dissented.

During the 1967 term the Court held that price fixing by musicians' unions did not violate the Sherman Act, thus further strengthening the antitrust immunity of unions. Justices White and Black dissented; the Chief Justice and Justice Marshall did not participate.[78]

The extent to which workmen's compensation benefits have, on occasion, been stretched was illustrated when an employee of a government contractor at a defense base in Korea drowned during a Saturday outing. A compensation commissioner found that death arose out of and in the course of his employment and awarded damages. The district court held the commissioner correct in finding that "the conditions of the deceased's employment created a zone where [he] had to seek recreation under exacting and unconventional conditions and that therefore the accident and death ... arose out of and in the course of employment."[79] In a per curiam opinion the Court said, "While this Court may not have reached the same conclusion ... it cannot be said that his holding ... is irrational or without substantial evidence."[80]

Justice Harlan, joined by Justices Clark and White, dissented, as did Justice Douglas. Justice Harlan said:

> I see no meaningful interpretation of the statute which will support this result except a rule that any decision made by a Deputy Commissioner must be upheld ... That interpretation, although meaningful, is unsupportable....[81]
>
> The injury did not take place on the actual job site, and it did not arise out of any special danger created by the job. In no sense can it be said that Ecker's job created any "special" danger of his drowning in a lake, or more particularly, of his loading a small boat with sand and capsizing it. Nothing indicates that

76 Local Union No. 189 v. Jewel Tea Co., 381 U.S. 676, 698 *et seq.* (1965).

77 Local Union No. 189 v. Jewel Tea Co., 381 U.S. 676 (1965).

78 American Fed. of Musicians v. Carroll; Carroll v. American Fed. of Musicians, 391 U.S. 99 (1968).

79 O'Keefe v. Smith Associates, 380 U.S. 359 (1965).

80 *Ibid.*, 363.

81 *Ibid.*, 366.

the lake was rougher, the boat tippier, or the sand heavier than their counterparts in the United States. If there were "exacting and unconventional conditions" in Korea it does not appear that the lake, boat, or sand was one of them.[82]

Justice Douglas said: "I would not be inclined to reverse a Court of Appeals that disagreed with a Deputy Commissioner over findings as exotic as we have here."[83]

[82] *Ibid.*, 369.
[83] *Ibid.*, 372.

CHAPTER XXV

Antitrust and Other Issues

THE EARLY CONFUSION respecting the Sherman Antitrust Act and the subsequent Clayton Act was not cured by the broader application of the commerce clause. Thus a later Court could not agree when the Associated Press was charged with violating the Sherman Act in three cases which came to the Court.[1]

Justice Black, delivering the opinion of the Court, held that the Associated Press, a co-operative organization of newspapers engaged in gathering and disseminating news for and to its members, violated the Sherman Antitrust Act. In one of the cases all sitting judges concurred; in two others Justices Reed, Douglas, Frankfurter, and Rutledge concurred, and the Chief Justice and Justices Roberts and Murphy dissented.

Justice Murphy said:

> Today is ... the first time the Sherman Act has been used as a vehicle for affirmative intervention by the Government in the realm of dissemination of information. ...[2]
>
> The nub of the complaint ... is that its by-laws (1) allow discrimination in the condition of admission based upon the factor of an applicant's competition with a present member, and (2) enforce such discriminatory exclusion through a nontrading agreement among members. ...
>
> It may be conceded that these by-law provisions ... are restrictive. ... But ... they may be regarded on this record as nothing more than the exercise of a trader's right arbitrarily to choose his own associates and to protect the fruits of his own enterprise from use by competitors.[3]

A majority of the Court held that the New York Stock Exchange, in denying its members the right to give direct-wire telephone connections to two nonmembers of the Exchange, without notice and a hearing, left the Exchange

---

[1] Associated Press v. United States; Tribune Co. v. United States; United States v. Associated Press, 326 U.S. 1 (1945).

[2] *Ibid.,* 51.

[3] *Ibid.,* 54.

liable to the nonmembers for damages under the Sherman Act.[4] Justice Clark concurred; Justices Stewart and Harlan dissented.

Justice Stewart said: "I think the Court errs in using the anti-trust laws to serve ends they were never intended to serve—to enforce the Court's concept of fair procedures under a totally unrelated statute."[5]

In an antitrust suit by the government against a large pharmaceutical manufacturer, six members of the Court, with the concurrence of Justice Stewart, stated their agreement with Colgate, a prior decision,[6] which held that a manufacturer could refuse to sell his products to a dealer who failed to maintain prices fixed by him. However, they held, in accordance with subsequent decisions,[7] that the manufacturer could not, by contracts or combinations, express or implied, unduly hinder or obstruct the free and natural flow of commerce in order to effect adherence to his resale prices, without violating the Sherman Act.[8]

Justice Harlan, supported by Justices Frankfurter and Whittaker, dissented, saying that the Court had overruled the Colgate case though it professed not to do so. He maintained that the subsequent cases vitiated only "cooperative group action."[9]

Later, upon remand of the case, the defendant demonstrated to the satisfaction of the district court that it had ended the practices complained of, whereupon it entered an order denying that the defendant had violated the law. Seven members of the Court reversed, saying the government was entitled to judgment in its favor. Justices Harlan and Frankfurter voted to hear argument.[10]

With the concurrence of Justices Douglas, Harlan, Stewart, White, and Fortas, Justice Black, writing for four members of the Court, held that the Pabst Brewing Company, the nation's tenth largest brewery, must divest itself of the acquired assets of the Blatz Brewing Company, the eighteenth-largest brewery, upon the ground that the effect of the acquisition might be to lessen competition or create monopoly nationally, in the state of Wisconsin, or in the area of Wisconsin, Illinois, and Michigan.[11]

Justice Douglas, concurring, said:

While I join the Court's opinion, I add only a word in support of the Court's

---

[4] Silver v. New York Stock Exchange, 373 U.S. 341 (1963).

[5] *Ibid.*, 370.

[6] United States v. Colgate, 250 U.S. 300 (1919).

[7] Federal Trade Commission v. Beechnut Co., 257 U.S. 441 (1922); United States v. Bausch & Lomb Co., 321 U.S. 707 (1944).

[8] United States v. Parke, Davis & Co., 362 U.S. 29 (1960).

[9] *Ibid.*, 55–56.

[10] United States v. Parke, Davis & Co., 365 U.S. 125 (1961).

[11] United States v. Pabst Brewing Co., 384 U.S. 546 (1966).

description of the anatomy of the "relevant geographic market" for purposes of the Clayton Act. The alternative leads to a form of concentration whose ultimate *reductio ad absurdum* is described in the appendix to this opinion:

APPENDIX TO CONCURRING OPINION OF MR. JUSTICE DOUGLAS

Every time you pick up the newspaper you read about one company merging with another company. Of course, we have laws to protect competition in the United States, but one can't help thinking that, if the trend continues the whole country will soon be merged into one large company.

It is 1978 and by this time every company west of the Mississippi will have merged into one giant corporation known as Samson Securities. Every company east of the Mississippi will have merged under an umbrella corporation known as the Delilah Company.

It is inevitable that one day the chairman of the board of Samson and the president of Delilah would meet and discuss merging their two companies.

"If we could get together," the president of Delilah said, "we would be able to finance your projects and you would be able to finance ours."

"Exactly what I was thinking," the chairman of Samson said.

"That's a great idea and it certainly makes everyone's life less complicated."

The men shook on it and then they sought out approval from the Anti-Trust Division of the Justice Department.

At first the head of the Anti-Trust Division indicated that he might have reservations about allowing the only two companies left in the United States to merge.

"Our department," he said, "will take a close look at this proposed merger. It is our job to further competition in private business and industry, and if we allow Samson and Delilah to merge we may be doing the consumer a disservice."

The chairman of Samson protested vigorously that merging with Delilah would not stifle competition, but would help it. "The public will be the true beneficiary of this merger," he said. "The larger we are, the more services we can perform, and the lower prices we can charge."

The president of Delilah backed him up. "In the Communist system the people don't have a choice. They must buy from the state. In our capitalistic society the people can buy from either the Samson Company or the Delilah Company."

"But if you merge," someone pointed out, "there will be only *one* company left in the United States."

"Exactly," said the president of Delilah. "Thank God for the free enterprise system."

The Anti-Trust Division of the Justice Department studied the merger for months. Finally the Attorney General made this ruling. "While we find some drawbacks to only one company being left in the United States, we feel the advantages to the public far outweigh the disadvantages.

"Therefore, we're making an exception in this case and allowing Samson and Delilah to merge.

482

"I would like to announce that the Samson and Delilah Company is now negotiating at the White House with the President to buy the United States. The Justice Department will naturally study this merger to see if it violates any of our strong anti-trust laws."[12]

The 1960 Bank Merger Act passed by Congress was interpreted by the Court in two cases. In one, six members of the Court held that the Clayton Act did not exclude bank mergers.[13] Justice Harlan, joined by Justice Stewart, dissented, saying:

> ...this holding, which sanctions a remedy regarded by Congress as inimical to the best interests of the banking industry and the public, and which will in large measure serve to frustrate the objectives of the Bank Merger Act, finds no justification in either the terms of the 1950 amendment of the Clayton Act or the history of the statute.[14]

This and the second case[15] moved Congress to supersede the 1960 Act with the 1966 Bank Merger Act, which was interpreted by the Court in two subsequent cases. Here five members of the Court held, over the dissent of Justices Harlan and Stewart (Justices Fortas and Marshall not participating), "that the Bank Merger Act provided for continued scrutiny of bank mergers under the Sherman Act and the Clayton Act, but had created a new defense," i.e., whether the merger offended the antitrust laws, whether it nonetheless was justified by the convenience and needs of the community to be served. However, it reserved all questions concerning the substantive meaning of the latter phrase.

In the second case five judges, over the dissent of Justices Harlan and Stewart (Justices Fortas and Marshall not participating), held that the district court had erred in concluding that the anticompetitive effects of the merger under the Clayton Act were outweighed by the benefits to the community.[16] Justices Harlan and Stewart, concurring in part, felt that the district court on remand should determine which element preponderated.

Writing for eight members of the Court (Justice Clark not participating), Justice Douglas held that it was the Court's judgment, not the comptroller's, that would determine the legality of the merger and that it was the banks' burden to prove that the effect of the mergers "clearly outweighed" their anticompetitive consequences.[17]

The decision also determined a controversy between the Comptroller of

---

12 *Ibid.*, 553–55, quoting newspaper columnist Art Buchwald.
13 United States v. Phila. National Bank, 374 U.S. 321 (1963).
14 *Ibid.*, 374.
15 United States v. First Nat'l Bank of Lexington, 376 U.S. 665 (1964).
16 United States v. Third National Bank in Nashville, 390 U.S. 171 (1968).
17 United States v. First City National Bank of Houston, 386 U.S. 361 (1967).

the Currency, who approved the merger, and the Attorney General and the Board of Governors of the Federal Reserve System Board, who opposed it. This led the *Wall Street Journal* to comment that the decision "nailed down, hard and fast," its conclusion that bank mergers can be blocked by the Justice Department's antitrust division and would increase the difficulty of "banks whose mergers are challenged to win an antitrust suit."[18]

Subsequently two Philadelphia banks, whose merger had been opposed by the Justice Department abandoned the prospective merger, saying the last-mentioned decision made it impossible "to merge two sizable commercial banks in any metropolitan area under the Bank Merger Act of 1966, regardless of the improved service and convenience to the public."[19]

It might be noted too, as further evidence of antitrust confusion in government departments that, according to a September 7, 1967 dispatch to *The New York Times,* the Justice Department was asking the Court of Appeals for the District of Columbia to void a merger of the International Telephone and Telegraph Corporation and the American Broadcasting Companies which had been approved by the Federal Communications Commission.

In a following 1966-term case,[20] argued and decided with five others,[21] the Court considered the ICC approval of the merger of the Pennsylvania and New York Central Railroads. Justice Clark wrote for four members of the Court, remanding the case to the ICC for inclusion of additional protective conditions for the Erie-Lackawanna, Delaware & Hudson, and Boston & Maine Railroads.[22]

Justice Brennan joined the Court's opinion, as did Justice Douglas, who dissented in part because he believed there were underlying issues concerning the adequacy of the commission's findings that should be determined.[23] Justice Fortas wrote, dissenting, joined by Justices Harlan, Stewart, and White. He maintained that "the Court's order . . . is insupportable as a matter of law and of sound administration of the principles of judicial review of decisions of administrative agencies." He defended the method adopted by the Commission to protect the three smaller roads while criticizing the Court's method, as being productive of delay.[24]

During the subsequent 1967 term, the ICC having complied with the

---

[18] *Wall Street Journal,* March 5, 1968.

[19] *Ibid.,* March 15, 1968.

[20] Baltimore & Ohio R.R.; Delaware & Hudson R.R.; Erie-Lackawanna R.R.; City of Scranton; Shapp; Chicago and E. I. R.R. v. United States, 386 U.S. 372 (1967).

[21] Delaware & Hudson R.R.; Erie-Lackawanna R.R.; City of Scranton; Shapp; Chicago & E. I. R.R. v. United States, 386 U.S. 372 (1967).

[22] Baltimore & Ohio R.R. v. United States, 386 U.S. 372, 392 (1967).

[23] *Ibid.,* 438.

[24] *Ibid.,* 471–72.

Court's directions, the Court ordered immediate issuance of judgment approving the Penn-Central merger.[25]

Writing for six members of the Court, Justices Stewart and Fortas not participating and Justice Harlan concurring, Justice Douglas held that by acquiring the assets of the Clorox Chemical Company, the leading manufacturer of liquid household bleach, the Proctor & Gamble Company had effected an illegal "product-extension merger."[26] The Federal Trade Commission had coined this phrase to designate a merger which was not "vertical," "horizontal," or "conglomerate" but which, because of the size and prestige of the acquiring company, entailed "the reasonable probability of a substantial increase in barriers to entry and of enhancement in pricing power" in the industry occupied by the acquired company.[27] This venture by the Court into the field of so-called conglomerate acquisitions may well have constituted the opening of a Pandora's box of subsequent questions.

Justice White wrote for six members of the Court, the Chief Justice not participating. He held that, in a suit by a bakery company against three large competitors, a jury was entitled to conclude that, where the evidence showed a drastically declining price structure which could be attributed to continued or sporadic price discrimination, the effect of such discrimination may be to lessen, injure, destroy, or prevent competition. Thus the plaintiff was entitled to a recovery under the Clayton Act.[28]

Justice Stewart, joined by Justice Harlan, dissented, maintaining that the respondents' action did not have the anticompetitive effect required by the statute. He said the Court had fallen into the error "of reading the Robinson-Patman Act as protecting competitors, instead of competition."[29]

On March 4, 1968, the Court handed down an antitrust decision which, as Justice Stewart put it, "stands the Sherman Act on its head,"[30] where in lieu of disapproving of minimum-price fixing, as it had invariably done, it held that newspaper publishing companies could not fix a maximum price that independent distributors might charge for home delivery of newspapers.

Justice White adhered to a prior decision which held that agreements to fix a maximum price cripple the freedom of traders and thereby restrain their ability to sell in accordance with their own judgment,[31] while Justice Harlan, dissenting, appeared to read that case "as prohibiting only combinations of suppliers to squeeze retailers from the top."[32]

[25] Penn-Central Merger, 389 U.S. 486; 390 U.S. 913 (1968).
[26] Federal Trade Commission v. Proctor & Gamble Co., 386 U.S. 568 (1967).
[27] *Ibid.*, 604.
[28] Utah Pie Co. v. Continental Baking Co., 386 U.S. 685 (1967).
[29] *Ibid.*, 705.
[30] Albrecht v. Herald Co., 390 U.S. 145, 170 (1968).
[31] *Ibid.*, 149.
[32] *Ibid.*, 152 n.8.

A unanimous Court (Justice Marshall not participating) held that the Federal Maritime Commission could apply antitrust doctrines to invalidate rules adopted by conferences of steamship lines furnishing Atlantic passage which prohibited travel agents from selling passage on competing nonconference lines and limiting maximum rates of commission to travel agents.[33]

In a later case,[34] over the dissent of Justices Harlan and Stewart, the Court ruled that manufacturers may not help underwrite advertising and other promotional costs of large retailers who buy directly from the manufacturers unless they make the same concessions to small retailers who buy through wholesalers. Justice Marshall did not participate. The Court remanded the case to the FTC so that it might prepare rules and guides for situations such as those found in the instant case, finding both the FTC and the appellate court, which had reversed it, in error; the latter for concluding that the FTC was entirely incorrect.

The decision caused the *Wall Street Journal* to comment editorially on March 29, 1968:

> When Congress passed the Robinson-Patman Act three decades ago, its intention surely was honorable; in practice, however, the law is an administrative monstrosity that often works against its alleged aims.
>
> Robinson-Patman was designed to prevent manufacturers and other suppliers from discriminating against some of their customers and in favor of others. In the ensuing years the Federal Trade Commission, which is responsible for the law's enforcement, and the courts have had all sorts of trouble trying to apply the statute to actual business situations.
>
> With the Government so confused, businessmen obviously have been puzzled too. According to some critics of the law, many companies have simply refrained from engaging in discounting and other forms of price competition to avoid running the risk of Robinson-Patman charges. This tends to defeat the supposed purpose of the anti-trust laws: Assuring consumers of the lowest possible prices.
>
> But avoidance of discounting does not guarantee businessmen safety from Federal prosecution, since Robinson-Patman is only one of the anti-trust statutes. If companies maintain relatively uniform prices they may be suspected of violating the Sherman or Clayton acts by engaging in collusion on prices.
>
> One of the sharper critics of Robinson-Patman is the US Supreme Court, which has to be the final arbiter as to just what the law means. Calling the act "confusing, inconsistent and misdirected," the Justices have urged Congress to overhaul it, and a new decision by the court should give the law-makers a push in that direction.

---

[33] Federal Maritime Commission; American Society of Travel Agents v. Aktiebolaget (Swedish American Line), 390 U.S. 238 (1968).

[34] Federal Trade Commission v. Meyer, 390 U.S. 341 (1968).

The editorial commented further:

> The court did not spell out procedure and a producer who works with whole-salers to allocate aid among retailers—or who bypasses wholesalers to work with retailers—just may find himself in trouble with other anti-trust laws.
>
> The likely upshot, once again, is fewer discounts for consumers. Congress should not find it too hard to improve on a law that manages to be both anti-competitive and almost unintelligible.

Although in resisting Justice Black's thesis that the Fourteenth Amendment incorporates the Bill of Rights the Court has not held the Eighth Amendment applicable to the states, as it has held some others, there can be no doubt that, under the Palko decision, the "cruel and unusual punishment" phrase in the Eighth Amendment prevents such infliction by the states under the implications of the Fourteenth Amendment. Despite the recurrent agitation for the abolition of the death penalty, it still does not come within the definition of "cruel and unusual punishment."[35]

The Court affirmed its position when four justices joined in an opinion by Justice Reed, holding that the purpose of Louisiana to electrocute Willie Francis, a Negro convicted of murder, after he had once before been placed in the electric chair but was removed therefrom when a mechanical failure ensued, did not involve cruel and unusual punishment.[36] Justice Frankfurter concurred upon the ground that "no matter how strong one's personal feeling of revulsion against a State's insistence on its pound of flesh," he could not enforce his "private view rather than that consensus of society's opinion, which, for purposes of due process, is the standard enjoined by the Constitution."[37]

Justice Burton, joined by Justices Douglas, Murphy, and Rutledge, dissented, urging that the case be remanded to the state court to determine the question of whether a new attempt would constitute cruel and unusual punishment, a question that the state court did not consider since it believed the issue was an executive, not a judicial, one.

However, during the 1968 term, the Court indicated its dislike of the death penalty when a majority, in an opinion by Justice Stewart, maintained that persons who admitted they had scruples against the death penalty could not automatically be barred from serving on juries in capital cases. He tempered the ruling by saying they could be excluded if, having made such a statement, they could not make an impartial finding of guilt and could not vote for a death penalty.[38] Justice Douglas disagreed only with Justice Stewart's

---

[35] *In re* Kemmler, 136 U.S. 436 (1880); Rudolph v. Alabama, 375 U.S. 889 (1963).
[36] Louisiana v. Resweber, 329 U.S. 459 (1947).
[37] *Ibid.*, 471.
[38] Witherspoon v. Illinois, 391 U.S. 510 (1968).

qualification.[39] Justice Black, joined by Justices White and Harlan, dissented, taking the opportunity of criticizing the Court for "making law," overturning convictions of obviously guilty defendants on technicalities and weakening law enforcement "at a time of serious crime in our nation."[40] The Court stated that its ruling should be retroactive; hence its effect served to commute many sentences of persons convicted and awaiting execution.

The old saw that husband and wife were one and the protection of the marriage relationship by the law posed problems for the Court. A six-man majority held that a wife could be compelled to testify against her husband on the trial of a charge that, before their marriage, he had transported her across state lines for purposes of prostitution, in violation of the federal Mann Act.[41] The Chief Justice and Justices Black and Douglas dissented.

The former, writing in dissent, called attention to a prior case holding that a wife could not voluntarily testify against her husband in such a criminal prosecution, over his objection.[42] He said: "The only relevant difference is that here the wife herself was the person allegedly transported by the husband for purposes of prostitution. Morally speaking, this profanation of the marriage relationship adds an element of the utmost depravity to the ugly business of promoting prostitution. Legally speaking, however, this does not warrant the radical departure from the Hawkins rule."[43]

Six members of the Court held that a husband and wife may be indicted and convicted of engaging in a conspiracy.[44] The Chief Justice and Justices Black and Whittaker dissented. Justice Frankfurter, writing for the majority said:

> Considering that legitimate business enterprises between husband and wife have long been commonplace in our time, it would enthrone an unreality into a rule of law to suggest that man and wife are legally incapable of engaging in illicit enterprises and therefore, forsooth, do not engage in them. . . .
>
> Such an immunity to husband and wife as a pair of conspirators would have to attribute to Congress one of two assumptions: either that responsibility of husband and wife for joint participation in a criminal enterprise would make for marital disharmony, or that a wife must be presumed to act under the coercive influence of her husband and, therefore, cannot be a willing participant. The former assumption is unnourished by sense; the latter implies a view of American womanhood offensive to the ethos of our society.[45]

39 *Ibid.*, 523–24, 528.
40 *Ibid.*, 532.
41 Wyatt v. United States, 362 U.S. 525 (1960).
42 Hawkins v. United States, 358 U.S. 74 (1958).
43 Wyatt v. United States, 362 U.S. 525, 531–32 (1960).
44 United States v. Dege, 364 U.S. 51 (1960).
45 *Ibid.*, 52–53.

How far removed we were even nearly a century ago when Congress passed the original statute against criminal conspiracy. . . . from the legal and social climate of eighteenth century common law regarding the status of woman is pithily illustrated by recalling the self-deluding romanticism of Blackstone, whereby he could conscientiously maintain that "even the disabilities, which the wife lies under, are for the most part intended for her protection and benefit. So great a favourite is the female sex of the laws of England."[46]

The Chief Justice, writing in dissent, said that

if the 1867 statute is to be construed to reflect Congress' intent as it was in 1867, the Court's decision is erroneous. And I believe we must focus upon that intent, inasmuch as there is no indication that Congress meant to change the law by the 1948 legislation which re-enacted without material variation the old conspiracy statute. . . .[47]

It is not necessary to be wedded to fictions to approve the husband-wife conspiracy doctrine. . . . A wife, simply by virtue of the intimate life she shares with her husband, might easily perform acts that would technically be sufficient to involve her in a criminal conspiracy with him, but which might be far removed from the arm's-length agreement typical of that crime.[48]

The apothegm often repeated by the Court that equity and taxes have little consanguinity was illustrated when the Court overruled a prior case[49] in holding that embezzled money constituted income which a taxpayer was required to report and on which he was required to pay income taxes.[50] Justices Black, Douglas, and Whittaker dissented, saying the prior case should not be overruled.

The taxpayer, indicted for "willful" evasion of his tax obligation, pleaded, with the prior case as his authority, that he could not be convicted of "willful" evasion. The Chief Justice and Justices Brennan and Stewart agreed, Justices Harlan and Frankfurter said that was a question for the jury, and Justice Clark found no merit in the contention. The defendant, a union official, and another person had embezzled more than $738,000 over a period of three years from the official's employer union and from an insurance company with which the union was doing business. The Chief Justice said that when Congress amended the tax statute it had removed the word "lawful" from the definition of income, evidently with

the obvious intent . . . to tax income derived from both legal and illegal sources,

[46] *Ibid.*, 54.
[47] *Ibid.*, 56.
[48] *Ibid.*, 57–58.
[49] Commissioner v. Wilcox, 327 U.S. 404 (1946).
[50] James v. United States, 366 U.S. 213 (1961).

to remove the incongruity of having the gains of the honest laborer taxed and the gains of the dishonest immune.... These include protection payments made to racketeers, ransom payments paid to kidnappers, bribes, money derived from the sale of unlawful insurance policies, graft, black market gains, funds obtained from the operation of lotteries, income from race track bookmaking and illegal prize fight pictures.[51]

Justice Whittaker, dissenting, said:

An embezzler, like a common thief, acquires not a semblance of right, title, or interest in his plunder, and whether he spends it or not, he is indebted to his victim in the full amount taken as surely as if he had left a signed promissory note at the scene of his crime. Of no consequence...is the absence of such formalities.[52]

In two other tax cases, in which husbands claimed that marital litigation might have had an effect on their business interests, seven members of the Court held expenses incurred in such litigation could not be deemed "business" expenses deductible for income tax purposes. Justices Douglas and Black dissented.[53]

The Federal Trade Commission charged the Colgate Company with employing deception in television commercials in that they purported to give viewers visual proof that their shaving cream could soften sandpaper, though the "sandpaper" shown in the commercials was not sandpaper. The Court sustained the FTC cease-and-desist order, holding that the misrepresentation of any fact, so long as it materially induces a purchaser's decision to buy, is a prohibited deception.[54]

The Chief Justice, writing for the Court, said:

It has long been considered a deceptive practice to state falsely that a product ordinarily sells for an inflated price but that it is being offered at a special reduced price, even if the offered price represents the actual value of the product and the purchaser is receiving his money's worth....[55]

It is generally accepted that it is a deceptive practice to state falsely that a product has received a testimonial from a respected source. In addition, the Commissioner has consistently acted to prevent sellers from falsely stating that their product claims have been "certified."[56]

51 *Ibid.*, 218.
52 *Ibid.*, 251.
53 United States v. Gilmore, 372 U.S. 39 (1963); United States v. Patrick, 372 U.S. 53 (1963).
54 Federal Trade Commission v. Colgate-Palmolive Co., 380 U.S. 374 (1965).
55 *Ibid.*, 387.
56 *Ibid.*, 389.

With the support of Justice Stewart, Justice Harlan, dissenting, said:

> The only question here is what techniques the advertiser may use to convey essential truth to the television viewer. If the claim is true and valid, then the technique for projecting that claim, within broad boundaries, falls purely within the advertiser's art. The warrant to the Federal Trade Commission is to police the verity of the claim itself....[57]

> I do not agree that the use of "mock-ups" by the television advertiser is of itself a deceptive trade practice.... If the image he sees on the screen is an accurate reproduction of what he would see with the naked eyes were the experiment performed before him with sandpaper in his home or in the studio, there can hardly be a misrepresentation in any legally significant sense....[58]

> In short, it seems to me that the proper legal test in cases of this kind concerns not what goes on in the broadcasting studio, but whether what is shown on the television screen is an accurate representation of the advertised product and of the claims made for it.[59]

In the following term the Court had occasion to consider the practice of a paint company which advertised for sale its paints in cans at a stated price for one can, with the statement that another would be given "free." The Federal Trade Commission issued a cease-and-desist order upon the ground that the practice was deceptive. The court of appeals disagreed; the high court, over the dissent of Justice Harlan, reinstated the commission's order. One of the bases of Justice Harlan's dissent was the fact that the company did not represent that the "free" can represented "a temporary saving for the customer" since the company had "striven over a number of years to associate itself irrevocably in the public mind with the notion that every second can is free."[60]

In a late case the Court vacated a judgment of eviction of a tenant from an apartment in a low-rent, public housing building who claimed she was to be evicted because of her association with a tenants' organization.[61] The Court found it "unnecessary to reach the large issues stirred by these claims,"[62] because the Housing Authority had, since the commencement of the suit, required notice to the tenant and a hearing, with opportunity to be heard, in consequence of which the Court remanded the case for compliance with the directive.[63]

[57] *Ibid.*, 395.
[58] *Ibid.*, 396.
[59] *Ibid.*, 398.
[60] Federal Trade Commission v. Mary Carter Paint Co., 382 U.S. 46, 52 (1965).
[61] Thorpe v. Housing Authority, 386 U.S. 670 (1967).
[62] *Ibid.*, 671–73.
[63] *Ibid.*, 674.

Justice Douglas, concurring, said:

> Over and over again we have stressed that "the nature and the theory of our institutions of government, the principles upon which they are supposed to rest ... do not mean to leave room for the play and action of purely personal and arbitrary power ... and that the essence of due process is 'the protection of the individual against arbitrary action.' "[64]

Justice White dissented.

It is to be noted that, previously in the term, the Court denied certiorari where an indigent tenant complained that the Georgia eviction statute required the filing of a bond, with good security, for payment of such sums as the landlord might recover, as a condition of opposing the eviction suit. In dissenting from the denial, Justice Douglas said: "This Court of course does not sit to cure social ills that beset the country. But when we are faced with a statute that apparently violates the Equal Protection Clause by patently discriminating against the poor and thereby worsening their already sorry plight, we should address ourselves to it."[65] The Chief Justice concurred, while Justice Brennan expressed the opinion that the writ should be granted.

A reflection of the controversy that has been tearing apart current opinion in the United States came when Dennis Mora and others, draftees, brought suit in the federal court seeking a declaratory judgment holding that the military activity in Vietnam was "illegal." From adverse decisions Mora and the others sought certiorari from the Supreme Court. With Justice Marshall not participating, the draftees were able to gain the support of only Justices Stewart and Douglas.[66]

Justice Stewart, dissenting, supported by Justice Douglas, wrote:

> There exist in this case questions of great magnitude. Some are akin to those referred to by Mr. Justice Douglas in Mitchell v. United States, 386 U.S. 972 ... But there are others:
>
> I. Is the present United States military activity in Vietnam a "war" within the meaning of Article I, Section 8, Clause 11 of the Constitution?
>
> II. If so, may the Executive constitutionally order the petitioners to participate in that military activity, when no war has been declared by the Congress?
>
> III. Of what relevance to Question II are the present treaty obligations of the United States?
>
> IV. Of what relevance to Question II is the joint Congressional ("Tonkin Bay") Resolution of August 10, 1964?

[64] Ibid., 678.

[65] Williams v. Shaffer, 385 U.S. 1037, 1041 (1967).

[66] Mora v. McNamara, 389 U.S. 934 (1967), citing Mitchell v. United States, 386 U.S. 972 (1967).

(a) Do present United States military operations fall within the terms of the Joint Resolution?

(b) If the Joint Resolution purports to give the Chief Executive authority to commit United States forces to armed conflict limited in scope only by his own absolute discretion, is the Resolution a constitutionally impermissible delegation of all or part of Congress' power to declare war? ...

We cannot make these problems go away simply by refusing to hear the case of three obscure Army privates. I intimate not even tentative views upon any of these matters, but I think the Court should squarely face them....[67]

Justice Douglas, with the concurrence of Justice Stewart, quoted Senator Fulbright, who quoted Thomas Jefferson, who said: "We have already given in example one effectual check to the Dog of war by transferring the power of letting him loose from the Executive to the Legislative body, from those who are to spend to those who are to pay."[68] He cited the five-to-four opposed views on the subject reflected in the Prize Cases, 2 Black 635.

Similarly, with Justice Douglas dissenting, the Court refused to review the conviction of David W. Brown for refusal to obey military orders after he had been denied conscientious objector status.[69]

Also, the Court denied certiorari to a group of students who contended that their arrest was discriminatory punishment for unpopular beliefs after they had gathered in various University of Wisconsin buildings to protest employment interviews in the buildings by the Dow Chemical Company, manufacturer of napalm.[70]

Then seven members of the Court joined in an opinion by the Chief Justice, affirming the conviction of David P. O'Brien, who burned his draft card and was therefore accused of violating the Selective Service regulation which prohibits one subject to the draft from knowingly destroying his registration certificate (draft card).[71] O'Brien contended that his burning of the card constituted "symbolic speech" protected by the First Amendment and that the provision in the Act was therefore unconstitutional. Justice Warren said: "This court has held that when 'speech' and 'nonspeech' elements are combined in the same course of conduct, a sufficiently important governmental interest in regulating the nonspeech element can justify incidental limitations on First Amendment freedoms."[72] Hence, he held, the regulation was within the con-

---

[67] Ibid., 934–35 (1968).

[68] Ibid., 937.

[69] Brown v. Clifford, 390 U.S. 1005 (1968).

[70] Zwicker v. Boll, 391 U.S. 353 (1968).

[71] United States v. O'Brien, 391 U.S. 367 (1968); see also Shiffman v. Selective Service, 391 U.S. 930 (1968); Zigmond v. Selective Service, 391 U.S. 930 (1968); Holmes v. United States, 391 U.S. 936 (1968); Hart v. United States, 391 U.S. 956 (1968).

[72] United States v. O'Brien, 391 U.S. 367, 376 (1968).

stitutional war power of Congress and that O'Brien was properly convicted.

Justice Douglas dissented, saying that he thought it time for the Court to rule upon the question of whether conscription is permissible in the absence of a declaration of war, though he admitted the question had not been briefed or argued.[73] Justice Stewart, who voted with the majority said he thought so too. Justice Marshall did not participate.

Scattered among these pages are evidences that criticism of the Court and its members is not confined to the bar or to the lay public. There are other such comments deserving of note:

In a case where the issue was a factual one of whether a decedent had committed suicide, Justice Frankfurter lectured his colleagues on the impropriety of having taken the case.[74] He said:

> Questions of fact have traditionally been deemed to be the kind of questions which ought not to be recanvassed here unless they are entangled in the proper determination of constitutional or other important legal issues....[75]
>
> Every time the Court grants certiorari in disregard of its own professed criteria, it invites disregard of the responsibility of lawyers enjoined upon the bar by the Court's own formal rules and pronouncements. It is idle to preach obedience ... to the bar year after year, if the Court itself disregards the code of conduct by which it seeks to bind the profession. Lawyers not unnaturally hope to draw a prize in the lottery.... laxity by the Court in respecting its own rules is bound to stimulate petitions for certiorari with which the Court should never be burdened.[76]

When the Court held the Federal Trade Commission empowered to stay a merger pending determination of its legality,[77] freshman Justice Fortas, dissenting and supported by three conservatives, Justices Harlan, Stewart, and White, said:

> This decision cannot be supported. Not a single one of the prior decisions of this Court cited as authority sustains it.... No statute of the Congress can be appropriately summoned to the Court's aid....
>
> Since 1956, the Federal Trade Commission has persistently requested the Congress to enact legislation giving the Commission itself the power to enjoin, or alternatively, to seek a district court order to enjoin mergers pending the outcome of the Commission's proceedings. Congress has just as persistently refused to do so....

[73] *Ibid.*, 389.
[74] Dick v. New York Life Ins. Co., 359 U.S. 437 (1959).
[75] *Ibid.*, 454.
[76] *Ibid.*, 460.
[77] Federal Trade Commission v. Dean Foods Co., 384 U.S. 597 (1966).

494

...it [Congress] has demonstrated over and over again that it has no interest in arming the Commission with the power today conferred upon it.[78]

In a case decided by a five-to-two vote during the 1966 term,[79] Justice Stewart, supported by Justice Harlan, said:

> The Court has decided this case on little more than repugnance for "the attitude or philosophy of the District Court" and the unjustified and extraordinarily opprobious conclusion that the Government "knuckled under." This is not a happy foundation for radical extensions of intervention doctrine....
>
> Finally, I must note my emphatic disagreement with the Court's extraordinary action in directing that further proceedings in this case must be conducted by a different district judge....[80] For this Court, on its own motion, to disqualify a trial judge in the middle of a case because it disagrees with his "philosophy" is not only unprecedented, but incredible.[81]

Justice Frankfurter filed a complaint when five members of the Court adhered to a previous decision to the effect that a taxpayer who desired to sue for an income tax refund must first pay the full amount of a deficiency assessment. Justices Whittaker, Frankfurter, Harlan, and Stewart dissented.[82] The disagreement among the judges turned on the construction of the statute.

Justice Frankfurter said in dissent:

> For one not a specialist in this field to examine every tax question that comes before the Court independently would involve in most cases an inquiry into the course of tax legislation and litigation far beyond the facts of the immediate case. Such an inquiry entails weeks of study and reflection. Therefore, in construing a tax law it has been my rule to follow almost blindly accepted understanding of the meaning of tax legislation, when that is manifested by long-continued uniform practice, unless a statute leaves no admissible opening for administrative construction.
>
> Therefore, when advised in connection with the disposition of this case after its first argument that "there does not appear to be a single case before 1940 in which a taxpayer attempted a suit for refund of income taxes without paying the full amount the Government alleged to be due," ... I deemed such a long-continued, unbroken practical construction of the statute controlling.... Once the basis which for me governed the disposition of the case was no longer available, I was thrown back to an independent inquiry of the course of tax legislation and litigation for more than a hundred years, for all of that was relevant to a true understanding of the problem presented by this case. This involved

---

[78] *Ibid.,* 613.
[79] Cascade Nat. Gas Corp. v. El Paso Nat. Gas Co., 386 U.S. 129 (1967).
[80] *Ibid.,* 160.
[81] *Ibid.,* 161.
[82] Flora v. United States, 362 U.S. 145 (1960).

many weeks of study during what is called the summer vacation. Such a study led to the conclusion set forth in detail in the opinion of my Brother Whittaker.[83]

Respecting two suits seeking recovery of damages on behalf of illegitimate children for the deaths of their mothers, the Court held a Louisiana statute which restricted such recoveries to legitimate kin unconstitutional as denying equal protection.[84] Justice Harlan, joined by Justices Black and Stewart, said:

> These decisions can only be classed as constitutional curiosities. . . . The question in these cases is whether the way in which Louisiana has defined the classes of persons who may recover is constitutionally permissible. The Court has reached negative answer by a process that can only be described as brute force. . . .
> The whole scheme of the Louisiana death statute, which is similar in this respect to that of most other States, makes everything the Court says about affection and nurture and dependence altogether irrelevant. . . . Louisiana has chosen, as have most other states in one respect or another, to define these classes of proper plaintiffs in terms of their legal rather than their biological relation to the deceased.[85]

In finding an alien ineligible for naturalization because he had not resided in the United States, Justice Jackson found that he had been mistaken in an opinion he had approved while attorney general.[86] So confessing, he wrote:

> Precedent . . . is not lacking for ways by which a judge may recede from a prior opinion that has proven untenable and perhaps misled others. See Chief Justice Taney, License Cases (U.S.) 5 How. 504 . . . recanting views he had pressed upon the Court as Attorney General of Maryland in Brown v. Maryland (U.S.) 12 Wheat. 419. . . . Baron Bramwell extricated himself from a somewhat similar embarrassment by saying, "The matter does not appear to me now as it appears to have appeared to me then." . . . And Mr. Justice Story . . . quite properly put the matter: "My own error, however, can furnish no ground for its being adopted by this Court." . . . Perhaps Dr. Johnson really went to the heart of the matter when he explained a blunder in his dictionary—"Ignorance, sir, ignorance." But an escape less self-depreciating was taken by Lord Westbury, who, it is said, rebuffed a barrister's reliance upon an earlier opinion of his Lordship: "I can only say that I am amazed that a man of my intelligence should have been guilty of giving such an opinion." If there are other ways of gracefully and good naturedly surrendering former views to a better considered position, I invoke them all."[87]

[83] Ibid., 177–78.
[84] Levy v. Louisiana, 391 U.S. 68 (1968); Glona v. American Guarantee, 391 U.S. 73 (1968).
[85] Glona v. American Guarantee, 391 U.S. 73, 76, 78, 79 (1968).
[86] McGrath v. Kristensen, 340 U.S. 162 (1950).
[87] Ibid., 177–78.

The Incidence of Dissent

DURING THE 1950 TERM, under Chief Justice Vinson, a conservative Court rendered a total of ninety-eight opinions, in sixty-four, or 65 per cent, of which dissents were filed. Fifteen of the dissents were rendered in five-to-four decisions, constituting some 23 per cent of the dissents and 15 per cent of the total opinions.

The following tables illustrate the dissents in the 1950 term:

Justice	Total	Sole	Vinson	Black	Douglas	Frankfurter	Clark	Minton	Reed	Burton	Jackson
Vinson	6*	0	x†	4	3	1	2	2	2	1	0
Black	32	6	4	x	18	12	5	5	2	6	7
Douglas	32	3	3	18	x	10	5	3	6	6	9
Frankfurter	21	1	1	12	10	x	2	3	2	6	11
Clark	8	0	2	5	5	2	x	1	1	2	3
Minton	10	0	2	5	3	3	1	x	2	3	4
Reed	11	1	2	2	6	2	1	2	x	2	4
Burton	13	0	1	6	6	6	2	3	2	x	3
Jackson	21	2	0	7	9	11	3	4	4	3	x

* The figures in this chapter make no claim to exactness, since a count of decisions and votes thereon necessarily varies with the inclusion or exclusion of decisions reported in the sections of the official reports headed "Decisions Per Curiam" and "Orders." For the present count, those decisions have largely been excluded, though from time to time, for one reason or another, the tabulator has succumbed to the temptation of inclusion. In any event, the figures as reported serve their purpose.

† x denotes none.

From these figures it appears that Black and Douglas, the liberals on a conservative court, were the principal dissenters and the principal collaborators. Each associated with Frankfurter, who with Jackson, constituted the second pair of dissenters with tendencies to liberality. The Chief Justice and Justice Clark found least cause for dissent. The rate of dissent was up to previously set standards.

The more important record of dissents are those which occurred from the 1953 term to date under the aegis of Chief Justice Warren. These figures appear in the following tabulation:

Term	Total opinions	Total dissents	Per cent of dissents to opinions	No. of 5-to-4 decisions	Per cent of 5-4 decisions to dissents	Percentage of 5-4 decisions to opinions	4-to-3 decisions	4-to-4 decisions
1953	77	50	65	8	16	10	2	1
1954	81	49	60	2	4	2	1	
8-man	49	13	26					
9-man	32	26	80					
1955	92	52	56	16	30	17	1	
1956	120	84	70	15	18	12	1	
8-man	32	26	80					
9-man	78	48	61	15	30	19		
1957	131	98	75	31	30	23		
1958	125	73	58	24	32	19	--	2
1959	129	90	—70	29	32	22	--	1
1960	127	84	66	26	40	20	1	
1961	109	76	69	6	8	5+	6	
1962	115	74	64	10	15	9	--	1
1963	141	83	58	16	19	11		
1964	110	80	72	9	10	8		
1965	156	109	70	16	22	14	--	1
1966	116	79	68	19	16	24		
TOTALS	1,629	1,171	72	227	—20	14		

A record of dissents during the various terms shows the following, beginning with the 1953 term:

Justice	Total	Sole	Warren	Black	Douglas	Frankfurter	Jackson	Reed	Burton	Minton	Clark
Warren	9	0	x	6	5	0	2	2	1	2	4
Black	24	2	6	x	20	3	2	0	0	5	2
Douglas	27	2	5	20	x	3	3	1	2	7	3
Frankfurter	8	0	0	3	3	x	6	0	1	3	1
Jackson	8	0	2	2	3	6	x	3	4	7	2
Reed	12	2	2	0	1	0	3	x	7	5	1
Burton	11	0	1	0	2	1	4	7	x	5	2
Minton	17	0	2	5	7	3	7	5	5	x	2
Clark	6	0	4	2	3	1	2	1	2	2	x

Here, as in the 1950 term, we find Black and Douglas leaders of the dissenters and collaborating with each other. The conservatives still appeared to dominate. The Chief Justice was evidently feeling his way. The Court was still dissenting in two out of three decisions.

The 1954 term witnessed the death of Justice Jackson on October 9, 1954, followed by the appointment of John Marshall Harlan of New York, aptly named for his forebear, who served with distinction during the term of Chief Justice Fuller. Justice Harlan was not sworn in until the end of March, 1955, so that for the greater part of the term the Court functioned with only eight justices.

The scorecard for the 1954 term shows the following:

Justice	Total	Sole	Warren	Black	Douglas	Frankfurter	Reed	Burton	Minton	Clark	Harlan
Warren	5	0	X	3	4	0	1	0	1	2	0
Black	13	0	3	X	10	3	2	0	1	2	0
Douglas	20	7	4	10	X	2	2	0	1	2	0
Frankfurter	11	0	0	3	2	X	3	5	2	0	2
Reed	22	1	1	2	3	3	X	11	11	3	2
Burton	14	0	0	0	0	5	11	X	4	1	2
Minton	13	0	1	1	1	2	11	4	X	1	2
Clark	5	0	2	2	2	0	3	1	1	X	0
Harlan	4	0	0	0	0	2	2	2	2	0	X

Here we find Reed, the conservative, leading the dissenters and co-operating with Burton and Minton in eleven of their respective fourteen and thirteen dissents. Black and Douglas joined in only ten of Black's thirteen dissents, while Douglas went off on his own seven times to make a total of twenty. The Chief Justice was inclined toward Black and Douglas but in a mild way.

The figures for the 1955 term are as follows:

Justice	Total	Sole	Warren	Black	Douglas	Frankfurter	Reed	Burton	Clark	Harlan	Minton
Warren	11	0	x	10	11	1	1	0	3	0	0
Black	13	0	10	x	13	1	1	0	4	0	0
Douglas	21	1	11	13	x	3	3	2	4	4	0
Frankfurter	20	2	1	1	3	x	4	8	2	12	4
Reed	19	1	1	1	3	4	x	12	4	5	11
Burton	19	1	0	0	2	8	12	x	3	9	10
Clark	11	0	3	4	4	2	4	3	x	2	4
Harlan	19	1	0	0	4	12	5	9	2	x	6
Minton	14	0	0	0	0	4	11	10	4	6	x

Here we find the Chief Justice moving into position with Black and Douglas, while Harlan begins his career as a conservative dissenter, joined by Frankfurter, who is shedding his liberal gown, in twelve of his nineteen dissents. Reed, Burton, and Minton are also allied in the conservative trend. The dissents register no overwhelming superiority in either camp.

Justice Minton retired at the beginning of the 1956 term, and Justice Reed resigned on February 25, 1957. They were replaced by William Joseph Brennan, Jr., of New Jersey, and Charles Evans Whittaker of Missouri. The 1956 term figures are as follows:

Justice	Total	Sole	Warren	Black	Douglas	Frankfurter	Reed	Burton	Clark	Harlan	Brennan	Whittaker
Warren	14	0	x	13	13	0	0	0	0	0	8	0
Black	24	1	13	x	13	0	0	1	0	2	8	0
Douglas	29	6	13	19	x	3	0	1	1	1	9	0
Frankfurter	33	3	0	5	3	x	4	15	3	22	5	4
Reed	7	0	0	0	0	4	x	2	3	4	0	0
Burton	33	2	0	1	1	15	2	x	12	17	2	4
Clark	20	2	0	0	1	3	3	12	x	4	0	1
Harlan	31	1	0	2	1	22	4	17	4	x	4	5
Brennan	13	0	8	8	9	5	0	2	0	4	x	0
Whittaker	4	0	0	0	0	4	0	4	1	5	0	x

In the 1956 term the liberal line was formed, with the Chief Justice and Justices Black and Douglas firmly entrenched, while Justice Brennan demonstrated his tendency to become a fourth. At the other side, we find Justices Harlan, Frankfurter, and Burton, with a conservative tendency manifested by Justice Clark. One consequence of the division during this and the subsequent three terms was the increased number of five-to-four decisions.

There was no change of personnel during the 1957 term, whose figures are as follows:

Justice	Total	Sole	Warren	Black	Douglas	Frankfurter	Burton	Clark	Harlan	Brennan	Whittaker
Warren	30	0	x	27	26	0	1	0	1	13	2
Black	33	1	27	x	28	0	2	1	0	13	2
Douglas	40	5	26	28	x	4	2	0	3	17	2
Frankfurter	32	3	0	0	4	x	12	6	26	4	13
Burton	30	1	1	2	2	12	x	14	18	1	15
Clark	23	1	0	1	0	6	14	x	11	0	9
Harlan	36	0	1	0	3	26	18	11	x	3	19
Brennan	18	0	13	13	17	4	1	0	3	x	0
Whittaker	30	1	2	2	2	13	15	9	19	0	x

Here we have a liberal bloc of four; the Chief Justice and Justices Black, Douglas, and Brennan; opposed to a conservative bloc of five: Justices Harlan, Frankfurter, Burton, Whittaker, and seemingly, Justice Clark.

Justice Burton retired at the beginning of the 1958 term and was replaced by Potter Stewart of Ohio. The 1958 figures follow:

Justice	Total	Sole	Warren	Black	Douglas	Frankfurter	Clark	Harlan	Brennan	Whittaker	Stewart
Warren	29	0	x	24	28	0	1	0	20	0	1
Black	33	0	24	x	30	3	2	2	15	3	1
Douglas	43	2	28	30	x	3	2	1	20	5	2
Frankfurter	22	0	0	3	3	x	7	14	1	15	8
Clark	13	2	1	2	2	7	x	7	0	7	3
Harlan	21	0	0	2	1	14	7	x	1	12	8
Brennan	22	0	20	15	20	1	0	1	x	0	1
Whittaker	25	2	0	3	5	15	7	12	0	x	10
Stewart	14	0	1	1	2	8	3	8	1	10	x

There was no doubt that the Chief Justice and Justices Black, Douglas, and Brennan constituted a liberal bloc of four, with Justices Harlan, Frankfurter, and Whittaker a conservative three, with conservative indications on the part of Justices Clark and Stewart.

There were no changes of personnel during the 1959 term:

Justice	Total	Sole	Warren	Black	Douglas	Frankfurter	Clark	Harlan	Brennan	Whittaker	Stewart
Warren	21	0	x	21	16	2	2	1	15	1	0
Black	31	0	21	x	24	3	2	4	15	2	0
Douglas	35	3	16	24	x	2	0	2	15	0	3
Frankfurter	39	0	2	3	2	x	10	30	2	25	14
Clark	13	0	2	2	0	10	x	4	0	7	1
Harlan	37	2	1	4	2	30	4	x	2	24	14
Brennan	12	0	15	15	15	2	0	2	x	0	0
Whittaker	38	6	1	2	0	25	7	24	0	x	15
Stewart	15	0	0	0	3	14	1	14	0	15	x

In the 1959 term the previous alignment continued. The solidarity of the Chief Justice's bloc was manifested by the fact that in nine of his dissents he was joined by the other three, while in five others he was joined by two of the three. At the other end of the spectrum, Frankfurter was joined by Harlan, Stewart, and Whittaker nine times.

There were no changes of personnel during the 1960 term:

Justice	Total	Sole	Warren	Black	Douglas	Frankfurter	Clark	Harlan	Brennan	Whittaker	Stewart
Warren	23	o	x	17	19	o	o	o	16	2	2
Black	31	o	17	x	27	2	o	2	13	3	1
Douglas	48	9	19	27	x	2	1	2	15	8	7
Frankfurter	23	1	o	2	2	x	9	16	o	15	5
Clark	20	1	o	o	1	9	x	9	1	12	4
Harlan	21	1	o	2	2	16	9	x	o	14	7
Brennan	20	o	16	13	15	o	1	o	x	1	4
Whittaker	32	1	2	3	8	15	12	14	1	x	9
Stewart	19	1	2	1	7	5	4	7	4	9	x

The previous alignments continued in 1960.

Justice Whittaker resigned during the 1961 term and was succeeded by Byron R. White of Colorado:

Justice	Total	Sole	Warren	Black	Douglas	Frankfurter	Clark	Harlan	Brennan	Whittaker	Stewart	White
Warren	18	o	x	11	15	o	1	2	5	1	2	o
Black	24	3	11	x	16	2	2	2	4	1	2	o
Douglas	32	9	15	16	x	o	1	4	6	o	1	o
Frankfurter	10	o	o	2	o	x	2	9	o	2	1	o
Clark	16	3	1	2	1	2	x	9	o	o	3	1
Harlan	37	9	2	2	4	9	9	x	1	4	10	o
Brennan	6	o	5	4	5	o	o	1	x	o	o	o
Whittaker	6	1	1	1	o	2	o	4	o	x	2	o
Stewart	16	1	2	2	1	1	3	10	o	2	x	o
White	1	o	o	o	o	o	1	o	o	o	o	x

In 1961 there was no noticeable change in the lineup; Justice Harlan reached a peak of dissents, and the conservatives lost a strong adherent in Justice Whittaker. Justice Frankfurter's health diminished his activity and presaged his early retirement.

Justice Frankfurter retired before the opening of the 1962 term, and Arthur J. Goldberg of Illinois, formerly secretary of labor, was appointed to replace him. The substitution of Goldberg for Frankfurter strengthened the ranks of the liberals as it weakened those of the conservatives:

Justice	Total	Sole	Warren	Black	Douglas	Clark	Harlan	Brennan	Stewart	White	Goldberg
Warren	7	0	x	5	2	2	0	4	0	0	0
Black	17	1	5	x	7	6	2	2	2	1	2
Douglas	18	4	2	7	x	1	3	2	3	1	3
Clark	24	1	2	6	1	x	15	1	11	9	0
Harlan	42	10	0	2	3	15	x	0	19	10	5
Brennan	5	0	4	2	2	2	0	x	0	0	1
Stewart	24	0	0	2	3	11	19	0	x	8	7
White	12	1	0	1	1	9	10	0	8	x	0
Goldberg	9	0	0	2	3	0	5	1	7	0	x

The fact that Justice Harlan led the list with forty-two dissents, followed by Stewart and Clark, each with twenty-four, while the Chief Justice had only seven dissents, Justice Brennan but five, and Black and Douglas were in a moderate range—at least for them—spelled the emergence of the liberal bloc. Curiously enough, Justice Goldberg, to whom, with but nine dissents, the results were satisfactory, cast seven of these with Justice Stewart who consorted with Justice Harlan.

There was no change of personnel during the 1963 term:

Justice	Total	Sole	Warren	Black	Douglas	Clark	Harlan	Brennan	Stewart	White	Goldberg
Warren	9	0	x	6	6	2	1	2	0	0	5
Black	24	2	6	x	12	4	6	2	2	4	8
Douglas	20	2	6	12	x	2	3	2	1	3	8
Clark	27	0	2	4	2	x	22	0	15	8	0
Harlan	51	9	1	6	3	22	x	1	25	17	3
Brennan	5	0	2	2	2	0	1	x	2	1	6
Stewart	29	1	0	2	1	15	25	2	x	10	4
White	21	1	0	4	3	8	17	1	10	x	3
Goldberg	17	0	5	8	8	0	3	6	4	3	x

The lack of dissent by the Chief Justice and Justice Brennan, coupled with the more than one-third dissents cast by Justice Harlan and the considerable number registered by his associates, Justices Clark, Stewart, and White, bespoke victory for the liberals. Noteworthy was the falling off of association between Justices Black and Douglas and the surprising number of dissents filed by Justice Goldberg, although half were cast with Black and Douglas, six with Brennan, five with the Chief Justice, and a lesser number with each of the conservatives.

The bench remained constant during the 1964 term:

Justice	Total	Sole	Warren	Black	Douglas	Clark	Harlan	Brennan	Stewart	White	Goldberg
Warren	4	0	x	2	2	0	0	1	1	2	2
Black	29	4	2	x	13	5	8	1	5	5	4
Douglas	23	5	2	13	x	3	4	0	1	1	3
Clark	10	1	0	5	3	x	8	0	2	3	0
Harlan	29	6	0	8	4	8	x	0	14	6	4
Brennan	2	0	1	1	0	0	0	x	0	2	0
Stewart	21	2	1	5	1	2	14	0	x	5	7
White	9	1	2	5	1	3	6	2	5	x	0
Goldberg	12	0	2	4	3	0	4	0	7	0	x

Again, we find the Chief Justice and Justice Brennan content with the term's work, although Justices Black and Douglas matched Justice Harlan in dissent. Neither Justice Clark or Justice White seemed disturbed by majority rulings, although dissents were cast in 80 of 110 cases. Justices Harlan and Stewart joined in dissent even more often than Justices Black and Douglas.

Justice Goldberg's short tenure on the Court ended with his resignation at the beginning of the 1965 term. He was succeeded by Abe Fortas of Tennessee:

Justice	Total	Sole	Warren	Black	Douglas	Clark	Harlan	Brennan	Stewart	White	Fortas
Warren	5	0	x	1	5	0	1	3	0	0	2
Black	16	4	1	x	5	3	7	0	7	2	1
Douglas	15	2	5	5	x	0	4	4	3	1	5
Clark	7	0	0	3	0	x	6	0	4	4	0
Harlan	31	6	1	7	4	6	x	1	20	6	3
Brennan	4	0	3	0	4	0	1	x	0	1	0
Stewart	21	0	0	7	3	4	20	0	x	5	3
White	10	2	0	2	1	4	6	1	5	x	1
Fortas	7	0	2	1	5	0	3	0	3	1	x

Most noteworthy during the term was the evidence of Justice Black's drift to the right, attested by his lessened adherence to Justice Douglas and his increased co-operation with Justices Harlan and Stewart, who were most closely associated in dissent. Again, the key to the predominance of liberal thinking was to be seen in the lack of dissent by the Chief Justice and Justice Brennan. Once more, Justice Harlan was the principal dissenter.

There were no changes of personnel during the 1966 term, although Justice Clark announced his expected resignation at the end of the term:

Justice	Total	Sole	Warren	Black	Douglas	Clark	Harlan	Brennan	Stewart	White	Fortas
Warren	15	1	x	2*	10*	3	2*	7	1*	1*	12*
Black	21	4	2*	x	10*	2	9*	1	9*	1*	5*
Douglas	31	8	10*	10*	x	2	3*	9	5*	1*	15*
Clark	16	0	3	2	2	x	9	0	8	4	2
Harlan	39	3	2*	2*	3*	9	x	1	29*	9*	5*
Brennan	11	0	7	1	9	0	1	x	1	2	7
Stewart	33	1	1*	9*	5*	8	29*	1	x	8	3*
White	13	1	1*	1*	1*	4	9*	2	8	x	2*
Fortas	22	0	12*	5*	15*	1	4*	7	3*	2*	x

* In United States v. Wade, 388 U.S. 218 (1967), a five-to-four decision, Justice Brennan wrote for the Court and Justice Clark concurred. Every other justice dissented in part.

Outstanding during the term was the commitment of the new member to the Warren, Douglas, and Brennan forces while the association of Justices Harlan and Stewart continued, with support from Justices Clark, White, and Black. Thus the liberal dissents increased, although the conservative dissents did not lessen. Justice Fortas, a freshman, evidenced his partiality to the radicalism of Justice Douglas, joining him fifteen times, while the Chief Justice and Justice Black each joined him only ten times. At the end of the term Justice Clark resigned, and the President appointed in his place Solicitor General Thurgood Marshall, a Negro, who had seen service on the second circuit bench. According to *The New York Times* of August 22, 1967, five southern senators voted against confirmation; Senator Ervin of North Carolina wrote of his

> abiding conviction that Judge Marshall is by practice and philosophy a constitutional iconoclast, and thus his elevation to the Supreme Court at this juncture of our history would make it virtually certain that for years to come, if not forever, the American people will be ruled by the arbitrary notions of the Supreme Court Justices rather than by the precepts of the Constitution.

In any event, one could expect Justice Marshall's accession to the bench to strengthen the liberal bloc during succeeding terms, although his record during the 1967 term had been too scant to justify judgment, since, for one reason or another, principally because of previous activities as solicitor general in many of the 1967 term cases and, to a lesser degree, because of his prior involvement in civil rights cases, he failed to participate. An example of the latter resulted in a five-to-four decision, thus affirming the conviction in Tennessee courts of a Negro accused of rape, whose argument that no Negro had ever sat on a jury in Maury County where he was tried, duplicated the argument made by Justice Marshall in a 1946 case.[1]

Following the close of the 1967 term, Chief Justice Warren resigned, and the President nominated Justice Fortas to be Chief Justice and Circuit Court Judge Homer Thornberry to fill the vacancy. A Republican senatorial filibuster followed a somewhat protracted examination of Justice Fortas, who finally refused to attend another session of the Judiciary Committee. At length, since those favoring the approval of Justice Fortas were unable to muster a two-thirds vote of the Senate and thus end the filibuster, the nominations of Fortas as Chief Justice and of Thornberry as an Associate Justice were withdrawn by the President. Thus history repeated itself: a filibuster prevented one Johnson from making appointments, as a reduction of membership of the Court prevented a post–Civil War Johnson from making such appointments. Thereafter, following the election of President Nixon, Chief Justice Warren announced that he would retire at the end of the 1968 term.

The only change of personnel during the 1967 term was the substitution of Justice Marshall for retired Justice Clark. During the term, of a total of 257 decisions, Justice Marshall, owing to previous associations, as noted previously, failed to participate in 83, leaving those to be decided by an eight-man —and, on occasion, seven-man—Court. As a result, five cases found the Court equally divided, thus letting stand the decision below, while four cases, with Justice Marshall's participation, were decided by a five-to-four vote. These 257 decisions brought forth 280 dissents, which were handed down in 134 cases, a percentage of about 52 per cent.

[1] *The New York Times*, March 26, 1968.

The box-score for the term reads approximately as follows:

Justice	Total	Sole	Warren	Black	Douglas	Harlan	Brennan	Stewart	White	Fortas	Marshall
Warren	16	4	x	1	7	1	4	1	2	4	2
Black	55	9	1	x	14	21	1	7	24	7	0
Douglas	41	12	7	14	x	3	2	3	1	10	1
Harlan	67	13	1	21	3	x	0	14	19	2	1
Brennan	5	0	4	1	2	0	x	1	1	2	1
Stewart	26	2	1	7	3	14	1	x	5	3	1
White	49	5	2	24	1	19	1	5	x	0	0
Fortas	17	2	4	7	10	2	2	3	0	x	1
Marshall	4	0	2	0	1	1	1	1	0	2	x

The liberal tendency of the majority of the Court continued, attested by the lack of dissent by Justice Brennan and the lesser number of dissents filed by Justice Fortas and the Chief Justice. While Justice Douglas roved, his liberal stance was evident, as was that of Justice Marshall. The minority conservative wing was led by Justice Harlan, followed by Justices Black and White. Justice Stewart served as a middle-of-the roader.

President Nixon, having been critical of the Court during the Presidential campaign, might be expected not to disappoint the conservative senators who had opposed the confirmation of Justice Fortas in his choice of a Chief Justice and a successor Associate Justice to Chief Justice Warren. Hence the extremism of the Warren Court majority will undoubtedly be diluted during the Nixon incumbency, although, just as Justice Holmes proved to be a disappointment to President Theodore Roosevelt, only time can tell.

CHAPTER XXVII

The Final Term
of the Warren Court

WHETHER BECAUSE OF THE condition of the docket or because of the storm of
criticism evoked during the 1968 effort to seat Justice Fortas as chief justice of
the United States and during the following Presidential election, the closing
days of the Warren Court produced fewer radical innovations than those of
some of its earlier decisions. The more startling of those decisions met with
evasion, passive compliance, and, in some cases, active resistance. Of the
latter, according to *The New York Times* of March 26, 1969, the school-prayer
decisions have met widespread defiance, especially in northeastern states. The
segregation decisions have continued to meet token compliance and tug of war
in the South and growing ignorance in the North, where schools in urban
areas have largely continued to reflect the colors of their immediate communities. The police have apparently done whatever was needful to meet the
administrative criminal requirements, and compliance undoubtedly has been
but one of the expediencies.

With the blessing of activity by jailhouse lawyers, the earlier decisions in
criminal cases have called for a step-up in determinations of retroactivity. So,
in McConnell v. Rhay,[1] the Court declared retroactive the doctrine of Mempa
v. Rhay[2] and held the Sixth Amendment to require provision for counsel for
felony defendants in proceedings for revocation of probation and imposition
of sentence. Likewise, in Arsenault v. Massachusetts[3] the Court held White
v. Maryland[4] effective retroactively to grant postconviction relief for lack
of counsel.

In Fuller v. Alaska,[5] however, the Court held only prospective Lee v. Florida,[6] which held evidence obtained in violation of federal wiretapping statutes

[1] 393 U.S. 2 (1968).
[2] 389 U.S. 128 (1967).
[3] 393 U.S. 5 (1968).
[4] 373 U.S. 59 (1963).
[5] 393 U.S. 80 (1968).
[6] 392 U.S. 378 (1968).

inadmissible in state court trials. In this case Justices Black and Douglas dissented, as they had previously in cases involving retroactivity.

Similarly, in Desist v. United States[7] and Kaiser v. United States[8] the Court held that Katz v. United States,[9] which found wiretapping prior to the passage of the 1968 Crime Bill subject to the rigors of the Fourth Amendment, prospective only. In the Desist case Justices Harlan, Fortas, and Douglas dissented, and Justice Marshall did not participate. In the Kaiser case Justices Harlan, Fortas, and Douglas dissented.

In Smith v. Yeager[10] the Court in effect decreed Townsend v. Sain,[11] which expanded rights to evidentiary hearings in habeas corpus proceedings, to be retroactive. Justice White dissented. In Thorpe v. Housing Authority[12] the Court held that the notice of the reasons for the tenant's eviction from a housing development required by a previous decision[13] had to be given retroactively. Finally, the Court held[14] that Barber v. Page,[15] holding that the state was obligated to make a good-faith effort to produce a witness for confrontation at a defendant's trial, was to be applied retroactively.

In the area of crime the Court held that the definition of "extortion" includes "blackmail" and is not limited to its common law restriction to public officials.[16] The Court expanded the requirements for free transcripts to defendants to include the record of a previous unsuccessful habeas corpus proceeding in a subsequent proceeding, where an appeal from the first denial was impermissible.[17]

In Smith v. Hooey[18] the Court held that the Sixth Amendment required a state to make a diligent, good-faith effort to afford a defendant a speedy trial on a pending indictment, even though he was in jail in another state. Justice Harlan concurred, basing his agreement on the due process clause of the Fourteenth Amendment.

Over the dissent of Justices White and Stewart, with Justice Fortas not participating and Justice Harlan concurring because he felt bound by the prior Miranda decision, which, he said, he still considered unsound, six members of the Court reversed a murder conviction because the police had not delivered to the defendant the Miranda warnings at the time of his arrest.

[7] 37 U.S. Law Week 4225 (1969).
[8] 37 U.S. Law Week 4236 (1969).
[9] 389 U.S. 347 (1967).
[10] 393 U.S. 122 (1968).
[11] 372 U.S. 293 (1963).
[12] 393 U.S. 268 (1969).
[13] Thorpe v. Housing Authority, 386 U.S. 670 (1967).
[14] Berger v. California, 393 U.S. 314 (1969).
[15] 3390 U.S. 719 (1968).
[16] United States v. Nardillo & Weisberg, 393 U.S. 286 (1969).
[17] Gardner v. California, 393 U.S. 367 (1969).
[18] 393 U.S. 374 (1969).

Justice White said that the decision "draws the straitjacket even tighter" on law enforcement.[19] While holding that Orozco's admissions could not be held against him, the Court left open for the defendant, on a retrial, to contend that the gun found in his possession at the time of his arrest could not be received in evidence against him.

Also, by way of recognition of the rights of convicted defendants, the Court held that a convicted bank robber, serving a twenty-year sentence, could collaterally attack his conviction in habeas corpus proceedings upon the ground that evidence introduced at his trial was found by means of an unconstitutional search, even though the contention had not been made at his trial.[20] It also held that a federal district judge may require a state to answer interrogatories propounded by prisoners who challenge their convictions in habeas corpus proceedings.[21] Justices Black, Harlan, and Stewart dissented in both cases; Justice White dissented in the Harris case, and Justice Marshall did not participate in the Kaufman case.

Finally, five members of the Court held that unfair conduct of a police line-up may be such as to violate due process and thus render identification at the trial a nullity.[22] Justices White, Harlan, and Stewart disagreed with the result, and Justice Black wrote in dissent.

Wiretapping prior to the passage of the 1968 Crime Bill has given the Court great concern. Originally it accepted the government's assurance that convictions had not been obtained by the use of evidence procured by illegal wiretapping. However, in Kolod v. United States[23] the Court refused to accept such assurance and remanded the case so that the district judge could examine the logs or transcripts and come to his own conclusion. Then, on March 10, 1969, the Court seemed to rule[24] that the logs were to be turned over to defendants' counsel for inspection. To this ruling Justice Black dissented, and Justices Fortas and Harlan dissented in part, while Justice Marshall did not participate.

The government, fearing that the decision would compel it to make public the known fact that it had been engaged in wiretapping the telephones of foreign embassies, took the, for it, unusual step of seeking a rehearing. Thereafter the Court, as has been its custom, denied the motion but issued a statement, written by Justice Stewart, to the effect that the government had misread the previous opinion, that the rule of submitting the logs to the district judge still prevailed, and that it was only if he found the wiretapping illegal

[19] Orozco v. Texas, 37 U.S. Law Week 4260 (1969).
[20] Kaufman v. United States, 37 U.S. Law Week 4238 (1969).
[21] Harris v. Nelson, 37 U.S. Law Week 4219 (1969).
[22] Foster v. California, #47, issued April 1, 1969.
[23] 390 U.S. 136 (1968).
[24] Alderman v. United States; Ivanov v. United States; Butenos v. United States, 37 U.S. Law Week 4189 (1969).

(and the Court had never said that government wiretapping for security reasons was illegal), that he was to proceed to investigate further.

Concurrently the Court remanded more than a dozen cases, including the notorious convictions of Cassius Clay, the prize fighter, and of James Hoffa, the labor leader, so that the trial courts might proceed in conformity with the Court's explanation of its previous ambiguous decision. Simultaneously, it refused in two cases[25] to give defendants access to transcripts.

In two search-and-seizure cases, the Court voided convictions because it found the affidavits submitted for the issuance of warrants insufficient to establish the reliability of informants. In one case[26] Justices Black, Harlan, Stewart, and White dissented; in the other Justices Stewart, Fortas, and Black dissented, the latter saying in their dissent: "A policeman's affidavit should not be judged as an entry in an essay contest. It is not abracadabra. As the majority recognizes, a policeman's affidavit is entitled to common-sense evaluation."[27]

In this connection it might not be amiss to quote a *Wall Street Journal* editorial of March 21, 1969:

> An impressive number of prominent jurists have joined the complaint about the recent string of Supreme Court decisions on criminal procedure, which have made life easier for defendants and tougher for police and prosecutors. Some especially penetrating comments were offered recently by Chief Justice Joseph Weintraub of the New Jersey Supreme Court....
>
> In a 6–0 decision, the New Jersey court refused to suppress evidence arising from the law the high court had struck down....
>
> If remedies . . . are being discussed, a far more elegant and penetrating solution might be an Amendment guaranteeing that Courts may consider whatever relevant evidence is available.

As for the suggestion in the last paragraph above, it might be remarked that, as Chief Justice Taft and Justices Cardoza, Black, and others have said on occasion, there is nothing in the Fourth Amendment even suggesting an interpretation that excludes relevant evidence, that the exclusionary evidence rule has, in truth, no constitutional justification, and that it is a mere rule of evidence that can be disposed of by Congress without amending the Constitution.

Now that the Court has gone knee-deep into the political arena, we find it taking cognizance of the objection of minor political parties who found Ohio election laws too stringent to permit them to nominate candidates for the presidency and vice-presidency.[28] Ruling that those laws denied equal

[25] Giordano v. United States, #28; Taglianetti v. United States, #446; issued March 24, 1969.
[26] Recznik v. Lorain, 393 U.S. 166 (1968).
[27] Spinelli v. United States, 393 U.S. 410 (1969).
[28] Williams v. Rhodes; Socialist Labor Party v. Rhodes, 393 U.S. 23 (1968).

protection, the Court acted with Justices Stewart and White dissenting in the first case and the Chief Justice in both.

On the score of taxation the Court held[29] that a foreign corporation authorized to do business in a state may not thereafter be discriminated against taxwise by reason of its foreign source. Justice Black dissented. The Court also held[30] that, to avoid taxation of accumulated corporate earnings, the corporation had the burden of proving that shareholder tax avoidance was not the "controlling or impelling motive" for the accumulation. Justices Harlan, Douglas, and Stewart concurred in part and dissented in part.

In the area of First Amendment cases the Court held[31] that a state law that prohibited a teacher from explaining or teaching the truth of the Darwinian theory violated the establishment clause. Justices Black, Stewart, and Harlan concurred. In another case involving religion[32] the Court disclaimed jurisdiction of a suit involving the possession of church property, which concerned the interpretation of church doctrine.

In two cases involving railroads the Court held in one[33] that a state court could not enjoin picketing by striking employees of one railroad of a terminal and facilities also used by other, unaffected roads, thus approving a secondary boycott. Justices Douglas, Black, and Stewart dissented; Justices Fortas and Marshall did not participate. In another case the Court upheld the right of a state legislature to enact a full-crew railroad law.[34] Justice Douglas dissented; Justice Fortas did not participate.

The Court upheld the right of Negro members of a railroad union to seek damages and injunctive relief in the federal courts for alleged racial discrimination without exhausting their contractual or administrative remedies, when they alleged that such recourse would be futile since the union and the employer were collaborating to deny their rights.[35]

In furtherance of protection to Negroes, the Court held an amendment to a city charter voiding a fair-housing law to deny equal protection and thus to be unconstitutional.[36]

The Court upheld the power of a union to fine members who exceeded work quotas established by the union.[37] Writing for the Court, Justice White suggested that those who sought to do more work might quit the union;

[29] Whyy v. Glassboro, 393 U.S. 117 (1968).
[30] United States v. Donruss, 393 U.S. 297 (1969).
[31] Epperson v. Arkansas, 393 U.S. 97 (1968).
[32] Presbyterian Church v. M.E.B.H.M. Presbyterian Church, 393 U.S. 440 (1969).
[33] Brotherhood v. Jacksonville Terminal Co., 37 U.S. Law Week 4247 (1969).
[34] Brotherhood v. Chicago R.I.R.R., 393 U.S. 129 (1968).
[35] Glover v. St. Louis & S.F.R.R., 393 U.S. 324 (1968).
[36] Hunter v. Erickson, 393 U.S. 385 (1969).
[37] Scofield v. NLRB, #273, issued April 1, 1969.

however, he failed to suggest a remedy where the union shop prevailed and the dissenter would lose his job. Justice Black dissented; Justice Marshall did not participate.

In the antitrust area, the Court, after reviewing the previous cases pro and con,[38] held that exchange of price information violated the Sherman Act.[39] Justice Fortas concurred, saying that he did not so understand the majority opinion. Justices Marshall, Harlan, and Stewart dissented (Justice Marshall casting one of his rare dissents), saying that exchange of price information was not illegal per se.

While continuing to avoid taking jurisdiction of questions pressed upon it from time to time by Justices Stewart and Douglas concerning the legality of the Vietnam war in the absence of a declaration by Congress,[40] the Court held that a draft board could not use the regulation governing delinquency to deprive a draftee of his statutory exemption as a conscientious objector.[41] Justices Stewart, Brennan, and White dissented, holding that the Military Selective Service Act of 1967 prohibited action by a draftee at the preinduction stage and required him to await prosecution or seek habeas corpus later. Immediately thereafter, in a similar case, the Court followed the theory of the preceding dissent.[42]

In still another military case the Court held that a final judgment of the military courts could be attacked only by habeas corpus proceedings and expressed doubts that it could be challenged collaterally by a suit in the Court of Claims for back pay.[43]

[38] E.g., Maple Flooring Mfrs. Assoc. v. United States, 268 U.S. 563 (1925).

[39] United States v. Container Corporation of America, 393 U.S. 333 (1969).

[40] E.g., Mora v. McNamara, 389 U.S. 934–35, 37 (1967); United States v. O'Brien, 391 U.S. 367, 389 (1968).

[41] Ostereich v. Selective Service System, 21 L.Ed.2d 402 (1968).

[42] Clark v. Gabriel, 393 U.S. 256 (1968).

[43] United States v. Augenblick; United States v. Juhl, 393 U.S. 348 (1969).

CHAPTER XXVIII

Commentary

DESPITE THE EFFORT MADE in the preceding pages to permit the Court to speak for itself, particularly respecting recent decisions of import, it might not be amiss to add a brief note, in view of current controversies stirred by so many of the recent decisions. That the Warren Court consisted of a libertarian majority is open to little question. That, under the guise of interpreting the Constitution, the Court has been legislating and declaring policy for years, is and has been an accepted fact. How far and to what extent it should do so is another matter. On this score the words of Justices Black and Harlan in the recent Berger case are illuminating.[1]

A glaring example of the lengths to which the majority is prepared to go was given in the Griswold case[2] by the fluent tongue of Justice Douglas, who read "privacy" into the minds of the Founders when they formulated the First Amendment—a presumption which caused Justice Black's hackles to rise.[3] But that was not all; for the fertile mind of Justice Douglas conceived that, after a lapse of almost two centuries, the First Amendment has "penumbras"—a discovery that would enable this and future majorities to move its peripheries out boundlessly and at will.

Nor has the Court acted with an open mind in legislating and in declaring national policy, for it is demonstrable that its members, like most other members of the human race, come to their tasks with predictable predilections in many of the fields they traverse,[4] to say nothing of after-acquired prejudices.[5]

---

[1] Justice Harlan in Berger v. New York, 388 U.S. 41, 89 (1967): "Newly contrived constitutional rights have been established without any apparent concern for the empirical process that goes with legislative reform." Justice Black, *ibid.,* 77: ". . . simply gives this Court a useful new tool, as I see it . . . to usurp the policy-making power of Congress." . . . "In order to strike down the New York law the Court has been compelled to rewrite completely the Fourth Amendment" (*ibid.,* 86).

[2] Griswold v. Connecticut, 381 U.S. 479 (1965).

[3] *Ibid.,* 509–10.

[4] *See* Glendon Schubert, *The Judicial Mind: Attitudes and Ideologies of Supreme Court Justices* (Northwestern University Press, 1965); *and see* Chapter I.

[5] Stewart, J., dissenting in Cascade Nat. Gas. Corp. v. El Paso Nat. Gas Co., 386 U.S. 129 (1967).

The attitudes, ideologies, and practices of a majority of the Court, especially during the latter part of the term of Chief Justice Warren, when the liberal bloc controlled, have produced an unusual number of extracontroversial decisions. From a Court that ordinarily generates judicial dissent in the majority of the cases it decides, these extracontroversial decisions have indicated something more than the usual judicial differences that close questions engender. Instead, they have stirred public indignation to a point that proves they were rendered in areas where public opinion is largely unsettled, where there is doubt whether acquiescent majorities exist to support them, and where there is no doubt that substantial minorities exist to oppose them.

These extracontroversial decisions include those rendered (1) in the school prayer cases, (2) the apportionment and vote cases, (3) the Escobedo and Miranda cases, (4) the Aguilar case, (5) the Garrity and Spevack cases, (6) the Berger case, and (7) the obscenity cases.

Each of these decisions met with dissents, the pros and cons of which, as stated by members of the Court, are to be found in the preceding pages, as noted above. Some added comment and references may make a contribution to appreciating the strength and weaknesses of these decisions, some of which prevailed by the single vote of one or more predictable justices.

Aside from the presumption of fallibility that arises from a decision that provokes substantial dissent, one of the basic vices of many of the Court's decisions is the inflexible straitjacket of "constitutionality," often unnecessarily or unjustifiably applied. In its rigidity is wrapped policies the Court imposes upon an entire nation of states, regardless of the variant practicalities flowing from a variety of local conditions and problems affected by the decision. Of these underlying factors, in all their possible fifty-one variances, either the Court is uninformed, or the Court ignores them because to recognize them would challenge the effort to justify a uniform remedy.

Ordinary legislation, not disguised as constitutional interpretation, is flexible and subject to ready change in response to public opinion without the tug-of-war which rules of stare decisis generate. Nor need it overcome the obduracy of men with life tenure who, like most men, are not given to confess error. On the other hand, the Court's legislation, until a shift of ideological membership occurs, must undergo the tortuous paths laid down for its amendment by the Constitution, paths the Court deliberately bypasses by its pretense of constitutional interpretation, as witness Senator Dirksen's effort to overcome the Court's school prayer decision.[6]

[6] Justice Harlan in Berger v. New York, 388 U.S. 41, 89 (1967): "And overlying the particular decision . . . is the fact that, short of future action by this Court, their impact can only be undone or modified by the slow and uncertain process of constitutional amendment."

Senator Dirksen, the Senate minority leader, said in a press release, issued January 11, 1967: "On September 21, 1966, the Senate voted on an earlier version of this amendment" [to permit

The power to nationalize state enforcement of its criminal laws was not given by the states to the national government.[7] Nor did Justice Black's historical syllogism convince a host of prior judges that the Fourteenth Amendment was intended to make the Bill of Rights applicable to the states. The power to cure national, social, and political ills by judicial fiat was contemplated neither by the Founders nor by Chief Justice Marshall. Nor did they or he ever stand sponsor for the proposition that one branch of our government should supersede and exercise another's function or functions. Yet on Marshall's foundation of judicial power, the Court, in Justice Jackson's words, "is forever adding new stories to the temples of constitutional law, and the temples have a way of collapsing when one story too many is added."[8] And one may paraphrase the vernacular to say that Justice Jackson hadn't seen anything yet.

Besides evidencing an apparent certainty ofttimes denied by as many as four men of equal rank and talent, on important occasions a majority of the Court, where it cannot fabricate remedies, resorts to panaceas bearing uncertain and threatening consequences—a means of avoiding old problems by creating new ones. Such, for example, is the practice of "punishing" policemen who make searches and seizures that do not accord with the confused, intricate, and frequently varying patterns of the Court's decisions for enforcement of the Fourth Amendment. That the Court bars evidence not so obtained as "punishment" for the law enforcement officer who obtains it and because it can think of no other way of compelling enforcement of the Amendment is beyond doubt.[9] That the aura of "constitutionality" it wraps about the exclusion of such evidence is a miasma is made clear by Justice Black.[10] For want of a remedy, the Court turns the admittedly guilty criminal out to continue

---

voluntary prayer in public schools]. "The vote was 49 to 37 in favor of the Resolution but it was 9 votes short of the two-thirds required. . . . In this 90th Congress the fight for this amendment will be one for keeps both in committee and on the Senate floor. If the time ever comes when legalisms, cleavages, outmoded dogmas and misinterpretation of the Constitution can deny to the people the right to be heard on this fundamental issue then we have fallen to a low state indeed."

[7] Justice Harlan in Berger v. New York, 388 U.S. 41, 89 (1967): "The Court in recent years has more and more taken to itself sole responsibility for setting the pattern of criminal law enforcement throughout the country."

[8] Douglas v. Jeannette, 318 U.S. 157, 181 (1943).

[9] Murphy, J., in Wolf v. Colorado, 338 U.S. 25, 44 (1949): "Only by exclusion can we impress upon the zealous prosecutor that violation of the Constitution will do him no good." Learned Hand in United States v. Pollar, 43 F. 2d 911, 914 (1949); "Limitations upon the fruit to be gathered tend to limit the quest itself."

[10] Black, J., in Berger v. New York, 388 U.S. 41, 76 (1967): "Had the framers of this Amendment [the Fourth] desired to prohibit the use in court of evidence secured by an unreasonable search or seizure, they would have used plain appropriate language to do so. . . . Since the Fourth Amendment contains no language forbidding the use of such evidence I think there is no such constitutional rule."

to prey upon a crime-ridden, court-unprotected community. If this practice can be termed a "remedy," it proves remedial only for the convicted criminal.

That the use above of the phrase "confused and intricate patterns of the Court's decisions" is no mere rhetoric is demonstrated by the Court itself when we find it wrangling about such "constitutional issues" as the question of whether a policeman touched a door handle of a taxicab before the defendant, a narcotics pusher, sitting inside, threw a package of narcotics to the floor, while ignoring the proved guilt of the accused.

To employ an apt but outworn cliché, throwing the baby out with the bath water is the panacea of requiring the presence of counsel at the initial stages of a police investigation to meet and dispose of the sporadic issues respecting coerced confessions—a simple expedient which assures that there will be no coerced confessions, since there will be no confessions at all.

After reciting the requirements the Court laid down in the Berger case for eavesdropping, Justice Black said: "Now if never before, the Court's purpose is clear; it is determined to ban all eavesdropping.... the Court means to inform the Nation there shall be no eavesdropping—period."[11] True as this seemed at the time, the subsequent Katz decision demonstrated that at least some members of the Court had second thoughts on the subject.

However the Court gets the power it exercises, it must respect its limitations, remembering what de Toqueville said: "They are all-powerful so long as the people consent to obey the law; they can do nothing when they scorn it." Attempting to rule by judicial fiat in areas where a substantial minority of hard-core resistance exists can only bring the Court and its law into disrepute, without changing the conditions respecting which the Court seeks to legislate. Every judge must know how mistaken Justice Wayne proved to be when he induced Chief Justice Taney to believe the Court could legislate the slavery issue out of existence. And even schoolboys know the consequences suffered by Taney and his court by this arrogant assertion of power.

Efforts of the Congress to effectuate the provisions of the Fourteenth Amendment by the passage of civil rights legislation failed in the 1870's; the Eighteenth Amendment became a more recent dead letter, to cite only two outstanding examples. The Court's laudatory bid to end school segregation and its recent effort to advance the cause of "open housing" by striking down the will of the majority in California, can incite and encourage, and doubtless have incited and encouraged, radical racial resentment and revolt. But only time can tell whether the Court's estimates of the practical effects of its ad-

11 *Ibid.*, 86.

White, J., *ibid.*, 111: "The Court appears intent upon creating out of whole cloth new constitutionally mandated warrant procedures carefully tailored to make eavesdrop warrants unobtainable." White, J., in Escobedo v. Illinois, 378 U.S. 478, 495 (1964): "The Court's goal is to bar all confessions."

denda to the Constitution will prove correct. Or, perhaps, it made no such estimate in its bid to impose an indubitable moral attitude on a perhaps unresponsive people.

The Court's dictum that "separate educational facilities are inherently unequal" would seem to be justified by the fact that a refusal to permit a Negro to attend a white school tends to foster an inferiority complex and a consequent reaction. On the other hand, in practical operation, not only do many whites seek to "protect" their children[12] but a considerable number of black people seem to prefer a practical segregation, as do members of various races and religions, and make demand for control by Negroes of schools essentially Negro.[13]

Practical-minded men may wonder to what extent the demands of school desegregation and open housing come within the ambits of sumptuary legislation, with which the law invariably has demonstrated its inability to deal. If people are to be told by law with whom their children must associate or to whom they may or may not sell their houses or who are to be their neighbors, it becomes difficult to separate these requirements from attempts to control, by law, expression of natural tastes and prejudices, likes and dislikes, areas that have always been productive of poor legal harvests. We cannot effectively legislate against fear or hate or its consequences, the racial or religious discrimination that has moved people since time immemorial; these must be eradicated from the hearts and minds of the people.

It is axiomatic that revolt does not start with the oppressed. As Eric Hoffer points out,[14] mass movements are started by men of words who, having discredited the prevailing order, enable men of action to take over.[15] May it not be believed that the Court has been supplying the words? Again, to quote Eric Hoffer: "Quite often in history action has been the echo of words. An era of talk was followed by an era of events."[16]

As recently as June 12, 1967, in the face of riots occurring all over the country, we find four high court justices holding that Negroes could ignore an injunction issued by a state court to prevent demonstrations and marches that city officials alleged were "calculated to provoke breaches of the peace" and threatened "the safety, peace and tranquility of the City," and to litigate the issue of its validity in subsequent contempt proceedings.[17]

---

[12] E.g., Detroit Integration Drive Fails as Whites Quit 3 School Areas: *New York Times* headline, April 15, 1968.

[13] E.g., Group Plans Suit on Slum Schools; 'Separate' but 'Equal' Aim of Campaign in City: *New York Times* headline, April 23, 1968; Negroes Protest at Northwestern: *New York Times* headline, May 4, 1968.

[14] *The True Believer* (New York, Harper & Brothers, 1951).

[15] *Ibid.*, 129.

[16] *The Passionate State of Mind* (New York, Harper & Brothers, 1954–55), 44.

[17] Walker v. Birmingham, 388 U.S. 307 (1967).

Of the liberal majority, apparently, only Justice Black, who voted to make a majority, seems to have begun to see the light. Such a holding is, of course, an affirmation of the radical and anarchic view that it lies within the discretion of each person to determine to break a law with which he disagrees.

Departing from generalities, one may view briefly the controversial decisions previously mentioned. The first of the school prayer cases[18] involved the innocuous equivalent of saying grace at the table: "Almighty God, we acknowledge our dependence upon Thee, and we beg Thy blessings upon us, our parents, our teachers and our Country." Justice Stewart, dissenting, recited a long list of customary and more fervent supplications and pledges habitual to Congress, the courtrooms, and elsewhere, while a majority of seven members of the Court branded this recognition of "a God" unconstitutional.

The reapportionment decision[19] that vested in lower court judges the task and power of dictating to bodies politically elected and took the Court into political areas to lay down political policies which it had admitted for almost two centuries was none of its business surpasses the Fuller court's effort to be a superlegislature. It constituted a sterling example of one branch of government taking over the unperformed duties of another and giving its intrusion the colorable protection of constitutionality. For documentation, witness Justice Clark, who said,

> Although I find the Tennessee apportionment statute offends the Equal Protection Clause, I would not consider intervention by this Court into so delicate a field if there were any other relief available to the people of Tennessee . . .[20] It is said there is recourse in Congress and perhaps that may be. . . . To date Congress has never undertaken such a task in any State. . . .[21]

And Justice Frankfurter said that "there is not under our Constitution a judicial remedy for every political mischief, for every undesirable exercise of legislative power. The Framers carefully and with deliberate forethought refused so to enthrone the judiciary. . . ."[22]

When later[23] the Court called for equal population in congressional districts and Justice Douglas coined the "one person, one vote" phrase,[24] the Court was arrogating to itself and to subordinate judges, with neither training nor experience in the field, political policy judgments that our form of gov-

---

[18] Engel v. Vitale, 370 U.S. 421 (1962); also School Dist. v. Schempp, 374 U.S. 203 (1963); Murray v. Curlett, 374 U.S. 203 (1963).
[19] Baker v. Carr, 369 U.S. 186 (1962).
[20] *Ibid.*, 258.
[21] *Ibid.*, 259.
[22] *Ibid.*, 270.
[23] Wesberry v. Sanders, 376 U.S. 1 (1964).
[24] Reynolds v. Sims, 377 U.S. 533 (1964).

ernment has vested in the people and their representatives. It may well be that a decision should be made that we should level all inequalities in the exercise of the franchise, including those of literacy. The question remains, however, who should make that decision, an undemocratically selected court of nine men, or the people and their direct representatives. In making that decision, it may be well to consider, as the Court apparently has not, whether the consequences of one vote per person may, with the growth of slum-ridden cities, prove more harmful than rural control ever was, particularly in view of the insistence that literacy is no mark of intelligence. Those who make the decision might well feel that this consequence is too striking a departure from the theory this country has long held that the foundation of a successful working democracy is a sound educational system and an educated electorate.

The rulings in the Escobedo[25] and Miranda[26] cases have been discussed. They, and that in the Aguilar case,[27] emphasize the majority's general attitude of protecting rights while disregarding duties, of making a fetish of individual rights without reckoning the cost to society. Incidentally, Escobedo was later convicted on a narcotics charge and was sentenced to serve a prison term of twenty-two years.[28]

Despite widespread public resentment of some of these decisions (President Nixon, in a campaign statement, ascribed increase of crime to some of the decisions),[29] the activists on the Court continue to feed critical comment[30] in the face of FBI and police reports that 1967 major crimes had increased measurably over those of 1966.[31]

In addition, Senators McClellan and Ervin, saying "Our citizens are fearful, terrorized and outraged" and "demand and deserve relief from this scourge of lawlessness which today imperils our internal security," mustered sufficient support, with the aid of the reaction to the assassination of Senator Robert F. Kennedy, to tack onto the Administration's Crime Bill curbs on the Court's decisions in the Miranda, Mallory, and Wade cases and to permit wiretapping on a broader scale than the Administration proposed.[32] In addition, they induced the Senate Judiciary Committee to include in the bill revocation of federal court authority to review state court convictions of habeas corpus proceedings and abolition of federal authority to overrule state courts in the admissions of confessions and lineup identifications. While these

25 Escobedo v. Illinois, 378 U.S. 478 (1964).
26 Miranda v. Arizona, 384 U.S. 436 (1966).
27 Aguilar v. Texas, 378 U.S. 108 (1964).
28 *Miami Herald*, February 21, 1968.
29 *New York Times*, May 9, 1968.
30 E.g., *Wall Street Journal*, April 22, 1968.
31 E.g., *New York Times*, March 15, 1968; May 1, 1968; May 29, 1968.
32 *Ibid.*, April 28, 1968; May 2, 1968.

restrictions of federal court jurisdiction were stricken from the bill before its passage, their inclusion at the hands of the Judiciary Committee should serve as notice to the Court that further tampering with state court crime admin-istration in this era of increasing crime might well lead to congressional action to curb the Court's jurisdiction, an area well within the congressional power.

It might also be remarked that it is difficult to see why the right of privacy might not properly give way to permissive and restricted wiretapping, at least during a period when crime has reached proportions that constitute a threat to the "national security," which opponents of wiretapping concede justifies resort to such means.

The repercussions of these criminal decisions can be conjectured from the need of making them prospective, as in the Mapp and Escobedo cases, and from the fact that, following the Court's decision in Chapman v. California[33] on March 13, 1967, beginning with Hollis v. California,[34] on petitions for certiorari, the Court vacated judgments and remanded them for further con-sideration in light of the Chapman case in twenty-two cases. In twenty-one of these cases Justice Stewart voted to reverse. Similarly, on February 13, 1967, in twenty-one cases, the Court denied petitions for certiorari, while in ten of these,[35] Justice Douglas voted to grant certiorari and reverse the judgments below on Justice Brennan's dissent in Spencer v. Texas.[36] In eleven others he was joined by Justice Fortas and the Chief Justice on the basis of the latter's dissent in the Spencer case.

Thus we find a total of twenty-one convicted criminals who would have been turned loose in a single state if the dissenters had had their way. How many more were lined up behind them in Texas and elsewhere, no one could tell. And only Justice Black's swing vote made possible the majority that refused to unlock the cell doors of these inmates adjudged "habitual crimi-nals" by the Texas courts.

The decisions in the Garrity[37] and Spevack[38] cases put society at the mercy of crooked policemen and crooked lawyers through a sophistry that ignores the wisdom of Justice Holmes and a paraphrase of his wise words by a Cali-fornia court. The Garrity decision may not shock a citizen; the Spevack case is bound to shock any decent lawyer who takes pride in his profession. A later case denied certiorari to a lawyer who had been disbarred a quarter of a century before upon his conviction for larceny, and whom the bar association

---

[33] 386 U. S. 18 (1967).
[34] 386 U.S. 262 (1967).
[35] 386 U.S. 926, 927 (1967).
[36] Ibid., 927–29, 938.
[37] Garrity v. New Jersey, 385 U.S. 493 (1967).
[38] Spevack v. Klein, 385 U.S. 511 (1967).

had refused to reinstate after his conviction had been reversed.[39] Justices Black and Douglas dissented, ignoring the fact that after the criminal case had been dismissed a referee appointed by the Court found the testimony in the criminal case sufficient, if not to permit a conviction under rules of criminal law, at least to justify disbarment. Fortunately the majority of the Court was more concerned with the protection of society in this case than with the petitioner's right to pursue a vocation for which he had been found unfit.

The Spevack decision was criticized in an article written by W. Warren Cole, Jr., in the September, 1967, issue of the American Bar Association *Journal,* which was followed in the December issue by a spate of acclaiming letters from lawyers who agreed with Cole. One lawyer advocated a constitutional amendment "to exempt bar disciplinary proceedings from the requirements of the Fifth Amendment," bringing to mind Justice Cardozo's earlier pronouncement that "Justice . . . would not perish if the accused were subject to a duty to respond to orderly inquiry."[40]

The Berger majority decision that struck down the New York law permitting court-authorized eavesdropping needs no greater or more eloquent condemnation here than was rendered by Justices Black and Harlan in their dissenting opinions, and the Court's subsequent recantations.[41] Nor need one dwell on the Court's state of hopeless confusion in defining obscenity, akin to an amateur painting himself into a corner, beyond quoting Justice Black in the Curtis Publishing case: "It strikes me that the Court is getting itself in the same quagmire in the field of libel in which it is now struggling in the field of obscenity. No one, including this Court, can know what is or is not constitutionally obscene or libelous under this Court's rulings."[42]

This may be added: In dissenting from denial of a writ of certiorari to review a conviction for creating and offering for sale six fiberglass statues, held obscene under the Florida statute which made the test of obscenity "appeals to prurient interest," Justices Stewart, Black, and Douglas said that the language of the Florida statute could be traced to the Court's decision in the Roth case and that the phrase used was no longer a test of obscenity.[43]

And, it may be added too that under this Court's rulings freedom of the individual needs little protection; we have it to the point of license, as out-of-hand picketing, sit-ins, strikes (to say nothing of rioting), and other excesses attest. Perhaps our high court judges will ultimately awaken to the need of locking the stable before all the horses are stolen by giving heed to the Holmes-

[39] Felber v. Bar Assoc., 386 U.S. 1005 (1967).
[40] Palko v. Connecticut, 302 U.S. 319, 326 (1937).
[41] Berger v. New York, 388 U.S. 41 (1967).
[42] Curtis Publishing Co. v. Butts, 388 U.S. 130 (1967).
[43] Fort v. Miami, 389 U.S. 918 (1967).

Brandeis rule that calls for restraints only when clear and present danger looms.

Perhaps this may mute the voices of those who, like the "vehement Delphidius," exclaim: "Who will ever be found guilty?"[44]

44 Edward Gibbon, *Decline and Fall of the Roman Empire,* I, 632.

Table of Cases

Abbate v. United States: 16, 389
Abel v. United States: 306–307
Abendroth, Estate of v. Commissioner: *see* Maass v. Higgins
Abernathy v. Sullivan: *see New York Times Co. v. Sullivan*
Ableman v. Booth: 58
Adair v. United States: 103–104, 167, 168
Adams v. New York: 297, 298
Adams v. Tanner: 107–108
Adams v. United States: 231
Adams Mfg. Co. v. Storen: 245
Adamson v. California: 11, 118–19, 233, 458
Adderley v. Florida: 339
Adkins v. Children's Hospital: 107, 172, 178
Adler v. Board of Education: 70
Aetna Life Ins. Co. v. Haworth: 188
A. F. of L. v. American Sash Co.: 462–63
A. F. of L. v. Swing: 196, 461
Afroyim v. Rusk: 263, 293
Agnello v United States: 304
Aguilar v Texas: 313, 315, 521, 526
Alabama v. King & Boozer: 257–58
Alberts v. California: 402, 405; *see also* Roth v. United States
Albertson v. Subversive Activities Board: 127, 277
Albrecht v. Herald Co.: 485
Alcorta v. Texas: 393
Alderman v. United States: 516
Allen v. University System: 77
Allen Bradley Co. v. Local No. 3: 227, 228, 461, 477
Allison v. Greason: 126; *see also* Zuckerman v. Greason
Almeda County v. United States: *see* United Brotherhood of Carpenters v. United States
Amalgamated Assoc. v. Missouri: 465
Amalgamated Assoc. v. Wisconsin Board: 465
Amalgamated Union v. Logan Valley Plaza: 358

American Column & Lumber Co. v. United States: 133–34
American Com. Assoc. v. Douds: 68
American Committee v. SACB: 275–76
American Fed. of Labor: *see* A. F. of L.
American Fed. of Musicians v. Carroll: 478
American Mfg. Co. v. St. Louis: 244
American Ship Bldg. Co. v. NLRB: 477
American Society of Travel Agents v. Aktiebolaget: *see* Federal Maritime Commission v. Aktiebolaget (Swedish-American Line)
American Steel v. Tri-City: 105
Anastaplo, *In re:* 119
Anders v. California: 241
Anderson v. Abbott: 225
Anderson v. Martin: 346
Anderson v. Nelson: 122, 312
Andrews v. Andrews: 249
Angelet v. Fay: 397
Anonymous v. Baker: 378
Antoni v. Greenhow: 94
Apex Hosiery Co. v. Leader: 196
Appalachian Coals v. United States: 196
Aptheker v. Secretary of State: 286–87
Arizona Copper Co. v. Bray: *see* Arizona Copper Co. v. Hammer
Arizona Copper Co. v. Hammer (Arizona Employers' Liability Cases): 108
Arizona Employers' Liability Cases: *see* Arizona Copper Co. v. Hammer; Arizona Copper Co. v. Bray; Ray Cons. Copper Co. v. Veazey; Inspiration Cons. Copper Co. v. Mendez; Superior Copper Co. v. Tomich
Arizona Groc. Co. v. Atchison T. & S. F. R.R.: 172
Armstrong v. Armstrong: 250, 251
Arnold v. Booth: 58
Arrow-Hart & H. Co. v. Federal Trade Commission: 180
Arsenault v. Massachusetts: 514

531

Ashton v. Cameron County: 186
Ashton v. Kentucky: 446
Ashwander v. TVA: 185
Associated Press v. NLRB: 188
Associated Press v. United States: 188, 480
Associated Press v. Walker: see Curtis Publishing Co. v. Butts
Atlanta, The: 32
Austin v. Kentucky: see Redrup v. New York
Automobile Drivers v. Cline: see Teamsters Union v. Hanke
Avent v. North Carolina: 332
Avery v. Georgia: 345
Avery v. Midland County: 432–33

Baggett v. Bullett: 69
Bailey v. Alabama: 141
Bailey v. Drexel Furniture Co.: 135
Bailey v. Patterson: 332
Baker v. Carr: 418–24, 425, 426, 433
Bakery Drivers Local v. Wohl: 461
Baldwin v. Missouri: 116–17
Baldwin v. Payne: see Planters' Bank v. Sharp
Baldwin v. Seelig: 180
Ballard v. United States: 211
Baltimore & Ohio R.R. v. Baugh: 47
Baltimore & Orio R.R. v. Maryland: 88
Baltimore & Ohio R.R. v. United States: 191, 484
Baltimore & Ohio R.R., Delaware & Hudson R.R., Erie-Lackawanna R.R., City of Scranton, Shapp, Chicago & E. I. R.R. v. United States: 484
Bank of Augusta v. Earle: 46
Bank of United States v. Dandridge: 24
Bank of United States v. Deveaux: 34, 35
Bank of United States v. Primrose: see Bank of Augusta v. Earle
Bank Tax Cases: see People ex rel. Bank of Commonwealth v. Commissioners
Bantam Books v. Sullivan: 407
Barber v. Page: 235, 515
Barenblatt v. United States (1957): 282
Barenblatt v. United States (1959): 282, 355
Barr v. Columbia: 335
Barr v. Matteo (1957): 261
Barr v. Matteo (1959): 261
Barrows v. Jackson: 351
Bartels v. Iowa: 111–12
Bartkus v. Illinois: 9, 11, 389
Bartmeyer v. Iowa: 82
Bas v. Tingy: 21
Basham v. Pennsylvania R.R.: 25–26
Bates v. Little Rock: 354
Baumgartner v. United States: 262

Bay Counties v. United States: see United Brotherhood of Carpenters v. United States
Bayard & Wife v. Singleton: 33
Beauharnais v. Illinois: 443
Beck v. Ohio: 315–16
Beckley Newspaper Corp. v. Hanks: 447
Bedford Cut Stone Co. v. Journeyman Stone Cutters' Assoc.: 106
Beecher v. Alabama: 361
Beilan v. Board of Pub. Educ.: 125, 260
Bell v. Maryland: 334, 337
Benanti v. United States: 160
Berea College v. Kentucky: 142
Berger v. California: 515
Berger v. New York: 163–65, 520, 521, 522, 523, 528
Bethlehem Steel Co. v. Zurich Ins. Co.: 182, 188
Betts v. Brady: 231–32
Biggers v. Tennessee: 380
Bitter v. United States: 388
Black v. United States: 166
Black & White Taxi Co. v. Brown & Yellow Taxi Co.: 47–48
Blacque, Estate of v. Commissioner: see Maass v. Higgins
Blair v. Ridgely: 67–68
Blankenship v. Holding: 414
Block v. Hirsh: 110–11
Bloom v. Illinois: 385–86, 399
Blow v. North Carolina: 336
Board of Education v. Allen: 215
Board of Supervisors v. Bianchi: see Moody v. Flowers
Bohning v. Ohio: see Bartels v. Iowa
Bolling v. Sharpe (1954): 325–26
Bolling v. Sharpe (1955): see Brown v. Board of Education
Bollman, Ex parte: 27–28
Bond v. Floyd: 456–57
Boorman Lumber Co. v. United States: see United Brotherhood of Carpenters v. United States
Borden's Farm Prod. Co. v. Ten Eyck: 185
Bosley v. McLaughlin: 101
Boston Beer Co. v. Massachusetts: 54
Bouie v. Columbia: 334–35
Boutilier v. Immigration Service: 198–99
Bowden v. Fort Smith: see Jones v. Opelika
Bowman v. Chicago & N. W. R.R. (Original Package Cases): 89
Boyce v. Anderson: 55
Boyd v. United States: 297
Boynton v. Virginia: 248, 330
Braden v. United States: 283, 355

Bradley v. School Board: 328–29
Bradwell v. Illinois: 81
Braunfeld v. Brown: 448, 452–54, 455
Breard v. Alexandria: 245
Breithaupt v. Abram: 305
Bridges v. California: 155–56
Bridges v. United States: 156
Bridges v. Wixon: 156
Briggs v. Elliott: see Brown v. Board of Education
Brinegar v. United States: 314
Briscoe v. Bank of Kentucky (1834): 35
Briscoe v. Bank of Kentucky (1835): 35, 42
Briscoe v. Bank of Kentucky (1837): 17, 35–36, 45
Briscoe v. Louisiana: see Garner v. Louisiana
Brookhart v. Janis: 392
Brooks v. Florida: 361
Brooks v. United States: 247
Brotherhood v. Chicago R.I.R.R.: 518
Brotherhood v. Jacksonville Terminal Co.: 518
Brotherhood of Railway Clerks v. Allen: 471
Brotherhood of Trainmen v. Howard: 475
Browder v. United States: 200
Brown v. Board of Education (1954): 4, 325
Brown v. Board of Education (1955): 4, 325, 326, 327, 328
Brown v. Clifford: 493
Brown v. Louisiana: 338
Brown v. Maryland: 34, 43, 496
Brown v. Slaughter: see Groves v. Slaughter
Brown v. United States (1958): 263
Brown v. United States (1959): 157
Brown, Speller, Daniels v. Allen: 10
Brush v. Commissioner: 76
Bruton v. United States: 361–62
Bryant v. Helvering: see Helvering v. Hallock
Buchanan v. Warley: 142, 351
Buck v. Bell: 116
Buckstaff Bath House Co. v. McKinley: 196
Budd v. California: 394
Budd v. New York: 98
Bumper v. North Carolina: 323
Bunting v. Oregon: 9, 102
Burger, Ex parte: see Quirin, Ex parte
Burger v. Cox: see Quirin, Ex parte v. Cox
Burgett v. Texas: 14–15, 388
Burnet v. Coronado Oil & Gas Co.: 10, 39, 173–74
Burns Baking Co. v. Bryan: 112
Burstyn v. Wilson: 400
Burton v. Wilmington Parking Authority: 330
Butchers' Assoc. v. Crescent City Co. (1873): 79–80
Butchers' Assoc. v. Crescent City Co. (1884): 81

Butenos v. United States: 516
Butts v. Harrison: see Harper v. Virginia Board of Elections

Cafeteria & Restaurant Workers Union v. McElroy: 261
Cafeteria Employees v. Angelos: 461
Calais S. Co. v. Van Pelt's Adm'r: 63
California v. Central Pac. R.R.: see Santa Clara Co. v. Southern Pac R. R.
California v. Southern Pac. R.R.: see Santa Clara Co. v. Southern Pac. R. R.
California v. Stewart: see Miranda v. Arizona
California v. Thompson: 114
Camara v. Municipal Court: 16, 309–10, 321
Cameron v. Johnson (1965): 337–38
Cameron v. Johnson (1968): 339–40
Campbell v. United States (1961): 391
Campbell v. United States (1963): 391–92
Campbell v. United States (1966); see Hoffa v. United States
Campbell Painting Co. v. Reid: 126
Cantwell v. Connecticut: 204, 233
Carafas v. La Vallee: 399
Carcerano v. Gladden: 399; see also DeStefano v. Woods
Cardona v. Power: 435–36
Carey v. Atlanta: 142
Carlson v. California: 196, 461
Carlson v. Landon: 263–64
Carmichael v. Gulf States Paper Corp.: see Carmichael v. Southern Coal & Coke Co.
Carmichael v. Southern Coal & Coke Co.: 188
Carpenter's Union v. Ritter's Cafe: 461
Carrington v. Rash: 434
Carroll v. American Fed. of Musicians: see American Fed. of Musicians v. Carroll
Carroll v. United States: 304
Carson v. Roane-Anderson Co.: 258
Carter v. Carter Coal Co.: 186
Cary v. Commissioner: 196
Cascade Nat. Gas Corp. v. El Paso Nat. Gas Co.: 495, 520
Cassell v. Texas: 345
Cement Mfrs. Assoc. v. United States: 134, 196
Central Pac. R.R. v. Gallatin (Sinking Fund Cases): 87–88; see also Union Pac. R.R. v. United States
Chae Chan Ping v. United States (Chinese Exclusion Cases): 139
Champion v. Ames: 132
Chaplinsky v. New Hampshire: 204; see also Cox v. New Hampshire
Chapman v. California: 122, 312, 398
Charles River Bridge v. Warren Bridge: 42–43

Chaunt v. United States: 291

Cheff v. Schnackenberg: 158, 385, 386

Chemical Bank & Trust Co. v. Henwood: *see* Guaranty Trust Co. v. Henwood

Cherokee Nation v. Georgia: 10, 16, 39, 61

Chessman v. Teets (1955): 240

Chessman v. Teets (1957): 241

Chicago & E. I. R.R. v. United States: *see* Baltimore & Ohio R.R. v. United States

Chicago B. & Q. R.R. v. Chicago: 233

Chicago B. & Q. R.R. v. Iowa (Granger Cases): 83, 97

Chicago Board of Trade v. United States: 196

Chicago M. & St. P. Ry. v. Ackley (Granger Cases): *see* Chicago B. & Q. R.R. v. Iowa

Chicago M. & St. P. Ry. v. Minnesota: 98–99, 167, 223

Chicago R. I. & P. R.R. v. United States: 172

Chicot County Drainage Dist. v. Baxter State Bank: 396

Chinese Exclusion Cases: *see* Chae Chan Ping v. United States; Fong Yue Ting v. United States

Chisholm v. Georgia: 21, 94, 99

Choctaw & Gulf R.R. v. Harrison: 258

Christal v. Police Commissioner: 125

Chy Lung v. Freeman: 43

Cicenia v. Lagay: 365, 370

City of Scranton v. United States: 484; *see also* Baltimore & Ohio R.R. v. United States

Civil Rights Cases: 92, 97, 247, 353; *see also* United States v. Stanley; United States v. Ryan; United States v. Nichols; United States v. Singleton; Robinson v. Memphis R.R.

Clark v. Gabriel: 519

Clewis v. Texas: 361

Coe v. Coe: 249, 250

Cohen v. Hurley: 119, 120, 124

Cohens v. Virginia: 33–34

Cole v. Young: 260

Colegrove v. Green: 416–17, 417–18, 420, 422, 424

Coleman v. Alabama: 344

Coleman v. McGrath: *see* Harisiades v. Shaughnessy

Coleman v. Miller: 194

Colgate v. Harvey: 196, 481

Collecter v. Day: 76

Commercial Pictures Corp. v. Regents: *see* Superior Films v. Dept of Education

Commissioner v. Bosch Estate: 49

Commissioner v. Church: 258

Commissioner v. Wilcox: 489

Commissioners of Immigration v. North German Lloyd: *see* Henderson v. Wickham, Mayor of New York

Commonwealth of Pennsylvania v. Board of Directors: *see* Pennsylvania v. Board of Directors

Commonwealth of Pennsylvania v. Brown: *see* Pennsylvania v. Brown

Communist Party v. Catherwood: 289

Communist Party v. SACB: 274

Concordia Fire Ins. Co. v. Illinois: 180

Conley v. Gibson: 475

Connecticut Gen. Life Ins. Co. v. Johnson: 12, 192–93, 196

Continental Oil Co. v. NLRB: 199

Cook v. Cook: 250

Cook v. Fortson: 425

Cooke v. United States: 157

Coolidge v. Long: 172

Coombes v. Getz: 172

Cooney v. Mountain States Tel. Co.: 196

Cooper v. Aaron: 326–27

Cooper v. California: 311

Coppage v. Kansas: 102, 104, 167, 168

Coppedge v. United States: 240

Corbett v. Chandler: *see* Toolson v. New York Yankees

Corfield v. Coryell: 73

Corrigan v. Buckley: 351

Cosmopolitan Ship. Co. v. McAllister: 257

Costello v. United States: 292

County of Mineral v. Public Utilities Commission: *see* United States v. Public Utilities Commission

Cox v. Louisiana: 336–37, 339

Cox v. Peters: 425

Cox v. New Hampshire: 204

Cox v. United States: 256

Craig v. Missouri: 35, 36

Cramer v. United States: 255

Crandall v. Nevada: 71

Crooker v. California: 365, 370

Cummings v. Missouri: 67, 68

Cunningham v. Macon & Brunswick R.R.: *see* Louisiana v. Jumel

Cunningham v. Neagle: 154

Curry v. McCanless: 196

Curtis Publishing Co. v. Butts: 447, 528

Darkow v. United States: *see* Schaefer v. United States

Dartmouth College v. Woodward: 33, 43, 54

Davidson v. New Orleans: 85–86

Davis v. Mann: 428

Davis v. Massachusetts: 198

Davis v. North Carolina: 398

Davis v. School Board: 326; *see also* Brown v. Board of Education
Dayton v. Dulles: 286
Debs, *In re*: 102
Debs v. United States: 146, 147
DeGregory v. Attorney General: 285
Deitrick v. Greaney: 195
DeJonge v. Oregon: 233
DeJoseph v. Connecticut: 234
Delaware & Hudson R.R. v. United States: 484; *see also* Baltimore & Ohio R.R. v. United States
DeLima v. Bidwell: 159
Den, *ex dem.* Murray v. Hoboken Co.: 86
Dennis v. United States (1950): 289
Dennis v. United States (1951): 271–72
Dennis v. United States (1966): 278
Deputy v. Du Pont: 196
Desist v. United States: 515
DeStefano v. Woods: 399
Deutch v. United States: 284
Diamond Rings: *see* Fourteen Diamond Rings
Dick v. New York Life Ins. Co.: 494
Di Santo v. Pennsylvania: 114
Dixie Tea Co. v. United States: *see* Smyth v. United States
Dobbins v. Commissioners: 76
Dodge v. Woolsey: 53
Dombrowski v. Eastland: 285
Dombrowski v. Pfister: 284
Dooley v. United States: 159
Dorchy v. Kansas: 105
Dorr, *Ex parte*: 59
Douglas v. Alabama: 12, 235–36, 240
Douglas v. California: 238–39
Douglas v. Jeanette: 206–207, 522
Downes v. Bidwell: 159
Draper v. United States: 313–14
Draper v. Washington: 240
Drayton v. McGrath: *see* Joint Anti-Fascist Committee v. McGrath
Dred Scott v. Sanford: 55, 56, 61
Drews v. Maryland: 337
Dr. Miles Medical Co. v. Park: 133
Du Bois Clubs v. Clark: 277
Duddleston v. Grills: 431
Duncan v. Kahanomoku: 64, 65
Duncan v. Louisiana: 158–59, 384–85, 399
Duplex Print. Co. v. Deering: 103, 105, 106
Durham v. United States: 10
Dusch v. Davis: 432, 433
Dyke v. Taylor Implement Co.: 159, 312, 386–87

Eagle Glass & Mfg. Co. v. Rowe: 103, 168

Eaton v. Price: 309
Educational Films Corp. v. Ward: 38
Edwards v. California: 71–72
Edwards v. South Carolina: 233, 332, 389
Elfbrand v. Russell (1964): 69
Elfbrand v. Russell (1966): 69
Elkins v. United States: 233, 301–302, 307
Elliott v. Wiltz: *see* Louisiana v. Jumel
Endo, *Ex parte*: 201, 254
Engel v. Vitale: 215–18, 525
Entsminger v. Iowa: 241
Epperson v. Arkansas: 518
Epton v. New York: 149–50
Erie R.R. v. Tompkins: 47, 48–49
Erie-Lackawanna R.R. v. United States: *see* Baltimore & Ohio R.R. v. United States
Escobedo v. Illinois: 12, 364–66, 367, 370, 397, 398, 521, 523, 526, 527
Esenwein v. Pennsylvania: 249
Eskridge v. Washington State Board: 238, 239, 240
Est. of Flagler v. Commissioner: *see* Cary v. Commissioner
Estes v. Texas: 381–84
Estin v. Estin: 249
Evans v. Gore: 138
Evans v. Newton: 356–58
Everson v. Board of Education: 211–13

Fahy v. Connecticut: 312
Fairfax's devisee v. Hunter's Lessee: 32
Farmers Union v. WDAY: 448
Farrington v. Tennessee: 54
Fay v. New York: 232
Fay v. Noia: 359–60
Federal Baseball Club v. National League: 245
Federal Maritime Commission; American Society of Travel Agents v. Aktiebolaget (Swedish-American Line): 486
Federal Power Commission v. Hope Nat. Gas Co.: 223–24
Federal Trade Commission v. Beechnut Co.: 13
Federal Trade Commission v. Bunte Bros.: 199
Federal Trade Commission v. Colgate-Palmolive Co.: 490–91
Federal Trade Commission v. Dean Foods Co.: 494–95
Federal Trade Commission v. Mandel Bros.: 248
Federal Trade Commission v. Mary Carter Paint Co.: 491
Federal Trade Commission v. Meyer: 486
Federal Trade Commission v. Proctor & Gamble Co.: 485
Feiner v. New York: 443
Felber v. Bar Assoc.: 528

535

Feldman v. United States: 389
Ferguson v. Georgia: 390
Ferguson v. Moore-McCormack Lines: 17
Fire Assoc. v. New York: 87
First Agricultural National Bank v. State Tax Commission: 38
First National Bank v. Maine: 172, 258
Fiske v. Kansas: 170
Flagler v. Commissioner: *see* Cary v. Commissioner
Flagler, Est. of v. Commissioner: *see* Cary v. Commissioner
Flast v. Cohen: 215
Flemming v. Nestor: 269–70
Fletcher v. Peck: 29, 30–31
Fletcher v. Rhode Island (License Cases): *see* Thurlow v. Massachusetts
Flora v. United States: 495–96
Fong Yue Ting v. United States: 139, 265
Fontaine v. California: 312
Ford Motor Co. v. Beauchamp: 196
Fort v. Miami: 528
Fortson v. Morris: 432
Fortson v. Toombs: 432
Foster v. California: 516
Foster v. Illinois: 232
Fourteen Diamond Rings: 159
Frank v. Mangum: 144, 145, 168
Frank v. Maryland: 308–309, 321
Frazier v. United States: 289
Freedman v. Maryland: 402
Freeman v. Hewit: 244
Frost v. California: 113
Frost v. Corporation Commission: 191
Frothingham v. Mellon: 215
Frowerk v. United States: 146, 147

Gallagher v. Crown Kosher Market: 448, 450, 454
Galvan v. Press: 265
Gardner v. Broderick: 126; *see also* Uniformed Sanitation Men's Assoc. v. Commissioner of Sanitation
Gardner v. California: 515
Garland, *Ex parte*: 67
Garner v. Board of Pub. Works: 68, 71
Garner, Briscoe, Hoston v. Louisiana: 330–32
Garrison v. Louisiana: 445–46
Garrity v. New Jersey: 15, 124, 125, 126, 127, 521, 527
Gastelum-Quinones v. Kennedy: 270
Gault, *In re*: 377
Gayes v. New York: 232
Gebhart v. Belton: *see* Brown v. Board of Education

Gelling v. Texas: 400
Gelston v. Hoyt: 29
Gent v. Arkansas: *see* Redrup v. New York
Georgia v. Brailsford (1792): 21
Georgia v. Brailsford (1793): 20
Georgia v. Rachel: 338
Georgia v. Stanton: 66
Gerende v. Board of Supervisors: 68
German Alliance Ins. Co. v. Lewis: 107
Gibbons v. Ogden: 33, 34, 43, 45
Giboney v. Empire Storage Co.: 461
Gibson v. Florida Legislative Comm.: 282, 355, 356
Gideon v. Wainwright: 12, 233, 234, 235, 236, 238
Gilbert v. California: 379
Gilbert v. Minnesota: 150
Gilchrist v. Collector: 28–29
Giles v. Harris: 197
Giles v. Maryland: 7–8, 393
Gillespie v. Oklahoma: 38
Ginsberg v. New York: 408
Ginzburg v. United States: 410, 411, 412–14
Giordano v. United States: 517
Giordenello v. United States: 314
Girard College Trusteeship: 50, 356; *see also* Pennsylvania v. Board of Directors; Pennsylvania v. Brown
Girouard v. United States: 153–54
Gitlow v. New York: 12, 68, 149, 170, 233, 359
Glana v. American Guarantee Co.: *see* Levy v. Louisiana
Glasser v. United States: 230–31
Glover v. St. Louis & S.F.R.R.: 518
Go-Bart Importing Co. v. United States: 304
Gober v. Birmingham: 332
Gobillion v. Lightfoot: 346
Gojack v. United States: 283–84
Gold Clause Cases: *see* Norman v. Baltimore & Ohio R.R.; United States v. Bankers Trust Co.
Goldman, Martin v. United States: 161, 162
Goldman, Theodore v. United States: *see* Goldman, Martin v. United States
Goldwyn, *In re* v. Allen: 378
Gordon v. United States: 390
Gori v. United States: 389
Goss v. Board of Education: 328
Gouled v. United States: 317, 318, 321
Granger Cases: 83, 84, 85; *see also* Chicago B. & Q. R.R. v. Iowa; Peik v. Chicago & N. W. R.R.; Lawrence v. Paul; Chicago M. & St. P. R.R. v. Ackley; Winona & St. P. v. Blake; Stone v. Wisconsin; McIlrath v. Southern M. R.R.; Munn v. Illinois

536

Graves v. Elliott: 196
Graves v. New York: 23
Graves v. Texas Co.: 257
Gray v. Sanders: 424–25, 426, 428, 431, 432
Great Northern Life Ins. Co. v. Read: 7
Great Northern R.R. v. Sunburst Oil Co.: 49
Green v. School Board: 329
Green v. United States (1928): see Olmstead v. United States
Green v. United States (1958): 158, 273
Green v. United States (1961): 386, 389–90
Greene v. McElroy: 260–61
Greenwald v. Wisconsin: 361
Greenwood v. Peacock: 338–39
Griffin v. California: 12, 121–22, 398
Griffin v. Illinois: 236–38, 239, 240
Griffin v. Maryland: 334, 337
Griffin v. School Board: 326
Grisham v. Hagan: 65–66
Griswold v. Connecticut: 11, 457–59, 520
Groban, In re: 378
Grosjean v. American Press Co.: 233
Grosso v. United States: 126, 127
Group No. 1 Oil Corp v. Bass: 38–39
Groves v. Slaughter: 55
Grovey v. Townsend: 143
Guaranty Trust Co. v. Henwood: 182, 188
Guinn v. United States: 141–42

Haddock v. Haddock: 248
Hague v. CIO: 197–98
Hall v. DeCuir: 90–91
Hamashita, In re: 255–56
Hamm v. Rock Hill: 335–36, 337, 339
Hammer v. Dagenhart: 134–35
Hannah v. Larche: 346
Hannah v. Lawson: see Hannah v. Larche
Hans v. Louisiana: 69, 99
Hansberry v. Lee: 351
Harisiades v. Shaughnessy: 264–65
Harman v. Forsenius: 348
Harper v. Virginia Board of Elections: 348–51
Harris v. Nelson: 516
Harris v. United States (1947): 304
Harris v. United States (1965): 157
Harris v. United States (1968): 311–12
Harrison v. United States: 129
Hart v. United States: 493
Hartman v. Greenhow: 94
Hartsfield v. Sloan: 425
Haupt, Ex parte: see Quirin, Ex parte v. Cox
Hawaii v. Mankichi: 159
Hawkins v. Bleakley: 109
Hawkins v. United States: 488
Hayburn's Case: 20

Hayes v. Missouri: 87
Haynes v. United States: 126–27
Head & Amory v. Providence Ins. Co.: 21
Heart of Atlanta Motel v. United States: 247, 335
Hebert v. Louisiana: 118
Heinck, Ex parte: see Quirin, Ex parte v. Cox
Heiner v. Donnan: 172
Helvering v. Campbell: 196
Helvering v. Chester N. Weaver Co.: 196
Helvering v. Davis: 16, 188, 189–90
Helvering v. Eubank: 196
Helvering v. Fitch: 196
Helvering v. Fuller: 196
Helvering v. Gambrill: 196
Helvering v. Gerhardt: 76, 191
Helvering v. Hallock: 193, 196
Helvering v. Horst: 196
Helvering v. Knox: see Helvering v. Campbell
Helvering v. Leonard: 196
Helvering v. Mountain Producers Corp.: 39
Helvering v. Mulcahy: see Helvering v. Gerhardt
Helvering v. Reynolds: 196
Helvering v. Rogers: see Helvering v. Campbell
Helvering v. Squire: see Helvering v. Hallock
Helvering v. Wilson: see Helvering v. Gerhardt
Henderson v. Wickham, Mayor of New York: 43
Henderson v. United States: 324
Henneford v. Silas Mason Co.: 188
Henry v. Collins: 446
Henry v. Rock Hill: 334
Henry v. United States: 306
Hepburn v. Griswold: 74–75, 78
Herndon v. Georgia: 177–78
Herndon v. Lowry: 178
Hester v. Swenson: 239
Highland Farms Dairy v. Agnew: 188
Hines v. Davidowitz: 200
Hirabayashi v. United States: 252–53
Hitchman v. Mitchell: 102–103, 168
Hoeper v. Tax Commission: 172
Hoffa v. United States: 166
Hoffa, Parks, Campbell, King v. United States: 163, 319–20
Holden v. Hardy: 100
Holding v. Blankenship: 414
Hollingsworth v. Virginia: 21
Hollis v. California: 398, 527
Holmes v. Jennison: 44
Holmes v. United States: 493
Holy Trinity Church v. United States: 477
Holyoke Water Power Co. v. American Writ. Paper Co.: 182, 188

Home Bldg. & L. Assoc. v. Blaisdell: 179–80
Homma v. Patterson: 256
Hope Ins. Co. v. Boardman: 34
Hoston v. Louisiana: *see* Garner v. Louisiana
Houston & Texas R.R. v. United States: 199
Houston Contractors v. NLRB: 477
Howard v. Gipsy Oil Co.: 258
Howard v. Lyons: 261
Howat v. Kansas: 229
Hudgins, *Ex parte*: 157
Hudson Distributors v. Eli Lilly & Co.: 248
Huidekoper's Lessee v. Douglass: 26
Humphrey's Executor v. United States: 183
Hunt v. Crumboch: 227–28
Hunter v. Erickson: 518
Hurtado v. California: 86–87
Hust v. Moore-McCormack Lines: 257
Hyde v. Continental Trust Co.: *see* Pollock v. Farmers' Loan & Trust Co.

Immigration Service v. Errico: 271
Indian Territory Oil Co. v. Oklahoma: 258
Indiana *ex rel.* Anderson v. Brand: 191
Inspiration Cons. Copper Co. v. Mendez (Arizona Employers' Liability Cases): *see* Arizona Copper Co. v. Hammer
International Brotherhood v. Hanke: *see* Teamsters Union v. Hanke
International Harvester Co. v. Dept. of Treasury: 244
International Machinists v. Gonzales: 475
International Machinists v. Street: 467–69, 470
International Union v. Russell: 475
International Workers Order v. McGrath: *see* Joint Anti-Fascist Committee v. McGrath
Interstate Circuit v. Dallas: 407
Iowa v. Missouri: *see* Missouri v. Iowa
Isserman, *In re*: 272
Ivanov v. United States: 516

Jackson v. Denno: 361, 362
Jacobellis v. Ohio: 408–10
James v. Dravo Contracting Co.: 191–92
James v. Louisiana: 317
James v. United States: 489–90
Jamison v. Texas: 205
Jay v. Boyd: 265–67
Jencks v. United States: 390–91
Jenkins v. United States: 387
Jewell Ridge Coal Corp. v. Local No. 6167: 225
Jobin v. Arizona: *see* Jones v. Opelika
Johnson v. Eisentrager: 256
Johnson v. Gordon: 53
Johnson v. Muelberger: 250
Johnson v. New Jersey: 397–98

Johnson v. United States (1948): 305
Johnson v. United States (1957): 240
Johnson v. Virginia: 334
Joint Anti-Fascist Committee; National Council; International Workers Order; Drayton v. McGrath: 289
Jones v. Georgia: 344
Jones v. Mayer Co.: 353
Jones v. Opelika (1942): 204
Jones v. Opelika (1943): 205
Jones v. SEC: 185–86
Jones v. United States: 314, 321, 322
Jones v. Van Zandt: 56
Jordan v. Silver: 430–31
Julliard v. Greenman (Legal Tender Cases): 75

Kaiser v. United States: 515
Kansas v. Ziebold: *see* Mugler v. Kansas
Kansas City v. Singer: *see* Singer v. Union Pacific R.R.
Katz v. United States: 165, 515, 523
Katzenbach v. McClung: 248
Katzenbach v. Morgan: 434–35, 436–38
Kaufman v. Lee: *see* United States v. Lee
Kaufman v. United States: 516
Kaye v. Co-ordinating Committee: 15, 126
Kedroff v. St. Nicholas Cathedral: 290
Keegan v. United States: 255
Kelley v. Maryland: *see* Niemotko v. Maryland
Kemmler, *In re*: 487
Kendall v. United States: 46
Kennedy v. Mendoza-Martinez: 292–93
Kent v. Dulles: 286, 287
Kent v. United States: 286, 287, 376, 377
Kepner v. United States: 159
Kerling, *Ex parte*: *see* Quirin, *Ex parte* v. Cox
Kern Limerick v. Scurlock: 259
Keyishian v. Board of Regents: 70, 71
Kilgarlin v. Hill: 431
Kimm v. Rosenberg: 268–69
King v. Smith: 73
King v. United States: *see* Hoffa v. United States
Kingsley Books v. Brown: 405
Kingsley Pictures Corp. v. Regents: 401
Kinsella v. Krueger (1956): 65
Kinsella v. Krueger (1957): *see* Reid v. Covert
Kinsella v. United States *ex rel.* Singleton: 65
Kirschbaum v. Walling: 242
Klopfer v. North Carolina: 236
Knapp v. Schweitzer: 389
Knauer v. United States: 263
Knox v. Lee (Legal Tender Cases): 74, 75
Kolod v. United States: 166–67, 516
Konigsberg v. State Bar (1957): 119

Konigsberg v. State Bar (1961): 119
Korematsu v. United States: 253–54
Kovacs v. Cooper: 440
Kowalski v. Chandler: *see* Toolson v. New York Yankees
Kreiger v. Kreiger: 249
Kretske v. United States: *see* Glasser v. United States
Kuhn v. Fairmont Coal Co.: 47
Kunz v. New York: 442
Kunze v. United States: *see* Keegan v. United States

Lamont v. Commissioner of Motor Vehicles: 460
Lamont v. Postmaster General: 290, 459–60
Lane v. Brown: 240, 241
Lane v. Vick: 47
Lane v. Wilson: 197
Lanza v. New York: 162
Large Oil Co. v. Howard: 258
Largent v. Texas: 205
Lassiter v. Northhampton Elec. Board: 436
Lathrop v. Donahue: 469–71
Lawrence v. Paul (Granger Cases): *see* Chicago B. & Q. R.R. v. Iowa
Leach v. Carlile: 150–51
Lee v. Florida: 161, 514–15
Lee v. Washington: 329
Lee Joe v. United States: *see* Fong Yue Ting v. United States
Legal Tender Cases: 74, 78; *see also* Knox v. Lee; Parker v. Davis; Julliard v. Greenman; Norman v. Baltimore & Ohio R.R.; United States v. Bankers Trust Co.
Leisy v. Hardin (Original Package Cases): 89
Lemke v. United States: *see* Schaefer v. United States
Leng May Ma v. Barber: 268
Lerner v. Casey: 125, 260
Levy v. Louisiana: 496; *see also* Glana v. American Guarantee Co.
Lewis v. United States (1947): *see* United States v. United Mine Workers
Lewis v. United States (1955): 127
Lewis v. United States (1966): 317
Liberty National Bank v. Buscaglia: 38
License Cases: 23, 44, 60, 496; *see also* Thurlow v. Massachusetts; Fletcher v. Rhode Island; Pierce v. New Hampshire
Liggett Co. v. Baldridge: 113–14
Liggett Co. v. Lee: 172
Lincoln Union v. Northwestern Co.: 462
Linkletter v. Walker: 395–97, 398
Little v. Barreme: 24
Local No. 807 v. United States: 226

Local Nos. 8–6 v. Missouri: 464
Local Union No. 189 v. Jewel Tea Co.: 478
Local Union No. 10 v. Graham: 462
Lochner v. New York: 100–101, 167
Loewe v. Lawlor: 106
Lombard v. Louisiana: 332, 333
Long v. Iowa: 241
Lopez v. United States: 163, 319, 320
Lottery Case: 247
Louisiana *ex rel.* Gremillion v. NAACP: 233
Louisiana v. Jumel: 95
Louisiana v. Resweber: 12, 487
Louisiana v. United States: 346–47
Louisville Bank v. Radford: 183
Louisville Gas Co. v. Coleman: 115
Lovell v. City of Griffin: 202, 203, 204, 233
Loving v. Virginia: 345–46
Lucas v. Colorado Gen. Assembly: 428, 429–30, 431
Lucas v. Rhodes: 426
Lucy v. Adams: 327
Lumber Products Assoc. v. United States: *see* United Brotherhood of Carpenters v. United States
Lupper v. Arkansas: 337; *see also* Hamm v. Rock Hill
Lustig v. United States: 7, 300–301
Luther v. Borden: 59
Lynd v. Rusk: 288

Maass v. Higgins: 199
Macallen v. Massachusetts: 37
McAuliffe v. New Bedford: 124
McBride v. Smith: 277
McCabe v. Atchison T. & S. R.R.: 141
McCandless v. Furlaud: 176–77
McCarroll v. Dixie Lines: 196
McCart v. Indianapolis Water Co.: 192
McCollum v. Board of Education: 213–14
McConnell, *In re*: 157
McConnell v. Baggett: 428; *see also* Reynolds v. Sims
McConnell v. Rhay: 514
McCray v. Illinois: 317
McCulloch v. Maryland: 33, 34, 38
McDonald v. United States: 305
MacDougall v. Green: 420, 425
McElroy v. United States *ex rel.* Guagliardo: 66
McGhee v. Sipes: *see* Shelley v. Kraemer
McGoldrick v. Berwind-White Co.: 244
McGoldrick v. Compagnie Gen. Trans.: 196
McGoldrick v. DuGrenier: 196, 244
McGoldrick v. Felt & T. Mfg. Co.: *see* McGoldrick v. DuGrenier
McGowan v. Maryland: 448–52

McGrath v. Kristensen: 496
McGuire v. United States: 161
McIlrath v. Southern M. R.R. (Granger Cases): see Chicago B. & Q. R.R. v. Iowa
McInness v. United States: see Olmstead v. United States
McKane v. Durston: 238
McLaughlin v. Florida: 345
McLaurin v. Oklahoma Regents: 325
McLeod v. Dilworth Co.: 244
McLeod v. Threlkeld: 243
McNally v. Hill: 399
McNeese v. Board of Education: 327
McPhaul v. United States: 283
Madera v. Board of Education: 377–78
Maguire v. Commissioner: 196
Mahnich v. Southern S. S. Co.: 224
Maisenberg v. United States: 263
Mallory v. United States: 375–76, 526
Malloy v. Hogan: 12, 119–20, 120–21, 236, 366, 388
Manual Enterprises v. Day: 405–406
Maple Flooring Mfrs. Assoc. v. United States: 134, 196, 519
Mapp v. Ohio: 12, 233, 302–304, 367, 395, 396, 397, 527
Marbury v. Madison: 33, 459
Marchetti v. United States: 126, 127
Marconi Wireless Co. v. United States: 222–23
Marcus Brown Holding Co. v. Feldman: 110
Marine Ins. Co. v. Young: 16
Marron v. United States: 304
Marsh v. Alabama: 209
Martin v. Hunter's Lessee: 7, 16, 32–33
Martin v. Struthers: 206
Maryland Comm. v. Tawes: 428
Mascitti v. McGrath: see Harisiades v. Shaughnessy
Mason v. Haile: 37
Massachusetts v. Mellon: 215
Massachusetts v. Painten: 308
Massiah v. United States: 363–64
Mathis v. United States: 375
Matthews v. Commissioner: see Cary v. Commissioner
Maxwell v. Dow: 385
May v. Heiner: 258
Mayflower Farms v. Ten Eyck: 185
Maynard v. Hill: 346
Mayor v. Miln (1834): 35
Mayor v. Miln (1835): 42
Mayor v. Miln (1837): 43, 44
Memoirs v. Massachusetts: 23, 410–12, 414
Mempa v. Rhay: 234–35, 514
Mercoid Corp. v. Mid-Continent Inv. Co.: 224

Merryman, Ex parte: 61, 62, 64
Meyer v. Nebraska: 111
Michael, In re: 157
Mientke v. United States: 235
Miles v. Graham: 138
Milk Wagon Drivers v. Meadowmoor Dairies: 196
Miller v. California: 163
Miller v. Pate: 393
Miller v. United States: 323
Miller v. Wilson: 101
Milligan, Ex parte: 62, 64, 65, 66, 255
Mills v. Alabama: 351
Mills v. Louisiana: 389
Milwaukee Publishing Co. v. Burleson: 150, 151
Minersville School Dist. v. Gobitis: 18, 202–203, 204, 205, 207
Minneapolis & St. L. R.R. v. Beckwith: 99
Minnesota v. Probate Court: 198
Miranda v. Arizona: 12, 366–75, 376, 397, 398, 399, 515–16, 521, 526
Mishkin v. New York: 410, 411, 414, 415
Mississippi v. Johnson: 66
Missouri ex rel. Gaines v. Canada: 196–97
Missouri v. Gehner: 38
Missouri v. Holland: 115–16
Missouri v. Iowa: 13
Mitchel v. United States: 7
Mitchell v. United States (1941): 141, 200
Mitchell v. United States (1967): 492
Monroe v. Board of Commissioners: 329
Moody v. Flowers: 432
Mooney v. Holohan: 393
Moore v. Dempsey: 144, 145, 168
Moore v. New York: 232
Mora v. McNamara: 492–93, 519
Morehead v. Tipaldo: 107, 178–79
Morgan v. United States (1936): 186
Morgan v. United States (1938): 186–87
Morgan v. Virginia: 324
Mountain Timber Co v. Washington: 109
Mugler v. Kansas: 85
Mulford v. Smith: 135
Mullaney v. Anderson: 73
Muller v. Dows: 34
Muller v. Oregon: 8–9, 101
Munn v. Illinois (Granger Cases): 83–84, 85, 97, 99, 109, 192; see also Chicago B. & Q. R.R. v. Iowa
Murdock v. Pennsylvania: 205–206
Murray v. Curlett: see School Dist. v. Schempp
Mutual Film Corp. v. Ohio Industrial Comm.: 400
Myers v. Anderson: 142, 183
Myers v. Brown: see Myers v. Anderson

Myers v. Howard: *see* Myers v. Anderson

Napue v. Illinois: 393
Nardone v. United States: 160
Nash v. Illinois: 393
Nathanson v. United States: 314
NAACP v. Alabama *ex rel.* Patterson (1958): 353
NAACP v. Alabama *ex rel.* Patterson and Livingston (1959): 353
NAACP v. Button: 354–55
NAACP v. Livingston: *see* NAACP v. Alabama *ex rel.* Patterson and Livingston
NAACP v. Williams: 12
National Bellas Hess v. Dept. of Revenue: 244
National Council v. McGrath: *see* Joint Anti-Fascist Committee v. McGrath
National Dist. Prod. Corp. v. Glander: *see* Wheeling Steel Corp. v. Glander
NLRB v. Allis-Chalmers Co.: 476
NLRB v. Brown: 476
NLRB v. Columbian Co.: 196
NLRB v. Darlington Co.: *see* Textile Workers Union v. Darlington Co.
NLRB v. Express Pub. Co.: 196
NLRB v. Fainblatt: 245
NLRB v. Fansteel Metal Corp.: 196
NLRB v. Houston Contractors: *see* Houston Contractors v. NLRB
NLRB v. Jones & Laughlin Steel Corp.: 188, 245, 248
NLRB v. National Woodwork Mfrs. Assoc.: *see* National Woodwork Mfrs. Assoc. v. NLRB
NLRB v. Sands Mfg. Co.: 196
NLRB v. United Ins. Co.: 472
National Mutual Ins. Co. v. Tidewater Trans. Co.: 257
National Woodward Mfrs. Assoc. v. NLRB: 477
Neal v. Delaware: 92
Near v. Minnesota: 151
Nebbia v. New York: 180
Nebraska Dist. v. McKelvie: *see* Bartels v. Iowa
Nelson v. Los Angeles: 125, 261
Nereide, The: 5, 22, 31, 416
Neubauer, *Ex parte*: *see* Quirin, *Ex parte* v. Cox
Neuberger v. Commissioner: 199
Newberry v. United States: 143, 200
New Hampshire v. Louisiana: 95
Newman v. Piggie Park Enterprises: 343
New Orleans v. Earle: *see* Bank of Augusta v. Earle
New State Ice Co. v. Liebmann: 9, 111
New York v. Louisiana: *see* New Hampshire v. Louisiana
New York v. Miln: *see* Mayor v. Miln

New York v. United States: 77
New York Cent. R.R. v. White: 109
New York City Board of Elections v. Morgan: *see* Katzenbach v. Morgan
New York *ex rel.* Rogers v. Graves: 76
New York Times Co. v. Sullivan: 444, 445, 446, 447, 448
Niemotko v. Maryland: 442
Nippert v. Richmond: 244
Nishikawa v. Dulles: 291
Niukkanen v. Alexander: 268
Nixon v. Condon: 142
Nixon v. Herndon: 143
Norman v. Baltimore & Ohio R.R. (Gold Clause Cases): 76, 181, 182, 183
Norris v. Alabama: 177
Norris v. Boston: *see* Smith v. Turner
Northern Securities Co. v. United States: 6, 18, 131–32, 133
Norton v. Shelby County: 396
Nortz v. United States: 181
Noto v. United States: 275
Nowak v. United States: 263
Nye v. United States: 155

O'Brien v. United States (1967): 166
O'Brien v. United States (1968): 493–94
Ogden v. Saunders: 24, 36
O'Gorman & Young v. Hartford Ins. Co.: 172
Ohio v. Helvering: 77
Ohio v. Price: 309
Ohio Life Ins. Co. v. Debolt: 51–52, 60
O'Keefe v. Smith Associates: 478–79
Oklahoma v. Barnsdall Refineries: 258
Oklahoma Tax Commission v. Magnolia Petroleum Co.: *see* Oklahoma Tax Commission v. Texas Co.
Oklahoma Tax Commission v. Texas Co.: 258
Olmstead v. United States: 159–60, 164, 166
Olsen v. Nebraska: 108
O'Malley v. Woodrough: 138, 139
On Lee v. United States: 161–62
One 1958 Plymouth Sedan v. Pennsylvania: 304
O'Neil v. Vermont: 233
Original Package Cases: 89, 97; *see also* Bowman v. Chicago & N. W. R.R.; Leisy v. Hardin
Orozco v. Texas: 515–16
Osborn v. Bank of United States: 34–35
Osborn v. United States: 163, 317–18, 320–21
Ostereich v. Selective Service System: 519
Otis v. Parker: 6, 100
Overstreet v. North Shore Corp.: 243
Oyama v. California: 256
Ozark Pipe Line v. Monier: 196

Pacific Co. v. Johnson: 38
Pacific Ins. Co. v. Industrial Accident Commission: 196
Palko v. Connecticut: 11–12, 117–18, 145, 234, 235, 299, 385, 393, 458, 528
Palmals v. Pinar Del Rio: 224
Panama Refining Co. v. Ryan: 181
Panhandle Oil Co. v. Mississippi: 257
Paoli v. United States: 362
Pappadio v. United States: *see* Shillitani v. United States
Parker v. Davis: *see* Knox v. Lee
Parker v. Ellis: 399
Parker v. Gladden: 387–88
Parks v. United States: *see* Hoffa v. United States
Passenger Cases: 23, 43, 60; *see also* Smith v. Turner; Norris v. Boston
Patterson v. Alabama: 177
Paul v. Dade County: 456
Paul v. Virginia: 243
Peik v. Chicago & N. W. R.R. (Granger Cases): *see* Chicago B. & Q. R.R. v. Iowa
Penn-Central Merger: 485
Pennekamp v. Florida: 13, 156–57
Pennsylvania v. Board of Directors: 50
Pennsylvania v. Brown (1966): 50
Pennsylvania v. Brown (1967): 50
Pennsylvania v. Brown (1968): 50–51: *see also* Girard College Trusteeship
Pennsylvania v. Nelson: 273
Pennsylvania v. Wheeling Bridge Co.: 44
Pennsylvania Coal Co. v. Mahon: 114–15
Pensacola v. Western Union: 88–89
People v. Defore: 297–99, 300
People v. Williams: 8
People *ex rel.* Annan v. Walsh: *see* Budd v. New York
People *ex rel.* Bank of Commerce v. Commissioners: 37
People *ex rel.* Bank of Commonwealth v. Commissioners (Bank Tax Cases): 37
People *ex rel.* Pinto v. Walsh: *see* Budd v. New York
Perez v. Brownell: 291, 292, 293
Perry v. United States: 181–82
Peter v. United States: *see* United States v. Seeger
Peters v. New York: 310
Peterson v. Greenville: 332, 333, 334, 335
Pettibone v. United States: 102
Peyton v. Rowe: 399
Phelps Dodge v. NLRB: 105, 199
Pickering v. Board of Education: 448
Pierce v. New Hampshire (License Cases): *see* Thurlow v. Massachusetts
Pierce v. Society of Sisters: 112

Pierce v. Turner: 10
Pierce v. United States: 148–49
Pierre v. Louisiana: 345
Pinto v. Pierce: 361
Piqua Branch Bank v. Knoop: 51, 52, 53
Planters' Bank v. Sharp: 54
Plessy v. Ferguson: 4, 17–18, 139–40, 141, 142, 167, 200, 324, 325
Poe, Doe, & Buxton v. Ullman: 12, 233, 457
Pohl v. Ohio: *see* Bartels v. Iowa
Poindexter v. Greenhow: 95
Pointer v. Texas: 12, 235, 236
Pollock v. Farmers' Loan & Trust Co. (157 U.S. 429 [1895]): 18, 136, 137
Pollock v. Farmers' Loan & Trust Co. (158 U.S. 601 [1895]): 18, 137–38, 167
Pope v. United States: 129
Port of Mobile v. Watson: 95
Poulos v. New Hampshire: 442
Powell v. Alabama: 177, 232
Powell v. Pennsylvania: 85
Powell v. Texas: 395
Preciat, John Currie, Miller, William Currie v. United States (Prize Cases): 62
Presbyterian Church v. M.E.B.H.M. Presbyterian Church: 518
Preston v. United States: 311, 312
Price v. United States: 341, 342
Prigg v. Pennsylvania: 47, 56
Prince v. Massachusetts: 209, 458
Prize Cases: *see* Preciate, John Currie, Miller, William Currie v. United States
Prout v. Starr: 99
Puget Sound Co. v. Tax Commission: 196
Purviance v. Angus: 20
Pyle v. Kansas: 393

Quaker City Cab Co. v. Pennsylvania: 114
Quirin, *Ex parte* v. Cox: 255

Radovich v. National Football League: 247, 248
Railroad Commission Cases: *see* Stone v. Farmers' Loan & Trust Co.; Stone v. Illinois Cent. R.R.; Stone v. New Orleans R.R.
Railroad Commission v. Pacific Gas Co.: 191
Railroad Retirement Board v. Alton R.R.:182
Railroad Trainmen v. Virginia Bar: 355
Railway Employees' Dept. v. Hanson: 463–64
Raley, Stern, Brown, Morgan v. Ohio (1957): 282
Raley, Stern, Brown, Morgan v. Ohio (1959): 282
Raney v. Board of Education: 329
Rathbun v. United States: *see* Humphrey's Executor v. United States

Ray Cons. Copper Co. v. Veazey (Arizona Employers' Liability Cases): *see* Arizona Copper Co. v. Hammer
Reading R.R. v. Pennsylvania: 88
Reagan v. Farmers' Loan & Trust Co.: 99
Recznik v. Lorain: 517
Redrup v. New York: 408, 414
Reed v. Allen: 174
Reid v. Covert (1956): 65
Reid v. Covert (1957): 65
Reitman v. Mulkey: 351
Rent Law Cases: 110
Republic Steel v. Raimund Local: *see* Tennessee Coal Co. v. Muscoda Local No. 123
Resnicoff v. Assoc. of the Bar: 126; *see also* Zuckerman v. Greason
Reynolds v. Sims: 350, 428–29, 430, 432, 433, 525
Rhode Island v. Massachusetts: 13
Ribnik v. McBride: 108
Rice v. Rice: 250
Richmond v. United States: *see* Yates v. United States
Rideau v. Louisiana: 384
Riggan v. Virginia: 315
Riley v. Massachusetts: 101
Rinaldi v. Yeager: 239
Rios v. United States: 13, 307–308
Robbins v. Shelby County Tax Dist.: 88, 196
Roberts v. La Vallee: 241
Roberts v. Russell: 362
Roberts v. United States: 166
Robinson v. California: 233, 393–94
Robinson v. Florida: 335
Robinson v. Memphis R.R. (Civil Rights Cases): *see* United States v. Stanley
Rochin v. California: 305
Rockefeller v. Wells: 426
Rogers v. Guaranty Trust Co.: 175–76
Rogers v. Hill: 175–76
Rogers v. Paul: 329
Rogers v. Quan: 268
Roisum v. United States: *see* Cox v. United States
Rolston v. Crittenden: 99
Roman v. Sincock: 428
Roosevelt v. Meyer: 74, 75
Rose v. Himely: 26
Rosenberg v. United States (1952): 285
Rosenberg v. United States (1953): 286
Rosenblatt v. Baer: 444–45
Roth v. United States (1942): *see* Glasser v. United States
Roth v. United States (1957): 402–404, 409, 410, 411, 413, 414, 528

Rothensies v. Huston: *see* Helvering v. Hallock
Roviero v. United States: 391
Rowan v. Runnels: 55–56
Rowoldt v. Petfetto: 267
Royal Indemnity v. United States: 199
Rudolph v. Alabama: 487
Rugendorf v. United States: 314
Rule: 20–21
Rusk v. Cort: *see* Kennedy v. Mendoza-Martinez
Russell, Shelton, Whitman, Liveright, Price, Gojack v. United States: 283

Sabbath v. United States: 323
Sacher v. New York Bar Assoc.: 272–73
Sacher v. United States (1952): 272
Sacher v. United States (1957): 273
Sacher v. United States (1958): 273
Sackler v. Sackler: 304
Saia v. New York: 439–40
Sailors v. Board of Education: 432, 433
St. Amant v. Thompson: 444
Sandoval v. California: 319
Santa Clara Co. v. Southern Pac. R.R.: 99
Santa Cruz Co. v. NLRB: 191
Sartor v. Arkansas Nat. Gas Corp.: 192
Savings & Loan Assoc. v. Topeka: 95
Sawyer, *In re*: 277–78
Scales v. United States (1959): 274
Scales v. United States (1961): 274–75
Schaefer, Vogel, Werner, Darkow, Lemke v. United States: 148
Schechter v. United States: 183
Schenck v. United States: 146, 147, 148, 149
Schipani v. United States: 166
Schlesinger v. Wisconsin: 113
Schmerber v. United States: 305–306
Schneider v. Irvington: 203
Schneider v. Rush: 290–91
Schneider v. Smith: 277–78
Schneiderman v. United States (1943): 262
Schneiderman v. United States (1957): *see* Yates v. United States
School Dist. v. Schempp: 218–20, 525
Schware v. Board of Bar Exam.: 267
Schwegmann v. Calvert Distillers: 248
Scofield v. NLRB: 518
Scranton v. United States: *see* City of Scranton v. United States
Screws v. United States: 342
SEC v. Ralston Purina Co.: 248
See v. Seattle: 310
Senn v. Tile Layers Union: 188
Service v. Dulles: 260
Shapiro v. United States: 127

Shapp v. United States: 484; *see also* Baltimore & Ohio R.R. v. United States
Shelley v. Kraemer: 351
Shelton v. Tucker: 233, 273–74
Sheppard v. Maxwell: 381
Sherbert v. Verner: 454–55
Sherrer v. Sherrer: 249, 250
Shiffman v. Selective Service: 493
Shillitani v. United States: 158
Shulman v. United States: *see* Goldman, Martin v. United States
Shuttlesworth v. Birmingham (1963): 332
Shuttlesworth v. Birmingham (1965): 338
Sibbach v. Wilson: 199
Sibron v. New York: 311
Siebold, *Ex parte*: 154
Silber v. United States: 283
Silver v. New York Stock Exchange: 481
Silverman v. United States: 162
Simmons v. United States: 127–28, 321–23, 380
Simms & Wise v. Slacum: 26
Sims v. Georgia (385 U.S. 538 [1966]): 361
Sims v. Georgia (389 U.S. 404 [1967]): 344
Singer v. Union Pac. R.R.: 200
Sinking Fund Cases: *see* Union Pac. R.R. v. United States
Skinner v. Oklahoma: 346
Slagle v. Ohio: 284
Slaughter House Cases: 72, 79, 81, 82, 83, 89, 97, 233; *see also* Butchers' Assoc. v. Crescent City Co.
Slochower v. Board of Education: 124, 125
Sloss-Sheffield S. & I. Co. v. Sloss Red Ore Local: *see* Tennessee Coal Co. v. Muscado Local No. 123
Smiley v. Holm: 417
Smith v. Allwright: 10, 11, 143–44, 225–26
Smith v. Bennett: 241
Smith v. Hooey: 515
Smith v. Illinois: 236
Smith v. Turner (Passenger Cases): 43, 60
Smith v. Yaeger: 515
Smyth v. Ames: 99, 233
Smyth v. United States: 182
Snyder v. Massachusetts: 385
Socialist Labor Party v. Rhodes: 517
Socony-Vacuum Oil Co. v. United States: *see* United States v. Socony-Vacuum Oil Co.
Soloner v. Gartner: 475
Sonzinsky v. United States: 188
South v. Peters: 420, 425
South Carolina v. Katzenbach: 347–48
South Carolina v. United States: 77
Specht v. Patterson: 378

Speiser v. Randall: 69
Spencer v. Texas: 13–14, 388, 527
Spevack v. Klein: 15, 124, 125–26, 127, 521, 527, 528
Spiegel v. Commissioner of Int. Rev.: 258
Spinelli v. United States: 517
Standard Oil Co. v. United States: 106, 132–33, 196
Staub v. City of Baxley: 233, 456
Steele v. Louisville & Nashville R.R.: 475
Stein, Wissner, Cooper v. New York: 361
Stettler v. O'Hara: 9, 106–107
Steward Mach. Co. v. Davis: 188
Stewart v. United States: 122–23
Stirone v. United States: 227
Stone v. Farmers' Loan & Trust Co. (Railroad Commission Cases): 85, 98
Stone v. Illinois Cent. R.R. (Railroad Commission Cases): 85, 98
Stone v. New Orleans R.R. (Railroad Commission Cases): 85, 98
Stone v. Mississippi: 54
Stone v. Wisconsin (Granger Cases): 84; *see also* Munn v. Illinois
Stoner v. California: 312
Strauder v. West Virginia: 91, 345
Stunt v. Steamboat Ohio: 53
Sturges v. Beauchamp: 101
Sturges v. Crowinshield: 36
Sugar Inst. v. United States: 196
Sullivan v. Little Hunting Park, Inc.: 353
Summers, *In re*: 153
Superior Copper Co. v. Tomich (Arizona Employers' Liability Cases): *see* Arizona Copper Co. v. Hammer
Superior Films v. Dept. of Education: 400
Sutton v. Leib: 250
Swain v. Alabama: 343–44
Swann v. Adams (1966): 431
Swann v. Adams (1967): 431
Swartwout, *Ex parte*: *see* Bollman, *Ex parte*
Sweatt v. Painter: 325
Sweezy v. New Hampshire: 280, 281
Swenson v. Bosler: 239
Swift v. Tyson: 46, 47, 48, 49

Taglianetti v. United States: 517
Takahashi v. Fish & Game Commission: 256
Talbot v. Seeman: 21
Talley v. California: 456
Tarrance v. Florida: 344
Tax Commission v. Aldrich: 258
Taylor v. Louisiana: 332
Teamsters Union v. Hanke: 461
Tehan v. Shott: 239

Tehan v. United States: 398
Teitel Film Corp. v. Cusack: 402
Temple v. United States: 158
Tennessee v. Davis: 154
Tennessee Coal Co. v. Muscoda Local No. 123: 225
Terminiello v. Chicago: 440–41
Terry, *Ex parte*: 157
Terry v. Ohio: 310
Texas v. White: 74
Texas & Pac. R.R. v. United States (1914): *see* Houston & Texas R.R. v. United States
Texas & Pac. R.R. v. United States (1933): 172
Textile Workers Union v. Darlington Co.: 476
Thiel, *Ex parte*: *see* Quirin, *Ex parte* v. Cox
Thomas v. Collins: 228–29
Thompson v. Thompson: 250
Thompson v. United States: *see* Cox v. United States
Thornhill v. Alabama: 196, 461
Thornton v. Duffy: 109
Thorpe v. Housing Authority: 491–92, 515
Thurlow v. Massachusetts (License Cases): 44–45, 60
Tileston v. Ullman: 457
Time, Inc. v. Hill: 447
Times Film Corp. v. Chicago: 401–402
Times-Mirror Co. v. Superior Court: 13, 155; *see also* Bridges v. California
Toledo Newspaper Co. v. United States: 155
Toolson v. New York Yankees: 245, 246
Toombs v. Fortson: 431, 432
Toomer v. Witsell: 73
Torcaso v. Watkins: 455
Towne v. Eisner: 10
Townsend v. Sain: 515
Trade-Mark Cases: *see* United States v. Steffens; United States v. Witteman; United States v. Johnson
Travis v. United States: 288
Trebilcock v. Wilson: 74, 75–76
Tribune Co. v. Associated Press: *see* Associated Press v. NLRB
Tribune Co. v. United States: *see* Associated Press v. United States
Trop v. Dulles: 291, 292
Truax v. Corrigan: 105–106
Truax v. Raich: 115
Trupiano v. United States: 304, 305
Trustees of Dartmouth College v. Woodward: *see* Dartmouth College, Trustees of v. Woodward
Turman v. Duckworth: *see* Cook v. Fortson
Turner v. Louisiana: 387
Turner v. Memphis: 332

Twining v. New Jersey: 11, 72, 117
Two Guys v. McGinley: 448, 452
Tyson Bros. v. Banton: 109–10

Ulmann v. United States: 280
Uniformed Sanitation Men's Assoc. v. Commissioner of Sanitation: 126; *see also* Gardner v. Broderick
Union Pac. R.R. v. United States (1879): 87–88
Union Pac. R.R. v. United States (1941): 200
United Artists Corp v. Dallas: *see* Interstate Circuit v. Dallas
United Brotherhood of Carpenters v. United States: 230
United Gas, Coke & Chem. Workers v. Wisconsin Board: *see* Amalgamated Assoc. v. Wisconsin Board
United Mine Workers v. Coronado Coal Co. (1922): 106
United Mine Workers v. Coronado Coal Co. (1925): 106
United Mine Workers v. Illinois Bar Assoc.: 355
United Mine Workers v. Pennington: 477
United Mine Workers v. United States: *see* United States v. United Mine Workers
United Public Workers v. Mitchell: 456
United Railways v. West: 223
United States v. Abrams: 148
United States v. American Linseed Oil Co.: 134
United States v. American Tobacco Co.: 106, 132, 133, 196
United States v. Associated Press: *see* Associated Press v. United States
United States v. Augenblick: 519
United States v. Ballard: 209–11
United States v. Baltimore & Ohio R.R. (1931): 172
United States v. Baltimore & Ohio R.R. (1948): 248
United States v. Bankers Trust Co.: *see* Norman v. Baltimore & Ohio R.R.
United States v. Barnett: 327–28
United States v. Bausch & Lomb Co.: 481
United States v. Bekins: 191
United States v. Bland: 153, 154, 171–72
United States v. Booth: *see* Ableman v. Booth
United States v. Broughton: *see* United States v. Reynolds
United States v. Brown: 276
United States v. Butler: 184–85
United States v. Chicago, M., St. P. & Pac. R.R.: 172
United States v. Classic: 143, 199–200
United States v. Colgate: 481
United States v. CIO: 466

United States v. Container Corporation of America: 519
United States v. Cruikshank: 90
United States v. Darby: 135, 242, 248, 459
United States v. Dege: 488–89
United States v. Di Re: 305
United States v. Dodd: *see* United States v. Lovett
United States v. Donruss: 518
United States v. E. C. Knight Co.: 130, 132, 167
United States v. First City National Bank: 483
United States v. First National Bank of Lexington: 483
United States v. Fisher: 22
United States v. Gilmore: 490
United States v. Green: 226–27
United States v. Guest: 341–42
United States v. Harris: 91
United States v. Hudson: 188
United States v. International Boxing Club: 245–46
United States v. International Union: 465–67
United States v. Jackson: 129
United States v. Jakobson: *see* United States v. Seeger
United States v. Johnson: *see* United States v. Steffens
United States v. Juhl: 519
United States v. Kahriger: 127
United States v. Laub: 288
United States v. Lee: 95–96
United States v. Lefkowitz: 304
United States v. Lehigh Valley R.R.: 13
United States v. Lewis: *see* United States v. United Mine Workers
United States v. Lovett: 260
United States v. Machen: *see* Smyth v. United States
United States v. Macintosh: 151–52, 153, 154, 171–72
United States v. Mississippi: 346
United States v. Morgan: 201
United States v. Murdock: 200
United States v. Nardillo & Weisberg: 515
United States v. Nichols: *see* United States v. Stanley
United States v. O'Brien: 493–94, 519
United States v. Pabst Brewing Co.: 481–83
United States v. Parke Davis & Co. (1960): 481
United States v. Parke Davis & Co. (1961): 481
United States v. Patrick: 490
United States v. Philadelphia National Bank: 483
United States v. Pollar: 522

United States v. Public Utilities Commission: 257
United States v. Quarles: 65
United States v. Rabinowitz: 8, 304, 305, 321
United States v. Raines: 346
United States v. Reese: 90, 97
United States v. Reynolds (1914): 141
United States v. Reynolds (1952): 391
United States v. Robel: 277
United States v. Ryan: *see* United States v. Stanley
United States v. Schwimmer: 68, 151, 152, 153, 154
United States v. Seeger: 455
United States v. Singleton: *see* United States v. Stanley
United States v. Socony-Vacuum Oil Co.: 196
United States v. South-Eastern Underwriters: 243–44
United States v. Spector: 265
United States v. Stanley (Civil Rights Cases): 92–94
United States v. Steffens (Trade-Mark Cases): 96
United States v. Swift & Co.: 18
United States v. Third National Bank in Nashville: 483
United States v. Trans-Missouri Freight Assoc.: 130–31
United States v. Trenton Potteries: 196
United States v. Union Pac. R.R. (1875): 87
United States v. Union Pac. R.R. (1879): 87
United States v. United Mine Workers: 229–30
United States v. Ventresca: 315
United States v. Wade: 166, 379, 526
United States v. Watson: *see* United States v. Lovett
United States v. Wheeler: 72
United States v. Witkovich: 267
United States v. Witteman: *see* United States v. Steffens
United States v. Wood: 289
United States *ex rel.* Quirin v. Cox: *see* Quirin, *Ex parte* v. Cox
United States Mortgage Co. v. Matthews: 181
United Steelworkers v. NLRB: *see* American Com. Assoc. v. Douds
Universal Camera Corp. v. NLRB: 471
Uphaus v. Wyman (1959): 280–82, 355
Uphaus v. Wyman (1960): 282
Urbasek, *In re*: 378
Utah Pie Co. v. Continental Baking Co.: 485

Valley Unitarian Church, First Unitarian Church v. Los Angeles: 69

Vanderbilt v. Vanderbilt: 251
Vann v. Baggett: *see* Reynolds v. Sims
Veterans v. SACB: 276
Vidal v. Mayor of Philadelphia: 49–50
Viereck v. United States: 255
Vignera v. New York: *see* Miranda v. Arizona
Virginia, *ex parte*: 91–92
Virginia R.R. v. Federation: 188
Vogel v. United States: *see* Schaefer v. United States

Wabash R.R. v. Illinois: 85
Wainwright v. New Orleans: 310
Walker v. Birmingham: 229, 524
Walker v. Sauvinet: 86, 234
Walkling v. Washington State Board: *see* Mempa v. Rhay
Warden v. Hayden: 317–18, 321
Warren-Bradshaw Drill. Co. v. Hall: 242
Washington v. Texas: 392–93
Watkins v. United States: 280
Watson v. Memphis: 328
Watts v. Seward School Board: *see* Pickering v. Board of Education
Weaver v. Palmer Bros. Co.: 113
Webster Elec. Co. v. Splitdorf Elec. Co.: 191
Weeks v. United States (1914): 297
Weeks v. United States (1918): 248
Welch v. Henry: 196
Welton v. Missouri: 88
Werner v. United States: *see* Schaefer v. United States
Wesberry v. Sanders: 426–27, 428, 525
West Coast Hotel Co. v. Parrish: 17, 107, 179, 188, 189
Western Live Stock v. Bureau of Revenue: 196
Western Union Tel. Co. v. Lenroot: 135–36
Weston v. Charleston: 37, 38, 39
Westover v. United States: *see* Miranda v. Arizona
West River Bridge v. Dix: 23
West Virginia Board of Education v. Barnette: 17, 203, 207–209
Wheeling Steel Corp. v. Glander: 12–13, 16, 193, 256–57
Whitaker v. North Carolina: *see* Lincoln Union v. Northwestern Co.
White v. Maryland: 514
White v. Steer: *see* Duncan v. Kahanomoku
White v. United States: 196
Whitehill v. Elkins: 70
Whitney v. California: 170
Whitney v. Tax Commission: 196
Whitus v. Balkcom: 344
Whyy v. Glasboro: 518

Wickard v. Filburn: 242–43, 248
Wieman v. Updegraff: 69
Wilkinson v. United States: 283, 355
Williams v. Florida: 362; *see also* Roberts v. Russell
Williams v. Georgia: 345
Williams v. New York: 378
Williams v. North Carolina (1942): 248
Williams v. North Carolina (1945): 248–49
Williams v. Rhodes: 517
Williams v. Shaffer: 492
Williams v. United States: 342
Wilson v. Bohlender: *see* McElroy v. United States *ex rel* Guagliardo
Wilson v. Loews: 289–90
Wilson v. New: 136
Wilson v. Wiman: 388
Winona & St. P. v. Blake (Granger Cases): *see* Munn v. Illinois
Winters v. Beck: 234
Wisconsin v. J. C. Penney: 244
Wisconsin v. Minnesota M. & M. Co.: 196
Witherspoon v. Illinois: 487–88
WMCA v. Lomenzo: 426, 428
Wolf v. Colorado: 9, 233, 299–300, 301, 302, 522
Wolfe v. North Carolina: 330
Wong Quan v. United States: *see* Fong Yue Ting v. United States
Wong Sun v. United States: 26
Wood v. Broom: 416
Wood v. Georgia: 351
Wood v. United States: 235
Woodby v. Immigration Service: 271
Worcester v. Georgia: 39–40
Worthen v. Thomas: 180–81
Wright v. Georgia: 333
Wright v. Mountain Trust Bank: 188
Wyatt v. United States: 488
Wylie, *In re*: 378

Yarborough, *ex parte*: 94
Yasui v. United States: 253
Yates v. United States: 273
Yellin v. United States: 284
Youngdahl v. Rainfair: 461
Youngstown Co. v. Sawyer: 464

Zemel v. Rusk: 287–88
Zigmond v. Selective Service: 493
Zorach v. Clauson: 214–15
Zuckerman v. Greason (1967): 15, 126
Zuckerman v. Greason (1968): 126
Zwicker v. Boll: 493

Index

Abel, Rudolf: 306
Adams, President John: 218
Admissions: *see* confessions
Agricultural Adjustment Act of 1938: 135, 184
Agricultural Adjustment Administration (AAA): 242
Alabama: 73, 141, 181, 190, 273, 332; prison segregation in, 329; criminal trespass in, 332–34; gerrymandering statue struck down, 346; election day editorial rule invalidated, 351; NAACP in, 353; apportionment plans held invalid, 428
Alabama legislature: 428
Alabama Supreme Court: 229, 353
Alabama, University of, University, Ala.: 327, 447
Alaska: 73, 429
Alien and Sedition Laws: 275
Alien Registration Act: 263
"Ambulance chasing": 119, 124, 355, 378
American Bar Association: 122, 527; free legal counsel recommended by, 241
American Bar Association *Journal*: 311, 375, 384, 528
American Broadcasting Companies: 484
American Law Institute: 122
American Sugar Refining Company: 130
American Tobacco Company: 106, 133, 175–77
Anti-Ku Klux Klan Act of 1871: 91
Anti-Racketeering Act of 1934: 226
Antisegregation decisions: 4; *see also* Negroes
Anti-trust laws: 477, 481, 483–86, 519; *see also* Sherman Anti-Trust Act
Apportionment, legislative: *see* reapportionment, legislative
Arizona: 69, 72, 204, 376; peaceful picketing statute struck down, 105
Arizona constitution: 115, 462–63
Arizona legislature: 105
Arkansas: 274, 326; NAACP in, 354

Arkansas legislature: 326
Arlington Cemetery: 96
Arson: 341
Assembly, public: 197, 233, 336, 440–43, 462
Associated Press: 447, 480
Atheists: 219, 455
Atomic Energy Act: 258
Atomic Energy Commission: 258
Attainder, bills of: 67–68, 259, 274, 276, 278

Bakery workers: *see* Lochner decision
Baldwin, Justice Henry: 25, 35, 40, 46; dissent re invalidation of Georgia statute, 40; Marshall views on bills of credit held by, 45; slaves called property by, 55
Baltimore and Ohio Railroad: 88, 97, 181
Baltimore city code: 308
Baltimore Sun: 60
Bank Merger Act of 1960: 483
Bank Merger Act of 1966: 483–84
Bank of the United States: 34, 41
Bankruptcy: federal law needed, 36; New York statute held invalid, 36; National Bankruptcy Act, 183
Banks: taxing of, 34–35, 38, 51, 53–54; reopening of, 179; deposit taxes invalidated, 116; directors' claim denied, 117; holding companies held liable, 224; robbery of, 321, 378, 390–91; mergers of, 483–84; robber of, 516
Bar and Bench of Other Lands: 15
Barbour, Justice Philip P.: 35; police powers of state upheld by, 43; police powers defined by, 44; dissent re circuit court jurisdiction, 46; death of, 55
Barnett, Ross: 273, 328
Baseball, not subject to Sherman Act: 245–47
Battery: 384–85
Bentham, Jeremy: 100
Berger, Victor: 150

Bethlehem Steel Corp: 182

Beveridge, Albert J., *John Marshall*: 22, 28, 30–31, 33, 40

Beveridge, Justice Albert J.: 22; Marshall opinions appraised by, 33 & n.

Bible: 219–20

Bill of Rights: 9, 11–12, 118–19, 206, 208, 231, 235–36, 270, 290, 299, 317, 377, 386, 457–58, 487; made applicable to states, 12, 377, 385, 522

Birmingham, Ala.: 229

Black, Justice Hugo: 6, 10–11, 13, 16, 45, 118, 155, 201, 205, 223, 233, 285, 309, 359, 379, 455, 458, 475, 487, 498–504, 507–11, 520 & n., 525, 528; Fourteenth Amendment, thesis of, 9, 11–12, 487, 522; dissent in corporation case, 12; dissent in recidivist cases, 14, 388; Milligan case cited by, 65; court-martial trials opinion, 65; dissent on validity of Management Labor Relations Act, 68; dissent re loyalty oath by city, 68; opinion re Oklahoma loyalty oath, statute, 69; on commerce clause violation, 72; dissent in federal sales tax case, 77; Waite court rule challenged by, 99; contention re Fourteenth and Fifth Amendments, 118; dissent re California law ruling, 118; opinion on Bill of Rights application, 119; dissent re bar admittance ruling, 119; dissent on certiorari denials, 126; dissent on blacklisting decision, 126; dissenting opinion of, in testimony admissibility decision, 127–28; dissent on kidnap transport ruling, 128; dissent in telegraph message case, 135; dissent in Illinois lawyer decision, 153; civil contempt ruling by, 155; opinion re perjury, 157; dissent re criminal contempt, 157; concurs in civil contempt, 158; dissent in injunction violation, 158; dissent of, from certiorari denial, 158; dissent re wiretapping, 161; dissents re microphones, 163; dissent re eavesdropping, 165–67, 523, 528; dissent in livestock rate ruling, 187; replaces Van Devanter, 190–91; opposes Hughes appointment, 191; dissent in rates ruling, 192; corporation as "person" rejected by, 192–93; concurs re amendment, 194; as main dissenter in 1938; opinion in CIO ruling, 198; dissents with Douglas, 199–200; dissent on Elkins Act violation, 200; alien act rejected by, 200; on four unanimous rulings, 200; dissent on licensing, 2c̄ opinion in school transport ruling, 211–12; opinion re religion in schools, 213; dissent re religious teaching outside school buildings, 214; dissent on textbook lending, 215; opinion in school

prayer ruling, 215–16; feuds with Jackson, 221; dissent re Hobbs Act ruling, 227; Birmingham injunction upheld by, 229; dissent on UMW contempt, 230; jury trial waiver rejected by, 231; dissent on opinion on counsel denials, 231–33; lecture statements on Fourteenth Amendment, 233; dissent on certiorari denials, 234; opinion re right of confrontation, 235; opinion re record transcripts, 236–37; dissent re indigent's appeal, 241; dissent on state sales tax, 244; dissent on license tax, 244; dissent on gross sales tax, 245; dissent on canvasser ordinance, 245; civil rights law upheld by, 247; dissent in Nevada divorce ruling, 248; decision of, on alimony, 249; opinion re Ohio divorce, 250; dissent re treason, 255; dissent re propagandist, 255; dissent on draftee convictions, 256; concurs re land ownership ruling, 256; dissent re war crimes, 256; dissent on tax levy, 258; opinion in state tax, 258; dissent on teacher, conductor dismissals, 260; dissent in due process ruling, 261; concurs on officer report, 261; dissent on county firings, 261; concurs re naturalization, 262; dissent on contempt, 263; dissent on deportations, 263–64; dissent on deportation defiance, 265; dissent on deportation suspension, 266–67; concurs on lawyer ruling, 267; dissent re Chinese aliens, 268; dissent re alien perjury, 268; dissent re alien obligation, 268; dissent on benefits ruling, 269–70; dissent in Communist convictions, 271–72; dissent in lawyer contempt, 272; disbarment opposed by, 272; dissent re Communist contempt, 273; dissent on Communist registration, 274; dissent on Smith Act violation, 274–75; concurs vacating Noto conviction, 275; dissent on remand, 275–76; dissent on subversives act hearings, 277; dissent on conspiracy reversal, 278; dissent on Immunity Act challenge, 280; on due process violation, 280; dissent on contempt conviction, 281, 283; dissent on contempt review, 282; dissent on ex-teacher conviction, 282; witness-conviction vote of, 282; dissent re subpoenaed matter, 283; dissent on execution stay, 286; concurs on issuing passports, 286; dissent on passports to Cuba, 287; dissent re contempt of Congress, 289; dissent re jury service, 289; concurs on Communist list ruling, 289; concurs re church property statute, 290; dissent re voter's citizenship loss, 291; decision re deserter's loss of citizenship, 291; dissent on Costello denaturalization, 292; opinion on citizenship provisions, 292;

vote abroad upheld by, 293; concurs re federal rule, 300; concurs on Fourteenth Amendment ruling, 303; dissent on search without warrant, 305; dissent on blood in evidence, 305; dissent re withdrawal of blood, 305; dissent in spy ruling, 306; evidence in car held admissible by, 311; dissent re search for heroin, 313; dissent on search, 315; dissent on gambler ruling, 316; ruling on informer identity, 316; concurs on overruled fraud decision, 318; dissent on robber rule reversal, 321, 323; dissent on vacated conviction, 323; dissent on "breaking" extension, 323; concurs on bus integration, 324; dissent on court policy, 324; opinion re public school closing, 326; dissent on jury trial denial, 328; concurs on prison desegregation, 329; segregation view of, 329; dissent on park, restaurant trespass, 334; opinion reversing breach of peace ruling, 335; dissent on trespass reversal, 335; opinion re sit-ins, 335–36; concurs on rights leader reversal, 336; dissent on picketing, 336, 358; dissent re antipicketing statute, 337–38; trespass confirmed by, 339; concurs re rights, 342; opinion re Fourteenth Amendment violation, 342; concurs re jury selection, 343; dissent re rules, 346; dissent in part on voting injunction, 348; dissent on state poll tax ruling, 348–49; dissent on housing amendment, 352; concurs invalidating NAACP ordinance, 354; opinion on union lawyer hiring, 355; concurs on NAACP membership lists, 356; dissent re park segregation, 356; dissent re voluntariness of confession, 361; tax fraud conviction voided by, 375; dissent on waiver decision, 376; concurs on juvenile delinquent decision, 377; dissent re witnesses counsel, 378; dissent on investigators contempt, 378; concurs in part re robbery remand, 379; dissent on trial televising, 381; concurs re trial by jury, 385; dissent re jury trial rejection, 387; dissent re double jeopardy, 388; dissent re contempt, 389; dissent on defendant testimony ruling, 390; dissent on rape reversal, 393; dissent on Mapp rule opinion, 396–97; dissent re applying decisions retroactively, 397; concurs on voluntariness doctrine ruling, 398; dissent on state rule reversals, 399; concurs against film censorship, 400–402; dissent on film preshowing, 402; dissent on obscenity regulation, 403–404; dissent on obscenity suits, 405; magazines held not obscene by, 405–406; concurs re censorship action, 407; film board decisions rejected by, 407; dissent on "girlie" magazine ruling, 407–408; concurs reversing obscenity conviction, 408; concurs re obscenity ruling, 410; dissent on Ginzburg conviction, 412–13; dissent on bookseller conviction, 414; opinion re districting dismissal, 417–18; "one person one vote" opinion of, 426; opinion re gubernatorial decision, 431–32; permit requirement held invalid by, 442; dissent re speaker license, 442; concurs on free speech ruling, 442; dissent re disorderly conduct, 443; dissent on libelous leaflets, 443; concurs in libel decision, 444; concurs, dissents re libel, 444–45; concurs reversing defamation conviction, 445–46; concurs on *Life* libel ruling, 446–47; concurs on Walker decision, 447; concurs awarding damages, 448; dissent on Hatch Act, 456; dissent re contraceptives statute, 458–59; dissent on picketing injunction, 461; dissent re labor jurisdiction, 461; dissent in right-to-work violation, 462; concurs upholding right to work, 462; right-to-work amendment upheld by, 463; ruling against steel takeover, 464; dissent re utility seizure, 464; dissent on union indictment, 465; dissent re union funds in politics, 467–69; opinion re bar dues, 470; concurs on union refund, 471; white bargainers rejected by, 475; dissent on strikebreaker fine, 476; dissent on boycott, 477; concurs against UMW, 477; dissent re Sherman Act, 478; dissent re price-fixing, 478; opinion in Associated Press decision, 480; opinion re brewery assets, 481; dissent on jury exclusion, 488; dissent on wife testimony, 488; dissent on husband-wife conspiracy, 488; dissent on income tax ruling, 489; dissent on deductible item, 490; opinion on damages ruling, 496; dissent on retroactivity, 515; dissent on habeas corpus proceedings, 516; dissent on due process violation, 516; dissent on defense inspection of transcripts, 516; dissent re search and seizure, 517; on excluding relevant evidence, 517; dissent re foreign corporation tax, 518; concurs on evolution teaching, 518; dissent re picketing, 518; dissent on union fines, 519; on obtaining evidence, 522 & n.; dissent on lawyer disbarment, 528; dissent on obscenity, 528

Black & White Taxicab & Transfer Co.: 47–48
Blackmail: 515
Blackstone, William: 395–96, 449, 489
Blair, Justice John: 20
Bland, Marie Averil: 153–54, 171–72
Blatchford, Justice Samuel: 82, 98
Bollman, Eric: 27–28

Bond, Julian: 456–57
Bonded indebtedness cases: 94–95; tax exemption on revenue bonds denied, 96; *see also* taxation
Boston & Maine Railroad: 484
Boston, Mass.: 130
Boston Naval Shipyard: 261
Botts, Benjamin: 28–29
Boutwell, George S.: 5
Boutwell, George S.: *Reminiscences of Sixty Years in Public Affairs*: 6 & n.
Boxing: subject to Sherman Act, 245
Boycott: 103, 106, 518; *see also* labor
Bradley, Justice Joseph P.: 63, 76–78, 85, 94, 233, 331; appointment of, 74; dissent in specie payment case, 75, dissent in salary tax case, 76; dissent on Fourteenth Amendment application, 80; concurs in monopoly case, 81; opinion in law practice case, 81 & n.; concurs in Iowa liquor case, 82; dissent on Fifth Amendment due process violation, 88; dissent on railroad receipts tax, 88; opinion re civil rights application, 92; dissent in Virginia bond cases, 95; dissent in Arlington tax sale case, 96; dissent on legislative role, 99
Bradwell, Myra: 81
Brandeis, Justice Louis D.: 4, 8, 19, 77, 82, 102, 107, 111, 115, 135, 146, 148, 171, 178, 191, 228, 463, 529; in Oregon case, 8–9; technique of, 9; stare decisis upheld by, 10; dissent on invalidity of state tax on U.S. securities, 37; dissent on taxing oil, gas revenues, 38; dissent on invalidity of oil, gas income tax, 39; diversity of citizenship rule rejected by, 47, 49; dissent in taxicab case, 48; dissent in "yellow-dog contract" case, 103; dissent in nonunion strikes, 103; dissent on boycott, 103; some strikes called illegal by, 105; concurs in rule on peaceful picketing, 105; dissent on peaceful picketing reversal, 105; dissent in union injunction case, 106; employment agency abuses cited by, 108; dissent in employment agency fee case, 108; dissent on theater ticket price statutes, 109; observation re the depression, 111; dissent re bread weight regulation, 112; dissent in shoddy case, 113; dissent in licensing statute case, 113; dissent re chain drugstore decision, 113; dissent re licensing opinion, 114; dissent re tax discrimination ruling, 114; dissent in mortgage recording tax decision, 115; dissent re sterilization of imbeciles, 116; dissenting opinion re trade association cases, 134; dissent re child labor act unconstitutionality, 134; judges held taxable by, 138; formula re espionage,

146; dissent re garment worker conviction, 147–48; dissent re German publications, 148; dissent re pamphlet distributor conviction, 148; dissent in Socialist conviction, 149; dissent re war measure, 150; dissent re mailing privilege, 150–51; dissent re fraud order, 151; dissent in citizenship denial, 152; dissent in naturalization decision, 152; dissent in contempt ruling, 155; dissent re wiretapping, 160; on hardship case, 174; dissent re tobacco case, 176; dissent re insurrection, 178; opinion re Frazier-Lemke amendment, 183; dissent re taxing power, 184–85; dissent in SEC ruling, 186; opinion re coal act, 186; retirement of, 194; Japanese exclusion order upheld by, 253
Brandeis, Louis D.: 8
Branigan, Governor (Indiana): 474
Brennan, Justice William J.: 16, 162, 273, 275, 282, 502–504, 507–509, 511, 527; dissent in habitual criminal cases, 14; dissent on court-martial trials, 65; opinion in veteran tax exemption case, 69; New York statute re subversives held invalid by, 70; dissent re bar admittance ruling, 119; opinion re self-incrimination case, 119; dissent re criminal contempt, 157; injunction violation sustained by, 158; dissent on deportation, 198; concurs on religious exercises ruling, 219; dissent on Birmingham injunction, 229; opinion on vacated confession conviction, 236; dissent in football ruling, 247; dissent re teacher, conductor dismissals, 260; dissent on due process ruling, 261; dissent on libel, 261; dissent on officer report, 261; dissent on county firing, 261; dissent on contempt, 263; dissent re Chinese aliens, 268; dissent re alien perjury, 268; dissent on benefits payment, 269; dissent on Communist contempt, 273; reversal in lawyer suspension, 278; on due process violation, 280; dissent on contempt conviction, 281–82; dissent on ex-teacher conviction, 282; witness conviction vote of, 282; dissent re subpoenaed matter, 283; on definition of subversion, 284; concurs on postal violation, 290; opinion re congressional power, 291; concurs on citizenship provisions, 292; opinion re withdrawal of blood, 305; dissenting opinion in spy ruling, 306–307; opinion re certiorari denial, 309; dissent in fur search ruling, 314; dissent on informer ruling, 316; concurs on narcotics seller conviction, 317; opinion in robber conviction, 318; ruling re free choice of schools, 329; concurs on segregation protest, 338; dissent on picketing rule, 339; dissent on jail

trespass, 339; dissent in part re rights, 342; concurs on election day editorial ruling, 351; opinion re voluntariness of confession, 361–62; dissent re witnesses counsel, 378; dissent on investigators contempt, 378; bank robbery remanded by, 379; opinion re robber, 379; dissent re trial televising, 381, 383–84; dissent on double jeopardy, 389; dissent on defendant testimony ruling, 390; opinion re reports to FBI, 390–91; dissent on jailing alcoholics, 395; dissent on film preshowing, 402; opinion re mailing obscene matter, 403; dissent on suits against obscenity, 405; censorship rule held intimidating, 406; opinion forbidding "girlie" magazine sales, 408; opinion reversing obscenity conviction, 408; on obscenity requirements, 410; opinion in Ginzburg conviction, 412–13; ruling in bookseller conviction, 414; ruling remanding apportionment case, 418–20; dissent re gubernatorial decision, 432; Puerto Rican registration upheld by, 435; opinion in libel decision, 444; opinion reversing defamation conviction, 445; opinion in Life libel ruling, 446; concurred in Walker decision, 447; concurred awarding damages, 448; dissent on Sunday closing, 452–54; opinion upholding Seventh-Day Adventist, 454; concurs re contraceptives statute, 457; dissent re utility seizure, 464; opinion re union funds in politics, 467–68; bar dues upheld by, 469–70; opinion re union refund, 471; strike-breaker fine upheld by 476; employee lockout upheld by, 476; boycott upheld by, 477; decision re Sherman Act, 478; concurs in rail merger opinion, 484; concurs on income tax ruling, 489; certiorari favored by, 492; appointment of, 502; dissent re draftee, 519

Bridges, Harry: 155–56

Browder, Earl R.: 200

Brown & Yellow Taxicab Co.: 47–48

Brown, David W.: 493

Brown, Justice Henry B.: 18, 100, 159; dissent in Idaho strike case, 102; personal property income tax favored by, 136; opinion upholding segregation, 139–40

Brewer, Justice David J.: 9, 11, 98, 159, 233, 265; nephew of Justice Field, 63, 98; dissent in original package case, 89; dissent in eighthour-day case, 100; dissent in Idaho strike case, 102; dissent re alien deportation, 139 & n.

Buchanan, President James: 57

Buchwald, Art: 9

Burdick, William L.: 15

Bureau of Labor: 108

Burleson, Postmaster General Albert S.: 150

Burr, Aaron: 26–27, 29; tried, acquitted by Marshall, 28

Burton, Justice Harold H.: 65, 69, 77, 273, 280, 500–501, 503; Management Labor Relations Act of 1947 held valid by, 68; dissent re loyalty oath by city, 68; ruling in Bridges conspiracy, 156; dissent in transmitter use, 162; dissent on literature distribution, 209; dissent re jury lists, 211; dissent in school transport, 212; concurs re religion in schools, 213; dissent re labor disputes ruling, 230; opinion re counsel decision, 232; dissent re record transcripts, 236–38; dissent re transcript settlement, 241; concurs in boxing case, 245–46; appointment of, 251; dissent re war crimes, 256; dissent re estate tax, 258; dissent on denaturalization, 263; dissent on deportation, 263; dissent re alien indictment, 267; dissent on not deporting salesman, 267; disbarment favored by, 272; dissent on sedition reversal, 273; dissent on Smith Act violation, 273; dissent on due process violation, 280; dissent on withholding passports, 286; concurs on Communist list ruling, 289; dissent re deserter citizenship, 291; concurs on Japanese citizenship reversal, 291; dissent on complaint insufficiency, 314; dissent on bus integration, 324; concurs re FBI reports disclosure, 391; concurs overruling film censorship, 400; concurs dismissing districting complaint, 416; dissent on amplifier use, 439; dissent on public disturbance ruling, 440; concurs on picketing injunction, 461; steel takeover opposed by, 464; dissent re electrocution, 487; retirement of, 504

Butler, Justice Pierce: 19, 49, 107, 135, 171, 181, 193; dissent in corporate franchise tax case, 38; dissent on state tax on corporations, 38; dissent in HOLC tax, 76; dissent on Palko case, 117; dissent in telegraph message case, 135; dissent on judges tax, 138–39; dissent re wiretapping, 160; second tobacco case ruling of, 176; dissent re corporate assessments, 177; opinion in rape decisions, 177; on minimum wage law ruling, 178–79; dissent re amendment, 194; death of, 195; dissent in law school case, 196; announces CIO ruling dissent, 197–98; see also Four Horsemen

Butts, Wally: 447

Byrnes, Justice James F.: opinion in commerce clause violation, 71–72; dissent in Bridges decisions, 155; replaced by Rutledge, 205, 221; appointment, resignation of, 221

California: 43, 71–72, 86, 102, 118, 154–55, 203, 240, 366, 393, 403, 523, 527; licensing statute struck down, 113; rule invalidated in Griffin decision, 122; tax statute struck down, 192; land ownership statute invalidated, 256; fishing license statute struck down, 256; blacklisting dismissed in, 289; reapportionment in, 430–31

California constitution: 69, 121, 420

California legislature: 53, 352

California Supreme Court: 53, 240

Callanan, Lawrence: 472–73

Campbell, Justice John A.: 41, 53; dissent in corporate tax case, 51; insurance company taxation held valid by, 51; legislative pressures criticized by, 52–53; slavery views of, 55; resignation of, 61; opinion in slaughter house case, 79

Canons of Judicial Ethics: 355, 383

Cardozo, Justice Benjamin N.: 4–5, 9–11, 16–17, 111, 145, 183, 254, 287, 300, 302, 528; on writing opinions, 15; dissent on invalidity of oil and gas income tax, 39; double jeopardy claim overruled by, 117–18; Texas statute held invalid by, 143; on hardship case, 174; dissent re tobacco case, 176; opinion in corporate assessments, 176–77; dissent re insurrection, 177–78; act limited to intrastate by, 180; NIRA section upheld by, 181; dissent re taxing power, 184–85; opinion re coal act, 186; opinion re Social Security cases, 189–90; death of, 194; opinion re common law rule, 297–98; on excluding relevant evidence, 517

Cardozo, Benjamin N.: 15n., 17n.

Cardozo, Benjamin N., *The Nature of the Judicial Process*: 5n., 7n., 9–10n.

Catron, Justice John: 41, 47, 53, 57, 60; dissent re circuit court jurisdiction, 46; dissent in corporate tax case, 51; insurance company taxation held valid by, 51; opinion re tax exemptions, 52; slavery views of, 55; death of, 62, 64

Censorship: 151, 208, 302, 415, 448; of motion pictures, 400–402, 407; of written, printed matter, 402, 406, 411–14; of photography, 405–406, 408; of books, 410–12

Central Pacific Railroad: 87

Certiorari, writs of: 10, 13–14, 51, 126, 149, 179, 234, 240, 255, 309, 311, 315, 320, 337, 360, 378, 381, 394–95 & n., 527–28; refused to conscientious objector, 235; denied to Rosenbergs, 285; denied in heroin case, 319;

denied to tenant, 492; denied to students, 493

Chain stores: 113, 172

Charles Evans Hughes: 173 & n., 189n.

Chase, Chief Justice Salmon P.: 62, 64, 74, 78–79; dissent in loyalty oath cases, 67; dissent in stagecoach tax case, 71; opinion in Texas statehood case, 74; legal tender acts held unconstitutional by, 74; dissent in reargued legal tender acts, 74; dissent on Fourteenth Amendment application, 80–81; dissent in law practice case, 81; death of, 82

Chase Court: 88

Chase, Justice Samuel: 21–22, 32; writ of habeas corpus jurisdiction opposed by, 27

Chicago, Ill.: 201

Child labor: act of Congress held unconstitutional, 134; decision re telegraph company labor, 135–36; amendment proposed on, 194; Jehovah's Witnesses case of, 209; *see also* labor

Chin Foy: 161–62

Choate, Joseph H.: 136

CIO: 197–98

CIO News: 466

Circuit court of Pennsylvania: 22

Citizenship, loss of: 290–91; by Frank Costello, 292; provisions of acts for, struck down, 292–93; and citizenship clause of Constitution, 293; *see also* naturalization

Civil rights: 72, 80, 82, 90–92, 94, 97, 139–43, 151, 170–71, 177, 194, 229, 339, 341, 354, 435, 512; 1964 law upheld, 247–48; failure of 1870 legislation on, 523; *see also* Negroes

Civil Rights Act of 1866: 342, 353

Civil Rights Act of 1870: 143, 197, 523; *see also* civil rights

Civil Rights Act of 1875: 92, 247; *see also* civil rights

Civil Rights Act of 1957: 346, 536

Civil Rights Act of 1964: 335–36, 341, 343

Civil Rights Act of 1968: 353

Civil Rights Congress: 283

Civil War: 57–58, 63, 94, 465

Civil War Relocation Authority: 254

Clark, Justice Tom C.: 4, 12, 15, 126, 156, 265, 271–72, 289, 390, 498, 502–504, 507–10; dissent in Chinese narcotics case, 26; dissent in court-martial trials, 65; opinion in manslaughter cases, 65–66; opinion in veteran tax exemption case, 69; dissent on loyalty oath statute, 69; opinion re subversives statute, 70–71; dissent re self-incrimination ruling, 120; opinion in murder conviction reversal, 123; dissent in police officer conviction, 124; dissent in lawyer disbarment case, 124; dissent re overruled contempt, 157; civil contempt opinion of, 158; injunction violation sustained by, 158; opinion re microphones, 163–64; opinion on religious exercises ruling, 219–20; concurs overruling counsel decision, 234; dissent re indigent discrimination, 239; dissent re indigent, 240; dissent re transcript settlement, 241; ruling in football case, 247; civil rights law upheld by, 247; opinion re Ohio divorce, 250; appointment of, 259; dissent on summary discharge, 260; dissent on security clearance ruling, 261; dissent on denaturalization, 263; dissent re alien indictment, 267; concurs on lawyer ruling, 267; dissent on not deporting salesman, 267; dissent on deportation, 270; dissent re deportation evidence, 271; dissent on vacating lawyer conviction, 273; dissent on Smith Act violation, 273–74; dissent on teacher affidavit, 273–74; dissent on labor act section, 276; dissenting opinion on lawyer suspension, 278–79; dissent on committee inquiry, 280; dissent on due process violation, 280; opinion in contempt ruling, 281; witness conviction affirmed by, 282; dissent on vacating contempt convictions, 283; dissent on witness questions, 284; dissent on rule violation, 284; dissent re Louisiana statute, 284; dissent on withholding passports, 286; dissent re issuing passports, 286–87; dissent re loss of citizenship, 291; dissent re deserter's citizenship, 291; dissent on Japanese citizenship reversal, 291; dissent on denaturalization, 291; dissent re citizenship provisions, 292; dissent on vote abroad, 293; dissent re "silver platter" doctrine, 301; Fourth Amendment ruled applicable to states by, 302–303; blood in evidence ruling by, 305; dissent on radio theft conviction reversal, 306; dissent on vacated narcotics conviction, 307; dissent re inspectors' warrant, 309; dissent re warehouse inspection warrant, 310; concurs re evidence in car, 311; dissent re "harmless error," 312; dissent re heroin search, 313; dissent re complaint insufficiency, 314; dissent on search, 315; dissent on gambler ruling, 316; opinion on Hoffa review, 320; concurs re school closing ruling, 326; dissent on restaurant integration, 330; dissent on Negro protest ruling, 332; concurs on park trespass, 334; concurs on sit-in reversals, 335; concurs on rights leader reversal, 336; dissent on picketing, 336; concurs re rights, 341; reversal re nondiscrimination proof, 344–45; dissent on sheriff contempt reversal, 351; dissent on housing amendment, 352; dissent on NAACP

lawyer hiring, 354; dissent re NAACP membership lists, 356; dissent re murder conviction, 359–60; dissent re voluntariness of confession, 361; dissent re absence of counsel, 363; dissent on Escobedo reversal, 364; decisions involving police practices, 366, 369–70; opinion on trial televising, 381; dissent on murder reversals, 384, 387; dissent re jury coercion, 387; dissent on FBI reports disclosure, 391; dissent on vacating robber conviction, 391–92; dissent on rape reversal, 393; dissent on narcotics reversal, 394; opinion re application of Mapp rule, 395–96; concurs re applying decisions retroactively, 397; dissent on voluntariness ruling, 398; film preshowing upheld by, 402; dissent on magazine obscenity ruling, 406; concurs re censorship action, 407; dissent on obscenity rulings, 408, 410–11; concurs on remanding apportionment case, 418, 420–21, 525; concurs rejecting Georgia unit rule, 424; dissent on "one man one vote," 426; Alabama apportionment rejected by, 428; concurs invalidating California apportionment, 430; Texas reapportionment upheld by, 431; concurs re libel case, 444; dissent on Life libel ruling, 447; dissent re solicitation permit, 456; dissent on handbill ordinance ruling, 456; concurs on picketing injunction, 461; steel takeover opposed by, 464; bar dues upheld by, 469; dissent on boycott, 477; concurs against UMW, 477; dissent re Sherman Act, 478; dissent on compensation, 478; concurs re damages, 481; opinion re rail merger, 484; resignation of, 511-12

Clarke, Justice John H.: dissent on taxing oil and gas revenues, 38; dissent in 1920 case, 72; dissent in nonunion strikes, 103; dissent on boycott, 103; dissent on peaceful picketing opinion, 105; dissent on peaceful picketing reversal, 105; replaced by Sutherland, 106; dissent in employment agency fee case, 108; garment worker conviction upheld by, 148; dissent re German publications, 148; resignation of, 169

Classic decision: 143, 225

Clay, Cassius: 517

Clayton Act of 1914: 103, 105, 130, 227, 480, 482; bank mergers not excluded by, 483; damages under, 485

Clemens, Samuel L.: 275

Cleveland, President Grover: 102, 218

Clifford, Justice Nathan: 54, 78, 90–92, 235; dissent on stagecoach tax case, 71; dissent in reargued legal tender acts, 74; replaced by

Gray, 82; dissent re due process, 86; concurs in Negro voter case, 90; dissent in Negro murder conviction, 91; dissent re trial transfer, 154; dissent in deputy marshal ruling, 154

Coal: mining of, 114; Guffy Coal Act struck down, 186; portal to mine face pay upheld, 225

Coast Guard, U.S.: 277

Code, Napoleon: 15

Cole, W. Warren, Jr.: 528

Collected Legal Papers (Oliver Wendell Holmes): 7

Collective bargaining: 464–65, 471, 477

Columbia Law School, New York, N.Y.: 233

Commerce clause: 29, 34, 43, 54–55, 242–47, 335, 480; potentialities noted, 71; California violation of, 71–72; national powers broadened under, 82; case totals re clause, 88; impact of, 130; narrow scope of, 131

Communist Control Act of 1950: 289

Communists: 68–70, 119, 156, 200, 259, 355–56; not required to register, 126; in insurrection case, 177; in labor movement, 259, 390; decisions re Communist issues, 260–92; required to register, 274; failure to register, 276–77; registration order reversed, 277

Complete Works of Abraham Lincoln: 61 n.

Confessions: 342, 359, 375–76, 378, 384, 395, 526; voluntariness of, 361–62, 367, 398; presence of counsel in, 363, 523; absence of counsel in, 363–66; of kidnap, rape suspect, 372; of juveniles, 377

Congress: 27, 31, 33–34, 36, 42–44, 56, 59, 71, 74, 77, 87–88, 90, 92, 96, 103–104, 107, 114, 131–32, 134, 139, 146, 149–54, 165, 172, 179, 181–84, 189–90, 194, 200, 217–18, 225, 229, 242–44, 247, 252, 257, 259, 273, 276, 278, 280, 287–88, 290, 292–93, 307, 324, 346, 417–22, 427, 436–38, 443, 462–63, 465, 468–69, 477–78, 483, 489, 494–95, 517, 519–20, 523–25; powers upheld in immigration cases, 43; powers increased by use of commerce clause, 44; slavery debated by, 56–57; military laws enacted by, 66, paper currency legalized by, 74; Webb-Kenyon Act passed by, 89; tax exemption on revenue bonds denied by, 96; labor statute struck down, 103; rent control statute of, 110; powers under Sherman Act, 130 & n.; lottery ticket transport prohibited by, 132; child labor act held unconstitutional, 134; eight-hour day legislation upheld, 136; judges tax exemption vetoed by, 138; crime bill passed by, 160–61; court packing killed in Senate, 190; contempt of, 289; Civil Rights Act of 1968

passed by, 352–53; prearraignment time limited by, 376; at-large elections barred by, 433–34

Connecticut: 73, 87, 117, 192, 204, 234, 458

Connor, Eugene ("Bull"): 229

Conscientious objectors: 455, 493, 519

Constitution, U.S.: 9, 17, 30, 33–35, 42–43, 49, 51, 55–56, 64–65, 67, 71, 74–75, 77, 79, 85–88, 90, 110, 112, 114, 116–17, 120, 143, 156, 165, 177, 179–81, 194, 203, 210, 216, 218, 225, 231, 234, 248, 254–56, 261, 281, 298, 300, 302, 304, 307, 320, 342, 365, 367, 397, 401, 417, 422–23, 426–27, 457–59, 462, 487, 517, 520–21, 524–25; called color blind, 18, 325; Eleventh Amendment passed, 18; held supreme by President Jackson, 40; article 4, section 2 applied, 72–73; amendment attempt failure, 135; amendment sought re court, 189; primary voters protected by, 200; Twenty-fourth Amendment adopted, 348

Contempt: 34, 61, 102, 119, 154, 228–30, 280–85, 353, 386, 389, 524; conviction sustained, 155, 157, 263, 328, 351; criminal contempt rule upheld, 157; lawyers convicted for, 272; Communists convicted of, 273

Cornell University, Ithaca, N.Y.: 284

Coronado Coal Company: 106, 173

Corporations: 12–13, 16, 36, 38, 46, 79, 83, 87, 130, 175–77, 182, 257–58, 281, 330, 375, 454, 466; defined, 33; early diversity rule of, 34; powers resented, 41; Kentucky case, 47–48; Tennessee corporation, 48; tax exemption cases of, 51–53; held "person" by Waite court, 99; constitutional privilege not available to, 126; "person" concept questioned, 192–93; tax on foreign, 518

Costello, Frank: 292

Counterfeiting: 301

Cramer, Anthony: 255

Credit, bills of: 35; Marshall, Taney courts clash on, 45

Credit Mobilier Company: 87

Crescent City Company: 81

Crime Bill of 1968: 160–61, 167, 374, 515–16; counsel at lineup vetoed by, 379–80; court decision curbs added to, 526

Criminal Code: 199, 342

Criminal prosecution: 10, 206, 253ff., 277, 286, 292, 359, 365, 375, 384, 390, 393, 399, 527

Crosskey, Professor William W.: on Marshall court opinions, 25

Counsel: 177, 231–32, 361, 380, 384, 388, 390, 392, 395, 523; required for indigents, 234, 369; in Hoffa case, 320; fees of, 343; presence at confessions, 363–66; right to, 367–74,

385; for juveniles, 377; for students, 377–78; for witnesses, 378; for sex offender, 378; in robberies, 379; relief for lack of, 514; *see also* lawyers

Cuba: 287–88

Cummings, John A., in loyalty oath case: 67–68

Curtis, Justice Benjamin R.: 57–60

Cushing, Justice William: 22

Custis, George Washington Parke: 96

Dade County, Fla.: 456

Danbury Hatters' Union: 106

Daniel, Justice Peter V.: 41, 44, 53–54, 60; dissent in corporate tax case, 51; insurance company taxation held valid by, 51; opinion on legislative powers, 52; slavery views of, 55; death of, 61

Dartmouth College case: 33, 43, 51, 54

Davis, Justice David: 62, 64, 78; martial law rule defined by, 64; dissent in loyalty oath cases, 67; dissent in Hepburn decision, 74; succeeded by Harlan, Sr., 82; dissent in freight tax case, 88

Day, Justice William R.: 159, 297; dissent in Lochner decision, 101; dissent re Kansas statute invalidity, 104; opinion in Georgia civil rights ruling, 142; resignation of, 169

Death penalty: 128–29, 177ff., 240; imposed on Julius and Ethel Rosenberg, 285–86; agitation for abolition of, 487

Debs, Eugene V.: 102, 146–47

Debt, imprisonment for: 36–37

Declaration of Independence: 49, 424

Delaware: 330

Delaware constitution: 92

Delaware & Hunson Railroad: 484

Denaturalization: *see* naturalization

Deportation: ordered for Bridges, 156; validated, 263–65; order defiance rejected, 265; order suspension denied, 265–67; invalidated, 267, 270; of Chinese aliens, 268; perjury upheld in, 268; burden of proof in, 268; prevention of, 271; evidence in, 271

Depression: 111, 176, 179, 181, 184

Desperate Hours, The (play): 447

DeWolfe, Mark: 103 & n., 109 & n., 114 & n., 117 & n., 146n., 147 & n., 149n., 151 n., 153n.

Dies, Congressman Martin: 259

Dillard, Irvin: 6n.

Dirksen, Senator Everett: 521 & n.

Discount houses: 133

District of Columbia: 110–11, 257, 277, 288–89, 345, 348, 378; schools ordered desegregated in, 325; prearraignment questioning in, 376

District of Columbia Court of Appeals: 484

District of Columbia minimum wage law: 107

Dissent: 6, 9–10, 13, 15, 19, 47, 108, 136, 143, 146, 193, 224, 521; meaning of, 3–5; justification for, 4, 16–17; undesirability of, 18; prior to 1789, 20; totals in court, 18–19, 40–41, 78, 96–97, 167–70, 174–75, 194–96, 221–23, 251–52; English practice followed, 20–21; none, 1801–1805, 21; none in Marshall landmark constitutional decisions, 33; record in obscenity cases, 415; record, 1950–66, 497–511; record in 1967, 512; *see also* under names of justices

Dissenters: 7, 12–14, 17, 20, 44, 78, 89, 108, 174–75, 194–95, 251–52, 497–511, 527; in legal usage, 3–5; increase of, 191, 221; Black and Douglas as, 498–99, 501, 502; Frankfurter and Jackson as, 498; Harlan, Jr., as, 507, 510; Goldberg as, 508; *see also* under names of justices

Diversity of citizenship rule, applied in taxicab case: 47–48; rejected in damages case, 48–49

Divorce actions: 248–51, 304

Dorr, Thomas W.: 59

Double jeopardy: 117–18; pleas overruled, 388–89

Douglas, Justice William O.: 6, 9, 11, 12n., 13, 15–16, 19, 120, 191n., 193, 196–98, 205, 207, 218, 233, 240, 289, 305, 309, 311–12, 359, 379, 461, 498, 501–504, 507–11; dissent in corporation case, 12; dissent in habitual criminal cases, 14; dissent in certiorari denials, 14; dissent in inheritance tax case, 49; opinion in court-martial trials, 65; dissent re city loyalty oath, 68; opinion re loyalty oath statutes, 69; Maryland loyalty oath held vague by, 70; opinion on commerce clause violation, 72; dissent in federal sales tax case, 77; dissent re California law ruling, 118; dissent re bar admittance ruling, 119; opinion in murder conviction reversal, 121; decision vacating police offer convictions, 124; dissent in certiorari denials, 126; dissent on blacklisting decision, 126; dissent in telegraph message case, 135; dissent in anarchy ruling, 149–50; dissent in Illinois lawyer decision, 153; opinion in overruled citizenships, 154; dissent re criminal contempt, 157; dissent in injunction violation, 158; dissent in wiretapping policy, 162; dissent in Hoffa case, 163; dissent in microphone use, 164; Brandeis replaced by, 194; concurs re amendment, 194; dissent on deportation, 198–99; dissents with Black, 199–200; dissent in voter ruling, 200; dissent in Elkins

Act violation, 200; alien act rejected by, 200; in four unanimous decisions, 200; dissent on civil liberties, 201; dissent on licensing, 204; "I Am" decision of, 209, 211; opinion re religious teaching outside school buildings, 214; dissent on textbook lending, 215; concurs in school prayers, 215–17; concurs on religious exercises ruling, 219; opinion in FPC ruling, 223; dissent re Hobbs Act ruling, 227; dissent on Birmingham injunction, 229; dissent on UMW contempt, 230; jury trial waiver rejected by, 231; dissent on counsel denial, 232; concurs overruling counsel decision, 233; dissent from certiorari denial, 234; indigents' rights upheld by, 238–39; dissent re transcript settlement, 241; dissent on state sales tax, 244; dissent on gross sales tax, 245; dissent on canvasser ordinance, 245; civil rights law upheld by, 247; dissent in Nevada divorce rule, 248–49; decision on alimony, 249; opinion re Ohio divorce ruling, 250; concurs on Japanese student ruling, 252–53; opinion on Japanese deportation, 254; dissent re treason, 255; dissent re Bund ruling, 255; dissent re propagandist, 255; dissent on draftee convictions, 256; concurs on land ownership ruling, 256; dissent re war crimes, 256; dissent on district courts rule, 257; dissent on tax levy, 258; dissent on teacher, conductor dismissals, 260; dissent on due process ruling, 261; dissent on libel, 261; dissent on county firings, 261; concurs on naturalization ruling, 262; dissent on contempt, 263; dissent on deportations, 263–65; opinion on deportation defiance, 265; dissent on deportation suspension, 266–67; dissent re Chinese aliens, 268; dissent re alien perjury, 268; dissent re alien obligation, 268; dissent on benefits ruling, 269; dissent on Communist convictions, 271–72; dissent on lawyer contempt, 272; disbarment opposed by, 272; dissent on Communist contempt, 273; dissent on Smith Act violation, 275; concurs vacating Noto conviction, 275; dissent on remand, 275; dissent on subversives act hearings, 277; remarks re Magnuson Act, 278; dissent on conspiracy reversal, 278; dissent on Immunity Act challenge, 280; opinion on due process violation, 280; dissent on contempt conviction, 281; dissent on contempt review, 282; dissent on ex-teacher conviction, 282; witness conviction vote of, 282; dissent re subpoenaed matter, 283; concurs on vacating contempt convictions, 283; views on witness rights, 285; execution stay granted

by, 285; dissent on vacating execution stay, 286; concurs re issuing passports, 286; dissent re Cuba passport denial, 287–88; concurs on Communist list ruling, 289; dissent re writer blacklisting, 289; concurs re church property statute, 290; opinion re loss of citizenship, 290; dissent on voter's citizenship loss, 291; decision re deserter's loss of citizenship, 291; dissent on Costello denaturalization, 292; opinion on citizenship provisions, 292; dissent re federal rule for states, 299–300; dissent on blood in evidence, 305; dissent re withdrawal of blood, 305; radio theft conviction ruling by, 306; dissent in spy ruling, 306; dissent re rodent search, 308–309; dissent re frisking suspects, 310, dissent re evidence in car, 311; dissent on narcotics convictions, 314, 319; dissent on fur search ruling, 314; dissent on informer ruling, 316; dissent on narcotics seller decision, 317–18; dissent on overruled fraud ruling, 319; opinion on Hoffa review, 320; dissent on wiretapping, 321; dissent on jury trial denial, 328; concurs on sit-in reversals, 330–31, 335; dissent on remand, 334; concurs on trespass reversal, 335; dissent in amusement park case, 337; concurs on breach of peace reversal, 338; concurs on segregation protest, 338; dissent on picketing rule, 339; dissent on jail trespass, 339; dissent on Mississippi statute, 340; dissent in part re rights, 341; dissent re jury selection, 343; concurs on miscegenation statute, 345; dissent re rules, 346; state poll tax held invalid by, 348–49; concurs on election day editorial ruling, 351; housing amendment held invalid by, 352; concurs invalidating NAACP ordinance, 354; concurs on NAACP lawyer hiring, 354; concurs on NAACP membership lists, 356; opinion on park segregation, 356–57; dissent re witnesses counsel, 378; dissent on investigators contempt, 378; dissent re remand, 379; concurs re television invalidity, 382; concurs re trial by jury, 385; opinion in recidivist reversal, 388; dissent re double jeopardy, 388; dissent re contempt, 389; dissent on defendant testimony ruling, 390; concurred on narcotics reversal, 394; dissent on alcoholism case, 395; dissent on jailing alcoholics, 395; dissent on Mapp rule opinion, 397; dissent re applying decisions retroactively, 398; dissent on state rule reversals, 399; concurs against film censorship, 400–402; dissent on film preshowing, dissent on obscenity regulation, 403–404; dissent on obscenity suits, 405; magazine held not obscene by, 405; concurs re censorship action, 407; film board decisions rejected by, 407; dissent on "girlie" magazine ruling, 407–408; concurs reversing obscenity conviction, 408; concurs on obscenity ruling, 410; dissent on Ginzburg conviction, 412–13; dissent on bookseller conviction, 414; opinion re districting complaint, 417; concurs remanding apportionment case, 418, 420; opinion on Georgia unit rule, 424; "one person one vote" opinion of, 424, 525; concurs rejecting Texas reapportionment, 431; dissent re gubernatorial decision, 432; concurs on Puerto Rican registration, 435; dissent re literacy requirement, 435–36; opinion re public disturbance, 440–41; dissent re speaker license, 424; dissent re disorderly conduct, 443; dissent on libelous leaflets, 443; concurs in libel decision, 444; concurs, dissents re libel, 444–45; concurs reversing defamation conviction, 446; concurs in *Life* libel ruling, 446–47; concurs in Walker decision, 447; dissent on Sunday closing, 448, 451–52, 454; concurs on "Supreme Being" term, 455; dissent on atheist certiorari, 455; dissent on Hatch Act, 456; opinion invalidating contraceptives statute, 457; dissent re labor jurisdiction, 461; dissent on right-to-work violation, 462; opinion on union-shop agreements, 463–64; concurs against steel takeover, 464; dissent on union indictment, 465; dissent re labor indictment, 466–67; concurs re union funds for politics, 467–68; dissent on bar dues, 469–71; dissent re expelled union member, 475; dissent on strike-breaker fine, 476; dissent on boycott, 477; concurs against UMW, 477; dissent re Sherman Act, 478; dissent on compensation, 478–79; concurs re Associated Press, 480; concurs re brewery assets, 481; appendix to opinion of, 481–83; concurs, dissents re rail merger opinion, 484; ruling on expansion merger, 485; dissent re electrocution, 487; argument with Stewart, 487; dissent on wife testimony, 488; dissent on income tax ruling, 489; dissent on deductible item, 490; concurs against tenant eviction, 492; dissent from certiorari denial, 492; dissent in draftee ruling, 492; dissent on draft card burner ruling, 494; dissent on retroactivity, 515; dissent on prospective holding, 515; partial dissent re corporate earnings tax, 518; dissent re picketing, 518; dissent on full crew (railroad) law, 518; on First Amendment, 520; certiorari vote in 21 cases, 527; dissent on lawyer disbarment, 528; dissent re obscenity, 528

Dow Chemical Company: 493
Draftees: 146; convictions affirmed, 256; certiorari denied, 492; exemption of, 519
Due process (amendment clauses): 12, 69, 80–81, 98–99, 114, 144, 149, 179–80, 191–92, 198, 202, 231–32, 235–38, 241, 256, 267, 280, 287, 292, 299, 305, 307–308, 325, 335, 338, 341, 345–46, 354, 366, 377–78, 381–82, 384, 387, 392–93, 450, 458–59, 462, 515–16; not applicable in Iowa liquor conviction, 82; defined, 85–87; of Fifth Amendment, 88; invoked by corporations, 99; of Fifth Amendment applied, 103–104; of Fourteenth Amendment violated, 104, 390; *see also* Fourteenth and Fifth Amendments
Dunham, Allison: 25, 55
Duvall, Justice Gabriel: 24–25, 33; dissent on New York bankruptcy law validity, 36

Eastland, Senator James O.: 285
Eavesdropping: evidence held inadmissible, 161; electronic, 161–67, 320, 363; Black statement on, 523 & n.; law on, struck down, 528; *see also* wiretapping
Eighteenth Amendment: 110, 523
Eighth Amendment: 12, 233, 291, 394; cruel and unusual punishment phrase of, 487; never held applicable to states, 487
Eisenhower, President Dwight D.: 218
Eleventh Amendment: adoption of, 21; suit prohibition of, 94–95; refuge provided by, 94–95; applied to state officers, 99
Elkins Act: 200
Embargo Act of 1808: 28
Employment agencies: 107–108, 110
Equal protection clause: 80–81, 141, 179, 191, 239, 252, 257, 290, 325, 341, 345–46, 348–50, 356, 417–24, 428–30, 436–38, 442, 462, 492, 496; denied, 180; violated, 196–97, 236, 256, 518; Sunday closing not violative of, 448; *see also* Fourteenth Amendment
Erie-Lackawanna Railroad: 484
Erie Railroad Company: 48, 395
Ervin, Senator (N.C.): opinion on Marshall, 511; on lawlessness, 526
Escobedo, Danny: 364–67, 370, 527; in decision on retroactive rule, 397–98; controversy on decision, 521; convicted on narcotics charge, 526
Espionage Act of 1917: 146–47, 150, 201; conviction of Rosenbergs, under, 285–86
Estes, Billie Sol: 145, 381
Evidence: 297–300, 315, 318–23, 375, 387, 390, 393, 485, 514, 517, 522 & n.; unlawful seizure of, 302, 516; illegally obtained, 304,

312, 516; blood sample in, 305, 379; swallowed morphine in, 305; in espionage, 306; narcotics in, 307, 313–14, 523; burglary tools in, 311; found in car admissible, 311; auto registration card in, 311; air rifle inadmissible in, 312; revolver inadmissible in, 312; heroin in, 313; gambling slips inadmissible in, 315–16; rifle in, 323; in Escobedo trial, 364, 366; handwriting in, 379; circumstantial, 393; see also search and seizure

Ex post facto laws: 67–68, 275

Extortion: 515

Fair Labor Standards Act: 135, 225; ruling under, 242–43

Fair trade laws: 133

FBI: agents, 166, 305, 321, 390; in espionage case, 306; crime rise reported by, 526

Faubus, Governor Orval: 326

Federal Commission on Civil Rights: 346

Federal Communications Act: 161, 448

Federal Communications Commission: 484

Federal Maritime Commission: 486

Federal Power Commission: 223

Federal rules of Criminal procedure: 314, 375

Federal Trade Commission: 158, 180, 183, 199, 485–86, 490, 494

Field, Cyrus W.: 63

Field, David Dudley: 63

Field, Justice Stephen J.: rule re diversified citizenship attacked by, 47; California court ruling reversed by, 53; dissent in bank tax increase, 54; appointment of, 62–63; background of, 63; opinion in loyalty oath cases, 67; dissent in reargued legal tender acts, 74; dissenting opinion on peacetime legal tender notes, 75; dissents in 1866–67, 78; dissenting opinion on Fourteenth Amendment application, 80; concurred in Iowa liquor case, 82; dissenting opinion in price fixing, 84; dissent in oleomargarine case, 85; dissent re due process, 86; nonparticipant in due process case, 87; dissent on Fifth Amendment due process violation, 88; dissent on railroad receipts tax, 88; dissent in peddler tax case, 88; dissent in telegraph company case, 88–89; opinion in interstate commerce case, 89; dissent in Negro murder conviction, 91; opinion on civil rights act, 92; opinion on Fourteenth Amendment re discrimination, 92; dissent in Virginia tax remedy, 94; concurring opinion on income tax, 137; dissent re alien deportation, 139; dissent in trial transfer, 154; dissent in deputy marshal ruling, 154; clash with

Judge Terry, 154; referred to by Douglas, 233–34

Fifteenth Amendment: 79–80, 89–90, 142, 197, 324, 424–25, 437; statute violative of, 346; voting registration tests invalidated under, 347

Fifth Amendment: 9, 11–12, 88, 103–104, 117, 127–29, 161, 231, 233, 260–61, 268, 274, 277, 281–83, 287, 292–93, 298, 303, 319, 322, 325, 359, 377, 379, 388–89, 398, 463, 528; thesis re Fifth and Fourteenth Amendments, 118; privilege of, made applicable to states, 119–21, 366, 388–89; violation of, 183; privileges taken by writers, 289; not applicable to states, 298; withdrawal of blood not violative of, 305

First Amendment: 12, 69, 149, 151, 207, 214, 228, 233, 268, 270, 274–75, 281–82, 184–85, 288, 290, 339, 354–55, 359, 404–405, 408–409, 412–14, 439, 442–43, 445–48, 453, 455, 457, 463–64, 467–69, 493; upheld in school transportation, 211; invalidated by religious teaching, 213; in school prayer ruling, 215–18; establishment clause of, 216, 449–50, 454, 518; free exercise clause of, 216, 219–20, 454; violation of, by post office, 290; editorial statute violative of, 351; motion picture protection of, 400–402; obscenity held not protected by, 403; amplifier use protected by, 439; rights violated under, 454; atheist denied certiorari under, 456; Julian Bond statements protected by, 457; "privacy" read into, 520

Flag pledge: 217; see also schools

Fletcher, Robert: 30

Florida: 88, 249–50, 528; sit-in convictions in, 335; miscegenation statute invalidated, 345; NAACP membership lists in, 355–56; reapportionment in, 431

Florida legislature: 355, 431

Florida State Penitentiary: 375

Ford, Paul Leicester: 23

Forrester, Mrs. Viola: 375

Fortas, Justice Abe: 14–15, 233, 320, 379, 483, 485, 511, 515, 518; dissent in habitual criminal cases, 14; dissent in inheritance tax case, 49; injunction violation sustained by, 158; dissent on deportation, 198; dissent on textbook lending, 215; dissent on Birmingham injunction, 229; opinion re inquiry reversal, 284; concurs in gun case dismissal, 308; dissent on informer ruling, 316; concurs on narcotics seller conviction, 317; concurs on overruled fraud decision, 318; concurs on breach of peace reversal, 338; concurs on segregation protest, 338; dissent on picketing rule, 339; dissent on jail trespass, 339; dissent on Mississippi statute, 340; concurred re rights, 341; opinion on violation of Fourteenth Amendment, 342; opinion re waiver, 376; opinion re juvenile delinquent, 377; dissent on alcoholism case, 394–95; dissent on jailing alcoholics, 395; opinion he habeas corpus, 399; dissent on "girlie" magazine ruling, 408; concurs on obscenity requirements, 410; dissent re gubernatorial decision, 432; dissent on state apportionment extension, 432–33; dissent on literacy requirement, 436; dissent re libel case, 444; dissent on *Life* libel ruling, 447; concurred re brewery assets, 481; dissent on rail merger opinion, 484; appointment of, 510; chief justice nomination of, 511, 514; nomination withdrawn, 512; dissent on prospective holding, 515; partial dissent on transcript inspection, 516; dissent re search and seizure, 517; concurred re price information, 519; certiorari vote in 11 cases, 527

Four Horsemen: 19, 107, 111, 143, 171, 195; *see also* Justices Sutherland, McReynolds, Butler, Van Deventer

Fourteenth Amendment: 9, 11, 63, 82–83, 85–87, 92–94, 198–99, 101, 107–108, 110, 112–13, 116–21, 124, 141–44, 149, 151, 173, 178–79, 191–92, 196, 198, 202, 204, 207, 213, 231–36, 256–57, 268, 274, 281, 284–85, 293, 299, 305, 307–308, 324, 330–31, 335, 338, 341–343, 346–47, 350–52, 354–55, 357–58, 361, 365, 367, 377–78, 381, 383–85, 387–88, 392–95, 400–401, 404, 406, 408–409, 417, 420, 422–24, 426, 428–31, 434, 436–38, 443, 450, 455, 458, 469, 487, 515, 523; not applicable to corporations, 12–13; discrimination forbidden by, 50; privileges and immunities clause of, 72–73, 81, 117; intended role of, 79; opinions on application of, 79–80; in Crescent City Company monopoly rule, 81; law practice right not defended by, 81; not applicable in Iowa liquor conviction, 82; state powers enlarged under, 82; civil rights negated under, 82; in price-fixing, 83–84; case totals, 1873–88, 86; only actions of state protected by, 90–91; equal protection provision violated, 105, 115; as "shorthand summary of first eight," 118–19, 235, 299; Bill of Rights incorporated by, 119, 522; provisions re Negroes, 139; violated by ordinance, 202; in school prayer case, 216; in religious exercise cases, 219–30; not applicable to states, 298–99; school desegregation

under, 324–29; obscenity not protected by, 403; rights violated under, 454

Fourth Amendment: 9, 12, 16, 120, 127–28, 159, 161–64, 233, 299–300, 303, 307–309, 313, 315, 317–19, 321–23, 359, 459, 522 & n.; seized evidence violative of, 297–99; not applicable to states, 298; believed applicable by Douglas, 300; ruled applicable to states, 302, 367, 395; withdrawal of blood not violative of, 305; search warranted under, 306; applicable by Fourteenth Amendment, 315

Francis, Willie: 487

Frank, Leo M.: 144–45

Frankfurter, Justice Felix: 4 & n., 7–10, 17 & n., 18, 65–66, 69, 73, 98, 118–19, 197, 206, 209, 215–24, 280, 283, 315, 332, 351, 362, 390, 393, 498, 501–507, 525; seriatim practice favored by, 23; opinion on court-martial trials, 65; dissent in manslaughter case, 65; Management Labor Relations Act of 1947 held valid by, 68; dissent re city loyalty oath, 68; opinion in federal sales tax case, 77, 98n.; brief submitted by, 102; concurred re California law ruling, 118; dissent, opinion in murder conviction reversal, 122–23; dissent in overruled citizenships, 153–54; dissent in Bridges decisions, 155; dissent re Bridges deportation, 1456; concurs re contempt reversal, 156–57; dissent in transmitter use, 162; opinion re stare decisis issue, 193; Cardozo replaced by, 194; concurs re amendment, 194; dissent in negligence case, 199; ruling on FTC case, 199; opinion on NLRB power, 199; dissent on civil liberties, 201; opinion re flag salute, 202–203, 207, 209; dissent re solicitation fee ordinance, 205–206; dissent re "I Am" decision, 209; dissent re jury lists, 211; dissent in school transport, 212; opinion religion in schools, 213–14; dissent on religious teaching outside school buildings, 214; dissenting opinion re radio patents, 222–23; dissent in FPC case, 223; dissent in liability ruling, 224–25; dissent on second miner pay ruling, 225; dissent on union member solicitation, 229; concurring opinion re UMW contempt, 230; dissent on labor disputes ruling, 230; opinion re counsel decision, 232; opinion re record transcripts, 236–37; opinion re labor act application, 242; dissent re insurance regulation, 243; opinion in gross income tax case, 244; dissenting opinion on boxing case, 246; dissent in football ruling, 247; Nevada divorce ruling by, 248; dissent in Florida, New York divorces, 249; dissent in Vermont decree, 250; dissent on alimony jurisdiction, 251; concurs in Japanese exclusion order, 253; concurs on draftee convictions, 256; dissent on district courts rule, 257; opinion re utility rate case, 257; dissent re estate tax, 258; concurs on bill attainder ruling, 260; concurs re security clearance, 260–61; dissent re naturalization cancellation, 262; dissent on deportation, 263; opinion on deportation order, 264; dissent on deportation defiance, 265; dissent on deportation suspension, 266; concurs on lawyer ruling, 267; Communist convictions upheld by, 271, 273; disbarment opposed by, 272; dissent on teacher affidavit, 274; Communist registration upheld by, 274; dissent on lawyer suspension, 278; opinion on due process violation, 280; witness conviction affirmed by, 282; dissent on witness questions, 284; dissent re execution stay, 286; dissent re contempt of Congress, 289; dissent re jury service, 289; concurs on Communist list ruling, 289; concurs re church property statute, 290; dissent re deserter citizenship, 291; concurs on Japanese citizenship reversal, 291; Fourteenth Amendment argument rejected by, 299; reversal opinion on federal search, 301; dissent re "silver platter" doctrine, 301; dissent on Fourteenth Amendment ruling, 302–304; dissent on search without warrant, 305; dissent on vacated narcotics conviction, 307; opinion re rodent search, 308; opinion re narcotics affidavit, 314; concurs on bus integration, 324; concurs rejecting integration suspension, 327; dissent re restaurant integration, 330; concurs on sit-in reversal, 330; witnesses counsel right rejected by, 378; opinion on defendant testimony, 390; concurs on FBI reports inspection, 391; concurs overruling film censorship, 400–401; opinion re obscenity regulation, 405; opinion on districting complaint, 416–17; dissent on remanding apportionment case, 418, 421–23; dissent on amplifier use, 439; dissent on sound tracks use, 440; dissent on public disturbance ruling, 440; speaking permit held invalid by, 442; concurs re free speech ruling, 442; concurs on disorderly conduct conviction, 443; opinion re libelous leaflets, 443; dissent on radio-television libel, 448; concurs re Sunday closing, 448, 450–52, 454; concurs voiding officeholder requirement, 455; dissent re solicitation permit, 456; dissent on handbill ordinance ruling, 456; concurs upholding Hatch Act, 456; opinion sustaining picketing injunction, 461; concurs upholding right to work, 462; right-to-work amendment upheld by, 463; opinion re union-shop agreements, 463–64; steel takeover opposed by, 464; dissent re antistrike law, 465; opinion upholding union indictment, 465–66; dissent re union funds for politics, 467; bar dues upheld by, 469; concurs re Associated Press, 480; dissent on drug resale prices, 481; concurs re electrocution, 487; opinion on husband-wife conspiracy, 488–89; concurs on income tax ruling, 489; dissent re tax refund, 495; retirement of, 507

Fraud: 150–51, 156, 209, 231, 262, 271, 290, 318; found in Bund case, 263; in income tax, 375

Frazier-Lemke amendment (to Bankruptcy Act): 183–84

Freedom of contract: 100–104, 172

Friends of the Lincoln Brigade: 203, 276

Fugitive Slave Law of 1793: upheld by court, 56, 58; declared unconstitutional by Wisconsin court, 58; see also slavery

Fulbright, Senator William: 493

Fuller Court: policy of, 11, 117; excesses of, 82–83; nationalistic powers proclaimed by, 99, 111; states' rights attitude of, 130; status of possessions argued by, 159; dissents in, 167; superlegislative efforts of, 525

Fuller, Chief Justice Melville W.: 19, 89, 132, 159, 500; appointment of, 98; death of, 98, 167; opinion re income tax ruling, 137; dissent in U.S. marshal decision, 154

Galileo: 3

Gallup poll: 323

Gamblers: 119, 162; conviction of, reversed, 316

Gangsters: 226

Garland, A. H., in loyalty oath case: 67–68

Garner, William: 90

Gas, natural: 38–39, 192, 223

Gault, Gerald: 376–77

Georgia: 95, 144, 357, 390, 492; civil rights challenged in, 247; poll tax in, 349; grand jury probe in, 351; county unit voting system invalidated, 424–26, 432, 525; apportionment statute struck down, 426; gubernatorial election in, 431–32

Georgia constitution: 431, 457

Georgia legislature: 29–31, 431–32; in Cherokee Indian case, 39, 61; act re Indian territory invalidated, 39–40; reapportionment of, 426; in Julian Bond case, 457

Georgia, University of, Athens, Ga.: 447

German-American Bund: 255

German newspapers: 148

Gibbon, Edward: 529n.

Ginzburg, Ralph: 411–12

Girard, Stephen: 49–50; will of, contested by relatives, 50–51

Gold: payments of, repudiated, 181–82; called in, 181; other litigation, 181–84, 188

Goldberg, Justice Arthur: concurs in religious exercises ruling, 219; concurs on right of confrontation, 235; ruling on indigent, 240; civil rights law upheld by, 247; concurs re issuing passports, 286–87; dissenting opinion re passports to Cuba, 288; concurs on postal violation, 290; concurs re citizenship provisions, 292; ruling re heroin search warrant, 313; dissent on fur search ruling, 314; opinion sustaining warrant, 315; dissent on jury trial denial, 328; concurs re trespass rulings, 334–35; opinion on rights leader reversal, 336; dissent re jury selection, 343–44; decision re NAACP membership lists, 355–56; opinion re Escobedo reversal, 364–65; concurs re television invalidity, 382; ruling on reversing obscenity conviction, 408; concurs in libel decision, 444; concurs re contraceptives, 457–58; nonparticipant in refund ruling, 471; employee lockout upheld by, 476–77; temporary layoff upheld by, 477; concurs against UMW, 477; decision re Sherman Act, 478; appointment of, 507; dissents by, 508; resignation of, 510

Grain elevators: 83–84

"Grandfather clause": see Negroes

Grange: 83–84, 96

Grant, President Ulysses S.: 63, 74

Gray, Justice Horace: 82, 85, 94, 159; dissent in peddler tax case, 88; dissent in interstate commerce case, 89; dissent in original package case, 89; dissent in Virginia bond cases, 95; dissent in Arlington tax sale, 96; dissent re legislative role, 99; replaced by Holmes, 100; death of, 131

"Great Dissenter": see Justice Oliver Wendell Holmes

Great Northern Railroad: 131

Greenglass, David: 286

Greenville, S.C.: 333

Gregory, Charles Noble: 63n.

Grier, Justice Robert C.: 51, 57, 60, 78; dissent in Texas statehood case, 74; resignation of, 74

Griffin, Eddie Dean: 121–22

Griffin, Ga.: 202

Habeas corpus, writ of: 27, 58–59, 61, 64–65, 91, 94, 102, 119, 228, 238, 240, 254–55, 359–61, 515–16, 519; denied to murder suspect, 144; sustained for U.S. marshal, 154; granted to Bridges, 156; denied to German nationals, 256; increase in applications for, 360; for Escobedo, 364; in federal courts, 399, 526

Habitual criminal statutes: 14; see also recidivists

Hague, Mayor Frank: 197

Hamilton, Alexander: opinion in Yazoo land cases, 30

Hand, Judge Learned: 6, 522n.

Harding, President Warren G.: 147

Harlan, Justice John Marshall, Jr.: 12, 14–15, 25, 66, 121, 126, 158, 236, 273, 313, 332, 494, 501–505, 507–11, 520 & n.; dissent in recidivist cases, 14; dissent in state tax collection case, 38; dissent in inheritance tax case, 49; opinion on court-martial trials, 65; dissent on manslaughter case, 65; dissent on loyalty oath statute, 69; Maryland loyalty oath defended by, 70; opinion re subversives statute case, 70–71; opinion re bar admittance ruling, 119; dissenting opinion in self-incrimination ruling, 120–21; concurs in Griffin murder reversal, 121; dissent re "harmless error" rule, 122; dissent in murder conviction reversal, 122; dissent in police officer convictions, lawyer disbarment cases, 124–25; opinion in testimony admissibility decision, 127; dissent re overruled contempt, 157; injunction violation sustained by, 158; dissent re jury trial for contempt, 158–59; dissent on wiretapping, 161; dissent re microphones, 163, 165; dissent re eavesdropping, 166, 528; dissent re taxpayer suit, 215; concurs re overruled counsel decision, 234; concurs on right of confrontation, 235; dissent on right of cross-examination, 236; dissenting opinion on record transcripts, 236, 238; dissent re indigents, 239–41; dissent re transcript reimbursement, 239; dissent in footfall ruling, 247; dissent re alimony, 251; concurs re security clearance, 261; concurs on lawyer ruling, 267; dissent on not deporting salesman, 267; opinion re benefits payment, 269; dissents on deportation, 270–71; dissent re deportation evidence, 271; opinion re Communist contempt, 273; opinion on Smith Act violation, 273; dissent on teacher affidavit, 274; dissent on remand, 275; dissent on labor act section, 276; dissent on Communists in defense plants, 277; dissent on lawyer suspension, 278; on due process violation, 280; witness conviction affirmed by, 282; dissent on vacating contempt convictions, 283; dissent on witness questions, 284; dissent on rule violation, 284; dissent re Louisiana statute, 284–85; dissent on withholding passports, 286; dissent re issuing passports, 286; concurs on postal violation, 290; dissent re loss of citizenship, 291; dissent re deserter's citizenship, 291; dissent on Japanese citizenship reversal, 291; dissent re citizenship provisions, 292; dissenting opinion on vote abroad, 293; dissent re "silver platter" doctrine, 301; dissent on Fourteenth Amendment ruling, 302–304; concurs on withdrawal of blood, 305; dissent on vacated narcotics conviction, 307; dissent re inspectors' warrant, 309; concurs re evidence in car, 311; dissent on robbery conviction reversal, 312; dissent on "harmless error," 312; dissent on search, 315; dissenting opinion on gambler ruling, 316; robber conviction reversal explained by, 321–23; concurs on school closing decision, 326; dissent on segregation avoidance, 327; concurs on prison desegregation, 329; dissent on restaurant integration, 330; concurs on sit-in reversal, 330–33, 335; dissent re demonstration, 334; dissent on park trespass, 334; dissent on restaurant trespass, 334; dissent on trespass reversal, 335; dissent on sit-in reversal, 335–36; dissent on picketing, 336–37; dissent on antipicketing statute, 337; opinion re rights, 341–42; concurs re jury selection, 343; concurs on miscegenation statute, 345; concurs on voting rights complaint, 346; concurs invalidating registration tests, 347; Twenty-fourth Amendment held constitutional by, 348; dissent on state poll tax ruling, 348, 350; concurs on election day editorial ruling, 351; dissent on sheriff contempt reversal, 351; dissent on housing amendment, 352; dissent on property discrimination, 353; dissent on NAACP lawyers, 354–55; dissent re union lawyer hiring, 355; dissent re NAACP membership lists, 356; dissent re park segregation, 356–58; dissent on picketing, 358; dissent re murder conviction, 359–60; dissent re voluntariness of confession, 361; dissent re confession, 362; dissent re absence of counsel, 363–64; dissent on Escobedo reversal, 364–65; dissent involving police practices, 366, 370–73; Miranda decision criticized by, 372–73; dissent on tax fraud reversal, 375; dissent on waiver decision, 376; partial dissent on juvenile ruling, 377; witnesses counsel rejected by, 378; concurs in part re remand, 379; dissent re robber, 379; concurs on tele-

vision invalidity, 382; dissent on murder reversal, 384; dissent re trial by jury, 384–86; dissent re jury coercion, 387; dissent re second degree murder reversal, 388; dissent on recidivist reversal, 388; concurs on FBI reports disclosure, 391; dissent on vacating robber conviction, 391–92; concurs on coparticipant testimony, 392–93; dissent on rape reversal, 393; concurs on narcotics reversal, 394; concurs re applying decisions retroactively, 397; dissent re voluntariness ruling, 398; concurs re habeas corpus, 399; concurs invalidating censorship, 401; dissents, concurs re obscenity regulation, 403–404; concurs on obscenity suits, 405; magazines held not obscene by, 405–406; dissent re censorship action, 407; dissent re film board decisions, 407; dissent on obscenity rulings, 410–12; dissent on Ginzburg conviction, 412, 414; dissent on remanding apportionment case, 418, 423–24; dissent re Georgia unit rule, 424–26; dissent re "one man one vote," 427; dissent on Alabama apportionment rule, 428–29; concurs invalidating California apportionment, 430–31; dissent on Florida, Texas reapportionment rule, 431; dissent on state apportionment extension, 432–33; dissent on serviceman's voting rights, 434; dissent on Puerto Rican registration, voting, 435–38; dissents, concurs re libel case, 444–45; concurs reversing criminal libel, 446; opinion in Walker decision, 447; opinion awarding damages, 447–48; dissent on radio-television libel, 448; concurs on Sunday closing, 448, 452, 454; dissent on Seventh-Day Adventist rule, 454–55; concurs voiding officeholder requirement, 455; concurs invalidating handbill ordinance, 456; concurs re contraceptives, 457–58; dissent re union funds for politics, 467; bar dues upheld by, 469–70; dissent on union refund, 471; dissent on strike-breaker fine, 476; concurs against UMW, 477; decision re Sherman Act, 478; dissent on compensation, 478–79; dissent on damages, 481; dissent on drug resale prices, 481; concurs re brewery assets, 481; dissent re merger exclusion, 483; dissent re bank merger act, 483; dissents, concurs re merger, 483; dissent on rail merger opinion, 484; concurs against expansion merger, 485; dissent re competition, 485; dissent on price-fixing, 485; dissent re underwriting costs, 486; dissent on jury exclusion, 488; concurs on income tax ruling, 489; dissent on FTC order, 491; dissent re paint company ruling, 491; dissent re tax refund, 495; opinion on damages ruling, 496; appointment of, 500; dissent on prospective holding, 515; concurs on speedy trial ruling, 515; concurs on murder reversal, 515; dissent on habeas corpus proceedings, 516; dissent re due process violation, 516; dissent re transcript inspection, 516; dissent re search and seizure, 517; partial dissent re corporate earnings tax, 518; concurs on evolution teaching, 518; dissent re price information, 519

Harlan, Justice John M., Sr.: 4, 17–18, 85, 159, 233, 325, 353; monopoly rejected by, 81; appointed in 1877, 82; dissent in due process case, 87; dissent on foreign insurance company tax, 87; dissent on challenges, 87; dissent in U.S. case against railroads, 87; opinion in interstate commerce case, 89; dissent re original package case, 89; dissent re civil rights act application, 92–94; civil rights dissents of, 97; dissent in Lochner case, 101; freedom of contract upheld by, 103; dissent re Sherman Act application, 130–31; on "rule of reason," 132–33; dissent re real estate income tax, 136; personal property income tax favored by, 136; opinion re income tax, 137; dissent re segregation ruling, 140–41

Harlan Fiske Stone: Pillar of the Law: 15, 17, 172n., 185n., 221 n.

"Harmless error" rule: 122, 312, 379

Hatch Act: 456

Hawaii: 159, 278, 429, 434

Hay, John: 61 n.

Hendrick, Lillie Shaver: 248

Henry, Patrick: 3

Hepburn decision: 74–76, 78; *see also* legal tender

Hill, George Washington: 175–76

Hiss, Alger: 259

Hobbs Act: purpose of, 226–27

Hoffa, James R.: jury bribe attempt of, 163, 319; conviction of, 319–20; case remanded, 517

Hoffer, Eric: 524 & n.

Holmes, Justice Oliver Wendell: 4, 6–7 & n., 10–11, 13, 39, 77, 82, 107, 109, 111, 124–25, 133, 145–46, 150, 155–56, 159, 171, 178, 191, 228, 246, 308, 446, 463, 527–28; called "The Great Dissenter," 3, 18–19, 167; dissent on invalidity of state tax on U. S. securities, 37; oil and gas revenues held not taxable, 38; oil and gas income held taxable, 39; succeeded by Cardozo, 39, 171; diversified citizenship rule attacked by, 47; dissent in taxicab case, 48; appointment of, 100; extremists challenged by, 100, 116; Lochner

decision dissent of, 100–101; dissent, opinion in nonunion strikes, 103; dissent on boycott, 103; dissent on congressional statute ruling, 104; dissent re Kansas statute invalidity, 104; concurs on peaceful picketing, 105; dissenting opinion re peaceful picketing reversal, 105; dissent in union injunction case, 106; dissenting opinion in minimum wage case, 107; dissent in employment agency fee case, 108; dissenting opinion in employment agency regulation, 108; concurs re workmen's compensation act, 108; dissent re ticket price statute, 109, 180; rent control decisions of, 110–11; dissent re foreign language teaching, 111–12; dissent re bread weight regulation, 112; dissent on opinion re gifts statute, 112–13; dissent on shoddy decision, 113; dissent in licensing statute ruling, 113; dissent re chain drugstore ruling, 113–14; dissent re licensing, 114; opinion in coal mining decision, 114; dissent in mortgage recording tax decision, 115; Migratory Bird Treaty act held valid by, 115–16; sterilization of imbeciles upheld by, 116; dissent in rail merger, 131–32; dissent on invalidated agreements, 133; dissent in trade association cases, 134; dissent, opinion re child labor act, 134–35; judges held taxable by, 138; dissent re peonage case, 141; concurs in second peonage case, 141; concurs re separate but equal rule, 141; dissent, opinion in murder suspect case, 144; opinion re Negro trials, 144; formula re espionage, 146, 201; Debs conviction justified by, 147; dissent re garment worker conviction, 148; dissent re German publications, 148; dissent in pamphlet distributor conviction, 149; dissent in Socialist conviction, 149; dissent re mailing privilege, 150–51; dissent on fraud order, 151; dissent in citizenship denial, 152, 154, 262; dissent in naturalization decision, 152, 154; dissent re contempt ruling, 155–56; quoted by Black, 155; dissent re wiretapping, 160

Holmes and the Constitution: 4 & n., 17n.

Holmes-Pollock Letters: see Mark DeWolfe

Home Owners' Loan Corporation: 76; *see also* taxation

"Hot oil": 181, 183–84

House Special Committee to Investigate Campaign Expenditures, 1945 report of: 466

House Un-American Activities Committee: 259, 268, 282–84; Hollywood writers before, 289

Housing Authority: 491

Housing, open: 110, 351, 435, 491, 518, 524; California legislation invalidated, 352, 523;

discrimination in sales, rentals banned, 353; discrimination in sales, rentals upheld, 353; eviction from, 515

Houston Police Department: 312

Hughes, Chief Justice Charles Evans: 4, 11, 17, 188, 195–96, 199, 202, 221; joined in voiding Missouri tax statute, 37; tax on school land income upheld by, 39; dissent re Kansas statute invalidity, 104; minimum wage law held valid by, 107; concurs in ice sale licensing decision, 111; separate but equal rule applied by, 141; Texas statute held invalid by, 143; dissent in murder suspect case, 144; ruling in newspaper case, 151; dissent in citizenship denial, 152–53; dissent in overruled citizenship, 154; resignation of, 168, 171, 201; both liberal, conservative, 171–73; 177; decision re fire insurance statute, 172; tax statutes rulings by, 172; ICC overruled by, 172; on hardship case, 174; vote on tobacco company case, 176; concurs in corporate assessments, 176–77; vote re insurrection, 177; on minimum wage rulings, 178–79; opinion re mortgage case, 179–80; milk law upheld by, 180; gold payments repudiated by, 181; dissent re retirement act, 182; 1934 record of, 183–84; decision on coal act, 186; opinion in livestock rate ruling, 186–87; decision in law school case, 196; dissent in railroad line case, 200; vote re alien act, 200

Hughes Court: 111, 116, 151, 171–73

Humphrey, Vice President Hubert H.: 474

Hunter, David: 32

Hunt, Justice Ward: 82; dissent in railroad receipts tax, 88; dissent in Negro voter case, 90

"I Am" (religious movement): 209–11

Ice: sale licensing of, 111, 180; in nonunion sales, 461

Idaho: 102

Illinois: 56, 81, 83, 119, 153, 236, 355, 378, 386, 416, 481; state child labor law approved, 102; tax statute struck down, 180

Illinois Supreme Court: 355

Imbeciles: 116

Immigration: 43, 306; statutes voided in New York, Louisiana, California, 43

Immigration Act of 1917: 265

Immigration and Nationality Act of 1952: 198, 267, 271, 292; provision invalidated, 290, 292

Immigration and Naturalization Service: 156

Immunity Act of 1954: 280

Income tax: 76–77, 490, 495; held unconstitutional, 136–37; decisions re judges, 138–

39; statute struck down, 172; fraud in, 375; on embezzled money, 489; see also taxation

Indiana: 240, 244, 431

Indiana circuit court: 64

Indians: in Georgia land sales case, 29, 31; cases re Cherokees, 39–40, 61; moved to Indian Territory, 40; minerals tax on lands of, 258

Informers: 313–16, 320

Inheritance tax: 116, 199; statutes struck down, 172; see also taxation

Injunctions: 102–103, 105, 141, 260, 405, 461, 464; union injunction upheld, 106; violation upheld, 158; CIO upheld, 197; upheld in Birmingham case, 229; violated by Mississippi officials, 327–28; on voting rights, 347–48

Insanity, legal: 10, 394

Insurance Workers International Union: 471

Integration: in schools, 196–97, 325–29; in interstate travel, 247, 324, 330, 332; in parks, 328, 337; of public accommodations, 248, 329–32, 335; see also Negroes and schools

Internal revenue: 154

Internal Security Act: 263, 275

International Boxing Club: 246

International Telephone and Telegraph Corporation: 484

Interstate commerce: 72, 84–85, 88–90, 102–103, 106, 132–34, 136, 199, 243, 305, 324, 332, 341; coal marketing in, 186; truckers in, 227–28; travelers in, 247–48

Interstate Commerce Act: 330

Interstate Commerce Commission: 172–73, 201, 242, 484

Intrastate commerce: coal mining held intrastate business, 106; Fifth Amendment in intrastate law, 118; monopoly of intrastate production, 130; milk control act under, 180; Negro travel in, 332

Invasion of privacy: 314, 457–58, 520

Inventions: 96

Iowa: 13, 63, 82, 109

Iredell, Justice James: 20

I.W.W.: 170

Jackson, Justice Howell E.: 18; income tax favored by, 136–37

Jackson, Justice Robert H.: 4 & n., 10, 12–13, 16, 18, 28n., 69, 73, 156, 209, 221, 226, 230, 255, 351, 395, 418, 456; views on federal court decisions, 4, 10; Management Labor Relations Act of 1947 held valid by, 68; opinion on commerce clause violation, 72; opinion in telegraph message ruling, 135–36;

transmitter use upheld by, 161–62; opinion re gas litigation, 192; dissent on civil liberties, 201; dissent re solicitation fee ordinance, 205; dissent re literature distribution, 206; dissenting opinion re religious literature, 206–207; opinion in flag salute ruling, 207; dissenting opinion re "I Am" decision, 209–11; dissent re jury lists, 211; dissenting opinion in school transport, 211–13; concurs re religion in schools, 213; dissent, opinion re religious teaching outside school buildings, 214–15; feud with Black, 221; dissent in FPC case, 223; dissent in liability ruling, 224; dissent in second miner pay ruling, 225; dissent re trucker unionization, 227–28; concurs on union member solicitation, 228–29; concurs re UMW contempt, 230; opinion re counsel decision, 232; opinion re penalty under AAA, 242–43; dissent in commerce case, 243; opinion re insurance regulation, 243–44; dissent in Nevada divorce, 248; dissent on New York divorce, 249–50; Nuremberg trials prosecutor, 252; dissenting opinion re Japanese exclusion order, 253–54; decision re treason, 255; dissent re Bund, 255; dissent on fishing license statute, 256; war crimes ruling of, 256; opinion re utility rates, 257; dissent on corporate share tax, 258; rule re estate tax, 258; rejoins court, 259; deportation upheld by, 264; dissent on deportation defiance, 265; Communist convictions upheld by, 271; disbarment opposed by, 272; concurs re jury service, 289; concurs on Communist list ruling, 289; dissent re church property statute, 290; dissent on search without warrant, 305; concurs overruling film censorship, 400; dissent on amplifier use, 439–40; dissent on sound tracks use, 440; dissent on public disturbance ruling, 440–42; dissent re free speech ruling, 442–43; dissent on libelous leaflets, 443; concurs on picketing injunction, 461; steel takeover opposed by, 464; error admitted by, 486; death of, 500; on judicial power, 522

Jackson, President Andrew: Marshall opinion resented by, 40, 61; Indians moved by, 40; court defied by, 40; nullification proclamation issued by, 40, 42; opinion of court actions, 42; injunction sought against, 66

Japanese: World War II decisions on, 252–56; California land ownership of, 256; citizenship loss of, 291

Jay, Chief Justice John: 20

Jefferson Papers: 22

Jefferson, President Thomas: 3, 21–23, 26–27, 31, 212, 422; seriatim opinions favored by, 23–24; in Aaron Burr treason case, 27–28; seizure of ship challenged, 28–29; Johnson action criticized by, 34; quoted, 493

Jehovah's Witnesses: 18, 201, 440; litigation on permits for, 202, 204–205, 442; flag salute forbidden by, 202; literature distribution by, 204–205, 209; licensing cases of, 204–206, 442; child labor law violation of, 209

Johnson, Justice William: 7, 22, 24–25, 34, 36, 40, 178; first of noted dissenters, 16, 26; seriatim opinions favored by, 23–24; appointment of, 26; clashes with Jefferson, 26, 28–29; first dissent of, 26; death of, 26, 35; habeas corpus jurisdiction opposed by, 27; writ of mandamus granted by, 28; legislative superiority upheld by, 28–29; commerce clause upheld by, 29; dissent in Yazoo land cases, 29–30; Nereide case decided by, 31–32; legislative over judicial power upheld by, 31–32; dissent in U.S.–Virginia court clash, 32; dissent in bank tax case, 34–35; dissent re bills of credit, 35; dissent re New York bankruptcy law validity, 36; opinion on taxed federal indebtedness, 37

Johnson, President Andrew: appointee seating avoided by Congress, 62; Reconstruction policies of, 64, 66; Garland pardon signed by, 67; out of office, 1870, 74; appointments prevented, 512

Johnson, President Lyndon B.: court appointments of, thwarted by Senate, 62–63; wiretapping directive of, 160; appointments withdrawn by, 512

Judicial Code: 360

Judicial Mind, The: Attitudes and Ideologies of Supreme Court Justices: 520 n.

Juries, grand and petit: 14, 87, 91–92, 126, 128–29, 157, 177, 209ff., 231, 236, 289, 297, 330, 345, 351, 361, 383, 394, 399, 447, 473, 485, 487, 489; grand jury witness held in contempt, 157; grand jury civil contempt upheld, 158; bribe attempt on, 163, 319–20, 345; Negroes excluded from, 177, 343; question in "I Am" decision, 211; service by government employees, 289; Mississippians, denied trial by, 328; prejudices of, 341; trial by, 384–88, 405

Juveniles: 376–77; Fortas decision on, 377; in lower courts, 377–78

Kansas: 85, 104; insurance rate regulation upheld, 109; on child labor amendment, 194

Kansas City stockyards: 186

Kansas-Nebraska Act: 56

Kennedy, President John F.: 217, 472
Kennedy, Senator Robert F.: 160–61, 167, 374, 376, 379–80, 474, 526
Kentucky: 35, 45, 47–48, 63; mortgage recording tax struck down, 115; tax question raised by judge in, 138
Kidnaping: 122, 128–29, 372
King, Martin Luther: 229, 352–53
Korean War: 259, 464
Korematsu, Fred (Japanese American): 253
Ku Klux Klan: 191, 341; leader sentenced, 343
Kurland, Philip B.: 25, 55

Lady Chatterley's Lover (film): 400–401
Labor: Lochner decision, 8, 100–101; Oregon ten-hour law defended, 8; eight-hour day for miners upheld, 100; freedom of contract defined, 101; Oregon ten-hour law approved, 101; child labor law approved, 101; fifty-four hour week approved, 101; Oregon hours for men approved, 101; contracts, 102–103; non-union strikes not permitted, 103; rule on boycott by pickets, 103; Sherman Anti-Trust Act applied to, 106; union held liable for damages, 106; employment agencies for, 107–108; eight-hour day wages upheld, 136; labor act held invalid, 134; Bridges in labor movement, 156; minimum wage law struck down, 178; minimum wage law upheld, 179; coal act struck down, 186; CIO upheld, 197; union cases decided, 225–27, 229–30; injunction forbidden, 229; Communists on, boards, 276; injunctions sustained, 461; right-to-work laws, 462–63; in politics, 467–69, 471–75; unfair practices argued, 476–77
Labor-Management Reporting and Disclosure Act: 259, 276
Lamar, Justice Joseph R.: 109; concurs re separate but equal rule, 141; death of, 168
Lamar, Justice Lucius Q. C.: 82; dissenting opinion re legislative role, 99; dissent in U.S. marshal decision, 154
Lausche, Senator Frank: 474
Law: 7–8, 10, 24, 46, 49, 63, 67, 101, 105, 113, 143, 160, 179, 182, 193, 197, 210, 224, 230–31, 236, 262, 285–86, 314, 394, 396, 441, 488, 525; lag of, 8; statutory, substantive law viewed, 46–49; international, 264; criticism of, 278; criminal law enforcement, 359, 365–66, 368, 375–80, 394, 405, 522 & n., 528; common law rule, 390, 395, 515; postal, 403; of libel, 444
Law and Literature: 15n., 17n.
Lawyers: 63–64, 127, 153, 157, 183, 231, 240, 292, 320–21, 363–64, 378, 395, 469, 514,

527–28; loyalty oath case of, 67; bar admittance rulings on, 119, 267; disbarment upheld, 119; disbarment overruled, 124–25; denied certiorari, 126, 527; convicted for contempt, 272–73; disbarred, 272–73; woman's suspension reversed, 278; furnished by NAACP, 354–55; new rules for, 354; dues upheld, 469
Lee, General Robert E.: 96
Lee, George W. P. C.: 96
Legal tender: acts challenged, 74; acts held constitutional, 74; Hepburn decision further followed, 75–76; notes upheld for peacetime, 75; specie payment in lieu of notes upheld, 75; dissents on, 78
Legislative action: 11, 29, 35, 83, 85, 95, 98, 103, 108–109, 111, 192, 257, 285, 493, 521; clash with judicial power, 83; landmark cases cited, 84; 228 acts set aside by court, 98; "yellow-dog contracts" not invalidated by, 102; foreign language teaching forbidden by, 111; ineffective, 524
Legislature: 51–63, 67, 71, 75, 81, 83, 86, 98–100, 107–108, 110, 113, 115, 143, 179, 202–203, 239, 282, 350, 408–409, 424, 449, 451, 465, 475, 518; reapportionment of, 418, 426–27, 429–31
Letters and Other Writings of James Madison: 24
Lewis, John L.: 230
Libel: 261, 443, 528; of public officials, 444–45; *New York Times* rule of, 444; radio-television station in, 448
Liberals, liberalism: 4, 15, 119, 124, 148, 152, 157, 170–74, 178–82, 188, 190, 196, 229, 251–52, 274, 395, 498, 525; 1931–32 court tally of, 173; 1943–45 court tally of, 251–52; in Warren Court, 520–21
License cases: 23, 59, 73, 88, 108, 113, 278, 442; fees for hunting and fishing, 73; Oklahoma licensing statute invalidated, 111, 114; Jehovah's Witnesses fee upheld, 203–204; fishing license statute invalidated, 256; of film showings, 400–402
Life Magazine: 447
Lincoln, President Abraham: 5, 57–58, 61–62, 64, 218
Lindberg, Charles A.: 128
Lipscomb, Andrew A.: 24
Liquor: 89, 159; control board seizure of, 304
Little Rock, Ark.: 201, 326
Little Rock, Ark., School Board: 326–27
Living Law, The: 8
Lochner decision: 8, 100; *see also* labor
Lord's Prayer: 219

Los Angeles, Calif.: 456

Los Angeles County, Calif.: 261

Lotteries: 54, 110; lottery ticket transport prohibited, 132

Louisiana: 36, 43, 90, 95, 284–85, 330–33, 338, 487, 496; statute forbidding discrimination invalidated, 90–91; Civil Rights Act of 1870 violated by, 143; election officers indictment upheld, 199–200; registration tests invalidated, 346–47; penalty for battery in, 384–85

Louisiana constitution: 90

Louisiana subversive activities law: declared unconstitutional, 284

Louisville and Nashville Railroad: 47

Lovell, Alma: 202–203

Lovers, The (film): 408

Loyalty oath: 67–68, 153, 259; World War I cases of, 68; security program re government employees, 68; city ordinance upheld, 68; required of political candidate, 68; Arizona statute struck down, 69; minority opinion on Arizona statute, 69; Oklahoma statute struck dawn, 69; in Julian Bond case, 457

Lurton, Justice Horace H.: dissent in peonage case, 141; death of, 168

Luther, Martin: 3

Lynch law: 144

McCarran Internal Security law: 259

McCarthyism: 68

McCarthy, Senator Eugene: 474

McCarthy, Senator Joseph: 259

McClellan, Senator John: 526

MacIntosh, Douglas: 151–54, 171–72

McKenna, Justice Joseph: 104, 109, 159; dissent in employment agency fee case, 108; dissent in rent control decisions, 110; replaced by Stone, 111, 134; dissent in trade association case, 134

McKinley, Justice John: 45–47, 55

McLean, Justice John: 23, 25, 35–36, 40–41, 55–57, 59–60; opinion on court jurisdiction, 42; federal rights in extradition of foreigners upheld by, 44; corporate tax exemption upheld by, 51; death of, 62

Macon, Ga.: 356–57

McReynolds, Justice James C.: 19, 39, 49, 107, 109, 112, 135, 138, 171, 195, 221; dissent in HOLC tax case, 76; dissent in Oregon labor case, 102; opinion upholding fees from workers, 107; dissent in rent control decisions, 110; dissent in licensing statute decision, 113; dissent in trade association ruling, 134; dissent re hour, wage regulation, 136; concurs re separate but equal rule, 141;

murder case cited in dissent of, 144; dissent re corporate assessments, 177; dissent re rape case, 177; dissent on milk ruling, 180; dissent re gold, 182; dissent on TVA project, 186; decision on bankruptcy act, 186; dissent on stare decisis issue, 193; dissent re amendment, 194; retirement of, 195; dissenting opinion in law school case, 196–97; dissent in registration ruling, 197; dissent in CIO ruling, 198; vote on alien act, 200; concurs re flag salute, 202; *see also* Four Horsemen

Madison, President James: 23–24, 31, 218, 426

Magnuson Act: 277

Maine: 188, 429

Management Labor Relations Act of 1947; provisions of, 68; held valid, 68

Mandamus, writs of: 28, 32, 91, 194, 353

Mann Act: 488

Marchetti (gambler): 127

Marconi, Guglielmo: 222–23

Marshall, Chief Justice John: 5-7, 10, 32, 34–36, 40–41, 43, 55, 60–63, 78, 131, 416; court concept of, 11, 32, 522; on opinions seriatim, 21; court control by, 22–23; dissent deprecated by, 23–26; two dissents by, 24; dissent avoided by, 25; treason defined by, 27–28; opinion in Yazoo land cases, 31; opinion in Nereide case, 31; case deferred by, 35; death of, 35, 41; state bankruptcy law upheld by, 36; dissent on New York bankruptcy law validity, 36; opinion in Cherokee Nation case, 39; compared with Taney, 42; Dartmouth College case doctrine followed by, 43; slavery views of, 54–55; majority of four rule of, 74

Marshall, Justice Thurgood: 126, 128, 236, 311, 321, 343, 399, 432, 478, 483, 486, 494, 511–12, 515–16, 518–19; dissent on state tax collection ruling, 38; Mississippi statute upheld by, 339; film board decisions negated by, 407; appointment of, 511–12; nonparticipation of, 512; dissent on price information, 519

Marshall land syndicate: 32

Maryland: 13–14, 56, 68, 70, 88, 181, 231, 448–50, 452; school religious exercises in, 218–20; park picketing in, 334; disorderly conduct convictions in, 337; censorship statute struck down, 402

Maryland constitution: 455

Maryland, University of, College Park, Md.: 70

Mason, Alpheus Thomas: 15, 17, 172n., 185n., 221 n.

Massachusetts: 13, 38, 44, 102, 203, 249, 308, 450; Sunday laws in, 454

Mathews, Justice Stanley: 82, 86–87, 94; opinion in Virginia bond case, 95

Meaning of Meaning, The: 9

Meany, George: 474

Memoirs of a Woman of Pleasure (Fanny Hill): 410–12, 414

Memorandum decisions: 78; by Frankfurter, 285

Memphis, Tenn.: 328

Meredith, James: 328

Mergers: of breweries, 481–82; of banks, 483–84; of communications systems, 484; of railroads, 484–85; conglomerate, 485

Messages and Papers of the Presidents: 40, 42, 46, 58

Michigan: 143, 481

Migratory Bird Treaty Act: 115

Military Selective Service Act of 1967: 519

Military, U. S.: 29, 61, 64, 89ff., 150, 153, 255, 492ff.; military tribunal cases of, 64–66, 519; laws enacted for, 66; chaplains of, 218; in decisions re Japanese, 253–54; troops in Little Rock, 326

Milk Control Board: 180

Miller, Justice Samuel F.: 62–63, 75, 78, 82, 89, 98; background of, 63; chief dissenter after Johnson, 63; dissent in loyalty oath cases, 67; dissent in Texas statehood case, 74; dissent in Hepburn decision, 74; dissenting opinion in specie payment case, 75–76; opinion on Fourteenth Amendment in slaughter house case, 79–81; due process defined by, 85–86; opinion in U.S. case against railroads, 87; dissent on railroads receipts tax, 88; dissent in B&O charter case, 88; dissent in Virginia bond cases, 95; Arlington estate sale held invalid by, 96; opinion on legislative role, 98–99

Miller, Phineas: in Yazoo land speculation, 30

Milligan decision: 61, 64; held inapplicable to belligerents, 64; other applications of, 64–66

Milwaukee Leader: 150–51

Minersville, Pa.: 202, 204

Minimum wages: 106–107, 178–79

Minnesota: 150–51; psychopathic statute upheld, 198

Minnesota mortgage moratorium law: 179–80

Minton, Justice Sherman: 65, 500–501; dissent in Bridges conspiracy ruling, 156; dissent on record transcripts, 236; dissent on boxing case, 246; opinion re Ohio divorce, 250; appointment of, 259; dissent on summary discharge, 260; disbarment favored by, 272;

dissent on sedition reversal, 273; dissent on Communist list ruling, 289; dissent re disorderly conduct, 443; dissent on picketing injunction, 461; dissent re steel takeover, 464; dissent re trainmen bargainers, 475; retirement of, 502

Miranda decision: one of four reversals, 366–76; Harlan review, criticism of, 372, 515; new rule established by, 372; White criticism of four reversals, 373–74; rule challenged by Congress, 374, 526; McChan case affected by, 374–75; defended by Black, 375; in decision on retroactive rule, 397–99; controversy on, 521, 526

Mirsky, Jeanette: 29

Miscegenation: 345–46

Mississippi: 66, 85, 339, 342; voting rights complaint upheld, 346

Mississippi constitution, held ineffectual in slavery issue: 55

Mississippi, University of, University, Miss.: 327, 447

Missouri: 13, 32, 35, 37, 56–57, 67, 87–88, 465; inheritance tax claims denied, 116

Missouri Compromise Act: 56–57; held unconstitutional, 57

Missouri legislature: 35, 37

Missouri, University of, Columbia, Mo.: 196–97

Mr. Justice: 25, 55

Mr. Justice Holmes and the Supreme Court: 98n.

Mr. Justice William Johnson and the Constitution: 22, 24–26, 28, 30–31, 34

Mobile, Ala.: 95

Monopolies: 79, 81, 88, 130; Crescent City company monopoly invalidated, 81; by breweries, 481

Montgomery, Ala.: 444

Moody, Justice William H.: 117

Mora, Dennis: 492

Morgan, Donald E.: 22, 24–26, 28, 30–31, 34

Mortgages: 179, 181

Municipal Bankruptcy Act of 1934: 186

Murder: 65–66, 86–87, 91, 144, 154, 341 ff., 359, 361, 378, 384, 387, 393, 398, 487; Palko contention overruled, 117–18; of civil rights workers, 342–43

Murphy, Justice Frank: 65, 77, 200, 205–206, 223–24, 233, 245, 456; concurs on commerce clause violation, 72; dissent re California law ruling, 118; dissent in telegraph message case, 135–36; dissent in Illinois lawyer decision, 153; opinion re Bridges deportation, 156; concurs in contempt reversal, 156; Butler replaced by, 195; opinion on tax ruling, 199; dissent in negligence case, 199; dissent in interest ruling, 199; dissent on licensing, 204; dissent re child labor case, 209; dissent re antitrust violations, 227; dissent on UMW contempt, 230; jury trial waiver rejected by, 231; dissent on counsel denials, 231–32; dissent on state sales tax, 244; concurs in Nevada divorce ruling, 248; dissent in Florida divorce, 249; concurs in Japanese student ruling, 252; dissent in Japanese exclusion order, 253; concurs re Japanese detention, 254; dissent re Japanese hanging, 255–56; dissent on draftee convictions, 256; concurs in land ownership ruling, 256; concurs on fishing license invalidity, 256; death of, 259; opinion re naturalization cancellations, 262; dissent on denaturalization, 263; dissent re federal rule for states, 299–300; opinion re districting complaint, 417; dissent re sound tracks use, 440; concurs on right to work, 462; dissent on right-to-work amendment, 463; dissent re Associated Press, 480; dissent re electrocution, 487

NAACP: 353–56; see also Alabama, Arkansas, Virginia, Florida, lawyers
Narcotics: 26, 307, 312–14, 317, 319, 363, 523; opinion on addiction, 393
National Bankruptcy Act: 183, 186
National Day of Prayer: 218
National Firearms Act: 126–27
National Football League: 246
National Industrial Recovery Act: 181–85
National Labor Relations Act: 278, 461, 465, 471, 475–77
National Labor Relations Board: 194–95, 229, 461, 471–72
Nationality Act of 1940: 291–92
Natural Gas Act: 223
Naturalization: 151–52, 154, 156, 290, 496; cancellation revoked, 262; Bund member denaturalized, 263; decisions reversed, 263; denaturalization judgment vacated, 291; Costello denaturalized, 292; see also citizenship, loss of
Neagle, David: 154
Nebraska: 108, 112, 463; bread weight regulation struck down, 112; right-to-work laws upheld, 462
Negroes: 4, 50–51, 56–57, 63, 82, 90, 94, 140–44, 229, 326, 329, 339, 341–45, 351, 384, 443–44, 456, 487, 512; discrimination in voting, 90, 142–43, 197, 225–26, 340, 346–51; beaten by mob, 91; Virginia jury service of, 91; excluded from Delaware juries, 92; Fourteenth Amendment implementation for,

139; Louisiana segregation upheld, 139; separate but equal accommodations for, 141, 201; literacy test invalidated, 141–42; "grandfather clause" voided, 142; segregated neighborhoods rejected by court, 142; segregated education upheld, 142; rape cases of, 177–78; rights upheld, 194; law school admittance upheld, 196–97; in interstate travel, 247, 324, 330, 332; in restaurants 248, 329–33, 335–36, 341; in school integration, 325–29; in park integration, 328, 334, 337; protests of, 332–33, 336, 338, 352; in trespass, 332–38; in breach of peace, 336–38; in miscegenation, 345–46; in open housing, 351–53, 518; attacks on organizations of, 353–56; in trainmen bargaining dispute, 475; in railroad union, 518; segregation preferred by, 524 & n., injunction ignored by, 524
Nelson, Justice Samuel: 57, 60, 76, 78; dissent in reargued legal tender acts, 74
Nelson, Steve: 273
Nevada: 71, 248, 250
Nevins, Allen: 29
Newberry, Truman H.: 143
New Deal: 6, 178–79, 181, 194–95, 221; acts voided, 182–84; acts approved, 188–89, 194
New Hampshire: 36, 44, 95, 201, 268, 280–82, 285, 444
New Jersey: 108, 110, 125, 172, 203, 211, 272, 304
New Jersey Committee for the Right to Read: 415
New Jersey legislature: 239
New Mexico: 72, 434
New Orleans, La.: 333
Newport, Ky.: 311
Newsweek: 15
New York: 36, 43, 48, 70, 76, 92, 109–10, 114, 119, 125, 149–50, 176, 178, 215, 218, 245, 251, 275, 359, 408; minimum wage law struck down, 107–108; Communist party as employer in, 289; Fourteenth Amendment violated by, 426; Puerto Rican registration in, 435–36; literacy test in, 435–38
New York Central Railroad: 484
New York City, N.Y.: 126, 214, 405
New York civil rights law: 297
New York court of appeals: 38, 171, 297, 304, 360, 400, 447
New York Journal of Commerce: 60
New York legislature: 43, 110, 290, 475
New York milk law: 180, 185
New York penal law: 414
New York Rent Control Act: 110
New York Stock Exchange: 231, 480

New York Times: 61, 241 n., 304n., 323, 343n., 374–76, 384n., 385, 393n., 395n., 399n., 434n., 511, 514; obscenity poll reported by, 415; in libel action, 444–46; on unions in politics, 473–75

Nicolay, John: 61 n.

Nineteenth Amendment: 424–26

Ninth Amendment: 458–59

Nixon, President Richard M.: 512, 526

Norris–La Guardia Anti-injunction Act: 103, 229; not applicable to government, 230; union member liability under, 230

North Carolina: 248, 332, 436, 511; right-to-work laws upheld, 462

Northern Pacific Railroad: 131

Northwest Territory Ordinance of 1787: 56

North Vietnam, passports "off limits" in: 288

Noto, John Francis: 275

Nuremberg war crime trials: 252

Obligation of contract: 36–37, 51, 53–54, 94–95, 180–81

O'Brien, David P.: 493

Obscenity: 10, 24, 151, 404, 528; in literature, 302, 402, 410–12, 414; in motion pictures, 400–402, 407–408; mailing of, 402–403, 405–406, 412; in written, printed matter, 402–407, 411–14; in photography, 405–406, 408; court confusion on, 408–10; hard-core pornography, 404, 409, 411, 414; test of, 410; pandering evidence in, 411–14; Oklahoma statute struck down, 414; controversy on decisions, 521

Office of Strategic Services (OSS): 268

Of Law and Men: 4n.

Ogden, C. K.: 9

Ohio: 58–59, 109, 242, 250, 302, 309, 315, 378, 397, 408; tax statute invalidated, 256; election laws in, 517

Ohio legislature: 34; bank tax legislation of, 51

Ohio Life Insurance Company: 51

Ohio Supreme Court: 51–53, 302, 311

Ohio Un-American Activities Commission: 282

Ohio Un-American Activities Committee: 284

Oklahoma: 69, 111; Negro literacy test for voters invalidated, 142; mineral rights tax validated, 258

Oleomargarine: 85

Opinions seriatim: 5, 15, 20–21, 23–25, 59; urged by Jefferson, 23–24; opposed by Marshall, 23–26

Opium: 161

Oregon: 8–9, 101, 107, 112, 302

"Original package" doctrine: 34, 89, 97

Orthodox Jews: 450; in Sunday closing litigation, 452–55

Osborn (attorney): 163; conviction of, 320

Pacifism: 150, 152

Paine, Thomas: 3

Palko case: 11, 117–18, 145, 234–35, 359, 487; cited by Frankfurter, 299; cited by Harlan, Jr., 393, 458

Pandering: 411–13; no statute on, 414

Parnell, Congressman: 259

Partin (Hoffa associate): 319–20

Passenger cases: 23, 43, 60

Passionate State of Mind, The: 524 & n.

Passport Act of 1926: 287–88

Passports: 286–87; denied travelers to Cuba, 287–88

Patents: 96, 222–23

Paterson, Justice William: 22, 26

Path of the Law, The: 7n.

Peck, Robert: Georgia land speculation of, 30–31

Peckham, Justice Rufus W.: Lochner opinion written by, 100; bloc vote of, 159

Pennsylvania: 48, 130, 218–19, 447, 450; fugitive slave case in, 56; oleomargarine case of, 85; freight tax struck down, 88; chain drugstore regulation struck down, 113; steamship ticket sale licensing invalidated, 114; tax discrimination struck down, 114; teacher discharge sustained, 260; Sunday closing laws in, 452–53

Pennsylvania Alien Registration Act: 200

Pennsylvania legislature: 50; shoddy prohibition struck down, 113

Pennsylvania Railroad: 484

Pennsylvania Sedition Act: 273

Pennsylvania Superior Court: 304

Pennsylvania Supreme Court: 50

Pepper, Senator George Wharton: 171

Per curium opinions: 13, 21, 127, 239, 275, 311, 336–37, 343, 361, 387–88, 399, 430, 478; Black dissent from, 192, 235; in integration cases, 332, 335; on censorship, 402; in libel, 446

Perjury: 69, 157; in deportation ruling, 268

Petty crimes: 385–87

Philippine Islands: 159, 255

Philips, Wendell: 3

Phoenix, Ariz.: 372

Pickets, picketing: 103, 334, 336–37, 339–40, 461–62, 475, 528; peaceful picketing upheld, 105; peaceful picketing decision reversed, 105; outside supermarket, 358; of railroad terminal, 518; *see also* labor

Pitney, Justice Mahlon: dissent on taxing oil and gas revenues, 38; opinion barring non-union strikes, 103; opinion voiding Kansas statute, 104; dissent on peaceful picketing reversal, 105; opinion sustained by Holmes, 108; workmen's compensation opinions written by, 109; dissent re Migratory Bird Treaty Act, 115; resignation of, 169; dissent on district courts rule, 257

Plessy decision: 4, 91, 139, 141–42, 201; overruled in 1954, 167, 324–25; doctrine of, upheld, 197

Poland, Albert: 375

Police officers: 123, 127, 300–301, 307, 310–13, 315–19, 323, 337–38, 364, 379–80, 523, 526–27; practices of, 366–68; interrogation of Miranda, 372; court "punishment" of, 522

Police powers, state: 42–44, 49, 81–83, 85, 89, 98–100, 117, 173, 443, 465; broadening of, 79; opinion on state v. national powers, 80; intrastate production monopoly curbs by, 130; upheld re segregation, 139

Pollock, Sir Frederick: 47, 109, 114, 117, 146–47, 149, 151, 153

Port of Mobile, Ala.: 95

Port of New York Authority: 76; see also taxation

Postal Service Act of 1962: 290

Post Office: 290; mailing of obscene matter, 402–406, 412

Poultry code: 183

Precedent: see stare decisis

Press, freedom of: 6, 149, 161, 205, 210, 233, 245, 381, 384, 400, 447–48; violated by Georgia ordinance, 202; New York Times libel rule applied in, 444–48, 457; violated by handbill ordinance, 456

Price fixing, legislative: 83–85, 192, 257; employment agency rate fixing held unconstitutional, 108; insurance rate regulation upheld, 109; theater ticket price regulation struck down, 109; employment agency rate regulation invalidated, 110; wage regulation upheld, 136; on livestock marketing, 186–87, 201; approved for FPC, 223; by musicians' union, 478; on newspapers, 485

Price We Pay, The (pamphlet): 148

Prince Edward County, Va.: 326

Pritchett, C. Herman, The Roosevelt Court: 190, 191 & n., 194–95n., 221–22n., 224

Privileges or immunities clause, Fourteenth Amendment: 72–73, 81, 85, 117, 198

Progressive party: 280

Prohibition: 85

Property rights: 11, 49, 106, 112, 115–16

Publicity: 28–29, 145; in Dr. Sheppard trial, 381; in Estes trial, 381; in murder case, 384

Puerta Rico: 159

Pullman Company: 102

Pusey, Merlo J.: 173 & n., 189n.

Quakers: 152

Racial discrimination: see segregation

Radovich, William: 247

Railroad Retirement Act of 1934: 182, 184

Railroads: 83–85, 87–88, 98, 104, 200, 324, 518; rail merger struck down, 131; hours, wages regulated by Congress, 136; segregation challenged, 139; Retirement Act of 1934, 182; merger of, 484–85; full-crew law enacted, 518; see also under names of railroads

Railway Labor Act: 463, 467, 475

Rape: 92, 177–78, 372, 375–76, 393, 512; Negro conviction for, 343, 398; Georgia conviction reversed, 361

Reapportionment: court jurisdiction argued, 416–18; in Tennessee, 418–24, 426, 525; county unit system in, 424, 432; one person one vote rule in, 424–26; court powers in, 426, 525; in Georgia, 426–27, 432; in Alabama, 428; in California, 430–31; in Florida, Indiana, Texas, 431; for local governments, 432–33; congressional reaction to rulings on, 433–34; controversy on decisions, 521

Reapportionment Act of 1929: 416

Reardon, Justice Paul C.: 384

Recidivists: 14, 388, 527

Reconstruction Acts: 66, 82, 89ff., 96

Reed, Justice Stanley F.: 7, 49, 77, 243, 265, 324, 351, 500–501; dissent in court-martial case, 65; Management Labor Relations Act held valid by, 68; opinion upholding California law, 118; dissent in overruled citizenships, 153–54; dissent in Bridges conspiracy ruling, 156; appointment of, 191, 194; opinion re CIO ruling, 198; dissent in FTC ruling, 199; dissent in railroad line case, 200; opinion re licensing, 203–204; dissent re solicitation fee ordinance, 205; dissent re literature distribution, 206, 209; dissent re flag salute, 207; dissent re religion in schools, 213; dissent in FPC case, 223; dissent in liability ruling, 224; dissent on union member solicitation, 229; opinion re counsel decision, 232; concurs in boxing case, 245–46; dissent re treason, 255; dissent re Bund, 255; concurs on draftee convictions, 256; dissent on fishing license statute, 256; dissent re estate tax, 258; concurs re bill of attainder, 260; dissent on summary discharge, 260; opinion on deportation, 263; disbarment favored by, 272; concurs re jury service, 289; dissent on Communist list ruling, 289; opinion re church property statute, 290; witnesses counsel rejected by, 378; concurs overruling film censorship, 400; concurs dismissing districting complaint, 416; dissent on amplifiers, 439; dissent on libelous leaflets, 443; dissent on picketing injunction, 461; dissent re steel takeover, 464; dissent re trainmen bargainers, 475; concurs re Associated Press, 480; opinion re electrocution, 487; resignation of, 502

Religion: 50, 150 ff., 153, 202–10, 233, 440, 442, 448, 518, 524; teaching in school buildings invalidated, 213; outside teaching validated, 214; school prayers struck down, 215–18; school Bible reading struck down, 218–20; in Sunday laws, 448–55; Seventh-Day Adventist case in, 454–55

Res judicate, rule of: 173–74

Restaurants: discrimination decision on, 248, 352; segregation efforts in, 329; in bus terminal, 330; integrated in leased buildings, 330; sit-ins, 330–31, 333–36; in airports, 332; in drugstores, 334, 352; *see also* Negroes, segregation

Retroactivity: application of, 397–99, 514–15

Revenue Act of 1919: 138

Rhode Island: 13, 44, 59, 406–407

Richards, L. A.: 9

Richardson, James D.: 40, 42, 46, 58

Right to work: 289–90, 462–63; laws upheld in North Carolina, Nebraska, 462

Riots: 149, 440–41, 447, 524, 528

Rives, William Cabell: 24

Roane, Judge Spencer: 32; *see also* Virginia court of appeals

Robbery, robbers: 311–12, 318, 359, 376, 388, 390, 516

Roberts, Justice Owen J.: 10, 39, 143–44, 159, 162, 176, 188, 201, 209, 223, 226, 243; corporate franchise tax upheld by, 38; dissent on invalidity of oil and gas income tax, 39; minimum wage law held invalid by, 107; concurs in ice sale licensing decision, 111; marketing provisions of act upheld by, 135; Texas statute held invalid by, 143; convention rule re Negro voters upheld by, 143; concurs in citizenship denial, 152; dissent in Bridges decisions, 155; dissent re Bridges deportation, 156; as dominant court figure, 171–77, 185; decision re fire insurance statute, 172; tax statutes decisions by, 172; ICC over-

ruled by, 172; on hardship case, 174; vote re insurrection, 177; opinion in rape decision, 178; vote on minimum wage law rulings, 178–79, concurs re mortgage ruling, 179; milk law upheld by, 180; gold payments repudiated by, 181; New Deal decisions of, 182–84; 1934 record of, 183–85; decision on coal act, 186; decision on bankruptcy act, 186; switch to liberalism, 189; end of dominance, 191; dissent on stare decisis issue, 193; concurs re amendment, 194; opinion in CIO case, 198; dissent on tax ruling, 199; dissent, Elkins Act violation, 200; dissent re literature distribution, 206; dissent re flag salute, 207; dissent re "I Am" decision, 209; dissent re radio patents, 222; remarks re admiralty ruling, 204; dissent on liability ruling, 224; dissenting opinion on miner pay cases, 225; dissent on Negro voting rights, 225–26; dissent re trucker unionization, 227; dissent re union member solicitation, 228; opinion re counsel denial, 231–32; dissents re labor act application, 242; dissent in commerce case, 243; resignation of, 251; concurs re Japanese detention, 254; dissent on corporate shares tax, 258; dissent on naturalization cancellation, 262; dissent re Associated Press, 480

Robinson-Patman Act: 485

Rogers, Richard Reid: 175–76

Roosevelt, President Franklin D.: 6, 179, 218; election of, 175; re-election of, 188; court packing threatened by, 189–91

Roosevelt, President Theodore: 6, 18, 167; disappointed by Holmes, 131; judicial decisions recall asked by, 131

Rosenberg, Ethel (Mrs. Julius Rosenberg): 285–86

Rosenberg, Julius: 285–86

"Rule of reason": 132, 148

Russian Orthodox Church: 290

Rutledge, Justice Wiley B.: 77, 221, 233, 244, 255, 351; dissent in telegraph message case, 135; dissent in Illinois lawyer decision, 153; concurs in contempt reversal, 156; Byrnes replaced by, 205; opinion re child labor case, 209; dissent in school transport, 212–13; dissent, opinion re radio patents, 222; union member soliciting upheld by, 228; dissent re UMW contempt, 230; dissent re counsel denial, 232; dissent on state sales tax, 244; decision re alimony, 249; concurs in Japanese student ruling, 252; dissent re Japanese hanging, 255–56; dissent on draftee convictions, 256; concurs in land ownership ruling, 256; concurs on fishing license invalidity,

256; death of, 259; concurs on naturalization ruling, 262; dissent on denaturalization, 263; dissent re federal rule for states, 299–300; concurs on bus integration, 324; concurs dismissing districting complaint, 417; concurs upholding right to work, 462; right-to-work amendment upheld by, 463; concurs re Associated Press, 480; dissent re electrocution, 487

Sabotage: 252, 254–55, 263
Sacco-Vanzetti case: 285
Samuel Freeman Miller: 63n.
Sanford, Justice Edward T.: death of, 38; critical of Van Deventer, 107; concurs in voiding rate-fixing statute, 108; dissent re theater ticket price statute, 109; dissent in mortgage recording tax decision, 115; dissent in trade association ruling, 134; writing on freedoms, 149; dissent in naturalization denial, 152; replaced by Roberts, 171
San Francisco, Calif.: 92
Saratoga Springs, N.Y.: 77
Saturday Evening Post: 447
Saturday Press: 151
Savannah, Ga.: 333
Scales, Julius Irving: 274
Schenck, Charles T.: 146–47
Schneiderman, William: 262–63
Schools: 50, 112, 357–58, 377–78, 435, 448, 457, 524–25; segregation upheld in, 91; foreign language teaching bans invalidated, 111–12; law school admittance upheld, 196–97; flag salute in, 202–203; flag salute in, overruled, 207–208; parochial school transportation upheld, 211–13; religious teaching invalidated in, 213; religious teaching outside schools validated, 214; textbook lending held valid, 215; prayers invalidated, 215–18; Bible reading struck down, 218–20; desegregation of, 324–27, 523; public schools reopening ordered, 326; integration suspension rejected, 326–27; Negroes in University of Alabama, 327; segregation avoided in, 327; Meredith case in, 328; racial basis faculties in, 329; student transfers in, 329; freedom of choice in, 329; prayers ruling defied, 514, 521; overriding efforts re prayer decision in, 521 & n.; segregation preferred in, 524
Schubert, Glendon: 520 n.
Schwimmer, Rosika: 151–52, 154, 262
Scott, Dred, decision: 55–57, 61, 140
Search and seizure: 13, 29, 162, 165–66, 233, 297, 299–303, 307, 315–16, 318, 321–23, 385, 397, 459, 522; federal officers in, 300–302; unlawful evidence admitted, 302; without warrant, 304–306; in espionage case, 306; in narcotics cases, 307, 313–14, 317, 319; of guns, 308; in frisking suspects, 310; limits of, 311; of burglary tools, 311; of air rifle, 312; of revolver, 312; "harmless error" in, 312; gambling slips in, 315; weapons, clothing in, 318; Harlan opinion on claims of, 321–22; "breaking" requirements extended, 323; convictions voided, 517; *see also* warrants, search

Seattle Fire Department: 310
Secret Service, U.S.: 301
Securities and Exchange Commission: 175, 194; power denied, 186
Sedition Act of 1798: 446
Segregation: 50, 90–91, 324, 332, 443, 523–24; challenged by Plessy, 139; rejected for neighborhoods, 142; upheld in education, 142; avoiding of, 327, 514; by school transfers, 328; in parks, 329, 334, 337, 356; in restaurants, 248, 329–32; protests, 331–33, 336, 338–39; in public accommodations, 245, 329–32, 335–36, 341, 343; in library, 338; *see also* Negroes, schools, housing
Selective Service: 493
Self-incrimination: 117–20, 126–27, 129, 263, 274, 280, 282, 322, 359, 366, 377, 385, 398; *see also* Fifth Amendment
Senate Judiciary Committee: 190, 526–27
Sermon on the Mount: 152
Seventeenth Amendment: 424–25
Seventh Amendment: 9
Seventh-day Adventist: 454–55
Shanker (president, New York teachers union): 474–75
Sheppard, Dr. Samuel: 145, 381
Sherman Anti-Trust Act: 106, 130, 230, 243, 246–47, 478, 481, 483, 485; agreements held void under, 133; keyed to interstate commerce, 134; convictions affirmed under, 196, 227; union guiltless under, 227; Associated Press cases under, 480; New York Stock Exchange violation of, 480; price information exchange violative of, 519
Shiras, Justice George: dissents, concurs on income tax, 136–37; bloc vote of, 159
Shoddy (in bedding): 113
"Silver platter" doctrine: 300–301, 307
Sixteenth Amendment: 136, 138
Sixth Amendment: 9, 12, 129, 158, 231–32, 234–36, 292–93, 319, 359, 379, 382, 384–85, 388, 392–93, 514–15; held inapplicable to states, 232; held applicable to states, 236; with-

drawal of blood not violative of, 305; jury trial assured by, 384–85

Slaughter house cases: 79, 81–83, 85, 89, 97, 234; *see also* Fourteenth Amendment

Slaughter house doctrine: 72

Slavery: 41, 54, 61, 353, 523; slaves as persons or property questioned, 55; power of states upheld in, 55; fugitives from, cause controversy over, 155–56; debate by Congress, 56–57; slaves freed by Justice Miller, 63; Thirteenth, Fourteenth, Fifteenth Amendments applied to, 79–80

Smith Act: 259, 273, 281; convictions vacated under, 273

Socialists: 146–47, 149–50

Social Security: 189–90, 267–70

Social Security Act: 269

South Carolina: 21, 26, 61, 66, 332–34; voting rights injunction dismissed, 346–48; Seventh-Day Adventist case in, 454–55

Spanish American War: 159

Speech, freedom of: 6, 69, 146–51, 178, 205, 210, 233, 272, 336, 351, 400–402, 456, 462, 467; violated by Georgia ordinance, 202; amplifiers, sound tracks in, 439–42; city ordinances violative of, 440; in public disturbances, 440–42; in public parks, 442; libelous material in, 443–48; violated by handbill ordinance, 456

Spirit of Liberty, The: Papers and Addresses of Learned Hand: 6n.

Standard Oil Company: 106

Stare decisis: 7, 10–11, 173, 247; issue in tax decision, 193; effects of, 521

"Star-Spangled Banner, The": 217

State Orphans' Court (Pennsylvania): 50

State Public Accommodations Act (Pennsylvania): 50

State University of New York, Albany, N.Y.: 70

Steamship tickets: 114

Stevens, Thaddeus: 64, 66

Stewart, Justice Potter: 4, 14–15, 65–66, 126, 163–64, 236, 282, 353, 387, 402, 485, 494, 507–11; dissent on state tax collection case, 38; dissent on loyalty oath statute, 69; Maryland loyalty oath defended by, 70; opinion re subversives statute, 70–71; dissent in self-incrimination ruling, 120; dissent, opinion in Griffin murder reversal, 121; dissent re "harmless error" rule, 122; death penalty clause held unconstitutional by, 129; concurs in anarchy case, 149; dissent re overruled contempt, 157–58; injunction violation sustained by, 158; opinion in Hoffa cases, 163; dissent re eavesdropping, 166; dissent, opinion on school prayers, 215–18, 524; dissent, opinion on religious exercises ruling, 219–20; Birmingham injunction upheld by, 229; dissent on certiorari denials, 234; concurs on right of confrontation, 235; dissent re indigents, 239–41; dissent on libel, 261; dissent on deportations, 270–71; deportation evidence decision of, 271; dissent on labor act section, 276; dissent on Communists in defense plants, 277; dissent on rule violation, 284; dissent re contempt, 285; dissent on denaturalization, 291; dissent re citizenship provisions, 292–93; dissent on vote abroad, 293; rule rejecting "silver platter" doctrine, 301–302; dissent on Fourteenth Amendment ruling, 302–304; concurs re withdrawal of blood, 305; ruling re narcotics seizure, 307; dissent re inspectors warrant, 309; concurs re evidence in car, 311; dissent on "harmless error," 312; dissent re heroin search, 313; dissent on search, 315; gambler conviction reversed by, 315; opinion re Fourth, Fifth, Sixth Amendments violation, 319–20; recorder use upheld by, 320–21; concurs on prison desegregation, 329; concurs on restaurant integration, 330; dissent on sit-ins reversal, 335; dissent on antipicketing statute, 337; opinion on civil rights act, 338–39; opinion re rights, 341; concurs on miscegenation statute, 345; dissent on state poll tax ruling, 348; dissent on housing amendment, 352; dissent on NAACP lawyer hiring, 354; dissent re NAACP membership lists, 356; dissent re park segregation, 356–57; dissent re murder conviction, 359; dissent re voluntariness of confession, 361; on Escobedo reversal, 364–65; dissent involving police practices, 366, 370; dissent on tax fraud reversal, 375; dissent on waiver decision, 376; concurs in part re remand, 379; dissent re robber, 379; dissent re trial televising, 381–83; dissent re trial by jury, 384–86; ruling re defendant testimony, 390; dissent on vacating robber conviction, 391–92; in circumstantial evidence reversal, 393; dissent on rape reversal, 393; opinion on narcotics addiction, 393–94; dissent on jailing alcoholics, 395; concurs re applying decisions retroactively, 397; concurs re habeas corpus, 399; censorship statutes held invalid by, 400–401; magazines held not obscene by, 405; dissent on obscenity ruling, 409; concurs on obscenity ruling, 410; dissent on Ginzburg conviction, 412; dissent on bookseller conviction, 414; concurs remanding apportionment case, 418; concurs rejecting Georgia unit rule, 424; dissents in part on apportionment statute, 427; opinion rejecting Alabama apportionment, 428–30; dissent on Florida, Texas reapportionment rule, 431; dissent on state apportionment extension, 432; dissent on Puerto Rican registration, voting, 435–36; dissents, concurs re libel case, 444; dissent on radio-television libel, 448; dissent on Sunday closing, 452–54; concurs on Seventh-Day Adventist ruling, 454–55; dissent on contraceptives ruling, 459; bar dues upheld by, 469; dissent on strike-breaker fine, 476; dissent on boycott, 477; concurs against UMW, 477; decision re Sherman Act, 478; dissent on damages, 481; concurs in Colgate decision, 481; concurs re brewery assets, 481; dissent re merger exclusion, 483; dissent re Bank Merger Act, 483; dissents, concurs on merger, 483; dissent on rail merger opinion, 484; dissent re competition, 485; dissent re underwriting costs, 486; opinion on jury service exclusion, 486–87; concurs on income tax ruling, 489; dissent on FTC order, 491; dissent on draftee ruling, 492–93; opinion against draft card burner, 494; dissent re tax refund, 495; opinion on damages ruling, 496; appointment of, 504; dissent on murder reversal, 515; dissent on habeas corpus proceedings, 516; disagrees on due process violation, 516; wiretapping decisions explained by, 516–17; dissent re search and seizure, 517; dissent on Ohio election law ruling, 518; partial dissent on corporate earnings, 518; concurs on evolution teaching, 518; dissent re picketing, 518; dissent re price information, 519; dissent re draftee, 519; reversal vote in 21 cases, 527; dissent re obscenity, 528

Stone Court: 242, 248

Stone, Justice, Chief Justice Harlan Fiske: 4, 15, 17, 19, 65, 77, 111, 134, 171–73, 199, 221, 242; dissent in Jehovah's Witnesses case, 18; dissent on invalidity of state tax on U.S. securities, 37; corporate franchise tax upheld by, 38; state tax on corporation upheld by, 38; dissent in taxicab case, 48; concurs in union injunction case, 106; dissent in employment agency regulation, 108; dissent re theater ticket price statute, 109; dissent in shoddy case, 113; dissent in mortgage recording tax decision, 115; fair labor act upheld by, 135; dissent in citizenship denial, 152; dissent in Bridges decisions, 155; dissent re Bridges deportation, 151; dissent re wiretapping, 160; dissent in tobacco case, 176; dissent re insurrection, 178; dissent on minimum wage ruling, 179; dissent re taxing power, 184–85; dissent on SEC ruling, 186; opinion on coal act, 186; opinion in CIO case, 198; dissent in railroad line case, 200; vote on alien act, 200; dissent re flag salute, 202–207; opinion re overruled decision, 202–203; dissent on licensing, 204; dissent on literature distribution, 209; dissent re "I Am" decision, 209; succeeded by Vinson, 211, 259; opinion in radio patents case, 222; dissent in second miner pay ruling, 225; dissent on labor union ruling, 226; dissent in trucker unionization, 227; dissent on insurance regulation, 243; Japanese student conviction upheld by, 252; dissent re treason, 255; dissent re Bund, 255; dissent on naturalization cancellation, 262; death of, 418; dissent re Associated Press, 480

Story, Justice Joseph: dissent justified by, 5, 17, 23–25; Nereide case dissent by, 31; national court supremacy asserted by, 32; dissent re certificates of indebtedness, 35–36, 45; dissent on New York bankruptcy law validity, 36; dissent in Cherokee Nation case, 39; Dartmouth College case doctrine followed by, 43; dissent in immigration case, 43; federal right in extradition of foreigners upheld by, 44; lack of court test deplored by, 45; decision on diversified citizenship rule, 47–49; will contestants' objections overruled by, 50; dissent in Mississippi slave sale case, 55; opinion in fugitive slave cases, 56

Strikes: 23, 102–103, 276, 528; averted by legislation, 136; threat of, 155, 227; by coal miners, 230; presidential move against, 464; of public utilities, 464–65; strike-breaker fine upheld by, 476; against railroads, 518; *see also* labor

Strong, Justice William: 54, 75; appointment of, 74; dissent in price-fixing cases, 83; dissent on Fifth Amendment due process violation, 88

Struggle for Judicial Supremacy, The: 4 & n., 28n.

Subpoenas: 283, 297

Subversive Activities Control Act: 259, 274–76; bar on hearings of, upheld, 277; ban on defense jobs unconstitutional, 277; section declared unconstitutional, 286

Subversive Activities Control Board: 126; inactivity, scandal of, 276–77

Subversives: 70, 263, 277, 280

Sugar: 120; *see also* Sherman Anti-Trust Act

Summary Suspension Act of 1950: 260

Sunday closing laws: 100, 448–55

Supreme Being: 455

Supreme Court, U.S.: 4, 7–8, 10–14, 18, 20, 22–23, 26, 34, 37–38, 42–43, 48, 54, 56–58, 62–65, 67–68, 73, 78, 117, 231, 272, 298, 375, 377–78, 387, 427, 492, 511, 517; superlegislative function of, 11; jurisdiction in habeas corpus upheld, 27; state act first declared unconstitutional, 31; controversy with Virginia court, 32; supremacy upheld, 32; six judges in 1835, 35; decision in Giraud school case, 50–51; jurisdiction refused in political dispute, 59; unpopularity of, 61; war defined by, 62; blockade sanctioned by, 62; membership raised to ten, 62; reduced to nine, 62; reduced to eight, 62, 195, 221; injunction against Johnson denied by, 66; on loyalty oaths, 67–70; stagecoach passenger tax held invalid by, 71; reduced to seven, 1870, 74; increased to nine, 74; move from nationalistic attitude, 79; phases of, 82–83; drummer tax struck down by, 88; mob indictments invalidated by, 80; state judge denied habeas corpus by, 92–93; Virginia bond case ruling invalidated by, 94; Virginia bond remedy held not unconstitutional by, 94; conservative, nationalistic views of, 98; due process of Fourteenth Amendment emphasized by, 98; injunction against union upheld by, 106; employment agency fee statute upheld by, 108; workmen's compensation act approved by, 108; disagreement in, 111, 223–24, 256; foreign language teaching ban invalidated by, 111; public school attendance decision of, 112; bread weight statute struck down by, 112; coal mining statute voided by, 114; Arizona employment statute invalidated by, 115; decision on self-incrimination in Fifth Amendment, 117, 119; Cardozo compromise followed by, 118; murder conviction reversed by, 121–22; immunity waivers held unconstitutional by, 126; company blacklisting upheld by, 126; gambler convictions voided by, 126; kidnap transport conviction set aside by, 128; second trial testimony held inadmissible by, 129; clash with legislature, 130; Sherman Act inapplicable in monopoly decision, 130; antitrust law violation decision of, 133–34; treaty violations re aliens sustained by, 139; Louisiana segregation statute upheld by, 139; Negro literacy test struck down by, 142; Maryland "grandfather clause" voided by, 142; espionage conviction upheld by, 146; pamphlet distributor conviction upheld by,

148–49; Minnesota statute upheld by, 150; mailing privilege denied by, 150; fraud order upheld by, 151; citizenships denied by, 152–54; lawyer denied practice by, 153; three citizenship cases overruled by, 153–54; contempt sustained by, 155; Bridges convictions, conspiracy reversed by, 155–56; contempt ruling reversed by, 156–57; criminal contempt ruling upheld by, 157; criminal contempt overruled, 157; civil contempt upheld by, 158; criminal contempt jury trial required by, 158; petty case trial denied by, 159; status of possessions argued by, 159; wiretapping, eavesdropping argued by, 160–67; Roberts dominant on, 171–77, 185; 1939 box score of, 171–72; rape decisions reversed by, 177, 361; insurrectionist conviction voided by, 178; minimum wage law voided by, 178; minimum wage law upheld by, 179; NIRA section invalidated by, 181; New Deal acts voided by, 182–84; Guffey Coal Act struck down by, 186; livestock rate case decided by, 186–87, 201; score of 1935 term, 187; attitude changed, 188–89; New Deal acts approved by, 188; packing threatened, 188–90; increase in dissents of, 191, 221–22; amendment rejection affirmed by, 194; 1938 term of, 194; 1939–40 term of, 195; 1940–41 term of, 195; deportation sustained by, 198–99; Browder convicted by, 200; Jehovah's Witnesses cases argued by, 202–10; parochial school transportation upheld by, 211–13; religious teaching in schools invalidated by, 213; religious teaching outside schools validated, 214; public school textbook lending held valid by, 215; school prayers invalidated by, 215–18; religious exercises invalidated by, 218–20; admiralty case overruled by, 224; extortion ruling upheld by, 227; UMW contempt upheld by, 230; counsel denial upheld by, 231, 233; counsel denial overruled by, 233; ruling in pauper appeal by, 235; confession conviction vacated by, 236; murder conviction vacated by, 240, 359; Iowa transcript ruling reversed by, 241; nationalization in, 242–43, 359; insurance regulation upheld by, 243; gross income tax invalidated by, 244–45; NLRB held constitutional by, 245; 1964 civil rights law upheld by, 247; Bund conviction set aside by, 255; state tax overruled by, 257; conservative bloc on, 259; security clearance reversed by, 260; Communist convictions upheld by, 271; Communist conviction reversed by, 273; screening struck down by, 277–78; certiorari denied Rosenbergs by, 285; special session of, 286; freedom of travel philosophy of, 288; Communist employer status upheld by, 289; Fourth Amendment violation rejected by, 297; Fourth Amendment ruled applicable to states, 302; fraud conviction reversed by, 318; fraud reversal overruled by, 318; public disfavor of, 323, 526; schools desegregated by, 325; integration warning by, 328; trespass convictions reversed by, 332–36; miscegenation invalidated by, 345–46; 1957 civil rights act validated by, 346; candidate's race designation rejected by, 346; voting rights complaint upheld by, 346; registration tests invalidated by, 346–47; Virginia statute invalidated by, 353; NAACP ordinance invalidated by, 354–55; convictions after confession reversed by, 361; absence of counsel ruling of, 361; criticism of, 364, 514; Miranda confession held inadmissible by, 372–73; rape conviction reversed by, 375; liberalization followed elsewhere, 377–78; division re robber, 379; May 20, 1968, decisions of, 399; prior decision overruled by, 399; attitude on censorship, 400; film censorship ordinance invalidated by, 400; confusion re obscenity, 408, 414; Florida, Indiana, Texas reapportionment rejected by, 431; reapportionment jurisdiction limited by, 432; congressional objection to decisions of, 433; atheist denied certiorari by, 456; Julian Bond decision reversed by, 457; contraceptives statute struck down by, 457; right of privacy review denied by, 459–60; action in public utility strikes, 464–65; union attitude of, 465, 471; *Wall Street Journal* on activities of, 471–72; confusion re antitrust acts, 480; drug ruling reversed by, 481; Penn-Central merger approved by, 484–85; decision on price fixing by, 485; decision on Maritime Commission case, by, 486; dislike of death penalty, 487–88; criticized for "making law," 488; students denied certiorari by, 493; criticized by Frankfurter, 494–96; Fortas opinion on decision of, 494–95; criticism of, by Stewart, Harlan, Jr., 495; conservative under Vinson, 497; concern on wiretapping, 516; in politics, 517–18; legislation, policymaking of, 520 & n.; prejudices of, 520; controversial decisions of, 521; state variances not considered by, 521

Supreme Court in the United States, The: 17

Supreme Court in United States History, The: 21 & n., 29 & n., 34 & n., 45–46, 52n., 56–61 & n., 66n., 86n., 88n., 94 & n.

Supreme Court of Appeals of Virginia: 315

Supreme Court of Missouri: 464

Supreme Court of the Philippines: 255

Sutherland, Justice George: 17, 19, 171, 181, 183; dissent on invalidity of state tax on U.S. securities, 37; dissent on corporate franchise tax case, 38; dissent on state corporation tax, 38; union injunction decision by, 106; opinion striking down minimum wage law, 107; opinion in ice sale licensing decision, 111; dissent re foreign language teaching, 111; dissent on invalidating Texas statute, 143; murder case cited in dissent of, 144; opinion re citizenship denials, 151–53; on hardship case, 174; dissent re corporate assessments, 177; dissent on minimum wage law, 179; dissent re gold payments, 181; decision on coal act, 186; retirement of, 191, 194; *see also* Four Horsemen

Swarthout, Samuel: 27–28

Swayne, Justice Noah H.: 54, 62, 78, 233; dissent in loyalty oath cases, 67; dissent in Texas statehood case, 74; dissent in Hepburn decision, 74; dissenting opinion on Fourteenth Amendment application, 80; replaced by Matthews, 82; concurs in Iowa liquor case, 82; dissent in U.S. case against railroads, 87; dissent in freight tax case, 88

Taft, Chief Justice William Howard: 98, 106–107, 134; peaceful picketing upheld by, 105; peaceful picketing statute held invalid by, 105; dissent in minimum wage law case, 107; dissent in rent control decisions, 110; wiretapping opinion of, 159–60; appointed after presidency, 169; succeeded by Hughes, 171; on excluding relevant evidence, 517

Taft Court: 82–83, 117, 133–34, 170

Taft-Hartley law: 259, 465, 471

Taft, Justice Kingsley A.: 311

Taney, Chief Justice Roger B.: 5, 18, 35–41, 47, 53–54, 57, 60, 64, 138; dissent on court's jurisdiction, 13; advocate of powerful court, 41; compared with Marshall, 42; opinion on police powers of state, 42; federal right of extradition of foreigners upheld by, 44; police power defined by, 44–45; dissent re circuit court jurisdiction, 46; dissent in corporate tax case, 51; insurance company taxation held valid by, 51; opinion re corporate charters, 51–52; opinion on state sovereignty, 52–53; views of on slavery, 54–55, 523; opinion on fugitive slave legislation, 56; judicial supremacy asserted by, 58; criticism of, 61–62; writ suspension rejected by, 61; death of, 62

Taney Court: dissent not overstressed by, 41; state police powers recognized by, 41–42; Taney, Marshall views clash, 43, 45; bloc voting in, 59; fears held re pursuit of war, 62; divisions in, 83; states' rights attitude of, 130

Tariff acts of 1828 and 1832: 40

Taxation: 18, 34–35, 37–38, 54, 94–96, 114, 173, 184, 193–94, 196, 199, 212–13, 375, 440, 453, 468, 489–90; state tax on U.S. securities held invalid, 37; corporate franchise tax upheld, 38; Massachusetts state tax collection overruled, 38; oil and gas revenue tax held invalid, 38; oil and gas income held taxable, 39; federal tax on oil and gas income invalidated, 39; inheritance taxes, 49; corporate tax exemptions upheld, 51–53; insurance company exemption rejected, 51; bank's state tax increase held void, 54; veteran tax case reversed, 69; on stagecoach passengers, 71; state judicial salary tax invalidated, 76; HOLC tax upheld, 76; Port of New York Authority tax upheld, 76; federal sales tax upheld, 77; foreign insurance company tax upheld, 87; freight tax struck down, 88; drummer, peddler taxes struck down, 88; exemption on revenue bonds denied, 95; mortgage recording tax struck down, 115; inheritance tax claim denied, 116; income tax held unconstitutional, 136–37; judges held taxable, 138; statutes struck down, 172, 180, 192; state sales tax invalidated, 244, 258; intangibles tax invalidated, 256; AEC contractor tax denied, 258; national v. state, 258; on corporate shares, 258; decision on estate tax, 258; on foreign corporation, 518; on accumulated corporate earnings, 518

Teachers: 69–70, 448; affidavit requirement for, invalidated, 273–74; racial basis allocation of, 329; of Darwinian theory, 518

Telegraph messages: 135–36

Television: 145, 381–84, 448, 465, 490

Tennessee: 48, 53, 225, 512; apportionment in, 418, 525

Tennessee Apportionment Act of 1901: 418, 421

Tenth Amendment: 459

Terry, Justice David S.: 53, 154

Terry, Mrs. David S.: 154

Texas: 14, 74, 142–43, 393, 429, 527; Negro voting rights validated in, 225–26; recidivist statute of, 358; censorship statute of, invalidated, 400; reapportionment rejected, 431; serviceman's voting right upheld in, 434

Texas legislature: 143

Texas Supreme Court: 228

Theater ticket agency: 108–10

Thirteenth Amendment: 79–80, 92–94, 139, 141, 353

Thompson, Justice Smith: 24–25, 35–36, 40; dissent on federal indebtedness tax case, 37; dissent in Cherokee Nation case, 39; Dartmouth College case doctrine followed by, 43

Thornberry, Judge Homer: nominated associate justice, 511; nomination withdrawn, 512

Times-Mirror (California): 155

Toledo News Bee (Ohio): 155

Toomey, John F., Jr.: 391

Trade associations: 133–34

Trademarks: 96

Traffic tickets: 123

Transportation: 98, 102, 113, 330; of oil, 181; of Negroes, 247, 324, 332

Trespass: 161, 332–38

Trials, criminal: 359, 361–62, 375–78, 380, 382–84, 388, 392–93, 399, 516; of Escobedo, 364; of Miranda, 372; of Dr. Sheppard, 381; of Estes, 381, 383; by jury, 384–88, 405; of recidivist, 388; of union official, 390; fair, 390–92; free transcripts of, 515; speedy, 515

Trimble, Justice Robert: 24

True Believer, The: 524 & n.

Truman, President Harry S: 68, 259, 277; action of, averting steel strike, 464

Trust-busting: 131

Tucker, Rev. Irwin St. John: 148

Twain, Mark: *see* Samuel L. Clemens

Unemployment: 189–90

Unemployment compensation: 289

Unemployment insurance: 454

Union of Philadelphia (Federalist newspaper): 22

Union Pacific Railroad: 87; amended charter act called due process violation by, 88; Elkins Act violated by, 200

Unions: 100, 102–104, 199, 226, 278, 280, 390, 461, 463–64, 467, 489; held liable in boycott, 106; coal, sued, 106; held liable for damages, 106; injunction against, upheld, 106; antitrust cases against, 227–28; membership solicitation upheld, 228–29; UMW fined, 230; attorney hiring by, 355; supermarket picketing upheld, 358; right to work violated by, 462; union-shop agreements of, 463; collective bargaining of, 464–65, 471, 477; dues use in elections, 465, 467–69, 471–75; House complaint on campaign funds of, 466; whites bargaining for Negroes, 475; alleged discrimination in, 518; fining members of, 518–19

United Insurance Company of America: 471
United Mine Workers: 230, 477
United States Circuit Court: 48
United States Judicial Code: 323
Utah: 100

Van Buren, President Martin: 46
Van Deventer, Justice Willis: 19, 107, 109, 171; dissent on corporate franchise tax case, 38; dissent on state corporation tax, 38; dissent in Oregon labor case, 102; dissent in rent control decisions, 110; dissent re Migratory Bird Treaty Act, 115; concurs in corporate assessments, 176; dissent on milk ruling, 180; replaced by Black, 190–91; *see also* Four Horsemen
Vermont: 188, 250
Veterans: 69
Vick (officer): 320
Viereck, George Sylvester: 255
Vietnam War: 62, 68, 288; Julian Bond's statements on, 457; questions raised on, 492–94; legality of, 519
Vinson, Chief Justice Fred M.: Management Labor Relations Act of 1947 held valid by, 68; dissent in Bridges conspiracy ruling, 156; dissent re criminal contempt, 157; succeeds Stone, 211; dissent re jury lists, 211; dissent on labor disputes ruling, 230; opinion re counsel decisions, 232; dissent on canvasser ordinance, 245; dissent on district courts ruling, 257; appointment of, 259; dissent on deportation suspension, 266; Communist convictions upheld by, 271; disbarment favored by, 272; dissent on Communist list ruling, 289; equal protection clause invoked by, 351; dissent re damages, 351; dissent on public disturbance ruling, 440; permit requirement held invalid by, 442; concurs in picketing injunction, 461; dissent re steel takeover, 464; few dissents by, 498
Vinson Court: 400, 497
Virginia: 32, 91, 315, 324, 334, 353; anti-miscegenation statute invalidated, 345; federal, state poll taxes struck down, 348–50; statute in NAACP lawyers, 354–55; right-to-work law in, 462
Virginia Court of Appeals: 32, 345; *see also* Supreme Court U.S.
Virginia General Assembly: 94–95
Voluntariness of confessions: 361–62, 367; doctrine applied, 398; *see also* confessions
Voting: 53, 59, 68, 85, 90, 94, 99, 188, 200, 431–32, 434; indictment invalidated in vote conspiracy, 90; literacy test for Negroes in-

validated, 142; Negro vote denial invalidated, 142–43; convention rule re Negro vote upheld, 143; Negro registration upheld, 197; Negro rights upheld, 225–26; voter abroad, 291; discrimination in, 340, 346–51; poll tax abolished, 348–50; election day editorial statute invalidated, 351; Illinois complaint dismissed, 416; election restraints in Tennessee, 418; in Georgia, 424; "one person one vote" rule, 424–27, 521, 525; in gubernatorial election, 431–32; right of Texas serviceman, 434; of Puerto Ricans, 435–36; literacy requirement for, 435–38
Voting Rights Act of 1965: 347–48, 434–35

Waite, Chief Justice Morrison R.: 11, 82–83, 92, 99, 202–203; court concept of, 11; appointed in 1874, 82; opinion in price-fixing cases, 83–85; decision on Fifth Amendment due process, 88; dissent in drummer tax case, 88; dissent in interstate commerce case, 89; opinion on rights, 90; dissent in Arlington tax sale case, 96; death of, 98; quoted, 192
Waite Court: policy of, 11; 1886 rule of, 13; duration of, 86; B&O Railroad charter held valid by, 88; unanimity in, 96; corporation held "person" by, 99; civil rights attitude of, 139; judicial restraint of, 191
Waivers: 231, 368, 376
Walker, General Edwin A.: 447
Wall Street: 177
Wall Street Journal: on Supreme Court activities, 471; on unions in politics, 471–74; on bank merger rules, 484; editorials of, 486–87, 517
Warrants, arrest: 301, 306
Warrants, search: 16, 165, 304, 308, 315, 318, 323, 517; for rodent inspection, 13, 308; in espionage case, 306; for building inspectors, 309; for warehouse inspection, 310; for searching suspects, 310; for car search, 311; for narcotics, 312–14; for furs, 314; for accused gambler search, 315; *see also* search and seizure
Warren, Charles: 21 & n., 29 & n., 34 & n., 45–46, 52n., 56–61 & n., 66n., 86n., 88n., 94 & n.
Warren, Chief Justice Earl: 4, 14–15, 162–63, 241, 275, 309, 379, 478, 498–500, 502–11; dissent in habitual criminal cases, 14; dissent re bar admittance ruling, 119; opinion re voiding part of firearms act, 126–27; injunction violation sustained by, 158; dissent on Birmingham injunction, 229; opinion re speedy trial right, 236; ruling on boxing, 245;

opinion re Ohio divorce, 250; dissent on tax levy, 258; dissent on teacher, conductor dismissals, 260; dissent on due process ruling, 261; dissent on libel, 261; dissent on officer report, 261; dissent on contempt, 263; dissent re Chinese aliens, 268; dissent re alien perjury, 268; dissent re alien obligation, 268; dissent on benefits ruling, 269; dissent on Communist contempt, 273; opinion on labor act section, 276; on due process violation, 280; dissent on contempt conviction, 281; dissent on contempt review, 282; dissent on ex-teacher conviction, 282; witness conviction vote of, 282; dissent re subpoenaed matter, 283; dissent on voter's citizenship loss, 291; decision on deserter's citizenship loss, 291; dissent on blood in evidence, 305; dissent re withdrawal of blood, 305; dissent on radio theft reversal, 306; dissent in spy ruling, 306; dissent on fur search ruling, 314; dissent on informer ruling, 316; narcotics seller conviction affirmed by, 317; concurs on overruled fraud decision, 319; dissent re Hoffa appeal, 320; school desegregation ruling of, 325; dissent on jury trial denial, 328; sit-in convictions reversed by, 330–31; opinion in trespass decision, 333; opinion re desegregated restaurant, 333; concurs on trespass rulings, 334–35; opinion re amusement park, 337; dissent on picketing rule, 339; dissent on jail trespass, 539; dissent in part re rights, 342; antimiscegenation statute invalidated by, 345–46; opinion re voting rights, injunction, 347; opinion re four reversals, 367–69; dissent re witnesses counsel, 378; dissent re remand, 379; concurs on revision invalidity, 382; reversal in recidivist case, 388; dissent re double jeopardy, 389; dissent on contempt, 389; dissent on defendant testimony ruling, 390; opinion on coparticipants testimony, 392–93; opinion on applying decisions retroactively, 397; voluntariness doctrine applied by, 398; opinion re habeas corpus, 399; dissent on film preshowing, 402; concurs re mailing obscene matter, 403; dissent on suits against obscenity, 405; dissent on obscenity ruling, 409–10; concurs on obscenity requirements, 410; Alabama apportionment rejected by, 428; dissent re gubernatorial decision, 432; dissent on *Life* libel ruling, 447; concurs awarding damages, 448; dissent on Sunday closing, 448–50; Sunday closing upheld by, 452–53; opinion reversing Julian Bond finding, 457; opinion re contraceptives statute, 457; dissent re labor

jurisdiction, 461; dissent re utility seizure, 464; dissent on union indictment, 465; bar dues upheld by, 469; dissent re trainmen bargainers, 475; dissent re expelled union member, 475; employee lockout upheld by, 476; temporary layoff upheld by, 477; decision re Sherman Act, 478; dissent on wife testimony, 488; dissent on husband-wife conspiracy, 488–89; opinion on income tax ruling, 489–90; opinion on FTC order, 490; concurs on certiorari denial, 492; opinion against draft card burner, 493; resignation of, 512; dissent on Ohio election law ruling, 518; certiorari vote in 11 cases, 527

Warren Court: 17, 28, 418, 514, 521

Wartime Suspension of Limitations Act: 156

Washington: 107–109, 179

Washington, Justice Bushrod: dissent explained by, 21–22, 24; nonparticipant in court clash, 32; dissent in debt imprisonment regulation, 36–37; state, federal court conflicts viewed by, 46–47

Washington, President George: 217–18

Washington, University of, Seattle, Wash.: 252

Watch Tower and Bible Tract Society: 205

Wayne, Justice James M.: 35, 56–57, 60; federal right in extradition of foreigners upheld by, 44; slavery views of, 55, 165, 523; death of, 67

We, the Judges: 12n., 191 n.

Webb-Kenyon Act of 1913: 89

W. E. B. Dubois Clubs of America: 277

Weintraub, Chief Justice Joseph (N.J.): 517

Welfare: 73

Western Union Telegraph Company: 88, 136

West Virginia: 91

Wheeler, Senator Burton K.: 189

White Court: 18, 82, 111, 168–69, 171, 191; new alignment more liberal, 141

White, Justice Byron: 4, 14, 16, 126, 158, 215, 236, 275, 283, 290, 308, 320–21, 351, 365, 375, 494, 508–509, 511; dissent in recidivist cases, 14; dissent re loyalty oath statute, 69; Maryland loyalty oath defended by, 70; opinion re subversives statute case, 70–71; dissent in self-incrimination ruling, 120; dissent, opinion in Griffin murder reversal, 121; dissent in testimony admissibility decision, 127; dissent in kidnap transport ruling, 128; dissent re overruled contempt, 157; dissent re microphones, 163; textbook lending upheld by, 215; dissent re indigent, 240; dissent on deportations, 270–71; dissent on labor act section, 276; dissent on rule violation, 284; dissent re contempt, 285; dissent re issuing passports, 286; dissent re loss of citizenship, 291; dissent re citizenship provisions, 292; dissent on vote abroad, 293; opinion re inspectors warrant, 309–10; concurs re evidence in car, 311; dissent on "harmless error," 312; dissent on robber ruling reversal, 321; dissent on vacated conviction, 323; dissent on park trespass, 334; dissent on restaurant trespass, 334; dissent on trespass reversal, 335; dissent on sit-ins reversal, 335–36; concurs on rights leader reversal, 336; dissent on picketing, 336; dissent on antipicketing statute, 338; concurs on segregation protest, 338; opinion re rights, 341; opinion re jury discrimination, 343–44; miscegenation statute held invalid by, 345; housing amendment held invalid by, 352; dissent re property discrimination, 353; concurs in part on NAACP lawyers, 354; dissent re NAACP membership lists, 356; concurs re park segregation ruling, 356–57; dissent on picketing, 358; opinion re voluntariness of confession, 361; dissent re confession, 362; dissent on Escobedo reversal, 364, 366; dissent involving police practices, 366, 370, 373–74; newspaper headline on, 375; dissent on tax fraud reversal, 375; concurs in part re remand, 379; dissent re robber, 379; dissent on television invalidity, 381, 383; concurs re trial by jury, 386; jury trial right rejected by, 387; dissent on recidivist reversal, 388; dissent on narcotics reversal, 394; concurs reversing obscenity conviction, 408; opinion re book censorship, 412; rule extending state apportionment, 432; concurs in Walker decision, 447; concurs awarding damages, 448; dissent on Seventh-Day Adventist ruling, 454; concurs re contraceptives statute, 457–58; concurs on strike-breaker fine, 476; dissent in employee lockout, 476; temporary layoff upheld by, 477; opinion against UMW, 477; decision re Sherman Act, 478; dissent on price-fixing, 478; dissent on compensation, 478; concurs re brewery assets, 481; dissent on rail merger opinion, 484; opinion re competition, 485; opinion on price-fixing, 485; dissent on jury exclusion, 488; dissent on tenant eviction ruling, 492; appointment of, 506; dissent on retroactivity, 515; dissent on murder reversal, 515–16; dissent on habeas corpus proceedings, 516; dissent on due process violation, 516; dissent re search and seizure, 517; dissent on Ohio election law

ruling, 518; ruling on union fines, 518–19; dissent re draftee, 519

White, Justice, Chief Justice Edward D.: 18, 109, 132–33, 147, 159; dissent in Lochner decision, 101; dissent in Oregon labor case, 102; Idaho indictment ordered quashed by, 102; dissent on real estate income tax, 136; income tax on personal property favored by, 136; concurs separate but equal rule, 141; opinion in literacy test rule, 142; death of, 169

Whitney, Eli: gin's effect on land speculation, 30

Whittaker, Justice Charles E.: 65–66, 267, 273, 280, 391, 394, 418, 503–506; dissent in murder conviction reversal, 122–23; dissent re free transcripts, 238; concurs on security clearance reversal, 261; dissent on denaturalization, 263; dissent on not deporting salesman, 267; dissent on vacated lawyer conviction, 273; dissent on teacher affidavit, 274; dissent on lawyer suspension, 278; witness conviction affirmed by, 282; dissent on witness questions, 284; dissent on withholding passports, 286; dissent on voter's loss of citizenship, 291; decision on deserter's loss of citizenship, 291; dissent on denaturalization, 291; dissent re "silver platter" doctrine, 301; dissent on Fourteenth Amendment ruling, 302–304; dissent on vacated narcotics conviction, 307; opinion re rodent search, 308; opinion re narcotics conviction, 314; dissent re complaint insufficiency, 314; dissent on restaurant integration, 330; concurs voiding Alabama statute, 346; dissent on radio-television libel, 448; dissent on handbill ordinance ruling, 456; concurs re union funds in politics, 467; dissent on drug resale prices, 481; dissent on husband-wife conspiracy, 488; dissent on income tax ruling, 489–90; dissent re tax refund, 495; appointment of, 502; resignation of, 506

Who's Who: 148

"Wild horses" (Chief Justice Stone's associates): 15, 221

Wilkinson, General James: 27

Williams, O. B.: 248

Wilson Dam: 185

Wilson, President Woodrow: 168, 218

Wiretapping: 159, 165–66, 320–21; Senate investigation of, 160, 166; held illegal, 160; permitted for national security, 160, 517; scope broadened, 160, 167, 526; evidence held inadmissible, 514–15; held prospective, 515; log inspection in, 516–17; decisions explained to government, 516–17; need for, 527; *see also* eavesdropping

Wisconsin: federal Fugitive Slave Act declared unconstitutional by, 58; literature ordinance invalidated, 203; strike law struck down, 464–65; monopoly in, 481

Wisconsin legislature: 58

Wisconsin State Bar: 469

Wisconsin, University of, Madison, Wisc.: 493

Witnesses: 157–58, 235–36, 280 ff., 380, 387, 390–92, 473; right of confrontation, 235, 377, 385, 392, 515; convictions of, 281–84; conviction reversals of, 281–85; in fire mar-shal probe, 378; in "ambulance chasing" probe, 378; contempt convictions upheld, 389

Woodbury, Justice Levi: 23, 56, 59

Woods, Justice William B.: 81, 94; dissent in Arlington tax sale case, 96

Workmen's compensation: 478–79

Workmen's compensation acts: 108–109, 355

World of Eli Whitney, The: 29

Writings of Thomas Jefferson, The: 23, 24

Wyoming Coal Company: 87

Yazoo land cases: 29–31

"Yellow-dog contracts": 102, 104